The Grand Design

THE
GRAND
DESIGN

Strategy and the U.S. Civil War

DONALD
STOKER

OXFORD
UNIVERSITY PRESS

2010

OXFORD
UNIVERSITY PRESS

Oxford University Press, Inc., publishes works that further
Oxford University's objective of excellence
in research, scholarship, and education.

Oxford   New York
Auckland   Cape Town   Dar es Salaam   Hong Kong   Karachi
Kuala Lumpur   Madrid   Melbourne   Mexico City   Nairobi
New Delhi   Shanghai   Taipei   Toronto

With offices in
Argentina   Austria   Brazil   Chile   Czech Republic   France   Greece
Guatemala   Hungary   Italy   Japan   Poland   Portugal   Singapore
South Korea   Switzerland   Thailand   Turkey   Ukraine   Vietnam

Copyright © 2010 by Donald Stoker

Published by Oxford University Press, Inc.
198 Madison Avenue, New York, NY 10016

www.oup.com

Oxford is a registered trademark of Oxford University Press

Library of Congress Cataloging-in-Publication Data
Stoker, Donald J.
The grand design : strategy and the U.S. Civil War / by Donald Stoker.
p.   cm.
Includes bibliographical references and index.
ISBN 978-0-19-537305-9
1. United States—History—Civil War, 1861-1865—Campaigns.
2. Strategy—History—19th century.   3. United States—Military policy.
4. Confederate States of America—Military policy.   I. Title.
E470.S87 2010
973.7'13—dc22   2009045427

1 3 5 7 9 8 6 4 2
Printed in the United States of America
on acid-free paper

To Carol and Sarah

"You appear to be much absorbed, my venerable Spartan,"
says I to the General, as I handled the diaphanous vessel he
was using as an act-drop in the theatre of war.

The General frowned like an obdurate parent refusing
to let his only daughter marry a coal-heaver, and says he:

"I'm absorbed in strategy. Eighteen months ago, I was
informed by a contraband that sixty thousand unnatural
rebels were intrenched somewhere near here, and having
returned the contraband to his master, to be immediately
shot, I resolved to overwhelm the rebels by strategy. Thun-
der!" says the General, perspiring like a pitcher of ice-
water in June, "if there's anything equal to diplomacy it's
strategy."

—ROBERT NEWELL, Union humorist,
from his *Orpheus C. Kerr Papers*, 1862

Contents

Maps

Acknowledgments

AUTHORS ARE ALWAYS INDEBTED to great numbers of people; that is no less true in my case. My debts fall into several categories; none can be repaid.

My research was greatly facilitated by the time the U.S. Naval War College's Monterey Program gave me during my non-teaching terms. I am grateful to Fred Drake and Hal Blanton for this. The Washington Navy Yard Library and the Dudley Knox Library at the Naval Postgraduate School provided the foundational materials. Two indispensable helpers were the Dudley Knox Library's Zooey Lober and Irma Fink. They always went out of their way to fulfill my many interlibrary loan requests.

I am indebted to my agent at POM Inc., Dan Green, for initially whipping the book into shape. My editors at Oxford University Press, Tim Bent, Dayne Poshusta, and Joellyn Ausanka, and publicist Susan Fensten, have proven wonderful to work with and made the product far better.

Many people read all or part of the manuscript and offered helpful comments or material: George Baer (who was especially encouraging), John Dunn, Mark Elam, John Griffiths, Mike Jones, Gary Ohls, Keith Poulter, Craig Symonds, and Steven Woodworth. Maria Sigala kindly took the jacket photo. Thank you all.

Last, and most important, I thank my wife, Carol, and daughter, Sarah, for putting up with my frequent absences. I dedicate this book to you. S.D.G.

The Grand Design

Introduction

Great men, my boy, are never so great but that they can profit
occasionally by a suggestion from the humblest of the species.

—ROBERT NEWELL, Union humorist

THE AMERICAN CIVIL WAR does not lack for stories, nor for books that
tell them. A generation ago, James McPherson noted in his monumental *Battle Cry of Freedom* that fifty thousand different books on the Civil War had
rolled off the presses. Historian Brian Holden Reid writes that by 2002 this
had become more than sixty thousand, a figure not including six thousand volumes on Abraham Lincoln.[1] This number will climb as we reach the conflict's
150th anniversary. Some of these books stand out in a field amply blessed
with superb writers and researchers. We have the masterly volumes of Bruce
Catton and Shelby Foote, biographies such as David Herbert Donald's beau-
tifully rendered *Lincoln*, the theater command studies of Steven Woodworth,
the naval studies of Raimondo Luraghi and Craig Symonds, and innumerable
others.

One of the enduring themes of Civil War writing involves the quest to
determine why the North won and the Confederacy did not. They range from
serious considerations, such as edited volumes and books by David Donald,
Gabor Boritt, Herman Hattaway, Archer Jones, and a great host of others, to
more popular, counterfactual accounts, or "alternative history," such as chap-
ters from Robert Cowley's *What If* series of books and Newt Gingrich's novels about Gettysburg and the what-might-have-been of a Southern battlefield
triumph. What these latter efforts tend to have in common is the idea that the
battle—Gettysburg in particular—was the pivot, the turning point.

Indeed, battles dominate Civil War literature, in part because they make
great narrative and provide the most dramatic possible setting, one over-
awed by individual acts of heroism and where momentous decisions—by the
Grants, Lees, and Stonewall Jacksons—are played out with immediate consequence. They offer the war in miniature and give us tales of pathos, bravery,
cowardice, and even the miraculous. Estimates are that there were roughly
ten thousand "clashes" (an admittedly vague term) during the Civil War, a

conflict that claimed 620,000 lives, and in which more than a million became casualties. Again, the three-day engagement we refer to as Gettysburg leads the way, followed by the Seven Days, Chickamauga, Chancellorsville, the Wilderness, and Antietam. There are wonderful books on all of these battles. Battles excite readers. And battles sell books.

Another reason for the battle focus is no doubt related to the fact that Civil War generals themselves, like Robert Newell's "venerable Spartan," thought them so crucial to their cause. And indeed they were correct. The Napoleonic notion of a "decisive battle" is often touted as something pursued by Civil War generals. There is certainly some truth to this. References to Austerlitz, Napoleon's epic victory over the combined forces of Russia and Austria-Hungary in 1805, fall from many of their pens. One could compare the nineteenth-century fascination with the Napoleonic era to the twenty-first-century fascination with World War II (and the Civil War, for that matter). Sun Tzu called "winning without fighting" the "acme of skill," but he knew this was rare. War is fighting; battle is at its heart. Delivering success in battle has always been part of the general's job. The Civil War was no different. But generals, particularly commanding generals, have to do more than fight (and win) battles. They have to win the war. This is why strategy matters.

All of this may help explain why none of the more than three score thousand books on the Civil War is dedicated to looking at the war's strategy, meaning the larger uses of military power. Historians are generally not taught to think in terms of strategy. Other related academic fields, such as political science and international relations, occasionally address strategic issues, but its practitioners are usually not interested in the Civil War. (The one exception seems to be in the study of Abraham Lincoln as a wartime leader.)[2] This general academic disinterest in strategic thinking is occasionally tinged with disdain; some historians equate focus on the military aspects of any war, particularly the Civil War, with avoidance or even ignorance of warfare's greater meaning in the American story.

But Civil War strategy, too, has a story, and it is one I try to tell in this book. To the mid-nineteenth-century American mind, strategy largely meant the maneuvering of forces (thus Newell's bumbling commander could indeed seek to "overwhelm the rebels by strategy").[3] Essentially, this simplified it to mean what we would today call a combination of tactics, meaning the use of military forces in contact with or near contact with the enemy, and operations, the military campaigns mounted to prosecute the strategy. And indeed, most of the studies of Civil War strategy, even the ones that interject theory, and despite insistence to the contrary, invariably focus upon tactics, or at best

campaigns. Worse, these efforts have too often been based upon the misreading or misunderstanding of the theoretical teachings they profess to use.

But strategy is bigger than tactics, as I hope this book will reveal, and demands a broader view, one that uses a framework based upon current definitions of relevant concepts, as well as the application of military theory, particularly concepts from Carl von Clausewitz and Antoine-Henri de Jomini, two of the most influential military thinkers of the last two centuries. Those who teach military theory generally find Clausewitz's *On War* the most useful of such works. The Prussian-born military theorist, veteran of the Napoleonic Wars and advisor to kings, penned a number of other volumes as well, including many on military campaigns and politics. He enjoyed scant readership in the United States before the Vietnam War but since then has been all but canonized by many American strategic studies programs.[4] A large part of this is due to the accessibility of a modern English translation of *On War* by Michael Howard and Peter Paret.[5]

The core of Clausewitz's theory is that war is driven by a trinity of forces: chance, passion, and rationality. These are respectively governed (usually) by the military, the people, and the government. Their interrelationships dictate the nature of the war to be waged.[6] Clausewitz defines strategy as "the use of the engagement for the purpose of the war." We go beyond this in our definition, as does Clausewitz when he develops his concept by giving us the general's job in relation to this: "The strategist must therefore define an aim for the entire operational side of the war that will be in accordance with its purpose. In other words, he will draft the plan of the war, and the aim will determine the series of actions intended to achieve it."[7]

Jomini's work provides another plank.[8] The Swiss-born veteran of Napoleon's campaigns, and the emperor's first real interpreter, was the military theorist with whom Civil War leaders were most familiar. Jomini was for generations a favorite of the American military profession before being supplanted by his Prussian rival and fellow Napoleonic-era veteran. Jomini's most important work, for our purposes, was his *The Art of War*, first published in 1837 as *Précis de l'Art de la Guerre*.[9] This, as well as Jomini's many other books, was accessible to nineteenth-century West Point–schooled officers, who knew French. It made its first appearance in English in a bad translation in 1854.[10]

For military and political leaders of the Civil War era, Jomini was the source of technical vocabulary. When they write about strategy and its related issues, it is generally in Jominian phrases. Jomini, in his short definition, wrote, "Strategy is the art of making war upon the map, and comprehends the whole theater of operations."[11] This, as the late Michael Handel pointed

out in *Masters of War*, is clearly a reference to the operational level of war. Clausewitz's *On War*, Handel also noted, suffers from the same limitations, as much of the time when he says "strategy" he means what is currently called operations, meaning what the military does to implement strategy.[12] Jomini's expansive definition encompassed thirteen points, but only the first two relate directly to the strategic realm: "the selection of the theater of war, and the discussion of the different combinations of which it admits" and "the determination of the decisive points in these combinations, and the most favorable direction for operations."[13] Jomini's other planks deal with the operational level of war and are addressed below.

The debate over how and to what degree Jomini's writings influenced the military events of the Civil War has raged for years and probably will never be settled. But we do know his works had an impact on such leaders as Henry W. Halleck, who wrote his own version of Jomini's *The Art of War* and translated Jomini's multivolume biography of Napoleon.[14] Jomini's thought, or a form of it, was taught at West Point by Dennis Hart Mahan beginning in 1832, where, of course, many of the military leaders on both sides of the Civil War received their training. But his lessons focused primarily upon battlefield tactics.[15] Jomini is often charged with trying to reduce conflicts to what might be called "warfare by calculus and algebraic formula," while Clausewitz is accused of arguing that the only proper way to wage war is with "total," complete, and "absolute" violence.[16] Both of these are caricatures.

What I hope this book will do is reveal how Civil War leaders—especially the two commanders in chief, Abraham Lincoln and Jefferson Davis—construed strategy, revealing the development of their large-frame thinking about how to prosecute the war. Civil-military relations, the respective roles of the military and civilian leaders and their ability to work with each other, had a significant impact on the creation of strategy as well as its implementation. Both groups have critical roles to play in waging a conflict. The quality of their interaction is often a determinant of the efficiency and effectiveness with which a nation fights. The Civil War provides an almost incomparable illustration of this. Each side was led by a native Kentuckian who had strong views about the role of the chief executive in wartime and was extremely protective of his wartime purview. Moreover, as we shall see, both were then plagued by professional officers who refused to do their jobs.

This book is therefore not a complete history of the conflict, nor will it offer a blow-by-blow examination of individual battles. Readers will find very little of the smoke of rifles and cannons or the gleam of bayonets. Battles are imperative in any study of war, including this one, but I treat them mainly

as the result of the strategic and operational efforts at prosecuting the war. The larger military and political objectives the combatants sought are what I endeavor to show. In short, *how* a battle was fought is the realm of tactics. *Why* a battle was fought is the arena of strategy. In the end, for good or ill, strategy, rather than just battles, determines the result of all wars, as it did in America's Civil War.

I WILL NOT BELABOR our study of theory, though it is important, but below is a diagram that I have found useful in my teaching that provides a solid foundation for our story:

What it shows is that strategy—located in the precise middle of this inverted pyramid—is only a piece of the puzzle that is warfare, the most confusing and complex of human endeavors, and cannot be studied apart from its critical accompanying factors. The most important of these is policy, meaning the political objective or objectives sought by the governments in arms (these are sometimes described as war aims). Policy should inform strategy, provide the framework for its pursuit, but not dictate it.[17] The term *policy* is often used when what is really being discussed is strategy or operations. Civil War leaders often spoke of "military policy" when today we would speak of military strategy or operational strategy, depending upon the context. Strategy defines how military force is used in pursuit of the political goal.[18]

Understanding the political objective is critical because it determines so much of where and how the war will be fought. Here, Clausewitz is particularly useful when he discusses determining the "nature of the war." As he writes in *On War*: "The first, the supreme, the most far-reaching act of judgment that the statesman and commander have to make is to establish by that test the kind of war on which they are embarking; neither mistaking it for, nor trying to turn it into, something that is alien to its nature. This is the first of all strategic questions and the most comprehensive." One of the key elements here is "by that test." Clausewitz explains that the most important element determining what the war will be like is the political objective or objectives sought by the belligerents.[19] Directly acting upon this is what he calls the value of the object, meaning that the importance the parties place upon the object (the political objective) will determine the duration of the war. Clause-witz argues that when one side is no longer willing to pay the costs of the war (blood, treasure, prestige, etc.), it will stop. This also influences the extremes to which a nation will go to prosecute the contest. The more valuable the object, the more willing the people and the state are to sacrifice.[20]

Related to this is the fact that the Civil War is sometimes called the first "total war." Often the arguments for this are not grounded upon a clear expla-nation of this phrase. Tangled in this definitional mess is the whole purpose, or political objective, for which the war is being fought. The standard modern response is to brand a war "total" based upon its scale. A big war is thus a total war. But just what *big* means is vague. Does it apply to the mobilization of resources, the destruction meted out, or both? And where do we draw the line so that we know the war is total?

A better approach to defining conflicts is found in *On War*. Clausewitz argues that all the wars upon which nations embark can be characterized as two types: wars fought for a limited political aim, such as taking a province, and ones waged for an unlimited political aim, such as the overthrow of the opposing government or bending it to one's will. He goes on to note that this is usually a major, national war necessitating extensive mobilization of the state's human and material resources.[21] In other words, to Clausewitz, the conflict type is determined by the objective sought. The scale of its waging is an accompanying factor.

During the Civil War the Union sought the complete destruction of the Confederacy's government, an unlimited objective. The Confederates, on the other hand, a had more limited aim. They did not fight for the total destruction of the United States; they sought to secede and take with them some provinces.

Connected to this is the touting of the Civil War as one of the first mod-ern wars, if not the first. Several factors combine to produce this assessment. The first, once again, is the scale of the conflict. The Civil War was indeed a big war in many ways. It was a major conflict between two democracies in which both sides mobilized large segments of the population, sometimes via conscription. The second element was industrial mobilization. Fielding mass armies necessitates large quantities of equipment and supplies. Northern industry expanded to meet these demands; the South industrialized, at least in regard to arms and many of the accoutrements of war, in an effort to do the same. A third plank to the modernity argument revolves around technology. The Civil War is the war of the railroad, the steam engine, armored ships with turrets, telegraph communications, rifles, observation balloons, and trench warfare. None of these was the decisive element of the conflict, but all contributed to its character and influenced how it was fought. Most of these elements, though, affected only the tactical level; they exerted almost no influence on strategy.

Military power is but one of many tools nations use to achieve their political objectives. To pursue their goals in wartime, states tap their economic, political, and diplomatic resources. These nonmilitary components are sometimes lumped under the rubric *soft power*. All of these (including military strategy), are therefore elements of grand strategy. Implementing grand strategy requires the coordination of the various elements of national power with military strength. The term *grand strategy* is sometimes used to describe a major campaign or the broad sweep of a war (William Tecumseh Sherman used it this way), but that is too limited in scope.[22]

For the purposes of this book, the key term is *strategy*, specifically military and naval strategy. Indeed, it is my departure point. As I've suggested, by strategy I mean the larger use of military force in pursuit of a political objective.[23] Some examples include implementing blockades, attrition (wearing down the enemy's forces), exhaustion (depleting his will and/or ability to fight), a Fabian approach (protracting the war by avoiding a fatally decisive battle and preserving one's forces), and applying simultaneous pressure at many points.

Of course, military strategy was deeply affected by the social dimension of the struggle, which involves just how serious both sides were about fighting the war (pretty serious, as it turned out) and their respective misperceptions of this. For example, each side looked at the opposing government as a tyranny holding its people in thrall. This was hardly the case (unless you were a slave, something possible both in the North and in the South). Emancipation is the most obvious aspect of this social dimension and the most critical. Both sides spilled much ink and blood deciding what the roles of black Americans should be in this war (and, of course, afterward). I have had numerous discussions with colleagues over whether the Emancipation Proclamation was an element of Union strategy or a Union political objective. We will see how it begins as one and becomes the other. The South also debated this question, eventually reaching a logical conclusion, but too late for it to have any impact upon its fight.

Clausewitz proposes many useful concepts for analyzing and waging war at the strategic level. One was what he called "the center of gravity," which he describes as "the hub of all power and movement, on which everything depends." He then advises that this "is the point against which all our energies should be directed." In other words, the center of gravity is the source of the enemy's strength. This is what should be broken, if possible, because its collapse can lead to the end of the war. Clausewitz's centers of gravity include the army, public opinion, the capital city, the political leadership, and any allies. Destroying the enemy's army is almost always the quickest way to achieve your political objective, Clausewitz believes. But he also cautions that every enemy is different and that, depending upon the situation, there might be more than one center. Here Clausewitz is often misread. He's accused of arguing that the *only* path to success consists of destroying the enemy's army. What he actually says is to do what works.[24]

Ideally, once strategy is determined, it is then executed. Here we enter into the operational level of war. Operations are what military forces do in an effort to implement military strategy. Importantly, this includes the activities of military forces before and after combat.[25] The conduct of these operations is known as operational art or operational warfare, or, if one prefers, operational strategy. While no one from the Civil War era would have been familiar with this exact terminology, they often thought this way.

The remaining eleven points of Jomini's baker's dozen definition of strategy largely deal with the operational level of war and its execution. They also explain some expressions that commonly arise in Civil War writing. For example, to Jomini, the operational commander should determine the "fixed base and the zone of operations." Then he decides "the objective point, whether offensive or defensive." From this flows the placement of the forces for offense and defense, and the routes (or lines) directed at the objective point. He also talked of optional lines of advance, supporting and alternative bases of operations, logistical requirements, fortresses and entrenched camps (here he is drifting into the tactical), and any efforts at diversions.[26]

Jomini, with his exposition of strategy and his histories of the Seven Years' War and the Napoleonic era, therefore taught military commanders to think in terms that today we would define as operational. Nonetheless, many of the better commanders thought and fought according to our hierarchy, differentiating between the levels and realms of the inverted pyramid. For example, though most called their operations "campaigns," they understood the linkage between the operational and strategic levels of war. The operations (or campaigns) should have clear objectives themselves that contribute to the achievement of strategic goals as well as the accomplishment of the government's political objective. Robert E. Lee, George McClellan, and Ulysses S. Grant all thought this way, or learned to. Joe Johnston, Don Carlos Buell, Henry Halleck (though a deep reader of Jomini), and many others never understood.

How the respective leaders planned their campaigns and what operational objectives they sought with them are core parts of this story. As we'll see, too often those concocting the plans did not take into consideration the realities of terrain, logistics, capabilities, and, perhaps most important, time.

Tactics govern the execution of battles fought in the course of operations. In much military literature the words *tactics* and *strategy* are used interchangeably and indiscriminately, even though they differ starkly.

So these are the realms. Political policy—the larger reasons a nation goes to war—gives shape to grand strategy, the merging of political, economic, and military thinking, which supports and influences the nature of strategy, the use of military forces, which is in turn implemented by operations, which is characterized at the point of the spear by tactics. An example: In the summer of 1863 the Confederacy sought to achieve its political objective—independence. Robert E. Lee launched a strategic offensive in an effort to accomplish this aim. His strategy was to attack the North's will to fight by decisively defeating the Union on its own territory; his operational goals included throwing the Union Army back over the Potomac; his initial tactical plan was to defeat the opposing Union army in detail, "in detail" referring to the tactic of bringing a large force to bear on a part of the enemy's, destroying it, and then repeating this against the remaining elements of their army.

Here is another example, but in reverse: the men landing on French beaches during the Normandy invasion of June 1944 were executing the tactical elements of an immense Allied military operation (Overlord) designed to implement a strategy (a "Second Front" in Europe) as a means of achieving the political objective (the unconditional surrender of Germany).

A number of other terms arise repeatedly in this story, most of them involving operations and tactics—the elements of a specific campaign. Again, many of them stem from Jomini's work. While at times *Art of War* does reach into the strategic realm, it is largely a treatise on how to conduct operational and tactical warfare. Indeed, it was at this level that his influence on the thinking of Civil War leaders was greatest. For example, Jomini very often mentions the importance of bases of operation, meaning the area or point from which armies draw supplies and reinforcements, as well as a place to which to retreat safely if needed (he and Clausewitz agree here).[27] He also stresses the need to protect the lines of communication that develop when an army advances away from its base.

Related to this is Jomini's preoccupation with an army's possession of the central position and with interior and exterior lines of advance. "Interior lines" refers to one side's advancing army or armies having shorter distances to traverse in order to concentrate than the enemy, who, suffering the disadvantage of having a greater distance to cover, is moving on the "exterior line." The force acting along interior lines thus has the advantage of holding the interior or central position and is therefore more able to unite and defeat, in detail (meaning one at a time; in this sense *detail* is used operationally), the several forces of the enemy. This is also considered a method by which a force that is smaller overall can defeat a more numerous opponent.[28]

Yet another term, again from Jomini, that frequently appears in the correspondence of the combatants is *demonstration*. To Jomini this was using forces to "draw the enemy in a direction where you wish them to go in order to facilitate the execution of an enterprise in another direction." In other words, mounting a demonstration was a method of deceiving the enemy, of masking one's true intentions.[29] Jomini also stressed concentration of forces, particularly in relation to his writing on interior and exterior lines.[30] (Clausewitz did as well, noting that "the best strategy is always *to be very strong*; first in general, then at the decisive point.")[31] The principle of concentration is applicable to all levels of war.

Finally, a tactical concept derived from Jomini's teachings that saw wide usage during the Civil War was the *offensive-defensive* (or its inverse). Some historians of the war have used this term to contend, inaccurately, that the South pursued an offensive-defensive strategy, particularly as concerns Jefferson Davis, or Lee and his decision to take the fight into the North.[32] But Jomini discussed this in a tactical sense, and its Civil War–era usage invariably points to tactical events.[33] Examples from both sides abound and can be found in the correspondence of such grandees as P. G. T. Beauregard, Leonidas K. Polk, Braxton Bragg, Edmund Kirby Smith, Grant (who later confessed that he had never read Jomini), and others.[34]

With these terms as our base, this book will tell the story of the "how" of strategy in the war—its evolution and the attempts at implementation—as well as show why certain strategic decisions were made and their impact. It is not an exercise in inevitability, but it is sometimes one in contingencies.

There were countless decision points along the way where different outcomes were possible. By this I do not simply mean that the South could have won, though this was certainly true. In my view, however, what is underevaluated, and therefore worth stressing, is that the North could and should have won sooner. The main reason behind the Union's victory in the Civil War is that its leaders eventually developed a military strategy capable of delivering the political end they desired. The question is not just how the North won, but why it took so long.

The framework I've sketched, I hope, offers a clean canvas upon which to outline the Civil War's policy, strategy, and operations—and their interconnection. (Tactics belong in the battle books, of which this is not one.) It's derived from my decade of experience teaching various versions of the U.S. Naval War College's course Strategy and Policy, primarily in the college's Monterey Program. Not content with the texts we were using to teach the Civil War, I began searching for more suitable works. From this came a short piece drawn from secondary sources on Confederate grand strategy for the 2002 West Point summer seminar on teaching military history.[35] But this was far from sufficient. I began examining some of the commonly cited primary sources while simultaneously thinking of writing a short book on the subject from published works. But this only revealed more problems with the Civil War literature and the subject of strategy. More primary research followed, and the eventual decision to write a book based largely upon the documentary record.

My belief is that this may be the first book to focus exclusively on the subject of strategy and the Civil War. My hope is that it will not be the last.

I

Policy and War

*The political horizon looks dark and lowering; but the
people, under Providence, will set all right.*

ABRAHAM LINCOLN, 1860

COLD AND DRIZZLE greeted President-elect Abraham Lincoln on the
morning of February 11, 1861. The next day he would be fifty-two, one of
the youngest men chosen to sit in the White House. Lincoln and his party
of fifteen gathered for the eight o'clock train in the station's waiting room.
Somberness characterized the retinue, despite the crowd of nearly a thousand
well-wishers. The party boarded the train's single passenger car; the crowd
lingered, enduring an icy downpour—waiting. Lincoln stood at the railing
before an audience he referred to as "friends." He thanked them, professed his
inability to complete the task laid before him without the help of the Divine
Being, and said goodbye. He would never see Springfield again.[1] The same
day, Jefferson Davis boarded a boat for Vicksburg, headed for Montgomery,
Alabama, and his swearing in as the Confederacy's provisional president.[2]

Lincoln knew he faced a hard row. War had been in the offing before his
election, and his inauguration made it all but inevitable—not because of war-
mongering on his part, but because of Southern fears of his intentions. To
many in the South, Lincoln's election meant abolition and slave revolt. They
saw the Republicans, not themselves, as the party of revolution. Lincoln often
insisted he had no intention of upsetting the slave system, but to the radicals
and hysterics his words meant nothing. There arose a convergence of fear,
antagonism, and sectionalism.[3]

So Lincoln went to face the growing crisis. Many, including Winfield
Scott, the general in chief of the Union army, feared it would worsen before
Lincoln took his oath of office. On October 29, 1860, the general had warned
President James Buchanan that Southern "rashness" could lead to attempts to
seize one or more of the forts the U.S. government still held in the South; he
recommended their reinforcement. Scott feared the worst but also believed
that if for the next year the president followed a path "of firmness and moderation," there was reason to hope that "the danger of secession may be made to

pass away without one conflict of arms, one execution, or one act of violence."
He suggested that exports be unimpeded and "to avoid conflicts all duties on
imports be collected outside of the cities, in forts or ships of war."[4] Here Scott
provided the first strategy for countering Southern secession.

Strategic thinking is useless, though, if no one wants to hear it, and initially Buchanan and his administration showed disinterest in Scott's suggestions.[5] The vain, three-hundred-plus-pound septuagenarian may have lost
much of his physical vigor (except at mealtime), but his mind remained sharp
and active.[6] When Scott's comments were revealed to the press, they encouraged some Southern radicals to declare reconciliation dead.[7]

Buchanan, though, was not quick to do anything except vacillate. He first
decided that reinforcement of the threatened outposts would be provoca-
tive, then changed his mind in early December 1860.[8] The North made no
preparations for war; Jefferson Davis saw this as proof that the Union did not
expect a fight.[9]

General Scott certainly had no itch for one; he had seen his share of war,
against the British during the War of 1812, against the Creeks and Semi-
noles, and, most famous, against Mexico. Nevertheless, he did believe the
government had to act. With Buchanan's permission, Scott decided that
Major Robert Anderson and his command at Fort Sumter, one of the Union's
remaining outposts in the emerging Confederacy, should be resupplied. By
January 5 the steamer *Star of the West* was on its way south, loaded with matériel and troops, only to be driven off on the ninth by fire from guns manned
by Citadel cadets. Scott also moved to reinforce Fort Pickens, Florida.[10] And
he made sure a copy of the aforementioned October 29 memo to Buchanan
reached Lincoln's hands; the incoming executive was grateful.[11]

As Buchanan dithered, pursuing his "after-me-the-deluge policy," others
sought to defuse the crisis.[12] Congressional committees formed to discuss the
situation. Some of Lincoln's supporters believed his party should participate.
Lincoln did not disagree, but he set limits, forbidding any compromise on the
extension of slavery. "If there be," he said, "all our labor is lost, and, ere long,
must be done again." He was also unwilling to surrender principle to appease
dissatisfied elements. "Stand firm," Lincoln insisted. "The tug has to come, &
better now, than any time hereafter."[13]

Lincoln's ideas on the proper military response began to jell during the
period between his election and his inauguration. After receiving an account
of a discussion with General Scott, Lincoln wrote on December 21, 1860,
"According to my present view, if the forts shall be given up before the inauguration, the General must retake them afterwards."[14] This approach was only

partially in line with Scott's thinking. Scott could agree with Lincoln's desire to hold the forts, particularly since such firmness had worked before when, at his suggestion, President Andrew Jackson had dispatched troops to Fort Moultrie and Charleston harbor to counter the Nullification Crisis of 1832. Retaining the forts had the added benefit of placing South Carolinians in the same position as had Jackson: the government was not making war on them, but if they acted, they would be making war on the United States.[15] Lincoln though, had already moved beyond Scott's thinking. On December 21, through a third party, the president passed to Scott word that "I shall be obliged to him to be as well prepared as he can to either *hold*, or *retake*, the forts, as the case may require, at, and after the inauguration."[16] *Retake* is the key term. If need be, Lincoln would use force.

Though he directed preparation for a firm response if one should prove necessary, Lincoln also sought to reassure his potential foes. He had no intention of attacking slavery upon taking office and told Alexander H. Stephens, the future Confederate vice president, "The South would be in no more danger in this respect, than it was in the days of Washington." But Lincoln had no illusions about the big sticking point. "I suppose, however, this does not meet the case," he wrote Stephens. "You think slavery is *right* and ought to be extended; while we think it is *wrong* and ought to be restricted. That I suppose is the rub. It certainly is the only substantial difference between us."[17]

As 1860 swept to its end, a New York journalist asked the president-elect how he would deal with secession. Lincoln said, "I think we should hold the forts, or retake them, as the case may be, and collect the revenue."[18] Clearly, Lincoln's mind was made up on the North's initial strategic response, and just as clearly, he followed Scott's lead, at least in part.

With the new year the crisis intensified. Several compromise proposals were floated, but to Lincoln there was nothing about which the government should or could compromise. And he feared bending too far. "What is our present condition?" he wrote in response to a complex agreement suggested by a group of congressmen from the border states. "We have just carried an election on principles fairly stated to the people. Now we are told in advance, the government shall be broken up, unless we surrender to those we have beaten, before we take the offices. In this they are either attempting to play upon us, or they are in dead earnest. Either way, if we surrender, it is the end of us, and of the government. They will repeat the experiment upon us *ad libitum*. A year will not pass, till we shall have to take Cuba as a condition upon which they will stay in the Union. They now have the Constitution, under which we have lived over seventy years, and acts of Congress of their own framing, with no prospect of their being changed; and they can never have a more shallow pretext for breaking up the government, or extorting a compromise, than now. There is, in my judgment, but one compromise which would really settle the slavery question, and that would be a prohibition against acquiring any more territory."[19]

When Lincoln left Springfield for Washington he was clear in his own mind about how to deal with the crisis. A reading of his correspondence in this period does not reveal any use of the term *secession*, and he refused to debate the issue of the right of the South to secede, hanging his political hat on the president's constitutional duty to defend the rights, property, and possessions of the U.S. government. But Lincoln possessed no illusions about what faced him, remarking in his rain-drenched farewell address at Springfield that "I go to assume a task more difficult than that which devolved upon General Washington."[20] One cannot accuse him of hyperbole.

LINCOLN SAID IN A SPEECH made in Philadelphia during his trip to Washington that he did not want "war and bloodshed."[21] Many in the North had similar hopes, in spite of the growing tension and the departure of the seven "Cotton States" by Lincoln's inauguration in March. They hoped the Union could be saved without violence and that these ungrateful children would find survival away from the nest impossible. The new secretary of state, Henry Seward, urged moderation, despite a previously more radical bent, and even made promises to former senators who had gone south that troops would soon be withdrawn from Fort Sumter. He did not let his lack of authority on such matters hinder his action.[22]

Seward believed that war could be averted and the South convinced to stay. He found in General Scott a temporary ally for a political strategy of conciliation. Scott also sought a cautious, moderate approach to the burgeoning crisis. At Seward's urging, Scott composed a letter to Lincoln detailing four options available to the new administration. It went out on March 3, the day before Lincoln's inauguration. Seward gave Lincoln the letter "and made sure that his colleagues, both in and out of government, were made aware of the general's written support" of the secretary of state's view.[23]

Scott offered up four choices. The first was to abandon former party designations for a new one, "Union party," and to "adopt the conciliatory measures proposed by [Senator John] Crittenden or the peace convention." Scott insisted this would not only prevent any further secession but also result in the return of some or all of the absconders. Barring this or some other act of conciliation, Scott predicted, the secession of the remaining slave states

would occur within sixty days. Second, Scott suggested the government collect the importation duties outside the ports it no longer controlled, "or close
such ports by act of Congress and blockade them." His third option: war. To
Scott this meant a war of conquest that, even if ably led, would take two or
three years and require 300,000 men, "estimating a third for garrisons, and the
loss of yet a greater number by skirmishes, sieges, battle and Southern fevers."
He predicted this path would produce enormous losses in Southern life and
property for which the North would gain nothing but $250 million in debt
and fifteen ruined states that it would have to hold down for "generations"
with large numbers of troops. His final option was to "say to the seceded
States, Wayward Sisters, depart in peace!"[24]

Lincoln made no comment upon the letter, but its wide circulation caused
a stir, as well as unfounded speculation because of its last line, which some
read as Scott recommending letting the South secede. But Scott was merely
presenting options, not advice, to the incoming president.[25] The letter's contents were also quickly relayed to Southern leaders.[26]

The first option was where Scott's heart lay. He and Seward were among
those of Lincoln's inner circle who believed that Union restraint would give
latent Unionism in the South time to bloom and reassert itself.[27] Seward
wrote, "The policy [strategy] of the time has seemed to me to consist in conciliation, which should deny to disunionists any new provocation or apparent
offense, while it would enable the Unionists in the slave States to maintain
with truth and with effect that the alarms and apprehensions put forth by the
disunionists are groundless and false."[28] Lincoln himself also adhered to this
view, at least in the beginning.[29]

Scott, as noted earlier, certainly did not want a war; he held that it would
be bloody and inflict untold suffering upon his native state of Virginia.[30] Scott
believed in the power of dormant Southern Unionism. But he also thought
that if the North invaded the South, the struggle would be no farther along a
year after the invasion than when it began.[31]

Smoothing over the broken places guided the thinking of both Scott and
Seward. Kentucky senator John J. Crittenden offered as a compromise "an
unamendable amendment to the Constitution" allowing slavery below the
latitude 36°30'. The measure died quickly from lack of support but was still
before the Kentucky legislature when Scott composed his letter. This certainly
aligned with Seward's strategy of "concessive delay," meaning to put off taking
any action against secession. It also fit with Scott's and Seward's belief in the
existence of deep wells of Southern Unionism. The Confederate attack on
Fort Sumter finally shifted Seward from this stump.[32]

Lincoln saw neither the first proposal in Scott's letter nor the fourth—
letting the "Wayward Sisters" "depart in peace"—as options. Nor was simply collecting the government's import duties outside the ports themselves,
as proposed in point two. This same point's second section, which suggested
blockade, however, revealed part of the strategy Lincoln eventually adopted
for suppressing the rebellion. Nonetheless, the only sure way to bring the
Union's "Wayward Sisters" back to the path of righteousness was to pursue
the rough road of point three: conquer the South. Lincoln soon chose this,
not because he wanted to, but because the South forced his hand. Scott's
estimation of the men and money necessary to do the job—staggering at the
time—would prove wildly optimistic; the Union dead eventually numbered
more than the 300,000 troops Scott had projected as necessary. His predic-
tion of devastation certainly came true. Indeed, devastating the South became
one of the paths by which the North won the war.[33]

When Lincoln stepped up to the podium on March 4, 1861, to deliver his
inaugural address, he had already firmly settled in his mind his actions with
regard to secession. He also made every effort to assuage Southern fears of
the arrival of his Republican administration. He had no intention of assaulting "their property, their peace, and personal security." "There is no necessity
for it," Lincoln avowed. "I am not in favor of such a course, and I may say in
advance, there will be no bloodshed unless it be forced upon the Government. The Government will not use force unless force is used against it." He
also quoted his own previous speeches wherein he promised to leave slavery
undisturbed and stated that he had no legal proviso for touching it. Moreover, he cited his party's political platform, which endorsed the right of states
to manage their own affairs and on which his election had been fought, and
denounced "the lawless invasion by armed force of any State or Territory, no
matter under what pretext, as among the gravest of crimes." One must note
here the caveat "lawless"; this would not have passed unobserved by any mind
as sharp as Lincoln's.[34]

Lincoln also insisted upon the perpetuity of the Union, noting, "It is safe
to assert that no government proper, ever had a provision in its organic law
for its own termination." The Union could not be destroyed "except by some
action not provided for in the instrument itself." No state could voluntarily
depart the house to which it had joined itself, and any violent acts "against
the authority of the United States, are insurrectionary or revolutionary,
according to circumstances."[35] Lincoln believed it his duty to protect the
Union and see its laws enforced, and assured his listeners that the Union
"*will* constitutionally defend, and maintain itself." He also committed him-

self to a peaceful solution, promising he would hold the posts belonging to the government but take no forceful action "beyond what may be necessary for these objects."[36]

Lincoln closed by giving the South the choice between peace and war: "In *your* hands, my dissatisfied fellow countrymen, and not in *mine*, is the momentous issue of civil war. The government will not assail *you*. You can have no conflict, without being yourselves the aggressors. *You* have no oath registered in Heaven to destroy the government, while *I* shall have the most solemn one to 'preserve, protect and defend' it."[37]

THE FIGURES IN THE ENORMOUS CROWD stood in mud up to their ankles, Richmond's heavy rains pounding them. It was February 22, 1862, and they were awaiting the arrival of their president. A little after noon, Jefferson Davis descended from his carriage onto a covered platform, Vice President Alexander Stephens and other Confederate notables in his train. He and Stephens had just been inaugurated, officially taking up posts held informally for slightly more than a year, and Davis had come to deliver his speech to the Confederate Congress. One witness observed that the Confederacy's government was birthed in a storm.[38] It would die in one as well.

Davis's address was shockingly honest, brazen even, and he held forth on Confederate strategy in a manner that must have appeared both an enunciation of the obvious and a blow to the guts of the congenitally optimistic and jingoistic figures dominating the Southern hierarchy. Since his last address to the body, Davis admitted, "events have demonstrated that the Government had attempted more than it had power to successfully achieve," and that "hence, in the effort to protect by our arms the whole of the territory of the Confederate States, Sea-board and inland, we have been so exposed as recently to encounter serious disasters."[39]

Davis succinctly described the strategy the Confederates implemented at the beginning of the Civil War and the basic problem with it. The South had chosen a cordon strategy, or cordon defense, meaning they tried to protect everything. This is understandable. The Confederacy needed to retain all the territory of the seceding states as grounds for recruitment and sources of supply for its armies. Just as important, demonstrating sovereignty over a clearly defined realm could help the cause of foreign recognition.[40] Failing to protect everything was unacceptable politically. The seceding states screamed states' rights but still expected the central government to protect the new nation's borders.[41] The Confederates also *wanted* to retain everything. They had no desire to surrender even one unplowed field to the North.

The Confederacy, or at least some of its leaders, had imperial ambitions as well. Jefferson Davis certainly stood among these. In an earlier time he had "dreamed of a new slaveholding republic that should expand into Mexico, Yucatan, and Cuba," a vision blocked by the Compromise of 1850, which halted the tide of Southern nationalism by, among other things, allowing the new territories created from land taken from Mexico to decide for themselves the fate of slavery within their borders. The compromise's tenets cut the feet out from under rabid secessionists such as Davis, at least for a while.[42] He didn't abandon his expansionist dream over the following decade. In a February 1861 speech he marked out two areas for Southern expansion: the West Indies and the northern reaches of Mexico.[43] In March 1861, he noted what was in his view the general Southern desire for Cuba, uniting this with the mistaken assumption that the North wanted Canada, projecting onto his opponents a version of his own imperial aims.[44] The next year, in further evidence of the South's ambitions, the Confederate Congress authorized the creation of a Southern version of the Union's Arizona Territory and then launched an ultimately failed offensive to win it.[45] Other Confederates believed there could be no clear victory over the North until Kentucky, Maryland, and Missouri rested comfortably in the Southern fold.[46]

Confederate ambitions flew beyond just the territorial, though territory certainly provided one of the primary objects for which the South drew its sword. In some respects, Confederate leaders saw themselves as revolutionaries. In his 1861 inaugural speech, stressing the South's right to secede, Davis insisted that "it is by abuse of language that their act has been denominated a revolution." But the playing of the French revolutionary anthem "La Marseillaise" after the speech, as well as many subsequent statements and actions, shows that Davis did not quite understand Southern feelings, or perhaps even his own, and certainly did not comprehend that they were indeed attempting revolution.[47]

In this same 1861 speech, Davis also insisted that the South was "anxious to cultivate peace and commerce with all nations" and that, being "an agricultural people[,]…our true policy is peace, and the freest trade which our necessities will permit."[48] Later, in an April message to Congress in Richmond, in which he echoed in some measure the Declaration of Independence, he presented a clear and high-minded-sounding accounting (if not a complete one) of the Confederacy's wants, declaring that the South desired "peace at any sacrifice save that of honor and independence; we seek no conquest, no aggrandizement, no concession of any kind from the States with which we were lately confederated; all we ask is to be left alone; that those who never held power over us shall not now attempt our subjugation by arms. This we will, this we must, resist to the direst extremes."[49]

How, then, does one reconcile the contradictions between the objectives of territorial expansion, revolt against the Federal government, and the "we only want peace" rhetoric of the Confederate commander in chief? The simple answer is that one cannot, and the Confederates themselves never bothered to do so. And from here grows one of the great problems with the Confederacy's political objectives: they were inherently contradictory. The Confederacy wanted "to be left alone," yet at the same time it wanted huge swaths of territory belonging to a number of other powers, particularly the Union. Moreover, Southerners wanted to foment revolution against the U.S. government, but they did not view themselves as revolutionaries. Sometimes night shone as day to the political leaders of the Confederacy.

In spite of these contradictions, the Confederates possessed a clear view of their primary political objective—independence—and pursued it zealously. But what they did not quite agree upon was what independence meant.

2

The Sinews of War

Strategy, my boy, is a profound science, and don't cost more than two millions a day, while the money lasts.

—ROBERT NEWELL, Union humorist

ON FEBRUARY 11, 1861, Davis received word that the Confederate Provisional Government had unanimously elected him president two days before. "Oh God, spare me this responsibility," he cried upon hearing the news. "I would love to head the army." Previously, Mississippi had named him a major general, "the career suited to his taste," and in a speech delivered the day he received word of being named president he had thanked Mississippi for the office and promised to take the war to the North—if war came. But duty called, and as historian Steven Woodworth aptly observes, "Jefferson Davis would never shirk his duty as he saw it."[1]

Woodworth's observation is critical. Davis's sense of obligation drove him to accept the highest office in the Confederacy, placing him at the core of its strategy making. How Davis saw things would govern much of the way the Confederacy fought its war. Fundamental to this was Davis's vision of what being president meant in regard to military matters. The Confederate constitution, like its U.S. model, designated the president commander in chief of the armed forces. Today, this is understood to mean that the president decides whether to use military force, where, for how long, and for what political purpose (within the strictures of the War Powers Act). Davis had a more expansive view of the president's military prerogatives, one he spelled out before his elevation to the office: "If the provisional government gives to the chief executive such power as the Constitution gave to the President of the U.S. then he will be the source of military authority and may in emergency command the army in person." In July 1861, Davis signed a letter to Lincoln, "Presdt. & Commander-in-Chief of the Army & Navy of the Confederate States of America," a clear indication of what he saw as his task: leading the nation *and* the military.[2] To Davis, the Confederate president was not only *commander* in chief; he was also *general* in chief, a view harking back to the Napoleonic example of the political leader who also led the army in the field. This refusal to separate the two in an era when industrialization and the increasing scale and power of the nation-state were making war a more complex endeavor, one requiring clearer divisions between civilian and military labor, hobbled the South's war effort. Moreover, it also prevented the much-needed appointment of a Confederate general in chief until 1865, when it was too late. The Confederate Congress had passed such a law in 1862; Davis vetoed it, insisting that it undermined the president's role as commander in chief of the army by allowing the general in chief to replace general officers appointed by the president. This was also one of the reasons for his May 1864 pocket veto of a bill to create an army general staff.[3]

Here is one of the driving and most problematic elements of Davis's personality: his tendency toward legalism, sometimes stretching to pedantry. He enjoyed showing others not only how *he* was correct but also how *they* were wrong. Davis seemed to have at least some awareness of this, once remarking to his wife in a letter that he wished he could "learn to let people alone who snap at me." Worse was Davis's general difficulty communicating with the people of the Confederacy.[4]

Shortly after his inauguration, Davis conceded that the South faced an unequal military contest, but he also sought to overcome this imbalance. The inequality began on the population front. The 1860 census numbered the inhabitants of the eleven Confederate states at 9,103,332. Slaves made up 3,521,110, more than a third. The Union retained a population of 22,339,991. This included those in the critical border states of Delaware, Kentucky, Maryland, and Missouri as well as the District of Columbia and the New Mexico Territory, whose combined population was 3,305,557, including 432,586 slaves. There were 525,660 people in the Rocky Mountain and Pacific coast areas, but they contributed little to Union military strength.[5]

The South's large slave population produced in many white Southerners a fear of slave unrest, particularly if the war went on for some time. On the other hand, in the early stages of the struggle, slavery enabled the South to mobilize a large percentage of its white manpower for its armed forces, as the slave population kept the economy going.[6]

The Confederacy was also outmatched industrially. In 1860, there were 128,300 industrial firms in the United States. The eleven states of the Confederacy had only 18,206, and these were generally small concerns. The value of the South's industrial output was but 7.5 percent of the American total. The North's agricultural production also outstripped the South's. Additionally, Tennessee, the Confederacy's meat-producing larder, lay not far from the frontier. Taking skilled men from their workbenches and putting them in

the ranks further undermined the South's limited industrial capacity. Moreover, there was no powder mill in the South, and the Confederacy had few
stocks.[7]

The disparity in strength also carried over to railroads, one of the era's
indicators of industrial might. The Union had 22,085 miles of rails, the South
only 8,541. Railroad personnel were generally Northerners with a distinct
lack of enthusiasm for the Southern cause. Railroads—their locations as well
as carrying capacity—heavily influenced the prosecution of the war. General
William Tecumseh Sherman compared the value of rail and wagon transportation in his 1864 Atlanta campaign, using as a measure a single-track railroad running 160 cars of supplies a day for 100,000 men and 35,000 animals.
He concluded that the campaign could not have been mounted without the
railroad because to supply the aforementioned force would have required
36,000 wagons, each pulled by six mules (220,800 mules) and hauling
two tons per day for 20 miles. This would have been impossible because of the
condition of the area's roads.[8]

River transport also proved key for both sides, particularly in the West.
Railroads had to be guarded; rivers did not. Railroads had a limited capacity;
only the number of vessels and the water level limited river transport. About
1,000 steamboats worked Western waterways when the war began. The Confederates took a few, though no one knows how many; the Union built hundreds. They provided invaluable logistical support. One 500-ton steamboat
could carry enough matériel per trip to provide nearly two days' supplies for
40,000 men and 18,000 animals.[9]

But the South was not without advantages, including the soldierly tradi-
tions of many of its people. Davis boasted that Southerners were "a military
people…We are not less military because we have had no great standing
armies. But perhaps we are the only people in the world where gentlemen go
to a military academy who do not intend to follow the profession of arms."[10]
This gave the South an unusually large percentage of its male population with
basic military skills and training. They were also eager to serve. Nearly 80 percent of the adult white male population of the Confederacy between the
ages of fifteen and forty would put on butternut or gray, an unprecedented
scale of mobilization. This translated into nearly 900,000 of 1,140,000 men.
The North still held the advantage in numbers, with 4,010,000 men between
fifteen and forty, but a smaller percentage rallied to the colors. As many as
2.8 million men served in Union armies.[11]

Both the North and the South generally raised troops at the state level,
which increased the rapidity by which they gathered forces. A local politician

might muster a company of around 100 men and then offer the unit to the state's governor, who would then send it to a camp of instruction where it would be combined with other companies to create a regiment. Junior and midgrade officers, particularly in the beginning of the war, were often elected. Both sides also drew upon local militias, but again the South's percentages—if not numbers—were more impressive. So many men flocked to the colors that initially both sides had more volunteers than they could arm.[12]

The antagonists had to pay these volunteers as well as finance the war and manage their respective economies. While the Confederate dollar held its value during the war's first two years, it did not thereafter. And officials refused to tax their population. The South raised approximately 1 percent of its funds via taxes, a smaller percentage than any other modern wartime government. The solution: print money, lots of it, backed by nothing except faith in a government that had been in existence not much longer than its currency. The result: rampant inflation that destroyed the economy. The figures for its sources of income up to October 1864 give a clear picture of Confederate finances: paper money, 60 percent; the sale of bonds, 30 percent; taxation, about 5 percent; miscellaneous, 5 percent. No one knows how much paper money eventually circulated in the Confederacy. The various states, municipalities, banks, corporations, and even individuals also printed notes. The Union did a much better job on the economic front. By the same month of 1864 it had derived only 13 percent of its income from paper money; bonds generated 62 percent, taxes accounted for 21 percent, and 4 percent came from other sources.[13]

BEFORE RESORTING TO THE SWORD, Davis's government attempted to achieve its political objective of independence through peaceful means. On February 27, 1861, shortly before Lincoln's inauguration, the Confederates dispatched former Georgia congressman Martin J. Crawford to Washington in an eventually forlorn effort to convince Buchanan to recognize the Confederacy before he left office, Davis having had word that Buchanan was willing to receive such a representative. Crawford found Washington overrun with large crowds hoping to catch a glimpse of the arriving Lincoln. Davis insisted later that these frightened Buchanan, who refused to see the Confederates.[14] He gave Buchanan too much credit.

After Lincoln's inauguration, John Forsyth, an Alabama newspaperman, and A. B. Roman, of Louisiana, joined Crawford. The trio sought an unofficial interview with Seward on March 11, 1861. Seward refused. They left a letter explaining that the Confederacy was de jure and de facto a nation and sought the establishment of amicable ties with the Union. Moreover, they also wanted Seward to set a date for presenting their credentials to Lincoln. Seward would have none of it, and delayed. Finally, in early April, a huffy Seward told them that the U.S. government would not recognize the Confederacy and that he saw "not a rightful and accomplished revolution and an independent nation…but rather a perversion of a temporary and partisan excitement."[15]

Davis saw this as treachery. Moreover, Seward's actions genuinely shocked him, a foolish and naive response.[16] Davis's representatives were there to prosecute a revolution against Seward's government. It was Seward's *job* to thwart them. Doing less would have meant he wasn't doing his duty. Davis should have understood this.

SECURING THE NEW COUNTRY dominated the Confederacy's actions in the chaotic and heady days following secession. Despite some high-flown rhetoric about taking the war to the North, the new nation's leaders concentrated on guarding their territory. Davis endured persistent demands from governors and local grandees for troops. Initially, adopting a version of an inherited system, he divided the country into eight military departments, each of which had at least two districts. Soon, small detachments were stationed along the coast from Cape Henry, Virginia, to Galveston, Texas.[17]

Politically, Davis had no choice but to protect everything. He did not have the luxury of trading space for time, as George Washington had in the Revolutionary War. A successful defense of the Confederacy's territorial holdings would prove that the Confederates had forged a nation, thereby helping the cause of recognition while also protecting the logistical support and recruiting base necessary for waging the war.[18]

The South also needed to maintain control over all of its territory because of its "peculiar institution"—slavery. Davis feared that once the Union army took over an area within the Confederacy, that area would then become useless to the South. The North would carry off the slaves, destroying the social structure and making that area unredeemable. A military strategy not founded on the preservation of the entire Confederacy, it was thought, would ultimately result in the destruction of the South, even if it won victories on the battlefield.[19]

The initial Confederate military strategy contained two defective elements. First, Davis supported the dispersal of forces for a cordon, or perimeter defense, leaving the South weak everywhere. Second, he established the aforementioned departmental system, meaning the division of the Confederacy into supposedly militarily self-supporting entities.[20] This increased the dispersion and created an unnecessary and inefficient compartmentalization of forces—though, as we will see, this was not as injurious as some writers have argued. The number of departments and their limits were also constantly altered.

Many Southerners' demands for a more aggressive, offensive strategy complicated Davis's situation. Southern newspapers pushed as hard as their Yankee counterparts for a thrust at the enemy's capital.[21] Davis refused to take this path. The Confederacy lacked the strength. Moreover, an attack against the North could have injured the South's struggle for international recognition by painting it as the aggressor.

Davis had a high view of his own military abilities. He had graduated from West Point with such future Confederate notables as Albert Sidney Johnston and Leonidas K. Polk, left Congress to serve in the Mexican War as a colonel of volunteers, and was secretary of war in the Franklin Pierce administration. Davis kept a tight grip on the nation's war effort, especially the Confederate War Office, essentially functioning as his own secretary of war. Five such secretaries served him, but his interventions generally reduced them to glorified clerks. Davis also exhibited a tendency to get down into the military weeds, too often losing sight of the big picture. Indeed, it appears that he could not distinguish between the tactical and strategic levels of war, and made the mistake of thinking his tactical success at the Battle of Buena Vista in the Mexican War automatically translated into a larger realm. The Confederate system, leadership, and strategic environment all contributed to its eventual defeat, something we will see as our story unfolds.[22]

WHEN THE WAR BEGAN, many military and political leaders on both sides failed to realize it would become as much an economic struggle as a military one. This crowd included Davis. The Confederate president, like many of his Southern brethren, placed great weight on the power of "King Cotton" and its allure to the European powers. Davis and his advisors regarded the fiber's pull as so strong that they could almost assume British and French recognition. The myth of King Cotton gripped Davis before the war began. In a February 1861 conversation, he insisted to a fellow railroad passenger that the South could achieve foreign recognition if it stopped the export of cotton for ninety days. His companion disagreed, whereupon Davis asked if the man would concur if it were six months. He still disagreed, telling Davis: "You must remember there is over one million of bales surplus now in the Liverpool warehouses." The president replied that therefore nine months would do it. The man countered that even that wouldn't suffice. "Well then," Davis said, "we'll give them twelve months—that must bring their affairs to a crisis."[23]

Faith in the power of cotton and the foreign necessity of obtaining it made the Confederacy's diplomatic and economic strategies inseparable. Inextricably entwined with the cotton issue was Davis's only significant foreign policy objective: recognition of the Confederacy. He believed economic and military support would follow, thus guaranteeing Confederate independence. Moreover, Davis believed that British recognition alone would discourage the North from prosecuting the war, and that the Union would withdraw from the fight from a fear of British intervention. Abroad, Davis and his diplomats built an image of a Confederacy fighting not for slavery but for freedom. The effort enjoyed some success in France and Britain before the Emancipation Proclamation.[24]

Like Davis, much of the Southern populace believed that foreign nations could not live without Southern "staples," meaning, of course, cotton. An unofficial embargo on cotton exports stemmed from this belief, much of it driven by local vigilance committees, or Committees of Public Safety, in Southern ports, though there were also supportive governors, such as Georgia's Joseph E. Brown.[25] The Confederate cabinet did not think an embargo the best means of influencing policy in European capitals, but it did nothing to hinder the movement.[26] Davis opposed the cotton embargo and kept Congress from making it law. The Confederate government purchased the fiber for export, as well as to lay a foundation for internal credit at home to enable the purchase of overseas supplies.[27] Officials such as Judah P. Benjamin stressed that the government had instituted no restrictions on exporting cotton, despite Union claims. Nonetheless, Davis never undertook any effort to make interference with the cotton trade illegal.[28]

The result of this chaotic policy on cotton was that the South failed to make effective use of its most valuable asset. The cotton crop of 1861 amounted to 4.5 million bales, worth $225 million in gold, almost ten times the value of all the gold in the South. Vice President Stephens proposed using $100 million in Confederate bonds to buy 2 million bales from both the 1860 and 1861 crops. They would then purchase fifty ironclad steamers to take the cotton to Europe, storing it until the price hit 50 cents per pound. He anticipated a profit of $800 million.[29]

This quixotic idea had a number of flaws, the most glaring being that there simply weren't 2 million bales remaining from the 1860 crop. By the end of May 1861, about 3.6 million bales had already been exported to New England and Europe. By the time the Confederate government was fully organized,

probably only a few hundred thousand remained. Moreover, getting the owners to part with the cotton for government bonds, obtaining Stephens's fifty
ships, and ensuring that the price of cotton climbed to 50 cents a pound when
all knew that 4 million bales sat in storage were insurmountable obstacles.
By the time the 1861 crop came in, the embargo and Union blockade were
in place. The cotton could not be generally exported, and regular commerce
had ceased.[30]

It took the Confederates until 1862 to realize that the Europeans were
not willing to enter the war merely to regain a supply of cotton.[31] After July 1,
1862, opposition to its export seems to have declined because its shipping vol-
ume increased.[32] The Davis government took control of cotton exports in the
war's third year and began to press them. Doing so sooner might have given
Confederate finance a surer footing.[33] Davis's administration never developed
a comprehensive policy for the use of cotton. One million bales were shipped
past the blockade, but another 2.5 million went up in smoke to keep them
out of Union hands. An unknown number were smuggled out, traded to the
enemy, or used by minor Confederate officials to meet government needs.[34]
Many others fell into Union possession and were sold.

In trying to use cotton as a tool of economic blackmail in exchange for recognition, the Confederates made a critical mistake. The impromptu embargo
actually had the opposite of its intended effect: it discouraged British entry
into the war.[35] No Parliament could stomach the humiliation of bowing to
what amounted to extortion. Moreover, politically, Britain found it beneficial
to comply with a blockade that initially was not particularly effective. This
could prove useful in a future conflict. And the British were dependent not
only upon Confederate cotton but also upon Union grain.[36] Davis's belief
in the lingering myth that King Cotton would encourage foreign intervention slowed Southern farmers' shift from cotton to food crops.[37] Clausewitz's
insistence that nations fight for political goals again proved correct.[38] Politics
trumps trade.

The right course would have been for the South to export its cotton as
quickly as possible, before the blockade became firmly established, thus raising money for the war effort. But this had its own set of problems. The South
lacked sufficient shipping and had to rely on foreign vessels coming to Confederate ports. This meant risking the blockade.[39]

Davis was correct in assuming that the lack of Southern cotton would
damage Britain's economy, particularly its textile industry. After British mills
exhausted their accumulated stocks, tens of thousands of workers were turned
out into the streets and reduced to poverty. The British government provided

public relief on a massive scale. Further support for the stricken came from across the British Empire, as well as from Haiti and Japan. In December 1863, 180,000 Britons were receiving relief. This number dropped to 130,000 by December 1864. In spite of this, there was no cry for Southern recognition or British intervention. The industrial laborers of Lancashire and other areas detested slavery.[40]

Other economic forces conspired to prevent British recognition and intervention. By 1863, cotton was flowing from Egypt, Brazil, India, and the West Indies, while British and French munitions makers, iron and steel firms, manufacturers of wool and linen products, and producers of many other items did brisk business in war-related matériel. An increasing percentage of seaborne trade moved to the British flag, and for a short time blockade running became "one of the most profitable businesses in the world," producing returns of up to 500 percent.[41]

Additionally, the working classes of Britain were not alone in loathing slavery. The growing British middle class also disdained it, and the Emancipation Proclamation brought that group firmly into the Union camp. The government, dominated by Lord Palmerston and John Russell, feared crossing this segment of the population, even with the advantage they enjoyed by virtue of the limitations on British suffrage, and in spite of their open sympathy for the South and its leaders. The French people also disliked slavery. Their favor fell on the North for that reason and also because they saw a strong American republic as a check on British power.[42]

Finally, Davis lessened the South's chances of gaining European intervention by appointing two poorly chosen representatives: William L. Yancey to London and Pierre A. Rost to Paris. Yancey, a prominent politician and one of secession's great "fire-eaters," was a rough, gruff character unsuited to London's diplomatic milieu. Rost lacked any prewar political fame, and his primary qualifications were French ancestry and a perceived mastery of French. The first made some influential Frenchmen wonder whether or not the South possessed native men of stature competent to represent its interests abroad, an impression no doubt confirmed by Rost's poor grasp of the Gallic tongue. The pair accomplished very little. No European government officer would see them officially, and they spent most of their time protesting the blockade. Later Confederate diplomatic representatives, such as former Democratic congressman John Slidell, proved more effective, but there was only so much they could do.[43]

ONE INCIDENT EARLY IN THE WAR raised Southern hopes of European intervention. On November 8, 1861, Captain Charles Wilkes of the Union

warship *San Jacinto* stopped the Royal Mail packet *Trent* and removed James
M. Mason and the aforementioned John Slidell, the recently named Confederate replacements for Yancey and Rost. The angry British ordered 14,000
men to Canada, prepared the fleet for war, and demanded an apology, as
well as the return of the prisoners. There is some suspicion that the two were
dispatched as agents provocateurs whose arrest would provoke war between
Britain and the Union. Their itinerary was widely publicized, and they had
mingled with the crew of the *San Jacinto* in Havana, glibly discussing their
intent. Lincoln replied with his famous "One war at a time" comment and
placated the British by releasing the prisoners. This defused the situation,
which was probably not as dangerous as many at the time believed. Britain
had very little to gain, and much to lose, by going to war with the Union.[44]

Though this raised Southern hopes of foreign intervention, it remained
little more than a "chimera," as historian Russell Weigley pointed out. Lee,
for one, held out no chance that the so-called *Trent* Affair would prove the
South's salvation, telling his wife not to count on war between the North and
Britain. He predicted that if the Union leaders had to choose between war
and freeing their captives, they would certainly let the men go. The South
would have to win its independence alone, and it was capable of doing so.
"But we must be patient," Lee wrote. "It is not a light achievement & cannot
be accomplished at once."[45]

Despite Southern hopes and Northern fears, only during a short period in
1862 was British and French intervention even a possibility. After this, Union
strength became increasingly apparent, and Union military forces had demonstrated progress. The French were keen to recognize the South—if the British
went first. But the British refused to lead. Indeed, after the summer of 1862,
even if the Europeans intervened, it was not likely that they could save the
South. It would have required the assumption of commitments the European
powers were unwilling to bear, while also threatening their possessions and
economic interests in the Western Hemisphere.[46] In the end, the decision to
intervene was a matter of clear cost-benefit analysis. The cost of intervention
was steep and promised little in return except for the chance to buy Southern
cotton. To Britain, the cost simply outweighed what it could possibly gain.

DESPITE CONFEDERATE PRESSURE, the North refused to abandon a
number of installations that Union troops held in parts of the South. Davis
insisted that the South wanted peace, which it did, but it also wanted control
of the entirety of the new Confederacy. The small concentrations of Northern
troops in places stretching from Texas to the Key West forts angered Davis,

as did a Union ship, *Star of the West*, trying to bring supplies to Fort Sumter. The continuing Union presence at Fort Sumter proved particularly galling, a thorn demanding removal.[47] The Confederate effort to win control over these Union outposts in the South turned secession into civil war.

Most Southerners cheered the Confederacy's bombardment of Fort Sumter on April 12, 1861, though not all believed it wise. Secretary of State Robert Toombs had warned of the consequences of firing on the fort, believing it would "inaugurate a civil war greater than any the world has yet seen.... You will wantonly strike a hornet's nest which extends from the mountains to the oceans, and legions now quiet will swarm out and sting us to death. It is unnecessary; it puts us in the wrong; it is fatal." Ralph Waldo Emerson wrote that "the attack on Fort Sumter crystallized the North into a unit and the hope of mankind was saved."[48]

Not only was Toombs correct regarding the effects of the bombardment, both immediate and long-term, he was also insightful regarding its futility. The South did not need to attack Sumter when it did, but its leaders believed they had no other choice. On April 6, Lincoln dispatched a messenger to inform South Carolina's governor, Francis W. Pickens, that the Union would resupply Fort Sumter but not try to "throw in" men and matériel. Fearing that a lack of action would "revive Southern Unionism," Davis, after consulting with his cabinet, decided the Federal presence had to go. Major Robert Anderson, the garrison's commander, refused the initial demand to surrender, but remarked that he only had food for a few more days. This sparked more communication between the administration and Brigadier General Pierre Gustave Toutant Beauregard, the Confederate military commander in Charleston. A Louisianan often referred to as the "Creole General," Beauregard was in his early forties, small, energetic, and vain. A subsequent Confederate request for the date of Anderson's capitulation followed, as well as an offer not to fire before then if the Union would take the same line. Anderson refused, realizing this would tie his hands in the event of the arrival of a relief expedition, but he committed to withdrawal by noon on April 15—unless he received new orders or more supplies. This didn't assure the Rebels, who worried about the very resupply possibility Anderson raised. On April 12, 1861, at four-thirty in the morning, the Confederate guns opened on Sumter. Allowing the post to surrender without a shot being fired would not have produced the dramatic effect upon the North Emerson described.[49]

Deciding *when* to begin a war is crucial. Launching a conflict too early can be as fatal as launching one too late. The South went to war too early. The Confederacy should have suffered the indignity of the Yankees holding on to a small piece of South Carolina for a bit longer, exported their cotton through blockade-free ports, and used the money to import the needed myriad of weapons and military supplies. The Confederacy acted impetuously when patience would have helped it more—and suffered for it. They brought upon themselves a war for which they were unprepared while emboldening a reluctant foe. They ignited a Northern *rage militaire* when waiting might have made secession a fait accompli.

Many see in the handling of the Fort Sumter imbroglio the first glimmers of Lincoln's genius. To support this some cite Lincoln's remarks to Gustavus V. Fox, who became the first assistant secretary of the navy, about their assessment that trying to resupply the garrison would be to the nation's benefit, even if it failed. Sending supplies to Sumter put the South in an awkward situation. In order to stop the delivery of provisions the Confederacy would have to fire on the boats ferrying supplies, thus making the South the aggressor. This is indeed probably what Lincoln expected to happen.[50]

The Confederates, though, chose to reduce the fort to prevent its resupply, taking the first bloody step in an even more violent and spectacular way. Davis insisted that he authorized the bombardment because he believed the Union intended to use the guns of both the fort and a supporting fleet against the Confederate besiegers. Part of Lincoln's response came in the form of his April 15 proclamation calling for 75,000 volunteers to enforce the laws of the United States. Davis considered this a declaration of war (he was basically right) and issued his own call for volunteers as well as for privateers. Davis dispatched three commissioners empowered to seek recognition from, and make treaties of friendship and trade with, Belgium, Great Britain, France, and Russia. Davis also wanted emissaries sent to the nations south of the Confederacy. In the wake of Lincoln's call for troops, four states in the upper South seceded and joined the Confederacy: Arkansas, North Carolina, Tennessee, and, most important, Virginia.[51]

On May 6, 1861, the Confederate Congress passed an act recognizing that a state of war existed between itself and the Union.[52] Though in many measures inferior to the North, the Confederacy still possessed a solid strategic position: it had clear control over nearly all of the territories of the secessionist states, a clearly defined government, and a significant and growing army. Its position was a historical anomaly, as rebels usually have to fight to establish control over territory and governmental structures.[53] The problem was, of course, that it had launched the war before it was strong enough to ensure that it could keep everything it held. It could not match its political ends with sufficient military means—and it never would. Significant as this was, it did not guarantee Confederate failure. The Union would have to uphold its end—or fail.

The United States during the Civil War. Adapted from Russell F. Weigley,
A Great Civil War: A Military and Political History, 1861–1865 (Bloomington:
Indiana University Press, 2000), xxx.

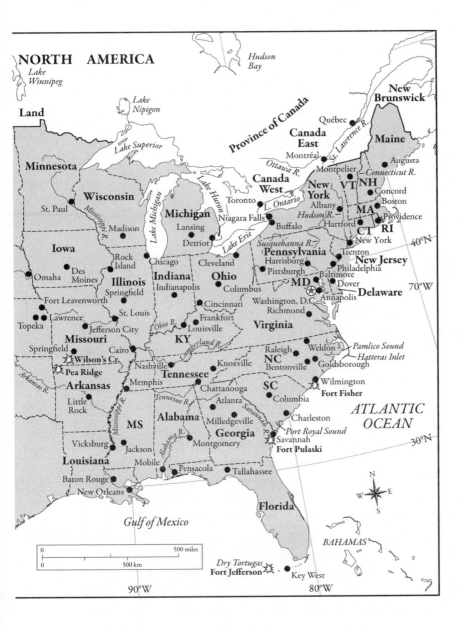

NORTH AMERICA

Lake
Winnipeg

Land

Minnesota

Wisconsin

St. Paul

Lake Nipigon

Lake Superior

Michigan

Lansing

Detroit

Iowa

Des Moines

Omaha

Rock Island

Chicago

Madison

Mississippi R.

Fort Leavenworth

Lawrence

Topeka

Springfield

Missouri

Jefferson City

St. Louis

Illinois

Indiana

Indianapolis

Springfield

Cincinnati

Ohio

Columbus

Cleveland

Frankfort

Louisville

KY

Cumberland R.

Hudson
Bay

Province of Canada

Québec

Canada
East

Montréal

St. Lawrence R.

Ottawa R.

Canada
West

Toronto

L. Ontario

Niagara Falls

Buffalo

Lake Erie

New
York

Albany

Hudson R.

Maine

Augusta

Connecticut R.

Montpelier

VT NH

Concord

Boston

MA

Hartford

Providence

CT RI

New York

New
Brunswick

40°N

Pennsylvania

Harrisburg

Pittsburgh

Susquehanna R.

Trenton

Philadelphia

Baltimore

MD

Dover

New Jersey

70°W

Delaware

Washington, D.C.

Annapolis

Richmond

Virginia

Ohio R.

Wilson's Cr.

Pea Ridge

Arkansas

Little Rock

Arkansas R.

Nashville

Tennessee

Memphis

Raleigh

NC

Bentonville

Weldon

Goldsborough

Pamlico Sound

Hatteras Inlet

Knoxville

Chattanooga

Tennessee R.

SC

Columbia

Wilmington

Fort Fisher

ATLANTIC
OCEAN

MS

Vicksburg

Jackson

Alabama

Alabama R.

Montgomery

Atlanta

Milledgeville

Georgia

Savannah R.

Charleston

Port Royal Sound

Savannah

Fort Pulaski

30°N

Louisiana

Baton Rouge

New Orleans

Mobile

Pensacola

Tallahassee

Florida

Gulf of Mexico

BAHAMAS

0   500 miles

0   500 km

Dry Tortugas

Fort Jefferson

Key West

90°W   80°W

3

Mr. Lincoln Goes to War

The war may last 10 years.
—ROBERT E. LEE, April 30, 1861

THE UNION HAD NO REAL STRATEGY when the war began. Lincoln quickly approached his professional military leaders for guidance, a decisive difference between him and Jefferson Davis. Even in the conflict's opening days, Lincoln was asking Winfield Scott what plans he had for winning the war. Lincoln always pondered how to achieve victory, and, as we will see, he was willing to do what was required. Davis, historian David Potter argued, "always thought in terms of what was right, rather than in terms of how to win." Lincoln tried to get his generals to figure out the path to victory. If they could not, he would try to figure it out for them. By contrast, "there is no evidence in all the literature that Davis ever at any one time gave extended consideration to the basic question of what the South would have to do in order to win the war."[1] This is perhaps the most important difference in how these men led.

On April 19, 1861, Lincoln instituted an element of Union strategy that endured throughout the course of the war: a blockade of southern ports. Initially, the blockade affected only South Carolina, Georgia, Florida, Louisiana, Mississippi, and Alabama. Later, as secession expanded, Lincoln included Virginia and North Carolina. In August, he forbade trade with the rebellious states.[2]

Lincoln expressed his first ideas on prosecuting the war on April 25, 1861. He would bolster Fort Monroe in eastern Virginia, blockade Southern ports, secure Washington, D.C., and then "go down to Charleston and pay her the little debt we are owing her."[3] This plan only applied to one theater, and historian T. Harry Williams speculated, probably correctly, that "at this stage Lincoln apparently did not envision operations in the Mississippi Valley."[4] The fact that Lincoln's plan intended to strike Charleston, the perceived heart of secession (if not its head), strengthens Williams's assessment.

Lincoln, though, does not appear to have been suffering from the disorder afflicting most of the civilian and military leaders on both sides: an inability to look beyond what today would be defined as the operational level of war.

In the Civil War, as in many conflicts pre-dating World War I, the method of differentiating the levels of war—tactical, operational, and strategic—did not exist in the manner in which we understand this today. Most leaders looked only at the prospective battle (tactical issues), not at how each individual engagement fit into a campaign (the operational level of war) and then at how this related to the nation's military strategy. Few could envisage an extended campaign (or operation), and almost none could see beyond their theater.[5] Their education had not prepared Civil War officers to think strategically.[6] Modern wars, of which the Civil War was arguably the first, because of the depth of resources and manpower brought to bear, require broader vision to prosecute successfully. Lincoln would sometimes fall victim to this same flawed thinking, but he threw off the shackles and encouraged his subordinates to do the same.

Lincoln was not the only Union leader trying to determine how to win the war, though he was undoubtedly among the first. On April 27, 1861, Major General George B. McClellan sent a letter from his headquarters in Ohio to Winfield Scott containing two plans for securing Union victory. "Communications with Washington being so difficult," he wrote, "I beg to lay before you some views relative to this region of country, & to propose for your consideration a plan of operations intended to relieve the pressure upon Washington, & tending to bring the war to a speedy close." The first plan involved securing Cairo, Illinois, and then crossing "the Ohio at or in the vicinity of Gallipolis and move up the valley of the Great Kanawha on Richmond." McClellan believed that a detachment in Gallipolis and a "prompt movement" on Louisville or the heights opposite Cincinnati would hamstring Kentucky. "The movement on Richmond should be conducted with the utmost promptness, and could not fail to relieve Washington as well as to secure the destruction of the Southern Army, if aided by a decided advance on the eastern line."[7]

If this proved impractical—because Kentucky abandoned its neutrality— McClellan suggested crossing the Ohio at Cincinnati or Louisville with 80,000 men, marching straight on Nashville, and "thence act according to circumstances." If the Union forces broke the military strength of Kentucky and Tennessee, they could push on to Montgomery, supported by eastern action against Charleston and Augusta. This would then permit Union drives against New Orleans, Mobile, and Pensacola.[8] As we will see, some of this resurfaced in McClellan's later plans.

General Scott forwarded McClellan's plans to Lincoln, pointing out that they could not be fulfilled before the expiration of the three-month terms of enlistment of the available men. "Second," Scott noted, "a march upon Richmond from the Ohio would probably insure the revolt of Western Virginia, which if left alone will soon be five out of seven for the Union." Scott believed McClellan was ignoring the possible use of the Ohio and Mississippi rivers "in favor of long, tedious, and break-down (of men, horses, and wagons) marches." Last, Scott argued that the plan offered a "piece-meal" approach rather than an enveloping one—"a cordon of posts on the Mississippi to its mouth from its junction with the Ohio, and by blockading ships of war on the seaboard."[9]

Scott replied with his own plan for prosecuting the war, one his previous reply foreshadowed, and one that, when its contents became known, the Union press derisively dubbed "Anaconda." The foundational element of Scott's "Great Snake" was a blockade of Confederate ports on the Atlantic and Gulf coasts. Tied to this would be the movement of 60,000 well-trained men down the Mississippi River. Supported by navy gunboats, they were to conquer their way to New Orleans, establishing secure posts along the way, and clearing the river for Union use. This combination of actions would "envelop the insurgent States and bring them to terms with less bloodshed than by any other plan."[10]

Scott provided a framework for the Union's war, but one based upon the false assumption that a great well of Union sentiment in the South only needed to be tapped. He believed that the North should not undertake an invasion of the South because this would provide unwanted impetus to anti-Union sentiment. Scott was not completely wrong: there were areas of the Confederacy with pro-Union feeling, but none had the depth necessary to provide a base for a Southern counterrevolution. T. Harry Williams brands Scott's plan "more a diplomatic policy than a plan of strategic action," while his fellow historian Archer Jones deems it a "political strategy," but they misunderstand. Scott's Anaconda was a military strategy; it counted upon military power to deliver the Union's objective.[11]

Lincoln did not adopt the Anaconda Plan. He sought a quicker end to the war. He also believed that victory would require more than a single operational drive down the Mississippi. Scott's proposal *did* provide grist for the mill of Lincoln's evolving thoughts on the prosecution of the struggle, particularly the importance of the Mississippi River.[12] It failed, though, to address the politically touchy, and as yet unresolved, status of the border states, something weighing heavily on Lincoln's mind.

But to suppress the rebellion the Union needed a large army. Initially the new Federal army arose from the individual states, which usually supplied much of the equipment as well. A way to encourage recruitment was to give military positions to popular political figures, such as those who became known as "War Democrats"—members of the Democratic Party, including Benjamin Butler and John A. McClernand, who had opposed Lincoln but supported the Union. Another reason Lincoln employed them was to avoid the partisan rancor that had distracted President James K. Polk during the Mexican War (Lincoln had been a part of the antiwar campaign). Both sides also appointed popular border states political leaders as military commanders in order to garner support in these regions.[13]

To fight the war, Lincoln needed a government as well as an army. One of the key figures we have already met: William H. Seward, the secretary of state. A former governor and senator from New York known for his antislavery stand, he would later become most famous for "Seward's Folly," the purchase of Alaska from Russia in 1867. So dedicated was Seward to preserving the Union that in April 1861 he advocated a foreign war as a means of bringing back the Confederate states. Lincoln rebuffed his overly ambitious secretary of state, and Seward's primary task became keeping Europeans out of the war.[14]

Seward started out overly bellicose but soon developed a fine diplomatic hand, as reflected in his handling of the *Trent* Affair. He also knew when to take a hard line and did not shy away from blunt talk. He assured the British and French that, if provoked, the United States government would not hesitate to prosecute a war against them if it deemed it necessary to preserving the Union. Interference in the struggle meant war. His stance achieved the desired effect. Seward also assured the Europeans that the Union wanted nothing but good relations with them.[15]

IN COMPOSING HIS PLAN for the war, Scott revealed to McClellan his great fear of "the impatience of our patriotic and loyal Union friends" who "will urge instant and vigorous action" before Union forces were properly trained and before autumn returned to kill the Mississippi River Valley's fevers.[16] In some respects, Scott proved correct. The Union papers cried, "On to Richmond!" and public pressure for action mounted. This did not produce the North's first advance, and when it did take place, it did not come down the Mississippi. Lincoln forced Scott to mount an offensive aimed at Manassas, Virginia, because he considered it militarily feasible.[17] Lincoln also wanted a quick war.[18] In his July 4, 1861, address to a joint session of Congress, one laying out the Union's legal arguments for war and the military actions Lincoln had taken while Congress was not in session, Lincoln asked for "the legal means for making this contest a short, and a decisive one." He also needed the physical means: $400 million and "at least" 400,000 more troops.[19]

Major General Robert Patterson commanded the Union forces operating against the Confederates in the Shenandoah. An elderly Pennsylvania militia officer and veteran of the War of 1812 and the Mexican War, Patterson was not known for speed; his troops branded him "Granny." Brigadier General Irvin McDowell led the main Union force. McDowell was a West Point graduate, a professional army officer, and a friend of William T. Sherman. Later he acquired a reputation as a trencherman due to his prodigious feats at the dinner table, which left little time for conversation and convinced many of his fellow officers that he was no leader. The troops in the ranks, for reasons unknown, unfairly branded him a traitor. McDowell took to wearing a self-designed summer hat resembling a coal scuttle. The men attributed a malevolent purpose to its easily recognizable distinctiveness. But these things lay in the future. In July 1861, McDowell still had the chance to make a good reputation for himself, though, like most of his contemporaries, he had never commanded any significant body of troops and never in battle.[20]

When the Union forces began their advance in July 1861, the Confederates had two armies in northern Virginia. Facing Patterson's Federals at the mouth of the Shenandoah Valley were 12,000 men under Major General Joseph Eggleston Johnston. Joe Johnston possessed a tremendous amount of military experience. After finishing at West Point in 1829, he saw service against the Black Hawks and then in the Seminole War, where he was wounded twice. Distinguished action in the Mexican War followed: Johnston commanded the key companies in the assault on Chapultepec in September 1847, "the decisive engagement of the war," and was wounded an astounding five times. The other Confederate force was led by Beauregard, recently arrived from Charleston. (Beauregard, incidentally, had been with Johnston at Chapultepec.)[21]

McDowell composed the Union operational plan, which consisted of Patterson's men pinning the Confederate forces at the mouth of the Shenandoah Valley while McDowell simultaneously met the roughly 20,000 Confederates at Manassas with 30,000 Union troops and defeated them. He also counted on Benjamin Butler, who commanded at Fortress Monroe, to keep his Rebel opposition from joining their brethren. McDowell wrote: "The objective point of our plan is Manassas Junction."[22]

Scott opposed the offensive, branding it "war by piecemeal." He insisted that "bloodshed would stop the rise of Union sentiment in the South" and instructed McDowell to resist launching the offensive.[23] McDowell had his own concerns. At a White House meeting in late June he insisted that he could not defeat the forces of both Beauregard and Johnston. He also believed that his column and Patterson's were too distant to support each other.[24]

The South's countermove to a Union advance had come up in Confederate correspondence the month before the battle. Beauregard, in the face of what he believed was a Union thrust against Harpers Ferry, insisted that the South needed to concentrate its forces in Virginia, and he presented Davis with a pair of convoluted plans based upon when, and whether, Beauregard could unite with Johnston. One of these included Johnston's army retreating on foot and concentrating for an attack against the enemy to defeat his advancing columns.[25] Davis replied that he hoped to reinforce Beauregard's force, bringing it up to the 35,000 men Beauregard believed necessary to take the offensive. He also said that if any of the Confederates' "forward elements" (Johnston's) had to move, it made much more sense for these forces to use the railroad.[26]

In mid-July, Patterson's movements altered the Confederacy's thinking on its deployments in Virginia. They worried Johnston, who had warned Davis that a retreat would have injurious effects. Davis replied that the "evil consequences" of such an event could be repaired only by "a vigorous attack" against the Union that "would drive them across the Potomac & by threatening the Capitol…compel the withdrawal of Patterson." But he doubted the success of such an operation, and feared that its failure would result in the enemy occupying the Shenandoah Valley and cutting the lines of communication between the Confederate army and Richmond.[27]

Despite objections from the Union generals, the campaign went ahead. As Scott expected, Patterson made no energetic moves and failed to pin Johnston's army. The Confederates discovered McDowell's advance on July 16, and Patterson's hesitation enabled the South to utilize its railroads and the telegraph to unite Johnston's forces with Beauregard's, as well as a third force under Theophilus Holmes, and meet McDowell with superior numbers.[28]

In the midst of the movement, McClellan, commanding troops in western Virginia, wired Scott. He did not know his commander's plans but offered to move on Staunton, Virginia, to support the Union operation.[29] Scott found this admirable.[30] McClellan, though, lost his three-month enlistees within a few days, leaving him with insufficient manpower for any significant act.[31] McDowell, meanwhile, was losing what became known as the Battle of First Manassas, or First Bull Run.

The contest took place at Bull Run Creek on July 21. Johnston arrived at Beauregard's command at noon on the twentieth and told his colleague that he expected Patterson to join with the main Union force by the twenty-second at the latest. They decided to attack before the enemy could link its forces and drew up a plan to do so. But McDowell's advance on the twenty-first contributed to the plan's abandonment.[32] The battle, fought with unskilled and partially trained troops on both sides, produced a Confederate victory. Davis appeared on the field during the last stages of the contest. He had wanted to come the day before, but his speech at the opening of the Confederate Congress had delayed his departure. Johnston noted later that "victory disorganized our volunteers as utterly as a defeat." The lack of discipline in the Confederate force meant it required several days to reassemble the units in action.[33] Pursuit of the fleeing enemy was impossible. Such became a common result of Civil War battles. In the wake of the battle, a stalemate ensued in the eastern theater that lasted until the spring of 1862.[34]

After the battle, Davis failed to give proper credit to Johnston and Beauregard for their success, and a poor working relationship between Davis and these two generals soon became the norm. Davis had clashed with Beauregard even before First Bull Run, the Confederate president having refused to approve any of Beauregard's high-flown daydreams for invading the North. Beauregard and his staff became openly critical of Davis, Beauregard believing his genius trumped all. Their relationship completely collapsed in the battle's aftermath. Davis's quarrel with Johnston was based on Johnston's resentment at the president placing him beneath three other Confederate generals in terms of seniority—this despite the fact that Johnston had held higher rank in the prewar army. A man prickly in regard to his reputation, Johnston couldn't bear such a perceived insult.[35]

Davis, though, did buy into another daydream in the summer of 1861, but it was one that cost the Confederacy very little to indulge. On July 8 a note went out to Henry Hopkins Sibley approving his ambitious scheme for a strategic offensive (albeit a weak one). Sibley, a West Point graduate, had served for many years in the West before offering his services to the Confederacy. Sibley had big ideas: he aimed to take California and everything in between. "On to San Francisco," Sibley hoped. Davis gave him nothing but permission—he had nothing else to give—and sent him on his way. After raising troops in Texas, Sibley joined the forces of John R. Baylor, who had already led Confederate forces into the New Mexico and Arizona Territories. Sibley's expedition, which didn't begin until February 7, 1862, was plagued by Sibley's drinking, his incompetence (particularly in regard to logistics), and enemy action. Marching from El Paso, Texas, with 3,500 men, Sibley, despite Union resistance, took Santa Fe, New Mexico, on March 4. At the end of the month, though, oncoming Federal troops destroyed eighty wagons of Sibley's supply train. The Confederates had no choice but to withdraw. The hungry retreat began on April 12. Half of Sibley's men didn't return with him, and the South never mounted another campaign for this inhospitable realm.[36]

THE RESULT OF BULL RUN provoked Lincoln into composing another plan for fighting the war. He ordered the rapid intensification of the blockade, the training of the forces under Benjamin Butler in the vicinity of Fort Monroe, and the securing of Baltimore. He also called for rebuilding the units defeated at Manassas, reinforcing the troops at Harpers Ferry, and getting rid of the "three-month men" as quickly as possible. Forces were gathered around the District of Columbia, and operations were launched in Missouri by John Charles Frémont and in western Virginia by McClellan. Lincoln also entered into the operational realm: when the army was reorganized he wanted the establishment of secure railroad lines between Washington and Manassas and from Harpers Ferry to Strasburg, Virginia, "the military men to find the way of doing these." "This done," he wanted "a joint movement from Cairo on Memphis; and from Cincinnati on East Tennessee."[37]

Here was Lincoln the maturing strategist. He was beginning to see the broad sweep of the war, not just defaulting to a single campaign against Richmond or down the Mississippi. He established strategic goals— blockades, securing Union possessions—as well as operational objectives, and envisioned campaigns in the East and West. Moreover, we also see something else that became characteristic of Lincoln's leadership, at least until the appointment of Ulysses S. Grant as general in chief. Lincoln designated the objectives but advised "the military men to find the way" of reaching them. The president was establishing separate spheres of responsibility for civilian and military leaders while simultaneously blurring them as he began partially assuming the de facto mantle of general in chief. He muddied the line between the strategic and operational realms, but this is often unavoidable. The role that Lincoln was carving out for the presidency in military affairs, though, soon would be challenged.

4

The Border States

POLICY, STRATEGY, AND CIVIL-MILITARY RELATIONS

*I think to lose Kentucky is nearly the same as to lose
the whole game.*
—ABRAHAM LINCOLN, September 22, 1861

CRITICAL TO THE SUCCESSFUL PROSECUTION of any war is separation of
power between the military and political realms. The military and the government each have distinctive roles to play to ensure that the war is waged
efficiently, effectively, and at the least cost. If the government fails to lay out
clear policy objectives, or clear rules determining when and where military
commanders may act, the war may develop in unwanted ways. If military
leaders exceed their responsibility and begin to make policy decisions, they
can unnecessarily widen a conflict. How Union and Confederate military and
political leaders dealt with the border states in the opening year of the Civil
War provides a clear picture of the problems caused by weak and indecisive
government oversight, generals overstepping their bounds, military leaders
not understanding their larger roles, and political leaders failing to exercise
their authority.

THE BORDER STATES—Missouri, Kentucky, Maryland, and Delaware, all
slave states—did not secede in the immediate wake of Fort Sumter's bombardment and Lincoln's call to arms. They all had residents eager to carry
their states into the Confederacy as well as many who favored the Union.
Where they fell out bore important consequences. Winning over Missouri,
Kentucky, and Maryland "would have added 45 percent to the white population and military manpower of the Confederacy" and increased its industry
by 80 percent.[1] This might have proven decisive.

More was at stake than men and matériel. Missouri joining the South
would give the Confederacy the crucial city of St. Louis and potentially fed
pro-Southern sentiment in the region around Cairo, Illinois. Gaining Kentucky would establish a defensible Confederate frontier on the Ohio River
and thwart Union use of the Tennessee and Cumberland rivers, two great
highways into the South.[2] A neutral Kentucky provided a valuable Southern

buffer against Union invasion. Federal forces could still move down the Mississippi—and indeed, Lincoln intended this—but this would be more difficult with an uncooperative enemy controlling its banks. Delaware, the smallest of the slave states, with only 1,800 slaves, never seriously envisaged secession; its legislature condemned it.[3]

Davis believed that the North's desire to win over the border states restrained them from attacking, as doing so would kill support in these critical areas. Indeed, he thought it advantageous to create a situation in which the North would be forced to move against the South. But he also wrote that when the Confederacy was ready to remove the Union garrisons from Southern territory, this would outweigh other considerations—remarks clearly betraying his belief that the border states were "Southern territory."[4]

Some in the border states favored an "armed neutrality" designed to exclude Union troops. In his July 4, 1861, address to a joint session of Congress, Lincoln battered this camp: "Figuratively speaking, it would be the building of an impassable wall along the line of separation. And yet, not quite an impassable one; for, under the guise of neutrality, it would tie the hands of the Union men, and freely pass supplies from among them, to the insurrectionists, which it could not do as an open enemy."[5]

Nonetheless, Lincoln exercised restraint in regard to border state neutrality. This proved especially true in the case of Kentucky, the linchpin of his border states policy. "I think to lose Kentucky is nearly the same as to lose the whole game," he wrote. "Kentucky gone, we can not hold Missouri, nor, as I think, Maryland. These all against us, and the job on our hands is too large for us. We would as well consent to separation at once, including the surrender of this capitol."[6] Sorting out Kentucky would test both Lincoln and Davis, but events drove them to deal first with the other border states.

MARYLAND EXHIBITED SUBSTANTIAL secessionist enthusiasm, many in the state identifying with Virginia. During the crisis in the spring of 1861, Thomas Hicks, Maryland's governor, prevented a secession vote simply by refusing to summon the legislature to sit. Lincoln moved troops into Maryland to ensure it remained loyal. When they did meet in May, the lawmakers urged not secession but neutrality.[7]

Davis certainly hoped Maryland would join the Confederacy.[8] In fact, he believed it *was* part of the Confederacy. "The border State of Maryland was the outpost of the Southern frontier first to be approached by Northern invasion," he wrote. Davis even received a request from Marylanders for an "army of liberation." He declined. "I am restrained by principles of high political necessity from sending an army into Maryland," he replied, "or invading or violating the sovereignty of her soil."[9] A year later, when Lee wanted to go into Maryland, Davis proved less squeamish.

Because the Confederacy did not interfere, Lincoln's dispatch of troops kept Maryland in the Union. This was critical. Maryland's secession, combined with that of Virginia, would have isolated Washington, forcing the government's evacuation.[10] One could even argue that keeping Maryland saved the Union, or at least helped lay the foundation for saving it. Robbed of its national capital, and with its prestige shattered, would Lincoln's fledgling government have been able to overcome the appeasement sentiments of many in the North? Perhaps not. Holding Maryland may have been the first step on the path to Union victory.

EVEN BEFORE HE ISSUED his July 23 memorandum on fighting the war, Lincoln took action to ensure the conflict's prosecution in the West. On July 1, 1861, he created the Department of the West, which began in Illinois, crossed the Mississippi River, and stretched to the Rockies. On July 3 he named John C. Frémont a major general and put him in charge. Frémont owed his position to prewar fame won as the "Pathfinder"—for exploring the West and being part of the Mexican War conquest of California—and to political realities. Important factions—the Republican Party's antislavery branch, German Americans, the politically powerful Blair family—all wanted Frémont, and he wanted the job.[11]

Scott and Lincoln agreed that Frémont should raise an army and, when he felt secure enough, push down the Mississippi, aiming at Memphis. Lincoln gave Frémont a free hand in his command, leeway the general took too far.[12] He didn't understand the difference between military strategy and political policy, nor their interconnectedness, nor the president's prerogative in the construction of the latter. His authority extended to military measures, not those that contravened the president's policies. Lincoln would be forced to educate him on this.

Frémont took up his command in St. Louis on July 25, 1861.[13] He inherited a mess. Having been hip deep in Kansas's pre–Civil War civil war, Missouri had suffered severe sectional violence even before the secession crisis. Davis, for his part, feared for Missouri as he did for Kentucky.[14] In the wake of the election in February 1861 of an overwhelmingly pro-Union convention, both sides began hurriedly forming military units. The Confederates rallied around Governor Claiborne F. Jackson and former Missouri governor and Mexican War veteran Sterling Price, the Unionists around Republican congressman Francis Blair Jr., brother of Lincoln's postmaster general, and army captain Nathaniel Lyon. Lyon's forces struck first. The Confederate response included launching a guerrilla struggle, which its leaders believed would have an effect beyond Missouri's borders by bringing Kentucky into the Confederacy while providing a valuable diversion for Rebel forces in Virginia. A short truce was arranged, one soon undermined by Blair. Open warfare combined with the guerrilla operations, and Union forces suffered defeat near Springfield on August 10. Later, on October 31, 1861, Governor Jackson and a "rump" legislature carried Missouri out of the Union.[15] Frémont's appointment appeared to be Lincoln's effort to reassert control over Union policy and strategy in Missouri. But the job quickly became too much for Frémont. He did little to improve the Union position in the state, and his managerial incompetence quickly alienated the general's former supporters. Worse, he began making policy.[16]

On August 30, 1861, Frémont issued a proclamation in an effort to address the many problems in his area of command. One provision caused a stir: "The property, real and personal, of all persons in the State of Missouri who shall take up arms against the United States, or who shall be directly proven to have taken an active part with their enemies in the field, is declared to be confiscated to the public use, and their slaves, if any they have, are hereby declared freemen."[17]

Those last ten words brought down upon Frémont the presidential hammer, though initially it was velvet-wrapped. Frémont's war measure had crossed the line from a military matter to a political one, and Lincoln, though he did not initially order a reversal, resolved to rein in his general. Lincoln and Scott feared the proclamation's negative effect on the work of Union loyalists in Kentucky, whom the administration had "pretty successfully coaxed along...to keep their state loyal."[18] Lincoln immediately sent a special messenger to alert Frémont to the fact that his promise to confiscate and free slaves would undermine Southern Unionist support in Kentucky, possibly even pushing the state into the Confederacy's arms. He asked the general to reverse himself and issue a new proclamation on confiscating property used to support the rebellion that aligned with a congressional measure, which Lincoln enclosed.[19]

Frémont replied that he would retract the offending part, but only if ordered. Doing so under any other terms would imply that he thought he was wrong, and he did not. He insisted that taking the slaves was necessary. "This," he said, "is as much a movement in the war as a battle."[20] Indeed, in little more than a year, Lincoln would agree, but not yet. For now, the issue was too sensitive politically. Lincoln wasted no time. He ordered Frémont to rescind the part of his proclamation regarding the seizure of slaves.[21]

Frémont's act is partially explained by his having been a member of the Republican Party's Radical section, which wanted abolition made a goal of the war. Indeed, to them, it already was. But it was Lincoln who made policy, not his generals, not wings of his own party, nor even members of his cabinet. Making the war about abolition would upset his delicate dance with the border states, particularly Kentucky. Lincoln refused to let this happen. Eventually, as an army and theater commander, Frémont proved beyond his depth. Lincoln relieved him in November.[22]

Lincoln assigned Major General David Hunter to succeed him, and sent along his ideas on what Hunter should do. Since the Confederates under Sterling Price were withdrawing from Missouri and controlled only a part of the state, Lincoln suggested that Hunter give up the chase, dividing his main force into two "corps of observation" based at Sedalia and Rolla, at the ends of the railroad lines. Pushing any farther would needlessly overextend the Union forces. If pressed, these units could easily unite with the Union troops in Kansas and repel the enemy. More important, once they secured their positions, Hunter could take troops out of Missouri and use them on other fields. Both Scott and McClellan gave their approval.[23] Lincoln was learning.

THE LINCOLN ADMINISTRATION came under pressure in late May 1861 from a trio of western governors to seize various vital points in Kentucky. Colonel Robert Anderson, of Fort Sumter fame, had already been named head of the Department of Kentucky, and McClellan in Ohio had earlier received orders to provide military aid to Union men in the state. He had been given the freedom to take Columbus (Kentucky) if he desired, but had heeded the advice of pro-Union Kentuckians that doing so would likely drive the state into the Confederate camp. Scott disagreed with others who pushed for Memphis's seizure, believing it premature, and stuck to his earlier strategy of restraint.[24]

The lack of Unionist restraint had contributed to the eruption of civil war in Missouri; Lincoln insisted things go differently in Kentucky. When the Bluegrass State declared its neutrality, Lincoln adopted a wait-and-see approach. He refused to concede the state's right to neutrality, but he did agree to observe it. As we've seen, Lincoln considered possession of Kentucky "the whole game," critical to eventual Union success because of its position along the Ohio and Mississippi rivers, as well as the possible influence it might exert on the other border states. Also, Lincoln saw a chance to test the Union's strategy of reconciliation toward the South. If the North made no aggressive moves, suppressed Southern Unionism might have time to revive. Patience was Lincoln's watchword. In June 1861, the state's congressional elections rewarded him by producing Unionists "in nine of Kentucky's ten districts."[25]

In August, Beriah Magoffin, Kentucky's governor, wrote Davis about Kentucky's declared neutrality, requesting that the Confederacy respect the wishes of the state's residents. Several things motivated him: anxiety over the raising of a Union unit in the state (one he asked the North to remove), the possible Confederate reaction, and fears about Confederate forces on the state's frontier. He sought to reassure residents by obtaining Davis's promise that the Confederacy would observe Kentucky's neutrality.[26] Davis agreed—as long as Kentucky followed a truly neutral course. He reserved the right to act in self-defense.[27]

As Davis struggled to assuage Kentuckians' fears, his generals plotted the state's invasion. On the same day Davis penned his reply to Magoffin, Brigadier General Gideon J. Pillow insisted that the time had come for Confederate forces to occupy Columbus, Kentucky. Pillow, then with his forces at New Madrid, Missouri, held a fortified position that he not only found untenable but believed would not block a Union descent down the Mississippi River. Leonidas K. Polk, Pillow's superior, an Episcopal bishop and an old friend of Davis's, held Fort Pillow (named for the general), the best Confederate emplacement south of Columbus. But Pillow, his gaze fixed upon Columbus, had already established positions at Union City, Missouri, in preparation for an attack. Convinced of Northern preparations to seize the town, Pillow urged Polk to act. The South had to have Columbus immediately in order to prevent the Union from taking it, Pillow insisted. "If we do not move now," he wrote, unencumbered by any facts, "we never can." He branded it "a *paramount military necessity*."[28]

Polk needed no convincing. He wrote Magoffin on September 1, 1861: "I think it of the greatest consequence to the Southern cause in Kentucky or elsewhere that I should be ahead of the enemy in occupying Columbus and Paducah."[29] On the night of September 3, Pillow's troops landed at Hickman, Kentucky, south of Columbus, because Union guns on the western side of the river prevented a more direct approach.[30] Governor Isham Harris of Tennessee was not pleased, especially since both Harris and Davis had promised to respect Kentucky's neutrality. Harris hoped for a quick Confederate withdrawal, unless the move had been absolutely necessary.[31] It was not, but Polk insisted that it was, as well as that he had never received any word about Confederate policy regarding Kentucky.[32] Later, Davis said that the Confederates had gone into Kentucky to take key strategic points because the Union was about to invade. He called it a self-defense measure and something done from "a desire to aid the people of Kentucky."[33]

Acting under Davis's direction, Confederate secretary of war Leroy Pope Walker ordered Polk's withdrawal on September 4 and asked Governor Harris to assure Magoffin that Pillow's move had been unauthorized and the troops ordered out. Meanwhile, writing to his old friend Davis, Polk underscored the correctness of his actions on the grounds of military expediency. The Confederate president replied: "The necessity justifies the action."[34] Davis was pressured by prominent Kentuckians and Tennesseans to reverse his withdrawal decision. He made the offer, as did Polk, Davis admitting the possibility if it could be done safely, and Polk wanting guarantees of simultaneous Northern withdrawal and subsequent noninvolvement.[35]

Compounding the disaster was that Polk, so desperate to move into Kentucky to gain a tactical advantage, failed to do even this. He took Columbus but hesitated to do much else. Opposing Polk were the troops of an unknown general named Ulysses Simpson Grant. Sam, as Grant was known to his friends, was in many ways typical of the generals of both sides. He had attended West Point and served with distinction in the Mexican War. After the war, the loneliness and boredom of army life, exacerbated by the fact that his pay wasn't enough to allow his family to live with him, led to his resignation in 1854. Grant's next seven years were marked by a succession of business failures. He tried farming but made so little money that he was reduced to hauling firewood; once he pawned his watch to buy Christmas presents for his wife and children. He went broke in 1858 and then entered into a real estate firm in St. Louis selling homes and doing what today we would call property management. This lasted nine months. The outbreak of the war found him an unenthusiastic clerk in his father's leather goods business in Galena, Illinois. He was thirty-eight years old. He was also in possession of what had just become a very marketable commodity: professional military experience. He was soon wearing a star.[36]

Grant may have not been much of a businessman, but he very well understood a military opportunity when he saw one, and moved on Paducah, Kentucky.[37] The loss of this city made Polk's Columbus position untenable the moment Union forces decided to advance; it also neutralized the benefits Pillow had hoped to achieve for the South through Columbus's seizure.[38]

The Kentucky legislature and governor ordered the removal of all Confederate forces from the state. Albert Sidney Johnston, another of Davis's old friends, newly appointed to command Confederate forces in the West, asserted the impossibility of the withdrawal of Polk's troops (as well as others that had moved into the eastern part of the state under Felix Zollicoffer), contending that doing so would make Tennessee vulnerable to invasion. He expanded the Confederate occupation by ordering 5,000 of Polk's men to occupy Bowling Green, calling it "an act of self-defense, rendered necessary by the action of the government of Kentucky and by the evidences of intended movements of the Federal forces."[39] Johnston extended the Confederate cordon north into Kentucky, but even before his men marched on Bowling Green, Johnston warned Davis of the vulnerability of the Confederate position in the West, writing that "we have not over half the armed forces that are now likely to be required for our security against disaster. I feel assured that I can command the requisite number of men, but we are deficient in arms."[40]

In the end, Davis sided with Polk. "It is true that the solution of the problem requires the consideration of other than the military elements involved in it," he wrote, "but we cannot permit the indeterminate quantities, the political elements, to control our action in cases of military necessity. Such I regarded your occupation of Columbus to be."[41] In the case of Kentucky, Davis put the military cart before the political horse, ignoring that "political elements" are a part of war and that a conflict, effectively waged, is governed by political policy and necessities. Moreover, Davis allowed a general, Polk, to decide policy and invade the purview of a nation's leader. The result: Rebel impetuosity and lack of firm direction from the top broadened the war to a theater the South could not adequately defend. Having Kentucky remain a buffer between itself and the North would have been the best that the Confederacy could have hoped for. Lincoln had no immediate intention of invading the state, and its continued neutrality would have secured Tennessee against any Union moves except those launched down the Mississippi or through the inhospitable regions of Missouri.

Invading Kentucky proved a cataclysmic strategic mistake nearly comparable to bombarding Fort Sumter. The state declared for the Union, vindicating Lincoln's prudence.[42] Polk's blunder undermined the South's position and opened numerous pathways for Union invasion. It eased strikes down the Mississippi or overland and opened the door to the Tennessee and Cumberland rivers, waterways penetrating deep into the southern interior. The Confederates needed to forestall Union offensive action as long as possible so they could gather strength. Waiting, while preparing a riposte to a Union invasion, would have done this. On November 6, 1861, Polk offered his resignation. Davis refused.[43] He should have accepted it.

5

McClellan on Top

UNION STRATEGY, JULY 1861–OCTOBER 1861

I can do it all.

—GEORGE B. MCCLELLAN

*We have no news in the army way.... we scarcely know that
we are at war.*

—JUDAH P. BENJAMIN

TO SAY THAT GEORGE B. MCCLELLAN was an enigma is a great under-
statement. In the nearly century and a half since he held sway over the Union
army, his personality and actions have inspired hatred and adoration—mostly
the former. Biographies include hagiographies, ad hominem attacks, and
everything in between. The primary foci of McClellan study have been his
military campaigns, especially that on the Peninsula and the one culminating
in the Battle of Antietam.[1] But something critical has received short shrift:
McClellan the strategist.[2]

It is not often that a former child prodigy ends up as the general in chief of
a nation's army, but in the case of McClellan, that is exactly what happened. He
matriculated at the University of Pennsylvania at thirteen; two years later, despite
being below the minimum age, he entered West Point. He graduated second in
the class of 1846, a group that included George Pickett and Thomas J. "Stonewall"
Jackson. In the Mexican War, McClellan won three brevet promotions for bravery. In 1855, the secretary of war, Jefferson Davis, included McClellan among the
three officers dispatched on a European tour of military installations, one that
included an inspection of Crimean War battlefields. McClellan acquired a good
reputation both inside and outside the army, so good that the Illinois Central
Railroad hired him as its chief engineer. Within a year, he was vice president of
the railroad. A year after that, he left to become president of the Ohio and Mississippi Railroad's Eastern Division. McClellan returned to the army in 1861 and
rose rocket-like through the ranks. When the Confederates bombarded Fort
Sumter, he was a civilian. Six months later he was general in chief.[3]

McClellan arrived in Washington late on July 26, 1861; a rapturous crowd
greeted him at the railroad station, believing he brought the remedy for the

Union debacle of First Bull Run and all the Union's other military woes. He owed his elevation to Winfield Scott, who, like McClellan's peers, held the young Pennsylvanian in high regard. McClellan had received command of Ohio's volunteers only three months before. Now he was in Washington at the head of what became the Army of the Potomac. People expected much of the "young Napoleon" who had delivered victories in western Virginia.[4]

McClellan's arrival was subsumed by adulation. Few could have avoided the ego-inflating impact of the Olympian hero worship heaped upon the thirty-five-year-old McClellan. He had his faults: as historian Joseph Harsh says, McClellan was indeed "stubborn, strong-willed, inflexible, and occasionally self-righteous." But the press turned McClellan into a hero, à la Douglas MacArthur eighty years later.[5] Ulysses S. Grant, who found McClellan "one of the mysteries of the war," sympathized regarding the great burden heaped upon the shoulders of so young a man. He also believed McClellan had risen too quickly for his own good. "If McClellan had gone to war as Sherman, Thomas, or Meade," Grant said, "had fought his way along and up, I have no reason to suppose that he would not have won as high a distinction as any of us."[6]

McClellan's new assignment went immediately to his head. He wrote to his wife, Mary Ellen, "I find myself in a new & strange position here—Presdt, Cabinet, Genl Scott & all deferring to me—by some strange operation of magic I seem to have become *the* power of the land. I almost think that were I to win some small success now I could become Dictator or anything else that might please me—but nothing of that kind would please me—*therefore* I *won't* be Dictator. Admirable self denial!"[7] Here is great egotism, but also some truth: the country *was* calling upon him to save it. He immediately set about trying to do so, instilling order and discipline in the Union forces around Washington and turning the disorganized rabble bequeathed by McDowell into serious soldiers.[8] For all his faults that manifested later, McClellan forged the core of, and then built, one of the finest armies the United States has ever fielded. In the end, however, he proved unable or unwilling to employ it properly. Others used his magnificent army to win the war. Lincoln, and history, eventually branded McClellan "slow." It could have been otherwise.

MCCLELLAN BROUGHT A MASSIVE EGO with him to Washington; he acquired a bigger one upon arrival. But he did bring something (or, more accurately, someone) with him that would prove just as injurious to the Union cause. Allan J. Pinkerton ran a detective agency before the war. He worked for McClellan during the general's railroad days and escorted Lincoln to

Washington before the inauguration. He returned to McClellan's employ when the general had his Ohio command, working for the army under contract. The bureau he ran specifically for the gathering of intelligence was McClellan's innovation.[9]

Before the conflict the U.S. War Department possessed no intelligence service. The only system for collecting information from the enemy arose from the field. There was not even a modern understanding of the term *intelligence* as denoting the gathering of information on a subject. Nor was there yet a national Secret Service. McClellan had Pinkerton doing two types of intelligence work: interrogations and espionage, with Union spies focusing on gathering information in Richmond. McClellan, though, was generally too busy to assimilate what came into his hands.[10]

Pinkerton played a key role in McClellan's campaigns and thus in the Union war effort. Unfortunately for both, Pinkerton was incompetent, and his intelligence-gathering apparatus provided McClellan with a constant stream of bad information. His numbers were consistently inflated. For example, he credited regiments with their full complement when they generally possessed only half. He fed McClellan's growing uncertainties by presenting a picture of Confederate forces as massive in size. From the time he assumed command until his removal in the wake of Antietam, McClellan's heartfelt belief was that he *was* outnumbered by the Rebel forces facing him.[11] This guided his strategic, operational, and tactical thinking.

In Washington, McClellan stepped into a military and civilian chain of command marked by confusion. On the military side was General Scott, who, though general in chief, did not truly exercise the full powers of his office. During the three months between Bull Run and Scott's retirement, Scott gave McClellan no instructions, nor did he submit another strategic plan. Scott even proved a hindrance to accomplishing some of the things McClellan considered necessary, such as building fortifications around Washington.[12]

On the civilian side, the problem was Lincoln, who failed to establish clear lines of communication between himself, Secretary of War Simon Cameron, Scott, and McClellan. Lincoln angered Scott by bypassing the old general and going directly to McClellan. He also cut the secretary of war out of the loop. Lincoln's actions forced McClellan to act outside the chain of command (perhaps even accustoming him to doing so). Cameron, for his part, did not firmly assert his control over the army, but neither did he keep his hands out of military matters. Occasionally he dispatched orders via Adjutant General Lorenzo Thomas, usually only producing confusion. Scott also gave orders, adding to the disarray.[13]

Domestic political realities imposed another layer of context. Lincoln's party suffered from fractiousness. The Radical Republicans wanted abolition—to them, the whole point of the war. War Democrats, and some elements of the Republican Party, differed. Congress also demanded a say in the war's conduct. The issue of congressional oversight—or interference, depending upon your point of view— arose in the establishment of the Joint Committee on the Conduct of the War. Created in December 1861 to investigate Union defeats at Manassas and Ball's Bluff, it took as its mandate overseeing the war. Radicals controlled it, and they distrusted generals who did not endorse abolition, such as McClellan.[14] Overall, the committee seems to have done little more than make Lincoln's already tough job even more difficult while further poisoning the political environment.

Though he would prove slow to move against the enemy, McClellan was quick to plan. He was encouraged to do so because upon his arrival in Washington Lincoln went directly to the young general seeking a proposal for winning the war. McClellan set to work, his ideas on how to wage the conflict having been formed by his experiences in the West.[15] A week after he assumed command of the Eastern Department, he gave Lincoln a grand strategic plan encompassing military, diplomatic, and political strategies directed at winning the war in one campaign.[16] It was perhaps the first such plan in American history.

Militarily, McClellan outlined a multipronged offensive. The key operational area would be Virginia. His reasoning: "The rebels have chosen Virginia as their battle-field, and it seems proper for us to make the first great struggle there." Simply put, the Union should follow the enemy, meeting concentration with concentration. This allowed the enemy to dictate the primary field of battle. "But, while thus directing our main efforts, it is necessary to diminish the resistance there offered us by movements on other points both by land and water." McClellan envisioned a drive against Virginia, the primary movement, supplemented by subsidiary land and water operations. The troops in Missouri would push out the Confederates there and secure it. He wanted an advance down the Mississippi River with 20,000 men, plus those raised in Kentucky and eastern Tennessee "if Kentucky assumes the right position" (it was still neutral). Moreover, with Kentucky on the Union side, the forces from eastern Tennessee could secure that area, push on Nashville, and take the Volunteer State's eastern lands and railroads. He also wanted the seizure of the rail lines from Memphis to eastern Tennessee. Holding these, McClellan insisted, in conjunction with the Mississippi River thrust "would go far towards determining the evacuation of Virginia by the rebels." He also advised guarding the passes in western Virginia and the arming of troops there.[17]

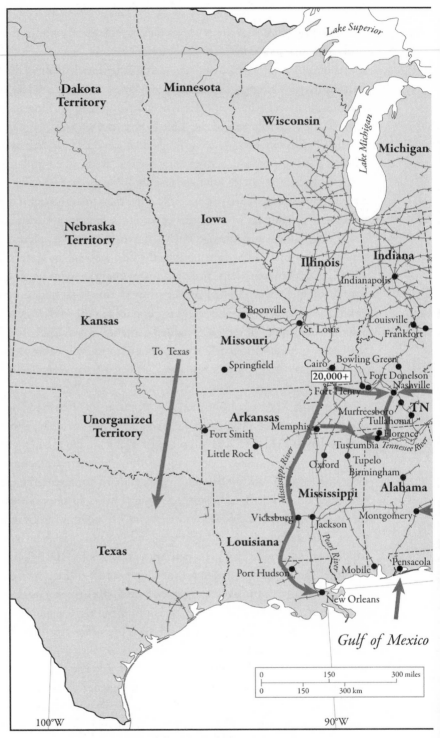

McClellan's Grand Plan, August 1861.

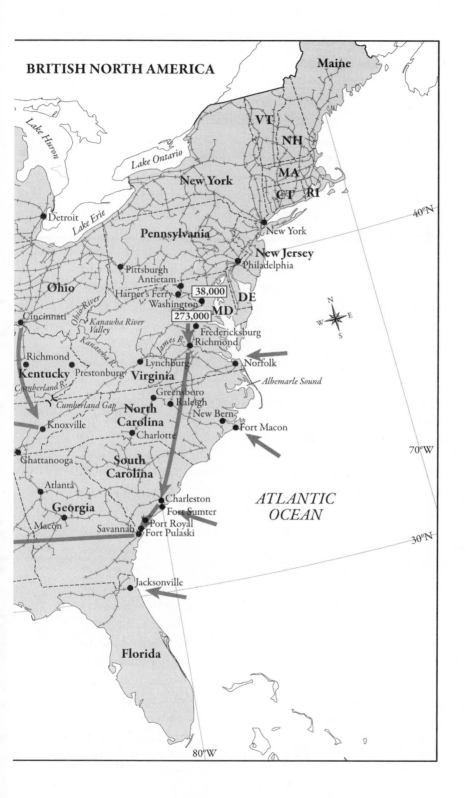

BRITISH NORTH AMERICA

In the East, after garrisoning Washington, Baltimore, Fortress Monroe, and other critical points with a total force of 38,000 men, he called for the creation of a 273,000-man army for field operations. This did not include manning the naval vessels needed to assist this force and escort transports laden with troops for capturing the Confederacy's coastal cities. Seaboard landings would serve two purposes: acting as diversions, thus siphoning away troops from Confederate main forces for city protection, and forming coastal lodgments that could be developed as circumstances allowed. McClellan also thought these units could act in conjunction with his primary field army in attacks on Rebel coastal cities.[18]

McClellan considered the South's ability to utilize its railroads to concentrate forces at key points, arguing that this could be countered by seizing railroads in the rear of Confederate "points of concentration" while simultaneously threatening their coastal cities, thus forcing each state to focus on local defense and decrease its contribution to the South's main armies.[19] McClellan's thinking on coastal operations aligns very well with the ideas Sir Julian Corbett presented in his seminal 1911 work on naval theory, *Some Principles of Maritime Strategy*. The landings fit Corbett's description of "operations more or less upon the [Confederate] seaboard designed not for permanent conquest, but as a method of disturbing our enemy's plans and strengthening the hands of our allies and our own position."[20]

All the various prongs, McClellan insisted, would dissipate Southern strength. "The proposed movement down the Mississippi will produce important results in this connection," he wrote, "that advance and the progress of the main army at the East will materially assist each other by diminishing the resistance to be encountered by each." A move from Kansas and Nebraska against the Red River and west Texas was intended to take advantage of supposed free state sentiment as it provided more support. He also recommended consideration of an offensive across New Mexico from California, though he confessed that this he had "not sufficiently examined to be able to express a decided opinion." Nonetheless, he suggested an alliance with Mexico, or at least some kind of accommodation that gained for the Union the use of Mexican ports and roads that could support a column into New Mexico or forces sent across the Rio Grande. "To what extent, if any, it would be desirable to take into service and employ Mexican soldiers," he added, somewhat oddly, "is a question entirely political, on which I do not venture to offer an opinion." He did not seem to understand that all of his ideas regarding Mexico were "entirely political," stretching beyond the military realm.[21]

McClellan did mention that a smaller force than what he had proposed might do the job, but he intimated that this would not fulfill what he understood was the government's task: reestablishing order as quickly as possible. "The question to be decided is simply this: Shall we crush the rebellion at one blow, terminate the war in one campaign, or shall we leave it as a legacy for our descendants?" McClellan planned to use his *grande armée* "not only to drive the enemy out of Virginia and occupy Richmond, but to occupy Charleston, Savannah, Montgomery, Pensacola, Mobile, and New Orleans; in other words, to move into the heart of the enemy's country and crush the rebellion in its very heart." This was the core of McClellan's strategic plan. He wanted to deliver one great, multifaceted blow at the Confederacy, destroying it in a single grand campaign. The strikes of the various tentacles were important, but the arm *he* intended to swing was the most critical. The others were merely subsidiary, and, though he didn't say this in his first proposal, he later intended them to be weaker in order to supply men for his thrust.[22]

Both the plan and the outline upon which it was based foreshadowed a later conflict between McClellan and Lincoln: a disagreement on the level of violence that should be used to conduct the war. McClellan argued for light measures against civilians and their property. Initially Lincoln did not disagree, but as the war dragged on and grew deadlier, his attitude hardened. McClellan wanted a "soft" war (inasmuch as there is such a thing), recommending "a rigidly protective policy as to private property and unarmed persons."[23] His peers and superiors came to prefer something else.

In his proposal, McClellan insisted that to win the war the North had to defeat the Confederacy's armed forces, take its strong points, and demonstrate the futility of resistance (while protecting private property). He also urged the reassertion of government authority through "overwhelming physical force." Taken together, these seem a contradiction. The North could not hope to fully protect people and property while using "overwhelming physical force." He wanted to wage a war that under the circumstances (though most did not yet realize it) could not be waged. This demonstrated one of McClellan's problems: he did not understand the nature of the war. "The contest began with a class; now it is with a people," he wrote.[24] In fact, however, it had always been with "a people." The only masses in the South being held in thrall were the slaves. The bulk of white Southerners supported the war. McClellan, like many Union leaders, chased the mirage of a Southern Unionism suppressed by a violent minority.

Would McClellan's plan have worked? If given a maneuver army of 273,000 men, would he have been able to win the war? It had weaknesses, the biggest being the small numbers of troops in the western prongs, particularly the one intended for the Mississippi River advance. But, executed by someone with the talent for implementation, McClellan's plan would have stood an excellent chance of success. What Grant proposed for the 1864 campaign echoed parts of McClellan's 1862 idea. Nonetheless, McClellan, for all his many gifts, lacked the ability to use the army tactically or operationally. The Peninsula Campaign showed this, as did Antietam. But the obvious problem would be the raising and provisioning of his 273,000-man force. This, though difficult, was not beyond Union means.

There has been much misunderstanding of McClellan's strategic plan. Some historians oversimplify it. Most overlook it, or dismiss it in a single paragraph. Others give it a little weight. As we will see, it haunted McClellan's military actions thereafter, becoming the basis for his other plans and an excuse for failure.[25]

This document landed on the president's desk on August 2, 1861. Lincoln read it to his cabinet the next day but made no known comments about it, as in the case of Scott's Anaconda Plan.[26] Afterward, pleased, McClellan wrote to his wife: "I shall carry this thing on 'En grand' & crush the rebels in one campaign—I flatter myself that Beauregard has gained his last victory."[27]

IN ADDITION TO TRAINING THE ARMY and delivering his strategic plan, McClellan turned on his former mentor Scott, launching a successful campaign to undermine the old general and force his retirement. Paranoia also struck McClellan: he soon became fearful that administration officials sought to undercut *him* as he had Scott. A pointed manifestation of his fear focused upon the Confederate army, both its intent and its size. On August 8, 1861, McClellan insisted that the enemy had 100,000 troops ready to attack Washington. He believed his force insufficient and wanted 100,000 men to defend the capital, insisting that Washington faced "*imminent danger.*"[28] Thus began his delusions regarding the size of Confederate forces, a marked change from his behavior in western Virginia, where he refused, correctly, to believe intelligence reports of large enemy forces. Scott saw no such emergency and told Secretary of War Cameron so. He also requested his placement on the retirement list, citing his age, his health, and being undermined by his protégé.[29] But the administration proved unready for him to go.

By mid-August McClellan, fearing an attack on Washington, asked the navy to provide forces to block the Potomac to prevent any Confederate crossing.[30] His estimate of the size of the Confederate forces opposing him climbed. By August 19 he thought 150,000 Confederates opposed his

55,000.[31] By September, he believed he faced 170,000 Rebels. Peak Confederate strength opposite Washington that month was actually 45,000.[32] How McClellan reached such numbers remains a mystery.[33] McClellan biographer Stephen Sears suggests "delusion" beyond even the errors of Pinkerton and his gang.[34]

McClellan's friends and detractors have long searched for a key to deciphering his actions. Clausewitz offers one in his essay "On Military Genius." "Intelligence alone is not courage; we often see that the most intelligent people are irresolute," he wrote. "In short," he continued, "we believe that determination proceeds from a special type of mind, from a strong rather than a brilliant one. We can give further proof of this interpretation by pointing to many examples of men who show great determination as junior officers, but lose it as they rise in rank. Conscious of the need to be decisive, they also recognize the risks entailed by a *wrong* decision; since they are unfamiliar with the problems now facing them, their mind loses its former incisiveness."[35] The bravery and decisiveness McClellan demonstrated in Mexico and at the beginning of the Civil War vanished under the tremendous responsibility thrust upon him. The Union, and indeed the entire nation, paid the price for this.

By early September, McClellan believed he could predict the enemy's future offensive actions. Assessing the Confederate forces at no less than 130,000, he insisted that "it is well understood that although the ultimate design of the enemy is to possess himself of the City of Washington, his first efforts will probably be directed towards Baltimore, with the intention of cutting our lines of communication and supplies as well as to arouse an insurrection in Maryland." He believed the Confederates would launch their offensive with 100,000 men, crossing the Potomac north of Washington. Their other 30,000 men would create diversions, enabling the main army to march on Baltimore unopposed. To counter this, McClellan insisted upon being reinforced at once with the best soldiers in the Union, including the elements of the prewar army, and that the Union should stay on the defensive, reinforcing the Army of the Potomac with everything it had. "The fate of the nation and the success of the cause in which we are engaged must be mainly decided by the issue of the next battle to be fought by the army now under my command," he told Secretary of War Cameron. Cameron, convinced a great battle was nigh, asked what he could do to help. McClellan asked for all available troops and insisted that the Army of the Potomac needed to be "not less than three hundred thousand men."[36] Trying to gather the totality of Union military strength under his direct control, he harked back to his idea of the 273,000-man force. It was not the last time.

McClellan built his army, and the "Phony War" in the East (as historian and former intelligence officer Edwin Fishel calls it) continued. By September 27, 1861, McClellan had 168,318 men under his command in the Washington area. He did not act, his excuse being that he needed to train them.[37]

AS MCCLELLAN TRAINED "his" army (and with a skill matched by few generals in American history) and considered campaign alternatives, Lincoln issued his own strategic plan. He ordered, "on or about the 5th. of October (the exact date to be determined hereafter)," the seizure of a spot on the Tennessee-Virginia railroad near the Cumberland Gap. He also wanted troops concentrated in five primary commands stretching from the Western Theater to the Eastern: Missouri, under Frémont; Louisville, Kentucky, under Robert Anderson, of Fort Sumter fame; western Virginia; Cincinnati, under O. M. Mitchel (these to support Anderson); and the East, under McClellan. Lincoln wanted simultaneous attacks along the coast and against the Cumberland Gap. The force for the attack on the Gap was to result from a rapid concentration of the units from Louisville and Cincinnati at Lexington, Kentucky, these troops then joining other Union forces under George Thomas at nearby Camp Dick Robinson. Lincoln believed that the Confederates could not hold Cumberland Gap because of their "greatly inferior force." Moreover, he seemed to have believed that such action would open up opportunities, writing that "the Coast and Gap movements made, General's McClellan and Fremont [sic], in their respective Departments, will avail themselves of any advantages the diversions may present."[38]

The order for preparations for a push against Cumberland Gap went out on October 10, 1861. Although the subsequent movement was partially thwarted by a Confederate advance, Lincoln's order demonstrates his growing grasp of military affairs.[39] He was learning from his generals, particularly McClellan. Most important, he had taken a step on the road to his future strategy for conducting the war: simultaneous advances.

In early October, in response to a request from Lincoln for a report on his army and what was being done to improve it, McClellan proffered another plan, one that future Lincoln secretary of war Edwin M. Stanton helped compose. It called for a much-reduced (at least in comparison to his prior proposal) eastern field army of 150,000 men but a total force of 208,000. He was disappointed that the government had not taken to heart his suggestion to sit on the defensive elsewhere (something he does not seem to have made clear to them) while reinforcing his army around Washington and focusing all efforts "upon this as the vital point where the issue of the great contest is to be decided." In spite of this, victory could be achieved "by introducing unity of action and design among the various armies of the land," reducing the "superfluous strength" from other armies, and reinforcing his main army, "whose destiny it is to decide the controversy." Moreover, he urged "unity in councils, the utmost vigor and energy in action," and that "the entire military field should be grasped as a whole, and not in detached parts." "One plan," he continued, "should be agreed upon and pursued; a single will should direct and carry out these plans. The great object to be accomplished, the crushing defeat of the rebel army (now) at Manassas."[40]

McClellan prefaced his new proposal by writing that "so much time has passed & winter is approaching so rapidly that but two courses are left to the Government, viz: Either to go into winter quarters, or to assume the offensive with forces greatly inferior in numbers to the army I regarded as desirable & necessary" (perhaps meaning his 273,000-man force). He advised advancing by November 25.[41]

In addition to being an exercise in self-aggrandizement, the letter reveals that McClellan's fears had mastered him. His insistence upon unity and "vigor" were commendable, but what he was truly urging was stripping other commands in order to strengthen his theater and placing all forces under his personal direction. The plan was also contradictory. He called for multiple supporting actions but wanted the other commands weakened to make his force stronger. Finally, he had digressed from the goals of his original grand proposal. Initially he had sought to crush the rebellion. Now he fixated on defeating the Confederate *army* immediately opposite him, not the Confederate *cause*. Confusing the levels of war, he was proposing a tactical solution to a strategic problem. In other words, he was chasing after a victory in battle, a tactical result, not victory in the war.

Despite these flaws, McClellan's ideas, as always, had merit. He recognized some of the keys to Union success: unity of command and planning, coordinating various armies, vigorous action, viewing the various fields of conflict as parts of a contiguous whole. These were some of the ingredients of the eventual Union victory, and, indeed, of most victories. He was also correct to think of targeting the Confederate army; Lincoln would come to the same conclusion. This was the Confederate center of gravity, the source whence it derived its strength. But to think that he would destroy this army, even the one directly opposing him, in one encounter was to chase the ghost of the Napoleonic decisive battle, and this in contradistinction to his earlier conclusion that he would have to seize a number of key Southern points, necessitating much bloodshed. But perhaps it was this very realization of the necessary bloodshed that drove this line of thought.

McClellan was also doing something beyond the vision of the bulk of his contemporaries: exhibiting an understanding of what today would be called the operational level of war and how this contributes to the achievement of strategic ends. His emphasis on various offensive thrusts, aimed at various objectives, highlighted the operational elements of a larger strategic plan. What McClellan meant by vigor remains a mystery.

Would this plan have worked? Under another commander, perhaps. The size of the army itself was not the problem. The problem was *time*. The political situation demanded action. The longer McClellan delayed, the more he became a political liability to an administration that had far too many of these already. Delay fed doubts about McClellan that reached even to the conspiratorial; a few bandied the word *treason*.

AFTER BEING FIRED McClellan would write, correctly, that by the time he assumed the role of general in chief "the whole country, indeed, had now become the theater of military operations from the Potomac to beyond the Mississippi." He now faced added tasks, including helping the navy strengthen the blockade, which meant joint army-navy operations against coastal areas. He also discovered the Union armies in the West to be as shabby as the one he had inherited in the East. However, McClellan saw more than just new responsibilities: "The direction of the campaigns in the West and of the operations on the seaboard enabled me to enter upon larger combinations and to accomplish results the necessity and advantage of which had not been unforeseen, but which had been beyond the ability of the single army formerly under my command to effect."[42] McClellan had advocated operations in areas beyond his control since his arrival in Washington, but now he controlled the other tendrils of Union military power.

In his examination of potential operations between naval and land forces McClellan thought in a very modern manner. Such operations are often referred to in the Civil War literature as "combined." Today, *combined* implies a multinational force. *Joint* describes operations conducted jointly by two or more service arms. Modern military practitioners call this—somewhat awkwardly—*jointness*.

McClellan's more immediate job was working with Lincoln. Initially, McClellan held a good opinion of his boss, being particularly happy that he and the president agreed on what McClellan called "the nigger question," meaning that the North fought to maintain the Union, not to destroy slavery.

McClellan worried that this issue would be revisited. He insisted that *he* was fighting to save the Union, and that the notion of freeing the slaves would prevent the achievement of this objective. Unlike Lincoln, he had also begun to believe that the war would be decided by the next battle, rather than on many fronts, and that duty dictated that he not move until fully prepared. His opinion of Lincoln quickly soured. In one week he went from calling him "perfectly honest" to branding him with Stanton's derisive *"the original gorrilla"* [*sic*]. Soon McClellan would be fighting—in his mind—not only the Confederates but the president and much of his cabinet as well. Eventually there would be no trust on either side. Nonetheless, McClellan purchased a house in the capital, telling his wife, "I think we can make up our minds to residing in Washington for some years."[43]

On November 1, 1861, General Scott retired. McClellan replaced him. Lincoln expected aggressive, offensive action from his new general in chief.[44] McClellan answered with reorganization. He broke the Western Theater into two departments, placing the Department of the West under Henry Wager Halleck. The new Department of the Ohio went to Don Carlos Buell.[45] Halleck, much older than his superior, had graduated from West Point in 1839. He made a name for himself outside the army as an engineer, lawyer, and military intellectual, penning, among other books, *Elements of Military Art and Science*, and translating Baron Antoine-Henri Jomini's multivolume study of Napoleon. Some contemporaries despised him. Others found him irritating, put off by his appearance and his impatience toward those less bright. He also had an odd habit of crossing his arms over his chest and scratching both elbows when pensive or pressed by cares. Hemorrhoids, exacerbated by stress, fueled his natural irascibleness; the opium he sometimes took to fight the pain fueled his irresoluteness.[46]

His counterpart in the Ohio Department, Don Carlos Buell, also did not inspire great love. He was querulous, fierce-looking, and chilly in manner; few liked him, and about this he cared not at all. On the other hand, few worked harder than Don Carlos, and he was not without intelligence and some talent for operational planning, as his letters reveal. Like most of his brethren on both sides bearing stars, he attended West Point (class of 1841) and served with distinction in the Mexican War.[47]

After appointing Halleck to his new position on November 9, McClellan tasked him with sorting out the organizational mess in Missouri, ordering him to fortify and hold Rolla, Sedalia, "and other interior points...and concentrating the mass of the troops on or near the Mississippi, prepared for such ulterior operations as the public interests may demand."[48] Lincoln had given similar advice to David Hunter, Halleck's predecessor, orders McClellan had approved.[49]

McClellan's instructions to Buell also owed much to Lincoln, who wanted an advance made on eastern Tennessee and Knoxville. Lincoln saw political and military advantages. He believed operations in eastern Tennessee would cut Confederate railroads in the area and separate the South from its "hog and hominy," robbing the Confederates of valuable food sources while fulfilling what became Lincoln's cherished goal of liberating the large, pro-Union region. McClellan believed taking Knoxville would provide a flanking threat against Confederate Virginia, forcing the South to weaken its forces opposing the Army of the Potomac.[50] Moreover, in early November the administration faced pressure to act in support of Kentucky and promised to do so.[51] McClellan stressed to Buell the need for a move into eastern Tennessee as quickly as possible. Agreeing with Lincoln, he also told Buell, "It is absolutely necessary that we shall hold all the State of Kentucky." But he also gave Buell freedom of action if these orders proved impractical.[52]

McClellan had clear ideas about what he wanted done in the West. His early orders, especially to Buell, show this. He knew why: "political and strategical considerations" necessitated an immediate advance into eastern Tennessee. McClellan also had clear operational objectives: severing "communication between the Mississippi Valley and Eastern Virginia," protecting Tennessee Unionists, and reestablishing Union government in East Tennessee. He wanted Buell to advance on Knoxville "if it is possible to effect it."[53]

The severing of the state's rail lines recalled his first great plan. The new general in chief had a problem, however: Buell refused to act. McClellan quickly lost patience with his old friend, telling him to move "at once" unless it was impossible.[54] Buell had quickly discovered that the lack of suitable railroads made a direct drive on Knoxville logistically unfeasible.[55] He responded to McClellan's prodding as McClellan did to Lincoln's: he gave his superior an alternative operational option.

Buell suggested first putting enough troops before Bowling Green to pin the Confederate forces there led by Simon Bolivar Buckner. Then the Union could push a column into eastern Tennessee via Somerset, or drive on Nashville down the "pike road" through Gallatin, or take both these routes. "The choice of these must depend on circumstances," Buell insisted. Either course would be supported by naval forces bringing troops up the Cumberland and Tennessee rivers "so as at least to land and unite near the State line, and cut off communication between Bowling Green and Columbus, and perhaps run directly into Nashville." Supporting all of this would be a "strong demonstration" against Columbus via the Mississippi River.[56]

Buell's plan aimed at the liberation not merely of eastern Tennessee but of the entire state and suggested a multipronged invasion. His proposed advance on Nashville, combined with movements down the Cumberland and Tennessee, would have isolated the Confederate positions in eastern Tennessee, forcing the Confederates either to fight or abandon the area.[57] Moreover, by advocating strikes down the Cumberland and Tennessee, Buell had identified two critical invasion routes.

In his *Lincoln and His Generals,* historian T. Harry Williams argues that McClellan saw little merit in Buell's proposal.[58] The correspondence shows otherwise. McClellan heartily approved the plan and told Buell to consider two advances, one into eastern Tennessee with 15,000 men, and a second on Nashville with 50,000. This move into eastern Tennessee was critical, and McClellan wanted it done first, before Buell took Nashville. McClellan also told Buell to keep him informed so that their actions could be "simultaneous." McClellan had "other heavy blows to strike at the same time" but doubted that all would be ready in less than a month or six weeks. He told his subordinate to act when ready, even if McClellan was not, and promised to "at once take the necessary steps to carry out your views as to the rivers."[59] McClellan's instructions to Buell were an operational implementation of his overarching strategic idea: land blows in concert at a number of different places—but in support of McClellan.

The general in chief meant Buell's drive into eastern Tennessee to be a part of his larger plan. Again, however, McClellan had a problem with which Lincoln became intimately familiar: a subordinate who would not advance despite incessant prodding. Both McClellan and Lincoln wanted Buell to march on eastern Tennessee as ordered. Buell sat. McClellan repeated the command on December 3 and again on the fifth. Lincoln wanted McClellan to follow this course, and McClellan himself believed that helping the hard-pressed Union men of the region was the honorable course. Additional pressure fell on Buell from Tennessee officials such as Governor Andrew Johnson.[60] Still Buell sat.

Halleck proved no more ambitious. With his new post he inherited disarray. He described the situation under his command as "complete chaos"— the troops were sick, poorly organized, poorly led, and poorly trained. He counseled McClellan to wait before ordering any action in the West, insisting that pursuing an on-to-Richmond strategy would bring on another Bull Run and "imperil" Missouri. Moreover, Halleck said, he could not spare some of the troops McClellan wanted.[61] This disappointed McClellan, who intended to have Halleck move in conjunction with Buell. Loath to weaken Halleck, however, McClellan decided that Buell's advance had to be postponed, or undertaken by some other means.[62] Buell's great idea died.

Additionally, McClellan intended to reinforce Major General David Hunter, who became head of the Department of Kansas on November 20, 1861, when the Department of the West was split into the Departments of the Missouri and Kansas. Hunter did not think this reorganization a good idea, but no one asked him. McClellan foresaw his new departmental commander launching yet another support operation, moving against the Indian Territory west of Arkansas and into northern Texas in conjunction with an offensive against Texas from the Gulf of Mexico. Hunter insisted he needed 20,000 additional men to act.[63]

McClellan also posed to Halleck an important question: "Can you yet form any idea of the time necessary to prepare an expedition against Columbus or one up the Cumberland and Tennessee rivers, in connection with Buell's movements?"[64] Here, influenced by Buell's plan, an idea was growing, but it would take someone else to bring it to fruition. Buell returned to this in his correspondence with McClellan on December 10, saying that the preparations were complete for the "demonstrations."[65] Still, nothing happened.

6

Union Strategy

NOVEMBER 1861–MARCH 1862

The soldiers must be directed and guided; in short there must
be political interference with strategy.

—SIR FREDERICK MAURICE

UNION FORCES IN THE EASTERN THEATER nonetheless did undertake active military measures during the period between McClellan's arrival in July and Scott's departure on November 1, 1861. In mid-August, McClellan ordered a campaign to clear the eastern Chesapeake Bay regions of Virginia and Maryland; this lasted until late November. More important was the Port Royal Expedition. Planned before McClellan came to Washington, it was initiated by the Blockade Board, which was searching for ways to increase the blockade's effectiveness. The move began life through the acquisition of a much-needed coaling station for Union warships, a station that evolved into an enclave, probably because of McClellan. It then became a plank of his strategy.[1]

The Blockade Board was one of the few Civil War institutions to thoroughly study a problem and offer sound advice. It also provided the framework for how the Union navy would first institute and then conduct its blockade. In three months, beginning in late June 1861, it developed a strategic concept the navy would use throughout the war to implement the blockade. This boiled down to the construction and deployment of squadrons and the seizure of Southern ports to provide the necessary logistical bases, subjects addressed in more detail in the next chapter. It also provided accurate and indispensable information on the Confederacy's coastline. The board's demise after filing its last report in September 1861 damaged the Union war effort, for it had a great and positive impact on Union strategy. Union military successes in the fall of 1861 on the Confederate coast can be directly attributed to its recommendations. The first military operation conducted on the board's advice was the August 28–29, 1861, descent upon Hatteras Inlet, under the command of Flag Officer Silas H. Stringham and Major General Benjamin F. Butler. The captures of Port Royal and Ship Island would follow in November and the capture of Fernandina, Florida, in March 1862.[2]

When he became general in chief, McClellan inherited some ideas and operations that had originated with the Blockade Board. He agreed with its concept of joint army-navy operations, and its suggestions proved not only daring but productive. McClellan had thought similarly since the early days of the war. In the first week of September 1861, he asked Secretary of War Cameron for permission to create what he called a "Coast Division," a virtual floating branch of the army for operations on the Potomac and Chesapeake.[3] The idea for the unit came from Ambrose Burnside, a generally well-liked Indianan, graduate of West Point, and veteran of the Mexican War. McClellan intended to use the troops to establish toeholds on the Southern coast that could be used as bases for forays into the interior against Southern rail lines. The August 1861 seizure of Cape Hatteras laid the foundation for this. By November, McClellan was also talking with prominent naval officer David Dixon Porter about future moves against New Orleans.[4]

On January 7, 1862, McClellan implemented Burnside's operation aimed at Roanoke Island and the surrounding area. He also put Burnside in command of the Department of North Carolina, which included Hatteras Inlet. Though they didn't accomplish everything McClellan sought, or as quickly, the operations went very well. In February, Union forces captured Roanoke Island, which dominated Albemarle Sound. Later landings took New Bern in March and Fort Macon and Beaufort at the end of April. McClellan had hoped to capture Goldsborough, Raleigh, and, if Burnside was reinforced, perhaps even the key port of Wilmington.[5]

By launching coastal operations, as historian William L. Barney writes, the North embarked upon an enclave strategy. Union leaders did not define it this way, though they did have the examples of British operations in the American Revolutionary and Napoleonic wars. Seizing and holding points along the Confederate coast proved advantageous. It had not, as Barney points out, "provided the North with a militarily feasible method of conquering the South," but it did produce other benefits he described. The Union gained bases for launching raids against Southern resources, railroads, and industries. The enclaves tied down large numbers of Confederate troops and could potentially draw them into battles. They also established a Union presence that destabilized the slave system, undermining the South's social structure. Descents such as that upon Port Royal Sound in South Carolina in November 1861 provided valuable ports for strengthening the blockade and helped seal off or impede traffic into Southern ports.[6]

HOWEVER, ALL THESE OPERATIONS and proposed operations paled before the great question of the day: what was McClellan going to do with the Army of the Potomac? Union officials demanded an answer. McClellan was not without a reply, indeed giving several, one after the other, over a number of months.

As we've seen, as 1861 wore on McClellan grew convinced that he needed more troops to move against the Confederate forces at Centreville and Manassas. Moreover, even if it worked, this would not deliver what he wanted: a crushing, decisive defeat of the Rebel army. He believed the Confederates would simply fight from line to line all the way to Richmond, increasing the war's cost and protracting it. By this time, the idea for a decisive use of the Army of the Potomac that could lead to a Union victory in the war was taking shape in McClellan's mind. His experience with joint army-navy operations clearly influenced what became the Peninsula Campaign.[7]

On November 6, 1861, Brigadier General Rush Hawkins, the commander of the Union forces holding Hatteras Inlet, met with Lincoln to discuss his garrison's situation. At the president's bidding he spoke to the cabinet, stressing the value of Union action in the Hatteras area because it dominated North Carolina's internal waterways. McClellan also attended, sitting at one end of the lengthy table. "After I had finished," Hawkins wrote of McClellan, "he drew me into conversations about operations in the Department of Virginia, and as I had often urged upon General [John E.] Wool the importance of making Fort Monroe a base for operations against Richmond, I was fully prepared to answer his questions or to combat opposition." McClellan, though, had nothing but interest in Hawkins's ideas, and "at his request I made a rough drawing showing the old road up the peninsula, with a waterway on each side for gun-boats and general transportation. He listened attentively to all I had to say, talked but little himself, and put my drawing in his pocket. I have always suspected that my animated advocacy of that route may have had something to do with his change of base from Washington, and the undertaking of his unfortunate Peninsular Campaign."[8] Hawkins was a little hard on himself here at the end; responsibility for McClellan's "unfortunate Peninsular Campaign" lay with McClellan (and perhaps Robert E. Lee), but he did provide valuable underpinning data for an idea already jelling in McClellan's mind.

In late November, McClellan approached John G. Barnard, a former member of the Blockade Board and now chief engineer of the Army of the Potomac, for advice regarding an amphibious operation aimed at circumventing the Confederate positions in northern Virginia and forcing the enemy out of their fortifications.[9] Barnard quickly delivered a detailed study, noting that "the idea of shifting the theater of operations to the James, York, or Rappahannock has often occurred." Barnard proposed a number of embarkation and debarkation points, including Fort Monroe, and even suggested the use of multiple columns and multiple landing sites, as well as the use of Burnside's Coastal Division.[10]

Barnard also warned of the potential danger to Washington: "In cutting the enemy's line of operations you expose yourself, and a bold and desperate enemy, seeing himself anticipated at Richmond, might attempt to retrieve the disaster by a desperate effort upon Washington." To prevent this, he advised placing a garrison of 100,000 troops in the capital for as long as the enemy could threaten it, and the manning of the fortifications by men who knew their business.[11]

As McClellan considered this, Lincoln grew impatient. Around December 1, the president proposed an advance in northern Virginia that became known as his Occoquan Plan. He suggested moving 50,000 men of the Army of the Potomac against the Confederate forces at Centreville. Another force would cross the Occoquan River along the Alexandria-Richmond road. A third element would be brought across the Potomac and landed south of the mouth of the adjoining Occoquan. It would push inland, linking up with the crossing force. These two arms would be mutually supporting, enabling each to hit the rear of an enemy force blocking the other. "Both points will probably not be successfully resisted at the same time," Lincoln wrote. Meanwhile, the force facing Centreville, if pushed too hard by the Confederates, could retreat to the safety of the works to its rear. He sent the note to McClellan, asking when such a move could take place and how many men could be used.[12]

Lincoln's plan was not implemented, but it spurred McClellan to activity, if not action. McClellan told the president that the advance could occur between December 15 and 25, and supplied him with the numbers. But McClellan believed that any movement in northern Virginia would be met with nearly equal forces; he had a way around this, and wrote Lincoln, "I have now my mind actively turned toward another plan of campaign that I do not think at all anticipated by the enemy nor by many of our own people." He had an alternative, but was struck by typhoid before producing it.[13]

MCCLELLAN'S FALLING ILL added to Lincoln's worries and contributed to his increasingly more aggressive insistence upon active military efforts. He did not interfere in the movements of the Army of the Potomac (at least not yet), but he began pushing Halleck and Buell to act upon the various proposals floating around. If Buell was marching on Nashville via Bowling Green, Lincoln wanted Halleck to provide a demonstration against Columbus to prevent the Confederates from reinforcing in Buell's front. He wanted them to act "in concert," and, in a manifestation of his growing frustration with the war effort, told Halleck, "Please do not lose time in this matter."[14]

McClellan did not hold long to his sickbed. By January 3, 1862, he was back at his post and pushing Halleck to comply with Lincoln's orders. McClellan believed it critical to prevent Confederate forces in Kentucky from reinforcing their brethren opposing Buell. To stop this, he wanted one to two divisions, supported by gunboats, sent up the Cumberland River. He also wanted a demonstration against Columbus to pin its defenders, and even capture the city if the enemy withdrew enough of their force to allow it. McClellan further suggested a feint on the Tennessee River and insisted that because Union "success in Kentucky depends in a great measure on our preventing re-enforcements from joining Buckner and [Albert Sidney] Johnston, not a moment's time should be lost in preparing these expeditions."[15]

Buell believed it necessary to take Columbus because it was the center of the Confederate defensive network. He told Halleck so and recommended the dispatch of gunboat-supported expeditions down the Tennessee and Cumberland to destroy the railroad bridges over these rivers, thus hindering the Confederate ability to concentrate troops against any Union drive. Buell's conclusion revealed something that Lincoln surely wished his generals understood about the nature of the war. At the time, however, none did, not even Buell, the author of this truth: "Whatever is done should be done speedily, within a few days. The work will become more difficult every day."[16]

Lincoln grew more anxious. He demanded an answer from Buell as to whether or not he had moved into eastern Tennessee. Buell replied that he was preparing to march on the Cumberland Gap, but that transportation problems and the need to make repairs to imported arms had delayed him. The combative Buell disagreed with the movement into eastern Tennessee and told Lincoln so, adding that he was going along with it only because it was the wish of the president and the general in chief. He preferred an advance "against the great power of the rebellion in the West, which is mainly arrayed on the line from Columbus to Bowling Green, and can speedily be concentrated at any point of that line which is attacked singly."[17]

Lincoln did not applaud Buell's gruff independence. "Your dispatch of yesterday has been received," he began, "and it disappoints and distresses me." He struck back on two fronts. Militarily, he "would rather have a point on the railroad south of Cumberland Gap than Nashville—first, because it cuts a great artery of the enemy's communication, which Nashville does not; and, secondly, because it is in the midst of loyal people, who would rally around it, while Nashville is not.... But my distress," he continued, "is that our friends in East Tennessee are being hanged and driven to despair, and even now I fear are thinking of taking rebel arms for the sake of personal protection. In this we lose the most valuable stake we have in the South." Having outlined the politics involved, Lincoln turned McClellan loose.[18]

The unhappy general in chief inveighed about the dire political consequences of failing to move into eastern Tennessee and relieving its Unionists. Additionally, he "was extremely sorry to learn from your telegram to the President that you had *from the beginning attached little or no importance* to a movement in East Tennessee." McClellan said Buell's failure to advance interfered with McClellan's own master plan for prosecuting the war. McClellan saw Bowling Green and Nashville as secondary in importance to the occupation of eastern Tennessee and believed he could not advance before this took place. "If that is not possible," he continued, "a complete and prejudicial change in my own plans at once becomes necessary." McClellan believed it more useful to the Union cause to free the pro-Union areas of eastern Tennessee, western North and South Carolina, and northern Georgia and Alabama. This, he insisted, would result "from the movement I allude to." McClellan suggested that, since Halleck said he could not yet support Buell by moving up the Cumberland, Buell should make his advance alone.[19]

Here, McClellan made the same mistake with Buell as Lincoln had, and on the same matter. "I do not intend this to be an order in any sense," Lincoln scratched in a frustration-drenched note to Buell, "but merely, as intimated before, to show you the grounds of my anxiety."[20] McClellan also merely *suggested* that Buell move. Neither *ordered* him to do so—at least not at this point. (McClellan gave his subordinate an out by allowing him discretion as to whether to act.)[21] One or both of them should have ordered a move. Had he refused yet again, he should have been relieved of his command. Had Buell truly believed he could make no move because of transportation problems, he should have tendered his resignation, forcing his superiors to acknowledge the seriousness of his claim. But neither the president nor the general in chief forced Buell to act.

Then Halleck made things worse. Lincoln had also been pressuring him. On January 6, 1862, Halleck awoke. "It would be madness to attempt anything serious with such a force," he insisted, "and I cannot at the present time withdraw any from Missouri without risking the loss of this State." He had 10,000 men to hold down a Missouri virtually in flames. He tried to pass some blame on to his superiors and fellow departmental commander, protesting he had not been told of Buell's campaign plans. Halleck invoked military history and theory to defend his inaction, insisting that "if it be intended that his column shall move on Bowling Green while another moves from Cairo or Paducah on Columbus or Camp Beauregard it will be a repetition of the same strategic error which produced the disaster of Bull Run. To operate on exterior lines against an enemy occupying a central position will fail, as it always has failed, in ninety-nine cases out of a hundred."[22]

Halleck calls "strategic" what we would today define as operational because the movements were intended to achieve certain limited military objectives. He also missed the point: it was not comparable to Bull Run. The great distance between Columbus and Bowling Green undermined his analogy. More important, the disparity in troop strength heavily favored the Union. Buell's force alone was almost as large as what the Confederates had in the theater—35,000 to around 40,000.[23] "It is exceedingly discouraging," a despondent Lincoln wrote. "As everywhere else, nothing can be done."[24] Lincoln did do something: he began trying to force his subordinates to act. On January 7, he told both Buell and Halleck to name dates when they could move south in unison. "Delay is ruining us," he declared, "and it is indispensable for me to have something definite."[25]

However, some things had finally begun happening in the West. On December 29, Buell had issued orders for troops under George H. Thomas to march into eastern Tennessee. This proved easier said than done, but by January 13, 1862, Thomas had around 14,000 men moving to oppose the Confederates under Brigadier General Felix K. Zollicoffer.[26] On January 8, 1862, Ulysses S. Grant received Halleck's order to mount a demonstration and to get the gunboats under Flag Officer Andrew H. Foote to help if they could, the point being to keep the Confederates from reinforcing Buckner in Bowling Green, a response to McClellan's order of January 3.[27] Grant complied.[28] On January 13, he dispatched General C. F. Smith up the Tennessee River to threaten the forts straddling the waterway, Heiman and Henry. Grant went with John A. McClernand's command into western Kentucky. He later wrote, "The object of the expedition was accomplished. The enemy did not send reinforcements to Bowling Green, and General George H. Thomas fought and won the battle of Mill Springs before we returned."[29]

More important, the expedition produced information that led to bigger things. Smith reported the possibility of capturing Fort Heiman, on the high ground across the river from Fort Henry, which dominated the position. Grant sent this information to Halleck. Smith believed that with support from Union gunboats, Fort Henry would quickly fall. Grant wrote in his memoirs that Smith's report agreed with what he believed—that the Tennessee and Cumberland rivers were their "true line of operations." He knew that if Union forces controlled these rivers, the Confederates would be forced to retreat out of Kentucky. Moreover, the arrival of Smith's report corroborated information Grant had received during the demonstration from a spy in Buell's employ. Grant also advocated a thrust down the two rivers.[30] Here was opportunity. Grant sought to grasp it.

So certain had Grant become about the promise of this line of advance that on January 6, even before the demonstration, he had asked for permission to come to Halleck's headquarters to discuss it with his superior. Halleck refused. Grant tried again on January 20. This time he succeeded, at least in being allowed to make the pilgrimage. He found curt, chastening denial, and on the twenty-sixth he "returned to Cairo very much crestfallen."[31]

But none of this was the offensive action Lincoln knew the Union needed. The president grew more depressed. McClellan had suffered a relapse, and Lincoln was under pressure from Congress's Joint Committee on the Conduct of the War to separate the offices of commander of the Army of the Potomac and general in chief.[32] On Friday, the tenth of January, he walked into Quartermaster General Montgomery Meigs's office and sat down in a chair in front of the fire. "General," Lincoln said, "what shall I do? The people are impatient; [Treasury Secretary Salmon] Chase has not money and tells me he can raise no more; the General of the Army has typhoid fever. The bottom is out of the tub. What shall I do?"[33]

A sympathetic Meigs suggested calling a council in case the Confederates attacked while McClellan was ill. Lincoln agreed, summoning a group that included Seward, Chase, and two of McClellan's divisional commanders, McDowell and William Franklin, to the White House on the evening of January 10 for an eight o'clock meeting. Lincoln wanted, indeed *needed* action, famously saying that if McClellan wasn't going to use the Army of the Potomac, "he would like to *borrow it*, provided he could see how it could be made to do something." He asked the military men about the feasibility of action by the Army of the Potomac and what they would do with it. McDowell said he would organize the army into four corps, placing three of these in a line covering Vienna, Fairfax Station, and Fairfax Courthouse. These would press the opposing Confederates, encouraging them to commit more troops. Meanwhile, the remaining corps, with accompanying artillery, would sail down the Potomac and land below the Occoquan River, capture Aquia, and, supported by cavalry assigned to wreck the bridges, march down the railroad from Manassas to the Rappahannock River.[34] This is almost exactly like the plan Lincoln had drawn up the month before.

General Franklin, well aware of McClellan's thinking, initially replied that he knew too little of the state of the rest of the army to comment. When pressed by Lincoln on whether he had given any thought to how he would use the army if in command, Franklin replied that he would take all the troops unnecessary for the protection of Washington and land them on the Peninsula, at the mouth of the York River, and march on Richmond.[35]

More talk and questions followed, particularly concerning the availability of river transport, but nothing came of this. McDowell and Franklin couldn't answer some of Lincoln's questions on the state of the army. Lincoln told Franklin and McDowell to do a little fact-finding and meet with him at 8:00 p.m. the next day.[36]

In his conversations with Franklin the following morning, McDowell successfully argued against the York landing, saying the Union would meet the same obstacles on the Peninsula as it faced near Manassas, but that it would just cost more money and, worse, more *time*, while allowing the Confederates to concentrate their forces against the Union move. Moreover, politically, particularly in the international realm, McDowell believed the clearing of the virtual blockade of Washington by driving back the Confederates vitally important; not doing so demonstrated "impotence." They gathered the needed information from various government bureaus and joined Lincoln, those from the night before, and a new addition, Postmaster General Montgomery Blair. McDowell and Franklin recommended operations against the Confederate army around Manassas, and a rambunctious discussion ensued. Blair led the dissenters; he favored a Peninsula movement and likened McDowell's proposal to the Union plan of the year before that produced the defeat at Manassas. Despite much back-and-forth, no decision was forthcoming. Lincoln wanted Meigs present to consult on water transportation, so they adjourned until three o'clock the next day.[37]

When Meigs joined the growing party he promised he could provide the necessary water transport in six weeks, and they talked more about attacking near Washington. But by this time McClellan had stirred from his sickbed, had visited Lincoln, and was ready to again take up his command. Lincoln dismissed them until the next day, having been told McClellan would be well enough to join them then.[38]

When the group reconvened on the thirteenth, McDowell briefed the attendees on his plan, saying the army could be ready for the overland march in three weeks; the water move needed four to six. Meigs bid a sullen McClellan to promise some type of movement toward Manassas. McClellan insisted the enemy was too strong, possessing 175,000 men to McClellan's nearly 200,000. Meigs continued to press: "The President expects something from you." McClellan replied, "If I tell him my plans they will be in the New York Herald tomorrow morning. He can't keep a secret, he will tell them to Tadd [Lincoln's son]." "That is a pity," Meigs replied, "but he is the President,—the Commander-in-Chief; he has a right to know."[39]

Meigs kept applying the prod, and the mountain finally moved, a little. McClellan revealed no details of the plans for his army but did express his belief in the utility of Buell's central line of advance. "Well," Lincoln said, "on this assurance of the General that he will press the advance in Kentucky, I will be satisfied, and will adjourn this Council."[40]

The next day McClellan himself gave the details of his plan to a reporter from the *New York Herald* in a warped effort to gain Democratic political support and counter Republican criticism, something Lincoln never knew.[41] Nonetheless, McClellan had also been correct about how loose-lipped Lincoln could be with military information.[42] Meigs left the meeting with the impression that "McClellan would prefer to send forward any other troops than those under his present command."[43] Meigs may have been right, and may have identified one key to McClellan's personality: an insufficiency of what Clausewitz defined as the courage to bear the responsibility for tough decisions.[44] Some call this "moral courage." McClellan had no lack of Clausewitz's other brand, the physical—his three brevets for bravery under fire during the Mexican War attest to a surfeit of this. But commanding literally hundreds of thousands of men and leading them into a fight that would result in the death and maiming of untold scores was a different matter. Few would not have hesitated under the weight of the responsibility that McClellan bore daily. He could train and build an army. He could plan. He could, when given no other choice, lead the force into battle, but he lacked the decisiveness Clausewitz believed necessary for good leadership at the topmost rung.

The meeting did produce action. Though he seemed to have taken away some understanding of how much public opinion was weighing upon the president, McClellan offered proof of Meigs's assessment by ordering someone else to advance. "You have no idea of the pressure brought to bear here upon the Government for a forward movement," McClellan told Buell. "It is so strong that it seems absolutely necessary to make the advance on Eastern Tennessee at once." McClellan, always a respecter of civilian property (critics would say especially of Confederate property), even told Buell to take the wagons he needed from civilians if those the government provided proved insufficient. Unsurprisingly, McClellan also intended for the movement to produce effects relative to his own operational area of command by possibly drawing away some of Joe Johnston's strength.[45]

Lincoln's conference sparked other activity. McClellan's order forced Buell to acquiesce to Lincoln. The president replied to Buell with a letter (of which Halleck also received a copy) that became well known because it revealed Lincoln's view of *how* the war should be fought. It was an idea that had been jelling in Lincoln's mind, one he had related to his friend Senator Orville Browning the day before, in a conversation where Lincoln also confessed that "he was thinking of taking the field himself."[46] It also showed a Lincoln absorbing the ideas of his military-related reading and of his military chiefs—then taking them further. "I state my general idea of this war to be that we have the *greater* numbers," the president began, "and the enemy has the *greater* facility of concentrating forces upon points of collision; that we must fail, unless we can find some way of making *our* advantage an overmatch for *his*; and that this can only be done by menacing him with superior forces at *different* points, at the *same* time; so that we can safely attack, one, or both, if he makes no change; and if he *weakens* one to *strengthen* the other, forbear to attack the strengthened one, but seize, and hold the weakened one, gaining so much."[47]

Lincoln then gave operational suggestions for implementing his proposed strategy of simultaneous pressure. Halleck should "menace Columbus" while Buell did the same to Bowling Green and eastern Tennessee. "If the enemy shall concentrate at Bowling-Green," Lincoln continued, "do not retire from his front; yet do not fight him there, either, but seize Columbus and East Tennessee, one or both, left exposed by the concentration at Bowling Green."[48]

The roots of Lincoln's strategic concept can be seen in his earlier memorandum, which called for multiple, concurrent movements against the enemy, including coastal operations.[49] In his letter to Buell, Lincoln proposed one of the best methods of fighting the war yet put forward by a Union leader. He broached a strategic idea (simultaneous movement) and then applied it to an operational area (Tennessee and Kentucky). His generals rejected Lincoln's idea, insisting that it violated the teachings on concentration of the famous military theorist and interpreter of Napoleon, Baron Antoine-Henri Jomini, and deeming it "the product of a mind that did not know the rules of war."[50] They failed to grasp the distinction between the strategic and operational (or what they might have branded a campaign). The implementation of a Union strategy along the lines of Lincoln's idea would be plagued by generals unwilling or incapable of carrying it out—at least until 1864. The Union commanders in 1861–62—Buell, Halleck, McClellan—stressed their lack of readiness and refused to move.[51] Halleck, for one, simply did not understand the necessity for action any more than did McClellan and Buell. Nor did he think the army leadership bore any blame for the continued inactivity of the bulk of Union forces. On January 20 he wrote McClellan that he had "received no information in respect to the general plan of campaign," and because of this felt "much hesitation in recommending any line of operations for these and other troops which I may be able to withdraw from Missouri." He believed his actions should be part of "some general plan." He also blamed others for the situation. "I take it for granted, general," he wired McClellan, "that what has heretofore been done has been the result of political policy rather than military strategy, and that the want of success on our part is attributable to the politicians rather than to the generals."[52] In truth, blame could only be laid at the feet of the general in chief and his subordinates, such as Halleck.

Halleck went on to give his own analysis of the Union's strategic errors, which was scattering troops to the point of making them incapable of attacking in great numbers. Again, the politicians received the blame for Union military failures: "I am aware that you, general, are in no way responsible for this, these movements having been governed by political expediency and in many cases directed by politicians in order to subserve particular interests."[53]

One thing that Halleck did not seem to understand was that McClellan *was* responsible for the dispersion of Union forces. He was the general in chief. Moreover, this had not weakened the Union strategically because it possessed greater strength. Halleck saw only the operational and tactical pictures. He also denounced any push down the Mississippi as premature, favoring lines of advance up the Tennessee and Cumberland rivers, Nashville the objective. This, he noted, would turn Columbus and force the Confederates to abandon Bowling Green, preventing a costly siege of the well-fortified Columbus. "This line of the Cumberland or Tennessee is the great central line of the Western theater of war," Halleck wrote, adding that success here would give the Union two great navigable rivers into the heart of the Confederacy.[54]

He also believed that this should not be attempted with fewer than 60,000 men. Supporting this would be a column of 10,000 men launched into Arkansas to cut off Sterling Price's Confederate army from its supplies and force it to withdraw. This would then allow the capture of New Madrid, Missouri, making Cairo, Illinois, safe and freeing up its garrison, while ensuring that Johnston and Buckner would not dare cross the Green River. To accomplish his plan, Halleck believed it necessary to gather troops from various places and cancel any peripheral operations, such as those being proposed for western Arkansas and Texas, and put "a small force" on the Green River.[55]

Despite all of this planning, Halleck himself admitted that he had not chosen any definite line of advance. "That must be a matter of further study if the general idea should be approved."[56]

MCCLELLAN, THOUGH, *WAS* TRYING to figure out what to do. In late January, he considered shifting the main front of the Union army from the Eastern Theater to the Western and even had Stanton make a study of the necessary rail and water transport. Nothing came of this.[57] In the end, McClellan stuck to his view that the Eastern Theater was where the war would be decided. In late January he described his strategy, as well as the Union's strategic priorities, writing, "The great points from which important operations are to be conducted are, first, the Department of the Potomac, in front of which is posted and strongly intrenched the largest and best-armed body of the insurgents guarding the approach to Richmond; second, the Department of the Ohio, opposed to the next great body of the rebels in Kentucky; third, the Department of the Missouri, the army in which, besides the clearing of the State of Missouri, has for a prime object the control of the Mississippi River and operations against New Orleans." Simultaneously, while troops from the Department of Kansas supported the movements from Missouri, there would be subsidiary operations against the Confederate coast "designed to draw off and distract the enemy." He wanted Thomas W. Sherman's force in Port Royal, South Carolina, "to attack Charleston or Savannah or both," while Ambrose Burnside pushed into Albemarle Sound and struck southern Virginia or North Carolina. Meanwhile, there would be Gulf of Mexico operations to seize Confederate positions in the Tortugas, Key West, and Pensacola, "together with demonstrations against the Florida coast."[58] Any other "outside operations" were to be undertaken only in support of the main plan.

McClellan was drawing upon the proposal he had submitted when first arriving in Washington, as well as the ideas advanced for coastal operations. He also advocated only the operations most likely to divert pressure from *his* advance, which he considered the most important, a point about which he was probably correct. By this time, though, Lincoln had grown even more frustrated with the Union armies' lack of progress. He was particularly eager for the Army of the Potomac to produce results. When it had 200,000 men under arms it cost the U.S. government $600,000 per day, not counting the expense of the necessary supporting steam transports. Lincoln needed

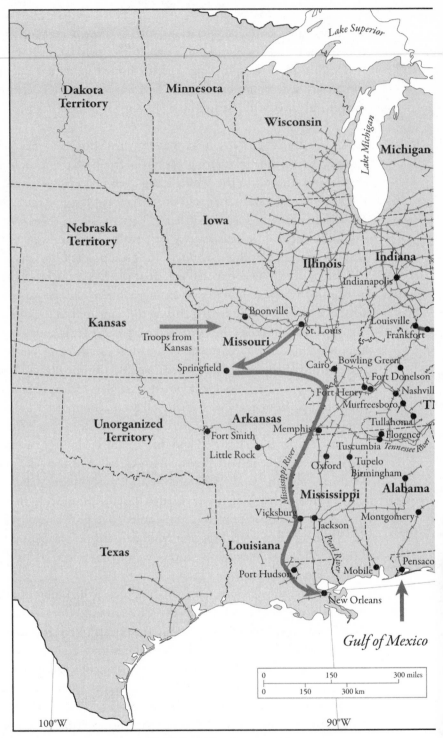

McClellan's Plan, January 1862.

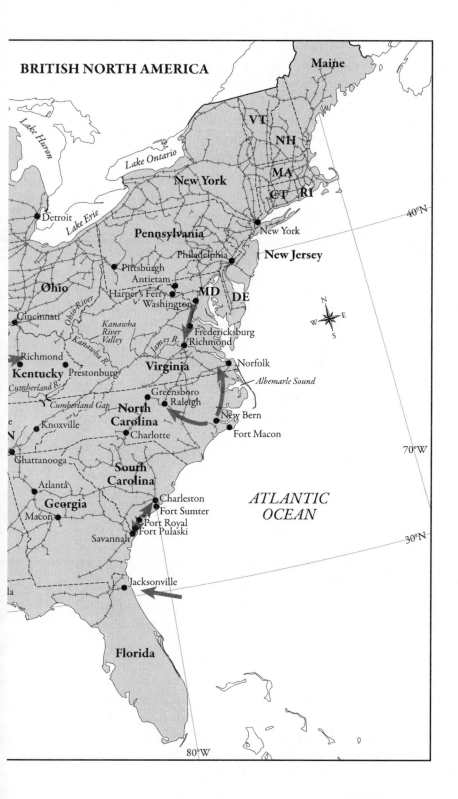

successes to encourage the people's willingness to sacrifice such great amounts of wealth.[59] In an effort to ensure that things began to happen militarily, Lincoln promulgated his General War Order No. 1 on January 27, 1862. This designated February 22, 1862, as "the day for a general movement of all the land and naval forces of the United States against the insurgent forces."[60] He issued this without consulting McClellan and from this point took an even greater interest in McClellan's actions.[61] The president had also just begun. To ensure that McClellan moved, Lincoln issued Special War Order No. 1. This commanded the Army of the Potomac to advance to take "a point upon" the railroad southwest of Manassas Junction on or before February 22.[62] Lincoln's orders half worked. He got a response out of McClellan, but not the one he wanted.

McClellan was not happy with Lincoln's order to move against Manassas Junction, though he was aware of the political and public opinion pressure also mounting against the general himself to do something with the Army of the Potomac other than march it in parades. Shortly after Stanton's elevation to secretary of war, he and McClellan discussed a campaign idea that had been jelling in the young general's mind for some time: attacking Richmond via the Chesapeake. McClellan had submitted his idea; Lincoln had rejected it and immediately issued his aforementioned Special War Order No. 1, ordering McClellan to move.[63]

McClellan responded by not moving. Instead, he asked for a chance to make his case. Lincoln bowed, and McClellan produced a detailed discussion of the Union's strategic options in the Eastern Theater, including a breakdown of what would become known as his Urbana Plan. But before delineating the North's options, McClellan launched into the reasons behind the Union Army's inactivity. He reminded Lincoln of the poor state of the Union forces in the East when he had come to town, as well as the shoddy condition of the Union armies in the West, which delayed operations there.[64] In all of these things McClellan spoke the truth, but these factors were not responsible for the strategic paralysis gripping the Union; it was an issue of leadership.

McClellan reached back again to his original grand plan, always a handy excuse. "I asked for an effective movable force far exceeding the aggregate now on the banks of the Potomac," he wrote. "I have not the force I asked for." McClellan also insisted, sincerely, that he had hoped to make a general advance in December but had been mistaken in believing this possible. "My wish was to gain possession of the Eastern Tennessee Railroads as a preliminary movement," McClellan wrote, "then to follow it up immediately by an attack on Nashville & Richmond as nearly at the same time as possible."[65]

McClellan had already clearly expressed to Stanton his idea of what the North should do to win the war: "I have ever regarded our true policy [strategy] as being that of fully preparing ourselves & then seeking for the most decisive results;—I do not wish to waste life in useless battles, but prefer to strike at the heart."[66] He believed it would take hard fighting, which he wished to avoid at virtually any cost (perhaps including, one could argue, even that of winning the war). He wanted to prosecute the struggle in one great, multi-pronged campaign, the main tentacle striking at Richmond. Every foreseeable preparation would be made preliminary to launching this clump of offensive operations intended to strike at the guts of the Confederacy, delivering a quick Union victory with the lowest possible cost in lives.

McClellan's operational plan for prosecuting the war in the East comes through clearly in the options he laid out for Stanton. One thing stressed by the military theorist Jomini was the importance of solid bases from which to mount operations. In Jominian fashion, McClellan presented two such potential anchors for an advance by the Army of the Potomac.[67] The first was Washington, from which the army could attack "the enemy's entrenched positions at Centreville, Manassas etc, or else a movement to turn one or both flanks of those positions, or a combination of the two plans." This was not the course McClellan wanted to take, and he gave a detailed analysis of why.[68] Most important, McClellan thought this move would not be decisive. He believed that while it might bring a victory, as well as some other positive results, it would not win the war nor destroy the main Confederate army, which could fall back when pressed by Union forces and fight "again & again, should the condition of his troops permit." Even if the enemy was not able to fight outside of the Richmond trenches, the Union forces would find it difficult to "follow" them to the capital because the Confederates would destroy the rail lines and bridges as they retreated. This would force the Union, in the end, to change "the entire theatre of war, or seek a shorter land route to Richmond with a smaller available force & at an expenditure of much more time than were we to adopt the short line at once."[69] Or, in other words, unless Lincoln did what McClellan had wanted to begin with.

McClellan concluded his soliloquy against a direct movement by noting that the result would simply be to force "the enemy to concentrate his forces & perfect his defensive measures at the very points where it is desirable to strike him where least prepared," meaning, of course, Richmond.[70] In this, despite all else, McClellan proved absolutely correct. Any direct attack against Confederate forces in northern Virginia necessarily forced the South to concentrate at or near Richmond to protect their lines of communication and supply. Such proved the Confederate response in 1862 and in 1864–65.

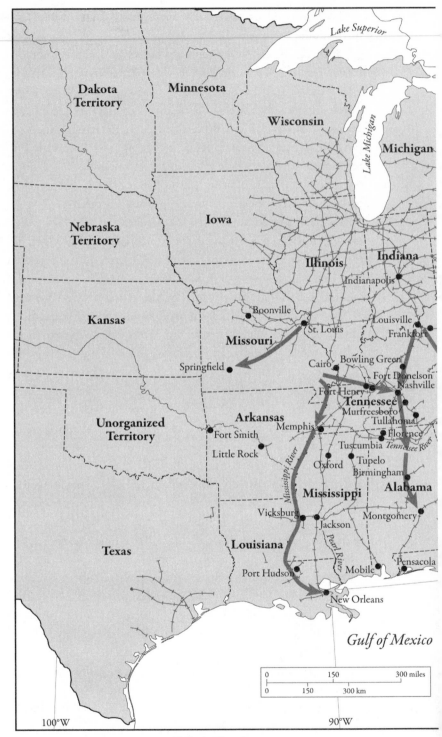

McClellan's Plan, Spring 1862.

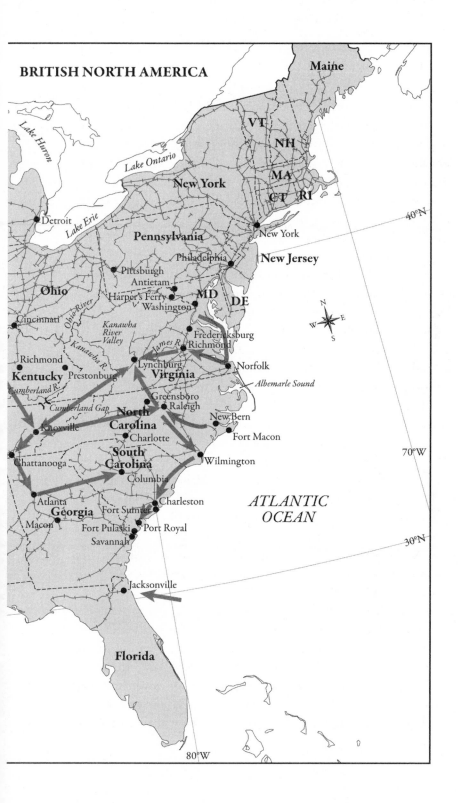

Then McClellan presented his alternative. "The second base of operations available for the Army of the Potomac is that of the lower Chesapeake Bay," he wrote, "which affords the shortest possible land routes to Richmond, & strikes directly at the heart of the enemy's power in the East." The roads were better here, McClellan said, the terrain generally more favorable, and spring arrived a few weeks earlier. Moreover, landing here would force the enemy to flee from their lines around Manassas to cover Richmond and Norfolk. McClellan promised big results, decisive ones, if success graced the movement: the capture of Richmond and Norfolk, the capture of the Confederate supply and communications lines, control of Chesapeake Bay, the securing of all of Virginia, and the Confederate abandonment of Tennessee and North Carolina.[71]

McClellan also argued that this plan provided better Union alternatives in the event of a defeat, giving the army a path of retreat down the Peninsula to Fortress Monroe, one made secure on its left flank by water and on its right by distance. Moreover, Union naval power could be brought to bear as well.[72]

If successful in battle, McClellan promised, he would produce dramatic operational and strategic results, and he intended that the other Union forces would be moving as well. His Virginia offensive was meant as an operational element of a larger strategic plan, one that again reached back to the original idea he had presented to Lincoln. Afterward, the Union "position would be—Burnside [in North Carolina] forming our left, Norfolk held securely, our centre connecting Burnside with Buell, both by Raleigh & Lynchburg, Buell in Eastern Tennessee & Northern Alabama, Halleck at Nashville & Memphis." Following this would be movements to link up with Thomas Sherman's troops in South Carolina by capturing Wilmington and Charleston, while the forces in the Union center drove into South Carolina and Georgia, Buell toward Montgomery, Alabama (or perhaps toward the main army in Georgia), and Halleck southward, down the Mississippi, to join hands with Union troops at New Orleans.[73]

All this would allow for the occupation of the South's ports, use of the Mississippi River, and reassertion of Union control over Arkansas, Louisiana, and Texas, permitting the Union "to force the slaves to labor for our subsistence instead of that of the rebels"; it would also bid "defiance to all foreign interference."[74] Again, McClellan was reaching back to his earlier proposal, insisting, "Such is the object I have ever had in view; this is the general plan which I have hoped to accomplish."[75] As always, everything was subsidiary to his Virginia drive.

After making his strategic arguments, McClellan went into the operational details. He planned to land the Army of the Potomac at Urbana on the lower Rappahannock River, though he also had two alternative landing sites, Mob Jack Bay and Fortress Monroe. "A rapid movement from Urbana would probably cut off [John] Magruder in the *Peninsula*, & enable us to occupy Richmond before it could be strongly reinforced." If this failed, they could use the navy to cross the James River and put the army "in the rear of Richmond, thus forcing the enemy to come out & attack us—for his position would be untenable, with us on the southern bank of the river." He hoped to land 110,000 to 140,000 troops, preferably the higher number, and promised that his operation would not leave Washington unprotected. He assumed a rapid movement on his part that would allow the seizure of Richmond before the enemy could sufficiently react. McClellan strongly urged the adoption of his second proposal. "If at the expense of 30 days delay we can gain a decisive victory which will probably end the war," he insisted, "it is far cheaper than to gain a battle tomorrow that produces no final results, & may require years of warfare & expenditure to follow up." McClellan believed engaging the enemy at Manassas would at best produce a battlefield victory from which it would be difficult, if not impossible, to derive any profit. McClellan, to his credit, then asked a question that virtually no other Civil War military or political leader had or would: if this was done, what next?[76]

McClellan refused to guarantee victory at Manassas (a wise move) but insisted that "on the other line I regard success as certain by all the chances of war.... Nothing is *certain* in war—but all the chances are in favor of this movement." The young general concluded his argument for his Urbana Plan by stating: "I will stake my life, my reputation on the result—more than that, I will stake upon it the success of our cause."[77]

McClellan gave his plan to Stanton on February 3, 1862, but before the secretary of war could send it to the president, Lincoln compared his Occoquan Plan with McClellan's Urbana operation via a short list of questions:

You and I have distinct and different plans for a movement of the Army of the Potomac—yours to be down the Chesapeake, up the Rappahannock to Urbana, and across land to the terminus of the railroad on the York River; mine to move directly to a point on the railroads southwest of Manassas.

If you will give me satisfactory answers to the following questions I shall gladly yield my plan to yours:

1st. Does not your plan involve a greatly larger expenditure of *time* and *money* than mine?

2d. Wherein is a victory more *certain* by your plan than mine?

3d. Wherein is a victory *more valuable* by your plan than mine?

4th. In fact, would it not be *less* valuable in this, that it would break no great line of the enemy's communications, while mine would?

5th. In case of disaster, would not a retreat be more difficult by your plan than mine?[78]

McClellan believed his letter to Stanton basically answered these questions, and he did not bother to reply.[79]

Lincoln was not convinced by McClellan's case for the Peninsula Campaign. Underlying McClellan's plan was a belief that working from a base on the Chesapeake was the only way for his inferior Union army to defeat Confederate general Joseph E. Johnston's supposedly larger force. Indeed, all of McClellan's plans for the Peninsula, as we've seen, had as a basis this false perception of Union numerical inferiority. Moreover, McClellan banked upon surprise and hoped to beat the Confederate forces to Richmond. Here he assumed quick Union moves and an enemy caught off-kilter that remained so. But what if the Union failed to move faster than the enemy? He gave insufficient consideration to what Clausewitz termed "interaction" and what many in the military define as "the enemy gets a vote." Reluctantly, Lincoln accepted McClellan's proposal.[80]

Union veteran and writer George Bruce argued that Lincoln's idea was better than the one McClellan subsequently proposed because McClellan's exposed Washington to a possible Confederate attack. In some respects Bruce was correct. Committing the bulk of the Union armies in the East to the Peninsula created opportunities for the Confederates, who had generals not averse to risk.[81] One can also understand Lincoln's faith in his idea by recalling that McDowell, a professional soldier, had developed substantively the same plan.

During the winter of 1861–62, more of McClellan's views on how the war should be fought bubbled to the surface. He told Lincoln he wanted to prosecute the war without enraging the civilian population of the South. He also hoped to avoid head-on assaults and the embittering casualties that would result, and instead pursue a war of maneuver that would still accomplish the defeat of the Confederate armies. McClellan wanted to fight while conciliating, which demonstrated a marked lack of awareness of the determination of his enemy. The result (in McClellan's mind): an advance on the fortifications of Richmond via the Peninsula, the capture of the capital, and a quick end to the war.[82]

McClellan's plan, in both its strategic and operational elements, was not doomed to fail. Conceptually, an operational move to the Peninsula and a quick drive on Richmond were not bad ideas. Indeed, it came staggeringly close to success.[83] McClellan's arguments for his case were cogent, logically presented, and convincing. But they also were in many ways self-serving and sometimes drifted into the grandiose. His plan depended upon too many things going his way, such as expecting the roads and weather to be better on the Peninsula than along the invasion route from Washington, and that the enemy would be surprised.

IN THEIR FOCUS on eastern Tennessee, both Lincoln and McClellan were misguided by their genuine sympathy for the plight of persecuted Unionists, to whose rescue they felt obligated to come. This region, however, had little strategic importance. Moreover, its lack of railroads and rivers made it a difficult place in which to mount any sustained campaign with a significant force. Lincoln wanted action for political reasons, as part of a political balancing act to keep the various factions of his party together. And there were also the War Democrats to please, some of whom hailed from eastern Tennessee. To McClellan what was important was that action in this arena supported his planned efforts in Virginia. But any Union action in the West depended upon weak reeds, Buell and Halleck, who refused to do their jobs.

Historian Joseph L. Harsh paints a picture of a McClellan who wanted to pursue a limited war in terms of the means utilized as well as the objective sought.[84] But for the Union the Civil War was not a limited war. The Union government sought the destruction of the Confederate political system, an unlimited objective. Moreover, if it was to win, the Union could not restrict the means it was willing to commit, nor tie its hands too much regarding the level of violence and destruction it would use against its foe; the enemy was simply too strong and determined for this. Harsh suggests, correctly, that McClellan wanted to fight the war with a minimal level of violence and to avoid escalation, and therefore wanted to take his time, prepare, and win in one grand campaign. In short, McClellan wanted a slow, methodical war.

But McClellan ignored the internal and foreign political ramifications of not moving quickly. He also ignored what Clausewitz taught about the tendency of wars to escalate. Moving too slowly gives the other side time to prepare as well. It drags out the war, and the longer a war goes on, the more likely each side is to throw in more and more of its resources. By delaying, and by not forcing his subordinate commanders to advance, McClellan destroyed any hope that his strategy of minimal escalation, or "soft war," would succeed. McClellan hoped, as he put it, to "dodge the nigger question" and keep the destruction of property to a minimum. But his hesitation forced the North to raise the level of violence and destruction in order to break the South's war-making capability, as well as its will, and led Lincoln to emancipate the South's slaves in order to use them against their former masters. Despite his talents (of which there were undoubtedly many), McClellan failed in Clausewitz's supreme test: he did not understand the nature of the war in which he was involved. In this he was hardly alone.

The Foundations of Naval Strategy

Nor must Uncle Sam's Web-feet be forgotten. At all the
watery margins they have been present.

—ABRAHAM LINCOLN

AS MUCH AS THE UNION and the South were unprepared for war on land, they were even more unprepared for war at sea. The Union had little naval power; the South had none. But both embarked upon vigorous efforts to correct this.

At the start of the war the U.S. Navy had ninety ships, a deceptively large number, given that only forty-two were commissioned vessels and exactly three of these plied American waters. It was also the wrong navy for the war the Union had to fight. A high-seas force, it lacked the equipment, doctrine, and training for the operations in coastal and inland waterways that dominated its employment during the struggle. The two figures most influential in the development and operations of the Union navy were Secretary of the Navy Gideon Welles and Assistant Secretary Gustavus V. Fox. Welles brought organizational ability and good personnel judgment to the job (and a beard rivaled only by that of German admiral Alfred von Tirpitz); Fox added professional naval experience and superb administrative skills. Together they built an effective naval force.[1]

The Confederate secretary of the navy was Stephen R. Mallory. A former Florida senator, he had chaired the Senate Naval Affairs Committee, overseeing some modern ship programs. He also kept a keen eye on European ironclad development. To help him build a Confederate navy he had the services of around 300 former U.S. naval officers, but he lacked the equivalent of a Fox.[2]

Union Naval Strategy

LINCOLN'S BLOCKADE SET WELLES the task of watching 3,500 miles of Confederate coastline. "Father Neptune," as Lincoln called him, not only had to enforce the blockade but had to build the navy to do it with.[3]

Politically, it was critical work. Under international law, the nation proclaiming a blockade had to enforce it or it did not constitute a true blockade.

The Confederacy branded it a "paper blockade" that violated the rights of the
Confederacy's potential trading neutrals, an argument aimed particularly at
Great Britain. The British eventually subscribed to the Union's view and gave
it official recognition in February 1862. Porous the blockade may have been,
but British recognition of it spilled over to other countries, creating a cumulative effect. Confederate secretary of state Benjamin wrote in April 1862 that
"the dearth of cotton, in Europe, so far from being caused by the blockade, is
due solely to the respect to which neutral powers have yielded to the proclamation of Mr. Lincoln interdicting commerce with our coast."[4]

To get the vessels necessary to institute the blockade, Welles recalled most
of the Union ships on overseas stations. He then began buying and leasing
craft and taking them from other Federal agencies. The navy grew exponentially. In nine months the Union commissioned 76 ships, bought 136, and
had 52 built. Inside a year there were 300.[5]

Welles faced an immediate problem involving basing. The Union lacked
ports close to the critical zones of operation. Ships spent too much time in
transit, sometimes more than on station, which cut down the time available
for executing their missions. The navy also needed bases for repair, supply, and
coaling, and the sheer size of the areas under the respective responsibilities
of the initial two commands made communication difficult. Supplying the
geographical information so critical to the Union's coastal operations was the
government's Coastal Survey office, headed by Alexander D. Bache, a scientist
and a "great-grandson of Benjamin Franklin." To manage the various issues
related to the navy's blockading squadrons, and to protect this office, which
he feared would be destroyed by the war and the South's secession, Bache proposed the Blockade Board in May 1861, a temporary panel to examine the
various issues surrounding the blockade. Welles agreed.[6]

Captain Samuel F. Du Pont, a member of the famous explosives-manu-
facturing family, chaired the board. An experienced naval officer, Du Pont
had served on blockade duty during the Mexican War and knew very well
what such work entailed. He believed blockading the extensive coastline was
unnecessary, arguing that the Union only had "to cover the ports of entry—
that is all the foreign interest has to require." Others on the board were Bache,
Major John G. Barnard, an army engineer who despite being "deaf as a post"
was in charge of the capital's defenses, and Charles Henry Davis, a good friend
of Bache's and a veteran of both the navy and the Coastal Survey.[7]

On June 25, 1861, Welles outlined the board's duties, which began with
an order to study all the government's information on coastal areas of the
South useful to the blockading squadrons. He stressed the necessity of seizing

at least two ports on the Atlantic seaboard, suggested Fernandina, Florida, and Port Royal, South Carolina, and wanted advice on this. He also encouraged the board to come up with other recommendations, including some for the Gulf of Mexico.[8] Originally the board was supposed to function as an information-gathering and -sifting operation, but Welles expanded its role to actual planning of operations in support of the blockade, including seizing useful ports as well as figuring out means of closing channels.[9]

The board wasted little time, quickly concluding the impossibility of keeping the blockading squadrons properly coaled unless the Union seized a port in South Carolina and another in either Georgia or Florida. In July 1861 it advocated the capture of Fernandina and Port Royal, as Welles had suggested. The recommendations went to Lincoln and his cabinet on July 26, in the wake of the defeat at Bull Run. The president approved the two operations. Lincoln had issued a memorandum on strengthening the blockade three days before, probably as a result of reports from the board.[10]

Overall, the board offered excellent advice, but it was not flawless. It advocated tightening the blockade of New Orleans on August 6 but mistakenly believed that blocking sea traffic to the city would have the same effect as capturing it, which, the board believed, the Union did not have the resources to do because of the city's fortifications. Instead, it recommended taking Ship Island, located halfway between Mobile and New Orleans, and using it as a base. This happened on September 17, 1861, and Ship Island served as a jumping-off point for the eventual capture of New Orleans in 1862. The board's biggest failing, however, was never determining the number and type of vessels needed for the blockade.[11]

Welles placed Du Pont in command of the naval forces assigned to attack Port Royal. General Thomas W. Sherman commanded the army troops. Du Pont was given his choice of objectives, but Fox probably convinced him that Port Royal was the best target. After Du Pont's departure for North Carolina, the board members began going their separate ways. The September 6, 1861, memorandum on Ship Island constituted its last formal report. By October, the board was defunct.[12]

Its continuance would have been a good thing for the navy. An army version—a forerunner of a general staff—also could have proved eminently valuable.

Confederate Naval Strategy

THE FIRST PLANK of Confederate naval strategy was put in place by Jefferson Davis. Replying to Lincoln's initial call for volunteers, Davis issued a call for privateers, a traditional response of weaker naval powers.[13] Some answered Davis's call, but the approach met with immediate problems, not the least of which being that European states had outlawed privateering in April 1856. The British Proclamation of Neutrality of May 13, 1861, effectively granted de facto recognition to the Confederate government but did not establish diplomatic ties. The French later followed suit. To the British, this meant that the Confederates had to abide by the treaty against privateering, while the Union had to construct an effective blockade. Moreover, early on, the British, French, and Spanish forbade privateers from bringing prizes into their respective ports. Meanwhile, the Union had tightened the blockade, leaving no place to sell prizes. Taken together, these factors killed Confederate privateering.[14]

Confederate secretary of the navy Stephen Mallory had his own ideas on naval strategy, ones driven by weakness. He sought the integration of new technologies to overcome the Confederacy's inferior naval position. The South lacked the North's industrial capacity and skilled mechanics; they would have to develop these, often from scratch. As Alfred Thayer Mahan pointed out, the South also suffered from having an extensive and accessible coastline, with a population too small to protect it.[15] The Union would take advantage of this.

After the Confederate Congress allocated money for a navy on March 16, 1861, Mallory began trying to buy suitable ships anywhere he could. This netted a few vessels. But Mallory believed that it would eventually be possible to construct ships in Confederate yards, and he knew what he wanted first. "I propose to adopt a class of vessels hitherto unknown to naval services," he wrote. Mallory craved fast, steam-powered raiders with rifled cannons. "Small propeller ships with great speed, lightly armed with these guns, must soon become, as the light artillery and rifles of the deep, a most destructive element of naval warfare." He had also already bought two steamships, *Sumter* and *McRae*, which he dispatched as raiders.[16]

On May 8, 1861, James D. Bulloch, a former U.S. naval officer, met with Mallory in Montgomery to discuss the role of the Confederate navy. "It was thought to be of prime importance to get cruisers to sea as soon as possible," Bulloch later said of the conversation, "to harass the enemy's commerce, and to compel him to send his own ships-of-war in pursuit, which might otherwise be employed in blockading the Southern ports."[17] Mallory sent Bulloch to Europe to buy or have built six propeller-driven ships, preferring they be powered by both steam and sail, and insisting they have long endurance. He wanted speed above all and armament of only a few guns. Smaller was better because they would be cheaper and allow the South to purchase more, but would still be capable of taking on enough supplies for a six-month voyage when launched.[18] Mallory's approach foreshadowed the submarine commerce warfare of both world wars.[19] Bulloch soon signed contracts for two such ships, Confederate finances having reduced the number, and despite the fact that his plans were revealed in the Northern press at about the time he arrived in Britain.[20]

Bulloch's deal produced the deadly Confederate raiders CSS *Florida* and CSS *Alabama*. *Florida* left Liverpool in March 1861 with a British crew, bound for a rendezvous in the Bahamas with a vessel carrying its weapons. Here the Confederates took over the ship and armed it, but an outbreak of yellow fever among the crew forced Captain John A. Maffit to take the *Florida* into Mobile for more men. They slipped through the blockade in January 1862. An eight-month cruise followed, one in which the *Florida* took twenty-two Union ships before finding temporary refuge in the French port of Brest for much-needed repairs. *Florida* sailed again on February 10, 1864, taking another thirteen Union ships on this cruise. The North finally destroyed the raider on October 7, 1864, when Napoleon Collins, the captain of USS *Wachusett*, rammed *Florida* at three o'clock in the morning in the neutral Brazilian port of Bahia, then hauled her out to sea.[21]

Fresh from a successful command of the raider CSS *Sumter*, during which he captured or burned eighteen Union ships, Raphael Semmes, a veteran of thirty years in the U.S. Navy, became *Alabama*'s commander. After sailing from Liverpool on May 15, 1862, Semmes rendezvoused in the Azores with a Confederate merchantman and took on his weapons. He spent the next two years terrorizing Union shipping, taking sixty-five ships worth $6.5 million. *Alabama* was sunk off Cherbourg on June 19 by Captain John Winslow's USS *Kearsarge*. Winslow and Semmes had shared a cabin as young lieutenants during the Mexican War.[22]

Mallory also wanted another type of ship for something far different from commerce raiding, one inspired by the old ship-of-the-line but possessed of some modern twists: an ironclad, steam-powered warship with rifled guns. He believed technological superiority would allow the South to overcome the disparity in numbers. "Such a vessel at this time could traverse the entire coast of the United States," Mallory insisted, "prevent all blockades, and encounter, with a fair prospect of success, their entire navy." They would allow the South to seize the naval initiative from its hidebound opponent. He eventually followed two routes to obtaining ironclads—buying them abroad and building them at home.[23]

The Confederate Congress proved very receptive to Mallory's ideas, voting $3 million to buy warships, including $2 million for ironclads.[24] Mallory dispatched Lieutenant James North to Europe with instructions to try to buy a ship of the *Gloire* class, the innovative French ironclad commissioned in 1858. If this proved impossible, he should try to have one built.[25] North, though, proved more interested in sightseeing than in doing his job. Mallory's agents tried buying ironclads in Europe from May to July 1861, without success. The Confederate navy secretary decided to build them at home and signed deals for a few ships.[26] Mallory also decided to build flotillas at various ports for their defense and gunboats for the Mississippi.[27]

Building ironclads consumed most of the South's naval effort. Mallory began studying the possibility of their construction in Southern yards in early June 1861. The first one arose from the burnt-out hulk of the USS *Merrimack* at Hampton Roads. The Confederacy had to do it this way because the South lacked the ability to build the ship it wanted from scratch. Mallory planned to use this new vessel, which became CSS *Virginia*, to clear the Union navy from Hampton Roads and Virginia's ports. He generally believed that ironclad rams (which *Virginia* became) would be most useful for coastal defense. By late 1861, the Confederates had five ironclads in the works.[28]

The Confederacy built ironclads to compensate for the enemy's great numbers of warships. The South could not build oceangoing armored ships like Britain's *Warrior* and France's *Gloire*, but it could build slower, coastal ones like *Virginia*. These would, Mallory insisted, "enable us with a small number of vessels comparatively to keep our waters free from the enemy and ultimately to contest with them the possession of his own."[29] Mallory envisioned great but ultimately unrealistic achievements for *Virginia*. He believed that with a calm sea it could sail up the coast and attack New York City, causing such a panic that it would end the war. The *Virginia's* success at Hampton Roads—ramming and sinking the USS *Cumberland*, then setting ablaze and driving aground the USS *Congress*—spurred Mallory to press the building of the CSS *Louisiana* in New Orleans, remarking that the "ship, if completed, would raise the blockade of every Gulf port in 10 days."[30]

Mallory also faced pressure to protect the Confederacy's harbors and rivers. This intensified as the Union began launching landings in the summer of 1861 and coastal defense became a priority. The Confederate army played a key role. Robert E. Lee, a son of Henry "Light Horse Harry" Lee, a prominent American cavalry commander during the Revolutionary War, ranked second in the West Point class of 1829. He served in the Mexican War, where he was wounded, and acquired a reputation as a superb officer. Later, he was superintendent of West Point, and commanded the U.S. Marines and militia that suppressed John Brown and his raiders at Harpers Ferry in October 1859.

Lee was offered command of a Union army at the outbreak of the war but declined; he would not raise his hand against his native Virginia. After service in his home state, including an unsuccessful campaign in its western parts, he took command of a new military department covering South Carolina, Georgia, and the Atlantic side of Florida in November 1861. He realized that Confederate coastal fortifications could not stand up to Union naval bombardment, so he evacuated all of them—except those protecting major cities—and built others inland, out of the range of Union shipboard guns. He had certain waterways blocked and concentrated the troops inland so that they could be shifted to threatened areas. Historian Raimondo Luraghi assesses Lee's system by comparing it with German defenses during World War II: "The strategic rationale upon which this defensive structure was founded was so well conceived that it did not fall until almost three years later, when it was taken from the rear by troops coming overland, whereas the so-called German Atlantic Wall, based on the idea of last-ditch defense on the seashore, fell to the first formidable blow from the sea."[31] This is true as far as it goes. But the Union never pushed the Confederate defensive system with a heavy hand. If it had, it probably would not have survived.

Mallory again turned to technology to provide an answer to the problem of coastal defense. The Confederacy invested heavily in what were called "torpedoes," which today are known as mines. Mines pre-dated the Confederacy, but the South would be the first nation to make them a staple of its naval defense. The man first put in charge of mining the South's waters was Matthew Fontaine Maury, a prickly former naval officer famous internationally for his scientific pursuits, particularly in oceanography and navigation. Others in the Confederacy also began making torpedoes in late 1861 and early 1862. Davis believed them the South's most effectual form of naval defense. Confederate mine warfare probably sank or damaged more than fifty Union navy ships, perhaps equaling 30,000 tons.[32]

The other technology involved submarine development. The Confederates began studying this in late 1861 and started building an unnamed submarine at the Tredegar Iron Works in Richmond before the year was out. It was decided to use the final product in Texas. Another such boat may have been built there and still others in Shreveport, Louisiana, though many of the details have been lost in the historical mists.[33]

The most famous Confederate submarine was the *H. L. Hunley*, the product of New Orleans–based inventors funded by Horace L. Hunley, a marine engineer and former Louisiana legislator. James McClintock, a former riverboat captain, and Baxter Watson supplied the ideas. They built their first boat in the fall of 1861, but it handled so poorly they abandoned it and built a second craft, CSS *Pioneer*. They successfully tested it just before the North attacked New Orleans, but then scuttled it to keep it out of Union hands. They went back to work, soon producing another vessel that sank during an attempt to attack a Union ship off Fort Morgan in Mobile Bay. Their fourth attempt produced the *Hunley*, which was 40 feet long, powered by a hand crank, and armed with a spar-mounted torpedo. Constructed in Mobile, it came to Charleston via rail, and killed most of its four crews before being lost after sinking the *Housatonic* on February 17, 1864, the first such submarine success.[34]

Matthew Maury—former U.S. Navy officer and later called the "father of modern oceanography"—had other ideas as well. In October 1861 he made some proposals that laid the foundation for another plank of Confederate naval strategy. Maury urged Virginia to create its own naval force (many Confederate states did), insisting that the Davis administration did not intend to have a navy. His plan, he said, could be fulfilled for what the Union paid for one large steamer and would create a naval force "sufficient to clear him [the Union] out of the Chesapeake and its waters" and "liberate the people of Maryland." "Big guns and little ships" were the essence of his strategy, and he sought "to construct a navy for the Chesapeake. In a few words it consists of rifled cannon of the largest caliber, mounted on launches propelled by steam, and floating just high enough to keep the water out." Rifles would outrange most of the guns on current Union ships, and the cost of a hundred such craft would amount to $10,000 per boat. "The Potomac Fleet of the enemy would find in a fleet of 100 such launches a perfect hornet's nest," Maury wrote.[35]

The proposal ended up before the Confederate Congress, and, with the help of the governor of Virginia, Maury got $2 million in December 1861. Though the plan was technically feasible, the weakness of Confederate industry made it a pipe dream. The arrival of the Union's *Monitor* and the later loss of the yards also helped kill Maury's plans.[36]

Maury's idea had its antecedents. Citing the European example of using gunboats and galleys in the Baltic and Mediterranean seas, Thomas Jefferson had advocated for a "mosquito fleet" of approximately 200 gunboats for the defense of America's coastline, most held in a reserve status. It was believed that small sail- and oar-powered craft armed with one or two cannon could harass larger enemy vessels, especially becalmed ones, in coastal waters, demoralizing the enemy crews with small arms and light cannon fire, while also preventing coastal descents.[37] Nothing came of Jefferson's idea, but steam power and better armaments made it more practical.

Maury's idea was also ahead of its time. The French Jeune École (Young School) of the later part of the nineteenth century pushed for the adoption of small, fast warships armed with self-propelled torpedoes. But the idea remained impractical for the same reason that Maury's proposal would have failed against Union naval power: before the advent of the steam-powered torpedo, the small ships lacked a weapon that enabled them to destroy larger armored warships. This development made small ships in littoral waters extremely dangerous threats to larger warships. Maury's plans would never be put to the test, but had the South been able to get these boats to sea, they would have been useless, being unprotected against the *Monitor* and other ironclad warships of the Union. Maury assumed Confederate innovation would remain unmet.

The Union's Reply

THE UNION CLOSELY EYED Confederate naval developments. Technologically, diplomatically, and militarily, the Union moved to counter them. On the technical side, in July 1861 Welles asked Congress for permission to establish a board to study ironclad development. Congress surprised Welles by giving him $1.5 million to build them. The Union navy picked three designs: USS *New Ironsides*, which was modeled after European vessels such as *Gloire* and HMS *Warrior*; USS *Galena*, an experimental vessel; and John Ericsson's now famous *Monitor*.[38] "His theory is impregnability in a vessel and immense caliber for his guns, which shall be irresistible," Welles wrote later.[39]

The Union possessed immense technical and industrial capability. This industrial weight would be felt soonest in the West. Not only could the Union outbuild the South in vessels for coastal and blue-water operations, it could also outbuild them in river craft. As early as April 1861 Union attorney general Edward Bates pointed out that a joint army and navy force could take control of the Mississippi "in such a way as to clench a noose about the South." Scott ordered ironclad gunboats built for the West in June 1861. The first was launched on October 12. They were not fully operational until January, when they joined other Union craft on the western rivers.[40]

The Confederates also built gunboats for the rivers, and in a July 30, 1862, meeting Mallory discussed building ironclads that could operate on both the rivers and the high seas.[41] But as was so often the case, the South could not produce sufficient numbers of boats quickly enough. Moreover, as the Union army began to make advances into Confederate territory, and not just in the West, the Confederacy began losing some of the few facilities it had for shipbuilding.

The Union's reply to the Confederate *guerre de course* was no less bold. Secretary of State Seward was not one to shrink from a foreign power or organization manifesting political sympathy toward the Confederates. The best way to combat Rebel raiders was to keep them from leaving the British and French yards in which they were being built. Seward applied political pressure on the British and French. Though he was not completely successful, his efforts produced the confiscation of a number of ships being built for the Confederacy (often secretly). Seward also did not shy from using methods that might offend the most delicate. This produced bitter complaints from James Bulloch about Union subterfuge in unmasking the South's ownership of two vessels seized in Britain.[42] In March 1863 Welles recommended an even tougher stance, telling Seward and Lincoln to inform the British "that our countrymen would not be restrained from active operations if Great Britain persisted in making war on our commerce under Confederate colors."[43] Lincoln let this pass.

Once at sea, Confederate raiders still needed ports for coaling and repairs. Seward took the initiative here as well, ordering all U.S. consuls to make sure Confederate vessels encountered every possible difficulty when they reached a neutral port.[44] In March 1863 Seward pushed for the issuance of letters of marque to Union privateers to nab blockade runners and chase down raiders. Lincoln thought the idea worthy. Welles found it impractical, branding it an "idle scheme of attempting to spear sharks for wool." He also feared it could cause war with Britain.[45] Interestingly, he made this remark at almost exactly the same time that he urged tougher action against Great Britain.

Union merchants found their own solution to Confederate commerce raiding: reflagging, or registering their vessels with different nations. The South did not want to risk alienating countries sympathetic to the South, or from which Richmond hoped to win recognition. This "flight from the flag" affected about half of the American merchant fleet.[46]

Mallory's plan to dispatch raiders did deliver on some of its strategic intent. It destroyed only about 5 percent of the Union merchant fleet, but it weakened the blockade by drawing Union warships from their stations, as intended. A single Confederate raider could make Welles order out squadrons to chase it down.[47] The small amount of effort the Confederates devoted to raiding commerce gave good strategic value for the dollar. If nothing else, it forced the consumption of a larger relative proportion of Union resources.

Finally, the Union response was to implement a blockade. While Welles and Fox procured the ships, men, and bases, they also worked to build an effective organizational structure. Welles created three naval squadrons—the Atlantic

Blockading Squadron, commanded by Silas H. Stringham; the Gulf Blockading Squadron, led by William Mervine; and the Home Squadron, based in the West Indies. Garret J. Pendergrast led the last, his job being the protection of the gold ships coming from California. Following the recommendations of the Blockade Board, Welles later divided the Atlantic Blockading Squadron, forming "the North and South Atlantic Blockading Squadrons."[48] L. M. Goldsborough became the commander of the northern squadron, replacing Stringham, who had resigned. Samuel F. Du Pont initially commanded the southern one.[49] Slowly, as more ships became available, Welles strengthened the blockade, ensuring that the bulk of Union naval attention fell on the most important ports.[50]

The Confederacy had only nine ports between Cape Charles and the Mississippi River with rail connections into the interior: New Bern, Beaufort, Charleston, Wilmington, Savannah, Brunswick, Pensacola, Mobile, and New Orleans. These were the most critical for Southern commerce. By May 1, 1862, six had been captured or closed. Only Charleston, Wilmington, and Mobile remained open. Writer and Union veteran George A. Bruce has insisted that all could have been closed by the middle of 1862 had the Union concentrated on doing so.[51] This is likely correct, especially given the weakness of Confederate coastal defense and the growing strength of the Union navy and army.

Key to the closure of Confederate ports such as New Orleans were joint navy-army operations to seize them, or to take and hold areas around them that would functionally close the routes of egress and ingress. On August 27–28, 1861, Union forces captured the North Carolina coastal fortresses of Hatteras and Clark. The seizure of Port Royal, South Carolina, followed on November 7. These early steps increased the blockade's impact by taking sites that effectively closed ports.[52] Soon the Union began taking the ports themselves, robbing the South of their benefits while providing bases for the Union navy, as well as ground forces, to operate against the Confederacy.

The Effects of the Blockade

THE UNION'S BLOCKADE was firmly established by mid-1862.[53] Just how critical it was to Union victory (or Southern defeat) continues to be debated. Some think it was one of the most important factors in the war's result. Others give it less importance.

First, as with every blockade, it did not prevent all trade. It remained porous in some measure until the end of the war (transshipment via Mexico contributed to this). Nonetheless, far more would have gotten through without it. Its effectiveness stemmed from the Union army's occupation of Confederate ports. One of the Confederacy's responses to the blockade was to build from the ground up (and nationalize) those industries necessary to supply and equip one of the world's largest armies. The Confederacy's chief of army ordnance, Brigadier General Josiah Gorgas, accomplished the amazing feat of building an internal Southern armaments industry.[54]

Blockade running was another response. Private enterprise, usually British-backed, encouraged early attempts to run the blockade. In the first part of 1863, a number of Confederate governmental departments used blockade runners to bring in needed goods. In the fall of the same year, the government began regulating the trade, guaranteeing for itself part of the shipboard space. February 1864 saw additional regulation that banned the importation of most luxury goods.[55]

Some believe that Confederate leaders were generally unconcerned about the blockade because they rarely mention it in their correspondence other than to denounce it as ineffective. The Confederates burned the bulk of their naval archives at the end of the war, undermining any hope of resolving this issue. Southern civilians certainly considered it a problem.[56] Mallory, for one, worried about it. In May 1861, as we've seen, he dispatched the dilatory Lieutenant North to Europe to buy an armored warship that could "prevent all blockades." In March 1862 he wrote of his hopes that the ironclad *Louisiana*, once completed, would raise the blockade. As late as July 1864 he told Bulloch to have six torpedo boats built because the Confederates had had success with them against Union blockade ships.[57]

What, then, can we say for certain about the effects of the blockade? Historian William Fowler argues that it resulted in the political isolation of the South. While it did not prevent Southern representatives from negotiating with foreign powers, it meant that any nation challenging the blockade, politically or militarily, potentially risked war with the Union.[58]

Moreover, it dramatically reduced the export and import trade through Southern ports. For example, in each of the years 1862, 1863, and 1864, cotton exportation via Southern ports was only one-tenth of prewar levels. The cotton crops were smaller because of Davis's 1863 call for farmers to grow foodstuffs instead of cotton. Still, the South's economy revolved around King Cotton; the inability to export knocked away one of its pillars.[59]

The blockade helped fuel inflation in multiple ways. First, blockade runners expected to be paid in specie, particularly gold. Such payments sapped the Southern economy, contributing to increasing prices. Second, it contributed to the scarcity of many products, becoming the primary cause of many shortages, particularly in luxury goods but also in indispensable items such as needles and shoes.[60] Scarcity fuels inflation, and the South suffered from the most savage kind, hyperinflation, which diminished its ability to wage the war, as well as the will of the average Southerner to endure its ravages. The price of flour, for example, increased 2,800 percent. The war was bound to shock parts of the economy, producing scarcity and some rise in prices. The blockade fueled an inflation already churning because of specie flight and the Confederacy's decision to finance the war by printing money. Moreover, combined with Union military successes, the blockade increasingly limited the South's ability to raise money overseas through the sale of bonds.[61]

And had there been no blockade? Greed and need soon would have overwhelmed the South's self-imposed cotton embargo, which did not stop some Southerners from trading cotton to the Union. Export on foreign ships—because the South possessed virtually none of its own—would have followed, along with the importation of everything the South needed to prosecute the war, also on foreign ships. This might have given the South the extra strength it needed to survive.

For the Union, the absence of a blockade might have been disastrous politically. If trading with the South presented no threat, the danger of Southern independence being recognized was increased, especially if the Confederacy grew stronger each day through foreign trade. Moreover, what nation would take seriously the threat of punitive action from a power not even willing to make the sacrifice necessary to blockade its secessionist sons? Foreign recognition of the Confederacy would not necessarily have led to intervention on its side, but undoubtedly it would have produced more forceful European efforts at mediation, and perhaps more substantial military aid. Failure to pursue the blockade also would have undermined Seward's efforts to thwart the construction of Confederate raiders in British and French yards. More raiders would have meant greater damage to the Union's ability to wage the war by robbing it of trade revenue and diminishing its own ability to import needed goods.

In sum, the blockade was a political, military, and economic necessity for the Union. It did not win the war, but it made it far more difficult for the South to achieve its political objectives. The Union devoted 5 percent of its military manpower to the blockade.[62] It received a good return on its investment.

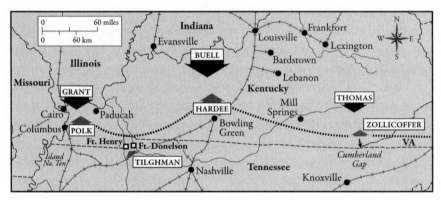

Johnston's Long Kentucky Line, Winter 1861–1862. Adapted from Shelby Foote,
The Civil War: A Narrative, vol. 1 (New York: Random House, 1958), 72.

8

The War in the West

I cannot possibly be mistaken in the strategy of the campaign.
—HENRY WAGER HALLECK, February 21, 1862

Forts Henry and Donelson

AT THE END OF DECEMBER 1861, Brigadier General Lloyd Tilghman, the Confederate commander of Fort Donelson in Tennessee, was worried. "I feel deeply solicitous about our condition on the Tennessee and Cumberland," he wrote Davis, "and believe that no one point in the Southern Confederacy needs more the aid of the Government than [these] points."[1] He was right to fret. Union eyes looked hungrily his way.

Albert Sidney Johnston now led the Confederate forces in the West. Johnston and Davis had attended Transylvania University and West Point together. Johnston had served in the Black Hawk War, headed the army of the Texas Republic, and served beside Davis in Mexico. He resigned his commission when the war began and made a daring ride from California to Virginia, crossing the Mojave Desert in the company of other would-be Confederates and dodging Apaches and Union troops along the way. Johnston arrived in Richmond on September 5, 1861. Five days later he received command of nearly all of the Confederate forces west of the Appalachians.[2]

But Johnston had problems. General Polk—another friend of Davis's—had destroyed Kentucky's neutrality while Johnston was returning to take up his command. Johnston believed Polk intended to take the key city of Paducah. But Polk had no such intent. Grant took the town on September 6, giving the Union control of the mouths of both the Cumberland and Tennessee rivers. Johnston did secure Bowling Green, which straddled the nexus of rail lines connecting Louisville, Nashville, and Memphis, by commissioning Kentucky native Simon Bolivar Buckner a general and hurriedly dispatching him from Nashville at the head of a small contingent of troops.[3]

Johnston's strategy for defending the region included fortifying Bowling Green, which marked roughly the center of his command, he and his generals agreeing that the key rail and road junction "was the most defensible point that could be selected to cover Nashville and our southern line of operations, extending from Cumberland Gap to the Mississippi River." While fortifying the city, Johnston hoped his army would grow large enough to mount an offensive. Columbus, Kentucky, situated on the Mississippi, anchored the western edge of the cordon. The series of fortified Confederate posts stretching across the state to the Cumberland Mountains became known as the Kentucky Line.[4] Operationally, the South's implementation of a cordon defense spread thin the South's inferior manpower, thus creating strategic weakness.

About 50,000 Confederates soon faced 90,000 or so Federals. Both sides daily increased in strength—indeed, Johnston did all he could to gather more troops, including the ultimately unsuccessful dispatch of a personal messenger to Davis to ask for men and arms from the East—but the Union forces grew much faster. Simply put, the Confederates did not have enough men to guard an area stretching Kentucky's length.[5] Moreover, Bowling Green proved less pivotal than the Rebels believed. Also, however deluded, belief in the power of King Cotton underpinned Johnston's strategic thinking. "Believing it to be of the greatest moment to protract the campaign," he wrote, "as the dearth of cotton might bring strength from abroad and discourage the North and to gain time to strengthen myself by new troops from Tennessee and other States, I magnified my forces to the enemy, but made known my true strength to the Department and the Governors of the States. The aid given was small."[6]

The Union had been considering how to breach the Kentucky Line (at this point in the war most of the Union generals proved superb at "considering" action) and discussing the possibility of advancing down the Cumberland and Tennessee rivers since at least as early as November 1861.[7] Talk of such a move became almost commonplace by late in the year.[8] Colonel Charles Whittlesey, Halleck's chief engineer, queried his superior about these waterways on November 20.[9] Halleck noted in a meeting with William T. Sherman and others that the natural place to break the Confederate defenses was along the Tennessee River.[10] In a January 20 letter Halleck insisted that the Cumberland and Tennessee rivers were lines of advance, though the "overly cautious" Halleck was in no more hurry than McClellan or Buell.[11]

The situation in Missouri played a part in persuading Halleck to postpone an advance aimed at Tennessee. Confederate forces under General Sterling Price stirred in the state, and Halleck believed he first needed to subdue them.[12] He warned that taking troops from his command sufficient for an advance down the Cumberland risked the loss of Missouri. Moreover, in early January he felt that the necessary gunboats would not be ready for one or two weeks. With some luck and additional arms, Halleck thought, he might be ready for a Cumberland thrust by early February 1862.[13]

The thoughts of General Ulysses S. Grant ran in a similar vein. He had twice unsuccessfully sought permission from Halleck to attack Fort Henry. Undeterred, and now joined by Flag Officer Andrew H. Foote, Grant again broached the subject with his superior on January 28, 1862.[14] His timing proved serendipitous. The next day, McClellan wired both Halleck and Buell that the Confederate general P. G. T. Beauregard had departed for the West with fifteen regiments.[15] The report was half right. Beauregard had indeed departed, but not the troops. Halleck, digging deeply, found some initiative (or at least the will to approve someone else's) and agreed to Grant and Foote's request, based on an inaccurate intelligence report.[16] Grant received his orders on February 1. Halleck instructed him to advance quickly enough to reduce the objective before the Confederates could significantly reinforce it. Grant and Foote sailed the next day.[17]

Simultaneously, Buell sent a letter to McClellan. He was still bucking Lincoln's orders, insisting upon the impossibility of moving into eastern Tennessee with units of any substantial size. Instead, he planned "to move at once against Bowling Green, in combination with an attack up the Tennessee and Cumberland and an effective demonstration against Columbus." Buell's plan was to take Fort Henry, Dover, and Clarksville and destroy the bridges. "These objects accomplished and Nashville in danger, the resistance at Bowling Green will give way; otherwise the struggle at that point will be protracted and difficult." "I am not unconscious of the magnitude of the work I propose," he added, "but it has to be done, and the sooner we can do it the better."[18] Buell advocated prompt action, but his lack of movement in the preceding months made it obvious that it would not come from him.

Some odd lines close Buell's letter. "While you were sick," he told McClellan, "by direction of the President I proposed to Halleck some concert of action between us. He answered, 'I can do nothing; name a day for a demonstration.' Night before last I received a dispatch from him, saying, 'I have ordered an advance on Fort Henry and Dover. It will be made immediately.' I protest against such prompt proceedings, as though I had nothing to do but command 'Commence firing' when he starts off. However he telegraphs me to-night that co-operation is not essential now."[19]

Buell had begun with a slap at Halleck, an unjust one because he was complaining that Halleck had said he could not move during the first week of January, but now he was saying he could at the beginning of February.[20] He followed this with further complaints that Halleck had enacted part of the operational

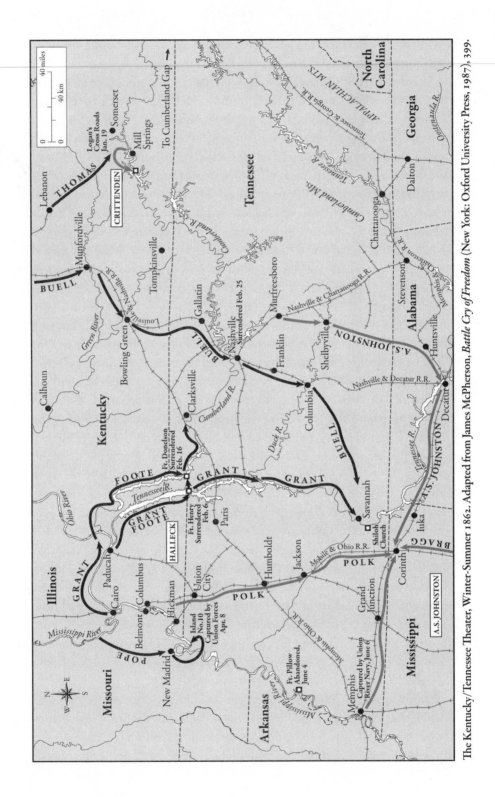

The Kentucky/Tennessee Theater, Winter-Summer 1862. Adapted from James McPherson, *Battle Cry of Freedom* (New York: Oxford University Press, 1987), 399.

plan Buell just suggested to McClellan in the very same letter. Buell seemed to want it both ways, refusing to move into Tennessee but presenting a new plan (which was in many ways an old plan), then criticizing the commander for putting an element of it into motion.

Meanwhile, Grant fought the war. He planned to take Fort Henry in a joint operation with Foote's naval forces. "The troops were to invest the garrison and the gunboats to attack the fort at close quarters," he wrote later. This took place on February 6. The night before, units under Brigadier General C. F. Smith landed across the river and moved behind Fort Heiman. They found it empty. General Tilghman, Henry's commander, had sent out the bulk of his force to keep them out of the range of Union gunboats, then dispatched them to Donelson before Foote's gunboats forced the fort's surrender.[21]

On February 5, Halleck asked Buell to make a diversion in support of Grant.[22] "My position does not admit of diversion," Buell snapped. "My moves must be real ones."[23] Such a great general could not merely provide support. Even before Henry's fall the Union high command wrangled over what to do next. "Considering" continued to plague the Union war effort.

On February 5 Buell announced his intention to begin his long-awaited march toward Bowling Green. The poor roads, he insisted, would slow him, and they *were* desperately bad. His troops also had to repair the broken rail line as they marched. Still, he declared, any move he made must amount to more than a "diversion."[24] The next day McClellan queried both Halleck and Buell about making the Cumberland and Tennessee rivers the main Union lines of advance, especially since they faced such miserable roads.[25] Buell initially replied by calling the move "right in its strategical bearing" while denouncing Halleck for going off half-cocked. He, too, had been thinking about shifting his forces to this line but would have to consider it a bit before taking action.[26]

Grant's advance awakened Halleck's ambitions. He promised McClellan that with 25,000 more men he could "threaten Nashville and cut off railroad communication." Halleck would then deliver Bowling Green bloodlessly because the Rebels would have to give up the town.[27]

On February 7, Halleck telegraphed McClellan that Fort Henry had fallen.[28] Grant lunged immediately for Donelson, unbidden, he insisted, by Halleck; the two never discussed it.[29] Halleck, having already moved to McClellan's side of the contest regarding the river drive, maintained that if McClellan agreed to the thrusts down the Cumberland and Tennessee, the general in chief should give him "everything you can spare from General Buell's command or elsewhere."[30] But McClellan had his own ideas. "Why not have Buell take the line of Tennessee and operate on Nashville," he wired Halleck, "while your troops turn Columbus? Those two points gained, a combined movement on Memphis will be next in order."[31] He suggested nearly the same course to Buell.[32]

Halleck had already begun prodding Buell about a combined march on Nashville, something for which Halleck believed he did not have enough troops. He suggested that Buell send his forces to the Cumberland and Tennessee rivers to move them against the Tennessee capital.[33] But Buell decided to continue his muddy march to Bowling Green.[34] The next day, he went back to considering.[35]

By now, Halleck had received McClellan's suggestion to put Buell in command of the forces advancing on Nashville. He was not happy about it.[36] However, never one to let an opportunity for personal advancement pass ungrasped, Halleck proposed the unification of all the Union forces in the West under one head, which, of course, meant his.[37] McClellan rebuffed him.[38]

Then Lincoln, via Stanton, chimed in. Lincoln had read Buell's February 1 letter outlining a plan of campaign for the West, liked it, and wanted his western generals to put their "two heads together" and do it.[39] Buell's plan, as we've seen, encouraged all the things the Union leaders had dithered about for months: moves into eastern Tennessee, down the Cumberland, and down the Tennessee, a "demonstration" against Columbus, and the seizure of Clarksville, all in preparation for an advance on Nashville.[40] On February 12, Buell finally decided that he would send part of his force via one or the other river while he kept up his march on Bowling Green.[41]

But the question of what to do next remained unsettled. Halleck told his superior that he had no firm plan for action past taking Donelson and Clarksville. "Subsequent movements must depend upon the enemy," he insisted.[42] Nevertheless, thanks to Grant, Halleck still held the initiative. The time to push had come. Not doing so risked losing momentum and surrendering an opportunity.

The general in chief decided for him. McClellan told Buell to support Halleck's forces by moving past Bowling Green and on to Nashville, overland or down the Cumberland.[43] "This is bad strategy," Halleck railed, preferring that Buell first help him reduce Donelson and Clarksville and then push on to Florence, Alabama, to cut the Decatur railroad. Halleck foresaw this forcing the Confederates to abandon Nashville and resulting in the liberation of Tennessee.[44] McClellan told him Nashville would be the objective. He believed (correctly) that this would force the Confederates out of Donelson anyway and gave Buell the leeway to instead support Grant if Buell's forces could not make an immediate march on Nashville. "The Decatur movement and one on Memphis are the next steps in my programme," he told Halleck, once again reaching back to the plan he had given Lincoln.[45] Buell had already decided to make Nashville his objective, and McClellan applauded the decision.[46]

Buell reached Bowling Green on February 14. Finding the Confederates gone, he reversed a decision he had made to send troops down the Cumberland and decided to push his whole force toward Nashville along the rail line.[47] Over the telegraph lines, Halleck pleaded with Buell to unite his forces with Halleck's to reduce Donelson and Clarksville first.[48]

Then Lincoln interfered, writing directly to Halleck and subverting the chain of command. The president worried about the enemy concentrating forces to try to break Grant's grip on Donelson. He wondered if Union cavalry could be sent to cut the rails from Knoxville and Union gunboats dispatched to destroy Clarksville's railroad bridge. "Our success or failure at Fort Donelson is vastly important," Lincoln wrote. He also revealed his distress: "I beg you to put your soul in the effort."[49] Lincoln's intervention was unwarranted—McClellan was on top of the situation—but the president simply no longer trusted his generals to do the smart thing.

Meanwhile, trying to undermine a good plan, Halleck again urged McClellan to stop Buell from driving on Nashville before Donelson's fall. Moreover, he thought Nashville of no importance now since the Union held Bowling Green. The idea was absurd. Nashville was the South's second-largest industrial center and the primary crossroads of the rail and river networks between the Appalachians and the Mississippi. McClellan put him in his place, telling him that the advance on Nashville "is the most important."[50] From his office in Washington, he saw more clearly the key nodes of the Western Theater than did one of the area's commanders. He also urged Buell on: "Time is now everything. If Nashville is open the men could carry their small rations and bread, driving meat on the hoof[.] Leave tents and baggage. If you can occupy Nashville at once it will end the war in Tennessee."[51] McClellan exaggerated slightly, but he saw an opportunity to make great gains and did not want it to slip away.

Halleck vigorously protested Buell's move.[52] McClellan struck him down again: "Give facts on which your opinion is based."[53] Then Donelson fell, and Halleck got greedy: "Make Buell, Grant, and Pope major-generals of volunteers, and give me command in the West. I ask this in return for Forts Henry and Donelson."[54] Halleck wanted a lot for something that he had not accomplished, which had not even been his idea in the first place, which he had in fact resisted, and to which he and Buell had contributed almost nothing. Buell also flashed his pettiness, delivering a long soliloquy on potential Union and Confederate moves that was in actuality only a smokescreen for asking Halleck to return some of Buell's troops.[55] Halleck, for his part, still tried to get Buell to move first on Clarksville.[56] Buell insisted that he could not do so because his only route was a boggy road.[57] Halleck persisted: "Help me, I beg of you."[58]

Halleck's ambitions rose with the tenor of his cries. The next day he reiterated to McClellan his request for the creation of a Western Division under his command. "Give it to me," he informed McClellan, "and I will split secession in twain in one month."[59] Simultaneously, he went around his boss and appealed to Thomas A. Scott, the assistant secretary of war, to have Buell sent to help him.[60] Lincoln parried this power grab, while McClellan remained in no hurry to give Halleck so much authority.[61] Halleck nonetheless persisted. "One whole week has been lost already by hesitation and delay," he told Stanton. "There was, and I think there still is, a golden opportunity to strike a fatal blow, but I can't do it unless I can control Buell's army."[62]

Halleck was right, though *he* was largely the cause of the delay. He had been trying to get Buell's army to advance against Clarksville instead of Nashville, intending to move on the Tennessee River while Buell advanced down the Cumberland. He wanted this so badly he had even gone over McClellan's head to try to get it.[63] The problem with Halleck's plan was that Nashville was not much farther from Buell's army than Clarksville was. Plus, threatening Nashville would mean flanking Clarksville, forcing its abandonment. Moreover, he had left Foote and Grant hanging, delaying their push for Nashville by ordering on February 18 that the all-important gunboats not go past Clarksville, which flabbergasted Foote.[64] Halleck then used Foote's and Grant's impatience to be off as an excuse for again trying to force Buell's line of advance on to the Cumberland.[65]

McClellan gripped the reins and gave Buell the choice of advancing on the Cumberland or overland. He would meanwhile direct Halleck's men against Columbus and Memphis.[66] Buell chose the overland route, leaving Bowling Green on February 22.[67] His pickets reached the outskirts of Nashville the next day.[68]

McClellan laid out the Union's next moves in the West. To Buell he wrote that he had requested Halleck "to give you all the aid in his power in your operations on Nashville." He believed "possession of railway junctions near Chattanooga would seem to be of next importance." "After we have gained

Nashville and can see our way to holding Chattanooga," he continued, "we must get possession of Columbus and Memphis.... We must not lose sight of Eastern Tennessee."[69] McClellan elaborated in a note to Halleck: "Buell will be in front of Nashville to-morrow evening. Best co-operate with him to the full extent of your power, to secure Nashville beyond a doubt; then by a combined movement of troops and gunboats seize Decatur. Buell will be directed to occupy and hold in three the railroad junctions in vicinity of Chattanooga and to re-establish the railroads from Nashville to Decatur and Stevenson. This will very nearly isolate A. S. Johnston from Richmond."[70]

By setting his sights on Chattanooga, McClellan had delineated the most important line of advance that the Union could choose. The city, on the south bank of the Tennessee River, held the key rail connection linking the eastern and western Confederacy, and was an ideal launching place for incursions into the Deep South. Meanwhile, he had not neglected pushing in other areas as well, such as down the Mississippi and into eastern Tennessee. But the main push was to be toward Chattanooga; taking Stevenson in northern Alabama would secure the railroad for this. Securing Decatur, Alabama, would give a rail and river junction on the Tennessee River. Both meant severing the Memphis and Charleston Railroad running between Chattanooga and Corinth, the only east-west Confederate rail link at the time, as the Confederates did not complete the gap on the line stretching across central Alabama until December 1862.[71] McClellan's plan would have all but cut the South in two.

The Confederate Response

THE SOUTH'S GENERALS, unlike their Northern counterparts, did not sit on their hands while Grant moved. With Fort Henry's fall, Johnston believed he had to defend Nashville at Fort Donelson, and on February 7, after a meeting with Beauregard and his other generals, he sent some 12,000 men to reinforce Donelson. He retained only 14,000; fatigue and sickness reduced that number to under 10,000 by the time they reached Nashville.[72] Johnston also ordered the evacuation of Bowling Green before the battle for Donelson began, telling Brigadier General John B. Floyd to save his army if he could not hold the position. Floyd failed at both.[73] He lost most of the army and Fort Donelson, whose surrender made Bowling Green untenable.

The fall of Henry, Donelson, and Bowling Green shattered the Confederacy's western perimeter and had far-ranging strategic consequences. To

Johnston, the loss of Donelson "was most disastrous and almost without remedy." Its surrender, coupled with the Union capture of Bowling Green, made Nashville vulnerable to Union forces.[74] It also opened up the Tennessee and Cumberland rivers to Union passage, making possible offensives against Clarksville, home of the second-largest ironworks in the South, and the important industrial center of Nashville, as well as thrusts into northern Alabama and Mississippi. Controlling these two rivers allowed the Union to force the Confederates from Kentucky and western Tennessee, depriving them of access to a large chunk of their war industry and the South's granary, as well as its greatest source of pork. Additionally, a third of the Confederate forces in Kentucky and Tennessee became casualties.[75]

Instead of taking advantage of the situation, Halleck quarreled with Grant, his more talented subordinate, and gave command of the Union advance to C. F. Smith. However, intervention from above, and the resolution of a communications problem, led to Halleck's reinstating the Union's thus far most successful military commander.[76]

Johnston replied to the enemy advance by beginning to assemble an army at Murfreesboro, Tennessee. He intended to strike back, but the weather turned inclement, ruining his plans. He then turned and crossed the Tennessee River to unite with Braxton Bragg at Corinth, Mississippi, and also join with Beauregard in defending the Mississippi Valley. He hoped to have 50,000 men assembled by March 20, 1862. "This," he wrote of his army, "must be destroyed before the enemy can attain his object."[77]

Davis offered his advice to Albert Sidney on repairing the Confederate situation in the West. His ideas were aggressive and optimistic despite the fact that he knew that the South's forces there were outnumbered and inadequately armed, the Confederates being forced to rely upon private weapons to make up the shortfall. "With a sufficient force," Davis wrote, "the audacity which the enemy exhibits would no doubt give you the opportunity to cut some of his lines of communication, to break up his plan of campaign, and, defeating some of his columns, to drive him from the soil as well of Tennessee as of Kentucky." He believed that the Union would aim at the Tennessee and Mississippi rivers in its next campaign and hoped Johnston could concentrate enough force to counter such a campaign. Additionally, Davis hoped a move by forces under Edmund Kirby Smith into eastern Tennessee would create a diversion. A Confederate fleet was also gathering on the Mississippi River. If the Union moved its gunboats up the Tennessee, it would give Johnston a chance to strike at Cairo, Illinois.[78] Davis correctly deduced the Union river campaigns, which were in some respects dictated by geography and logistics, but he was overly optimistic, indeed unrealistic, about the potential for a Confederate naval strike against Cairo.

Missouri

IN A NUMBER OF LETTERS to his superiors, Halleck expressed great concern about the situation in Missouri. He had cause to worry. In mid-December 1861 Confederate general Sterling Price, writing from his camp near Osceola, Missouri, asked Davis to ensure the cooperation of the Confederate forces in northwestern Arkansas. Price believed that this would allow him to collect 50,000 men and "to take and hold three-quarters of the state." He maintained that he could not gather more men to him because those who might join would likely choose to remain home to protect their property and families against marauders. He also believed that the Union's extended lines and occupation of all avenues of approach to the Confederate forces kept sympathizers from filling his ranks. Price would resort to tying down as many Union troops as he could.[79]

Price and Polk agreed to coordinate their actions and further agreed that Brigadier General Ben McCulloch deserved the blame for previous Confederate failures in Missouri. Largely because of McCulloch's refusal to cooperate, Price insisted, Price's forces had to fall back to southern Missouri, the result being that many who rallied to the Confederacy felt betrayed and abandoned and simply went home.[80] Price soon hoped to have 20,000 men under his command and to move against St. Louis in conjunction with Polk. Even if they failed, Price believed, the effort would show the people of Missouri that the Confederate government cared. It would also force the Union to move troops to St. Louis from other parts of the state, allowing Confederate recruiting in areas then currently held by the Union.[81]

By January 1862 Polk, for his part, wanted Price to take action. He urged him to keep the enemy guessing, believing that keeping Halleck's troops occupied would bar Halleck from uniting with Buell against Johnston, as well as against Polk's flank.[82]

Halleck responded, but slowly. Brigadier General John Pope pushed for action against Price on December 11, 1861. Until late January, however, Halleck stressed preparation, though he did scatter troops all over the state to encourage the formation of pro-Union militias. At the end of January, he ordered an advance from Rolla, Missouri, toward Springfield, by troops under Brigadier General Samuel R. Curtis.[83]

The Confederates also prepared. In February 1862, Secretary of War Benjamin told Price that he was trying to raise troops from North Louisiana,

Arkansas, and Texas to support him. He hoped to see Price's campaign under way by the middle of March.[84] Moreover, in mid-January, in an effort to sort out their situation in the Trans-Mississippi Theater, Davis appointed fellow Mississippian Earl Van Dorn, commander of a department that included Missouri, Arkansas, the Indian Territory, and parts of Louisiana. An aggressive, enthusiastic leader, Van Dorn began concentrating the region's dispersed forces and hoped to gather enough men to move by February 20.[85] The date came and went, and Van Dorn failed to accrue the numbers he hoped for. He eventually gathered 17,000 troops, including those under Sterling Price, Albert J. Pike, McCulloch, and others. He planned to have Pike's forces watch Kansas while he went on the offensive. "I design attempting Saint Louis.... This seems to me the movement best calculated to win us Missouri and relieve General Johnston, who is heavily threatened in Kentucky." His target date: April 1, 1862.[86]

Van Dorn never got the chance to put his plan into action. Halleck already had Curtis's men marching from Rolla, Missouri. On February 12 they pushed Price's forces from Springfield and drove them into Arkansas. Van Dorn, having finally achieved his desired concentration at Van Buren, Arkansas, moved to meet Curtis. The two forces clashed at Pea Ridge, or Elkhorn Tavern, on March 7 and 8. Van Dorn attempted a daring surprise double envelopment, a two-pronged attack, against the Union forces. Marching at night, Van Dorn sent half his force around to the north of the Union position, planning to strike the enemy in the rear at dawn in a tactical maneuver reminiscent of the Napoleonic era. He intended this move to draw in the defenders to his fore, and he would then strike the rear with the rest of his force. It failed, Curtis's 10,500 troops fighting Van Dorn's 17,000 to a standstill. Defeated (though he refused to admit it), Van Dorn withdrew. By March 23 he had his army again on the march, pushing for St. Louis. Orders from Richmond redirected him: he was to bring his force to Mississippi. Curtis, and the Confederate high command, had cleared Halleck's flank. The Confederates never again threatened to bring Missouri under their flag.[87]

9

A New Year—and a New Strategy

I regard Butler's Ship Island expedition as a harmless menace so far as New Orleans is concerned.

—CONFEDERATE MAJOR GENERAL MANSFIELD
LOVELL, February 27, 1862

A Strategy of Concentration

THE TWENTY-SEVENTH OF FEBRUARY 1862 was an active day for Confederate strategists. While General Lovell waxed so confident (and, as it turned out, so incorrect) about Union intentions, David J. Houston, a farmer from Natural Bridge, Virginia, penned a note to Jefferson Davis. Houston had five sons in the army and worried that Confederate forces were "defending *too much* territory." "Napoleon divided and conquered in detail," he said, and suggested concentrating forces at several towns in Virginia. He also advised defending only a few important sites along the Confederate coast, "stationing all forces on or near railroads for rapid movements." Davis sent the letter, the first of a number that he received during the war that in some respects forecast Confederate strategy, on to Lee.[1] At the time, big things were brewing strategically in the South. Fort Henry had fallen to Grant and Foote on February 6, and Roanoke Island fell to General Burnside two days later; Donelson surrendered on the sixteenth. These defeats deflated Rebel spirits; "the Cause" needed reviving. As Houston's missive made its way through the mails, the Confederacy prepared its riposte.

On February 22, 1862, Davis delivered an official inaugural address to the Confederate Congress in which he admitted to the error of trying to defend the entirety of the Confederate frontier and attributed the recent disasters at Donelson and Roanoke to this unfortunate decision. But, he insisted, "strenuous efforts have been made to throw forward reenforcements to the Armies at the positions threatened." He made a number of observations: that Maryland would join the Confederacy if given free rein, which was likely true, and that the Union would soon "sink under the immense load of debt they have incurred," which was less likely for the North than it was for the South. He also turned Clausewitzian in his expression of how much the South desired

its independence, revealing the depth of his dedication to "the Cause"—
something shared by the bulk of the South's white population (and some of its
black)—and an awareness of the bitter sacrifice the war would require: "But
we knew the value of the object for which we struggled, and understood the
nature of the war in which we were engaged. Nothing could be so bad as failure, and any sacrifice would be cheap as the price of success in such a contest."[2]
For the Confederacy, the *real* sacrificing had begun. Lincoln had taken the
gloves off, and the South was discovering that it was fighting above its weight.

Before Houston sent his note to Davis, advice came from the Western
Theater from the hand of Major General Braxton Bragg. A former U.S. Army
officer, Bragg had a reputation for quarrelsomeness in the prewar army. Later,
he would demonstrate great administrative skills that enabled him to weld
from a disorganized mass an effective organization that became the Army of
Tennessee. He would also suffer from divisional commanders who proved
habitually disobedient, a tendency exacerbated by Bragg's indecision and a
natural disputatiousness that led him to fight with everyone around him.[3] But
this was later. At this moment Bragg offered Secretary of War Judah Benjamin
the reasons for Confederate failure, as well as a new strategy: "Our means
and resources are too much scattered," he wrote. "The protection of persons
and property, as such, should be abandoned, and all our means applied to
the Government and the cause. Important strategic points only should be
held. All means not necessary to secure these should be concentrated for a
heavy blow upon the enemy where we can best assail him. Kentucky is now
that point." Bragg recommended abandoning all their posts on the Gulf of
Mexico except Pensacola, Mobile, and New Orleans, as well as all of Texas
and Florida, "and our means there made available for other service." "A small
loss of property would result from their occupation by the enemy," he continued, "but our military strength would not be lessened thereby, whilst the
enemy would be weakened by dispersion. We could then beat him in detail,
instead of the reverse. The same remark applies to our Atlantic seaboard. In
Missouri the same rule can be applied to a great extent. Deploring the mis-
fortunes of that gallant people, I can but think their relief must reach them
through Kentucky."[4] He also stressed the need for unity transcending local
interests. His later correspondence with Beauregard reinforced these views.
"We should cease our policy [strategy] of protecting persons and property, by
which we are being defeated in detail."[5]

This was perhaps the most cogent strategic plan offered by any Confederate leader during the course of the war. Bragg had identified the Confederacy's
key weakness—that it lacked the means to defend its far-flung regions—and

recognized that defending the vital core of the Confederacy, the area east of the Mississippi and north of Florida, was what mattered. Losing the rest would do little to injure the Confederacy's power. He wanted to mass Confederate military strength in its center and then move to offensive warfare. There was also a limitation to Bragg's thinking: it applied generally to the West, particularly Kentucky and Tennessee.[6]

Bragg's letter encouraged Benjamin to act. Many talked and wrote of "concentration" at this time, particularly in the West, and sometimes in fanciful discussions that included invasions of Ohio. Beauregard, in what was for him a typically unrealistic plan, proposed concentrating 40,000 troops, about half to be freshly furnished by states in the Mississippi Valley, and then, in conjunction with Confederate gunboats, capturing Cairo and Paducah (maybe even St. Louis) and closing the mouths of the Tennessee and Cumberland rivers.[7] Bragg, though, presented a rational case in strategic rather than merely operational or tactical terms. Benjamin wasted little time replying: "The heavy blow which has been inflicted on us by the recent operations in Kentucky and Tennessee renders necessary a change in our whole plan of campaign, as suggested in your dispatch of this date, just received."[8] As a response to the Confederate defeat at Fort Donelson, and the subsequent collapse of Confederate defenses in Kentucky, Davis and Benjamin began a massive movement of forces from around the South. The fall of Donelson upset Davis greatly. He wrote his brother: "I am making every effort to assemble sufficient force to beat the enemy in Tennessee, and retrieve our waning fortunes in the West." Benjamin and Davis's action followed Bragg's line of thought, but, as we will see, they took it to an extreme.[9]

Benjamin ordered Bragg to take his forces from Pensacola, Florida, and all but a small garrison from Mobile, Alabama, to the Tennessee state line. The Confederates gathered units from other areas, such as New Orleans and eastern Florida. An expected Federal attack on Savannah kept Confederate forces pinned there. But what was happening in the West remained unclear to the leaders in Richmond, Benjamin admitting that "we grope in the dark here, and this uncertainty renders our own counsels undecided and prevents that promptness of action which the emergency requires." However, they did believe that unless they had more weapons, the Confederacy would have no hope of defending its "exposed coast and frontier" and would be forced to abandon the entire Gulf region aside from the key port city of New Orleans. The surrender of Columbus, Kentucky, which Polk had believed so critical, was also feared, and the South's leaders worried that Confederate forces might have to retreat as far as Memphis.[10]

On February 23 Benjamin wrote to Brigadier General P. O. Hébert in Galveston, Texas: "Our recent disaster in Tennessee has greatly exposed our line of communication with the West, and the importance of this line is so great that it must be held at any sacrifice." He ordered the coast stripped of any troops not manning defensive guns; those men were to be dispatched to Major General Earl Van Dorn in Little Rock. Benjamin explained that "our entire forces must be thrown toward the Mississippi for the defense of that river and of the Memphis and Charleston Railroad," the critical east-west rail route that stretched from Memphis, Tennessee, across northern Mississippi and Alabama to Chattanooga, Tennessee.[11]

Benjamin soon learned that things were far worse in the West than he had thought. Johnston wrote that the fall of Fort Donelson had forced him to pull his troops from the north bank of the Cumberland River and to evacuate Nashville. Buell's army outnumbered Johnston's 40,000 to 11,000. Meanwhile, heavy rains had swollen the Cumberland River, allowing the Union to use gunboats and its troops at Donelson to cut off Southern communications. Albert Sidney Johnston determined he had to evacuate Nashville or lose the army. He retreated, as mentioned earlier, to Murfreesboro, Tennessee, uniting with Major General George B. Crittenden and the "fugitives" from Donelson; this gave him only 17,000 men. He sent another 2,500 under Floyd to Chattanooga to guard the approaches to northern Georgia and Alabama, as well as the communications between the Mississippi and the Atlantic. He hoped this force would be reinforced by the neighboring states.[12]

Johnston insisted that Tennessee's topography and the "great power which the enemy's means of transportation affords them upon the Tennessee and Cumberland" made it impossible for him to guard the whole line of the Union advance with the men under his command. The Union offensive had put the Confederates in a hard spot. "I am compelled to elect whether he shall be permitted to occupy Middle Tennessee," Johnston insisted, "or turn Columbus, take Memphis, and open the valley of the Mississippi." He believed that defending the Mississippi Valley was the most critical thing and intended to cross to the left shore of the Tennessee River near Decatur, joining Beauregard in the defense of Memphis.[13] Instead of moving to the important center, however, Johnston concentrated on the fringe, opening to the Union the road to Chattanooga, a key rail junction and the gateway into the Deep South. But could the North seize it?

Davis also answered Congress's request for information on the next year's anticipated military needs. This depended upon the Union, Davis replied, while also recommending increasing the army by 300,000. He outlined his suggested naval requirements: fifty ironclads for harbor and river defense "and a fleet of, say, ten of the most formidable war vessels to protect our commerce upon the high seas."[14]

March 1862 saw Davis veto a bill to create a commander in chief of the Confederate army. He had a number of reasons, the most important being that he believed it undermined the president's constitutional authority as commander in chief.[15] This was a pivotal decision and an unfortunate one for the South. In fact, the Confederacy desperately needed a true general in chief. Davis did establish the position of "military advisor," plucking Robert E. Lee from his obscure command along the South's eastern seaboard for the job. Lee had an anomalous post, one in which he appeared to be in command, even to those in the field, when in actuality he was not. Davis was; Lee acted where and as Davis allowed.[16] As we've seen, Davis served as his own secretary of war and general in chief, a cumbersome accumulation of duties he acquired not only because he wanted them but because he believed he should have them. His legalism injured the Confederate cause by denying it a clear chain of command and decisive leadership at the top.

The Road to Shiloh

ON MARCH 25, 1862, Albert Sidney Johnston told Davis, "My force is now united."[17] Johnston believed that Buell might be marching to join Grant at Pittsburg Landing, and he was determined to try to strike Grant before any such union occurred; he likely told Davis as much beforehand.[18] The Confederate operational solution was Napoleonic in concept: unite several Confederate forces to strike one Union army moving from the Tennessee River (Grant's), defeating it before the arrival of a second advancing from Nashville (Buell's). Davis certainly exhibited great confidence in his old friend's ability to pull the Southern chestnuts from the Union fire. He remarked that if Johnston could do this, "the future will be brighter," and if he could not, the "only hope is that the people of the South West will rally en masse with their private arms and thus enable you to oppose the vast army which will threaten the destruction of our country."[19]

Johnston's intelligence was correct, but it shouldn't have been. At best, he should have found only Grant's army on the banks of the Tennessee—on the opposite shore, the river between them—with no Buell on his way. But Halleck's slavish adherence to the principle of concentration meant that the Union forces sacrificed a chance to land a decisive blow at the South's heart. They got a bloodletting instead.

The presence of Grant's army at Pittsburg Landing was the result of weakness in the Union leadership. On February 25, reacting to unconfirmed reports that the Confederates had abandoned Nashville and fallen back on Murfreesboro, McClellan polled both Buell and Halleck for information on their respective commands. He asked Buell how long it would take him to move his army to the edge of Murfreesboro, the next way station on the railroad between Nashville and Chattanooga. McClellan sought cooperation between the two as he was trying to decide "whether we should turn Murfreesborough by line of Tennessee River or whether we can undertake that simultaneously with a movement to turn Columbus and seize Memphis." He also inquired about the forces pushing into eastern Tennessee, aiming for Knoxville.[20]

A portion of Buell's force entered Nashville on the twenty-fifth.[21] Three days later, he reported that his advance elements were 10 miles down the rail lines toward Murfreesboro. He promised to push on as soon as he could, but had not decided upon the direction.[22] He also generally deciphered the enemy's intentions: "Johnston will not stand at Murfreesborough; in fact is preparing to get out of the way. I hope to be able to crowd him a little. Their plan seems to be to get the rear of the Tennessee, and in positions to concentrate either on Halleck or me."[23]

McClellan now made his decision. He wired Halleck on March 2, "Buell thinks the enemy intends uniting behind the Tennessee River, so as to be able to concentrate either on you or Buell." He therefore emphasized that it was "doubly important" to hold Nashville and to take Decatur, Alabama, thereby isolating Memphis and Columbus and making them ripe to fall. Critically, he noted that "Chattanooga is also a point of great importance for us." "Arrange details with Buell," he added.[24] Buell received similar instructions, and McClellan told him to cooperate with Halleck.[25] McClellan reiterated the importance of seizing Decatur on March 3, telling Halleck, "Buell must then force Chattanooga," which would allow Halleck to take Memphis and, more important, establish his communications with Butler's forces, which he expected to take New Orleans in three weeks.[26] These notes contained the same flaw: McClellan was asking and emphasizing but failing to clearly *order* them to take certain specific actions.

Buell nonetheless seems to have gotten the point, though he had doubts about Halleck (echoing the same lack of confidence Halleck had in Buell): "I can't get exactly at what Halleck is doing, and therefore can't see how to assist him at this moment if he should need it."[27] (Halleck knew *exactly* what he was doing, and it had nothing to do with the wishes of his superiors.)

Buell, trying to be cooperative, asked Halleck how he could help support Halleck's push on Columbus, cautioning him to remember that the Tennessee River separated them. He also told Halleck that Johnston was "moving towards Decatur and destroying the bridges as he goes."[28]

Halleck responded by tempting Buell to stray from McClellan's intent, while telling him of new developments. "Why not come to the Tennessee and operate with me to cut Johnston's line with Memphis, Randolph, and New Madrid?" he wired Buell. "Columbus has been evacuated and destroyed. Enemy is concentrating at New Madrid and Island No. 10. I am concentrating a force of 20,000 against him.... Estimated strength of enemy at New Madrid, Randolph, and Memphis is 50,000. It is of vital importance to separate them from Johnston's army. Come over to Savannah or Florence and we can do it. We then can operate either on Decatur or Memphis or on both, as may appear best."[29]

A few days later, the Union high command cut the reins guiding its forces in the West. The Army of the Potomac had finally begun to move, and Lincoln, convinced that McClellan could not do it all, relieved him of his post as general in chief right at the moment when Union operations had finally gotten jump-started. McClellan was using the far-flung Union tentacles to squeeze the South into submission, even if he was avoiding the army camped outside Washington. Leaving him in the top position likely would have ensured better direction of the war than what followed after his immediate departure, especially in the West, where the Union effort spiraled out of control. This meant the abandonment of McClellan's plan to drive on Chattanooga. Rather than days or weeks, it took seventeen months of bleeding for Union forces to reach it.

Abraham Lincoln, General in Chief

WHEN HE RELIEVED MCCLELLAN of his position as general in chief, Lincoln created the Department of the Mississippi and put Halleck in charge. Halleck now controlled virtually all of the troops west of the Appalachians, including Buell's.[30] He had gotten what he most wanted. Now that Halleck commanded in the West, he could move Buell's troops to wherever he wanted them, and he wanted them united with Grant's. On March 10, Buell had troops in Columbia, Tennessee, only about 70 miles from Decatur, the fall of which would have severed the rail line between Chattanooga and where the Confederates were concentrating at Corinth, Mississippi.[31] Buell, meanwhile, believed it most important for the Union to secure the territory on the north

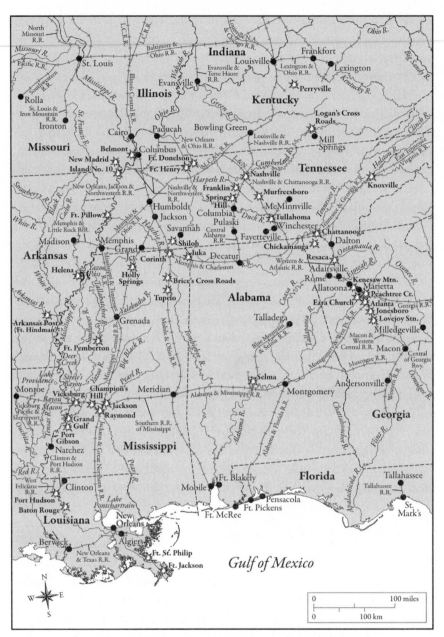

Area of the Western Campaigns. Adapted from Russell F. Weigley,
A Great Civil War: A Military and Political History, 1861–1865 (Bloomington:
Indiana University Press, 2000), 97.

bank of the Tennessee River, telling Halleck, "It enables us, with the Tennessee as a base, to operate east, west, or south. All our arrangements should look to a centralization of our forces for that object."[32] Moreover, he preferred concentrating their forces at Florence, Alabama, which would provide a firm base for moving against other Confederate positions. He feared that gathering their armies on opposite banks of the Tennessee invited disaster.[33]

Halleck did not immediately reject Buell's idea, and when he began exercising his new command on March 13 he queried Buell about his troop numbers and their disposition.[34] Buell had 71,233 men fit and not on attached duty out of a total of 101,737. A small column slogged its way toward the Cumberland Gap. Another had recently driven the Confederates from eastern Kentucky. Other regiments did occupation duty and guarded key spots. On hand Buell had about 50,000 troops, and he had his own ideas about what to do with them. He wanted to attack the Confederate positions on the Memphis and Charleston Railroad between Chattanooga and Corinth. The idea would be to continue pushing south with two prongs, gaining control of key river and railroad crossings and securing his central Tennessee base.[35]

Halleck disagreed. He believed the enemy had a firm line from Decatur to Island No. 10 on the Mississippi River, and that the best place to break it was in its middle, at Corinth, or perhaps Jackson, Mississippi. "This seems to be the best line of operations, as it leads directly to the enemy's center, and is easily supplied."[36] Buell preferred to march where he thought best, and also believed that at whatever point they chose to attack they would surely meet the enemy's main force.[37] They were at cross-purposes.

Halleck made his decision: Buell would unite with C. F. Smith's and Grant's forces at Savannah, Tennessee, on the banks of the Tennessee River, 9 miles from Pittsburg Landing. Old Brains had word that 60,000 Confederate troops had gathered at Eastport and Corinth.[38] Though he ordered Buell to march apace, Halleck kept Grant on a leash, insisting there be no battle before Buell arrived and success was certain.[39] Halleck paralyzed his subordinates. They ended up sitting at Pittsburg Landing, waiting for the enemy to hit them. And Buell even wired Halleck information (false at the time) that the Confederates were preparing a counterpunch against Smith, possibly even at Savannah, north of Shiloh.[40] "Move on, as ordered to-day," Halleck replied, "to re-enforce Smith. Savannah is now the strategic point. Don't fail to carry out my instructions. I know that I am right."[41]

But he was far from right. A great opportunity was slipping through his hands, one that, if snatched, might have helped end the war much sooner. Buell's information told him that Floyd's troops had left Chattanooga, leaving it defended by only "a few companies." Nonetheless, Buell obeyed Halleck's orders.

He dispersed his troops to watch the various Confederate approaches to Nashville, freeing up the bulk of his men to march for Halleck's concentration point at Savannah.[42] Halleck had not yet received Buell's note of March 14 delineating the multipronged southward push. He endorsed nearly all of Buell's ideas and ordered him to send what troops he could to "the vicinity of Savannah or Eastport."[43]

Shiloh and Its Wake

ON APRIL 3, 1862, Albert Sidney Johnston told Davis that he was moving his 40,000 men "forward to offer battle near Pittsburg" before Buell could arrive with his reinforcements.[44] "I hope you will be able to close with the enemy before his two columns unite," Davis replied. "I anticipate victory."[45]

The Confederates caught Grant napping at Shiloh Church, near Pittsburg Landing, at dawn on April 6. Johnston slammed into the breakfasting 40,000 enemy troops with a similar number of his own, hoping to destroy Grant's army before Buell could come up. A tenacious Union defense, particularly by units in a small wood that became known as "the hornets' nest," kept Grant's forces from being pushed into the Tennessee. But the Union held, Grant held, and Grant brought more troops across the river during the night (Buell's), stiffening his bridgehead. Grant counterattacked the next day, pushing back the exhausted Confederates. Both sides paid a heavy price: The Confederates suffered 13,000 casualties, the Union 10,700.[46]

At the close of the first day the South believed it had won a great victory, a desperately needed one, but it had not. Moreover, Johnston was mortally wounded leading the last of a dozen Rebel attacks on "the hornets' nest"—the one that finally broke its defenders. Johnston bled to death, having earlier sent his staff doctor to care for wounded Union prisoners. Though he had not demonstrated any particular brilliance as a commander, his death nevertheless weakened the Confederate war effort. His successors, starting with Beauregard, lacked Davis's supreme confidence, and also the ability to run a large command. A nearly continuous stream of disasters pummeled the South's western hopes for the rest of the war. In the aftermath of Shiloh, Lincoln received a letter insisting upon Grant's removal. Lincoln replied, "I can't spare this man; he fights," a succinct summary of what the president considered most important in a military leader.[47]

The Rebels withdrew to Corinth, Mississippi. Expecting a Union move against him with as many as 85,000 men, Beauregard begged for reinforcements. "If defeated here we lose the Mississippi Valley and probably our cause," he insisted, "whereas we could even afford to lose for a while Charleston and Savannah for the purpose of defeating Buell's army, which would not only insure us the valley of the Mississippi, but our independence."[48] As is too often the case in Beauregard's correspondence, the rhetoric climbs quickly into the ether. Despite this, Confederate leaders made every effort to assist him, including Davis, who instructed the governors of Alabama, Georgia, Louisiana, Mississippi, and South Carolina to send every armed man possible to Corinth.[49] They had ample time. Thanks to Halleck, it would take the Union thirty days to traverse the roughly 20 miles between Shiloh and Corinth.

Beauregard received broad freedom of action via Robert E. Lee, now serving as de facto chief of staff to Davis; Lee typically dealt with subordinates in this manner. Beauregard could retreat if he found it necessary, but "should it be inevitable, it is hoped you will be able to strike a successful blow at the enemy if he follows, which will enable you to gain the ascendancy and drive him back to the Ohio." Lee preferred that Beauregard hold his position as long as he could feed his army, considering this "preferable to withdrawing from it, and thus laying open more of the country to his ravages." But then he advised: "Unless by skillful maneuvering you can entice him to a more favorable position to attack."[50]

A WEEK AND A HALF before Shiloh, Buell had sent troops under the command of Brigadier General O. M. Mitchel deeper into the Confederacy to implement his idea for securing his Tennessee base.[51] Because it protected the railroads, this proved in line with the aforementioned renewed command from Halleck for Buell to support Grant.[52] Mitchel was undermanned; he shouldn't have been. By April 11 he had troops in Huntsville, Alabama, astride the Memphis and Charleston Railroad linking Chattanooga and Corinth.[53] By the sixteenth he had taken Decatur and was pushing units westward toward Tuscumbia, Alabama, in the direction of Corinth.[54] By the seventeenth, with only 7,000 men (including those guarding his supply lines), he controlled the railroad from Tuscumbia all the way to Stevenson, Alabama, on the rail line to Chattanooga.[55] He had dealt a heavy blow to Southern logistics and mobility. Union forces now controlled the Tennessee River and the railroad triangle Nashville/Decatur/Stevenson. Both routes could provide direct logistical support for a drive on Chattanooga. Mitchel realized the importance of his position, while Buell, his superior, did not.[56] Mitchel wrote Secretary of the Treasury Chase on April 19, 1862, that he controlled the railroad between Tuscumbia and Stevenson. Moreover, he had not burned the bridges over the Tennessee River near Stevenson "in the hope I might be permitted to march on Chattanooga and Knoxville." But his new instructions said to destroy them. "I do not comprehend the order, but must obey it as early as I can. This entire line ought to be occupied, in my opinion, and yet I fear it will be abandoned."[57]

Now, ears in the capital perked up and Stanton took notice of Mitchel's little army, ordering him to file daily reports with Washington.[58] Lincoln also gave this some attention.[59] But Halleck and Buell did not. Neither took any action to reinforce Mitchel, who began to despair of getting any significant help and worried that the important position he had taken would be lost.[60] Soon enemy pressure forced Mitchel's men out of Tuscumbia. He also had intelligence that placed the number of enemy troops in Chattanooga on April 21 at "not more than 1,000."[61]

The Rebels withdrew; Mitchel again put forces into Tuscumbia.[62] He begged Buell to reinforce it and pleaded for more men.[63] "I wish it were possible to give me force enough to strike a blow at Chattanooga. It was in the hope that this might be done that I spared the Tennessee Bridge," Mitchel wrote earlier.[64] With almost no support, Mitchel acted on his own. "I have decided to occupy Stevenson in force," he wrote.[65] By May 1 he had troops 12 miles from Chattanooga. But then things started to go sour as partisan bands began hitting his supply lines. "As there is no [hope] of an immediate advance upon Chattanooga," he told Stanton, "I will now contract my line."[66] Mitchel, exhausted and disillusioned, sent a despondent wire to Stanton: "This campaign is ended, and I now occupy Huntsville in perfect security, while all of Alabama north of Tennessee River floats no flag but that of the Union. If my recommendations pass to the hands of the Adjutant-General I deem them lost."[67] Stanton tried to reassure him. "Your spirited operations afford great satisfaction to the President," he wrote. This seems to have helped. Mitchel certainly found it pleasing, though it did nothing to improve a position that grew increasingly tenuous.[68] Confederate raiders under Colonel John Hunt Morgan attacked his supply depot at Pulaski, Tennessee, taking a number of Union prisoners, including Mitchel's son (whom the Union general planned to exchange for Morgan's brother). Mitchel also became dependent upon information from a network of slave sympathizers to keep his holdings.[69]

The Union let a critical opportunity slip through its hands. The panic on the Confederate side had already begun; Governor Joseph E. Brown of Georgia led the rout. He accosted the Richmond government: "Let me beg you to send heavy re-enforcements to Chattanooga without delay." He forecast dire consequences: if Chattanooga fell, and "the railroad bridges on both sides of it burned, we are cut off from the coal mines, and all our iron mills are stopped. We are soon to be driven out of Tennessee, it seems, and both armies fed on what little provision is left in the cotton regions. It cannot last long. Our wheat crop is ruined with rust, and all our young men not now under arms called from their fields under the conscription act, when you have not arms for them. If this policy is to be continued, hunger will at no distant day produce its natural result."[70]

He had good reason to worry. The Confederate departmental commander, Major General Edmund Kirby Smith, controlled Chattanooga and the Cumberland Gap, both of which faced imminent attack from small Union forces that he could not stop; his garrisons had been denuded for the concentration at Corinth.[71] The Confederate situation did not improve as May lengthened. Officially, Kirby Smith had 17,000 men in his department. But they were new regiments and, as was normal, largely down with sickness. This left him 8,000 men ready for duty, 3,000 of whom did not have weapons. Matters were even graver at the critical point. On May 28 Kirby Smith wrote: "The effective force at Chattanooga under Brigadier-General Leadbetter is about 900 infantry, 400 cavalry, and eight pieces of light artillery.... The inadequacy of the force at Chattanooga and my inability to re-enforce it is a subject of serious anxiety."[72] In early May, Mitchel reported to his superiors that the Confederates had not more than 2,000 men in the city.[73]

On May 27, Smith begged for reinforcements, especially for Chattanooga, which he believed faced imminent attack. Initially, he received encouragement.[74] On the seventh and eighth of June, Union troops shelled the city—then withdrew.[75] A few days later, Smith, who had gathered what force he could to meet the Union drive on the Cumberland Gap, asked Davis's advice on which way he should retreat from Chattanooga if he had to give up the city. South to Georgia, Davis replied.[76]

For the Confederates though, the danger had passed, at least for the moment. The Union high command had other things on its mind. Seizing Chattanooga in the spring or summer of 1862 would have enabled an immediate thrust into Georgia, the heart of the Confederacy. Instead, Halleck moved on Corinth, an objective of far lesser value strategically, having failed to seize the best chance he would ever have to land a staggering blow against the Confederacy.

HALLECK CELEBRATED THE VICTORY at Shiloh by coming to Pittsburg Landing and taking direct command of the Union forces, which he then concentrated for a push against Corinth.[77] He did not hurry, and he also turned tactician, forgetting that as a theater commander, he was supposed to be a strategist. In short, he swapped the forest for the trees. Halleck concentrated more than 100,000 men, pulling in the forces under Buell, Grant, and Major General John Pope, and waited until April 30 to advance. They neared Corinth's fortifications on the eighteenth. His progress was inexplicably slow, especially since he had been sent on April 14 a captured dispatch from Beauregard that gave Confederate strength at Corinth on April 9 as 35,000, though more reinforcements were expected. Historian John F. Marszalek writes in his biography of Halleck that "Old Brains" sought Corinth, a place, something he had written about in his work on military theory, rather than the destruction of enemy's army.[78] He also became focused on the next battle, ignoring larger operational and strategic issues. Corinth, as noted, was a mildly useful operational objective, but Beauregard's army was one component of a Confederate center of gravity. Destroying it would have won the Union the entire West. Meanwhile, Mitchel was two days' march from a nearly empty Chattanooga—an operational, indeed strategic objective of significant value—and begging for reinforcements.

Beauregard entrenched his forces around Corinth and sortied against Union fingers, stinging the Federals on two separate occasions. Halleck slogged on.[79] After a May 25 conference with his generals, Beauregard elected to withdraw. He wrote to Brigadier General J. B. Villepigue, the commander of Fort Pillow: "Wishing to take the enemy farther into the interior, where I hope to be able to strike him a severe blow, which cannot be done here, where he is so close to his supplies, I have concluded to withdraw on the 30th instant from this place for the present before he can compel me to do so by his superiority of numbers. The evacuation of this place necessarily involves that of your present position."[80] Beauregard then stole a march on the Federals, falling back 52 miles, to Tupelo, Mississippi.

Davis, of course, wanted further explanation. Beauregard responded that he had withdrawn toward Tupelo out of necessity—and after consulting with his other generals, who agreed unanimously. "In retiring toward Tupelo it was hoped the enemy would have followed the movement with a part of his forces," he wrote, "affording me the opportunity of taking the offensive with a lesser disparity of numbers and afforded me the chances of cutting off his line of communication. The retrograde movement was…approved by General R. E. Lee, acting general-in-chief, in his letter of the 26th ultimo." To Davis's question about his future movements, Beauregard, replied, Halleck-like: "The plan of future operations must depend to a great extent on the movements of the enemy."[81]

The loss of Corinth and Beauregard's retreat, like the fall of Donelson, further undermined the Confederacy's strategic position in the West. But in this last instance Beauregard made the right choice. Meanwhile, Davis queried whether it had ever been "practicable to have cut the enemy's line of communication, so as to compel him to abandon the Tennessee River or to permit us to reoccupy Nashville?" Beauregard replied that it had not and mentioned his two unsuccessful attempts to draw the enemy out of his works.[82]

Davis, obviously, was not pleased with the utter disaster that had befallen the Confederacy in the West. His assessment of Beauregard's motives reveals his view of the underlying problem: "Beauregard claims by telegram to have made a 'brilliant and successful retreat' and pleads his constant occupation as the cause of his delay to reply to the inquiry made through the Adjt. Genl. as to the reason for his retreat and the abandonment of the Memphis & Charleston R. Road—There are those who can only walk a log when it is near to the ground, and I fear he has been placed too high for his mental strength, as he does not exhibit the ability manifested on smaller fields."[83] His conclusions were not unlike those Lincoln had arrived at regarding McClellan.

Davis sent his aide-de-camp, Colonel William Preston Johnston, who was a nephew of Albert Sidney Johnston, west to investigate what had happened in the wake of Shiloh, discover the future plans of the region's Confederate commanders, and find out if the lost territory could be recovered.[84] Johnston did not give Beauregard and the other Confederate commanders high marks. He believed "the value of Corinth as a temporary base from which to attack the enemy was vast, but . . . it was untenable for permanent occupation on account of its unhealthfulness," which, as Johnston explained, arose from the poor quality of the town's water supply. He argued that the Confederate commanders should have tried a repeat of Shiloh from Corinth because they had accumulated approximately 50,000 men there, a third more than they had had for the earlier fight (this was really closer to 25 percent greater). Were they not going to attack, they should have left sooner.[85] Beauregard, though, considered his actions a success.[86]

Colonel Johnston regarding conclusions hardly mattered. Whatever Davis might have had in mind regarding Beauregard's future, the general himself decided it. Citing ill health, he repaired to Bladon's Springs, Alabama, turning his command over to Braxton Bragg and informing Davis not by telegram but by letter. Davis confirmed the transfer of the departmental mantle on June 20, 1862.[87] Beauregard's withdrawal provoked yet another caustic presidential assessment: "Beauregard left his command to seek rest, and restore his health. The sedentary life at Corinth must have been hard to bear as he reports himself exhausted and his army undergoing reorganization."[88] Davis never gave Beauregard another significant command, and the general spent most of the remainder of the war on the Carolina coast.

New Orleans and the Mississippi River

STRANGLING THE CONFEDERACY into submission remained an element of the Union strategy, one McClellan and subsequent Union leaders executed via various coastal operations on specific targets. One place was Savannah,

Georgia's principal port. Unable to take the city, McClellan elected to seize its approaches. Union successes against Henry, Donelson, and Roanoke Island had encouraged McClellan to push Brigadier General Thomas W. Sherman to reduce Fort Pulaski, control of which decided Savannah's access to the Atlantic. He also gave orders to seize Fernandina and St. Augustine in Florida.[89] This pair, as well as nearby Jacksonville, passed into Union hands in March. April saw Pulaski surrender to Union bombardment. From then on, of all the Confederacy's Atlantic ports, only Wilmington, North Carolina, enjoyed uninterrupted access to the sea.[90]

Union forces in the Gulf of Mexico did their share as well. Apalachicola, Florida, fell to the Federals in April; Biloxi and Pass Christian, both in Mississippi, also changed hands. The Gulf victories cost the Union no casualties. The Confederate troops from these areas had been sent to support Albert Sidney Johnston, illuminating the problem with the Confederate strategy of concentration.[91] The South had to strip some areas in order to mass enough troops to repel a Union advance, but doing so meant leaving those areas weak and thus susceptible to Union encroachment. The Union put Sir Julian Corbett's ideas about maritime strategy into practice, simultaneously revealing the efficacy of the logic behind the strategy for fighting the war Lincoln had presented to Buell: hitting the South in many places at once would eventually break it.

New Orleans proved the greatest loss resulting from Confederate concentration. The Union had looked upon it greedily for some time. Commander David Dixon Porter proposed its capture in November 1861 and sold the idea to Gideon Welles after finding two senators to carry him past the Navy Department's gatekeepers. Welles took Porter to see Lincoln, who also liked the idea. He in turn took Porter to McClellan and told McClellan to find the necessary troops and a general to administer the city once it fell, and to do it quickly. Porter and McClellan fell to making a plan. Lincoln returned at eight that same evening and McClellan greeted him with a promise of 20,000 men, whereupon Lincoln ordered the navy to prepare the necessary ships. The expedition needed a commander. Porter pushed for David Farragut, his foster brother, who eagerly took the job.[92]

When the operation finally began, Union timing could not have been better. To support Albert Sidney Johnston's counterattack, the Confederates had stripped New Orleans, the center of Southern banking and the South's most populous city. Moreover, to defend against Union naval incursions down the Mississippi, the gunboats protecting the city had been dispatched to Memphis—and then sunk by Union rams. By early April 1862, New Orleans's defense depended upon shore batteries in forts, 3,000 militia, a pair of unfinished ironclads, and a ragtag fleet. These proved insufficient preparations against a Union flotilla led by the skilled and aggressive Farragut, and a 15,000-man force under Major General Benjamin Butler, a prewar Democratic Party politician from Massachusetts. After a six-day mortar barrage of the defending forts, Union gunboats cut a path through the city's protective boom and Farragut fought his way past the forts with seventeen ships. The defending fleet was destroyed or scuttled, the garrison surrendered or fled, and the city fell, opening up another route for Union penetration into the Deep South.[93] Porter believed they should have taken New Orleans sooner "instead of wasting our resources in attacking Hatteras Inlet, Port Royal, and other places of less importance."[94]

But Welles and the others in the Union high command were not quite as unthinking as the hypercritical Porter implied. Farragut's orders to take New Orleans included instructions for follow-on operations. Welles had told him to push up the Mississippi River and join with another Union naval expedition that had launched from Cairo, Illinois. Welles also ordered Farragut to take Mobile's defensive works and give them to the army to garrison.[95] Farragut could not do both simultaneously, so he did the most immediate and obvious thing: he sent units north. The navy took Baton Rouge, Louisiana, on May 7, 1862. A squadron under Commander S. P. Lee was outside Vicksburg on May 18. Lee demanded the city's surrender. The Confederate commander promptly refused, replying "that Mississippians don't know, and refuse to learn, how to surrender to an enemy. If Commodore Farragut or Brigadier-General Butler can teach them," he added, "let them come and try."[96]

Vicksburg would prove a troublesome obstacle for the Union. It rests on a bluff 200 feet above a narrow bend in the Mississippi. New Orleans is about 400 miles to the south, Memphis approximately the same distance northward. When Farragut and General Butler arrived and surveyed the scene, they elected to withdraw. The navy's guns lacked the elevation to assail its defensive batteries, and the army lacked sufficient troops to assault it—they only had about 1,500 troops to face an estimated garrison of 8,000–10,000, theoretically supported by an additional 30,000 men located an hour's train ride away in Jackson, Mississippi. Their information was in fact inaccurate, as there were only about 3,600 men at Vicksburg. Not until the end of June did Vicksburg have 10,000 defenders.[97]

The administration, starting with Lincoln, was not happy with Farragut's withdrawal (oddly, they learned about it from false newspaper reporting announcing the retreat *before* Farragut had even arrived). To Assistant Navy Secretary Fox, everything else paled in comparison to pushing up the

Mississippi. "So soon as we heard of the fall of New Orleans, we notified
Foote and Halleck that you would be in Beauregard's rear at once," Fox wrote.
"This may be a fatal step as regards our western movements, since our advance
to Memphis would have been the means of forcing Beauregard to fight or
retreat, besides capturing all the enemy's gunboats, which have already made
one attack on our Western Flotilla, and are preparing another." Welles seconded this and told Farragut to link up with the river flotilla descending from
the north and commanded temporarily by Flag Officer Charles Henry Davis,
who had replaced the wounded Foote.[98]

Farragut gathered his forces, including the mortar boats under Porter and
troops under Butler, who committed to assembling around 7,000 men. Red
tape and incompetence delayed the mission, but by June 25, Farragut's forces
were poised outside Vicksburg. Butler, though, dispatched only 3,000 men, not
7,000; he simply lacked sufficient manpower to garrison New Orleans and the
other places the Union now held as well as supply troops for an attack on Vicksburg. Unable to assault the city, Farragut ran Vicksburg's guns with part of his
squadron and joined forces with the units under Flag Officer Davis. He wired
Halleck for help in fulfilling Lincoln's order to clear the Mississippi River.[99]

Halleck replied from Corinth on July 3, telling Farragut, "The scattered
and weakened condition of my forces renders it impossible for me at the
present to detach any troops to cooperate with you on Vicksburg. Probably
I shall be able to do so as soon as I can get my troops more concentrated. This
may delay the clearing of the river, but its accomplishment will be certain in
a few weeks."[100] Pressed by Stanton as to whether or not he was dispatching
troops to Farragut, Halleck replied he could not, as he was sending troops to
Arkansas, as well as to Buell in Kentucky and Tennessee.[101] Halleck missed
yet another opportunity. Arkansas mattered not at all. He had done nothing
since Corinth's fall and should have marched at least part of his 100,000-man
army to Memphis, which the Union Navy had taken on June 6, embarked
as much of it as Union transport allowed, and sailed for Vicksburg.[102] Once
again, with Halleck, theory substituted for action. Farragut was disappointed.
"I think now is the time for Halleck to act," he wrote Welles, "as [the Confederacy's] whole force is turned to Richmond. I don't believe they have 5,000
men here, and they conscripts, except the artillery." He told Welles that he
believed there was little he could do at Vicksburg and suggested that he might
be more effective back in the Gulf of Mexico. Orders from Welles to send
some of Porter's mortar boats to support McClellan's Peninsula offensive,
combined with fears regarding the effects of the falling river on Farragut's
larger vessels, forced his retreat.[103]

Welles gave his assessment of the situation. "The evacuation of Corinth has much lessened the importance of your continuing your operations on the Mississippi," he wrote Farragut. "The army has failed to furnish the necessary troops for the capture of Vicksburg, and has not at present, it is represented, an available force to send there to cooperate with you in its capture. Indeed, the place itself shall be of little consequence should the project of changing the course of the Mississippi meet with success." (His last reference was to a canal-building effort that was intended to divert the river around Vicksburg but which soon failed.) Welles ordered Farragut back to the Gulf, telling him to use his forces against what objectives he thought best.[104] Welles believed Vicksburg would have fallen by the beginning of June if the Union had sent enough troops. Later, he blamed Halleck.[105]

Half a Loaf

FROM FEBRUARY TO MAY 1862, Union forces in the West achieved a string of victories, taking 50,000 square miles of the Confederacy, including New Orleans, the South's largest city; Baton Rouge, Louisiana's capital; and Nashville, the capital of Tennessee. The North also now controlled more than 1,000 miles of navigable Southern rivers, mileage it soon exploited for further advances.[106] These gains were impressive, but they were in some ways hollow. Lincoln wanted to win the war as quickly as possible. The Union leadership was ensuring that such would not be the case. Aggressive leadership on the part of Halleck and Buell and better planning at the strategic level in regard to the Union's joint army-navy Mississippi drives could have gained the Union much more for only a little more effort. The North dealt the enemy heavy blows. These could have been heavier still. The worst culprit was Halleck. In the spring of 1862 he could have destroyed the Confederate army at Corinth or seized Chattanooga. Doing either would have destroyed the Confederate strategic position in the West and made possible an early conquest of the Deep South. He did neither. In the summer he compounded his failure by refusing to help Farragut take Vicksburg.

Grant wrote in his *Memoirs* that after the fall of Forts Henry and Donelson great opportunities lay before the Union. If a single general had commanded in the West, "he could have marched to Chattanooga, Corinth, Memphis and Vicksburg with the troops we then had." The volunteers who were then coming into the Union service would have provided forces for operating against any Confederate resistance from these key points, denying important areas to the Confederates and keeping out of the Rebel ranks the large numbers of men in these lands. Grant commented: "Providence ruled differently."[107]

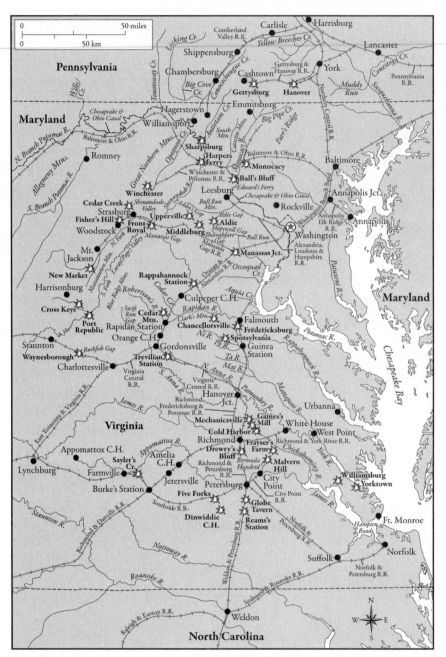

Area of the Virginia Campaigns. Adapted from Russell F. Weigley, *A Great Civil War: A Military and Political History, 1861–1865* (Bloomington: Indiana University Press, 2000), 59.

War in Virginia

I shall soon leave here on the wing for Richmond—which
you may be sure I will take.

—GEORGE B. MCCLELLAN, March 16, 1862

BY FEBRUARY 1862, both Jefferson Davis and Joseph E. Johnston had grown increasingly worried about the very forward position of Johnston's army in northern Virginia. The Confederates labored to raise more men for Johnston, hoping (vainly, it proved) to increase his force from 36,000 to as many as 100,000. Davis believed this would constitute a solid base for advancing against the enemy in conjunction with Confederate forces at Aquia Creek and in the Shenandoah Valley. But until Johnston could drastically reinforce his lines of communication he remained at risk. In a February 20 meeting, the Confederate leaders had agreed that their armies north, east, and south of Richmond should take up positions that allowed them to support one another. Johnston's men were spread from Dumfries on the Chesapeake to Leesburg on the Potomac, west of Washington; the Shenandoah Valley held about another 5,000; around 6,000 bivouacked close to Fredericksburg. Another 27,000 or so were to the east and south of Richmond, primarily at Norfolk and Yorktown.[1] A form of David Houston's suggestion—Houston being the farmer from Natural Bridge who had written to Davis—had come to pass.

Johnston had not been wasting his time. When McClellan became head of the Army of the Potomac, Johnston had posts in Centreville and Manassas, as well as batteries along the Potomac River. By early fall the Rebels had largely blocked the water route into Washington, D.C., the Union navy declaring at the end of October 1861 that the Potomac was effectively closed to unescorted vessels.[2]

But by the end of February, Davis believed Johnston's dispositions vulnerable. A defeat of his forces to the south, or of those east of Richmond, would see Johnston's lines of communication severed and an attack upon his rear. Davis considered this a real threat since the Union seizure of Roanoke Island and other victories in North Carolina menaced both Norfolk and Yorktown. Davis posed Johnston two questions: "First. How can your army best serve to prevent the advance of the enemy while the want of force compels you to stand on the defensive. Second. What dispositions can you and should you make, to enable you most promptly to cooperate with other columns in the event of disaster to their forces or to your's [*sic*], and of consequent danger to the Capitol."[3]

Johnston solved his positional dilemma by withdrawing from Manassas. "It was my intention in falling back to take a line on which the two bodies of troops could readily unite against the body of the enemy operating against either," he wrote of his operations. Moreover, he tried to follow Davis's orders to remain close enough to cooperate with the troops to Richmond's east and southeast. Enemy activity complicated things. The Union had a large force in the Shenandoah Valley, and Johnston also had to contend with the possible advance of McClellan's army. Initially, the former seemed to worry him more than the latter. He remarked that "the large [enemy] force in the valley and the good roads hence to Culpeper Court-House and Gordonsville make it not impossible that McClellan, who seems not to value time especially, may repair this railroad and advance upon both routes, uniting the valley troops with his own." Later, though, he chastised himself for having been "too confident of the slothful condition of our adversaries."[4]

Johnston was generally right to brand Union actions "slothful," especially in regard to McClellan, but now the Union forces in the East were finally on the move. On March 24, 1862, Confederate leaders received their first word of McClellan's landing at Fortress Monroe. Southern leaders, initially unsure of the Union's objective, deciphered it by April 4. Major General John B. "Prince John" Magruder's 15,000 men at Yorktown posed the immediate Union opposition. A West Point graduate and veteran of the Mexican War, Magruder had won his nickname for his "courtly manner and reputation for lavish entertainment" while stationed in Newport. Other Confederate forces still sat in penny packets all over Virginia.[5]

McClellan had decided to begin what became known as the Peninsula Campaign at Fortress Monroe on March 12, 1862. The site, 75 miles southeast of Richmond, anchored the tip of the peninsula lying between the York and James rivers. This had been his last choice of bases. Enemy actions forced the change. First, the Confederate ironclad CSS *Virginia* sortied from Hampton Roads. The timely arrival of the Union's USS *Monitor* contained the Rebel behemoth, but its presence threatened McClellan's supply line in Chesapeake Bay while blocking any possible Union advance on Richmond up the James River. Simultaneously, Johnston upset McClellan's plan to land at Urbana by pulling his army out of Manassas and placing it farther south, behind the

Rappahannock River, destroying McClellan's hope of inserting Union forces between Johnston's troops and the Confederate capital. Johnston also angered Davis, who wasn't informed of the movement beforehand.[6]

Lincoln gave official permission for McClellan's movement on March 8, 1862, but he wasn't happy about it. He imposed two strong caveats: that a sufficient force remain to guard Washington, and that no more than two Union corps leave for the Peninsula until the Potomac was cleared of Confederates between the capital and the Chesapeake.[7] The withdrawal of Johnston's army dealt with the second provision, but the first proved contentious, and Lincoln attached a string: McClellan had to secure Manassas as well.[8]

Stanton, though, wanted more. "The Department has nothing to show what is your plan of operations," the secretary of war wrote McClellan. "Will you be pleased to state specifically what plan of operations you propose to execute under the present circumstances?"[9] McClellan replied that he would use Fort Monroe "as the first base of operations" and advance via Yorktown and West Point toward Richmond, the Confederate capital "being the objective point." He thought Richmond's fall would ensure the capture of Norfolk as well as "the whole of Virginia." He expected "a decisive battle between West Point and Richmond, to give which battle the rebels will concentrate all their available forces, understanding as they will that it involves the fate of their cause." Because of this, McClellan insisted the Union should counter by gathering "all our available forces, and operate upon adjacent lines, maintaining perfect communications between our columns," and "that no time should be lost in reaching the field of battle." McClellan also believed it necessary to reach West Point, Virginia, as quickly as possible. Taking this city, located at the confluence of the York and Mattaponi rivers, would lead to the establishment of a base of operations and supply only 25 miles from the Confederate capital. He had two plans for doing this: an overland campaign from Fortress Monroe, which he believed would probably necessitate the sieges of Yorktown and Gloucester, and a combined land and naval assault on Yorktown, "the first object of the campaign." He believed this would lead "to the most rapid and decisive results," and he stressed "the absolute necessity of the full cooperation of the Navy," without which the operations would be needlessly prolonged. The army would have to take strong enemy positions, such as Yorktown, that could be easily turned with the navy's assistance.[10]

Stanton acquiesced, and McClellan continued his preparations, which included sorting out the situation around Washington and its approaches. While McClellan was on the Peninsula with 100,000 men, another corps of about 30,000 under McDowell was to sail down and join him when ordered. Major General Nathaniel Banks commanded Union forces in the Shenandoah Valley and was assigned to keep the Confederates from cutting the Baltimore and Ohio Railroad or invading Pennsylvania. McClellan's detailed instructions to Banks told him "to cover line of Potomac & Washington." Even farther west, in the mountain country of what would become West Virginia, was Frémont, who was supposed to move toward eastern Tennessee, taking advantage of the area's Union sympathies and perhaps cutting the Confederate railway through the area.[11] McClellan outlined for Stanton the numbers and dispositions of the troops that he left in and around Washington: 55,456, including 35,000 in the Shenandoah. He intended all of them to remain under his command after he departed for the Peninsula.[12]

Stanton also wanted McClellan's plans for cooperating with Burnside's Roanoke expedition. McClellan, realizing he possessed no clear knowledge of how deeply Burnside was engaged, did not give exact orders. He believed it best for Burnside to move no farther into the interior than New Bern and that he should immediately "reduce Beaufort." He should post troops at Fort Macon, then go back to Roanoke Island and make ready to assist the other Union forces via Winton or Fort Monroe, depending upon the circumstances.[13]

Burnside's potential supporting role evolved. The day after arriving on the Peninsula, McClellan told Burnside that events might make it necessary for the Army of the Potomac to cross the James River below Richmond and drive on Petersburg. Because of this, he wanted to maintain close communications with Burnside in North Carolina, and to know what Burnside could do about neutralizing the Confederate forces in Beaufort and Goldsborough while preventing the enemy's retreat from Richmond. After taking Richmond, McClellan planned to drive on Raleigh and link up with Burnside's forces through Goldsborough.[14]

Events in the Shenandoah Valley mangled McClellan's plan before he even departed for the Peninsula. Major General Thomas "Stonewall" Jackson had stirred up trouble. McClellan had assumed that Banks could deal with Jackson—if the Confederate general was not reinforced—and that Banks would not be able to detach any troops to garrison the key position of Manassas for some time, probably until McClellan had drawn the main Confederate force to Richmond. McClellan judged it unlikely that Johnston would reinforce Jackson and conduct offensive operations, it being too late to achieve anything by this. He told Banks that "the most important thing at present is to throw Jackson well back & then to assume such a position as to enable you to prevent his return." And after Banks rebuilt his rail communications he should move on Staunton as McClellan moved on Richmond so that the enemy could not concentrate against just Banks's force.[15]

In its defense, the objective of McClellan's operational plan is clear: Richmond. It was also an important one. McClellan had thoughtfully considered his lines of advance and the necessity and utility of cooperation with the navy, as well as the imperative of having secure lines of supply and communication. Furthermore, the plan took advantage of the extended enemy position. Davis had been right to worry about Johnston's dispositions; he was indeed exposed. McClellan had also provided for supporting forces in the Shenandoah Valley and eastern Tennessee.

But there were problems as well. Both McClellan and Stanton considered support from Burnside, but both failed to ensure it would arrive. Pressure from North Carolina certainly would have been helpful. Moreover, one wonders whether McClellan, in his discussions with Burnside about possibly crossing the James and attacking Petersburg, was doing contingency planning or immediately taking counsel of his fears. The fatal flaw lay in the necessity of quick execution. This might not have been a problem with a different commander.

Once a great ally of McClellan's, Stanton had become a bitter detractor. After McClellan's departure, the garrison commander in Washington insisted to Stanton that he lacked the troops to protect the city and his command area, especially since McClellan had ordered him to send 4,000 of them to Manassas and Warrenton (which had been Banks's purview). Stanton initiated a review that concluded that to obey Lincoln's order regarding the securing of Washington, the Union needed 30,000 men at hand; they had only 19,002. How they determined the number needed is unclear, and the whole situation seems odd. Pressure from Congress's Joint Committee on the Conduct of the War, combined with Lincoln's own fears for the capital's safety, resulted in direct intervention in McClellan's plans.[16] Lincoln took one corps, McDowell's, from McClellan's army.[17] Resorting to hyperbole worthy of Beauregard, McClellan deemed this "the most infamous thing that history has recorded."[18]

All this was indicative of the lack of trust inherent in the civil-military relationship within the Union high command, and in particular between civilian officials and McClellan. McClellan refused to grasp that the administration not only wanted action but, for domestic and foreign political reasons, *needed* it. McClellan's quiescence had so alienated his civilian masters that some wondered aloud if the general carried treason in his heart. For his part, McClellan saw in their every criticism deceit and ill will. Moreover, he labored under the delusion that wars could be fought in a political vacuum, and he never grasped Clausewitz's truth that war *is* a political act. This poisonous civil-military relationship might well have made anything McClellan tried impossible.

"All my arrangements are completely changed by recent orders," McClellan wrote on April 6, which was somewhat of an exaggeration. Nonetheless, the change did rob him of one corps that he had planned to have on the Peninsula, and of forces he had intended to use to help open the York River, thus easing, as well as encouraging, the cooperation of the navy with the northern elements of his forces on the Peninsula. Major General Erasmus D. Keyes, one of McClellan's corps commanders, rightly complained that they were now being required to execute a plan different from the one he had originally agreed to. To him, a good plan that might have won the war for the Union had become "a bad plan, with means insufficient for certain success."[19] In any case, McClellan never would have executed the plan as intended; doing so was simply beyond him, as we shall see.

McClellan's departure for the Peninsula created an opportunity for Lincoln to reorganize the Union armies. He relieved McClellan as general in chief, leaving him in command of the Army of the Potomac, and created the aforementioned Department of the Mississippi, under Halleck, and a Mountain Department, under Frémont.[20] Lincoln believed McClellan had enough responsibility, and felt he was doing the general "a very great kindness in permitting him to retain command of the Army of the Potomac, and giving him an opportunity to retrieve his errors." Lincoln did not immediately name a successor and instead tried to perform the duties himself, with Stanton's help.[21] Moreover, bending under pressure from Radical Republicans, Lincoln yanked another division from McClellan to stiffen the new command given their political darling Frémont.[22] Lacking a general in chief left more room for this kind of politically motivated shenanigans and robbed Lincoln of the ability to thwart such pressures by citing the general in chief's military requirements.

Also important to remember here is that McClellan had intended his Peninsula Campaign to be an element of a larger, multipronged Union offensive (albeit one that supported *his* movements). When Lincoln removed McClellan as general in chief, he destroyed McClellan's strategic plan. Worse, with no general in chief and Lincoln's subsequent absorption with events on the Peninsula, Union strategy spun out of control. There was now no one at the top to coordinate the Union prongs and to force the commanders to take advantage of the opportunities that opened to them in the spring and summer of 1862.

The administration also made another error. On April 3, 1862, it closed down the recruiting system used for raising volunteer regiments. McClellan pilloried the decision, as did William Tecumseh Sherman. Both insisted that this did not take into account the realities of attrition.[23]

War on the Peninsula

IMMEDIATELY FACING MCCLELLAN'S FORCES on the Peninsula were Magruder's men. The Union had not caught him completely by surprise. On January 10, he speculated that a landing on the Rappahannock seemed the most likely Union move, though he also saw an attack on his own section of the Peninsula (he made his headquarters at Yorktown) as possible and prepared for an enemy descent on the James River.[24]

Before McClellan arrived outside Yorktown, Magruder's superiors had already begun to act. On March 25, 1862, Davis, through Lee, ordered Joe Johnston to bring 30,000 troops—about half of the troops that Johnston wanted to shift southward—to Richmond if he did not expect an attack along the Rappahannock.[25] Johnston wanted the immediate concentration of all the units in his department. "We cannot win without concentrating," he wrote Lee.[26] Just as in the West, a focus on concentration would soon dominate the Confederate military response, though an internal debate swirled around where the concentration should be, and for what purpose.

Johnston had been told to begin moving only half his troops because the administration had not yet determined the objective of the Union advance and wanted to preserve some flexibility against the still-developing threat.[27] Moreover, Davis and Lee worried about a Union advance on Staunton that would sever Confederate rail communications with Tennessee and trap significant Southern forces. They were right to worry; McClellan had indeed ordered Banks to take Staunton. The weakening of Johnston's forces in the event of a Union advance against the Rapidan River would make this a possibility. Moreover, Davis viewed the loss of the rail connections to Tennessee as more hurtful to the Southern cause than the abandonment of Norfolk and the Peninsula.[28]

Lee had become Davis's military advisor on March 13; he and Davis then ran the Confederacy's war in the East.[29] Davis struggled to prioritize the defense of Virginia in the face of as yet unclear enemy movements. Davis, Johnston, and Lee had a number of meetings that began on March 31 and culminated on April 14. Johnston pushed again for the concentration of Confederate forces, but outside Richmond, not on the Peninsula. He believed Magruder's position at Yorktown untenable and easily turnable by Union gunboats (which was what McClellan had planned to do), and that beating McClellan on the Peninsula would only slow the Union advance. Lee thought differently. He saw the narrowness of the Peninsula as ideal terrain for defense. Lee's view won out. Davis ordered Johnston to the Peninsula.[30]

Realizing his inferiority to the enemy, Magruder took to his entrenchments and executed a bold bluff, which McClellan bought. McClellan elected to mount a siege of the Confederate positions in Yorktown, ones that the Union army could have carried immediately upon their landing because of their superiority in forces. McClellan saw more than what was there. His tendency to overestimate enemy forces, which had manifested itself on larger fields, grew exponentially on this smaller one. He argued for the necessity of a siege and asked for the return of McDowell's corps, or at least the division commanded by Brigadier General William B. Franklin.[31]

Lincoln would have none of it. His tolerance for McClellan's dallying lasted only five days. "I think you better break the enemies' line from Yorktown to Warwick River, at once," Lincoln wrote. "They will probably use *time*, as advantageously as you can."[32] Secretary of War Stanton also urged McClellan to storm the Confederate works.[33] "I was much tempted to reply that he had better come & do it himself," McClellan wrote his wife regarding Lincoln's goad.[34] Lincoln and Stanton probably should have come and done it themselves, or at least clearly and decisively *ordered* their subordinate to do it. Time, as Lincoln feared, would work against the Union as the Confederacy gathered its strength.

The day before Lincoln's note, McClellan concluded that the Rebel defense could only be breached by siege and requested the necessary train.[35] Historian and McClellan expert Ethan Rafuse insists that McClellan "had the foresight to" prepare for siege operations, which certainly seems the case. McClellan even made some of the necessary preparations before departing.[36] But McClellan may also have been discombobulated by Lincoln and Stanton taking away McDowell's corps. This forced the alteration of McClellan's operational plan for the Peninsula, just as Lincoln's refusal to endorse McClellan's grand strategic plan, the one that called for a field army of 273,000, had disrupted his vision and left him paralyzed. McClellan had constantly clutched at this grand plan, and in his mind, the administration's failure to give him what he deemed necessary became an excuse for inaction. A similar thing occurred with his operational plan for the Peninsula. Taking away McDowell's corps meant that McClellan no longer had what he insisted he needed. Thus the administration had made it impossible for him to do his task. Indeed, they had even betrayed him.

The Union reorganization of departments also raised complaints from McClellan as well as worries. On April 4 the administration created the Department of the Shenandoah under Banks and the Department of the Rappahannock under McDowell.[37] To McClellan, this forecast disaster: "The order in regard to new departments is received. I fear the movement it indicates of an advance on Richmond in two isolated columns is a mistake; it will probably enable the rebels to concentrate on one while he holds the other in check."[38] The danger that McClellan pointed out in such a step certainly existed, but prompt movement of the Union forces would have made any Confederate effort to defeat their advances in detail very difficult, as well as very risky.

By April 9, McClellan had not attacked. The president pushed again, in one of the most famous letters of the war:

> I suppose the whole force which has gone forward for you, is with you by this time; and if so, I think it is the precise time for you to strike a blow. By delay the enemy will relatively gain upon you—that is, he will gain faster, by *fortifications* and *re-inforcements*, than you can by re-inforcements alone.
>
> And, once more let me tell you, it is indispensable to *you* that you strike a blow. *I* am powerless to help this. You will do me the justice to remember I always insisted, that going down the Bay in search of a field, instead of fighting at or near Mannassas [*sic*], was only shifting, and not surmounting, a difficulty—that we would find the same enemy, and the same, or equal, intrenchments, at either place. . . .
>
> I beg to assure you that I have never written you, or spoken to you, in greater kindness of feeling than now, nor with a fuller purpose to sustain you, so far as in my most anxious judgment, I consistently can. *But you must act.*[39]

McClellan did not act, at least not in the way Lincoln wanted, which had by now become the general's pattern when dealing with his commander in chief. He prepared for his siege. He asked again for Franklin's division (which he received), and planned to take Cape Gloucester, on the opposite bank of the York River, in order to clear a passage up the waterway and then cut the Confederate communications via this route.[40] All of this took time, great amounts of time. Eventually McClellan allowed the Confederates to hold him at the tip of the Peninsula for an entire month.

The Confederates began their withdrawal from Yorktown on May 3, at the last possible moment before McClellan's bombardment.[41] Lincoln's dissatisfaction had greatly intensified in the days before. "Your call for Parrott guns from Washington alarms me," he wrote, "chiefly because it argues indefinite procrastination. Is anything to be done?"[42]

General Johnston's commander in chief was not happy with him either. Davis insisted that Johnston's pulling back from opposite the Union army had surprised him, despite warning notes to this effect. He accepted the action but asked if it could be forestalled.[43] "I determined to retire because we can do nothing here," Johnston explained. "The volunteers are demoralized by electioneering, & becoming sickly—the enemy will give us no opportunity. [W]e *must* lose. There is no chance to win. By delay we may ensure the loss of Richmond too."[44] Historian Steven Woodworth insists that Johnston "went to the Peninsula with every intention of retreating before a serious clash with McClellan's army."[45] Events bear out the truth of this.

The impact on the Confederate war effort proved disastrous. Johnston's retreat necessitated the abandonment of Norfolk, the best Confederate shipyard, on May 9 and the consequent destruction of the ironclad *Virginia*, as well as some unfinished gunboats. This Union success would not have occurred when it did without the direct intervention of Lincoln and Secretary of the Treasury Salmon Chase. These two, along with Stanton, disembarked at Fortress Monroe on May 4. The soldiers told them a landing near Norfolk was impossible. They disagreed, particularly Chase, who took a boat to the opposite shore of the James River and returned to tell Lincoln about it. The president had been poring over maps of the area and discovered the perfect landing place. He visited it that night, walking on the beach with Stanton as Chase watched from the protective cutter USS *Miami*. The next day, Chase with them, Union forces landed and marched into Norfolk. "So has ended a brilliant week's campaign of the President," Chase wrote.[46]

All of this left a bitter taste in Davis's mouth, and the events on the Peninsula shook his confidence in the prospects of a successful defense of Richmond.[47] Davis and Lee met with Johnston on May 12 at the general's headquarters at New Kent Courthouse but got nothing about the general's intentions other than that he planned to improve his position and wait for the Union forces to leave their gunboats, which would then open a chance to strike.[48] Davis urged Johnston to attack McClellan if he crossed the Chickahominy River, believing McClellan's "passage between that river and the James may furnish you the opportunity."[49] When Johnston reached the environs of Richmond, Davis insisted he confer with him on any future plans.[50] On the Peninsula, Davis had the same problem as Lincoln: a general who refused to fight.

But at least McClellan had finally begun moving, though largely because his counterpart was withdrawing. He tried but failed to block Johnston's retreat, then advanced toward Richmond, basing his operations at White House Landing, located on the Pamunkey River about midway between Richmond and the mouth of the York. Johnston, fearful of a waterborne thrust via the James directly at the Confederate capital, pulled back over the Chickahominy River on the sixteenth. The day before, the Rebel battery south of Richmond at Drewry's Bluff had repulsed an attack by Union ironclads, eliminating the chances of a Union naval ascent of the James reaching the Confederate capital. McClellan also began considering shifting his base to the James. This worried Johnston, who feared that if this was done, McClellan could beat Johnston's army to Richmond. Lee and Davis also fretted over this, and both unsuccessfully prodded Johnston to attack before McClellan touched the James.[51]

Lincoln and Stanton then intervened again, returning McDowell's corps to McClellan's control, while also changing the Union operational plan. McDowell was ordered to "move upon Richmond by the general route of the Richmond and Fredericksburg Railroad, cooperating with the forces under General McClellan now threatening Richmond from the line of the Pamunkey and York Rivers." Simultaneously, he was to "establish as soon as possible a communication between your left wing and the right wing of General McClellan," while ensuring that he protected the capital against any Confederate thrust. McClellan was instructed to keep the main Confederate army pinned to prevent it from attacking McDowell before he could join hands with McClellan.[52] Now the Union was enacting a plan that McClellan had earlier insisted was a mistake. It was also an inadvertent step toward McClellan's operational suggestion of May 8, nine days before, when he had told Stanton, "We ought immediately to concentrate everything and not run the risk of engaging a desperate enemy with inferior three [armies]. All minor considerations should be thrown to one side and all our energies and means directed toward the defeat of Johnston's army in front of Richmond."[53] McClellan saw things very much as Johnston did. Their face-off, though, conjures memories of a schoolyard taunt: "One is afraid to fight and the other is afraid the other might."

Lee had his own ideas, ones that aligned very well with McClellan's fears. When he arrived in Richmond in late April, he began examining the possibility of concentrating and striking the divided Union forces in Virginia.

Not yet sure where to attack, he began corresponding about it with Jackson and Major General Richard S. Ewell. "The blow wherever struck," he noted, "must, to be successful, be sudden and heavy."[54] Jackson replied with a trio of plans. Lee made some suggestions but gave Jackson his leash.[55] What followed is often called one of the most brilliant operations in military history: Jackson's Valley Campaign.

By mid-May, the situation had clarified and Lee knew what kind of movement he wanted made. Lee also knew that McClellan had called for reinforcements, and on May 16 he told Jackson to prevent Banks from reinforcing McClellan or moving to Fredericksburg. A "successful blow struck" at Banks "might also lead to the recall of the reinforcements" being "sent to Frémont from Winchester." "But," he added, "you will not, in any demonstration you may make in that direction, lose sight of the fact that it may become necessary for you to come to the support of Genl Johnston, and hold yourself in readiness to do so if required… Whatever movement you make against Banks do it speedily, and if successful, drive him back towards the Potomac, and create the impression as far as practicable that you design threatening that line."[56]

On May 23, Jackson defeated Banks's army at Front Royal and pushed north, toward the Potomac. This proved the catalyst for the Union once again to alter its operational plan. The events in the Shenandoah had two effects on Lincoln: they aroused his fear of a Confederate attack on Washington, and they presented him with what he saw as an opportunity. Lincoln and Stanton, acting together as general in chief, tried to trap Jackson between forces under Banks in the Shenandoah, Frémont in the Alleghenies, and others taken from McDowell near Fredericksburg.[57] Lincoln flogged his commanders with orders such as this to Frémont: "Much—perhaps all—depends upon the celerity with which you can execute it. Put the utmost speed into it. Do not lose a minute."[58]

Reluctantly, McDowell sent 20,000 of his men marching to the valley.[59] "This is a crushing blow to us," he wrote Stanton.[60] This also had other effects. First, it forestalled a poorly planned attack that Johnston intended to launch against McClellan before he could unite with McDowell, though the Union leaders didn't know this.[61] Second, it made worthless much of what McClellan's forces had been doing. McClellan insisted that the previously ordered junction had forced him "to approach Richmond from the north" because he had to establish a supply base on the Pamunkey River (not, as he had hoped, on the James), something that would have been unnecessary if McDowell's men had been sent by water, as McClellan then wanted and as originally intended. Moreover, to meet McDowell, McClellan had to put two corps north of the Chickahominy River, thus splitting his army and opening up an opportunity for the Confederates. And he had to do this even though much of McDow-ell's force would be unavailable for the next three weeks.[62] By grasping at an opportunity in the Shenandoah, Lincoln and Stanton increased the chance that the larger object of Richmond would slip through Union fingers. "If the enemy can succeed so readily in disconcerting all our plans by alarming us first at one point, then at another," McDowell aptly observed, "he will paralyze a large force with a very small one."[63] This was exactly what Lee intended. Jack-son's much smaller force now occupied three Federal armies. Moreover, in the end, Jackson slipped away, partly due to his own brilliance, partly because of the sheer incompetence of the Union commanders in the field, and partly because of the difficulty of coordinating their movements.

Both McDowell and McClellan judged taking the troops from McDowell a mistake.[64] As long as Washington remained safe, McDowell's force would have done more for the Union cause by driving on Richmond in support of McClellan. Weakening and delaying his advance played into Lee's hands. Moreover, Lincoln made the mistake of counting upon Frémont to fulfill part of his plan. Frémont had failed him before, something Lincoln well knew.[65] And on one occasion in May the general had the temerity to tell Lincoln: "If I am to understand that literal obedience to orders is required, please say so."[66]

While operations heated up in the Shenandoah, Davis hoped that John-ston would fight McClellan on the banks of the Chickahominy, savaging any crossing attempt. However, Johnston, determined to get what he had always wanted—the concentration of Confederate forces before Richmond—pulled back from the river on the seventeenth, unannounced, and under no imme-diate threat from McClellan. This stunned Davis. A disagreeable meeting between them ensued in which Davis asked Johnston whether he intended to fight for Richmond. Johnston proved evasive. Davis responded by threaten-ing to replace him if he wouldn't fight.[67]

On May 21, Davis demanded from Johnston specifics about his army and his plans. This apparently displeased Johnston, who wrote to Lee about the extent of his command authority. Lee assured him there was no problem on this front.[68] This was a harbinger of things to come. Later, when Johnston was sent to command in the West, this issue of command authority arose con-stantly—and with disastrous results. On May 28, Johnston returned again to his old saw, reminding his superiors: "I have more than once suggested a concentration here of all available forces."[69]

By now, the Union had provided a great opportunity for the Confeder-ates. To link with McDowell, McClellan had put two corps of his army across the Chickahominy River. Heavy rains pelted the Peninsula on May 30.[70] The next day, Brigadier General W. N. Pendleton relayed to Johnston some very useful local information about the Chickahominy and offered a suggestion: "It is said to rise immediately after a rain like this and to continue in flood some twenty-four hours. Would not this seem a providence to place all the Yankee force this side that stream almost certainly in your power? Might not an active, sudden, and adequate movement of troops to-night and at dawn in the morning so overwhelm the divisions confronting General Hill as to crush and capture them with next to certainty?"[71] Less than two hours later Johnston wrote, "If nothing prevents we will fall upon the enemy…early in the morning—as early as practicable. The Chickahominy will be high, passable only by the bridges—a great advantage to us."[72]

Johnston finally attacked on May 31. With part of his army he prevented the bulk of the Union forces from crossing the Chickahominy. The rest he threw at McClellan's exposed forces on the river's south bank. A good tactical plan quickly fell apart in the execution as Johnston and his subordinates, particularly James Longstreet, mismanaged what became known as the Battle of Fair Oaks (also called the Battle of Seven Pines). Longstreet, or "Old Pete," as he was known, graduated from West Point in 1842 and was wounded while serving in the Mexican War. Some consider his behavior here illustrative. He was particularly attached to his own views, an intransigence that led some to brand him "German in his mentality." Longstreet, though, could also be stolid and reliable when in command of a corps, as he would prove later in the war. Lee came to call him "Old War Horse" for good reason. But that would be later. In the end, Johnston's envisaged multipronged attack devolved into unsupported piecemeal assaults. The two days of fighting accomplished very little beyond bloodying both armies. Each had brought nearly the same numbers to bear, slightly less than 42,000. The Confederates suffered 6,134 casualties, the Federals 5,031. One very significant result arose from this contest: Johnston was grievously wounded, being shot in the shoulder and then hit by shrapnel when he was blown off his horse.[73] Robert E. Lee soon took his place.

Lee in Command

ON JUNE 1, 1862, DAVIS put Robert E. Lee in command of the Confederate forces in eastern Virginia and North Carolina.[74] It was a critical moment, and Lee brought a fresh, aggressive spirit to the leadership of the Confederate forces in the east, one few expected. His critics had derided his early war failure in western Virginia, branding him with such epithets as "Evacuating Lee" and "Granny Lee." Although the guns of the greatest American army yet to take the field stood within range of the Confederate capital, Lee sensed an opportunity. He also understood the situation facing the South in the East. He wrote Davis on June 5 of his hopes. "After much reflection I think if it was possible to reinforce Jackson strongly, it would change the character of the war. This can only be done by the troops in Georgia, South Carolina & North Carolina. Jackson could in that event cross Maryland into Pennsylvania. It would call all the enemy from our Southern coast & liberate those states." But Lee also expressed his fears. "McClellan will make this a battle of posts," he wrote the Confederate president. "He will take position from position, under cover of his heavy guns, & we cannot get at him without storming his works, which with our new troops is extremely hazardous. You witnessed the experiment Saturday. It will require 100,000 men to resist the regular siege of Richmond, which perhaps would only prolong not save it." But, as usual when a problem presented itself, Lee had a solution, one wrapped in his frustration: "I am preparing a line that I can hold with part of our forces in front, while with the rest I will endeavour to make a diversion to bring McClellan out. He sticks under his batteries & is working day & night.... Our people are opposed to work. Our troops, officers, community & press. All ridicule & resist it. It is the very means by which McClellan has & is advancing."[75]

Lee would try to "change the character of the war," or, as Clausewitz said, its nature. He believed the South too weak to sit on the defensive and await the methodical blows of a much stronger opponent. He wanted to launch a diversion with Jackson, draw off the enemy from its positions in the Deep South, build a defensive line to defend Richmond—if he could get the army and people "to work"—and attack.

In early 1862, Lee had grown increasingly aware of the escalation of the war's intensity and the determination of the Lincoln government to prosecute it through to its bitter, bloody end. When he later learned in February 1863 that the U.S. Congress had voted Lincoln $900 million and authorized raising 3 million men, Lee commented, "Nothing can now arrest during the present administration the most desolating war that was ever practiced, except a revolution among their people." He also realized that no such change in the North's public opinion could come about on its own. "Nothing can produce a revolution," he added, "except systematic success on our part."[76] When Lee became commander of the Confederate armies around Richmond, he set out to do his part in contributing to a shift in Union public opinion.

Lee ordered men collected at Staunton and sent to Jackson. Jackson's "plan is to march to Front Royal and crush Shields," Lee wrote. "It is his only course, and as he is a good soldier, I expect him to do it."[77] On June 8, 1892, Lee received Jackson's letter to Johnston telling him of his recent success against the enemy at Staunton. "I congratulate you upon defeating and then avoiding your enemy," Lee wrote Jackson. "Your march to Winchester has been of great advantage.... Should there be nothing requiring your attention in the valley so as to prevent your leaving it for a few days, and you can make arrangements to deceive the enemy and impress him with the idea of your presence, please let me know, that you may unite at the decisive moment with the army near Richmond. Make your arrangements accordingly, but should an opportunity occur for striking the enemy a successful blow do not let it escape you."[78]

Lee wanted Jackson reinforced after his victory at Staunton because this would allow him "to take the offensive again."[79] He hoped to make Jackson "strong enough to wipe out Frémont." Then Lee would pull in Jackson and have him "cut up McClellan's communication and rear" while Lee attacked from the front. "I can hold McClellan in his present position for a week or ten days during this movement, and be getting our troops from the south," he told Davis. "I think this is our surest move." Lee intended this to force McClellan out of his trenches and facilitate an attack against him, something not possible before because of "inferior" Southern numbers.[80]

On June 13 Jackson told Lee that "circumstances greatly favor my moving to Richmond in accordance with your plan." Lee asked Davis for permission to shift Jackson's force, wanting to strike before the Union forces in the Valley began to move and insisting that "the first object now is to defeat McClellan." Davis "concurred."[81]

With information that Frémont and Shields were retreating, reeling from Jackson's blows, on June 16 Lee ordered Jackson to join him for a simultaneous offensive, instructing him to keep his movements secret and to make an effort to deceive the enemy regarding his intentions. He also revealed the seriousness of the situation the South faced: "Unless McClellan can be driven out of his intrenchments he will move by positions under cover of his heavy guns within shelling distance of Richmond. I know of no surer way of thwarting him than that proposed."[82]

Because he judged McClellan's left wing too strong to attack, Lee built a line of fortifications to block McClellan's advance and crossed to the north bank of the Chickahominy with the bulk of his army to threaten McClellan's communications with the York River. Lee hoped to force McClellan to retreat, or fight outside his trenches. When the fortifications were complete, Lee ordered Jackson "to move rapidly and secretly from the Valley."[83] What ensued became known as "the Seven Days."

The Union could have prevented Lee's offensive. In the days immediately before the Battle of Fair Oaks, Lincoln pushed McClellan to attack Richmond. Desperation, or perhaps even panic, had tinged Lincoln's letters as Jackson's Valley Campaign unfolded in late May. "I think the time is near when you must either attack Richmond or give up the job and come to the defence of Washington," Lincoln wrote.[84] But McClellan did not act. Previously he had wasted a month at Yorktown. When the Confederates withdrew, it took McClellan another month to move his army to the Chickahominy River and throw his left over it. Richmond stood less than six miles away. The Battle of Fair Oaks took place on May 31, yet McClellan did not move against the Confederate forces until June 25, nearly a month later, and then in only a small way.[85]

Paralysis plagued the Union field command around Richmond. Incompetence dominated it in the Shenandoah. On June 8, Lincoln and Stanton once again ordered McDowell to join McClellan, the third time they had done so.[86] To make this possible, and to secure more troops for McClellan, they struggled to beat Frémont and Banks into taking up positions in the Shenandoah that would prevent Jackson from moving north, though Frémont had a very difficult time grasping the simplicity of his task, and the other Union generals in the area of operations did no better. Moreover, by mid-June, Lincoln agreed with McClellan's view that Jackson's efforts were indeed an attempt to divert reinforcements bound for McClellan.[87] Lincoln tried to gather more troops for McClellan because he wanted action on what was then the most critical front. "I could better dispose of things if I could know about what day you can attack Richmond," he wrote McClellan, "and would be glad to be informed, if you think you can inform me with safety."[88]

McClellan still refused to act. This gave Lee ample time to reinforce Jackson, then shift him from the valley, as well as prepare his own positions to free up sufficient forces to attack McClellan. Meanwhile, McClellan pleaded constantly for more reinforcements, dug defensive works, and fought rain, dysentery, malaria, and everything but Lee's army.[89]

On June 26, McClellan, based on information from a deserter, wrote Stanton that he believed he would be attacked the next day.[90] He was right. McClellan's minor assault at Oak Grove the day before inaugurated six days of heavy but piecemeal attacks against the Army of the Potomac (hence the "Seven Days"). After preparing for the security of Richmond, which Magruder ensured by launching a successful bluff, Lee commenced his offensive by massing most of his army on the north bank of the Chickahominy at Mechanicsville in an attempt to destroy the corps commanded by Major General Fitz-John Porter and then sever McClellan's connections with his supply base at White House Landing. Again, poor coordination plagued the attackers, and the Federal troops stopped the Confederates cold. McClellan, laboring under the delusion of superior enemy numbers, decided to pull back Porter's corps, as well as change his base of supply to Harrison's Landing on the James River.[91]

The next day, the twenty-seventh, at Gaines's Mill, Lee tried again, throwing almost 50,000 men at Porter's 35,000. Despite the late arrival of Stonewall Jackson's forces to the battle, Confederate troops under John Bell Hood broke the Union lines. Porter fell back across the Chickahominy. McClellan continued to transfer his base to the James River and commenced a fighting retreat. Confederate forces assaulted Garnett's (or Golding's) Farm on the twenty-eighth, Savage Station on the twenty-ninth, and White Oak Swamp (or Frayser's Farm, or Glendale) on the thirtieth. McClellan would have to be told of this last assault later: inexcusably, he was absent, despite having heard the gunfire. McClellan's forces, though, continued their withdrawal. The Confederates kept coming, launching a confused attack against the strong Union position at Malvern Hill on July 1. After repulsing the enemy, the Army of the Potomac again withdrew. During the fighting the Confederates consistently failed to properly concentrate their forces and Jackson proved habitually late. The Union also failed to do anything other than absorb the blows and then give ground, often when it didn't have to. The contest ended with McClellan's army 30 miles from Richmond, on the banks of the James River, at Harrison's Landing.[92]

Lee wrote of the bitter fighting, "Under ordinary circumstances the Federal Army should have been destroyed."[93] Some have taken Lee's remark to mean that he adopted a strategy of annihilation when he took command of the Army of Northern Virginia.[94] One would be hard pressed to draw this conclusion from the available evidence. Lee was certainly trying to destroy McClellan's army, but every general tries to destroy the enemy's army. Such is the general's job, particularly prior to the postmodern era. But concluding that this became the sole, driving, strategic concept behind Lee's prosecution of the war stretches the documentary band. Lee's comment to Secretary of War Seddon bears repeating: "Every victory should bring us nearer to the great end which it is the object of this war to reach."[95] In other words, Lee kept the political objective in view, as well as the military means of reaching it.

Others have argued that at this point the Confederacy began pursuing an "offensive-defensive strategy." The argument is based upon the misreading of a passage from Davis's memoir in which he described the onset of the Seven Days. "Thus was inaugurated the offensive-defensive campaign which resulted so gloriously to our arms," Davis wrote, "and turned from the capital of the Confederacy a danger so momentous, that looking at it retrospectively, it is not seen how a policy less daring or less firmly pursued could have saved the capital from capture."[96] Davis was discussing the Confederacy's *tactical* response, not its strategy. From this small seed grew a great myth.

Lee's victories during the Seven Days produced dramatic results. Lee likely saved Richmond; he believed that he did. Joe Johnston's passive war of posts—if he did not outright abandon the city—would have seen Richmond fall to McClellan's siege warfare, as Lee feared, though undoubtedly it would have taken a while. Lee also succeeded in throwing back the enemy host, inflicting significant casualties, and capturing large numbers of prisoners and valuable weapons and stores.[97] But Lee's army paid a price, a heavy one: more than 20,000 casualties, including more than 4,000 dead and missing. The Union suffered 16,000 casualties. The historian Russell Weigley argues that the South could not afford the cost of this offensive action in particular, nor the generally offensive strategy that Lee adopted.[98] The South indeed could not endure such casualties indefinitely, but at this point in the war, with Union forces crowding Vicksburg and Chattanooga, it might not have survived the fall of Richmond— not because the city exerted some mystical importance in the Confederate mind as the capital of the South but because it ranked first among the industrial sites of the Confederacy. The loss of its Tredegar Iron Works alone would have dealt a nearly fatal blow to the South's ability to arm itself.

But this was not the only reason for holding on to the capital. In Lee's mind Richmond had to be held because of its pivotal role as a logistics base. He believed that if he lost the city and its rail web, he would be forced to abandon all of Virginia and fight from a line in North Carolina because it would be from there that he would be compelled to supply his army. Had the Confederacy lost all of Virginia in the summer of 1862, combined with the fall of New Orleans and the Confederate defeats in Kentucky, Tennessee, and Mississippi, the war very well could have ended then and there. The remaining resource base would have been insufficient to continue the war much longer. Moreover, considering the propensity of Confederate troops to abscond when their homes fell to the Union, desertion could have decimated Lee's remaining Virginia troops.

In the wake of the Seven Days an ecstatic Davis wrote his wife: "Our success has been so remarkable that we should be grateful and believe that even
our disappointments were ordered for our gain." Both offered like-minded
assessments of McClellan. Davis noted that "McClellan certainly showed
capacity in his retreat, but there is little cause to laud a general who is driven
out of his entrenchments by a smaller and worse armed force than his own and
compelled to abandon a campaign in the preparation for which he had spent
many months and many millions of Dollars."[99] In an assessment of the entire
Peninsula Campaign, Varina Davis made an astute observation: "McClellan
is like Gen Johnston, great in retreat."[100]

McClellan had missed a huge opportunity in 1862. Taking Richmond,
added to the other disasters inflicted upon the South by Union forces, might
have ended the war. Lee soon would give him another chance, one he would
also prove unable to grasp, but only after Lee had ensured that his name, as
well as that of Stonewall Jackson, would enter the pantheon of history's great
generals.

The Evolving Union Strategy

IN MID-JUNE, THE UNION'S LEADERS had felt confident about their
situation. Union armies in the West had shattered the Confederate perimeter, cleared large parts of Kentucky and Tennessee, and penetrated into
Mississippi and Alabama. McClellan's army stood outside Richmond, poised
to deliver what many Unionists believed would be the final blow against
secession.[101]

Lincoln left Washington on June 23, journeying to West Point, New York,
to consult with General Winfield Scott about the military situation in Virginia. Scott, professing not to have followed things as closely as one should
to offer advice, took the president's brief on the situation and did as bidden.
He believed the commands under Banks and Frémont numerous enough to
shield Washington from any Confederate attack from the direction of the
upper Potomac, and that the forces at Manassas and in the capital's various
forts protected it from the other direction. The Union troops at Fredericksburg he pronounced "entirely out of position," as they could not offer timely
support to McClellan. He suggested shifting them to the mouth of the York
to help McClellan's push against Richmond (which McClellan wanted), or
to reinforce this army "in the very improbable case of disaster." Scott saw
promise in the taking of Richmond, believing its fall, combined with the
other Union victories, would put an end to the rebellion. He also believed

the Union needed to seize some other key points: Mobile, Charleston, and Chattanooga.[102]

By the end of June 1862, Lincoln concluded that the Confederacy had amassed too many troops around Richmond for McClellan to attack, stripping their other sectors, including the West, to do so. "But if we send all the force from here to McClellan, the enemy will, before we can know of it, send a force from Richmond and take Washington. Or, if a large part of the Western Army be brought here to McClellan, they will let us have Richmond, and retake Tennessee, Kentucky, Missouri &c." The Confederacy had not quite done what Lincoln feared, such as taking troops from the West, and his assessment of possible Confederate actions was incorrect, particularly in regard to Richmond. Nonetheless, his determination in the face of such a dismal picture comes through in his plan for continuing the war: "What should be done is to hold what we have in the West," Lincoln told Seward, "open the Mississippi, and take Chattanooga and East Tennessee" while protecting Washington and raising another 100,000 men, "which, added to McClellan directly or indirectly, will take Richmond without endangering any other place which we now hold, and will substantially end the war."[103] This letter revealed what Lincoln, at least in 1862, thought would deliver victory: the seizure of vital points of Confederate geography, including Richmond. Indeed, the Confederacy did possess vital points, but as the war progressed, Lincoln came to realize that the Confederacy's center of gravity, the true source of its strength, was not a particular place. On July 1, to provide the strength to mount this renewed effort, he called on the various governors to raise 300,000 men "so as to bring this unnecessary and injurious civil war to a speedy and satisfactory conclusion."[104]

A few days before, to support his idea of taking Richmond, Lincoln created the Army of Virginia under Major General John Pope, drawn from the forces of McDowell, Frémont, Banks, and those guarding the capital. Lincoln ordered them to protect Washington and western Virginia from Confederate depredations, particularly those of Jackson and Ewell (who, unknown to Lincoln, had already rejoined Lee's army). They would also provide another prong of a Union attack against Richmond. Lee's offensive, and McClellan's retreat to the James River, thwarted this.[105]

Pope was fresh from victories gained in the West under Halleck's command. Lincoln, on his own initiative, called him east. Immediately upon taking up his command, Pope raised Lee's ire by advocating harsh measures against disloyal civilians, and the ridicule of his own men by insulting eastern troops, saying such things as "I have come to you from the West, where we

have always seen the backs of our enemies." A bombastic statement to a journalist that his headquarters would be "in the saddle" provoked the riposte
that Pope's headquarters was "where his hindquarters should" be.[106] He also
seems to have been generally disliked in the prewar army, something that
undoubtedly contributed to his being held in contempt by fellow generals on
both sides of the line.

Lincoln ordered Burnside's troops from North Carolina to reinforce
McClellan.[107] Others followed. This was not enough for McClellan, who still
believed he faced as many as 200,000 Confederates.[108] Lincoln told McClellan
on July 4: "Save the Army—first, where you are, if you *can*; and secondly, by
removal, if you must."[109]

For the seven weeks after the arrival of his army at Harrison's Landing on
July 2 McClellan sat, arguing with the administration about what to do while
demanding more reinforcements.[110] Lincoln himself even journeyed to the
army and quizzed its corps commanders about whether or not it could be
safely withdrawn.[111] McClellan still refused to move.

MCCLELLAN'S ENEMY THOUGHT DIFFERENTLY. On May 3, 1862,
Joseph E. Brown, the governor of Georgia, recommended an aggressive campaign to "liberate Tennessee, penetrate Kentucky, and menace Cincinnati."
Davis replied that what he suggested had "been long desired. Its adoption is
a question of power, not of will." In a letter to his wife dated June 21, Davis
wrote that the Confederacy needed the total defeat of McClellan "and then
we must make a desperate effort to regain what has been abandoned in the
West."[112] The next few months would see the South undertake much of what
both men wanted, with varying degrees of success.

Davis received other exhortations to offensive action. During the second
week of July a letter reached the Confederate president from John Foster
Marshall, colonel of the 1st South Carolina Rifles. The Colonel wanted the
army to "march directly, promptly now if possible upon our enemy; not upon
them at Charles City…but to Maryland." Marshall was convinced that if
Jackson marched on Harpers Ferry with 50,000 men that "McClellans Army
on the James River would dissappear [*sic*] in thirty days." He also insisted that
the "North would be more likely to think of peace with war at their doorstep"
and that this would strengthen the Confederacy's negotiating position vis-à-vis
the European states.[113]

Davis's response revealed where his thinking on strategic matters was
tending. He insisted his own ideas coincided with those of Marshall, noting,
"Indeed, such has been my purpose for many months, and I have silently

borne criticism on the supposition that I am opposed to offensive warfare, because to correct the error would have required the disclosure of facts which the public interest demanded should not be revealed." Davis assured Marshall that they were preparing for future actions and that "General [Lee] is fully alive to the advantage of the present opportunity, and will, I am sure, cordially sustain and boldly execute my wishes to the full extent of his power."[114]

In early July, Davis gave one correspondent similar replies: "My early declared purpose and continued hope was to feed upon the enemy and teach them the blessings of peace by making them feel in its most tangible form the evils of war."[115] He went on, mixing his levels of war and making a case for offensive action while ensuring that no censure could fall upon the presidential pate. "The time and place for an invasion has been a question not of will," he insisted, "but of power. There have been occasions when it seemed to me possible to make aggressive movements upon detachments of the enemy and they were pointed out to our Generals, but they did not avail themselves of them, and it may be that their caution was wise, at least I have thought it proper to defer much to the opinions of commanders in the field, and have felt the hazard of requiring a General to execute, what he did not favorably entertain."[116] Davis's desire to give his generals freedom to act is certainly admirable. The question was whether he could *force* his generals to act.

Davis continued, insisting he had never "preferred defensive to offensive war," but looked forward to the time when the South could take the war to the Union.[117] By July 1862 Davis's military thoughts had clearly turned to the offensive. Moreover, he now had two generals willing and eager to give life to his intentions, Braxton Bragg and Robert E. Lee, and in fact they were already doing so without his prompting. There seems to have arisen nearly simultaneously among the three of them the idea that the South's poor strategic situation in July 1862 could be salvaged only by offensive action.

The Results of Union Failure on the Peninsula

ON JULY 11, 1862, LINCOLN APPOINTED Halleck general in chief; he took up the office on the twenty-third. Lincoln gave him carte blanche to deal with the military situation, especially the most pressing one, that on the Peninsula, as well as the Union's most problematic general. Lincoln also made clear his belief that no number of additional troops would pry McClellan from his stump.[118]

Halleck sailed to Harrison's Landing. There he found an ill-humored McClellan who wanted to attack Richmond's communications to the south.

Halleck disagreed and insisted McClellan join his army with Pope's and attack Richmond while keeping the force between the two capitals. Barring this, McClellan could attack with just his own army, plus the 20,000 additional troops that were on the way. McClellan said he would need 30,000. Halleck replied that there simply were not that many available and that therefore McClellan's only other option was withdrawal. Forced to choose, McClellan said he would attack.[119]

Satisfied, Halleck sailed back to Washington, whereupon he immediately received telegrams from McClellan demanding more men before he could advance. Instead of ordering him to act, Halleck pleaded with McClellan to move. After less than a week in his new position, Halleck was already demonstrating the lack of decisiveness that would plague his tenure as general in chief and undermine the Union's war effort.[120]

Halleck gave McClellan the same two choices: attack Richmond or evacuate and unite with Pope's army. McClellan demurred. On August 3, Halleck ordered him out. He planned to join McClellan's forces with Pope's and drive on Richmond. McClellan begged "that this order be rescinded." He forecast disaster: demoralization of his army, a blow to the hopes of the people of the North, and "the strong probability that it would influence foreign powers to recognize our adversaries."[121]

Halleck pushed back, citing military necessity, particularly the fact that Lee stood between the armies of Pope and McClellan with, at least according to McClellan, about 200,000 men. Moreover, Halleck had feared an attack by Lee upon Pope's forces. This concern was certainly a valid one, but Halleck exhibited no more decisiveness than did McClellan. The new general in chief failed to force McClellan either to drive on Richmond or to withdraw and concentrate. As John F. Marszalek so aptly puts it: "The commanding general cajoled but did not order compliance."[122]

McClellan, as well as many other Union generals, often remarked that the best way to defend Washington would be to attack Richmond. Had Lee been compelled to fight for Richmond, he would have been forced to concentrate the bulk of his forces around the city. While he still would have been willing to launch a daring raid down the Shenandoah Valley if it had been left improperly guarded, this would have involved only a small portion of his force and not constituted a decisive threat to the fate of the Union capital. Attacking rather than withdrawing would have forced the Confederates to fight; such was one of the paths to a Union victory.

McClellan's subsequent retreat from the Peninsula had political effects. Anti-Union sentiment in Great Britain rose to its highest point since the infamous

Trent Affair. Earlier, Confederate victories in the summer of 1862, particularly Jackson's in the Shenandoah, convinced many in London that the time for British intervention had arrived. Wiser heads, and Lee's retreat after the September 17 Battle of Antietam (which will be discussed shortly), convinced the British government that "this American question must be well sifted." Some in Britain, notably William E. Gladstone, the cabinet leader of the Liberals, carried on the fight. In October 1862, Gladstone argued that Britain had a moral obligation to intervene. He seemed to labor under the belief that British intervention did not mean war with the Union and that European pressure could end the conflict.[123] Seward, the most radical of the Union's defenders, had made it clear to British diplomats early in the war that intervention meant war with the Union.[124] Lincoln's determination to see the conflict through to a successful conclusion, regardless of the obstacles, leads inexorably to the conclusion that he would have pursued war with any European power he believed it necessary to fight. But his actions during the *Trent* Affair also demonstrate that he preferred, as he famously remarked, "one war at a time."[125] Later, in 1863, Gladstone would show his support for the Southern cause by speculating heavily in Confederate bonds sold as a result of a loan from the French bank Erlanger.[126]

Lee Strikes

NO GENERAL IN THE CONFEDERACY made the switch from defensive to offensive warfare more eagerly than Robert E. Lee. In July 1862, Lee bottled up McClellan's forces at Harrison's Landing. Typhoid and dysentery savaged the Union troops, and they evacuated 31,000 sick and wounded.[127] As July wore on, however, Lee remained unsure about McClellan's intentions. He worried about another attack aimed at Richmond and believed that McClellan was being reinforced.[128] Jackson had already been dispatched to meet the gathering threat of the new Union army moving south from Washington under Pope, but Lee remained circumspect about the developing situation in his theater, telling Jackson: "Under these circumstances I am reluctant to weaken the force around Richmond without seeing the prospect of striking a blow elsewhere. I am however ready to reinforce you as soon as that prospect is apparent."[129]

On July 27, Lee acted. He dispatched reinforcements to Jackson, having notified Davis the day before that he feared Jackson's forces too weak to meet the Union troops opposing him. "I want Pope suppressed," Lee wrote, and told Jackson to attack Pope and be prepared to rejoin Lee when it was over. Lee, meanwhile, promised to keep McClellan occupied.[130] Lee launched an effort to cut McClellan's communications to force him to "retire to the broad

part of the river. But if this cannot be done the attempt if partially successful will anchor him in his present position...so that I can reinforce Jackson
without hazard to Richmond, and thus enable him to drive if not destroy the
miscreant Pope."[131]

As Jackson went in search of Pope, Lee worked to establish a solid defense
of Richmond to enable him to take the offensive. As he did this he faced a
dilemma similar to one that had confronted George Washington. Washington
had struggled to keep his army intact and resisted attempts to siphon off elements for local defense. He realized that keeping the Continental army united
and in the field provided a clear political and moral focal point for the Revolution, while forcing the British to keep their forces concentrated to meet a
potential American attack.

Lee devotedly pursued the idea of concentration as well and consistently
struggled to unite forces under his banner, while resisting pleas for support
from what he considered less important or less threatened areas. He wrote
North Carolina's governor, Henry T. Clark: "But it is impossible with the
means at our command, to pursue the policy [strategy] of concentrating our
forces to protect important points and baffle the principal efforts of the enemy,
and at the same time extend all the protection we desire to give to every district." He also revealed his belief in the strategic importance of maintaining
Virginia, an idea he would return to in his letters. "The safety of the whole
State of North Carolina, as well as of Virginia, depends in a measure upon the
result of the enemy's efforts in this quarter, which if successful, would make
your State the theater of hostilities far more injurious and destructive to your
citizens than anything they have yet been called upon to suffer.... [S]ubdivi-
sion of our forces," he added, would produce "nothing but disaster."[132] While
Lee was doubtless protecting the size and integrity of his own forces in much
the same way as Washington when subjected to such requests, the practicality
and appropriateness of his approach seem undeniable.

Lee already had his eyes set on the "miscreant," and wrote on August 14
that he believed McClellan was withdrawing to reinforce Pope.[133] He put
Major General James Longstreet's troops in motion to reinforce Jackson the
same day and ordered Major General G. W. Smith to finish the defensive lines
they were constructing, watch McClellan, and hold Richmond in the event of
any attack.[134] He also warned Davis that the theater of war was changing.[135]

On August 17, Lee told Davis that McClellan had gone. The withdrawal
of the Union host removed any immediate threat to the Confederate capital,
giving Lee the freedom to maneuver. The passing of any immediate danger
to Richmond pleased Lee, though it disappointed him that McClellan had

escaped without first suffering greater damage. He remained uncertain of McClellan's destination but offered two possibilities: an ascent of the Rappahannock to land at Fredericksburg and renew his drive on Richmond from there, or the reinforcement of Pope. Regardless, Lee believed it time to begin moving his army north.[136]

Lee planned to cross the Rappahannock on the eighteenth and told Davis as much, but he was not ready until the twentieth. The delay robbed Lee of an opportunity. Pope had stuck his neck out by crossing the Rappahannock and placing his army between this river and the Rapidan. Lee tried to cut Pope's communications in combination with moving across the Rapidan, but Pope withdrew, assisted by the Confederate failure to destroy the Rappahannock bridges, as well as intelligence from one of McDowell's spies regarding Lee's intentions. Pope also had a captured copy of Lee's order to Major General J. E. B. Stuart about burning the bridges.[137]

By August 23 Lee was hoping to move the theater of the war north, from the James River to the Rappahannock. Doing so would enable the army to use the provisions and forage then being consumed by the enemy and lessen the logistical strains put upon other areas.[138] He soon expanded this to moving the front north of the Rappahannock for at least a season.[139]

As his information changed and he advanced, Lee asked for subsidiary supporting operations, something we'll see again. He had already dispatched Jackson north, reinforced him with Longstreet's forces, left a garrison in Richmond, and moved the bulk of his army northward, all with the intention of trapping Pope, whom he hoped to fight without exposing Richmond to attack. But he saw other chances to bruise the Union. He had intelligence that the forces of Brigadier General Jacob D. Cox were being withdrawn from the Kanawha Valley via Wheeling, in the western part of Virginia. He noted that "if the campaign could be pushed in this direction it would have the effect of relieving other parts of the country." He wanted reinforcements to make this happen.[140] When Cox's retreat was confirmed, he asked that Major General W. W. Loring's Shenandoah forces be directed to clear the Kanawha Valley, then move north and join Lee in the Valley of Virginia.[141]

During their advance the Confederates captured a letter dated August 20 from Halleck, revealing Pope's plan to hold the Confederates until he could be joined by McClellan's men on the lower Rappahannock. Lee sought to unite his whole army to face the Union forces.[142]

Halleck, still worried about the security of Washington, sought to concentrate the troops of Pope, Burnside, and McClellan to meet the Confederate

thrust. He failed to pull this off before Lee's blows fell. Halleck had not clarified the command situation: McClellan thought he would be in charge, while
Pope believed Halleck commanded; Halleck did not issue forceful orders,
and McClellan dragged his feet in reinforcing Pope, intentionally keeping
two corps out of the battle that developed. On top of this, pressure mounted
on Halleck to relieve McClellan. Halleck simply wilted under the weight.[143]

Despite all this, McClellan found time to offer Lincoln advice. On August 29,
he wrote, "I am clear that one of two courses should be adopted—1st To concentrate all our available forces to open communications with Pope—2nd To Leave
Pope to get out of his scrape & at once use all our means to make the Capital
perfectly safe. No middle course will now answer. Tell me what you wish me to
do & I will do all in my power to accomplish it."[144] Lincoln responded that he
believed the first course the best. McClellan's dismissive comment about Pope fed
his distrust of his former general in chief.[145] Lincoln found it particularly galling,
especially when troops that easily could have reinforced Pope at Second Manassas
were held back. Gideon Welles believed that McClellan's subsequent failure to
reinforce Pope came from "personal resentments."[146]

In any case, by this time any advice from McClellan on the current situation proved useless. Lee had moved, and even though he insisted to Davis
that he sought "to avoid a general engagement, being the weaker force, & by
maneuvering to relieve the portion of the country referred to" (meaning up
to the Rappahannock), he certainly did not shy from battle. By August 30, he
believed the Union had concentrated its forces between Manassas and Centreville. The same day he inflicted a humiliating defeat on Pope's forces at what
became known as Second Bull Run (or Second Manassas) in a battle against
what he thought was the combined forces of Pope and McClellan.[147]

Nearly a week before, on August 25, Lee had sent Jackson in a march
around the north flank of Pope's army; two days and 54 miles later, they broke
Pope's supply lines at Bristoe Station. The Union general headed north to
meet them. Meanwhile, Jackson took two of his three divisions to capture the
Union stores at Manassas Station, 3 miles away, leaving Ewell's division as a
blocking force. The advancing Pope pushed back Ewell's men on August 27,
whereupon Jackson, who had a smaller force than Pope's, formed his men on
some low hills, hid, and waited. When Pope's forces arrived, Jackson attacked,
and pushed back the Federal troops. Pope then attempted to launch a double
envelopment against Jackson's army, but he mismanaged the attack in a way
that reduced it to a frontal assault, one that became entangled with Jackson's
troops just as Longstreet arrived and brought 30,000 Confederate troops into
the fray on Pope's left flank. The Federal troops fell back, then executed a solid

fighting retreat. Fifty-five thousand Confederates had defeated 62,000 Union troops, inflicting 16,000 casualties for the 9,000 endured.[148]

In the wake of this victory Lee accurately assessed the military impact of his campaign: "The great advantage of the advance of the army is the withdrawal of the enemy from our territory, & the hurling back upon their capital their two great armies from the banks of the James & Rappahannock Rivers." In three months, Lee had indeed changed the theater of the war, just as he had wanted, as well as its character, something he had also sought. He had cleared the Union armies from most of Virginia, pushing the front lines back to where they had been early in the struggle. Small, scattered enemy detachments remained, but they posed no threat.[149]

There were also morale and diplomatic results. Public opinion in the South rode high with Lee's successes and the Union's failures. That in the North dipped with the same waves. John J. Nicolay, one of Lincoln's secretaries, noted this in describing the fecklessness of Congress in the wake of the Seven Days: "A single reverse or piece of accidental ill-luck is enough to throw them all into the horrors of despair."[150] Diplomatically, the British came exceedingly close to insisting upon mediation. As historian Howard Jones notes: "Indeed, if Lee had not followed his army's success at Bull Run [Second Manassas] with an immediate march north, the South might have won a mediation followed by recognition."[151] Lincoln never would have submitted to mediation under any imaginable circumstances; in his mind, there was no point on which he could give. But this very well could have been the closest the South came to achieving its primary and most cherished diplomatic goal.

What Could Have Been

ON THE EVENING OF JUNE 27, after the battle at Gaines's Mill, during the Seven Days, McClellan ordered the Army of the Potomac to retreat. Major Generals Phil Kearny and Joseph Hooker objected. The thin screen of Confederate forces at their front had not fooled them, and they browbeat their corps commander, Major General Samuel Peter Heintzelman, into taking them to McClellan. Kearny had believed they could break into Richmond and insisted he be allowed to launch an immediate attack. McClellan had refused. The retreat began. However wrongheaded, it was skillfully handled, with McClellan never giving Lee a chance to land a killing blow. Nonetheless, an opportunity to deliver a critical thrust had passed.

In April 1862, McClellan received word (mistaken, as it proved) that Robert E. Lee had assumed command on his front, with J. E. Johnston serving under him. "I prefer Lee to Johnston—," McClellan wrote, "the former is *too* cautious & weak under grave responsibility—personally brave & energetic to a fault, he yet is wanting in moral firmness when pressed by heavy responsibility & is likely to be timid & irresolute in action."[152] McClellan, of course, was offering a perfect description of his own problems commanding the Union forces on the Peninsula, as well as after, and the reasons why he could not grasp the opportunities presented.

Later, McClellan insisted that had McDowell not been diverted, the combined Union forces "would have driven the enemy within the immediate intrenchments of Richmond before Jackson could have returned to its succor, and probably have gained possession promptly of that place."[153] Maybe—had someone other than McClellan held the Union command.

The muddled nature of the interference of Lincoln and Stanton in McClellan's operational execution of his Peninsula Campaign did nothing to ensure its success and much to reduce its chances. They refused to make him act, while also failing to make him execute his plans in a timely manner. One of the commentators in Sun Tzu's *Art of War* writes: "No evil is greater than commands of the sovereign from the court."[154] Such was the case on the Peninsula.

On July 28, 1862, an irritated Halleck wrote his wife: "General McClellan is in many respects a most excellent and valuable man, but he does not understand strategy and should never plan a campaign."[155] As usual with Halleck, his assessment was off target. It was not that McClellan did not understand strategy, or operational or campaign planning. McClellan understood these perhaps better than any other Civil War general, as his correspondence makes clear. His failing was that he was incapable of executing the plan. McClellan possessed no flexibility and could not take risks. The better solution would have been replacing the commander of the Army of the Potomac with one who would indeed attack Richmond.

In the spring and summer of 1862 the war had been the Union's to win. Bad strategy, poor civilian and military leadership at the top ranks, and inadequate operational planning and execution meant that the Confederacy, though wounded, survived. And this made it more dangerous.

11

Confusion in the West

THE SUMMER OF 1862

*The order to send troops to Washington was certainly
a very inconsiderate one.*

—HENRY W. HALLECK, July 3, 1862

IN EARLY JUNE 1862, Halleck had not yet decided upon his next move.
He stressed to Buell the importance of opening up communications with the
long-suffering General Ormsby Mitchel—still deep in the South and knocking at the gates of Chattanooga—and warned that Buell's army might soon
be ordered in that direction.[1] Securing logistical lines, not fighting the enemy,
became Halleck's focus, though the spring retreat of the rivers from their winter heights certainly merited some attention to this, as the Union would soon
lose some of its ability to ship men and supplies via water.[2]

Indirectly, McClellan intervened to give Halleck some direction. Lincoln
passed to Halleck a note in which McClellan once more referred to his earlier
plans: "May I again invite your excellency's attention to the great importance
of occupying Chattanooga and Dalton by our Western forces? The evacuation of Corinth would appear to render this very easy. The importance of this
move and force cannot be exaggerated."[3] Some of McClellan's eagerness for
such a move undoubtedly related to his own position on the Peninsula.

Others also pushed Halleck eastward. Tennessee governor Andrew Johnson wanted him to move into eastern Tennessee to support Unionists there
and also pointed out a missed opportunity: "If there could have been more
forces left in the middle part of the State it would have convinced the rebels that there was no chance of a successful rising up, and by this time the
disunionists would have been put completely down, and the forces could
have entered East Tennessee by way of Chattanooga, while General [G. W.]
Morgan would have entered by way of Cumberland Gap, and the whole army
in East Tennessee would have been bagged and the people relieved."[4] The
failure by both Halleck and Buell to grasp the importance of Chattanooga
had compounded Buell's earlier failure to clear eastern Tennessee and push
forces to Cumberland Gap. Both objectives had been within reach. Mitchel
could have taken Chattanooga in April 1862. Union major general George

H. Thomas, who was not noted for his aggressiveness, believed that, properly supported, he could have taken eastern Tennessee in October 1861.[5] Accomplishing both of these things, particularly the capture of Chattanooga, would have laid the foundation for delivering a punishing and perhaps decisive campaign into the heartland of the Confederacy. Opportunities not grasped meant a longer war.

Halleck replied to Lincoln via telegram, insisting that he had made the decision to move against Chattanooga five days before and that the troops were already on the move.[6] Halleck had begun receiving rumors of the Confederates ordering forces to Chattanooga on June 6 and now considered it an operational objective.[7]

Whether Halleck was acting because he saw the need to take Chattanooga or because the intelligence reports convinced him he had to meet Confederate concentration in a like manner remains a difficult question to answer. His correspondence on the matter points more toward a primary concern with opening communications with Mitchel. Halleck was probably reacting to enemy movements rather than seizing the initiative. Two things support this conclusion. First, previously Halleck had sent Grant to take Fort Henry not because he had some desire to actually act against the enemy but because of information (which later proved false) about the Rebels reinforcing the fort. Second, a note Halleck had sent Buell about the misuse of engineering troops as pickets reveals a fear about the movements of the Confederate forces. "This is all wrong," Halleck had written, "his whole force not required in defense should work with all possible energy to open our communication with Mitchel, so that you can meet Breckinridge with superior numbers, as he has gone to Chattanooga."[8]

Meanwhile, Mitchel and his subordinates were still fighting the good fight for Chattanooga and its approaches. On June 5, some of his forces under Brigadier General James S. Negley defeated a Confederate detachment and united with other Union troopers at Jasper, about a dozen miles from Chattanooga. Mitchel gave Negley the freedom to take the city if he could.[9]

Lincoln asked Halleck whether he deemed it possible in his drive on Chattanooga to also push with the Union forces under Brigadier General George Washington Morgan into Cumberland Gap.[10] Halleck did not respond directly to Lincoln's suggestion regarding the Gap, but he did wire his intentions. He would send Buell with four divisions to unite with Mitchel, telling Stanton that this move would be slow and consume most of Halleck's logistical capability to keep it supplied.[11] Instead of pursuing the Confederates deeper into Mississippi, Halleck proposed sending some of the forces not required to

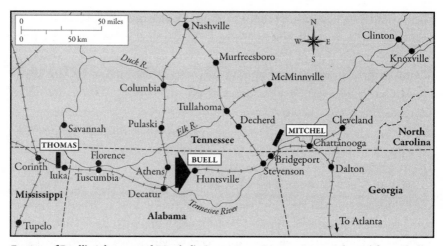

Region of Buell's Advance and Mitchel's Operations, Summer 1862. Adapted from Shelby Foote, *The Civil War: A Narrative*, vol. 1 (New York: Random House, 1958), 559.

hold the Memphis and Charleston Railroad to the relief of General Samuel Curtis, commander of the Union forces in Arkansas, and the others to eastern Tennessee.[12] Stanton replied immediately: "Your proposed plan of operations is cordially approved." But then he brought up another issue, one particularly pressing at that moment: "I suppose you contemplate the occupation of Vicksburg and clearing out the Mississippi to New Orleans. If it should in any contingency become necessary, can you lend a hand to Butler?"[13] At that very moment Farragut and Butler were making preparations for their second attempt at Vicksburg. Stanton could have directly ordered Halleck to support this move rather than merely inquired about it; he didn't. Halleck therefore charted his own course, which included operations in Arkansas and eastern Tennessee that contributed little to achieving the Union's political objective of forcing the South into line.

Halleck's immediate concern remained restoring his lines of communication, particularly with Mitchel. He told Buell to do this, while warning that Buell's entire army would "probably move west."[14] Mitchel had troops fighting on the outskirts of Chattanooga on June 7.[15] This displeased Buell, who thought Mitchel lacked the troops to march on Chattanooga, and wrote that even if he took the city "he would jeopardize the force sent there and expose Middle Tennessee."[16] Mitchel thought differently. "I am of the opinion that every effort should be made to maintain the position we now hold," he told Buell. "If we fall back we open the door to pour in troops at the exact point they are already determined to use, and if we once commence to fall back it is difficult to determine when we can halt." Mitchel worried about reports of a looming Confederate move against Murfreesboro, which sat astride the Union communications line between Stevenson, Alabama, and Nashville.[17]

Mitchel told Halleck what he believed was coming. "Since the fall of Corinth the enemy, being relieved from the necessity of concentrating all his strength at that point, will be at liberty to advance through Cumberland Gap into Kentucky from Knoxville, across the mountains, into Nashville, and from Chattanooga into Northern Alabama."[18]

In a reply to Stanton's letter announcing the extension of Buell's control over the eastern areas of Tennessee and Kentucky (and in which Stanton's and Lincoln's concerns about these areas were expressed), Buell gave his own view of the Union situation, a mirror image of Mitchel's except in the degree of concern.[19] Buell agreed it was time to act—and quickly—but saw no cause for worry because the enemy having its army in the vicinity of Corinth freed Union forces "for operations in Kentucky and Tennessee, where it is certainly very much needed." He also explained what he had been trying to do in his command area: "My disposition of the troops left in Tennessee had in view the defense of Nashville and Middle Tennessee against invasion by the way of Chattanooga and Stevenson or directly from East Tennessee, and finally active operations against the Memphis and Charleston Railroad between Decatur and Bridgeport, if circumstances favored it. The latter was very happily accomplished by General Mitchel's activity and energy." To Buell, the next things on the Union agenda should be making Tennessee safe and driving the Confederates entirely from the state. Moreover, instead of trying to take Chattanooga or help someone else do so, Buell criticized Mitchel for advancing to the city (arguing that doing so endangered Nashville) and then praised him for pulling back.[20]

On June 10, Halleck began the next phase of the war in the West. Abandoning his slavishness toward operational concentration, he split his army into three forces led respectively by Grant (Army of the Tennessee), Buell (Army of the Ohio), and Pope (Army of the Mississippi), the last of whom was almost immediately called to the Eastern Theater. They devoted the bulk of their time to repairing railroad lines.[21]

By mid-June Halleck began looking beyond Chattanooga, telling Stanton: "If the enemy should have evacuated East Tennessee and Cumberland Gap, as reported, Buell will probably move on Atlanta. It will probably take some time to clean out the guerrilla parties in West Tennessee and North Mississippi." Halleck also had a column moving on Memphis, and if the expected two-pronged naval attack on Vicksburg failed, he would send forces against this objective after he reinforced Arkansas.[22]

He also gave Buell a clear operational objective: Chattanooga. Halleck had decided that seizing the city would put Union troops in control of the most important rail connection to Atlanta and prevent Confederate generals Edmund Kirby Smith and P. G. T. Beauregard from uniting their forces. Smith would be forced to "abandon East Tennessee or be captured." Halleck also wanted Mitchel to leave troops at McMinnville, Tennessee, or along the railroad to Nashville to thwart any Confederate advance.[23]

These orders arrived too late. The day they came, June 11, Mitchel reported word of Confederate reinforcements in Chattanooga—more than 12,000—and warned (prematurely, it proved) of a Confederate offensive.[24] Moreover, as always (and as expected), Buell insisted he faced insurmountable problems.[25] Halleck urged him on.[26]

Lincoln, meanwhile, wanted to know how his cherished operations in east Tennessee were proceeding.[27] Finally things were moving. On June 18, the same day Lincoln inquired, Brigadier General G. W. Morgan took Cumberland Gap, which he called "the American Gibraltar."[28] Halleck expected the Confederates to leave eastern Tennessee.[29]

At this moment, though, McClellan's operations around Richmond were Lincoln's priority.[30] This resulted in an order during the last week of June for Halleck to detach 25,000 men and send them east.[31] Halleck had earlier resisted such demands from Washington, discounting reports that elements of Beauregard's army had been sent to Virginia.[32] In fact, he insisted that Beauregard would attack *him* if his forces were weakened.[33] Again, Halleck fought back, not like a lion, but like a mother hen protecting her nest: "I think under the circumstances the Chattanooga expedition better be abandoned or at least be diminished. If not, I doubt our ability to hold West Tennessee after detaching so large a force as that called for."[34]

This pleased neither Stanton nor Lincoln. "The Chattanooga expedition must not on any account be given up," Stanton wrote. "The President regards that and the movement against East Tennessee as one of the most important movements of the war, and its occupation nearly as important as the capture of Richmond."[35] Lincoln also personally reiterated the request for 25,000 troops, though he left Halleck an out, telling him, "Please do not send a man if it endangers any place you deem important to hold or if it forces you to give up or weaken or delay the expedition against Chattanooga." Moreover, the president stressed the importance of taking the railroads east of the key Tennessee city. Interestingly, in his hierarchy of strategic importance Lincoln ranked the seizure of pro-Union areas of eastern Tennessee, as well as the region's railroads, as being on a par with taking Richmond.[36] Yet in the larger scope of the war, eastern Tennessee mattered not at all; capture of the region's railroads would be helpful but not decisive. Richmond was the arms-producing capital of the South and the logistical and command hub of the Confederate armies in the east. Its fall meant the loss of Virginia, enabling Union armies to push into North Carolina. Chattanooga, though, was not only an easier target but also a critical one. Its possession would allow the severing of critical rail lines while giving the Union a springboard for throwing an army into the heart of the Confederacy.

Lincoln's orders angered Halleck. "The defeat of General McClellan near Richmond has produced another stampede at Washington," he wrote contemptuously. He planned for the movement of four divisions eastward while predicting disaster on his front: "The entire campaign in the West is broken up by these orders and we shall very probably lose all we have gained." He imputed to the Confederates immense powers of perception: "The enemy on Saturday advanced twenty-five regiments to Fulton and undoubtedly intend to cut that line. They know all." He went on to forecast the loss of Arkansas and western Tennessee, and revolts in Tennessee and Kentucky that would make these areas more difficult to control than Missouri.[37] Lincoln relented. He wanted reinforcements for the East, but not if they delayed the push against Chattanooga.[38] The irony, of course, is that had Halleck and Buell taken Chattanooga when they had the chance, they would have been able to reinforce McClellan, or to press the South at other points.

On July 4, Lincoln was again asking Halleck for men, but this time only 10,000.[39] Halleck polled his commanders. All agreed they could spare none. Halleck endorsed their decision, using against the president Lincoln's own argument about not giving up territory more important than Richmond and not abandoning a Chattanooga campaign. Halleck suggested Lincoln remove troops from the Shenandoah Valley, "which at this time has no strategic importance.... A week or two may change the aspect of affairs here."[40]

Lincoln bent again, telling Halleck not to send off any forces if it threatened his position or operations. He also sent Governor William Sprague of Rhode Island to talk to Halleck about coming east. Big changes were near for the Union high command.[41]

Bragg Decides

THE IMPENDING SHIFT in the Union military leadership was echoed in the South. When Braxton Bragg replaced Beauregard, Davis told him that his appointment to the West would probably be temporary.[42] It turned out to be a very long "temporary"—too long in the eyes of many in the Confederacy.

On the day of his confirmation to command, Bragg received a note from Brigadier General Daniel Ruggles, in Grenada, Mississippi, asking whether or not he should hold on the line of the Tallahatchie River. Bragg's response showed that some things, at least, had changed in the West. He ordered Ruggles not just to hold "but to take the offensive." Moreover, he ordered Brigadier General John B. Villepigue, whom Ruggles had ordered to stay put, to move on Memphis, insisting that Villepigue had the troops to take the city and "if he can ought to do it."[43]

Davis, for his part, was optimistic about the prospects afforded by the change of command, telling his wife, "Bragg may effect something since Halleck has divided his force and I hope will try."[44] W. P. Johnston, Davis's aide-de-camp, reported that Bragg was considering a number of options but had not yet set upon a plan of attack.[45] He would, but it would take some time, and be driven partially by the actions of the enemy, particularly Buell's. Moreover, though Bragg inclined toward offensive action, he had a difficult time deciding where to strike. He dithered between pushing northward from his base in Tupelo, Mississippi, and moving eastward. A picture of hesitation, or perhaps indecision, emerges.[46]

On July 14, Kirby Smith wrote from Tennessee urging concentration to oppose the growing danger from the force under Buell. He believed that this "overwhelming" Union element could not be resisted without help from Bragg. Bragg had dispatched 3,000 men on June 26. Smith added them to his forces. He also took some aggressive action. He sent 1,300 cavalry under Colonel John Hunt Morgan to raid into Kentucky and three additional regiments of cavalry under Brigadier General Nathan Bedford Forrest into middle Tennessee to delay Buell until Bragg arrived with help.[47] Morgan, in a twenty-four-day, 1,000-mile ride through Union territory, captured garrisons and supply depots and took more than 1,200 prisoners. Forrest, a six-foot-two Mississippian who combined natural military genius with utter ruthlessness, caused so much destruction to the rail lines that the Union had to allocate two divisions to their protection.[48] These raids inaugurated the beginning of a series of successful Confederate strikes at the extended Union supply lines—a key element of how the South would fight its war, especially in the West.

Buell began advancing with what Smith believed was 20,000–30,000 men. By July 19, Smith was convinced of the imminence of an attack on Chattanooga, as well as the impossibility of his holding it. He issued a number of pleas for help, telling Bragg, "Your co-operation is much needed. It is your time to strike at Middle Ten."[49] Meanwhile, Smith's dispatch of Morgan and Forrest continued to pay off for the Confederacy when Forrest captured Murfreesboro. Davis asked Bragg whether he could cooperate "to save that important position and perhaps crush the invading detachments."[50] Morgan's raid had also made a good impression on Lee, who wrote encouragingly to Davis about action by Bragg and Smith, as well as by W. W. Loring in Virginia's southwest, believing the time had come for them to act.[51] Lee's unfolding counteroffensive against Pope undoubtedly influenced his suggestion.

Bragg, who realized the importance of Chattanooga to the Confederate strategic position, also received pressure to move eastward from his most important superior. In March, April, and June, his wife, Elise Bragg, pressed him to take the offensive. In a June 8 note she insisted that the worst thing to do would be to pursue a Fabian strategy of avoiding battle. Railroads and steam navigation of rivers, she argued, had made this approach to war-fighting obsolete. "Why not…take your army round into Tennessee & thence into Kentucky. You leave the enemy in your rear—true, but is not that better than an enemy in your midst, starvation."[52]

A desire for offensive action, Buell's movements, Kirby Smith's pleas (some historians say manipulation), the successful raids by Forrest and Morgan, Davis's prod, and finally his wife's timely advice all combined to make up Bragg's mind. This also determined one of the primary theaters of Civil War combat over the next two years.

Bragg told Davis he could not push from Tupelo but would go to Chattanooga, leaving the Tupelo line well defended, and immediately advance from there. He left Major General Earl Van Dorn at Vicksburg and Major General Sterling Price at Tupelo and wrote to President Davis that "Obstacles in front connected with danger to Chattanooga induce a change of base. Fully impressed with great importance of that line, am moving to East Tennessee. Produce rapid offensive from there following the consternation now being produced by our cavalry."[53] Here, in cooperation with the cavalry raids against Union supply lines, the Confederates found an opportunity.

Bragg began concentrating his army in Chattanooga.[54] From Tupelo he also wrote to Beauregard, asking the sick-listed general's opinion of his plan. He was combining his 34,000 men with Smith's 20,000 to "take the offensive." To Bragg, it was a choice of doing nothing in Mississippi or positive action in

Tennessee. "My reasons are: Smith is so weak as to give me great uneasiness for the safety of his line, to lose which would be a great disaster. They refuse to aid him from the east or south and put the whole responsibility on me. To aid him at all from here necessarily renders me too weak for the offensive against Halleck, with at least 60,000 strongly intrenched in my front. With the country between us reduced almost to a desert by two armies and a drouth of two months, neither of us could well advance in the absence of rail transportation. It seemed to me then I was reduced to the defensive altogether or to the move I am making." Bragg had high hopes for the future, believing that "before they can know my movement I shall be in front of Buell at Chattanooga, and by cutting off his transportation may have him in a tight place. Van Dorn will be able to hold his own with about 20,000 on the Mississippi. Price stays here with 16,000."[55] Bragg relayed the same information to Richmond.[56] Davis, for his part, approved "heartily" of the plan and hoped that the combined columns of Bragg and Smith would destroy Buell, force the Union from Tennessee, and help the Confederates seize Kentucky.[57]

Smith also saw the same opportunities as Bragg, and even before Bragg's decision he had urged him to come to Chattanooga with the bulk of his forces, rather than just send reinforcements. "There is yet time for a brilliant summer campaign," he insisted. He offered to place himself under Bragg's command and, using Chattanooga as a base, support him in an advance aimed at recovering central Tennessee and possibly Kentucky as well.[58]

Bragg arrived in Chattanooga on July 30. He believed it would be ten days to two weeks before his troops could take the field, but he and Smith quickly drew up a plan for a counteroffensive. Smith's troops would attack Cumberland Gap. If he succeeded, they would throw their "entire force" into central Tennessee to isolate Buell's army. If the Union tried to help Buell by sending troops west of the Tennessee River, "then Van Dorn and Price can strike and clear West Tennessee of any force that can be left to hold it." Meanwhile, they counted on Confederate cavalry to keep the Union forces north of Tupelo, Mississippi, in check.[59]

Moreover, based upon information gathered during the raids by Forrest and Morgan, Bragg believed that there were deep wells of anti-Union feeling in middle Tennessee and Kentucky, "and nothing is wanted but arms and support to bring the people into our ranks, for they have found that neutrality has afforded them no protection."[60] Davis quickly developed high expectations for the Confederate counteroffensive, believing that if Buell's railway support was broken as reported, Bragg could "fight the enemy in detachments." With Buell defeated, Bragg, if he had the resources, could march on Nashville, forcing Grant either to retreat and give up central and eastern Tennessee or to pursue Bragg. "His Government will probably require the latter course," he added shrewdly. This, Davis thought, would deliver both Kentucky and Tennessee.[61]

The plan that came together so quickly fell apart at an even faster pace. Kirby Smith promptly forgot his promise to serve under Bragg and began making changes to support his own agenda, which was within his power because he and Bragg commanded different departments. (Davis had refused an earlier request by Bragg to place Smith officially under Bragg's command.) Instead of taking Cumberland Gap, Smith decided that he would simply cover it with part of his forces and march on Lexington, Kentucky, with the rest.[62]

Bragg now had to change his operational plan. He would push his forces into middle Tennessee, avoiding the strong Union positions at Murfreesboro (which was back in Union hands), Stevenson, and other spots, his army amid the forces of Smith and Buell. Bragg thought this would keep Chattanooga from Union hands because it would force Buell to retreat to cover his lines of supply. He warned Smith about the danger of moving too far into Kentucky when leaving Union troops in his rear before Bragg had met Buell's army, and he reiterated the roles of Price and Van Dorn in menacing western Tennessee with around 25,000 men drawn from their forces. These were to at least pin the enemy and, if possible, retake territory. In the interim, Bragg wrote, he trusted that Smith could deal with the Union forces at Cumberland Gap.[63]

Bragg, at first unsure about the operational objective of his own advance, contemplated both Nashville and Lexington, initially leaning toward Lexington. Later he decided to try to "occupy such position as to threaten Buell and prevent his moving any forces to the rear" and, at Smith's suggestion, to try to move behind Nashville. Optimistically, Bragg hoped to join hands with Smith, Price, and Van Dorn in Ohio. About Buell he echoed Davis's remarks: "By rapid movements and vigorous blows we may beat him in detail, or by gaining his rear very much increase his demoralization and break him up."[64]

Buell's Lament, Halleck's Rise

WHILE THE CONFEDERATES PLANNED his demise, Buell slogged on. This provoked his superiors in Washington, and Halleck passed along their criticism: "The President telegraphs that your progress is not satisfactory and that you should move more rapidly. The long time taken by you to reach Chattanooga will enable the enemy to anticipate you by concentrating a large force to meet you.... I communicate his views," added Halleck, "hoping that your movements hereafter may be so rapid as to remove all cause of complaint, whether well founded or not."[65] Buell offered extended excuses, including blaming his subordinate, Mitchel.[66] Halleck expressed sympathy, imputing Washington's attitude to a lack of understanding of the length of the operational and defensive lines maintained by Union commanders in the West, as well as being unnerved by events on the Peninsula.[67]

But the Confederates were now making what should have been the easy Union capture of Chattanooga much more difficult. Buell had to deal with the Rebel cavalry raiders and began receiving reports of heavy Confederate troop concentrations in the city.[68] Morgan's raid proved such a distraction that Halleck took his goggling eyes off the ball. "Do all in your power to put down the Morgan raid even if the Chattanooga expedition should be delayed," he told Buell.[69] Three days later, reluctantly, Halleck decamped for the East and a new job as general in chief of the Union army.[70]

AS WE'VE SEEN, after McClellan's removal from the post of general in chief, Lincoln and Stanton tried unsuccessfully to fill his shoes. Moreover, events on the Peninsula left matters in the West to Halleck (which meant that the Union campaign there lost energy and focus). Something had to be done. Lincoln consulted with Winfield Scott as well as with Pope, who served a short tenure as an advisor to Lincoln before returning to the field. Both gave the same answer: Halleck.[71]

The choice was in many ways understandable. Halleck had an excellent reputation among his peers. Moreover, despite the torpid nature of his drive on Corinth, in comparison to McClellan he seemed positively Mercury-like. His superiors congratulated him after Corinth's fall, but Lincoln wanted to know what he planned for a sequel. Halleck suggested pushing Buell into eastern Tennessee, which sat well with Lincoln's perceptions (somewhat misguided, as we've seen) about the region's importance.[72]

On July 2, 1862, Lincoln's summons to greater things reached Halleck. Old Brains grasped the chance slowly. He delayed his departure, insisting that Bragg would soon attack. But the pressure on him increased. Lincoln sent a messenger "to convince Halleck to come east with 50,000 troops for McClellan." Halleck agreed to come (without the troops), but only if he was given command over all the forces in the Eastern Theater. Lincoln did Halleck one better, making him general in chief of the Union army.[73]

Halleck's arrival in Washington coincided with the escalation of the war that followed the failure of the Peninsula Campaign. Union leaders and soldiers increasingly wanted to force the South to pay. On July 22, 1862, Lincoln issued an order that ratcheted up the Union army's ability to make the South feel the impact of the struggle. General Orders No. 109 reiterated permission to seize property and supplies in Southern states for use in the war, but raised the conflict's destructive tenor by allowing that "property may be destroyed for proper military objects." Lincoln also ordered the employment of blacks as laborers, though with careful records kept, so that compensation could be made to their owners.[74]

On July 25, 1862, Congressman Elihu B. Washburne wrote to Grant about the growing popular sentiment for a harsher and more aggressive war against Southerners and their property. "They want to see more immediate moving upon the 'enemy's works,'" Washburne wrote. "In fact they want to see *war*." Moreover, the administration had concluded that the contest had to be more forcefully and fully waged by all means possible, which meant using blacks as soldiers or laborers.[75] This aligned well with the tougher mind-set growing within the ranks of the Union army.

Also indicative of this hardening in attitude toward the South and its supporters was one of Halleck's August 1862 orders. He told Grant to "clean out West Tennessee and North Mississippi of all organized enemies," even imprisoning and expelling "active sympathizers," treating "that class without gloves" and seizing "their property for public use." Moreover, he told Grant to take as much of his supplies as possible from the enemy in Mississippi. "It is time that they should begin to feel the presence of war on our side."[76] This pleased Grant greatly.[77]

On the heels of this, on August 15, Halleck's General Orders No. 107 outlined procedures for seizing enemy property for government use and the organization and conduct of foraging parties. The order carefully defined the difference between pillage and "property lawfully taken from the enemy." Accurate inventories had to be kept of all property confiscated, and officers were responsible for the actions of foragers. The military could seize suitable "private property for the subsistence, transportation, and other uses of the army."[78]

UPON HIS ARRIVAL IN WASHINGTON Halleck got sucked into the increasingly desperate and confused Union situation in the East. "I have had no time to attend to matters in the West," he wrote his friend Sherman on August 25, "and they seem to be going on badly."[79] McClellan and Virginia exerted their twin influences, leaving Union forces in the West rudderless. Grant, writing from Corinth, tried to initiate action in his sector, telling Halleck that most of the Rebels to his fore had departed, and suggesting throwing the Confederates back to Columbus, Mississippi.[80] But nothing came of this, and Grant lapsed into a period of inactivity, one likely imposed by the fact that Halleck still officially controlled the Union forces Grant now led. Old Brains also kept Grant on a tight leash.[81]

Halleck eventually gave some thought to the West, contemplating a movement against Vicksburg as early as August 7. He also wanted to reorganize and focus Union forces for effective action. He was far from optimistic: "As Missouri and Tennessee are now seriously threatened and raids made into Kentucky, every available man in the West is required in the field. McClellan is barely able to hold his position, and the forces here are insufficient for the defense of Washington." He added, "I find our entire Army so divided and scattered that very little can be done till they are more concentrated or largely reinforced. I am trying to do both."[82] His solution, as always: concentrate— and wait.

But in Washington, Halleck found things worse than he had anticipated. This meant there would be no immediate offensive action. He told Sherman at the end of August that they would need to wait until the troops were organized. In the meantime, they should hold their positions and prepare.[83] Halleck was now looking toward the fall for any significant move.

He also had to immediately deal with the administration's anger. Should Buell fail to act, his removal would be imminent. "There is great dissatisfaction here at the slow movement of your army toward Chattanooga," he wired Buell. "It is feared that the enemy will have time to concentrate his entire army against you."[84] That was exactly what happened. Two months after the fall of Corinth, Buell had still not reached Chattanooga, despite inklings since the end of July that something was up. Instead, Bragg stole a march on the Union.[85]

Attacking Baton Rouge

AS BRAGG PREPARED HIS OFFENSIVE, Van Dorn, the Confederate commander at Vicksburg, fought his war. When Memphis fell and the Confederates abandoned Fort Pillow, the Union launched an attack against Vicksburg with a flotilla of more than forty gunboats. The bombardment began on July 12. Van Dorn sent the ironclad *Arkansas* against the Union vessels. By July 27 the Union's gunboats withdrew after more than two months of trying and failing to reduce the city.[86]

In the wake of this Van Dorn ordered an attack on the Louisiana capital, Baton Rouge, about 40 miles south of the mouth of the Red River. Van Dorn believed that it was critical to hold the Mississippi at two points in order to facilitate the supply of Vicksburg and guarantee communications with the Trans-Mississippi. Holding Baton Rouge and Vicksburg would provide these two points and open navigation on the Mississippi and Red rivers while increasing opportunities for an attack on New Orleans.[87]

Later, Van Dorn believed that had they had more troops, they potentially could have retaken New Orleans. His problem was that he had little chance of gathering more men. Even as early as 1862, the Confederacy was already stretched with regard to its manpower availability, particularly in the West. Van Dorn reported that there were plantations without any white males.[88] Davis replied that while "the importance of the object at which you aim cannot be overestimated," no more troops from Bragg's army would be forthcoming. Davis did promise to send him something and gave advice about where to obtain more men.[89]

Van Dorn put the Baton Rouge mission in the hands of the former vice president turned major general, John C. Breckinridge, with 6,000 men and some gunboats. They intended to mount a joint attack from the land and water.[90] Breckinridge began his offensive on July 30. Sickness quickly reduced the force by 3,000 men. Finding himself outnumbered and the Union forces supported by three gunboats, he appealed for help from the *Arkansas*. Promised that the *Arkansas* would appear on the morning of August 5, Breckinridge launched his attack in the dawn hours, certain that the *Arkansas* would soon arrive. It never did; it broke down on the way, only 4 miles from Baton Rouge, and ran aground. The attack failed. And so did a Confederate effort at joint warfare.[91] The next day, its crew destroyed the disabled ship, though not before giving her one last chance to engage the enemy. Lieutenant Stevens, her commander, "cut her from her moorings, fired her with his own hands, and turned her adrift down the river. With every gun shotted, our flag floating from her bow, and not a man on board, the Arkansas bore down upon the enemy and gave him battle. The guns were discharged as the flames reached them, and when her last shot was fired the explosion of her magazine ended the brief but glorious career of the Arkansas. 'It was beautiful,' said Lieutenant Stevens, while the tears stood in his eyes, 'to see her, when abandoned by commander and crew and dedicated to sacrifice, fighting the battle on her own hook.'"[92]

In the wake of his defeat Van Dorn ordered positions established at Port Hudson as Confederate troops held Baton Rouge "in menace." After two weeks of this, the Union abandoned the Louisiana capital to the Confederates. Control of Baton Rouge opened 200 miles of the Mississippi to Confederate navigation, as well as the Red River, which provided a water connection between the eastern and western parts of the Confederacy.[93]

The fact that this was going on at the same time that Bragg was shifting his forces to Chattanooga in preparation for a sweeping Confederate offensive demonstrates the divided nature of the Confederate command structure in the West, making cooperation more difficult and encouraging scattered responses. The South needed to concentrate its forces in the region. Instead, it frequently made poor use of them, mounting local attacks too often unrelated to any larger purpose. The Southern cause would have been better served by preserving the *Arkansas* for the defense of Vicksburg and sending Breckinridge's men to strengthen Van Dorn's prong of Bragg's coming offensive. By trying to do too much, the South accomplished too little.

Failures of Command

ON JUNE 29, 1862, BUELL ARRIVED in Huntsville, Alabama, with his army. Mitchel met him. Mitchel wanted to immediately push into eastern Tennessee, sending 10,000 men to take Chattanooga and the nearby railroads, while other similarly sized units attacked Rome, Georgia, and the railroads west of Knoxville. Meanwhile, Morgan, then at Cumberland Gap, would capture the rail lines "presumably around Knoxville." The pair argued for three days; Buell refused to decide. Fed up, Mitchel resigned. He was ordered back to Washington, given a new command at Port Royal, and, tragically, succumbed to yellow fever a few months later.[94]

The failure of Union commanders to follow through on the western tenets of McClellan's original grand plan in a timely manner, as well as the personal sloth, indecision, and general strategic and operational incompetence of Halleck and Buell, haunted Union offensive efforts in the West. The result: in the summer of 1862 great opportunities slipped through Union hands.

The Confederates had their own problems and their own failings. Their command structure sin the West was broken. No one ruled, so little got done, and what was accomplished was done slowly, such as Bragg's decision to move to Chattanooga, or done badly, as was the case with Van Dorn's attempt on Baton Rouge. The command problems so apparent in the summer would not be resolved in the fall, when they would matter even more.

The summer also produced something else: Lincoln decided that it was imperative to control the Mississippi. "I will tell you—I am determined to open it," he told Senator Orville Browning on July 24, "and, if necessary will take all these negroes to open it, and keep it open."[95]

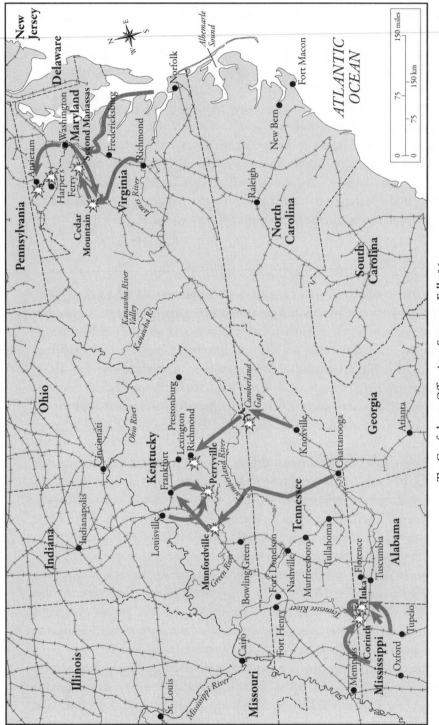

The Confederate Offensives, Summer–Fall 1862.

12

The Tyranny of Time

*I sincerely wish war was an easier and pleasanter business
than it is, but it does not admit of holidays.*

—ABRAHAM LINCOLN, October 8, 1862

Fall 1862

THE DEBACLE OF SECOND MANASSAS shook Lincoln's faith in his new commanders. Pope quickly found himself exiled to a command in Minnesota. Halleck, Lincoln concluded, was little better than a "first-rate clerk." As general in chief, he had proved incapable of coordinating the forces of Pope and McClellan. Fear that Washington might fall and reports of the poor state of the Union forces led Lincoln to place McClellan once again at the head of the Union troops around the city. His cabinet protested, but Lincoln did it anyway. He needed McClellan to reorganize the army, he told Secretary of the Navy Welles, despite McClellan's abandonment of Pope. "It is shocking to see and know this," Lincoln commented, "but there is no remedy at present. McClellan has the army with him." Moreover, although McClellan had failed to fight, Lincoln recognized his ability to make an army ready to fight and said, "We must use the tools we have." At this moment, it was what the Union's war effort demanded.[1]

Lincoln was right to prepare; the Confederacy planned to attack from the Mississippi Valley to Maryland. The concentration of the striking power of the Confederate armies had taken place over the preceding months. Defensive strategy was finished. The strategic and operational offensive would now drive the South's war—for a time.

Davis drafted for Generals Lee, Bragg, and Smith a proclamation to carry with them in their respective fall 1862 offensives into Maryland and Kentucky (though Lee had crossed the Potomac and delivered a similar one before Davis penned this version). Davis noted that since they would come "at the head of an invading army," the Confederates needed to explain themselves. Given that the Union refused to make peace, Davis insisted, "we are driven to protect our own country by transferring the seat of war to that of an enemy. . . . The Confederate army therefore comes to occupy the territory of their enemies and to make it the theatre of hostilities." In other words, the

Confederacy would take the war to the North in offensive moves that Davis insisted were defensive. They were hardly so. The Confederacy sought conquest, pure and simple. His letter is solid proof of this and also denotes the Confederate shift to an offensive strategy. Nothing *forced* the Confederacy to invade states that had not seceded (though many of their respective residents certainly tried to carry them from the Union). The fact that Davis referred to the Confederate forces as "an invading army" strengthens the argument that the Confederacy had moved to an offensive strategy.[2] In July 1861, Davis had said he would carry the war northward if the Union refused to let the South go. Now, at last, he would make good on his threat.[3]

Davis's proclamation insisted that the war continued only because the North continued to wage it and repeated his insistence that the South merely wanted to be allowed to control its own destiny. He told the people of Maryland and Kentucky that they had the power to force the Union to conclude a peace, or drive their respective state legislatures to make a separate peace with the Confederacy. By so doing they would "secure immunity from the desolating effects of warfare."[4]

Davis's words may have only been propaganda, but if he truly believed them, it shows his view of the war was that of a struggle between two coalitions of opposing states. By trying to separate Lincoln's Federal government from its allies, the states, he aligned his action with the teachings of both Clausewitz and Sun Tzu. But the proclamation accomplished nothing in either Maryland or Kentucky. Both it and the invasions were carrot-and-stick efforts, intended to damage the North's ability to prosecute the war while bettering the South's strategic position. The carrot lacked sweetness, and the stick, as we shall see, proved too small.

Davis's subordinates had already been thinking of heading north. Confederate leaders believed Maryland and Kentucky rightfully belonged to the South. To many in the South, success meant the detachment of these states from the Union and their attachment to the Confederacy. Lee was one of those who believed it was time to claim one of the missing stars.

Lee's aggressive-mindedness intensified in the wake of his victory at Second Manassas. He saw an opportunity that had to be grasped. He wrote Davis on September 3 that they now had their best opening since the beginning of the war to invade Maryland. The Union armies were weak, were demoralized from their recent defeat, and had not yet integrated their new troops. He also revealed one of the assumptions driving his offensive (one that also applied to the views of Bragg and Kirby Smith toward Kentucky): that the people of Maryland lived in Union thrall.[5]

Lee also wished to maintain the initiative he had so handily seized. Attacking Washington was out of the question. He had not the strength and could not have supplied his troops even had he had enough ammunition. He "therefore determined while threatening the approaches to Washington, to draw the troops into Loudoun, where forage and some provisions can be obtained, menace their possession of the Shenandoah Valley, and if found practicable, to cross into Maryland." Lee asked for troops from the West. If Bragg was not about to move, he insisted, they "could be advantageously employed in opposing the overwhelming numbers which it seems to be the intention of the enemy now to concentrate in Virginia."[6]

Lee soon found movement into Maryland very "practicable." He told Davis that he would advance "at once" unless Davis disapproved of the idea. Wisely, Lee kept the political picture in view as he prepared. He asked Davis to send Enoch L. Lowe, Maryland's pro-Confederate ex-governor, to accompany him (though Lowe never arrived), and told Davis that he planned to enter Pennsylvania "unless you deem it unadvisable upon political or other grounds." In marked contrast to events in Bragg's headquarters, Lee's decision to invade Maryland was reached rapidly. Pope pulled back into Washington's defenses on September 2. On September 3, Lee told Davis of his plan by letter. And on September 4, without waiting for a reply, he began his march. To support his move, he urged that W. W. Loring's force be sent down the Shenandoah to Martinsburg, something Lee had suggested earlier.[7] Lee had a number of strategic and operational objectives in mind. He wrote that his army entered Maryland to give "the people of that State an opportunity of liberating themselves. Whatever success may attend that effort, I hope at any rate to annoy and harass the enemy." Operationally, going north of the Potomac would draw McClellan's army out of its fortifications around Washington; Lee could then hope to fight them. As a bonus, he could feed his army on enemy soil.[8]

Lee seems to have had other, more ambitious objectives in mind as well. After the war, Brigadier General John G. Walker wrote that on September 7, Lee had told him that after taking Harpers Ferry he planned to concentrate the army at Hagerstown, march on Harrisburg, "the objective point of this campaign," and destroy the Pennsylvania as well as the Baltimore and Ohio railroads. Combined with the intended destruction of the Chesapeake and Ohio Canal, this would leave Washington with only one land communication route to the West, a long and cumbersome one via the Great Lakes. This done, Walker recalled Lee saying, the general would consider striking "Philadelphia, Baltimore, or Washington, as may seem best for our interests."

Lee believed McClellan's cautiousness would enable him safely to abandon his lines of communications for a time.[9] After he crossed into Maryland, Lee thought that the Confederates might have an opportunity to retake Norfolk as well.[10]

Many in the South continued to believe that Marylanders were simply waiting to have the yoke of Union oppression lifted from their shoulders and would thus welcome the Confederates. Whether or not Lee initially held this view—and the tenor of his letters casts doubt upon this—it took only a day to disabuse him of the notion. He quickly concluded that the state's residents would not rise against the Union.[11]

Nonetheless, Lee was also convinced that the time had arrived for the Confederate government to propose peace and advised Davis to do so. He noted the Union's failure to achieve the objective it had set out to accomplish more than a year before and believed that the South, by proposing to end the war at a time when it was in a position to hurt the enemy, would prove to the world that the Confederacy sought only its independence. A Northern refusal would be evidence that the "party in power" was responsible for continuing the war, not the South. A peace proposal would also impact the Union midterm elections, allowing Northern voters to choose between ending and continuing the war.[12] Lee had the political objective clearly in sight and considered his offensive in light of this. The possible flip side of his invasion, though, was the risk that it would rally the North while proving to foreign states that the Confederacy was bent on aggression, not conciliation.

The movement of Lee's army would be plagued by the worst straggling "in its history." Scores of men simply fell behind or dropped out of ranks. The problem was so great that Lee estimated it robbed him of one third to one half of his original complement. He had perhaps 55,000 infantry upon crossing into Maryland, but only 40,000 were available when it came time to fight. The loss was the result of wear from the previous campaign and the effect of the hard Maryland roads on the often barefoot soldiers of the South. Lee later ascribed his withdrawal from Maryland to the disparity in numbers, something contributable in part to "the usual casualties of battle," but more critically to straggling, something common in all conflicts. He was also well aware of the difficulty he faced in trying to simultaneously defend the Confederacy's frontier and operate in the enemy's country.[13]

When Lee reached Hagerstown, Maryland, he was undecided whether the path of his invasion should be to the east or the west of the Blue Ridge

Mountains. Moving to the east would threaten Baltimore and Washington and, Lee believed, would "insure the withdrawal of the mass of the enemy's troops north of the Potomac." Lee had also thought that when his army reached Fredericktown, the Union troops that had withdrawn from the Valley of Virginia to Martinsburg and Harpers Ferry would leave Virginia. "In this," Lee wrote later, "I was disappointed." As a result, he dispatched Jackson to reduce Harpers Ferry and sent Major General Lafayette McLaws against Martinsburg. These sat astride his communication and supply lines through the Shenandoah. He had to hold them before he could head north.[14]

Despite Lee and Davis's ambitions for the campaign, friction and chance would hinder its success. One of Lee's subordinates lost a copy of his Special Orders No. 191, which outlined Lee's operational plan.[15] "Here is a paper with which if I cannot whip 'Bobbie Lee,' I will be willing to go home," McClellan crowed. To "whip Bobbie Lee" McClellan had only to move rapidly and put his army between the forces of Jackson and Lee, giving him the chance to defeat each separately. But moving quickly was something McClellan could not do. He gave Lee time to concentrate his forces. Lee also fought a delaying action at Boonsboro, Maryland, giving Jackson time to complete the reduction of Harpers Ferry.[16]

Moreover, though it gave McClellan a great opportunity, getting his hands on Lee's order did not give him "much more than he already knew, or would know, considering the high quality of the information already reaching him from Maryland informants." In addition, the note's discovery by the North did not pass unnoticed by the South. A Confederate sympathizer who witnessed McClellan's celebration upon receiving the note immediately took horse for the Confederate forces then at South Mountain. By ten o'clock on the evening of September 13—the very day McClellan received the key papers—Lee knew the enemy possessed his plans.[17]

Lee's invasion culminated on September 17 at the Battle of Antietam, or Sharpsburg, the bloodiest day of the entire war. Lee, who chose to stand and absorb any assault, had perhaps 40,000 men (some sources say as many as 51,000), McClellan 75,000–87,000. Tactically, McClellan planned to hit Lee's left, then his right; then, having convinced Lee to pull forces from his middle to blunt the Union blows, McClellan would break the Confederate center. This last never came. McClellan, because of his numerical superiority, would have been better served to strike en masse. Instead, he made piecemeal attacks with only parts of his force. These had some success. Burnside's corps pushed back the Confederate right, but Confederate reinforcements under A. P. Hill, hurrying from their recent capture of Harpers Ferry, arrived on the field in time to save the Confederate position. Nightfall ended the fighting, and the next day the armies stared at each other, McClellan refusing to act even though he had two full corps that had not seen action. The ferocious contest cost the South between 10,000 and 14,000 casualties, the Union 12,400.[18] On the night of September 18, Lee withdrew back across the Potomac.[19] McClellan did not pursue. The historian Stephen Sears concludes that "Antietam was one of the very rare Civil War battles in which the war might have been decided in an afternoon. That it was not was due in equal measure to Lee's battlefield brilliance and McClellan's battlefield timidity."[20] One could also argue that the North's real opportunity arose after the battle.

By moving into the North, Lee was rolling the dice. Lee's army was far from its sources of supply and reinforcement, and Lincoln saw a chance to destroy it before it could safely withdraw—a chance that was promptly missed. He wrote later: "I confidently believed, last September that we could end the war by allowing the enemy to go to Harrisburg and Philadelphia." Panic in Pennsylvania, though, meant that the Union could not permit Lee to complete the overextension upon which he had embarked.[21] Lincoln would return to this line of thought.

Though repulsed, Lee remained reluctant to give up the preinvasion gains of his fall campaign and sought to hold the Union at the frontier. Lee wrote that "McClellan's army is on the north bank of the Potomac, stretching from Hagerstown to Harper's Ferry. I hope to be able to retain them on the Potomac, or, if they cross, to draw them up the valley." He also looked for ways to move the war back into the North, using his forces as well as those of Loring, who had recaptured western Virginia's Kanawha Valley while Lee was in Maryland. Lee suggested Loring strike northwards through the Monongahela Valley, attacking Union rail transportation, destroying tunnels and bridges, and perhaps even moving into Pennsylvania.[22] A revived Union threat against the Kanawha Valley and its all-important Confederate saltworks at Charleston, as well as the Virginia and Tennessee Railroad, forced the South to hold back Loring.[23]

Lee had also wanted to act immediately with his own forces: he had intended "to recross the Potomac at Williamsport, and move upon Hagerstown" and "endeavor to defeat the enemy at that point." The state of his army prevented this. He concluded that "the hazard would be great and a reverse disastrous. I am, therefore, led to pause."[24] Nonetheless, Lee consistently sought to keep the initiative, even in the wake of a retreat such as the one after Antietam. He had the same reaction the following summer.

As Lee reluctantly took his "pause," Davis filled him in on an element of Southern sentiment, offering a window on Southern public opinion: "The feverish anxiety to invade the North has been relieved by the counter irritant of apprehension for the safety of the Capitol in the absence of the Army, so long criticized for a 'want of dash,' & the class, who so vociferously urged a forward movement in which they were not personally to be involved, would now be most pleased to welcome the return of that Army. I hope," he added with some bitterness, "their fears are as poor counsellors as was their presumption."[25]

Relieving McClellan

LEE'S EXTENDED POSITION had briefly presented the Union with an opportunity, one that McClellan, as we've seen, refused to grab. By late September, even Halleck was questioning what McClellan was up to and insisted upon a plan from the head of the Army of the Potomac, one that involved moving across the lower Potomac and keeping Washington covered.[26]

Privately, McClellan agitated for the removal of his perceived enemies in the cabinet, Stanton and Halleck, through a meeting of Northern state governors and as well as for his own reappointment as general in chief. He despised Halleck. "I will *not* serve under him," he told his wife, and insisted that he would leave the army if Stanton remained and Halleck did not yield to McClellan his former post. He believed it was the least the nation could do given that he had saved the country twice. McClellan was now governed by ego and paranoia. When they met in Altoona, Pennsylvania, on September 24, 1862, the governors leaned more away from McClellan than toward him.[27]

Of course, differences between the general and his commander in chief had been brewing for some time. Among other things, their respective views of how to fight the war, and for what ends, had diverged. McClellan wanted to fight the war without enraging the civilian population of the South. He wanted to avoid head-on assaults and the embittering casualties that would result, and pursue instead a war of maneuver, which would result in the defeat of the Confederate armies. He wanted to fight and conciliate, a historical echo of the unsuccessful campaign the Howe brothers had waged in New York during the American Revolution. He insisted that the war be conducted

in a civilized manner, meaning fighting only the enemy's army. Lincoln's issuance of the Preliminary Emancipation Proclamation in the wake of Antietam
raised the specter that soon the North would be fighting not only for the
objective of union but also for the forcible abolition of slavery. This was not
something that appealed to McClellan.[28]

Lincoln visited McClellan at the beginning of October. He warned him
about "overcautiousness" and extracted a commitment to cross the Potomac.[29] After Lincoln's return to Washington, Halleck sent McClellan the
administration's orders: "The President directs that you cross the Potomac
and give battle to the enemy or drive him south. Your army must move
now while the roads are good. If you cross the river between the enemy and
Washington, and cover the latter by your line of operations, you can be re-
enforced with 30,000 men. If you move up the Valley of the Shenandoah,
not more than 12,000 or 15,000 ca[n] be sent to you. The President, advises
the interior line, between Washington and the enemy, but does not order
it. He is very desirous that your army move as soon as possible. You will
immediately report what line you adopt and when you intend to cross the
river."[30] Again, on October 7, McClellan agreed to move, and again he did
nothing.[31]

On October 13, Lincoln sent McClellan a long letter, expressing his frus-
trations and laying out his discontent. "You remember my speaking to you of
what I called your over-cautiousness," he wrote. "Are you not over-cautious
when you assume that you can not do what the enemy is constantly doing?
Should you not claim to be at least his equal in prowess, and act upon the
claim?" McClellan's lack of movement, based supposedly upon a fear that he
could not keep his army supplied at Winchester without the rebuilding of
the railroad (something the enemy, who was possessed of fewer wagons, was
already doing), "ignores the question of *time*, which cannot and must not be
ignored." Lincoln laid out McClellan's and Lee's respective problems, but also
provided an operational plan: "Again, one of the standard maxims of war, as
you know, is 'to operate upon the enemy's communications as much as possible without exposing your own.' You seem to act as if this applies *against*
you, but can not apply in your *favor*. Change positions with the enemy, and
think you not he would break your communication with Richmond within
the next twentyfour [*sic*] hours? You dread his going into Pennsylvania. But
if he does so in full force, he gives up his communications to you absolutely,
and you have nothing to do but to follow, and ruin him; if he does so with
less than full force, fall upon, and beat what is left behind all the easier." Lincoln added, "Exclusive of the water line, you are now nearer Richmond than

the enemy is by the route that you *can*, and he *must* take. Why can you not reach there before him, unless you admit that he is more than your equal on a march. His route is the arc of a circle, while yours is the chord. The roads are as good on yours as on his."[32]

Lincoln had wanted McClellan to move farther south because this would allow the seizure of Lee's army's communications if the Confederates did not react. If the Rebels went north, Lincoln advised a close pursuit and taking his communications. If Lee didn't allow this, or withdrew toward Richmond, Lincoln suggested McClellan stay on him and "fight him if a favorable opportunity should present, and, at least, try to beat him to Richmond on the inside track." If Lee elected to give battle at Winchester, McClellan should oblige him because of the inherent advantage of the Union fighting so near its supply centers. "If we can not beat the enemy where he now is," Lincoln insisted, "we never can, he again being within the entrenchments of Richmond." Lincoln told McClellan that he thought "it preferable to take the route nearest the enemy, disabling him to make an important move without your knowledge, and compelling him to keep his forces together, for dread of you. The gaps would enable you to attack if you should wish. For a great part of the way, you would be practically between the enemy and both Washington and Richmond, enabling us to spare you the greatest number of troops from here. When at length, running for Richmond ahead of him enables him to move this way; if he does so, turn and attack him in rear. But I think he should be engaged long before such point is reached. It is all easy if our troops march as well as the enemy; and it is unmanly to say they can not do it."[33] The gist of Lincoln's complaint, one he would level at other Union generals, was their inability to expect as much of their men as the Southern generals did of theirs.

Moreover, Lincoln pointed out the opportunity Lee had presented to the Union by coming north and which partially remained because of the forward position he maintained in Virginia. The Union troops were certainly up to the task, but too often they were lions led by lambs. Two days before Antietam, Lincoln told McClellan, "Destroy the rebel army, if possible."[34] After Antietam, it became one of the primary means he saw of winning the war.

Yet Lincoln still held back. He ended his great note of October 13 by saying, "This letter is in no sense an order." He refused to impose himself fully upon military strategy. The result was that McClellan responded as he always had—by waiting. He put his first troops over the Potomac on October 21. It took nine more days to cross the rest. A reluctant Lincoln waited until after the November election to relieve Little Mac. Lincoln's secretary, John Nicolay, wrote, "Defeat could scarcely be worse than the endless suspense to which McClellan has subjected us."[35]

The West

THE EASTERN CAMPAIGN had demonstrated the problems and weaknesses of both camps; the Western Theater placed them in even sharper focus. Similar issues plagued both sides: divided command structures, poor coordination, insubordinate subordinates, and commanders who refused to command.

On the Confederate side, confusion persisted. Moreover, the operational plan for the campaign continued to evolve, growing new prongs. This dissipated Southern efforts and made it more difficult to reach any operational objective, and indeed made it increasingly unclear what operational objectives they hoped to achieve. All of the fingers that eventually moved north, those of Bragg, Van Dorn, Breckinridge, Kirby Smith, Price, and Humphrey Marshall, might have accomplished something had they moved in unison. Separately, they achieved very little.

Van Dorn received instructions from Bragg on August 11 to launch an offensive against the North, but by this time his forces were greatly depleted. Breckinridge was at that moment preparing another attack on Baton Rouge, and Van Dorn only had about 5,000 men he could spare from his garrisons. He had wanted to move on New Orleans but said he would go where needed and gladly march on Louisville with Bragg and Price—should the government give him some exchanged prisoners as recruits and weapons with which to arm them.[36] Grant's army stood in his path.

Kirby Smith had strengthened the far eastern end of the Confederate thrust by securing the support of Brigadier General Humphrey Marshall, with whom he met in Knoxville in early August. Both agreed that the time was now ripe for an offensive into Kentucky. Marshall promised to push his troops through Pound Gap by August 15 and move via Maysville, Kentucky, bound for Cincinnati, while Smith advanced on Lexington.[37]

Smith began the Confederate offensive on August 14. Crossing the narrow neck of Tennessee, he quickly took Barboursville, Kentucky. He found no supplies on his march, the country having been picked clean. His situation critical, Smith believed he had but two choices: advance toward Lexington or withdraw. He was concerned that a retreat would damage Kentuckians' support for the Confederacy, so he elected to push on. He told Bragg, "I still cordially invite you to make this the line of your operations, so that you may act with our forces concentrated." "Should you be able to evade Buell and cross the Cumberland," he added later, "and Marshall succeed in reaching the productive portion of Kentucky the enemy will be so distracted that we might hope to reach the Ohio."[38]

As he marched, Smith wrote Davis to "strongly urge upon" him "to order General Marshall to advance at once through Pound Gap, and as it seems to me this is of all others the time to strike a decisive blow for our cause in the West."[39] He planned to move against Lexington on the twenty-seventh and wanted Marshall to threaten this city by pushing into eastern Kentucky at the same time.[40]

Though he later joined Bragg, Humphrey Marshall, like most of the other Confederate commanders, had plans of his own. He intended to move in support of Bragg with a small force and big ambitions. The month before, in July, encouraged by a note from Morgan about the possible ease with which eastern Kentucky could be seized, Marshall promised to take Kentucky—if he could gather 6,000 men.[41] By late August, he had calmed down a bit and insisted that he needed 10,000 men (he eventually gathered 5,000).[42] His ambitions, though, remained outsized: "My plan, submitted to General Bragg, is that I shall cut the Ohio at Maysville, Bragg at Louisville, while Smith holds Lexington, thus insulating Cincinnati, while Price cuts her off from Cairo by crossing at Evansville and seizing the Ohio and Mississippi Railroad in Illinois; thence bearing directly on Alton and Saint Louis." Marshall argued that they needed all the railroads and the capital, and could then install a provisional government.[43]

Once Kentucky belonged to the South, Marshall planned to force all men of military age either to join the Confederate Army or to depart northward and suffer the Union draft. Those remaining would be required to take a loyalty oath to the Confederacy or be treated as hostile. "The mild policy I pursued last winter will not win, I am convinced," he wrote, adding that "something must be done to arrest the feeling that our people are the only ones who are to suffer from the vicissitudes of war." No one in Richmond got this note until it was moot, however, it having gotten misplaced until early October, but it did forecast some of what the Confederates would do in Kentucky.[44]

Bragg finally began to move on August 28, much later than he had originally anticipated. But he was optimistic. His operational plan had evolved into an advance by his forces into Tennessee, Kirby Smith's drive on Lexington, and Marshall's thrust into eastern Kentucky from western Virginia. The combination, it was felt, would deal with Buell. Meanwhile, Bragg wrote to Sterling Price in Mississippi, "Sherman and Rosecrans we leave to you and Van Dorn...and we shall confidently expect to meet you on the Ohio and there open the way to Missouri." He sent a similar note to Van Dorn.[45] The Confederates were thinking in grand terms.

BY EARLY AUGUST, the Union had solid information that the Confederates were about to advance, but its leaders remained unsure of the enemy's plans. Buell believed they would aim at Nashville. Nonetheless, he wanted to keep his options open. "If they attempt to invade Kentucky it will not be with a very large force," he guessed. He also conceived a solid, practical response, one he should have acted upon: "In that case we should leave them to the management of the force we can collect to meet them there and devote everything against the main body of the enemy."[46] Buell relayed word of Kirby Smith's offensive before it began. Halleck responded in an unusual fashion— with clear orders: "If the enemy are concentrating in East Tennessee you must move there and break them up. Go where-ever the enemy is."[47] This proved a difficult command for Buell to obey.

By the middle of August, Buell had a clear view of his enemy's primary strategic objective, if not how they planned to achieve it. "It is undoubtedly true that they deem it of vital importance not only to hold East Tennessee but regain what they have lost," he wrote, "and that is said to be their present plan." He prepared by calling for reinforcements that had been promised from Grant.[48] Grant, headquartered at Corinth, did as ordered, but he sent a warning as well. "The best information I can get indicates that a feint only is intended here for the purpose to hold our troops, but, sending so many troops away, may it not be turned into an attack?"[49]

In the midst of trying to deal with the evolving Confederate offensive, Halleck informed Buell that the administration had lost patience. Buell snapped back, telling him to relieve him if he thought it necessary.[50] Halleck did nothing of the kind; doing so would have required him to make a decision.

Buell sent Major General William "Bull" Nelson, a giant of a man and a former naval officer who would later be murdered by a brother Union general with the unfortunate name of Jefferson Davis, to take command in Louisville, Kentucky, and organize the troops there. Once in Louisville, Nelson found that the Union had unnecessarily complicated the command structure in the West by creating the Department of the Ohio under Major General Horatio Wright.[51] Buell began pulling his troops in from all directions, trying to concentrate his forces, but unsure where his retreat would stop or where he could engage Bragg.[52] By August 25, he had decided he would give up some of the railroad lines to the enemy and concentrate troops around Nashville, "which will make the city secure against cavalry demonstration." He could then reestablish his communications with Louisville. He would still have about 30,000 men free, but thought this "altogether insufficient to render the State secure or exert much influence over the population." Guerrillas worried him as well. The key thing, he insisted, was to hold on to Huntsville, "the only foothold we have in Alabama."[53]

The problem was that this was not what the administration wanted him to do. Lincoln and his cabinet had grown tired of generals who demanded reinforcements and avoided the hard, bloody work of war. Only Halleck's pleas preserved him. "The Government seems determined to apply the guillotine to all unsuccessful generals," Halleck wrote. "It seems rather hard to do this where the general is not in fault, but perhaps with us now, as in the French Revolution, some harsh measures are required."[54]

On August 30, Buell, who thought he faced an army of 50,000–60,000 under Bragg, concluded that he needed to fall back on Nashville, where he believed he could gather a field force of 50,000.[55] His operational thinking exhibited the same problem as that of most of his brother Union generals, and it resulted in his advancing the wrong way. Bragg had left Chattanooga on the twenty-eighth, marching north. Buell certainly had long lines of communication and supply to hold, and faced an unknown and unfolding Confederate threat, but at the time of his writing, from Dercherd, Tennessee (northeast of Chattanooga), he was closer to Bragg's base of Chattanooga than to the enemy, which had taken the bulk of its army northward, across the picked-over regions of eastern Tennessee and Kentucky. Buell could have secured Nashville and pushed south for Chattanooga. Bragg, like Lee, had overextended himself and by so doing presented the enemy a great opportunity. Taking Chattanooga would have left Bragg's army adrift, with no place to go. And, of course, had he taken it the previous spring, he would have prevented Bragg's invasion altogether.

On September 1, having been besieged by one of Kirby Smith's divisions for a month, George Morgan's Union force at Cumberland Gap destroyed everything of use to the enemy and retreated nearly 200 miles to the Ohio River. Smith's men then rejoined their commander, who had marched deep into Kentucky and mounted demonstrations opposite Louisville and Cincinnati, throwing these cities into uproar. Smith found the inhabitants supportive, and, like Bragg, he issued proclamations applauding their liberation.[56]

When Bragg began his march northward on August 28, he unfolded his part of "the only multi-army offensive the Confederates ever launched." Three days before, he had told Van Dorn to move as soon as possible, instructing him to destroy the forces moving from Corinth to reinforce Buell as they crossed the rivers. Bragg planned to support Kirby Smith or to fight Buell if the Union general gave them the chance.[57]

On September 9, Bragg's army camped at Sparta, 40 miles to the east of Nashville. Bragg thought Buell was making for Louisville and told Smith, who had reached Lexington, to unite with him at Glasgow should Union forces press him. Together, Bragg insisted, they could defeat the Federals. Bragg's 300-mile thrust into Union territory resulted in the North abandoning the areas of northern Alabama and eastern Tennessee they had gained in the spring and summer. On the fifteenth, the Confederates reached Munfordville, which surrendered the next day without a fight, handing Bragg 4,000 prisoners and a great success.[58] Though no one knew it at the time, this proved the offensive's culminating point.

At the end of August, Buell began moving his troops toward Murfreesboro, but he remained unsure of Bragg's intentions. "March where you please," Halleck told him, "provided you will find the enemy and fight him." Buell marched. Pushing his troops northeastward, he shadowed Bragg, moving first to Nashville, then to Bowling Green, and then, after hearing of the surrender at Munfordville, to Louisville, all the while wondering what the Rebels intended. By the nineteenth, he was certain the enemy aimed at Louisville, believing Bragg and Smith would unite forces. Halleck rebuked him: "I fear that here as elsewhere you move too slowly, and will permit the junction of Bragg and Smith before you open your line to Louisville. The immobility of your army is most surprising. Bragg in the last two months has marched four times the distance you have." Buell slogged on, finally massing his forces at Louisville, Kentucky, on the twenty-fifth.[59]

Bragg's superiors were just as upset. The day before Halleck sent the administration's latest stinging critique to Buell, Jefferson Davis and George W. Randolph (the latest Confederate secretary of war; there would be five) also decided that something was wrong. "Telegrams from Tennessee and Mississippi indicate a want of co intelligence and cooperation among the generals of the several columns," Davis wrote Bragg. The administration knew nothing of their proposed movements, and Davis's concern was that if the Confederate generals—Van Dorn, Price, and Breckinridge—each acted "for himself" "disaster ... must be the probable result." Randolph told Van Dorn: "We fear that a serious misunderstanding exists with reference to the movements of Price, Breckinridge, and yourself."[60]

The intervention of Davis and Randolph did not provide the clarity of direction it was intended to give. Price and Van Dorn had been struggling to coordinate their efforts since early September and were still struggling. Apparently there were also problems exchanging messages between the two commanders. By September 19, Price agreed to Van Dorn's proposal that they unite at Rienzi, Mississippi, south of Corinth. Enemy presence there prevented this, and Van Dorn suggested Ripley, Mississippi, instead.[61]

Van Dorn was nonetheless very optimistic. He told Price that if Bragg and Smith were successful, "the enemy in our front will withdraw." He also gave his take on the general Confederate offensive that had developed across the entire eastern half of the continent: "If it becomes necessary to wait it will not be unfortunate, as we are holding a large force in check; later we will defeat them, free West Tennessee, and penetrate Kentucky or cross the Ohio. I do not think it necessary to act hurriedly. On the contrary, a little delay, attacking, as it were, *en echelon* from Maryland to West Tennessee and Arkansas, seems to me advisable."[62] Considering the entrenched positions held by the Union forces facing him, patience may have been Van Dorn's best approach.[63]

Van Dorn and Price also had the misfortune to face a defense led by the Union's most energetic commander—Grant. In mid-September, Grant wrote to Halleck that he believed the movement of Van Dorn and his subordinate Breckinridge was "covering a move to get General Price into East Tennessee." He intended to stop Price.[64] "Do everything in your power to prevent Price from crossing the Tennessee River," Halleck replied. "A junction of Price and Bragg in Tennessee or Kentucky would be most disastrous. They should be fought while separate."[65]

Price, though, thought it better to follow Bragg's orders and try to pin the forces of Major General William S. Rosecrans so that they could not reinforce Buell. He moved north, taking Iuka, Mississippi, on September 14. Grant engineered a two-pronged attack with forces under Rosecrans and Major General Edward Ord. Only Rosecrans delivered his blow, which fell on the nineteenth, inflicting 1,516 casualties on the Rebels for 782 of his own. Afterward, Price withdrew and joined Van Dorn.[66]

Van Dorn and Price united at Ripley, Mississippi, on September 28, 1862, Price insisting that the unexpectedly large Union force at Corinth had prevented him from carrying out Bragg's orders. Secretary of War Randolph ordered Van Dorn to take command of all Confederate forces in Mississippi, including Price's, to ensure "proper disposition for the defense of the Missis-sippi River, and also for an advance into Tennessee," and transferred Major General John C. Pemberton to the command of Van Dorn's department so that Van Dorn could lead an army in the field.[67]

Van Dorn had gone north with the intention of pushing to St. Louis. Then, as the situation evolved, he thought Paducah, Kentucky, a better objec-tive. Finally, Van Dorn decided that Corinth was the true point of attack, as if taking it from the Union would crack open their defensive line.[68]

AS VAN DORN AND PRICE tried to sort out what they were to do, Bragg and Kirby Smith continued their two-pronged advance into Kentucky. Bragg found much to disappoint him, particularly the reaction of the Kentuckians themselves, who failed to rally to the Confederate banner in the numbers that he had expected. He had only gathered about 2,500 men, which did not even replace the losses he had already suffered in the campaign. Bragg had 15,000 extra weapons but no recruits to use them; Van Dorn and Price had men they couldn't arm. Bragg believed the South could hold Kentucky and Tennessee only if he was supplied with 50,000 reinforcements. Bragg also thought that Van Dorn and Price had not moved, and that as a result he faced the Union forces from northern Mississippi as well. Overall, he was not confident of suc-cess. "In this condition any advance is impossible. I still hope the movement of Generals Price and Van Dorn may clear away our rear and open a base for us. Otherwise we may be seriously embarrassed."[69]

At Munfordville, Bragg knew that Buell and his army were at Bowling Green, a mere 40 miles away. Outnumbered, with his supply situation danger-ous and Kirby Smith off fighting his own war (as had been the case during the entire campaign), Bragg elected to withdraw. He marched to Bardstown in an effort to unite with Smith as Buell shifted his forces to Louisville.[70]

On September 26, Bragg issued his version of Davis's proclamation, one aimed at the Union residents of the "Northwest." Bragg informed them that they could protect their homes by declaring neutrality and appealed to their economic interests, arguing that their true ties of trade and commerce were with the South, not with the easterners who taxed them, and that these bonds would be quickly restored when hostilities ceased.[71] As with the proclama-tion issued by Lee in Maryland, the Confederates were trying to break apart the Union "coalition." It also produced the same result. Kentucky's inhabit-ants could see no gain in supporting a Confederate army that would not be around to protect them. Kirby Smith understood this. Bragg did not; he read their reluctance as cowardice.[72]

Lincoln made his own kind of proclamation: it was time for Buell to
go. The axe fell on September 29. Buell did not stay relieved, however. His
intended replacement, George Thomas, balked at taking the job, particularly
under such circumstances. Cries also arose from Ohio political grandees. Lincoln rescinded the order, and Buell agreed to continue to grace the Union
army with his presence.[73]

Halleck returned to hectoring Buell into moving.[74] Buell, surprisingly, had
already done so, and toward the enemy at that.[75] As Shelby Foote describes it:
"After four months of building and repairing roads and railroads, tediously
advancing and hastily backtracking, enduring constant prodding from above,
he was about to fight."[76]

Meanwhile, in an effort to overcome the reluctance of Kentuckians
to get behind the Confederate cause, Bragg staged a ceremony to inaugurate a Confederate governor of the state at Frankfort, Kentucky. This
would also give him the legal authority to institute conscription to fill his
ranks. The ceremony failed to have the effect he wished, and news of the
arrival of Buell's army upset plans for a celebration. On October 4, Bragg
ordered his troops concentrated at Harrodsburg. Bad intelligence reports,
combined with foot-dragging and outright disobedience by subordinates,
culminated in a sloppy but bloody struggle at Perryville. Buell's 55,000
troops made contact with the first of the 40,000 Confederates on October
7. Bragg sent orders for Polk to attack the oncoming Union force, which
Bragg did not realize at the time was a part of Buell's army. Polk, thinking there was more there than met the eye, hesitated. Bragg arrived the
next day and ensured that the attack went off. Polk's men, massed to the
north of Perryville, struck the Union's left, caving it in. But the Union
counterattack drove the Rebels back into Perryville. The Federals got the
worst of the fight, suffering 4,200 casualties to the Confederacy's 3,400.
Both fought with only part of their forces. Buell was absent from the fight
because the lay of the ground prevented the sound of the contest from traveling very far, a case of what is known as acoustic shadow. Night found the
Confederates in control of the field; they then withdrew. Buell followed,
on tenterhooks.[77]

Van Dorn and Price suffered as well. They met Rosecrans at Corinth, the
capture of which Van Dorn believed was "precedent to the accomplishment
of anything of importance in West Tennessee." The Confederates attacked
before the arrival of the exchanged prisoners they hoped would swell their
ranks because the Union forces continued to increase. Moreover, to Van Dorn
"it was very evident that unless a sudden and vigorous blow could be struck

there at once no hope could be entertained of driving the enemy from a base of operations so convenient that in the event of misfortune to Bragg in Kentucky the whole valley of the Mississippi would be lost to us before winter." Van Dorn's men broke into the city, his 22,000 facing 23,000 under Rosecrans. But the Confederates couldn't hold Corinth and were driven out with help from Union reinforcements sent by Grant. Rosecrans suffered 2,520 casualties. Van Dorn had 2,470 wounded and killed and 1,763 missing, some of the latter occurring after the battle.[78]

Retreating after Perryville, Bragg began leaning toward a complete withdrawal from Kentucky. When he received word of Price and Van Dorn's defeat and realized the poverty of his supply situation, he decided to quit the state and struck out for the Cumberland Gap on October 13.[79] John Euclid Magee, an artilleryman in Bragg's army, fretted during the retreat that Buell would cut them off. They were on short rations and some of the men went hungry. His worries soon faded. "The arrival of wagons from the Gap put an end to all fears about Buell cutting us off," he wrote on October 16. "He is certainly proving a traitor to his government, for he had it all but done, and has let us pass."[80]

Recriminations began almost immediately. Seemingly everyone connected (or not) to the campaign heaped blame upon Bragg. Even his wife criticized his generalship, as well as his failure to defeat Buell and clear Kentucky of Union forces. Supporters remained, though they proved not as noisy as the critics. He also still held the confidence of the only one (except perhaps for Mrs. Bragg) who mattered: Jefferson Davis. Bragg seemed to be getting a reputation similar to McClellan's: that of a general who could drill and train his army but not use it in the field.[81]

Leadership on both sides had been found wanting. Buell, McClellan, and Bragg all consistently sat when action and daring were called for, though Bragg was less guilty here. Bragg also would have benefited from having Kirby Smith under his direction. The split command structure, for which Davis bears the blame, may have doomed the Confederate western offensive from the start.[82] Halleck and Lincoln did little better. Halleck—a clerk, as Lincoln had judged, and not even a first-rate one—consistently refused to exercise his command. And leaving Buell in his post was undoubtedly a mistake. Lee's actions risked much—his entire army, and with this, the fate of the Confederacy—when he had only a small hope of accomplishing the operational objectives of his campaign, much less the strategic ones.

Lincoln did not leave his mistake in keeping Buell in command stand uncorrected for long. Once the Confederates withdrew into eastern Tennessee,

Buell insisted he could no longer pursue and that he would withdraw his men to protect Nashville, his base for defensive as well as offensive action. Simultaneously, he insisted that the only true security for Kentucky lay in seizing the very areas of eastern Tennessee that he had so consistently refused to free.[83] Halleck responded with fury and, surprisingly, even a little wisdom. "The great object to be attained is to drive the enemy from Kentucky and East Tennessee," he seethed. "If we cannot do it now, we need never to hope for it." He demanded Buell find some route to force the Confederates out of these areas. He stressed the occupation of Chattanooga and Knoxville, the seizure of which would keep the Rebels out of Tennessee and Kentucky. Plus, he pointed out that Buell stood nearer to both these cities than to his proposed base of Nashville. "The capture of East Tennessee should be the main object of your campaign," he wrote. "You say it is the heart of the enemy's resources; make it the heart of yours. Your army can live there if the enemy's can." He also relayed the administration's discontent, noting that Lincoln did not understand "why we cannot march as the enemy marches, live as he lives, and fight as he fights, unless we admit the inferiority of our troops and of our generals. Once hold the valley of the Upper Tennessee, and the operations of guerrillas in that State and Kentucky will soon cease."[84] Lincoln was no longer interested in excuses, and the instructions to live off the land reveal to what degree the war had escalated. In the beginning, almost no Union commander would have considered such an order. Halleck had given Pope a similar order in August, telling him, "Live on the country as much as possible till we can supply you."[85]

Buell gave his defense, though it wasn't much of one, and violated Henry Kissinger's rule of never coming off second-best in your own dispatch: "We can give good reasons why we cannot do all that the enemy has attempted to do, such as operating without a base, &c., without ascribing the difference to the inferiority of our generals, though that may be true. The spirit of the rebellion enforces a subordination and patient submission to privation and want which public sentiment renders absolutely impossible among our troops."[86]

But Lincoln's patience was gone. Buell's torpor, his blatant disobedience of orders, and political pressure upon the president from three governors whose states' residents made up the majority of Buell's army all combined to get him ousted. On October 24, 1862, Halleck placed William Rosecrans in charge of the Department of the Cumberland.[87] Eight days before, John Nicolay, one of Lincoln's secretaries, wrote: "Buell, after turning over and rubbing his eyes a little, week before last, suddenly [has] gone to sleep again more soundly than ever. It is rather a good thing to be a Major General and in command of a Department. One can take things so leisurely!"[88]

Cumulative Failure

THE FALL OF 1862 unfolded a story of dramatic failure and missed opportunities. Strategically, the Union had made particularly grave errors. In his *Memoirs* Grant wrote that after the fall of Corinth, Halleck had 80,000 men who could have been used for active operations against the Confederates, plus new troops coming into service. Instead, Halleck set Buell to repairing rail lines. "If he had been sent directly to Chattanooga as rapidly as he could march," Grant wrote, "leaving two or three divisions along the line of the railroad from Nashville forward, he could have arrived with but little fighting, and would have saved much of the loss of life which was afterwards incurred in gaining Chattanooga."[89] Bragg's offensive was only the beginning of this bitter harvest.

Buell failed dramatically. Operationally, he could have separated Bragg's army from its base of supply, leaving it to wither or flee, and he could have done this by seizing Chattanooga and its critical supporting rail net when Bragg struck out for the Ohio. An operational success of this magnitude could have laid the foundation for the destruction of Bragg's army, an achievement of strategic importance that, if not a war-winning one, was certainly a requirement for a final Union victory. Instead, he marched *north*. He failed to accomplish much here either and let the Confederates quietly withdraw when pursuit could have increased the injury done to Bragg's army.

McClellan failed tactically, operationally, and strategically. When Lee took the enormous risk of dividing his forces as he moved north, he gave McClellan the chance to defeat him in detail. But Lee had read his enemy correctly, and McClellan proceeded to miss opportunities to possibly destroy or at least severely maul Lee's army before Antietam, during the battle itself, and when Lee withdrew into Virginia. McClellan did not understand the enemy, the nature of the war, nor what was necessary for winning it.

Lincoln also failed. He had ended his famous note of October 13 to McClellan on the general's "over-cautiousness" by saying, "This letter is in no sense an order."[90] It should have been. As we have seen, Lincoln often interjected himself into the strategic and operational decisions of the army, but we have also seen something that flies in the face of most of the interpretations of Lincoln as a strategist: *none of his interventions was having any significant beneficial impact upon the strategic and operational course of the war.* Lincoln suggested. He did not order. The story of Union strategy in the summer and fall of 1862 is a litany of missed opportunities. These failures came from the top.

The Confederacy made its mistakes as well. In the West, the South would have been well served by closer coordination between all the attacking elements, especially those under Bragg and Kirby Smith, as well as the establishment of clearer operational objectives for all of the offensive prongs. Instead, too much of the operational plan boiled down to marching north and hoping good things happened. This is not good operational warfare. Moreover, both Lee and Bragg had stuck their heads into nooses, creating the potential for strategic disaster in the form of the destruction of the South's two primary armies. They were fortunate their enemies refused to tighten the knot.

Afterward, Bragg noted that his offensive had been founded on a flawed assessment. "The campaign here was predicated on a belief and the most positive assurances that the people of this country would rise in mass to assert their independence," he wrote Richmond. "Willing perhaps to accept their independence, they are neither disposed nor willing to risk their lives or their property in its achievement."[91] This applied equally to Lee's campaign in Maryland.

For all of their effort and bloodshed (the forces of Bragg, Van Dorn and Price endured more than 11,300 casualties; Lee suffered as many as 14,000 at Antietam alone), the Confederate invasions had gained very little. Secretary of War Randolph later commented that since Bragg's expedition brought out much loot—a million yards of cloth, 15,000 stand of arms, ammunition, horses, and other items—"it was not without its fruits."[92] This was true, and Bragg made a similar point. But this was hardly compensation for a wasted campaign season—and wasted lives. As Shelby Foote wisely observed, "What had been announced as a full-scale offensive, designed to establish and maintain the northern boundary of the Confederacy along the Ohio River, had degenerated into a giant raid."[93]

The Confederate western offensive did accomplish something, however. To meet it the Union had been forced to gather in most of its troops from northern Alabama, abandoning that area, as well as much of central Tennessee and the Cumberland Gap.[94] By comparison, Lee's invasion of Maryland had accomplished nothing and cost more. Worst of all, neither of these Confederate operations had moved the South any farther toward accomplishing its political objective. The shift to an offensive strategy had failed. Things might have been different, especially in the West, where poor coordination and operational ineptness greatly reduced the chances of Confederate success against a commander who proved one of the weakest of Union Western reeds.

The shattering of the Confederacy's cordon defense had proven that the South could not defend its borders. The South's offensive strategy of 1862 proved it could not project power beyond the areas it held. In early November 1862, Confederate Colonel William Thomas, the commander of the Legion of Indians and Highlanders, wrote Davis, "Summer is gone; fall has come. During the latter we came near losing East Tennessee. At present we have to look out for the future."[95]

13

Facing the Arithmetic

ESCALATION AND DESTRUCTION

*It is a great annoyance to gain rank and command enough
to attract public attention. I have found it so and would now
really prefer some little command where public attention
would not attract.*

—ULYSSES S. GRANT, October 24, 1862

BEFORE THE CONFEDERATE SUMMER OFFENSIVE unwound itself, and as it trudged to its pointless end, several things lay the foundations for the Union's next moves in the West. In August, following the Federal failure to reduce the Confederate bastion, Halleck had broached the idea of a drive on Vicksburg as soon as the troops were ready. Meanwhile, he had maintained Union forces in the field in Arkansas to keep the Confederates out of Missouri.[1] The next month, he initiated planning for a combined offensive by forces under Grant and Frederick Steele to attack Confederate gunboat-building operations on the Yazoo River. The immediate effect of this was to give birth to the idea of a two-pronged, joint army-navy drive on Vicksburg. A joint force would go down the Mississippi, supported by troops making an overland march along the Mississippi Central Railroad from Memphis.[2]

In October, Sherman chimed in. William Tecumseh Sherman graduated from West Point in 1840, sixth in his class of forty-two. His father died when he was nine, leaving the family destitute. He and some of his ten brothers and sisters were farmed out to relatives and friends, and "Cump," as he was called, was fortunate enough to make his new home with Thomas Ewing, a prominent Lancaster, Ohio, attorney. Sherman spent the Mexican War in California but left the army in 1853. He became a successful banker for a while, and then a mediocre lawyer, before landing at the head of a military school being established in Alexandria, Louisiana, one that later became Louisiana State University. He reentered the army when the war began and was a brigade commander at Bull Run.[3] Now a major general, he sent Grant his view of how the North should be waging the war in the West, as well as an astute assessment of the attitudes of Southerners, particularly those in his command area. He believed Union forces should take control of the Mississippi and not bother trying to garrison interior areas. Such units were vulnerable to destruction and did nothing to bring people back to the Union. "They cannot be made to love us," he wrote, "but may be made to fear us, and dread the passage of troops through their country." He then suggested a form of raiding that later became part of how the North fought the war: "With the Mississippi safe we could land troops at any point, and by a quick march break the railroad, where we could make ourselves so busy that our descent would be dreaded the whole length of the river, and by the loss of negroes and other property [they] would in time discover that war is not the remedy for the political evils of which they complained." He continued, "We know that all the South is in arms and deep in enmity, and we know that every man available for war in the North should now be in motion. We cannot change the hearts of those people of the South, but we can make war so terrible that they will realize the fact that, however brave and gallant and devoted to their country, still they are mortal and should exhaust all peaceful remedies before they fly to war. This is all I hope for, and even this will take time and vast numbers."[4] Sherman realized that public willingness to continue was a potential Southern center of gravity. One defeated a determined and implacable foe not by changing their hearts but by instilling fear. He understood his enemy. And he understood how to hurt them.

By the end of October 1862, Grant had grown frustrated with the lack of direction from his superior in Washington. "You have never suggested to me any plan of operations in this Department," he told Halleck. Grant offered his own, contending that the best chance for progress was the destruction of the railroads leading to Corinth as well as to Columbus, opening the railroad from Humboldt to Memphis, and uniting the forces from Bolivar and Corinth at Grand Junction. "With small reinforcements at Memphis I think I would be able to move down the Mississippi Central road and cause the evacuation of Vicksburg and be able to capture or destroy all the boats in the Yazoo river."[5]

In comparison to his latter proposals, Grant was offering a simple operational plan with limited, local goals. However, he did mention one objective that both sides had determined possessed strategic importance: Vicksburg. Grant was beginning the quest that would make him famous—and teach him how to win the war.

Halleck supported the move and began sending the necessary reinforcements, some of which he obtained by limiting the strategically pointless operations in Arkansas. These troops would be used to inflict a direct strike against the Confederates instead of a peripheral blow. "I hope for an active campaign on the Mississippi this fall," Halleck told Grant. He also planned to support the southward drive to clear the Mississippi with one launched northward from New Orleans.[6]

In November 1862, President Lincoln appointed Major General Nathaniel Banks commander of the Department of the Gulf and sent him to relieve Butler at New Orleans. Banks, before the war a Massachusetts politician, was one of the commanders who had failed so miserably in the Shenandoah Valley earlier in the year. Halleck gave Banks orders that were very specific, if also very contradictory, giving him two objectives—"opening of the Mississippi and the reduction of Fort Morgan or Mobile City, in order to control that bay and harbor." Halleck also provided help. The naval forces in the Gulf and on the Mississippi were to support Banks, and Halleck added that "a military and naval expedition is organizing at Memphis and Cairo to move down the Mississippi and cooperate with you against Vicksburg and any other points which the enemy may occupy on that river." He confided to Banks that Lincoln believed the opening of the Mississippi to be "the first and most important of all our military and naval operations, and it is hoped that you will not lose a moment in accomplishing it."[7] But if the Mississippi was so important, why did Halleck tell Banks to take Mobile and its defenses as well?

Halleck also gave his thoughts on future Union moves after clearing the Mississippi: the capture of Vicksburg; the destruction of key rail lines at Jackson and Marion to sever links between northern Mississippi, Mobile, and Atlanta; and an advance up the Red River.[8]

The scope and intent of the Union offensive in the Western Theater was becoming clear: "It is believed that the operations of General Rosecrans in East Tennessee, of General Grant in Northern Mississippi, and of General Steele in Arkansas," Halleck wrote Banks, "will give full employment to the enemy's troops in the West, and thus prevent them from concentrating in force against you. Should they do so, you will be re-enforced by detachments from one or more of these commands."[9]

Halleck, in all of this, was finally playing the role of general in chief. He gave his subordinates clear, obtainable operational objectives and attempted to coordinate actions over a wide area so that the Union moves supported one another. Properly, he also allowed the commanders on the ground the freedom to seek the objective as they wished. He wrote Banks: "These instructions are not intended to tie your hands or to hamper your operations in the slightest degree. So far away from headquarters, you must necessarily exercise your own judgment and discretion in regard to your movements against the enemy, keeping in view that the opening of the Mississippi River is now the great and primary object of your expedition."[10] Clear operational objective, yet freedom of action in achieving it; all of Halleck's communiqués should have been this way. Halleck's note also made clear what had now become the North's strategic priority: opening the Mississippi River.

Complicating the Union's plans for the West was Grant's troublesome subordinate, Major General John A. McClernand. A War Democrat and former Illinois politician, he journeyed to Washington to give his own campaign plan to Lincoln and Stanton. Late in the summer of 1862, McClernand argued that the administration had to open the Mississippi River to grain transportation or risk losing the political support of the upper Midwest— and had to do this as quickly as possible. Similar fears had been raised in an August 3 cabinet meeting. Halleck agreed that it should be cleared, but he had no enthusiasm to do it with the new troops the administration intended to raise for the purpose. McClernand, of course, intended to lead the expedition, and his willingness to actually fight earned him a sympathetic hearing among administration officials wearied by talking generals. Halleck, though, had no confidence in McClernand's ability to direct such an operation and told McClernand that he would not support the general's plan. Grant found McClernand insubordinate at best and didn't want him in his area of command; he was, however, given little choice.[11]

Lincoln and Stanton gave McClernand orders to recruit the necessary forces, but there were strings attached: General Grant had to not need them, and the general in chief had the discretion to decide their ultimate use. Lincoln had stacked the deck against McClernand. The Union would soon get the troops, and the better commander would end up leading them. The administration's show of support for McClernand had more to do with politics than anything else. Similarly, political concerns had driven Lincoln's approval of a Banks-led expedition to Texas, an expedition supported by New England free labor and textile interests but which was eventually abandoned in favor of the more important Mississippi River campaign.[12]

Before Banks's departure to take up his new command, Lincoln warned him, as he had done with so many of the general's colleagues, against making excessive preparations and the "piling up of *impedimenta*," which "has been, so far, almost our ruin, and will be our final ruin if it is not abandoned.... You must be off before Congress meets." Yet Banks failed to advance against the enemy in the fall of 1862, something that at this moment set him apart from the other Union field commanders. In fact, he did not even reach New Orleans to take up his new command until December 14.[13] Lincoln would have to wait for the Mississippi's opening.

Lincoln was far from being the only one fed up with Union generals who offered excuses instead of actions. Buell's old command had been taken up by

Grant's former subordinate, Major General William S. Rosecrans. Halleck instructed "Old Rosy," as he was called by his men, to "drive the enemy from Kentucky and Middle Tennessee" and then "take and hold East Tennessee, cutting the line of railroad at Chattanooga, Cleveland, or Athens, so as to destroy the connection of the valley of Virginia with Georgia and the other Southern States." Halleck told Rosecrans to travel light and quickly, foraging off the enemy. "The time has now come when we must apply the sterner rules of war, whenever such application becomes necessary," Halleck wrote. To support Rosecrans in middle and eastern Tennessee, Halleck sent another force up the Kanawha River. In early October, Halleck had begun massing troops at Point Pleasant, on what is now the Ohio–West Virginia border, for this move.[14]

The Union prepared for action in the East under the new commander of the Army of the Potomac, Major General Ambrose Burnside. Burnside had earlier led a successful independent command in North Carolina and then served as a corps commander under McClellan. He was best known for his luxuriant side-whiskers, which became known as *burnsides* and, later, *sideburns*. He insisted the job as commander was beyond him, and he was offered it three times before he finally bent.[15] If for nothing else, one must praise him for his honesty and self-awareness.

On November 5 Halleck told Burnside that upon taking up his new post he was to report what he planned to do with his men.[16] Burnside replied a few days later from Warrenton, Virginia: "To concentrate all the forces near this place, and impress upon the enemy a belief that we are to attack Culpeper or Gordonsville, and at the same time accumulate a four or five days' supply for the men and animals; then make a rapid move of the whole force to Fredericksburg, with a view to a movement upon Richmond from that point."[17]

To Burnside, this route to Richmond addressed the administration's great concern about the safety of the capital because the Army of the Potomac would always be closer to Washington than the enemy was. This line of advance also made it less likely that the Confederates could try to attack Washington or invade Pennsylvania. More important, this was the most direct route to Richmond, which he believed "should be the great object of the campaign, as the fall of that place would tend more to cripple the rebel cause than almost any other military event, except the absolute breaking up of their army."[18]

Lincoln quickly approved Burnside's plan with a caveat. "He thinks that it will succeed," Halleck wrote Burnside, "if you move very rapidly; otherwise not."[19]

This was the final major piece in the Union's strategic program for the fall of 1862: Grant and Banks on the Mississippi, Rosecrans in eastern

Tennessee, and Burnside against Richmond. The administration intended to do as McClellan had originally suggested in his grand plan, and what Lincoln had adopted as his philosophy for fighting the war—attack on several fronts at once. But the Union's operational planning remained focused on securing geographical objectives, the seizure of which would not deliver a decisive result. Clearing the Mississippi and taking Vicksburg would help the North in future operations but not destroy the South's war-making capacity or will. Some argued that clearing the river would strengthen the administration's political standing in the Northwest, a region that before the war depended upon the river to move its grain to foreign ports. Union railroads could do this, and did, though the farmers paid more, and Great Britain continued being a loyal customer for Yankee grain. But nothing would better solidify northwestern political support than winning the war. Even if it cleared eastern Tennessee as ordered, Rosecrans's campaign would not produce any substantial result. And even if Burnside took the Confederate capital, it would not bring an end to the war, though the blow would be severe.

In early November 1862, though, a burst of optimism struck Halleck. "Our prospect of an early movement down the Mississippi is improving," he wrote Banks. "In fact, while things remain almost in statu quo here: where Archimedes with his longest lever could not move the army, at the West everything begins to look well again."[20] Lincoln was not as buoyant, and worried that his new generals would prove no different from the old ones. "I certainly have been dissatisfied with the slowness of Buell and McClellan," he wrote Union general Carl Schurz, "but before I relieved them I had great fears I should not find successors to them, who would do better; and I am sorry to add, that I have seen little since to relieve those fears. I do not clearly see the prospect of any more rapid movements. I fear we shall at last find out that the difficulty is in our case, rather than in particular generals."[21]

The South's Response

THOUGH IT MADE GREAT USE of their resources to push the South at various points, Union planning did not give much consideration to the actions of the enemy. Recriminations followed Bragg from Kentucky, but Davis refused to relieve him. Unknowingly, he echoed the concerns of his counterpart across the Potomac, admitting, "That another Genl. might excite more enthusiasm is probable, but as all have their defects I have not seen how to make a change with advantage to the public service." He also appreciated Bragg's strengths, noting that "his administrative capacity has been felt by the army of Missi. [H]is knowledge of the troops is intimate and a new man would not probably for a time with even greater ability be equally useful."[22] To Davis, replacing Bragg would create more problems than it would resolve.

While his generals tried to avoid blame or attach it to someone else, Davis planned yet another attempt to recover the lost territory in the West. He had hoped for a combined offensive by Pemberton in Mississippi and, once Pemberton solidified his defenses, by Lieutenant General Theophilus H. Holmes in Arkansas. He thought that if Pemberton and Holmes drove the enemy from Arkansas and the occupied areas of Tennessee, this, in combination with the establishment of "strong batteries on the Mississippi," would make Confederate moves against Missouri and Kentucky more feasible. This he saw as important, insisting that "until this can be done the War cannot be driven from our interior and the resources of our country will rapidly decline to insufficiency for the support of an army."[23] Like Lee, Davis clearly saw the necessity of holding on to territory sufficient to provide the resources and personnel for waging a successful war. A Fabian strategy, particularly one necessitating the temporary abandonment of such territory, would erode the South's ability to fight.

Bragg's retreat from Kentucky and Van Dorn's defeat at Corinth changed the strategic situation in the West, and Davis told Holmes to abandon a planned move into Missouri. Davis believed that the North's continued possession of western Tennessee and the Mississippi River prevented any such advance. He also thought such an attempt would leave Holmes's force too much in danger from a rise in the waters of the Arkansas, White, and Francis rivers, which, if it happened, would enable the North to break his communications, take his base, "and reduce your army to an alternative which cannot be willingly accepted."[24]

His idea became a combined offensive by the Confederacy's western armies: Holmes in Arkansas, Pemberton in western Tennessee, and Bragg in central Tennessee. Davis hoped that if this could be done while the rivers were still low, Union forces could be driven from Tennessee and Arkansas, and sufficient fortifications built and garrisoned along the Mississippi to give the Confederates control of the river south of Memphis and north of Port Hudson. He saw this as preparing the ground for an advance into Kentucky and Missouri and insisted that "the recapture of Helena, of Memphis, and of Nashville involving the defeat of three armies, seems to me the objects for our present effort." He urged communication, cooperation, and coordination among the three commanders, as well as the "concentration of two or when practicable of all of the columns in the attack upon one of the enemy's armies."[25] Later, in response to a note about the defense of the Mississippi, Davis would remark that this would be "best affected by attacking & defeating the enemy's best army wherever formed."[26]

Davis's thinking was certainly in line with that of Bragg, who wrote to Davis on October 23 of his intent to occupy middle Tennessee as soon as possible and hold the area between the Tennessee and Cumberland rivers during the coming winter. His army needed the resources there, and he hoped to deny them to the Union. Bragg also saw a chance to conquer Buell by uniting Confederate forces and attacking while other Southern armies pinned Union forces in western Tennessee.[27]

Davis looked at an advance into middle Tennessee as a means of influencing Confederate public opinion, which had been injured by the failure of the recent Confederate offensive into Tennessee and Kentucky. He wrote Kirby Smith that he hoped for the Union's defeat, recruitment success, and supplies for the army. Moreover, he looked for a movement to Rosecrans's rear, whereupon "he shall be checked or compelled to retire," resulting in the "relief" of the territory east of the Mississippi River. "If on the other hand," Davis continued, "he should advance to cooperate in an attack on Mobile or Vicksburg your forces will have to aid in that quarter and abandon the less vital point of Middle Tenn. Holmes is getting a large army in Arks. And will I hope be able to attack the Enemy successfully on the west side of the Missi. and embarrass him in the use of the river." Davis believed that Bragg could not move into middle Tennessee unless Smith coordinated with him.[28]

Bragg journeyed to Richmond for a week of meetings with Davis and Secretary of War Randolph at the end of October. On November 1, he received the order to march, the president having approved Bragg's October 31 campaign plan, which was a movement aimed at taking Nashville. Bragg and Kirby Smith were ordered to advance, leaving sufficient forces to defend Cumberland Gap and the Tennessee Railroad east of Chattanooga.[29]

However, approving the plan did not mean movement against the enemy; Lincoln could certainly vouch for that. After leaving Richmond, Bragg quickly decided that his army was in no condition for an immediate offensive, especially against a more numerous enemy entrenched in Nashville.[30] He returned to his base at Tullahoma and concentrated on training and equipping the many ragged and barefoot troops in his ranks. He had 40,000 infantry and artillery and 10,000 cavalry. He dispatched 5,000 horsemen in two detachments under his raiders Colonel Morgan and General Forrest to do "partizan [sic] service, for which, and which alone, their commanders are peculiarly & specially suited." Morgan was to fight north of the Cumberland, attacking

Union communications and supply lines, while Forrest worked south of the river to Nashville's west. Using his guns, he was to attack enemy river transports and bridges along both the Cumberland and Tennessee rivers, then cross the Tennessee into the Union rear "and harass him generally." All of this cavalry activity, Bragg hoped, would "create a diversion in favor of Pemberton" and force the enemy to retreat from Mississippi.[31] Bragg's remark about "partizan service" recalled a mode of warfare from an earlier age. A common eighteenth-century practice was to send units on detached service to harass the enemy. The Colonials fought this way during the Revolutionary War.

Bragg then concentrated the rest of his army at Murfreesboro and its turnpike approach. He had his cavalry placed at his front, keeping the Union forces from foraging on the Confederate side of the Cumberland River. His information told him that the Union had 60,000 men in Nashville. Bragg knew he had no hope of assaulting the intensive Federal works but was confident of defeating them in the open—if he could draw them out, which was what the cavalry raiding was intended to do. Bragg's operations had some success, allowing him to gather supplies from a wide area, deny them to Rosecrans, and all but besiege the Union army in Nashville.[32]

War in Virginia

ANOTHER CONFEDERATE GENERAL also seemed to draw on Washington's example to help him fight the war. In the eastern theater, to defend the Confederacy's recovered Virginia, Lee adopted an operational Fabian strategy of avoiding battle. Union numerical superiority drove Lee to conclude that it was "preferable to attempt to baffle his designs by maneuvering, rather than to resist his advance by main force. To accomplish the latter without too great risk and loss, would require more than double our present numbers." He put Jackson's forces in the Shenandoah Valley, to threaten the Union's flank and rear if they decided to move east of the Blue Ridge Mountains. Lieutenant General James Longstreet's troops were left where they could hit the Union army's rear and cut its communications if it tried to penetrate the Shenandoah. Lee was attempting to "baffle the advance of the enemy and retain him among the mountains" until he could get him "separated" so that he might "strike at him to advantage." Lee sought to avoid battle, confuse the enemy, encourage him to separate his forces, and then defeat him in detail. He was trying to use aggressive maneuver to gain advantage over his more numerous foe. Lee, here and at other times, sought to wage his war in a manner similar to that of George Washington in the wake of his disastrous defeat in New York: avoid battle and wait, striking when it is advantageous to do so. But not all of his thinking in early November 1862 was defensive; he also considered a move into Maryland.[33]

When Burnside replaced McClellan as the head of the Army of the Potomac, Lee feared that the Union army would be put south of the James River. He didn't believe his army was in a state to advance against Burnside and feared doing so would impair its ability to conduct future operations. Nonetheless, as he wrote Randolph, "partial operations" were under way, "tending to embarrass and damage the enemy."[34] He urged an active defense of North Carolina, perhaps meaning one conducted in the spirit of his defense of northern Virginia, but he did not advise a direct advance against the enemy's forces.[35]

Burnside began moving the Army of the Potomac on November 16. Lee remained unsure of the Union's path of advance. By November 25, Lee thought Burnside was concentrating his army opposite Fredericksburg. He urged preparations for the defense of Richmond and unity of effort in resisting the Union thrust aimed at the capital, "which if defeated, may prove the last." Lee also had the advantage of good information on Burnside's plans from Northern newspapers, which reported that Burnside would advance on Richmond from Fredericksburg. Lee concluded that if Burnside could be forced to "change his base of operations the effect produced in the United States would be equivalent to a defeat." He also wrote that the longer "we can delay him and throw him into the winter, the more difficult will be his undertaking." Lee decided to make Fredericksburg his base and meet Burnside there.[36]

By November 28 Lee began wavering from his conclusion that Burnside would cross at Fredericksburg by considering a Union crossing lower down the Rappahannock, if at all, though it was difficult to cross below Fredericksburg at the time.[37] He also worried that Burnside's inaction meant his Union opponent was waiting for a subsidiary attack elsewhere, perhaps south of the James River. He asked that troops from quiet areas in the West and South be sent to Richmond to support him.[38] Davis agreed with the necessity of concentrating troops for the "impending struggle on the North and South side of Richmond."[39]

Burnside had hesitated, but it was not the general who shied from the whip; it was his president. Lincoln had serious doubts about Burnside's operational plan. On the twenty-fifth he asked for a meeting with the general.[40] Burnside believed the bulk of Lee's army lay across the river at Fredericksburg, and he thought to cross and push them away. Burnside saw this as "somewhat risky." Lincoln decided to mitigate the risk, and not only in this local attack. He believed it more important to make sure Lee's army didn't get away and simply get stronger as it fell back on its communications to Richmond's trenches.

"I therefore propose," Lincoln wrote Halleck, "that Gen. B. shall not move immediately." Lincoln wanted to first gather supporting forces on the Rappahannock's south bank: as many as 25,000 men at Port Royal, Virginia, southeast of Fredericksburg, supported by a gunboat or two, and another similar force, also with gunboats, as far up the Pamunkey River as possible. All three forces would then move in unison, with Burnside's army crossing at Fredericksburg, the Rappahannock force marching along the river's south bank, or if possible, toward Richmond, while the Pamunkey army pushed up its river, grabbing the bridges as it went, and maybe even marching far enough to destroy the railroad trestles along both the Pamunkey and Mattaponi. "Then," Lincoln continued, "if Gen. B. succeeds in driving the enemy from Fredericksburg, he[,] the enemy[,] no longer has the road to Richmond, but we have it and can march into the city. Or, possibly, having forced the enemy from his line, we could move upon, and destroy his army." All the units would have secure lines of supply and safe retreat routes, if needed. The smaller forces even had gunboat support to fall back upon. Lincoln thought his plan had the best chance for success, with the least risk, of any they then had.[41]

Since taking up residence at the White House, Lincoln had become a pretty good operational planner and a believer in simultaneous advances. The hallmarks of his strategic thinking were here applied operationally. Lincoln had supporting attacks designed to weaken the enemy and open up opportunities, alternative courses of advance so that if something favorable developed it could be taken advantage of, and secure communications for resupply or retreat. Most important, he believed in fighting not just to win a battle but to deal a heavy blow to the enemy's ability to fight further. To do this, he sought to strike a potential Rebel center of gravity: their army or their capital.

As we've seen abundantly, Lincoln's problem was that his generals did not view things this way. Halleck, undoubtedly scratching his elbows (which Gideon Welles said he did "as if that was the seat of thought"), pronounced the plan undoable, as did his subordinate Burnside. They felt it would take too long to raise the force necessary for the "Pamunkey thrust."[42] Halleck did try to get Major General John Dix, the commander of the Union forces at Fortress Monroe, to mount a diversion in support of Burnside. Dix insisted he could not, and Halleck, as usual, did not find it in him to order a subordinate to do his job.[43]

Lee had no cause to worry about subsidiary operations. Burnside would move exactly where Lee had guessed he would. Burnside began pushing the first elements of his 120,000 men across the Rappahannock at Fredericksburg on December 13, 1862. Unclear communications from Burnside, as well as Halleck's mishandling of the preparations, delayed the attack, giving Lee ample time to entrench his 75,000 men on the hills behind the town. This threw Burnside's tactical plan off-kilter. He had hoped to cross the Rappahannock and move through Fredericksburg before Lee arrived. Undeterred, Burnside decided to mount a two-pronged attack, one through the town and against the Confederates on Marye's Heights above it, the other 3 miles south against the enemy positions there. It took two weeks to complete the necessary bridges. Burnside then threw his men against the well-prepared enemy. His massed infantry attacks broke against Marye's Heights. Meanwhile Major General William B. Franklin, who commanded the southern prong, chose not to overwhelm the Confederates to his front and instead sent in a single division, led by George Gordon Meade, that serendipitously struck the only break in the Confederate line. But Franklin didn't support them, and the Confederates rushed to plug the hole. In the end the Confederates inflicted a gruesome defeat on the Army of the Potomac, and 13,000 casualties to the South's 5,000.[44]

Lee fought at Fredericksburg not only to keep the Union from advancing upon Richmond but because doing so would preserve a larger part of Virginia from which he could draw supplies for his forces. In the battle's aftermath, he concluded that the enemy's strength was so great that the best manner of fighting him was to "draw him further away from his base of operations."[45]

The Union had its own after-action assessment. Even though the Union lost 50 percent more men than the enemy, Lincoln said to one of his private secretaries that "if the same battle were to be fought over again, every day, through a week of days, with the same relative results, the army under Lee would be wiped out to its last man, the Army of the Potomac would still be a mighty host, the war would be over, the Confederacy gone." Lincoln went on to conclude that "no General yet found can face the arithmetic, but the end of the war will be at hand when he shall be discovered."[46] Lincoln was a bit off with his numbers (about 120,000 Yankees faced off against 75,000 or so Rebels), but he had made his point. Lincoln believed that the North needed to destroy Lee's army in order to triumph. He didn't see Richmond as what Clausewitz would term a center of gravity, the source of the Confederates' strength. Lincoln realized that the Confederacy did not derive its power from a single, fixed geographical point. Lee's Army of Northern Virginia itself provided one of the South's key centers. Indeed, Lincoln, in a later letter to Halleck, insisted that he had wished the Army of the Potomac to make Lee's army "its objective point" ever since the failure of McClellan's Peninsula Campaign.[47] Though no early order for such action seems to have survived, John Hay recorded in his diary that during the Second Manassas campaign, Lincoln "often repeated, 'We must hurt this enemy before it gets away.'"[48] Attrition was one of the keys to achieving this. And this comes from hard fighting.

Many people had advice for Burnside after the Battle of Fredericksburg. Quartermaster General Montgomery Meigs warned him of the potential monetary and logistical collapse of the Union if the army did not deliver victory on the banks of the Rappahannock. Meigs urged him to risk a major battle and to try to destroy the Rebel army, seeing to it that the offensive be mounted in such a way as to prevent the Confederates from retreating into their works around Richmond. Meigs also reached beyond reality by writing, "The rebel army will not fight if it is too much outnumbered, but, by retiring to North Carolina, will compel long lines of operations and exhaust us in enormous expenditures."[49]

In late December, a pair of Union generals urged Lincoln to concentrate the Union's eastern forces, raise an army of 250,000, and land it on either side of the James River. This would put them about 20 miles from Richmond, and they would get there without having to fight. The army would also throw off most of its baggage and advance "more like an immense partisan corps than a modern army." (Here is yet another allusion to eighteenth-century warfare.) They foresaw the forces striking at the capital and the railroads south of it. They did not know whether it would bring about the destruction of the Confederate army, but believed it would lead to the seizure of Richmond, thus materially damaging the Confederate ability to wage war. To get the necessary troops, they wanted to strip the Union forces in Florida, North Carolina, and South Carolina to the bare minimum. They made their proposal because they were convinced the current campaign had no chance of success, but Lincoln pointed out that they had revived the same old problem: leaving Washington uncovered. Realistic or not, the measure was a manifestation of an immense dilemma facing the Army of the Potomac: a loss of confidence in its commander.[50]

Their plan was not unlike one suggested in late November by John G. Barnard, the Army of the Potomac's chief engineer. Barnard believed the best approach was to support the overland drive on Richmond (which would pin the Confederate forces) with the landing of 50,000 men on the south bank of the James River. This force would then capture Richmond's communications lines to the south and try to take the city, thus destroying its war-making industries. Even if they could not take Richmond, he argued, the troops would force the Rebels on the Rappahannock to retreat, allowing the Union to sever the city's other rail connections.[51] Some believed this plan had merit.

After his defeat at Fredericksburg, Burnside remained determined to advance, but his subordinate commanders resisted. On New Year's Day, 1863, Lincoln told Halleck to talk to the other generals, examine the situation, and make a decision as to what should be done. He had brought Halleck to Washington for his military advice, he reminded the general in chief, and "if in such a difficulty as this you do not help, you fail me precisely in the point for which I sought your assistance." The president also revealed his frustration with the indecisive Halleck: "Your military skill is useless to me if you will not do this."[52] An offended Halleck tendered his resignation.[53] Lincoln refused it.

New Year's proved a rich day for resignations. Burnside gave his in a letter in which he revealed his lack of confidence in the secretary of war—as well as in Halleck—and his view that these feelings were shared not only by the army at large but also by the country in general: "It seems to be the universal opinion that the movements of the army have not been planned with a view to co-operation and mutual assistance." In addition, given that only one of his commanders supported his plans for movement south, Burnside felt it best to leave his post.[54] Lincoln didn't let him go then, or a few days later when he tried again to resign.

Halleck concluded that Burnside should push across the Rappahannock again by whatever route he deemed practicable. He also reminded him that "in all our interviews I have urged that our first object was, not Richmond, but the defeat or scattering of Lee's army, which threatened Washington and the line of the Upper Potomac." Moreover, he added, "the great object is to occupy the enemy, to prevent his making large detachments or distant raids, and to injure him all you can with the least injury to yourself."[55]

Burnside advanced again on January 20, but when he did, the skies unleashed a torrential downpour, trapping the Army of the Potomac in what became known as the "Mud March." Burnside abandoned the offensive two days later. Morale, weakened by Fredericksburg, had been further undermined by the petty and unprofessional behavior of Burnside's subordinates. Major General William B. Franklin brazenly and openly criticized Burnside's plan, demoralizing the men of his command, and also led a contingent of four generals to complain to Lincoln. Burnside told the president to remove the fractious (who numbered eight), or he would go. Lincoln did a bit of both. He relieved Burnside, exiled some of his detractors westward, and appointed one, "Fighting Joe" Hooker, as a replacement.[56]

WHEN HALLECK ISSUED HIS INSTRUCTIONS about foraging from the enemy, Rosecrans complied immediately. Unlike Buell, Rosecrans felt no impulse toward conciliation of the enemy. Yet even with this latitude his army found it difficult to accumulate enough supplies for offensive operations.[57] This, nonetheless, was what his superiors demanded.

Halleck did not expect Rosecrans to move unsupported and promised an advance on his Tennessee-Virginia flank that he hoped would attract some of Bragg's forces: "In connection with your proposed operations in Middle and East Tennessee, a column of about 20,000 men, under General Cox, is moving up the Kanawha River, and it is hoped that they will be able to cut the railroad near Newbern or Wytheville."[58] None of this got Rosecrans's Army of the Cumberland moving southward. The general did promise that if the Confederates fought for middle Tennessee, "we shall be able to crush them by decisive battle." But Rosecrans remained ensconced in Nashville. "I am trying to lull them into security," he wrote of the Rebels. This did not reassure his superiors.[59]

On November 27, Halleck echoed the warnings others had received against the "piling up of impediments," and told Rosecrans, "If you remain long at Nashville you will disappoint the wishes of the Government." He also told him how the Union armies should now conduct the war: "Take a lesson from the enemy. Move light, and supply yourself as much as possible with provisions, animals, forage, transportation, &c., in the country you pass through." By December 4, Halleck was telling him of Lincoln's discontent with his "long stay in Nashville" and threatening him with replacement. "'If you remain one more week at Nashville, I cannot prevent your removal."[60]

Rosecrans brushed off Halleck's counsel. "To threats of removal or the like I must be permitted to say that I am insensible," he replied and told Halleck that the government should either trust him or get someone else. "Our true objective now is the enemy's force," he continued, "for if they come near, we save wear, tear, risk, and strength; subject them to what we escape, and gain all the chances to be expected from a rise in the river."[61] Choosing to focus on the enemy's army was a worthy objective, but it wasn't the objective that his superiors had given him. Moreover, allowing the enemy to advance into Tennessee so that they could be struck more easily was politically unacceptable to the Lincoln administration. Indeed, Halleck believed that Lincoln's insistence upon Rosecrans's advance into Tennessee was motivated by the president's fear of the potential international political damage that would befall the Union cause if the British Parliament met in January and the Confederacy still held middle Tennessee, which had been in Union hands the previous July. Continued Confederate retention of this territory could be used, Halleck wrote, as "an argument in favor of intervention by England."[62] The political ramifications of all action, and inaction, remained firmly planted in Lincoln's mind.

He understood how military events affected domestic and foreign politics. Most of his generals did not.

In his December 5 note Halleck had reminded Rosecrans why he had received his command: "It was believed you would move more rapidly" than Buell, he wrote. "Hence the change."[63] Still Rosecrans did not advance, though by December 10 he repeated his promise of a key victory, one that would "virtually end the game."[64] He was chasing the will-o'-the-wisp of Austerlitz— the dream of the decisive battle.

Finally, on December 26, having accumulated enough "impediments" to prevent his offensive from being stopped by raids on his supply lines, Rosecrans advanced on Murfreesboro from his base at Nashville. Bragg also moved. He crossed the Tennessee and drew up his troops on the shallow Stones River near Murfreesboro, intending to cut the Union's communications in the rear of Nashville. This would, he thought, "seriously embarrass" the Union elements because the Cumberland's low waters would frustrate their resupply. Bragg had bolstered this advance by dispatching Morgan north to strike in Kentucky. He sent his other cavalry, under Forrest, to support the Confederate forces in Mississippi by cutting Grant's supply lines, about which we will hear more shortly.[65]

But first Bragg, with 35,000 men, had to deal with Rosecrans's 47,000. Both planned to launch attacks on December 31, but Bragg struck first, hitting the Union right at daybreak and rolling it up. Two Union divisions collapsed, but a third, commanded by Phil Sheridan, stood fast and counterattacked, retreating only after exhausting its ammunition. Bragg tried to finish the job with a second attack against the Union center, but this failed. The next day, New Year's Day, the combatants stared at each other. Rosecrans broke the temporary stalemate the morning of the second by seizing some high ground to the north of his line. Bragg attacked the position. His troops took it, but then withdrew in the face of fire from massed Union artillery. Convinced nothing more could be done, Bragg withdrew. In the bloody contest one-third of the Confederates, 12,000 men, became casualties. The Union suffered 13,000, but Bragg's retreat meant Rosecrans had delivered a victory, though not the decisive one he had promised. He didn't move for another six months, and Bragg's army still blocked the road to Chattanooga.[66] Politically, though, Rosecrans's victory at Stones River (or Murfreesboro) was much needed by an administration besieged by critics.[67]

ROSECRANS HAD LONG PROMISED MOVEMENT; Grant and Sherman quickly delivered it. On October 16, 1862, Grant became the head of the

Department of the Tennessee. He set about planning a two-pronged attack down the Mississippi River, with Sherman commanding the river-based elements. Their objective, of course, was Vicksburg. "The campaign against Vicksburg commenced on the 2d of November," Grant wrote later. He had a field army of about 30,000 men marching from Corinth, Mississippi, and Bolivar, Tennessee, and expected to face a Confederate force of about the same size. He also noted one of the hallmarks of the campaign: repairing the railroads as they advanced in order to guarantee their line of supply. The Confederates withdrew as he came on.[68]

Initially unsure as to exactly what would happen with the Mississippi River portion of the Union advance (because of the awkward situation with McClernand), Grant received permission to commence this advance and on November 8 put Sherman in command. He dispatched him to Memphis to link up with Admiral Porter. Together, they would push down the Big Muddy. Grant wrote Sherman: "My notion is to send two Divisions back to Memphis and fix upon a day when they should effect a landing and press from here with this command at the proper time to cooperate."[69]

Grant also outlined the operation for Halleck, informing him that Sherman would command the expedition down the Mississippi with 40,000 men. Sherman would land above Vicksburg and break the Mississippi Central Railroad and the lines running east from Vicksburg where they crossed the Big Black River. "I will co-operate from here, my movements depending on those of the enemy. With the large cavalry force now at my command I will be able to have them show themselves at different points on the Talahatchie and Yalabusha [*sic*], and where an opportunity occurs make a real attack. After cutting the two railroads General Sherman's movements to secure the ends desired will necessarily be left to his judgment." Grant also hoped that his force would succeed in pinning the advanced Confederate forces of Pemberton, the primary defenders of Vicksburg, so that Sherman could get behind them and seize the city. Both Grant and Sherman understood that if Pemberton fell back, Grant would follow, all the way to Vicksburg if necessary.[70]

Grant's offensive didn't last long. On December 18, Forrest's cavalry tore up large segments of the rail line Grant needed to feed his men. Earl Van Dorn finished the job of severing Grant's logistical support on December 20 by destroying the Union supply center at Holly Springs, Mississippi. Grant found it impossible to continue his advance.[71]

Confederate raiding again proved one of the most dangerous weapons in the South's arsenal. By using large, fast-moving cavalry formations led by daring commanders, the South took advantage of the Union's most vulnerable spot in the West: their supply lines. The South's raiding consistently proved more effective at stopping advances by Union forces than did conventionally deployed Confederate armies. Moreover, the raiders generally fed themselves on the enemy's captured provisions and often armed themselves with captured equipment. Successfully conducted, such raids were a means of making the enemy pay much of the cost of the war, while injuring their ability to inflict damage.

Grant drew a number of important lessons from the defeat of his campaign. In his memoirs he wrote that the raids "demonstrated the impossibility of maintaining so long a line of [rail]road over which to draw supplies for an army moving in an enemy's country." After being forced to abandon his offensive and retreat, Grant ordered his troops to live off the land. "I was amazed at the quantity of supplies the country afforded," he wrote later. "This taught me a lesson which was taken advantage of later in the campaign when our army lived twenty days with the issue of only five days' rations by the commissary." He also realized that he could have fed his men this way for as long as two months. This experience, according to Grant, inspired his move against Vicksburg the following year.[72]

Sherman and Porter, meanwhile, moved south, though Sherman had only 30,000 men, not the 40,000 Grant had expected. Sherman complained about the divided command system in the West, with two army commands and one navy. "All ought to be under one head," he insisted, "but thus far I meet the heartiest cooperation."[73] Sherman and his forces steamed down the Mississippi to the Yazoo River, then marched on Vicksburg, launching a failed attack on the nearby bluffs at Chickasaw Bayou on December 29. On January 2, 1863, Sherman's forces withdrew, abandoning the offensive.[74] He told his brother afterward, "The place is too Strong, and without the cooperation of a large army coming from the Interior it is impracticable."[75]

Though repulsed at Vicksburg, Sherman would gain something for the Union cause. After McClernand arrived to take command of the forces on the Mississippi, Sherman suggested they move their forces north and seize Arkansas Post. He had decided to do this after receiving word of Grant's failure and having no information on any advance from below Vicksburg by Banks. Porter, the naval commander, enthusiastically agreed. McClernand gave his approval, noting that it would "free the navigation of the Mississippi River "from the molestation inflicted" by Confederate forces launching sorties from Arkansas Post. The joint force descended upon the Confederates, who surrendered on January 11, 1863.[76]

The Emancipation Strategy

ON AUGUST 22, 1862, LINCOLN PENNED that famous note to Horace Greeley of the *New York Tribune* in which he eloquently explained the primary political objective of his government—preserving the Union—and what he was willing to do to achieve it. "I would save the Union," Lincoln wrote. "I would save it the shortest way under the Constitution. The sooner the national authority can be restored, the nearer the Union will be 'the Union as it was.' If there be those who would not save the Union unless they could at the same time save slavery, I do not agree with them. If there be those who would not save the Union unless they could at the same time destroy slavery, I do not agree with them. My paramount object in this struggle is to save the Union, and is not either to save or to destroy slavery. If I could save the Union without freeing any slave, I would do it; and if I could save it by freeing all the slaves, I would do it; and if I could save it by freeing some and leaving others alone, I would also do that. What I do about slavery and the colored race, I do because I believe it helps save the Union."[77] Lincoln approached slavery as a political matter rather than a purely moral one and examined all the options: toleration of it, abolition, or partial abolition. In the end, he chose abolition (or at least a form of it), convinced that destroying slavery was necessary to win the war. Lincoln, as he put it, became "pretty well cured of objections to any measure except want of adaptedness to put down the rebellion."[78]

The road to the Emancipation Proclamation and the Union's use of African American troops was a twisted one. Lincoln certainly did not intend to employ them when the war began. Indeed, in September 1861, in a private letter, Lincoln rejected the idea that military demands might drive emancipation. Prior to this, though, the Union had already begun using former slaves. In May 1861, Major General Benjamin Butler gave refuge to runaway slaves at Fort Monroe, Virginia, arguing that they were "contraband." Lincoln agreed, and so did Congress, which passed the First Confiscation Act, declaring the forfeiture of slaves used by the Confederates in support of the war.[79]

The Lincoln administration began seriously examining emancipation at the end of 1861. In March 1862, the president urged granting federal compensation to the slaveholders of any state adopting gradual emancipation. He hoped the measure would be taken up by the border states and was disappointed by their lack of support of what was at the time more a political measure than a military one. When Northern attitudes toward the South hardened in the wake of the failure of the Peninsula Campaign, Lincoln realized that he would have to risk losing the support of the border states because he needed the buttress of the Republican antislavery faction even more.[80]

Lincoln progressed to his goal incrementally. In April 1862, he signed the law ending slavery in the District of Columbia.[81] In July 1862, prior to the passage of the Preliminary Emancipation Proclamation, he altered the militia ordinance of 1795 to include provisions for black troops. In some respects, this merely legalized what some local commanders in Louisiana and South Carolina were already doing. The key section allowed the president "to receive into the service of the United States, for the purpose of constructing intrenchments, or performing camp service, or any other labor, or any military or naval service for which they may be found competent, persons of African descent."[82]

Earlier in the war, when abolitionist subordinates tried to push Lincoln beyond where he wished to go with the slavery issue, he took quick and decisive action. In early 1862, Simon Cameron, Lincoln's first secretary of war, was shunted off to Russia as ambassador because he had distributed a report urging the government to arm former slaves. Generals such as John Frémont in Missouri and David Hunter in South Carolina took it upon themselves to free the slaves in their command areas (and, in Hunter's case, to arm them). Lincoln had decreed restraint and forced them to repudiate their respective proclamations. He insisted that the North fought not to free the slaves but to retain the Union. Moreover, Lincoln wanted a more permanent, legally binding solution than that contained within such spontaneous emergency bills.[83]

Lincoln next suggested that the government buy the slaves, which would be much cheaper than prosecuting the war. He even proposed a plan of gradual emancipation to do this.[84] For a time, as we know, he also supported colonization of part of America's black population; Congress voted money for its beginnings.[85] This idea died because the Central American nations from which Lincoln hoped to obtain land for some of these former slaves were not interested in ceding territory for the emigration of U.S. blacks.[86]

In the wake of the battle of Antietam in September 1862, Lincoln issued the Preliminary Emancipation Proclamation. This was, he told his cabinet, something he had promised God he would do if Lee's army was driven back. The timing was critical. Secretary of State Henry Seward had argued for delaying its issuance until after a battlefield victory (which Antietam delivered), fearing that otherwise it would be viewed as a desperate act, the Union's "last *shriek* on the retreat."[87] Lincoln took his advice. The proclamation's opening paragraph stressed prosecuting the war to restore "the constitutional relation between the United States and each of the States," and announced his administration's intent to free slaves held in any area in rebellion on January 1, 1863. In a lawyerly manner, Lincoln established a sense of precedent for emancipation by citing two previous acts of Congress that dealt with the insurrection, including a July 1862 measure concerning the seizure of Rebel property. At the same time as he promised to take the Confederates' slaves, he held out a carrot to all "who shall have remained loyal," promising them "compensation for all losses by acts of the United States, including the loss of slaves."[88] Lincoln offered a chance at repentance—compensated repentance—but also, if there was no repentance, the promise of retribution.

On January 1, 1863, true to his word, Lincoln issued the Final Emancipation Proclamation, freeing the slaves in the areas in rebellion (which is critical to remember) "as a fit and necessary war measure for suppressing said rebellion."[89]

Why did Lincoln do this? His personal views certainly favored abolition, and some of his closest friends insisted that he came to Washington determined to kill slavery.[90] But as we've seen, Lincoln was more in favor of saving the Union than freeing the slaves. Therefore, the Emancipation Proclamation was a means rather than an end. In one of its last paragraphs, Lincoln makes very clear how he expects his act to contribute to the Union's war effort: "I further declare and make known that such persons of suitable condition will be received into the armed service of the United States to garrison forts, positions, stations, and other places, and man vessels of all sorts in said service."[91] Lincoln clearly intends to take the enemy's strength and add it to his own— something advised by Sun Tzu.[92] In 1865, during some failed negotiations for peace, Lincoln told Confederate vice president Alexander Stephens that the Emancipation Proclamation was "a war measure."[93]

After the proclamation, Lincoln's interest in using black troops grew. In March 1863, in a letter to Andrew Johnson, then governor of Tennessee, Lincoln argued that "the colored population is the great available and yet unavailed of force for restoring the Union." He continued, with a bit of hyperbole, that "the bare sight of fifty thousand armed and drilled black soldiers upon the banks of the Mississippi would end the rebellion at once."[94] To General Banks, Lincoln insisted that "to avail ourselves of this element of force is very important, if not indispensable."[95] Lincoln's willingness to free the slaves and then to bring them into the Union's armed forces demonstrated his determination to win the war. "I shall not hesitate to use all the means at my control to secure the termination of this rebellion," he wrote. Whatever measures this required became acceptable.[96]

Lincoln also intended for the Emancipation Proclamation to have an international effect. It did, though not the one many had expected. He had hoped it would influence Europe in favor of the Union. In fact, however, it did little to further the Union cause. Indeed, it actually increased the chances of foreign intervention, something Seward had feared. British leaders saw the Proclamation as an incitement to race war, a desperate and hypocritical measure. Tory leaders derided it. Liberals, workers, and abolitionists applauded it, but these groups had little political power. Only later did the British government seize upon emancipation as a reason to ensure that Great Britain stayed out of the war.[97]

More important was the reaction at home. Prior to the Civil War, the idea of freeing the slaves inspired terror and the fear of racial war in both the North and the South. The Emancipation Proclamation pleased abolitionists, as expected, and drove those who loathed Lincoln already to loathe him even more deeply. Secessionist Democrats in Congress shrieked, some branding it an incitement to insurrection, but fortunately for Lincoln, the Republicans held the majority. There were some desertions because of the proclamation. Of the 13,000 who walked away from Illinois regiments during the war, the largest number tramped off in the wake of the proclamation's publication. Overall, though, this was not a significant problem. Many in the border states became disaffected, some complaining that freeing the slaves in the rebellious states meant that they would flee northward, overwhelming the region.[98] The Emancipation Proclamation did as Lincoln intended: it added strength to the Union cause while taking it from the Confederacy. Moreover, Lincoln's casting of it as necessary for successful prosecution of the war was a political master stroke.

After January 1863, tens of thousands of slaves began walking away from their owners. Slavery collapsed even in areas where, technically, the slaves had not been freed. Approximately 186,000 blacks entered Union military service. At least half were in bonds at the beginning of the war. In 1865, blacks accounted for somewhere around 10 percent of Union military forces.[99] Lincoln considered these men critical to Union military operations. "Abandon all the posts now possessed by black men," he told a pair of Wisconsin Republicans in August 1864, "surrender all these advantages to the enemy, & we would be compelled to abandon the war in 3 weeks. We have to hold territory. Where are the war democrats to do it. The field was open to them to have enlisted & put down this rebellion by force of arms, by concilliation [sic], long before the present policy was inaugurated. There have been men who have proposed to me to return to slavery the black warriors of Port Hudson & Olustee to their masters to conciliate the South. I should be damned in time & in eternity for so doing."[100]

In 1864, Lincoln summed up his view of the relationship between the slaves and the Union war effort in a letter to Albert Hodges, a prominent Kentucky politician and Lincoln supporter. As he reveals to Hodges, Lincoln had stopped the efforts of Frémont, Hunter, and former secretary of war Cameron because at that point he did not yet deem freeing the slaves "an indispensable necessity." When he had pursued compensated emancipation in the border states in March, May, and June 1862, he believed arming the slaves would be necessary if this failed. "They declined the proposition;" Lincoln wrote, "and I was, in my best judgment, driven to the alternative of either surrendering the Union, and with it, the Constitution, or of laying strong hand upon the colored element. I chose the latter."[101]

Before January 1863, the slaves were truly Lincoln's "unavailed of" force. Afterward, they were one of the tools of Union victory.

Escalation's Drumbeat

BY JANUARY 1863, restraint in regard to fighting the war was dead. Union quartermaster general Montgomery Meigs wrote Burnside: "The war appears to me to be gradually assuming the aspect of a long one, to be settled by exhaustion, and every pressure we can put upon a rebel is so much toward the end."[102] What the Union could not take from the South for its own war effort it would now destroy. This was directed at two things: Southern resources and Southern will. The Union was now pursuing a strategy of exhausting the South. It never backed away from this.

Though the wisdom of escalating the war, particularly the issuance of the Emancipation Proclamation, is indisputable, other elements of Union strategy proved not so cogent. The most glaring mistake was the concentration on the Mississippi River. The "real" war was in Tennessee. It would take another year for the Union to figure this out. Meanwhile, Grant would wage a tenacious, brilliant, and ambitious campaign for something of secondary importance. The Union aimed to take territory, which it did. But this was not a Confederate center of gravity. The North needed to destroy Confederate armies, not merely take places. "The army," Lincoln wrote in November 1862, "like the nation, has become demoralized by the idea that the war is to be ended, the nation united, and peace restored, by *strategy*, and not by hard desperate fighting."[103] In other words, the war would be won not by movements, marching, maneuvers, feints, or lofty thinking, which were so much associated with the meaning of the word *strategy* in Lincoln's day, but by violence and bloodshed. Further escalation was coming.

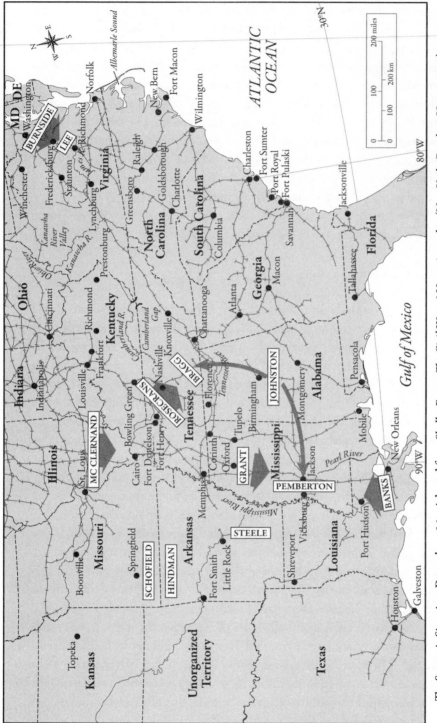

The Strategic Situation, December 1862. Adapted from Shelby Foote, *The Civil War: A Narrative*, vol. 1 (New York: Random House, 1958), 797.

14

The Enormous Proportions of War

*Time has convinced all reasonable men, that war in theory
and practice are two distinct things.*

—WILLIAM TECUMSEH SHERMAN, March 12, 1863

THE YEAR 1862 PROVED a disastrous one for the Confederacy. It suffered
more than 100,000 battle casualties and lost tremendous swaths of territory.
The historian Grady McWhiney provides a catalog: "Kentucky, Missouri,
New Mexico, Arizona, and Western Virginia, as well as parts of Tennessee,
Arkansas, Louisiana, North Carolina, South Carolina, Florida, and Mississippi." He noted that the South had done "somewhat better" in the East, but
that in the West its losses were "devastating."[1]

Southern resistance during the Peninsula Campaign had been greatly hindered by the poor relationship between J. E. Johnston and Davis. They were,
in some respects, too much alike. As Clifford Dowdy and Louis H. Manarin
have observed, "Each was a man who would rather prove himself right than
achieve effectiveness."[2] This is perhaps a bit too damning an opinion of Davis
considering the amount of effort he devoted to trying to achieve Southern
independence, but there is also some meat to it. Davis had some awareness of
his tendency to try to overcome his critics, justify his actions, and not only
have his own views triumph but be *seen* to have done so. Despite his dissatisfaction with Johnston's performance on the Peninsula, Davis appointed him
the new head of the Western Theater. The area's poor command structure had
injured Bragg's Tennessee offensive, "as a series of overlapping and often contradictory orders worked to deprive Bragg of reinforcements and supplies."[3]

The year 1862 had been better for Lee, who had delivered successes in the
East, saving Richmond by driving away McClellan and following up with the
defeat of Pope at Second Manassas and Burnside at Fredericksburg. However,
being driven from Maryland had spoiled his string of victories. In January
1863, he gave Secretary of War Seddon his views on how the South should
fight the war, the basis of them being his belief that Confederate armies were
too small and that more should be done to beef them up. "More than once have
most promising opportunities been lost for want of men to take advantage of
them," Lee wrote. He also realized the difficulty of destroying a Union army,

and of fighting them in general. To Lee, the Union's superior numbers had allowed its defeated armies to avoid being completely destroyed. Lee also did not want to suffer casualties for no reason. "The lives of our soldiers are too precious to be sacrificed in the attainment of successes that inflict no loss upon the enemy beyond the actual loss in battle. Every victory should bring us nearer to the great end which it is the object of this war to reach."[4] Few generals, in the North or South, understood the need for incremental successes leading to the accomplishment of their government's political objective. Too many focused simply upon the battle, one of the era's manifestation of the Napoleonic ideal, and could not see beyond it. Lee was an exception; he possessed broader, deeper insight.

IN A SPEECH AT JACKSON, Mississippi, on December 26, 1862, Davis insisted that he had been among those who "from the beginning, looked forward to a long and bloody war." Nonetheless, he was forced to admit that "its magnitude has exceeded my expectations. The enemy have displayed more power and energy and resources than I had attributed to them. Their finances have held out far better than I imagined would be the case." Davis was certainly not the only one surprised by the war's escalating carnage. It had become a conflagration feeding upon itself, one that increasingly strove to consume every vestige of human and material resources at the disposal of the state. Davis remained optimistic about ultimate Confederate success while also demonstrating a growing awareness of what the war was becoming. He also unknowingly forecast its ultimate result: "It is not possible that a war of the dimensions that this one has assumed, of proportions so gigantic, can be very long protracted. The combatants must be soon exhausted."[5] Exhaustion would become exactly what the North had in mind.

In a late December 1862 letter to Theophilus Holmes, the commander of the Confederacy's Trans-Mississippi Department, Davis provided an assessment of the South's strategic situation, his view of the Union's primary military objectives, and what the Confederacy needed to do to defend itself. He believed the North aimed at winning the Mississippi River and seizing Richmond. Of these two, he thought controlling the Mississippi the more critical for the South. If Richmond fell, it would be a blow to foreign public opinion and would result in the "destruction of manufactories and other resources very essential to our future efforts." But losing the Mississippi gained for the enemy a solid base for operations on both its banks, answered the cries of northwestern farmers who wished to utilize the river, and made New Orleans a profitable base for the Union war effort.[6]

Davis was half right about the Union's objectives. Lincoln indeed aimed at controlling the Mississippi, and his generals had set their sights on Richmond. But Lincoln believed the destruction of Lee's army was more important. Davis was also correct about the strategic advantages control of the Mississippi would give to the North, but he was incorrect about the Northwest's *need* for the river. As we've seen, the extensive railway (not to mention canal) systems in the North provided the region's farmers with means of moving their produce. The danger to the Union from the Northwest was political in nature; some of the region's antiwar Democrats were threatening to try to make their own peace with the Confederacy in order to reopen the Mississippi to Union trade.[7]

In any event, Davis's observation that the South needed to keep control of the Mississippi River to avoid "dismemberment" was on the mark. He announced that a large Union force was prepared to go down the Mississippi and attack Vicksburg, supported by another marching overland from Memphis. Meanwhile, other Union troops were to come up the river, aiming at Port Hudson. Davis saw holding Vicksburg and Port Hudson as critical for defense of the river, as well as maintaining communications with the Trans-Mississippi, and instructed Holmes to join forces with Johnston to counter the Union and "destroy his power for future operations against you." Moreover, after Holmes helped Johnston, Davis said, Johnston could then turn and reinforce Holmes, allowing the clearing of Arkansas as well as Holmes's desired offensive into Missouri. "We cannot hope at all points to meet the enemy with a force equal to his own," he wrote, "and must find our security in the concentration and rapid movement of troops." Davis predicted the results if the Confederates failed: a subsequent Union attack on the Trans-Mississippi. But he also had hopes for ultimate success: "Nothing will so certainly conduce to peace as the conclusive exhibition of our power to hold the Mississippi River."[8]

Davis's idea of how the war should be fought in the West came down to concentration and speed. By stressing these, Davis was trying to address the general problem of meeting any Union offensive in the West, where the Confederates had inadequate strength. When he penned this he did not yet know that Holmes would prove unable to support Johnston, though he was right to note that conquest of the Mississippi River would leave the Union free to concentrate its efforts against Holmes and the Trans-Mississippi if they so chose.[9]

Davis promised in his aforementioned Jackson speech that "Missouri will again be free" and that Kentucky was "still the object of the ardent wishes of

Gen. Bragg." But he also revealed that he no longer harbored illusions about foreign intervention. "This war is ours," he told his audience; "we must fight it out ourselves."[10]

Johnston's War

DAVIS HAD ALREADY ACTED to address his assessment that the Confederate forces in the West needed to cooperate better. On November 24, 1862, he sent Johnston to command the Western Department, comprising Tennessee, Alabama, Mississippi, and the eastern area of Louisiana.[11] Once again for the Confederacy, things would be different in the West—if not necessarily better.

Johnston responded instantly with his own operational plan. He believed that his forces were greatly inferior to the enemy's, while Confederate troops in the Trans-Mississippi Department outnumbered their Union opponents. He also observed that the Confederates east of the Mississippi River were separated not only by the Tennessee River but also by Grant's army, which was larger, "probably," than either of the two Confederate forces. The Confederate dispositions therefore imperiled Vicksburg. His solution was to suggest that Holmes and Pemberton's forces join together, and even to bring in Bragg's army if possible, and then "fall upon" Grant. Defeating him would enable them to keep the Mississippi and allow Holmes to advance into Missouri.[12]

Circumstances conspired to thwart Johnston. First, the Union had its own plans, and Federal armies under Grant and Sherman were then pushing southward, gunning for Vicksburg. Second, Holmes, the Confederate commander in the Trans-Mississippi, refused to dispatch the 10,000 troops he had been ordered to send over the Mississippi to Vicksburg. Holmes wrote to his superiors in Richmond on December 5 with the disappointing news, but the letter was not received until December 23. Davis had expected the Trans-Mississippi commander to move and told Johnston to keep in close contact with Holmes so they could attack Grant together.[13]

Johnston, realizing that his only chance of getting the necessary troops for a riposte would be to take them from the Confederate forces in Tennessee, quickly grew disillusioned and not a little bitter. On December 15, he wrote Senator Louis T. Wigfall that "this has blown away some tall castles in the air." Johnston had "been dreaming of crushing Grant" after combining the troops of Holmes and Pemberton with his own. Then he would have Holmes's army invade Missouri, unite the forces of Pemberton, Bragg, and Kirby Smith with his own, and march to the Ohio River. But "our troops beyond the Mississippi seem to be living in great tranquility," he added.[14]

Holmes certainly would have disagreed with Johnston. He replied that his orders reflected ignorance about the true state of affairs in the Trans-Mississippi and later explained to Johnston that at no time had he possessed more than 22,000 effective troops. Sickness, desertions, and battle casualties had reduced this number to slightly more than 16,000 by the end of September. Moreover, at the time of the request for troops to reinforce Vicksburg, the Union was moving on Van Buren and Fort Smith in Arkansas. Confederate major general Thomas Hindman had marched to stop them. This left Holmes with only McCulloch's division to send to Vicksburg. Doing so, he argued, would have robbed him of his only reserve, and it would have taken a month to move them, "during which time the enemy might be quietly taking possession of the valley of the Arkansas, the key of the department." Hindman's forces met the Union west of Fayetteville at Prairie Grove on December 7–8. Here 9,500 Yankees fought 12,000 Confederates to a standstill, whereupon the Confederates withdrew. Moreover, at the time of Holmes's writing he was facing a renewed Union drive against Van Buren with 20,000 men. Holmes doubted that Hindman's 10,000 troops could resist them. Holmes's situation was in some ways representative of that continuously faced by the commander of the Trans-Mississippi: he was too weak to help anyone without sacrificing the heart of his department. Moreover, any forces he dispatched would not reach Vicksburg in time. Holmes wrote that "such a diversion would enable the enemy to penetrate those portions of the Arkansas Valley where the existence of supplies of subsistence and forage would afford them leisure to overrun the entire State and gradually reduce the people to a dependence upon the Federal Government." In the end, Holmes used the discretion that Davis—who refused to issue an order—had granted him and did not transfer the troops from his department.[15]

By late December, Johnston, still angry about the lack of reinforcements, had assessed the situation in his department and developed a clear idea of his objectives for the Confederate forces in the West. "I firmly believe, however," he wrote to Davis, "that our true system of warfare would be to concentrate the forces of the two departments on this side of the Mississippi, beat the enemy here [meaning the Union forces moving on Vicksburg], and then re-conquer the country beyond it which he might have gained in the mean time."[16]

Actually achieving this, of course, was the rub. Johnston had the immediate problem presented by the forces of Banks, Sherman, and Grant, all of which were making their first attempts to take Vicksburg. Earlier in the month, Pemberton's forces had withdrawn in the face of Grant's advance. During this same time, against Johnston's will, Davis, having made a visit to Bragg's army and concluding that his position was tenable, ordered 10,000 troops taken from here to reinforce Pemberton at Vicksburg. To hold his department and the Mississippi River, Johnston believed that he needed a field army of 40,000 men, as well as garrisons at Port Hudson and Vicksburg capable of holding out against Union attacks until relieved by the field force. The problem was manpower. He thought 11,000–12,000 men were required to hold Port Hudson; he had only 5,900. He had 21,000 men for his field force, and about 9,000 more were being sent from Kirby Smith's command. He also expected a force from Holmes in the Trans-Mississippi of about the same size. The last, of course, would not be coming. There was also Bragg's command, though Johnston believed it dangerous to draw troops from Bragg because it would enable Rosecrans either to move against Chattanooga or to reinforce Grant. Johnston simply did not have enough men and needed more. "The 8,000 or 10,000 men which are essential to safety," he wrote Davis, "ought therefore, I respectfully suggest, to be taken from Arkansas, to return after the crisis in this department."[17]

"The country beyond the river is as much interested in that object as this," Johnston wrote, "and the loss to us of the Mississippi involves that of the country beyond it."[18] Holding the Mississippi became Johnston's great, immediate objective. Taking it from him became the Union's.

Johnston and Davis at War

THE PROBLEMS JOHNSTON FACED when taking up his new command manifested themselves early. As Grant and Sherman threatened Vicksburg in January 1863, Johnston, in his description of the situation to Davis, insisted, "Should the enemy's forces be respectably handled the task you have set me will be above my ability." This was not auspicious. Davis needed a commander with some optimism—and more faith in himself. Indeed, Johnston did face a tough situation, but the Union situation was difficult as well. The distances, terrain, and climate made a Union drive on Vicksburg challenging, even though Union forces controlled the inland waterways. Moreover, the Confederacy was not without its resources, and Bragg's intelligent use of his cavalry had entirely thwarted Grant's first attempt. The next warning sign came on January 6, in another of Johnston's dispatches to Davis: "The impossibility of my knowing condition of things in Tennessee shows that I cannot direct both parts of my command at once."[19]

While Johnston was struggling with his new command, Bragg fought the Union at Murfreesboro. However, in terms of its reflection on Southern strategy, what was even more significant than the fighting was what happened in its wake. The initial impression that Bragg had won a victory, combined with the repelling of the Union attack on Vicksburg, fed Davis's perceptions about the situation in the Union states in the Northwest. In a speech at Richmond he argued, "Out of this victory is to come that dissatisfaction in the North West that will rive the power of that section," causing the separation of the Northwest from the eastern states. The resulting discord, he believed, would "paralyze the power of both;—then for us future peace and prosperity."[20]

Despite Davis's hopes to divide the Union, the Confederate war effort was itself being undermined by the infighting and mutual recrimination among the generals in Bragg's command. After the battle of Murfreesboro, Bragg, learning that the opposing Union troops were being reinforced, withdrew. He asked for reinforcements from his commander, Johnston, who told Davis that he might be able to spare some for a few weeks if Sherman did not reappear. But he added a troublesome question: "Which is the most valuable, Tennessee or the Mississippi?" "To hold the Mississippi is vital," replied Davis, who told Bragg, "Fight if you can, and fall back beyond the Tennessee."[21] Only Rosecrans's torpor made it possible for Davis to offer this choice.

Bragg was unhappy both with not being reinforced and with Davis's instructions. "I told the President Grant's campaign would be broken up by our cavalry expeditions in his rear before Stevenson's command could meet him in front," he wrote Johnston with some bitterness, "but he was inexorable, and reduced me to the defensive, or, as he expressed it, 'Fight if you can, and fall back beyond the Tennessee.'"[22]

But some of the responsibility for Bragg's acidity must be put at the feet of Johnston. His question to Davis about choosing between protecting the Mississippi and reinforcing Bragg was a tough one. It is certainly true that he had the right—and even, one could argue, the responsibility—to seek Davis's advice before making a major decision. Nonetheless, Davis would not have placed him in command over the Western Department had he not expected Johnston to make the tough calls. In May Lee posed a similar question, asking Davis to choose between Virginia and the Mississippi.

Bragg's generals all but revolted, and his subordinates blamed him for the results of Murfreesboro. Bragg, in turn, accused them of failing to do their jobs during the Confederate attacks against the Union left flank and then for trying to tar him with their mistakes before the official reports could be filed. He offered to leave if his continued presence injured the army's effectiveness, noting, "Though I must say there is no man here to command an army."[23]

Davis sent Johnston to sort the thing out and take stock of the situation. Davis, for his part, had faith in Bragg's ability, though he worried that if Bragg's subordinates had lost confidence in him, it could lay the groundwork for a disaster in the face of the expected Union push.[24] Johnston agreed with Davis about Bragg's aptitude and did not want him replaced, believing that "the interest of the service *requires* that General Bragg should not be removed."[25]

Rousing the Slumbering Giant

ROSECRANS, THE MAN SITTING across the lines from Bragg, was in no better stead with his superiors and showed less inclination to decamp and take advantage of Bragg's withdrawal. Meanwhile, Halleck and Lincoln felt pressure from Tennessee politicians to push Union forces into eastern Tennessee and finally liberate that area.[26] This would have fallen to Rosecrans's army; indeed, it had been part of his initial orders.

In January 1863, Rosecrans expected the Confederates to strip whatever troops they could from Tennessee and Kentucky and mass for an offensive against him. But Rosecrans now faced the classic problem of all armies deep in hostile territory: his lines of supply and communication faced constant assault from guerrillas. Later, the Rebels would make his problems even worse by dispatching cavalry raids to tear up the railroads and burn bridges. He asked for reinforcements, telling Halleck, "We ought to hold the Tennessee River with a force adequate to cover the country south of Duck River, and cover that flank from cavalry, of which they have four to our one."[27]

In mid-January, Halleck decided upon the necessity of securing Kentucky, and he believed that the best way of doing this was by defeating Bragg's army. That Halleck had reached such a surprisingly clear conclusion shows that either he had learned something on his own or that Lincoln's hounding his generals in the east to destroy Lee's army had produced some spillover. Halleck nonetheless refused to stoop to the indignity of actually ordering his generals to do what he wanted them to do. He directed the two generals primarily responsible for this, Rosecrans and Wright, to concentrate their forces and secure their supply lines (which included the important rail line from Louisville to Nashville). These were certainly worthy objectives, but Halleck had earlier been paralyzed in the face of opportunities to seize equally urgent objectives when he commanded in the West; his successor proved little different.[28]

After a short illness, Rosecrans went to work securing his supply routes. He also revealed his new idea of military strategy: gone was his insistence upon a decisive battle. "This war must be conducted to annihilate the military power and exhaust the resources of the rebels. All our preparations should be promptly made firmly to advance and strongly to hold the country." Rosecrans's views reflected those under his command. Some of his officers had examined the problem of controlling the hostile population and holding large areas now under their control, and their reports to Rosecrans went to Halleck. One noted the Union's previous insistence on encouraging supposed loyal sympathy in the South, and wrote that this was pointless "because there is no Union sentiment in the rebel States (with here and there a noble exception) among that class of men who wield the political power of these States." To him the remedy was simple: to "despoil the rebels" and roust them out of the region, leaving room for the "return of loyal men." He also offered advice to anyone wishing to conduct successful counterinsurgency operations: "Let these loyal men feel that the country is once in their possession instead of being possessed by their oppressors. Aid them in its possession for awhile, and they will soon acquire confidence sufficient to hold it." Another Union officer supported him, pointing out that if it was a choice between a "conciliatory" policy and a "rigid" one, the latter should be adopted.[29]

Their recommendations fell on receptive ears. Halleck told Rosecrans that the policy of "a more rigid treatment of all disloyal persons within the lines of your army [is] approved.... No additional instructions from these headquarters are deemed necessary." Additionally, Rosecrans's army was to sustain itself by seizing whatever it needed in the occupied regions.[30] Thoughts of conciliation and preservation of Southern property had faded from the Union mind. All that war demanded, war would be given.

Halleck, though, was not pleased with other aspects of Rosecrans's war. He believed his general was trying to secure too many posts, thus leaving various endangered points for the Rebels to assail while also weakening his main force. But he was even less pleased with the situation in the East. The inaction of the Army of the Potomac, he wrote Rosecrans, had "very greatly embarrassed the Government" by not driving the Confederates from the vicinity of Washington or engaging them, as desired, "south of the Rappahannock." Halleck believed doing this might have enabled them to send troops to help open the Mississippi. "It is greatly to be feared that the time of many of our troops will expire without our having accomplished any important results."[31]

Opening the Mississippi had triumphed as an operational and, indeed, strategic objective in the Union high command, and Halleck told Rosecrans that because of reports that some of Bragg's forces had been sent west to reinforce Vicksburg, the general in chief had been asked to take some of Rosecrans's troops to bolster the Mississippi River campaign. Halleck thought this unnecessary, but he deemed it critical that Rosecrans press Bragg's forces "and, as far as possible, feel him and keep yourself informed of his strength."[32]

Rosecrans insisted that he held only the necessary places. He also had his own ideas of what was needed for his army's success: laying in sixty to ninety days' supplies in Nashville. This would allow them temporarily to ignore their lines of communication, except Nashville. Second, he wanted to put enough supplies up the Cumberland River to allow an advance into eastern Tennessee. Moreover, he told Halleck something that Lincoln surely didn't want to hear. "I believe the most fatal errors of this war have begun in an impatient desire of success," he wrote, "that would not take time to get ready; the next fatal mistake being to be afraid to move when all the means were provided."[33] Such were the words of all Union generals who refused to advance. His note conjures the image of McClellan, Buell, and Halleck himself. There would always be one more thing that needed to be done before the fight could be taken to the enemy.

By mid-February, Lincoln involved himself in the problem of the Confederate attacks by cavalry and irregulars against Union lines of communication and supply. Undoubtedly driven by reports from Rosecrans's army about mounting more troops, Lincoln asked Rosecrans about Union forces launching similar raids. He feared that as Confederate military strength declined, the Rebels would resort more and more to such attacks.[34]

Nonetheless, Rosecrans continued to push for concentration. He wrote to Major General Horatio Wright, the commander of the Department of the Ohio, based in Cincinnati, that they should mass their forces in Murfreesboro and Nashville under his command. "Every effort should be bent to keep the troops all here, and our rear covered by troops drawn from East as well as West. How comes it that the West not only fights its own battles, but sends troops East to aid them, yet we have only half the population they have?"[35]

Meanwhile Wright, whose confirmation to the rank of major general the Senate had refused, asked to be relieved. Halleck quickly obliged, and put Burnside in Wright's Cincinnati post as commander of the Department of the Ohio.[36] After warning of a potential Confederate offensive, Halleck gave Burnside some orders—if orders they can even be called. The general in chief outlined three possible courses of action for the general, shot down the third suggestion himself, then told Burnside it would probably be best to implement numbers one and two, "that is, to hold your main force in some central position, and at the same time to annoy the enemy and threaten his communications, by making cavalry raids into East Tennessee." Halleck then welded

Burnside to an anvil: "The movements of your own troops will depend in no small degree upon those of the army under General Rosecrans."[37] The challenge would be getting Old Rosy to act.

Rosecrans, Halleck wrote, was "to occupy and injure as much as possible the army in his front," but his more important objective was to come to the rescue of the "loyal inhabitants" in eastern Tennessee. Halleck reiterated his order to Rosecrans to keep the enemy under pressure, but Rosecrans didn't think an advance "prudent."[38]

Halleck then tried to clarify what he expected of Burnside by telling him to concentrate his forces in central Kentucky to meet an expected Confederate raid. Meanwhile, Rosecrans wasted no time in asking Burnside to move to the line of the Cumberland River, which he agreed to do, and wanted to know when Burnside could move into eastern Tennessee.[39]

Halleck kept his thumb on Rosecrans in late March and early April, telling him to stop enemy movements in the Kanawha Valley. Burnside, who had already seized the initiative, concentrated his forces at two points and drove the Confederates from Danville, Kentucky, effectively ejecting the Rebels from the center of the Bluegrass State. He then gathered his troops at half a dozen key posts and ordered the construction of fortifications along the railroads to keep them secure. "I hope to have enough force soon to make some diversions in your favor," he wrote Rosecrans in the first week of April.[40]

Raids would be the only thing that Rosecrans would do for many months. And raids were something Montgomery Meigs, the Union's quartermaster general, wholeheartedly embraced. "Compel your cavalry officers to see that their horses are groomed," he wrote Rosecrans in a letter filled with specific advice and guidance; "put them in some place where they can get forage, near the railroad, or send them to your rear to graze and eat corn." Meigs was extremely attentive to the needs and limits of the horses, upon which success for these raids naturally depended. "When in good order, start them, a thousand at a time, for the rebels' communications, with orders never to move off a walk unless they see an enemy before or behind them; to travel only so far in a day as not to fatigue their horses; never to camp in the place in which sunset found them, and to rest in a good pasture during the heat of the day; to keep some of their eyes open night and day, and never to pass a bridge without burning it, a telegraph wire without cutting it, a horse without stealing or shooting it, a guerrilla without capturing him, or a negro without explaining the President's proclamation to him."[41] Meigs's plea for action—"strike every detached post"—had as little effect on Rosecrans as had those of the president and general in chief.

Burnside kept in close contact with Rosecrans and supported him as well, but Rosecrans proved reluctant to execute the orders he had received. The pressure upon them both intensified in mid-May when Halleck sent them word of Joe Johnston's efforts to reinforce Vicksburg. Halleck believed the Confederates might support this by launching raids into Kentucky and Tennessee and told Rosecrans and Burnside that the best defense would be "to concentrate your forces and advance against the enemy," threatening eastern Tennessee if they could. Instead of advancing immediately, Rosecrans insisted that if he had sufficient cavalry, he "would attack Bragg within three days."[42]

Lincoln's patience, though long, became increasingly frayed. He prodded Old Rosy, telling him, "I would not push you to any rashness"—as if there were any chance of that—"but I am very anxious that you do your utmost, short of rashness, to keep Bragg from getting off to help Johnston against Grant."[43] Although Rosecrans replied that he would "attend to it," he did not.[44] He and Burnside continued to plan and talk and shuffle troops.[45] All the while, Burnside remained optimistic in regard to an advance into eastern Tennessee.[46]

On the last day of May, Rosecrans finally spurred Burnside to get his men into position. "I wish to make a forward movement within the next four days," Rosecrans wrote. He hoped Burnside's troops could, if needed, support his own by moving against McMinnville. He also suggested that if the circumstances were right, they could move in unison on Chattanooga.[47]

By this point, however, events elsewhere had overtaken them. Grant's offensive against Vicksburg became more important than what was happening in Tennessee. On June 3, Halleck ordered Burnside to send reinforcements to Grant. To Rosecrans, Halleck issued a warning: "Accounts received here indicate that Johnston is being heavily re-enforced from Bragg's army. If you cannot hurt the enemy now, he will soon hurt you." Burnside resisted Halleck's order, arguing that detaching some of his men would mean he couldn't support Rosecrans in a movement on eastern Tennessee. Surprisingly, Halleck acted decisively and ordered Burnside to send Grant 8,000 men.[48]

Rosecrans, for his part, polled his generals, asking whether or not they should advance. Almost to a man, Rosecrans's subordinates decreed a movement against Bragg pointless.[49] One of his crew of pessimists even identified the very reason that Rosecrans's army should attack as a reason not to: "It is now of vital consequence to the enemy that Bragg's army should be kept unbroken." Only cavalry commander Major General David S. Stanley thought it time to move; he also had the temerity to believe that they could defeat Bragg's army.[50]

The nearly universal doubts among his generals did not, however, discourage Rosecrans's chief of staff, Brigadier General James A. Garfield, the future president. To Garfield fell the task of summarizing and evaluating the responses. "No man can affirm with certainty the result of any battle," he informed Rosecrans, "however great the disparity in numbers. Such results are in the hand of God." Garfield, though, had no doubt their army would overwhelm Bragg's, particularly given the Union superiority in numbers. They should attack, Garfield wrote; "the most unfavorable course for us that Bragg could take would be to fall back without giving us battle, but this would be very disastrous to him.... Besides the loss of material of war, and the abandonment of the rich and abundant harvest now nearly ripe in Central Tennessee, he would lose heavily by desertion." He also identified a possible Confederate center of gravity and its western manifestation, writing, "Our true objective point is the rebel army, whose last reserves are substantially in the field, and an effective blow will crush the shell, and soon be followed by the collapse of the rebel Government." Defeating Bragg, in Garfield's view, "would be in the highest degree disastrous to the rebellion."[51]

Yet still Rosecrans delayed. Alluding to Grant's campaign against Vicksburg, he wrote Halleck that it was better to "observe a great military maxim to not risk two great and decisive battles at the same time."[52] Halleck snapped back, correcting Rosecrans's use of military theory by explaining to him that this applied to "a single army" fighting two battles at once, not to "two armies acting independently of each other." He reminded Rosecrans that Bragg and Johnston had the interior position, meaning their forces were between the Union armies, giving them the potential to combine against either Grant or Rosecrans. Therefore it was to the Union's advantage for Rosecrans to fight Bragg. Halleck also reminded him of another maxim: "councils of war never fight."[53]

Despite this, Halleck still refused to order Rosecrans to attack Bragg, continuing to believe—in the face of all the evidence to the contrary—that only the general on the spot could make such a decision. Instead, he told Rosecrans of the administration's dissatisfaction and asked if he could not at least "harass" Bragg.[54] Rosecrans argued theory and sat on his haunches.[55] Halleck pushed again. "Is it your intention to make an immediate movement forward? A definite answer, yes or no, is required."[56] But he still gave no order. An unintimidated Rosecrans responded the same day: "In reply to your inquiry, if immediate means to-night or to-morrow, no. If it means as soon as all things are ready, say five days, yes."[57]

By now, Lee's 1863 offensive in the Eastern Theater was beginning to have an effect in the West. Burnside had sent two raids into eastern Tennessee and western Virginia and considered moving his remaining force after them in an effort to support Hooker, who, Burnside believed, was moving to try to meet Lee. "What is your opinion?" Burnside asked Rosecrans. "Will it be of service to you if the move is made?"[58] "I think favorably of the proposed movement," Rosecrans replied; "it will help me very much."[59] The next day, June 18, Halleck chimed in, telling Burnside, "This seems the proper time for an advance toward East Tennessee."[60] Burnside certainly agreed and answered Rosecrans's query by saying he intended to push against Knoxville, Tennessee.[61]

Finally, on the twenty-third of June, like a giant rousing from a deep slumber, Rosecrans's army began moving south from Murfreesboro toward Bragg and Tullahoma, Burnside in support. The heavens opened on both armies, turning the roads into rivers of mud. Rosecrans's campaign would not be a brilliant one and, despite his earlier letters to Lincoln, would not be decisive, but it would prove successful. Over the next week his forces maneuvered Bragg's army out of its fortifications in Tullahoma. The Confederates withdrew behind the Tennessee River, Bragg electing to block the Union passage to Chattanooga. This also prevented him from sending additional troops to reinforce Johnston.[62] At this point, the major armies of the Union were all in motion at once. Finally, the idea of simultaneous pressure initiated by McClellan and Lincoln (or at least a form of it) was being implemented: Grant stood before Vicksburg; the Army of the Potomac marched after Lee; Banks moved on Port Hudson; and Rosecrans had finally marched.

Grant and Vicksburg

AT THE BEGINNING OF 1863, Halleck urged Grant to concentrate his forces so that he could either reinforce Sherman or work with Rosecrans against Bragg. News of Sherman's repulse at Vicksburg intensified Halleck's desire that Grant reinforce him. He also flogged Banks to assist.[63] But it was too late to effect any immediate changes in the situation in Vicksburg. "Sherman has returned to Napoleon," Grant told Halleck a few days later, referring to the small Arkansas town located at the mouth of the Arkansas River. "His loss was small. Will send you the particulars as soon as learned. I will start for Memphis immediately, and will do everything possible for the capture of Vicksburg."[64]

Grant responded to messages from Sherman and Porter, both of whom mistrusted their superior McClernand, and joined them. Halleck gave Grant the choice of appointing his ranking subordinate to lead the drive on Vicksburg or doing it himself. Grant preferred Sherman, but McClernand outranked him. Having no confidence in McClernand, Grant assumed overall command and ordered his subordinates south; he went back to Memphis "to make all the necessary preparation for leaving the territory behind me secure." Grant added troops from Arkansas to the expedition and also counted upon Banks to push up from south of Vicksburg.[65] "The real work of the campaign and siege of Vicksburg now began," Grant wrote in his memoirs, and by January 20 he had considered one of the key things that this "real work" would eventually entail: "What may be necessary to reduce the place I do not yet know, but since the late rains think our troops must get below the city to be used effectively."[66]

Grant thought it necessary to reorganize the Union command structure in the West. He asked for the consolidation of four small departments, while also relaying to his superiors the total lack of faith in McClernand among both army and navy leaders. The administration bent instantly to his request. Lincoln let him have as much of Arkansas as he wanted, as well as command over forces on both sides of the Mississippi River. Halleck warned him not to hold out much hope for help from Banks.[67]

McClernand, who all along had intended to command the Vicksburg drive, did not take his displacement kindly. He went above his commander's head for redress, appealing directly to Lincoln, who had been the original backer of his effort to raise troops in the Northwest for this mission. McClernand asked for what he had always wanted: an independent command. He didn't get it. The month before, he had written Lincoln, "I believe I am superseded."[68] For once, he proved correct.

In February 1863, Grant and his commanders had in motion three plans for skirting Vicksburg's defenses and putting Union troops below the "Confederate Gibraltar": diverting the flow of the Mississippi River by the digging of a canal; cutting a levee and moving via Lake Providence, Bayou Baxter, and the Red River into the Mississippi; and by breaking a levee not far from Helena, Arkansas, on the far northern reaches of the Big Muddy, and pushing ships and troops through the Yazoo Pass and the Coldwater, Tallahatchie, Yalobusha, and Yazoo rivers. All failed, victims of geography and Confederate countermoves. By the middle of March, another joined this list: an abortive attempt by Admiral Porter to reach the Yazoo above Snyder's Bluff through "Steele's Bayou, Black Bayou, Deer Creek, Rolling Fork," and finally the Sunflower River ended when fire from Confederate troops stopped the ships from going any farther.[69]

On March 20, Halleck made clear Grant's task, as well as the importance the administration placed upon it. "The great object on your line now is the opening of the Mississippi River," Halleck wrote, "and everything else must tend to that purpose. The eyes and hopes of the whole country are now directed to your army." He rated its opening more valuable "than the capture of forty Richmonds."[70]

The critical importance of Grant's task was made even clearer when, less than a week later, Halleck went further, effectively spelling out the administration's views on the role of slaves in the war effort and how to implement militarily what the Emancipation Proclamation made possible. Halleck ordered Grant to "withdraw from the use of the enemy all the slaves you can, and to employ those so withdrawn to the best possible advantage against the enemy." To Halleck this meant using them as teamsters, laborers, cooks—and soldiers. "Every slave withdrawn from the enemy is equivalent to a white man put *hors de combat*," Halleck insisted. "The character of the war has very much changed within the last year," he went on. "There is now no possible hope of reconciliation with the rebels. The Union party in the South is virtually destroyed. There can be no peace but that which is forced by the sword." Halleck finally saw the situation clearly: "This is the phase which the rebellion has now assumed. We must take things as they are."[71] The North would take resources from the enemy and use those against him. The war was escalating.

Grant had no difficulty obeying his orders or making sure his subordinates did the same. Not only would the Northern armies take the South's slaves, they would attack their overall ability to wage war. He wrote General Steele, "Rebellion has assumed that shape now that it can only terminate by the complete subjugation of the South or the overthrow of the Government....It is our duty, therefore," he continued, "to use every means to weaken the enemy, by destroying their means of subsistence, withdrawing their means of cultivating their fields, and in every other way possible."[72] Sherman had come to a similar conclusion, writing to Ohio's governor that the Union "must keep the War South, till they are not only ruined, exhausted, but humbled in pride and spirit."[73] Sherman had added another plank to what was becoming a Union strategy of exhaustion: undermining the South's will to fight.

By April 4, Grant had settled upon what became the solution to the Vicksburg problem, something he had been contemplating since the winter and which the high waters of a Mississippi that had burst its banks had thus far made impossible: he would run Vicksburg's guns and mount his campaign from below the city.[74]

Before Grant had sent word to his superiors of his intended movement, Halleck speeded him along. He urged Grant to join his forces with those of General Banks by whatever means possible, even sending troops to help him against Port Hudson if Banks could not support Grant. "I know that you can judge of these matters there much better than I can here; but as the President, who seems to be rather impatient about matters on the Mississippi, has several times asked me these questions, I repeat them to you." Halleck added a final shove, though one characteristic of his habitual failing to give direct orders: "As the season when we can do very little on the Lower Mississippi is rapidly advancing, I hope you will push matters with all possible dispatch."[75] Fortunately for the Union cause, Grant didn't require a direct order. He could take a hint.

A Confederate Crisis

IN ADDITION TO THE CONTROVERSY surrounding Bragg, another problem arose in the Confederate command in the West. On January 8, 1863, when Davis told Johnston that holding the Mississippi was "vital," he also addressed Johnston's complaint that he could not manage his command area. "The difficulty arising from the separation of troops of your command is realized," Davis said, "but cannot be avoided."[76]

Johnston returned again to his argument that the distances between the two armies in his department made it impossible for him to "maintain or exercise any general control. I must either take the immediate direction of one of these armies," he insisted, "thus for a time superseding its proper commander—which I believe was not intended—or be idle except on the rare occasions when it might be expedient to transfer troops from one army to the other." He worried that following the first course would undermine a fellow officer, causing harmful discontent. If he followed the second course, he would "generally be a distant spectator of the services of my comrades—a position which would inevitably disgrace me."[77]

Johnston's argument has a couple of weaknesses. First, he had been placed in command of the Western Department. The other generals therefore worked for him; it was his job to supplant them if he felt the need. Moreover, the other Confederate commanders, including the much-reviled Bragg, eagerly sought his leadership. Polk even suggested that Johnston take Bragg's place, arguing that if Lee could command both a department and an army in the field, Johnston could as well.[78]

Johnston's second remark demonstrates that he was far more concerned with elements of personal honor and reputation than with effective prosecution of the war. The remainder of his note drives this point home: he had "already lost too much time from service, and therefore can ill-afford to be inactive at any time during the remainder of the War." His concerns are certainly understandable in the context of the time, as he was competing against his brother officers for prestige and future assignments, but part of the era's code of personal honor involved doing what was asked of one by one's superiors. Johnston wanted to serve, but he did not want to serve in the capacity Davis wished, and so he requested another posting, one that might give him "better opportunity to render such service as I may be capable of."[79]

Davis attempted to reassure Johnston. "As that army is a part of your command, no order will be necessary to give you authority there, as, whether present or absent, you have a right to direct its operations and do whatever else belongs to the general commanding."[80] Johnston refused to be reassured, and the tensions between him and his civilian masters increased, something clear in his telegrams to Davis, as well as to others, including former U.S. senator and now Confederate congressman and Davis enemy Louis T. Wigfall. Johnston's words made their way to Richmond and the ears of James A. Seddon, the new secretary of war.[81]

Seddon wrote Johnston a flattering and often eloquent (as well as long-winded) letter that he had been appointed to his position because of his experience and the confidence he enjoyed in the eyes of his superiors. He answered the general's objections, explaining that one of the reasons he had been chosen was precisely to exercise direct command over his subordinates. Seddon asked Johnston about his preferences in regard to the Army of Tennessee: did he want to command it alone, or with Bragg as an assistant, making use of the other general's organizational and administrative skills?[82] Seddon, in short, gave Johnston carte blanche over his department. But the secretary also made the by now common mistake of trying to sweet-talk him into doing his job rather than issuing an outright order. Such lack of firm direction from the civilian authorities plagued the Confederacy as much as it did the Union. The thin-skinned nature of some of the generals made this unnecessarily worse.

Davis also told Johnston that his appointment had been made in a way that allowed him to travel from army to army in his department, taking command wherever necessary. He wrote that Johnston's personal honor would not be involved in the removal of Bragg because Johnston had nothing to gain from it. But, Davis added, "you shall not be urged by me to any course which would wound your sensibility or views of professional propriety."[83]

"I apprehend from some passages of your letter that I may not have fully understood my position here," Johnston replied, apparently still unmollified by either Davis or Seddon and their arguments that *he* was in command. He repeated his worries about upsetting fellow officers and reiterated his claim that his department was too large.[84]

This ridiculous situation dragged on into March, when Seddon tried again, though with no greater firmness than before. He repeated his belief that Johnston should take over Bragg's army and that if he felt any "delicacy" about "displacing" Bragg, Johnston should keep him, utilizing his skills as "organizer and disciplinarian." "I am sure this is what both the country and the Executive desire from you, and really in this vital struggle all considerations of scrupulous delicacy and generosity should, in my humble opinion, be disregarded to assume the position of greatest usefulness and effort."[85]

Seddon, so willing to urge Johnston to disregard "all considerations of scrupulous delicacy," should have taken his own advice and forced Johnston to do the job the government had given him and which he had agreed to take on. Seddon also saw Johnston's taking command of Bragg's army as a way of dealing with the popular discontent that had arisen against Bragg. Again, however, he merely suggested rather than order.[86]

Johnston's position was similar in some respects to that of a modern American combatant commander. For example, the head of Central Command controls forces in various places at the same time, including Iraq and Afghanistan, but there are generals on the ground commanding these units. The head of Central Command looks over their shoulder. Johnston needed to make the leap from commanding a single army to running a theater. This was something he lacked the mental liquidity to do. His complaints about his command area being too big had some legitimacy; it was indeed immense, far larger than what Lee controlled. But if he truly believed this beyond his ability he should have insisted that Davis replace him. Had Davis refused, Johnston should have tendered his resignation.

Davis and Seddon were complicit in this command debacle. The responsibility of the civilian chiefs was to ensure that their appointed military leader fulfilled his responsibilities. Johnston would not exercise his command, and Davis and Seddon failed to make him do so.

The War in the East

IN THE WAKE OF THE BLOODY Battle of Fredericksburg, a hard winter descended upon the opposing armies of the East. Lee's army fought as much against hunger as against the enemy in the early months of 1863 and also struggled to clothe and shoe itself and find enough forage for its animals.

During the winter, Lee dealt with these problems, as well as Union moves south of Richmond that endangered the areas of North Carolina from which the Army of Northern Virginia drew some of its supplies.[87]

North Carolina had heated up in December due to a Union thrust inland from New Bern. The Confederates bungled the defense, and the Union destroyed 4 miles of the important railroad connecting Wilmington, North Carolina, and Petersburg, Virginia. This led to further calls upon Lee for troops. He nearly always resisted such demands, seeking to keep his forces concentrated. He insisted that that the men of North Carolina could defend the state if they would "turn out" to do so.[88]

Lee also resisted calls on his force because he feared that the Army of the Potomac might be placed south of the James River and he wanted to have as much strength as possible to counter this. On February 17, word of Union transports sailing for the South led to the dispatch of Longstreet's corps of 16,000 to North Carolina. Two pointless Confederate operations against New Bern and Washington, North Carolina, followed, as did a far more useful collection of food supplies in southwestern Virginia. Lee wanted and needed the provisions they gathered, but he did not want Longstreet tangled up in any operations that hindered his quick recall. At winter's end, a quarter of Lee's forces were not available to meet the new Union push.[89]

The Union also tried its hand against Charleston, South Carolina, during this period. A small joint army-navy attempt on James Island near the city in June 1862 had failed, but this did not discourage the Union; they began planning again in September. Secretary of the Navy Gideon Welles harbored doubts regarding the utility of devoting so much matériel to taking a city he deemed of "no strategic importance." Simultaneously, Welles hoped his monitors would ensure Charleston's fall to sea power alone, as had happened at Port Royal. He believed that once Admiral Du Pont, the commander of the blockade off Charleston, was possessed of a squadron of monitors, he could sail past Fort Sumter and the port's other fortifications and force the city to surrender or face destruction from the sea. Such a victory would not only strike a blow at the symbolic heart of the rebellion but also represent the Navy Department's victory over its most important rival, the U.S. Army.[90]

One of the problems with Welles's plan was that Du Pont didn't believe in it. He doubted the little ships possessed the necessary offensive power, and even if they made it past Sumter, which Du Pont thought unlikely, they would find not safety but simply more enemy guns. However, Du Pont neglected to make his concerns sufficiently clear to his superiors. He also believed that to be successful, any attack against the city had to be a joint army-navy affair, a key concern that also got lost in the translation between the operation's commander and his overseers, who thought the troops Du Pont wanted were for occupation duty after the city's fall.[91]

Du Pont and Brigadier General John Gray Foster, the commander of the army troops, proceeded to plan a joint operation. Foster returned to Washington in February to brief the administration, including Lincoln, but found himself the subject of angry attack, particularly from Assistant Secretary of the Navy Gustavus Fox, who thought it was clear that Du Pont was to make a purely naval attack. Fox set about trying to put Du Pont straight. A critical report from an official sent to investigate Du Pont's actions, combined with what was already perceived in Washington as his McClellan-like delay, destroyed the administration's confidence in the admiral. Public pressure to effect something at Charleston also mounted.[92]

On April 7, Du Pont launched his attack, sending his ironclads against Fort Sumter. On April 11, Lincoln learned that Du Pont's assault had failed. With operations in progress on the Mississippi and in preparation on the Rappahannock, Lincoln told Du Pont to keep pressure on Charleston, at least in the form of a demonstration, to prevent Beauregard's troops from being sent to another theater. Du Pont, though, had already sailed for his base at Port Royal with his injured squadron.[93]

As Du Pont made his repairs, Lee fought off efforts to take men from his army to bolster Johnston, insisting that it would be more "natural" to use those reinforcements that had been sent west. He conceded that it was not as "easy for us to change troops from one department to another as it is for the enemy, and if we rely on that method we may be always too late."[94] The Confederates could not shift their men as easily as many in the North feared and as many historians have contended.

Moreover, Lee also had his own ideas about how best to help Johnston, as well as Beauregard's North Carolina forces. "Should Genl Hooker's army assume the defensive," Lee wrote, "the readiest method of relieving the pressure upon Genl Johnston & Genl Beauregard would be for this army to cross into Maryland. This cannot be done, however, in the present condition of the roads, nor unless I can obtain a certain amount of provisions and suitable transportation. But this is what I would recommend if practicable."[95] Again, Lee's offense-mindedness emerges. His solution for relieving enemy pressure was to knock the enemy off balance. We will soon see how this thought developed into the logic behind his summer campaign.

In mid-April, Hooker began to move. Lee remained unsure what his opponent intended. No matter, though; Lee knew what *he* intended. "We should assume the aggressive by the first of May," he wrote Davis, continuing along his path of reasoning that the best way to assist Johnston was through offensive action. He pointed out that Hooker's army would be weakened by the expiration of the term of service of his regiments and wouldn't have time to gain new recruits. A "vigorous advance" would clear the Shenandoah Valley, and the Union forces to his front would be "thrown north of the Potomac." The problem was that Lee lacked both forage and food for his army.[96]

Although he had no authority over any Confederate actions in the West, Lee had strategic views on that theater. In reply to a note from Adjutant General Samuel Cooper about sending reinforcements to central Tennessee Lee expressed his hope of stopping Fighting Joe Hooker and clearing the Valley, but added that he would send forces west if the government so decreed. He considered holding the Mississippi "vital" and believed that to do so it was necessary to keep back Rosecrans. While the enemy's superior numbers in practically every area made it difficult to decide from where to remove troops, he thought Johnston's best move would be to concentrate the troops in his department and "use them where they can be more effectively employed."[97] Tactically, operationally, and strategically, concentrate and attack would be Lee's solution to dealing with a numerically superior foe.

Despite the odds, Lee remained optimistic about eventual success against the Union, telling his wife, "If we can baffle them in their various designs this year & our people are true to our cause & not so devoted to themselves & their own aggrandizement, I think our success will be certain." He believed that Confederate success in 1863 would produce a dramatic change in Northern public opinion by the next fall, resulting in the demise of the Republican Party and the establishment of an administration dominated by "the friends of peace."[98] In late April, however, Lee had to leave such considerations and face another offensive by the Army of the Potomac.

On January 26, 1863, Lincoln sent a now-famous letter to Hooker, the Army of the Potomac's new commander. In it he reveals his obvious reservations about Hooker, reservations that stemmed in part from Hooker's undermining of Burnside's command. It also includes Lincoln's jibe at Hooker's protestation that what the country needed was a dictator. "Only those generals who gain successes can set up dictators," Lincoln remarked. "What I now ask of you is military success, and I will risk the dictatorship."[99]

Hooker's appearance inspired the kind of respect men want to feel for their leaders, but he was also arrogant and ceaselessly self-promoting. His fellow corps commander, Major General Samuel Heintzelman, noted in October 1862 that "General Hooker has said that he felt that he is the only General in the country competent to lead the armies of the Republic." Hooker combined such braggadocio with a reputation for drinking and whoring, though many would argue that these accusations were overdrawn. John Hay, Lincoln's secretary, insisted that Hooker would get flushed from even a tiny drink of alcohol and speculated as to whether this accounted for some of the lurid tales told of the general. Whatever the truth, Lincoln expected more than bluster from his generals; he expected action, wisely directed. "Beware of rashness," he wrote Hooker, "but with energy and sleepless vigilance go forward and give us victories."[100]

As a condition for his taking the command, Hooker succeeded in obtaining the right to communicate directly with the president. This move, the result of the frosty nature of the relationship between Halleck and Hooker (they had had some prewar business dealings that had gone sour), violated the chain of command and needlessly complicated the Union command structure. Halleck's failure to exercise his role of general in chief convinced Lincoln to allow Hooker this privilege.[101]

Hooker began whipping the demoralized Union army back into shape, exhibiting impressive leadership in the process. Halleck, meanwhile, reorganized the command structure in the East. He put the troops at Harpers Ferry and in the Shenandoah Valley under the command of Major General Robert Schenck. Hooker lost the 9th Corps to Major General Dix at Fortress Monroe, while Major General Heintzelman retained command of the capital's garrison. Halleck considered all of these forces too weak to protect themselves individually and told Hooker to help them if they were pressed. He also intended that they cooperate with Hooker. Lincoln had offered to place Heintzelman's troops under Hooker's orders, as well as those that became Schenck's command. Hooker declined. The Army of the Potomac provided work enough, he argued.[102]

Hooker would have a nearly free hand. "In regard to the operations of your own army," Halleck told him, in a refrain that now had become familiar, "you can best judge when and where it can move to the greatest advantage, keeping in view always the importance of covering Washington and Harpers Ferry either directly or by so operating as to be able to punish any force of the enemy sent against them." He did give some direction, however, in a copy of a letter he had sent Burnside on January 7 about the necessity of concentrating on fighting Lee's army, one that had been approved by Lincoln.[103]

Hooker took up a veteran command possessing a two-to-one advantage in numbers over its enemy. Moreover, 45,000 men under Heintzelman protected Washington, and Schenck led another 21,000 in the Shenandoah.

Nonetheless, Hooker mounted no operations for a very long time aside from small Union raids; the Confederates countered with the same, but more effectively. Rain, snow, mud—all of these mired the theater over the winter.[104]

At the end of March, Halleck pressed for action. The Union leaders knew that Lee had sent Longstreet's corps south of the James River to face the Federal forces on the coast, thus weakening the primary Confederate army. "It would seem, under these circumstances," Halleck observed, "advisable that a blow be struck by the Army of the Potomac as early as practicable." He added another reason as well—that the Confederates would be distracted by actions elsewhere. "It is believed that during the next few days several conflicts will take place, both south and west, which may attract the enemy's attention particularly to those points." Hooker sat on his hands. He had his own ideas about how to use his army.[105]

So did Lincoln and a great desire to see them prosecuted. Near the end of the first week of April, he visited Hooker; Halleck was among his entourage. Lincoln liked what he saw among the soldiery but thought Hooker overconfident. His operational intentions were also a source of fear. The argument among Hooker and his generals was whether the best route to Richmond entailed moving around Lee's right flank or his left. Lincoln proceeded to enlighten them on what the administration expected militarily, something Halleck's January conveyance of Lincoln's letter of instruction to Burnside obviously had not achieved. Lincoln gave them what today would be called the "commander's intent," something presidents should not have to do under ordinary circumstances. During the Second World War, President Franklin Roosevelt famously determined over the objections of the Joint Chiefs of Staff that U.S. troops would fight in the European Theater in 1942, a decision that led to the November landings in North Africa. But Roosevelt's intervention was *strategic* in nature. Lincoln's instructions, though addressing a strategic issue in regard to the Confederate army, dwelt more on operational and even tactical detail. These are the purview of the general, not the president, and an indication of Lincoln's lack of confidence in his commanders. As such, it is worth excerpting:[106]

> My opinion is, that just now, with the enemy directly ahead of us, there is *no* eligible route for us into Richmond; and consequently a question of preference between the Rappahannock route, and the James River route is a contest about nothing. Hence our prime object is the enemies' army in front of us, and is not with, or about, Richmond—at all, unless it be incidental to the main object.

What then? The two armies are face to face with a narrow river between them. Our communications are shorter and safer than are those of the enemy. For this reason, we can, with equal powers fret him more than he can us. I do not think that by raids towards Washington he can derange the Army of the Potomac at all. He has no distant opperations [*sic*] which can call any of the Army of the Potomac away; we have such operations which may call him away, at least in part. While he remains in tact [*sic*], I do not think we should take the disadvantage of attacking him in his entrenchments; but we should continually harrass [*sic*] and menace him, so that he shall have no leisure, nor safety in sending away detachments. If he weakens himself, then pitch into him.[107]

Lincoln was not finished. Underwhelmed by his generals and fearing they would repeat the same tactical mistake McClellan had made at Antietam and Burnside at Fredericksburg—keeping back too many troops—Lincoln wanted to prevent past failures from becoming future ones. Years later, Major General Darius N. Couch would note that after a dinner with the corps commanders, Lincoln asked to speak to Couch—who was second in command—and Hooker in private, saying, "Gentlemen, in your next battle, *put in all your men*."[108]

When he was ready, Hooker submitted his operational plan to Lincoln, having it delivered by Dan Butterfield, his chief of staff. Hooker believed he had "more chance of inflicting a heavier blow upon the enemy by turning his position to my right" and cutting Lee's communications with Richmond using his cavalry. He wanted to do this because he believed Lee would "escape being seriously crippled" by falling back toward the Confederate capital before Hooker could cross the Rappahannock. The cavalry sent to the Confederate rear would put themselves between Lee's army and Richmond, blocking a Rebel withdrawal until Hooker could "fall on his rear." Or, if this didn't work, Lee would be forced to "fall back by the way of Culpeper and Gordonsville, over a longer line than my own, with his supplies cut off." Moreover, Hooker wrote, "while the cavalry are moving, I shall threaten the passage of the river at various points, and, after they have passed well to the enemy's rear, shall endeavor to effect the crossing." The plan was in some respects similar to the one Quartermaster General Montgomery Meigs had proposed to Burnside in the wake of Fredericksburg.[109]

Lincoln approved Hooker's plan. The weather, however, did not. Major General George Stoneman's cavalry began their ride on April 13, but rains pounded them and the rivers bulged. Within two days, the weather stopped him. When told of problems with the advance, Lincoln reacted with strong skepticism. His generals had too often promised movement and not delivered. He wanted answers. Hooker did his best to ease Lincoln's fears. "No one, Mr. President, can be more anxious than myself to relieve your cares and anxieties, and you may be assured that I shall spare no labor and suffer no opportunity to pass unimproved for so doing."[110]

Meanwhile, Halleck had not completely abandoned involving himself in the operations of the Eastern Theater. In early February, from his post at Winchester, Virginia, at the mouth of the Shenandoah, Major General Robert H. Milroy received some intelligence that the Confederates intended to make a stab at taking back western Virginia. "I respectfully ask to be permitted to interfere with this arrangement," Milroy wrote his departmental commander, Major General Schenck. "If General Moor [sic] will advance on [Brigadier General John D.] Imboden by way of Huntersville and Warm Springs, and Mulligan will advance from New Creek by way of Petersburg, to Franklin, and I move on him up the Valley, by Staunton (brushing Jones out of the way), his forces can all be gobbled up, the base of guerrillaism and raids into West Virginia effectually cut off, and permanent peace given to that region."[111]

Halleck passed word of Milroy's concerns on to Hooker. "If General Milroy's suspicions are well founded, your cavalry should move so as to cut off the enemy or compel him to fall back." Hooker pooh-poohed Milroy's concerns and branded him a "stampeder."[112] Halleck immediately took up the sobriquet, even wondering by wire to Schenck whether Milroy should be replaced. A testy Halleck countered with one of his habitual rejoinders. "To move an army up the Shenandoah while Hooker operated from the Rappahannock," he replied, "would be to repeat the same old error of distant parallel lines, with the enemy between them, ready to concentrate upon and crush our divided forces."[113] A week later, Halleck received a report that the Confederates were planning a move against Winchester, Milroy's post.[114]

Milroy was right to worry. Lee, Seddon, and others in the Confederate high command had their gaze focused on old Virginia's northwest. Pressure from Confederate politicians with connections to the area had forced their hand. Various plans cooking since January resulted in a number of Confederate raids in the region to draw away Union troops from other areas, inspire recruitment, and strengthen the larder. But Lee, as always, thought of gaining more, and his "more" specifically meant an attack on Milroy's forces at Winchester. "I am very desirous to expel him from the Valley," he wrote, "and nothing but the immediate presence of General Burnside's large army (now commanded by General Hooker) and its threatened movements have prevented me from detaching a portion of the cavalry of this army to aid you in effecting that object."[115] But until the time was ripe for this, Lee contented himself with further raids in the area by Brigadier Generals John D. Imboden and W. E. "Grumble" Jones during April and May.[116]

By this time, Halleck had intelligence that Confederate forces were massing at Staunton, south of Milroy's post at Winchester. He even knew the objective of one of the raiding parties—the Baltimore and Ohio Railroad. He wanted Hooker to send cavalry to deal with them and protect this communications link. He also continued to fret about Milroy's competence and asked Schenck if he could put a better man there.[117]

Hooker reacted contemptuously to Halleck's missive, telling Stanton, falsely, that he had just been told that he was to send all of his cavalry to protect the Baltimore and Ohio Railroad. "I am not aware that any of your cavalry has been ordered to the Baltimore and Ohio Railroad," Halleck wrote. "It is expected, however, that you will not permit a very large cavalry force to pass from your front to destroy that road without intercepting or destroying it."[118] The Union's dysfunctional command situation was beginning to pay off for the Confederates.

For the next few weeks, to deal with the Confederate raids, Halleck communicated frequently with General Schenck and others.[119] The Confederate actions in western Virginia must have aroused Halleck's attention or ire, or perhaps it was the fact that Hooker had no interest in the area. Whatever the reason, Halleck changed his mind about operations in the valley. On April 19, Milroy was ordered to push up the Shenandoah when Hooker started his advance.[120]

Halleck also tried to arrange other supporting operations. He suggested to General Dix, the commander of the Federal forces at Fort Monroe, that Hooker's movement presented an opportunity for the Union. Believing Lee would mass his army between Richmond and the Rappahannock River, Halleck suggested Dix attack Richmond's railroad connections to the south. However, he could not simply propose something daring. "But would that be a safe operation? Moreover, would it not be contrary to principle?" The list of his fears went on until he asked whether it might be "more in accordance with principles" for Hooker and Dix to act simultaneously, Hooker striking the Rebels frontally while Dix proceeded to "threaten his flank and rear by the Pamunkey" and Mattaponi rivers. He finally decided that the best course was for Dix to take McClellan's old supply base at West Point and launch from there.[121]

Dix relayed his eager agreement, especially in taking West Point. In both of these supporting areas—Union operations in the Valley and Dix's in Virginia—Halleck was at his best (once he got to the point), as well as his worst. He continued his slavish dedication to Jomini's ideas, particularly the one involving operating on interior lines, meaning having a position in relation to the enemy's forces that allows one to concentrate separated forces more quickly than the opponent, but he also pointed out the advantages of Dix supporting Hooker. Moreover, Hooker himself had enjoined the Union navy to assist his efforts, and had received a promise of help.[122]

After the rains destroyed Hooker's initial plan, he developed another. He wrote Lincoln on April 27 that he would send three corps on a northward swing around the Wilderness. Three other corps, meanwhile, would cross the Rappahannock to pin the bulk of the Confederate forces opposite the Army of the Potomac. If the Confederates withdrew to meet the forces to the north, this element could then attack. Simultaneously with these movements, Hooker's cavalry would again try to sever Lee's communications. Hooker hoped to have a pair of supporting columns, trapping the Rebel forces between two stones. "While I am anxious," Lincoln replied, "please do not suppose I am impatient, or waste a moment's thought on me, to your own hindrance, or discomfort."[123]

When Hooker began his second advance, Lee was initially unsure of the enemy's game. This quickly changed. Faced with the possibility of being pinned between the two-pronged Union assault, Lee, always audacious, attacked. He left a thin screening force in Fredericksburg, met Hooker's northern turning movement near Chancellorsville with a part of his army, and sent the bulk of his forces, 25,000 men, in his own turning movement. This completely unhinged Hooker's attack and rolled up the northern flank of the Army of the Potomac. With about 60,000 men, Lee had successfully fended off an attack by a Union force twice his size and inflicted 16,800 casualties while suffering 13,000 of his own. Bloodied, Hooker's forces withdrew back across the Rappahannock by the end of the first week in May.[124]

While Lee had not needed Longstreet to thrash Hooker's army, it is impossible not to wonder what he might have accomplished had he had the added flexibility and punch of Longstreet's veterans. Indeed, Lee himself later told John Bell Hood that he believed that if he had "had the whole army...General Hooker would have been demolished." Many argue that Hooker lost his nerve, but it also could have been his wound. Hooker was injured by falling debris during the contest. Had Hooker "been killed by the shot which knocked over the pillar that stunned him," said Lincoln, "we should have been successful."[125]

After the battle, Heintzelman, the commander of the Union troops in Washington, complained in his journal that insufficient supporting operations had kept them from drawing off troops from Lee's armies. He believed that gunboats and men could have pushed up the James to take Richmond and that the various movements should have been simultaneous. "We never make our combinations sufficiently extensive." The observation was half true. To give Hooker credit, he had alerted the Union commanders on the Peninsula that the Army of the Potomac was moving, creating opportunities for them to seize.[126] And Halleck had made an effort to arrange support from other units. But the problem was that there was no one at the top coordinating these moves. Nothing had changed in the Union high command.

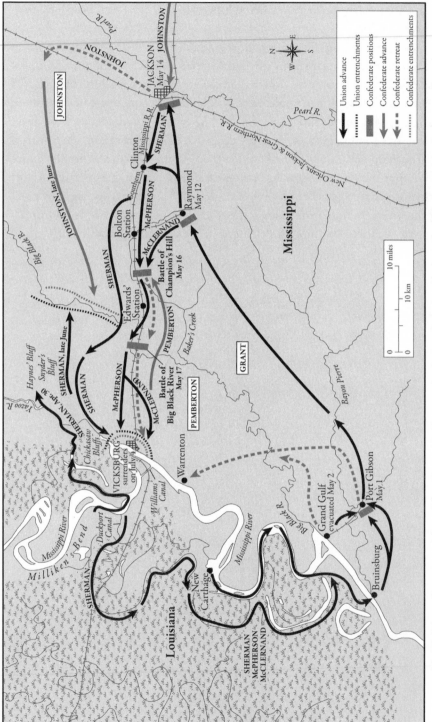

The Vicksburg Campaign. Adapted from James McPherson, *Battle Cry of Freedom* (New York: Oxford University Press, 1987), 632.

Vicksburg and Exhaustion

Vox populi—Vox humbug.

—WILLIAM T. SHERMAN, June 2, 1863

AS JOHNSTON, DAVIS, AND SEDDON wrangled about command responsibilities, Southern chances of success in the Western Theater became increasingly dim. Grant had started to move, and in February 1863, Joe Johnston grew concerned about the Union canal-digging effort across the river from Vicksburg. Grant ultimately abandoned this, but not before Johnston had told the Confederate president that if Grant succeeded, moved his army south of Vicksburg, and then invested Port Hudson with the combined Union forces, "it would be difficult for us to succour the place. Indeed we have not the means of forming a relieving army."[1]

As spring came on, Johnston requested reinforcements from Virginia. Davis declined, there being insufficient troops. Davis, for his part, wanted to know if Johnston could strengthen Bragg's army in Tennessee from units farther west.[2] Johnston pronounced this difficult because "at Mobile, in Mississippi, and in Middle Tennessee we cannot foresee attack long enough beforehand to be able to re-enforce the threatened army from either of the others." Moreover, the Confederates probably would not know about a Union attack on either of the first two until it actually happened. A Union push in middle Tennessee would give more warning, but only a few days—time enough to bring in reinforcements from eastern Tennessee but nowhere else. Johnston also pointed out the difficulty of temporarily shifting troops from Jackson, Mississippi, to Bragg's army at Tullahoma, Tennessee, as Davis wanted. Transferring 8,000–10,000 troops would take three weeks, with an additional two weeks for their necessary wagons and horses.[3]

Despite his lack of willingness to exercise his command, Johnston did understand the nature of the struggle in the West. "Our disadvantage in this warfare," he told Davis, "is that the enemy can transfer an army from Mississippi to Nashville before we learn that it is in motion. While an equal body of our troops could not make the same movement (the corresponding one rather) in less than six weeks."[4] Lee, as we have seen, drew similar conclusions about Northern mobility. This put the lie to the contentions of Halleck and others in the North that the South held an inherent advantage because of its interior position. The Union's ability to shift troops much more quickly via its superior railroads more than compensated for any geographical disadvantages. This also demonstrated the weakness in the arguments of Halleck and others that Lincoln did not understand theory. Intuitively, he grasped its shortcomings better than America's Jomini expert.

In May, Johnston was promised reinforcements and ordered to Mississippi to take matters there in hand. "I shall go immediately, although unfit for field service," he replied candidly and a little oddly.[5]

Grant, meanwhile, pushed south. In early April 1863, Halleck urged him to cooperate with Banks against Port Hudson should Banks not be able to reach Vicksburg.[6] Grant, however, already had his course set. As mentioned previously, he planned to get south of Vicksburg and begin his campaign from New Carthage, Louisiana, roughly a dozen miles southwest of his target as the crow flies. He sent Halleck his plan, which was for part of the naval fleet to "run the batteries of Vicksburg" while he moved the army to either Warrenton or Grand Gulf, both on the Mississippi side of the river. Warrenton was approximately 7 miles south of Vicksburg and had good roads to the city. Grand Gulf, which also sat on the banks of the Mississippi, though a farther dozen or so air miles below, had a road leading to Jackson, Mississippi's capital, and an important rail hub. "This is the only move I now see as practicable," Grant wrote, "and hope it will meet your approval. I will keep my army together, and see to it that I am not cut off from my supplies, or beaten in any other way than in fair fight."[7] Grant's staff and generals opposed the plan, particularly Sherman, who wrote his wife, Mary Ellen, that "though it is the plan it is not a good plan." He also branded it "one of the most hazardous & desperate moves of this or any war." Grant dismissed their fears and pushed along the campaign, demonstrating Clausewitz's higher form of courage, meaning the fortitude to make a decision and then take responsibility for whatever transpires.[8]

In late March, Grant had already dispatched troops under McClernand to New Carthage, south of Vicksburg, having previously explored the possibility of operating from here. McClernand took New Carthage on April 6 but did not move as quickly against Grand Gulf as Grant wanted. Moreover, Grant had planned to operate against Port Hudson, Louisiana, in conjunction with Banks, using Grand Gulf as a jumping-off point. Port Hudson was the other significant Confederate Mississippi River bastion. It was just north of Baton Rouge, about 140 miles due south of Vicksburg. After Port Hudson fell, the intention was to have Banks garrison it, then march the rest of his men north and join Grant in moving against Vicksburg.[9]

Grant could do none of this without support from the navy, aid that Admiral Porter eagerly supplied. Porter's vessels ran the guns of Vicksburg on the night of the sixteenth, losing a transport to enemy fire. Grant joined McClernand at New Carthage on the seventeenth, discovering for himself the hindering effects of bad roads and the flooding caused by broken levees. Reassessing the situation, he decided that it was now impossible to move against Port Hudson. He returned to his base at Milliken's Bend, Louisiana, a few miles northwest of Vicksburg, and once there issued Special Orders No. 110, announcing his intention "to obtain a foothold on the east bank of the Mississippi River, from which Vicksburg can be approached by practicable roads."[10] This was a turning point.

First, however, the Union had to discover a suitable landing place. Unable to find the right spot above Grand Gulf, they chose Hard Times Plantation on the Mississippi's west bank, nearly across the river from Grand Gulf. Union troops arrived there on the twenty-seventh.[11]

This was only part of Grant's plan. He kept Sherman's troops up the Yazoo River on the northeast of Vicksburg, on the eastern bank, with orders to take the city if Pemberton's position weakened sufficiently. To keep Pemberton guessing about what the Union was doing, Grant sent cavalry under Colonel Benjamin Grierson on a raid into the heart of Mississippi. Additionally, he had Sherman feint a sudden lunge at the Confederate fortifications at Haines's Bluff, about 15 miles northeast of Vicksburg, to pin Pemberton's troops in and around the city until Grant could secure a beachhead on the eastern shore.[12]

Grant's communications regarding Sherman's movements reveal his understanding of what effects the Northern press was having on public opinion and the army. He told Sherman that he did not want to order a "heavy demonstration" because that was all it would be, rather than a genuine invasion, and the "people at home would characterize it as a repulse." He therefore advised Sherman to publicize his order before he set off, making it clear that his was a reconnaissance mission and not an attack on Vicksburg.[13]

Sherman, who once threatened to hang all the reporters in his camp, showed his usual eagerness to get on with the job at hand. "We will make as strong a demonstration as possible," he replied to Grant. "The troops will all understand the purpose, and will not be hurt by the repulse." As for the people, he maintained that they "must find out the truth as they best can; it is none of their business." To Sherman, if a feint was what was necessary to help

Grant take Vicksburg, that was reason enough; there was no need to justify it before public opinion.[14]

Grant planned to have Porter bombard the Grand Gulf guns and then storm the town. But the gunboats' April 29 attack against the Confederate position failed, forcing Grant to abandon this idea. He wasted no time in finding another. He decided to cross his army below Grand Gulf, move inland, then head north, "cutting off Grand Gulf and taking it from its unprotected rear." On April 30, Grant's troops landed at Bruinsburg, 10 miles south of Grand Gulf and on the eastern side of the Mississippi. Grant saw this as a critical moment. "When this was effected I felt a degree of relief scarcely ever equalled since.... I was now in the enemy's country, with a vast river and the stronghold of Vicksburg between me and my base of supplies. But I was on dry ground on the same side of the river with the enemy. All the campaigns, labors, hardships and exposures from the month of December previous to this time that had been made and endured, were for the accomplishment of this one object."[15]

But Grant still didn't have his base at Grand Gulf, the capture of which he considered imperative; it was the place Clausewitz would have called "the key to the country." Grant wrote his wife that he looked upon taking Grand Gulf "as virtual possession of Vicksburg and Port Hudson and the entire Mississippi river." The terrain was difficult, hilly with heavy woods and scrub, with the roads along the ridges, ground that could enable a small force to hold off a much larger one. The Rebels took up strong positions on a pair of roads outside nearby Port Gibson. They numbered about 6,000. Grant had 23,000, and more coming. Grant attacked on May 1, overwhelming the defenders, and rode into Grand Gulf two days later.[16]

Originally, of course, Grant had planned to join Banks in smashing Port Hudson before moving on Vicksburg. Banks had dropped his end of the table by taking off down the Red River to Alexandria, Louisiana, in the opposite direction; Grant received word of this in Grand Gulf. Up to this point he had still intended to send McClernand's corps south to help Banks. But now he had to reassess yet again. He decided he would not bother with Banks or Port Hudson, believing this would take too long. "I therefore determined to move independently of Banks," Grant wrote in his memoirs, "cut loose from my base, destroy the rebel force in rear of Vicksburg and invest or capture the city." Vicksburg and Pemberton's army became his objectives. He wrote Sherman, whom he had ordered to join him, that the "enemy is badly beaten, greatly demoralized, and exhausted of ammunition. The road to Vicksburg is open. All we want now are men, ammunition, and hard bread." He told

Halleck that he thought the country would supply everything he needed for an "active campaign" and that he wouldn't stop until "Vicksburg is in our possession."[17]

Grand Gulf became Grant's base of supply as he moved inland.[18] He also made sure there would be subsidiary operations to keep the Confederates guessing, while wondering to Halleck whether Rosecrans could "at least make a demonstration of advancing."[19] His instructions to Major General Stephen Hurlbut on mounting cavalry raids demonstrate the continued escalation of the war, as well as the Union's emerging strategy of exhaustion. "Impress upon the Cavalry the necessity of keeping out of people[']s houses, or taking what is of no use to them in a Military point of view," Grant began. "They must live as far as possible off the country through which they pass and destroy corn, wheat crops and everything that can be made use of by the enemy in prolonging the war. Mules and horses can be taken to supply all our wants and where it does not cause too much delay agricultural implements may be destroyed. In other words cripple the rebellion in every way without insulting women and children or taking their clothing, jewelry & c."[20] Similarly, on April 11, 1863, Grant wrote a note to General Steele in which he revealed his view of the nature of the war: "Rebellion has assumed that shape now that it can only terminate by the complete subjugation of the South or the overthrow of the Government[. I]t is our duty therefore to use every means to weaken the enemy by destroying their means of cultivating their field, and in every other way possible."[21]

Grant's decision to abandon his base immediately after establishing it caused Sherman consternation; he lobbied against it, insisting that Grant would be unable to keep his army supplied down the single available road. Grant intended to bring up only basic supplies such as hardtack, salt, and coffee, and to make the enemy's countryside provide the rest. Already he had had no problem doing this.[22] The Union armies, particularly in the West, would now begin to try to exhaust the Confederacy's supplies. Logistically, Grant would make war pay for war. In effect, he was breaking the rules of how the war had been waged.

Grant broke the rules another way as well. He knew that the careful Halleck would not permit him to abandon his base, but he also knew that by the time his superiors found out, it would be too late. His plan would have already succeeded—or failed.[23]

However, Grant did not intend to strike directly for Vicksburg, though he did have troops stir up trouble in that direction to give this impression. He marched northeast for the Mississippi capital, Jackson, aiming at the railroad providing Vicksburg's supplies and communications. On May 10, 1863, he sent Banks a note telling him about the change of operational plans and asking for as much support as Banks could provide.[24]

The Confederates had by now awakened to the danger. As previously mentioned, Joe Johnston, who had been ill for a month, rose from his sickbed to take command in the field—spurred, no doubt, by a surprisingly direct order from Seddon. He reached Jackson on the evening of May 13 to find that Union troops under Sherman were at Clinton, located along the rail link to Vicksburg, thus interposing themselves between Johnston's and Pemberton's forces. "I am too late," Johnston told Seddon.[25]

Johnston tried to get Pemberton to attack Sherman's forces at Clinton before Sherman could combine with Grant's other advancing units. At first Pemberton agreed and sent Johnston word of this. But then, fearful of leaving Vicksburg vulnerable, Pemberton demurred. Moreover, his orders from Davis instructed him to hold the city.[26]

Meanwhile, Grant's forces fought and foraged their way to Jackson, taking the city on May 14 and forcing Johnston to retreat northward to Canton, Mississippi. "But by moving against Jackson," Grant later wrote in his memoirs, "I uncovered my own communication. So I finally decided to have none—to cut loose altogether from my base and move my whole force eastward."[27] Here was implementation of the lesson learned the previous fall when Confederate raiders had destroyed his bases of supply. Grant had discovered he could live off the land. Doing so came to characterize how the Union army did business in the West. It also undermined the plans of his opponents, who were intending to attack Grant's line of supply.[28]

Johnston still sought to unite his force with Pemberton's. When he received word that Pemberton had not yet moved toward Clinton, he reiterated that only by such a move could they link their forces. Pemberton got the note the next day, May 16, and marched toward Clinton. He was too late.[29] Grant was ahead of him.

On May 14, while still in Jackson, Grant received a captured copy of one of Johnston's dispatches pressing Pemberton to attack Sherman. Fearful that Johnston and Pemberton would unite on the railroad between Jackson and Vicksburg, Grant moved. This resulted in a battle three days later at Champion Hill, a gullied, overgrown, steep-banked, 140-foot-high rise along the railroad between Jackson and Vicksburg. Pemberton's troops held the ridgeline. The fighting quickly became a bloody back-and-forth melee, with positions falling, being retaken, and falling again. But in the midafternoon, Pemberton's forces broke and made a narrow escape back to their entrenchments around Vicksburg. The demoralized Confederates had suffered 3,800 casualties, the Union 2,400. The division of General Alvin P. Hovey, which had been the first Union force engaged, was hardest hit, losing a third of its men.[30]

Even before Pemberton had retreated to his entrenchments, Davis had become displeased with the response of his generals to the Union offensive. He could not understand "why a junction was not attempted," as he put it. He noted that it would have created a force "nearly equal" to the enemy's and might have led to their "total defeat" in a place where they could barely hope to retreat or receive reinforcements.[31] This had been Johnston's intent, but uniting Pemberton's forces and the other Confederate units proved difficult, a task not eased by the communication obstacles between the various Rebel forces caused by Union forces controlling much of the territory between them.[32]

On May 17, Johnston sent word that he was trying to join up with Pemberton. He quickly found this impossible, however, because by then Pemberton had withdrawn into Vicksburg. Johnston began preparing a relief effort and asked for reinforcements, though he also told Pemberton that if Haines's Bluff proved untenable, Vicksburg would consequently be of no value and he would be forced to surrender. "Under such circumstances, instead of losing both troops and place, we must, if possible, save the troops. If it is not too late, evacuate Vicksburg and its dependencies, and march to the northeast." Pemberton held a council of war with his generals. All agreed on the impossibility of withdrawal because of damage to morale and to the army's ability to fight. "I have decided to hold Vicksburg as long as possible," he wrote Johnston, "with the firm hope that the Government may yet be able to assist me in keeping this obstruction to the enemy's free navigation of the Mississippi River. I still conceive it to be the most important point in the Confederacy."[33]

Pemberton should have followed Johnston's advice and saved the army. It was, after all, the source of the Confederacy's strength. By comparison, Vicksburg mattered very little. In fact, one could make the argument that it did not matter at all. James Jones, a clerk in the Confederate War Department, wrote of Vicksburg's impending loss that "it would be a terrible blow, but not necessarily a fatal one, for the war could be prolonged indefinitely." Lee's adjutant Walter Taylor did not believe that the fall of both Vicksburg and Port Hudson mattered very much—as long as the Union did not "overrun" the rest of the West. "What the North is to be taught in order to secure peace is that a few military successes do not at all affect the ultimate result."[34] After

Vicksburg's fall, the Union would go back to fighting the war primarily in the same areas for which it had struggled in the spring of 1862—in Virginia and in central and eastern Tennessee.

Vicksburg was not incapable of withstanding a siege, having on hand two months' worth of supplies, but to save the city the Confederates would have had to provide relief from the outside. Davis noted, correctly, that "the vital issue of holding the Mississippi at Vicksburg is dependent on the success of General Johnston in an attack on the investing force." But he was not optimistic. "The intelligence from there is discouraging," he told Bragg.[35]

Grant's troops pushed on. On May 17 they crossed the Big Black River for the second time, this time en route to the Confederate citadel. Before abandoning Jackson, Grant had Sherman destroy the railroads and burn any industry of military value. "He did the work most effectually," Grant noted with satisfaction. On May 22, Grant attacked Vicksburg, believing its dispirited defenders would yield and not wanting to risk a siege. The position proved tougher than he thought; it was not simple trenches keeping out the onrushing Union troopers. The Confederates had turned the city into a fortress, with deep ditches and numerous hard points. The assault failed, and Grant settled down to a siege anyway.[36]

By this time, however, Grant's performance had impressed his commander in chief. In a letter, Lincoln wrote of the man who was quickly becoming his favorite general, "Whether Gen. Grant shall or shall not consummate the capture of Vicksburg, his campaign from the beginning of this month up to the twenty second day of it, is one of the most brilliant in the world."[37]

The Confederates continued gathering forces for a counterstroke: 10,000 troops were ordered from Charleston (the commander there, Beauregard, sent 6,500), and another 11,500 came from Bragg, with dribs and drabs from other places.[38] Johnston also ordered the garrison at Port Hudson to abandon a post they now had no hope of holding and unite with his army.[39] One of the ways Davis sought to provide Johnston with additional men was to tell Governor John J. Pettus of Mississippi to "levy the people...to join Johnston & attack the enemy in rear." Davis believed it was critical to not let the Union reach the river or "effect a junction with his reserves."[40] Pettus complied and ordered what was effectually a Confederate version of the French Revolutionary *levée en masse*—a mass conscription, such as that called for in 1793 by France's leaders, and heralding the age of the "people's war"—for the state of Mississippi.[41]

The troops came in slowly. Johnston maintained hope of success, but also unintentionally built a base for his indictment should he fail, remarking, "If army can be organized and well commanded, we shall win."[42] Davis remained worried. He counted on Pemberton to hold, and, like Johnston, was confident he would do so. But the concern was there, and Davis told Johnston that "the disparity of numbers renders prolonged defense dangerous. I hope you will soon be able to break the investment."[43]

As Johnston gathered his relief force he pled for more reinforcements, hoping to build an army of at least 30,000 to strike at what the Confederates estimated as 60,000–80,000 men under Grant.[44] Simultaneously, a ridiculous argument ensued between Johnston, Davis, and Seddon as to how many men Johnston had in his army, Seddon seemingly being unable to take seriously the accounts of the general in the field who actually led the forces when those reported numbers differed from his estimates.[45]

Davis hoped that Johnston would raise the siege. In late May, and in a better mood, Davis wrote Lee that "our intelligence from Missi. is, on the whole, encouraging."[46] Seddon felt differently. He wrote Johnston, "I feel intense anxiety as to your plans, and should be gratified to learn them as far as you deem safe to inform me." Johnston's intentions were not complex. "My only plan is to relieve Vicksburg," he replied, and then asked for more reinforcements to make this possible, noting, "The great object of the enemy for this campaign is to acquire possession of the Mississippi. Can you collect here a force sufficient to defeat the object?" But there was nothing to send. Already, in early June, Johnston pronounced the city doomed.[47]

The Confederacy also sought help for Vicksburg from the Trans-Mississippi Department. Previously it had been commanded by Theophilus Holmes, but in late January 1863, Edmund Kirby Smith, now a lieutenant general, was ordered to take over the department.[48] Smith arrived at his new command in early April. At the time, the Confederate situation in Arkansas had improved. "Disloyal" organizations had been suppressed. Federal troops held only Helena and Fayetteville, and Holmes insisted that merely a shortage of arms prevented him from making regular incursions into Missouri.[49]

Cooperation between the two departments of Johnston and Smith had the potential to produce good results. Johnston believed that the Mississippi Valley should be one command. In his mind, doing this would also free Bragg's Army of Tennessee to march where needed. This particular departmental line was never redrawn, but Smith, an old friend of Johnston's, tried to ensure close cooperation, even telling Senator Wigfall, a key Johnston supporter, that Smith would treat requests from Johnston as orders. Smith, for his part, wanted to act against Arkansas and Missouri, while his primary subordinate, Major General Richard Taylor (son of past president Zachary Taylor and

Davis's brother-in-law from Davis's first marriage), believed New Orleans should be their objective. Johnston and the Confederate president, at least in the spring and summer of 1863, believed Vicksburg and Port Hudson the decisive arenas.[50]

Because of poor communications with the Trans-Mississippi, Davis was generally uninformed about conditions there. It was also virtually impossible for the Richmond government to ship weapons and ammunition to the region. Because of this, Davis hoped Kirby Smith would finish the Shreveport foundry while bringing in powder on the Rio Grande. Davis also intended to reestablish communications with the area via the old water route—the Red River—should the Union attack on Vicksburg be repulsed and the Federals fail to occupy the waterway's lower reaches.[51] Furthermore, Davis had clear objectives for this department. In late February 1863, he wrote Holmes of his trust that they would recapture all of Arkansas not held by the Confederates and advance into Missouri. Davis believed that in order to do this it was necessary for the Confederates to retain the Arkansas River valley for the drawing of supplies.[52]

Though Holmes was pleased to see Smith, Smith was not pleased with the state of his inheritance. He found no departmental administration, despite two years of war, and had to build one from scratch. The department's armed strength had been exaggerated, and there were neither enough arms nor sufficient equipment. He immediately set out constructing the infrastructure necessary to supply his department's military needs, with the ambitious intent of making it self-sustaining. Smith had insufficient resources for any advance into Missouri and saw virtually no possibility of raising more men. In his mind, freeing Missouri would best be accomplished by Confederate success in the Mississippi Valley and removing enemy pressure upon Louisiana.[53]

On May 23, Seddon sought to "venture, with diffidence," that Johnston appeal to Holmes or Price in the Trans-Mississippi to "make diversions for you" in support of Johnston, or, if Vicksburg fell, to take Helena. Seddon would have sent such a message directly to the Trans-Mississippi, but Richmond could not communicate directly with the department.[54] Instead, Joe Johnston passed along Seddon's note while appealing to Smith to help relieve the now besieged Port Hudson and stressing the importance of keeping open communications across the Mississippi. Meanwhile, the secretary of war suggested the time was right for a move against Helena, Arkansas, which Johnston put to Smith as an option. But he also told Smith that his primary task should be to hold open the communications between the Trans-Mississippi and the rest of the Confederacy, and to prevent the Union from controlling the Mississippi River.[55]

Smith, however, had already begun acting on his own. On May 20, upon hearing from Pemberton about Grant crossing the Mississippi, he dispatched Taylor to the region of Louisiana opposite Vicksburg, aiming at the area from Milliken's Bend down to New Carthage. Taylor disagreed with his orders, thinking, as did Johnston, that Pemberton's forces should be withdrawn and that the move itself was nearly impossible. Moreover, he continued to believe that his objective should be New Orleans. He marched anyway, eventually launching two failed efforts at Union posts, including Milliken's Bend, in early June, after which he deposited around 4,000 troops across the river from Vicksburg.[56]

By this time, Smith had received a request from Johnston for help against Port Hudson. Smith sent Taylor, who marched in that direction with 3,000 men. He took Brashear City, Louisiana, on June 23 and then moved toward New Orleans, where he had wanted to go all along.[57]

Johnston, though he had originally wanted troops from the Trans-Mississippi concentrated against Port Hudson, was forced by events to change his mind. On June 26, he wrote Smith that the only thing that could prevent the fall of Vicksburg was Smith's men. This surprised Smith, and when he got the message he pronounced any effort from his side of the Mississippi impossible. He had already committed all of his disposable forces, sending Taylor's to try to relieve Port Hudson and the rest toward Vicksburg.[58]

On July 2, two days before Vicksburg's fall, Davis added his voice, asking Smith to move all his troops to the Mississippi River and cooperate in the relief of Vicksburg. "I am convinced that the safety of Vicksburg depends on your prompt and efficient co-operation," he said.[59] The request was far too late in coming. Even had it been sent quickly enough to allow Smith to do something, he had very limited troop strength, and the Union defenses opposite Vicksburg were too strong for him. Taylor had earlier found it impossible and gave up his attempt on June 7. Moreover, for the last two weeks of June, Smith had been trying to find some way of relieving Vicksburg, but to no avail. On the fifteenth, his forces at Richmond, Louisiana, were themselves attacked by a Union column.[60]

Smith responded to Johnston's plea to relieve Port Hudson by dispatching Taylor's small force. He also promised to inform Pemberton that he could expect no relief from the Mississippi's western bank, that his only hope was to cut his way out of Vicksburg, and that he should get out information about the date of his attempt so that Johnston could coordinate an attack. Smith promised he would advance at that time and make a demonstration to draw off what Union forces he could. But Smith wrote all this on July 4, the very day of Vicksburg's surrender.[61]

Bad news from the West continued for the Confederates. In another operation intended to relieve pressure on Vicksburg, Smith, at Seddon's suggestion, had launched an offensive aimed at Helena, Arkansas. Major General Theophilus Holmes bungled the July 4 attack against the city, while contributing nothing to the relief of Vicksburg.[62]

As the noose around Vicksburg tightened, Johnston returned to one of his old habits, thereby adding another layer of difficulty to the increasingly hopeless situation faced by the Confederate forces in the West. On June 12, he told Seddon that he had never considered himself commander of the troops in Tennessee since coming to Jackson and therefore didn't feel that he had the authority "to take troops from that department after having been informed by the Executive that no more could be spared. To take from Bragg a force which would make this army fit to oppose Grant, would involve yielding Tennessee. It is for the Government to decide between this State and Tennessee."[63] Again, Johnston refused to recognize the extent of his command authority. Moreover, by insisting that he did not consider himself the Confederate commander in Tennessee, he de facto decided to command what he wished and not what his government appointed.

Johnston also continued to refuse to decide whether troops should be pulled from Tennessee to save Vicksburg, insisting that he had no means of making such an assessment and that it was for the government to determine. He also grew increasingly testy, insisting to Seddon on June 15, "Without some great blunder of the enemy we cannot hold both. The odds against me are much greater than those you express. I consider saving Vicksburg hopeless."[64]

Seddon was not pleased. "Your telegram grieves and alarms me," he began. "Vicksburg must not be lost without a desperate struggle. The interest and honor of the Confederacy forbid it. I rely on you still to avert the loss. If better resources do not offer, you must hazard attack. It may be made in concert with the garrison, if practicable, but otherwise without, by day or night, as you think best."[65]

Seddon's note did not improve Johnston's mood or boost his confidence. He told Davis that this task of preserving Vicksburg was "above his ability." Moreover, he continued to maintain that he could not "command other remote departments." "No general can command separate armies."[66] Nonetheless, after accurately enumerating his difficulties, which included communicating with Pemberton, Grant's superior strength, and the Big Black River protecting Grant from attack, Johnston told Seddon, "I will do all I can, without hope of doing more than aid to extricate the garrison."[67]

Johnston had effectively refused to do his job and to accept the command given him. If he truly felt the task was beyond him, he should have offered his resignation. Davis might then have relieved him of his command and put Braxton Bragg in his place. For all Bragg's limitations and problems, the South needed a commander in the West who knew the area, its troops, and its myriad problems, and, most important, who wasn't afraid to do battle with the enemy. For better *and* for worse, that commander was Bragg. Putting the entire West under his command and telling him to do all in his power to relieve Vicksburg might have produced the best effort on the part of the Confederate forces in the area. Even this might have proved insufficient. By mid-June, the chances of saving Vicksburg were slim at best. Nonetheless, Bragg, despite his many personal failings, would have made a desperate effort to do so, and in the West, desperation was all the South had left.

But Davis did not fire Johnston; he tried to help him by further exploring the possibility of an offensive in Kentucky.[68] Meanwhile, Seddon acknowledged Johnston's great difficulties and urged him to attack. Seddon even offered to take upon himself the responsibility for any offensive action by Johnston in order to leave the general "free to follow the most desperate course the occasion may demand." He wanted Johnston to try to save Vicksburg and even asked whether it was possible for him to march to the relief of Port Hudson first, drive off Banks's besieging force, unite with the garrison there, and then move upon Vicksburg. Johnston insisted he simply lacked "the means of moving" and that marching on Port Hudson meant abandoning Jackson.[69] (Lincoln would later tell one of his generals almost exactly the same thing Seddon had told Johnston and get the same result.)

Meanwhile, Colonel E. J. Harvie, of Johnston's staff, tried to influence the situation in the West and justify his superior's stupidity. Harvie wrote to Joseph R. Davis, the nephew of the Confederate president, in an effort to get him to put pressure on his uncle. Harvie believed that Bragg's army could be brought to Mississippi and combined with Johnston's 24,000 men, and together the force could lift the siege of Vicksburg. He defended Johnston's inaction on this point by insisting that not only did Johnston lack the authority to do so before June 10, but by the tenth, when Johnston received such authority from the president, it was too late. Lifting the siege had become a political issue, not merely a military one, because it might involve the abandonment of the state of Tennessee to the enemy. Johnston deemed this decision so important that it could be resolved only in Richmond. Harvie thought Davis "ought to decide the question and take the responsibility. It may be that his decision involves the very fate of the Republic itself."[70]

Harvie was undoubtedly sincere in his beliefs about the situation, but he also appeared unaware of the extent of the command his superior held. Johnston controlled his department, indeed *commanded* his department, and had since his appointment; at least he had the authority to command his department if he would do so. He could move Bragg's troops if he desired. Had Davis not wanted them moved, he would have intervened. Davis never had to do so because Johnston refused to act. Instead, he quibbled.

Amidst all of this, Vicksburg held out. Grant ringed the city with 70,000 troops and began digging approaches. As the siege dragged on, the defending soldiers were reduced to one-quarter rations and afflicted with scurvy and other diseases. For the civilians, dog, cat, rat, and mule meat became staples.[71]

As June wore on, Johnston grew increasingly convinced of the impossibility of saving Vicksburg. The defenders now felt the same way. They had hoped and planned for Johnston's arrival, but hope failed, as Johnston failed. The Union works moved closer to the city, and on June 25 and July 1, Grant's men detonated underground mines and attacked the breaches; the city's starving, ragged defenders kept them out. Meanwhile, the best Johnston hoped for was that the garrison might escape, and he worked to achieve this. It was not a simple task. Communications with Pemberton were generally one-sided. Confederates floated down the river from Vicksburg with notes to Johnston, but there were few means of getting information in.[72]

Johnston had hoped to move on Vicksburg as soon as June 4, but he delayed because he lacked provisions, transportation, artillery, and virtually everything else. After three weeks of preparation, on June 28 Johnston finally felt ready and began a slow march from Jackson, believing Grant possessed 30,000–50,000 more men than he actually did. On July 3, he sent a note to Pemberton saying that he would try to mount an attack on the seventh—a note that Pemberton received after the city fell.[73]

Certain that he could no longer count upon any help from Johnston, Pemberton decided that he had two choices: surrender or try to fight his way out. He consulted with his generals, and they agreed to capitulate. On July 3 they asked Grant for terms. He responded as he had at Fort Donelson: unconditional surrender. Grant, though, bent on this. The Confederates had around 30,000 men in the city. Dealing with so many prisoners would have monopolized Grant's transports and paralyzed him for any immediate future moves. He followed the then accepted practice of paroling them instead, which meant they could not fight again until there had been an official exchange between the warring sides. Grant gambled that most of these men would never trouble him again. The Confederate force surrendered on July 4, and the subsequent application of the parole effectively destroyed Pemberton's army. Later, many of these men again bore arms for the Confederacy—against Grant.[74]

In surrendering, the civilians of the South's Gibraltar endured what was in their mind a great humiliation. Their only satisfaction was that the Union troops broke open the stores of Vicksburg's speculators and handed out the food and clothes to the starved, half-naked skeletons.[75] The city of Vicksburg did not celebrate Independence Day for a hundred years.

IN THE WAKE OF GRANT'S VICTORY, Lincoln wrote the general a congratulatory note. Its last line included a phrase that Davis never could have penned and which demonstrated one of the advantages Union leadership possessed. After outlining where his and Grant's thinking differed and why he had worried that the general was making a mistake by not going directly at Vicksburg rather than through the area around it, Lincoln wrote, "I now wish to make the personal acknowledgment that you were right, and I was wrong."[76]

But just how important was the Union victory at Vicksburg? The effects were certainly dramatic: Pemberton's army gone, tracts of Mississippi devastated, Confederate morale damaged, Union morale buoyed. The subsequent opening of the Mississippi gave the Union the base Sherman wanted, one it soon used. Grant certainly thought the fall of the so-called Confederate Gibraltar significant, writing, "The fate of the Confederacy was sealed when Vicksburg fell."[77] But this was not the case. Fighting to clear the Mississippi and take Vicksburg, which seemed to make so much sense at the time and to most observers afterward, was not the critical theater. The South did not collapse, despite the twin blows of Vicksburg and Gettysburg. Southern power was reduced and its strategic position injured, but the will remained unbroken and the power to resist still formidable. Indeed, the Union would come very close to losing the war in 1864. In the end, Grant had conducted a brilliant campaign against a secondary objective. He did remove Pemberton's army from the game (though many of these men would be back), which was of great benefit to the Union cause, but Tennessee was where he should have been fighting. His superiors would figure this out shortly. From then on, it would be Grant's war.

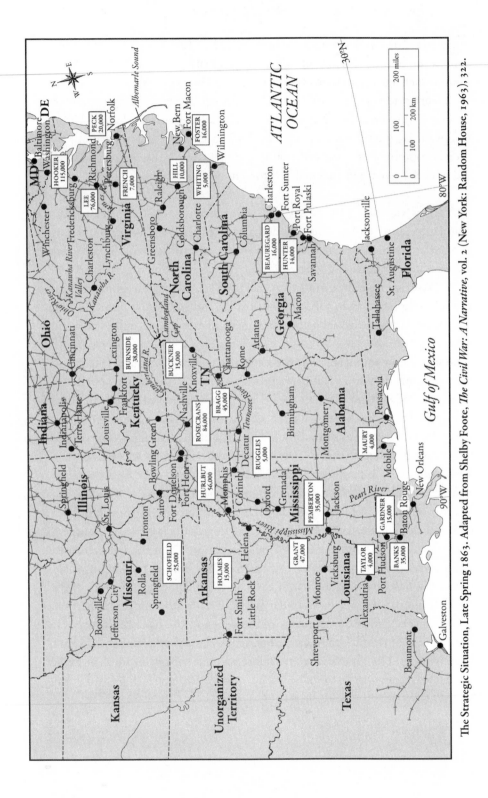

The Strategic Situation, Late Spring 1863. Adapted from Shelby Foote, *The Civil War: A Narrative*, vol. 2 (New York: Random House, 1963), 322.

Map labels

ATLANTIC OCEAN

Gulf of Mexico

Albemarle Sound

30°N
80°W
90°W

200 miles
200 km
0 100
0 100

States / Territories: MD, DE, Virginia, North Carolina, South Carolina, Georgia, Florida, Ohio, Indiana, Illinois, Kentucky, TN, Alabama, Mississippi, Missouri, Arkansas, Kansas, Unorganized Territory, Louisiana, Texas

Cities: Baltimore, Washington, Winchester, Norfolk, Richmond, Petersburg, Fredericksburg, Charleston, Lynchburg, Greensboro, Raleigh, New Bern, Fort Macon, Goldsborough, Wilmington, Charlotte, Columbia, Charleston, Fort Sumter, Port Royal, Fort Pulaski, Savannah, Macon, Atlanta, Rome, Chattanooga, Jacksonville, St. Augustine, Tallahassee, Cincinnati, Lexington, Frankfort, Louisville, Knoxville, Nashville, Bowling Green, Fort Donelson, Fort Henry, Decatur, Birmingham, Montgomery, Pensacola, Mobile, New Orleans, Baton Rouge, Port Hudson, Vicksburg, Jackson, Grenada, Oxford, Corinth, Memphis, Cairo, Ironton, St. Louis, Springfield, Indianapolis, Terre Haute, Springfield, Rolla, Jefferson City, Boonville, Fort Smith, Little Rock, Helena, Monroe, Alexandria, Shreveport, Beaumont, Galveston

Rivers: Ohio River, Kanawha River, Kanawha R., Cumberland R., Cumberland Gap, Tennessee River, Mississippi River, Pearl River, James River, Shenandoah Valley

Forces (boxed):
PECK 20,000
HOOKER 115,000
LEE 76,000
FRENCH 7,000
HILL 10,000
FOSTER 16,000
WHITING 5,000
BEAUREGARD 16,000
HUNTER 14,000
BURNSIDE 38,000
BUCKNER 15,000
ROSECRANS 84,000
BRAGG 45,000
RUGGLES 5,000
HURLBUT 56,000
MAURY 4,000
PEMBERTON 35,000
GARDNER 15,000
GRANT 47,000
TAYLOR 4,000
BANKS 35,000
SCHOFIELD 25,000
HOLMES 15,000

The Cruel Summer of 1863

THE GETTYSBURG CAMPAIGN

*Even if one tries to destroy the enemy completely, one must
accept the fact that every step gained may weaken one's
superiority*

—CARL VON CLAUSEWITZ

The Confederate Strategic Situation

"WE WERE NOW ENTERING upon the third summer of the war.... What
we had lost to the enemy so far was only of outlying provinces which we could
never have hoped to keep intact. But they were like wounds only skin deep &
not affecting our power of resistance. Indeed, as the territory occupied by our
principal armies became more compact, & the distances between these armies
was diminished our power of resistance, according to the rules & axioms of
the great Game of War, was approaching its maximum."[1] Confederate general
Edward Porter Alexander's apt assessment of the Confederacy's strategic situation in the summer of 1863 reminds us of Braxton Bragg's letter of February 1862. Bragg had argued for holding the Confederate heartland and little
else. Alexander's remarks drove this point home: a "compacted" Confederacy,
in many ways, was a stronger and more deadly Confederacy. The question
became, what to do with this strength?

In the spring of 1863 the South faced a gathering crisis in the West. Grant
had moved inexorably south, Vicksburg his ultimate aim. As Lee thrashed
Hooker at Chancellorsville, Pemberton, commanding at Vicksburg and feeling Grant's hot breath upon him, asked for reinforcements. Joe Johnston
insisted he could provide none without sacrificing Tennessee and asked Richmond if two brigades could come from the east.[2]

On May 9, 1863, Seddon wrote Lee about sending men west. Lee resisted,
arguing that even if they were dispatched, they wouldn't arrive before the
end of the month, which would be too late. Moreover, he wrote, "the uncertainty of its arrival and the uncertainty of its application cause me to doubt
the policy of sending it." Lee also fought, as always, the reduction of his own
army and cited the overwhelming preponderance of Hooker's opposing force,

which he estimated at 159,000, with another 30,000 on their way. "You can therefore see the odds against us," he told the secretary of war and then gave Seddon a hard choice: "decide whether the line of Virginia is in more danger than the line of the Mississippi."[3]

Here, once again, one of the major dilemmas facing the Confederacy reared its head: it could not easily defend all of its territory. Alexander's assessment was certainly correct, but the much-reduced Confederacy lacked the manpower necessary to protect its many vital points and could not stop the Union's application of simultaneous pressure—just as Lincoln had hypothesized in late 1861. The Union strategy devised by McClellan and refined by Lincoln was beginning to bear fruit. Once the Union possessed a general in chief with sufficient vision, it would reap victory.

Davis agreed with Lee's arguments against shipping troops west. Lee, as usual, had his own ideas about how to fight the war. In April he had advised a move by his forces into Maryland as the best way of assisting Johnston. By May, he believed that an advance beyond the Rappahannock, halfway between Richmond and Washington, and along the banks of which the Battle of Fredericksburg had been fought would draw the enemy's troops from the coast of the Carolinas.[4]

Lee's vision for his summer offensive continued to gestate as he called troops to his main army from Major General D. H. Hill's department south of the James River. Discussions about the situation in North Carolina coincided with Lee's push to build a case for an offensive. "There is always hazard in military movements," he told Seddon, "but we must decide between the positive loss of inactivity and the risk of action." He believed that there was nothing to be gained by "remaining quietly on the defensive." "Unless it can be drawn out in a position to be assailed," Lee said of Hooker's army, "it will take its own time to prepare and strengthen itself to renew its advance upon Richmond, and force this army back within the intrenchments of that city." Only a movement on his part, Lee was convinced, could force the Army of the Potomac into the field. But despite his hunger to take the offensive, he was willing to remain on the defensive—if the government wished it.[5]

Seddon quickly agreed with Lee's decision to advance. He saw the risks as necessary and worth the potential reward, believing "such action is indispensable to our safety and independence, and all attendant sacrifices and risks must be incurred."[6]

By early June 1863, Lee not only wanted to take the offensive but felt that he *had* to move or the South's position in the East would worsen. The question became what kind of move, and for what purpose? Lee planned an offensive with multiple objectives, strategic as well as operational. He hoped to do something that would impact the course of the war, but in a manner that reached beyond the thought of most of his contemporaries. Lee hoped to strike at Union public opinion, and thus its will to fight.

In a long letter to Davis, he discussed his view of Northern public opinion and the importance of encouraging the Union faction that desired peace. The declining strength of the Confederate armies, and the necessity that the South husband its strength, meant it was losing the battle of time. Meanwhile, as the South grew weaker, the North was growing stronger. "Under these circumstances we should neglect no honorable means of dividing and weakening our enemies that they may feel some of the difficulties experienced by ourselves. It seems to me that the most effectual mode of accomplishing this object, now within our reach, is to give all the encouragement we can, consistently with the truth, to the rising peace party of the North."[7]

There was disagreement over whether an offensive by Lee into the North would help the peace faction, or Copperheads, as they were often called. The *Richmond Enquirer* had no confidence in them and said the South had to rely on its own "peace party," the Army of Northern Virginia. The *New York Times* insisted that an invasion of the North would strengthen Union support for the war and surely spell the peace party's doom. One of the chief Copperheads, former Ohio congressman Clement L. Vallandigham, who had been expelled from the Union and subsequently campaigned for Ohio's governorship, agreed with the *Times*. Confederate vice president Alexander Stephens held the same opinion. But Davis and his cabinet did not; their thinking ran more along the lines of Lee's.[8]

What kind of strategy, though, if any, would Lee pursue? Lee's adjutant Walter H. Taylor described the foundation of Southern strategy as being "one of defense." The North's superior numbers and material resources forced the Confederacy to "husband its resources" and to hope that the "dissatisfaction and pecuniary distress" of a prolonged war would cause those in the North to "weary of the struggle."[9] Taylor argued that the South pursued a defensive strategy (though one should really apply his observation just to Lee), the intention of which was to protract the war and convince the North to quit; this comment aligns very well with Lee's desire to affect Northern public opinion. Taylor's view was supported by an April 1868 conversation between Lee and Army of Northern Virginia veteran William Allan wherein Lee insisted that "the South was too weak to carry on a war of invasion, and his offensive movements against the North were never intended except as parts of a defensive system."[10]

However, Taylor also offered the operational and tactical applications of this strategic approach, a course reflecting Lee's insistence upon seizing the operational and tactical initiative, as well as the way he chose to fight the war. According to Taylor, Lee believed that a "true defensive policy [strategy]" involved "delivering an effective blow to the enemy." Such a blow would "thwart his designs of invasion, derange" the enemy's "plan of campaign," and thus "prolong the conflict."[11] In other words, generally sit strategically on the defensive, but keep the enemy off balance with rapid offensive operational and tactical blows. This would enable the South to protract the war long enough to convince the North to quit.

Charles Marshall, another of Lee's adjutants, provided a similar interpretation. He argued that Lee pursued a defensive strategy based upon concentration, one that included taking the initiative against the enemy in order to keep them unbalanced. He also insisted that Lee did not intend to fight battles that did not help the South accomplish its political objective. Lee encountered problems with this approach, "but they did not deter him from pursuing steadily and in spite of all opposition the plan by which alone he believed the war might be prosecuted to a successful issue."[12] In other words, Lee would fight his own war.

Taken together, these comments indicate a generally defensive strategic bent, but one supplemented by operational and tactical offensive action as the situation warranted. In the end, though, these examples do not demonstrate proof of a larger, coherent Confederate offensive-defensive strategy (which, as we've seen, is often claimed for the South), nor do they fit the related mistaken interpretation of a South waiting for a Union move and then striking. Indeed, they demonstrate the very opposite.

Strategically, in 1863 Lee also hoped to fight his way to a Confederate victory if the opportunity arose. The picture on this, though, is contradictory. Davis wrote in his memoirs, "If, beyond the Potomac, some opportunity should be offered so as to enable us to defeat the army on which our foe most relied, the measure of our success would be full." Defeating the Army of the Potomac was one thing, but this was not the same as fighting one's way to victory. Allan recorded Lee as saying on this point that "he did not intend to give general battle in P.[ennsylvania] if he could avoid it." But Lee also revealed to Allan that he had no delusions that he could move north and not give battle. Indeed, Lee wrote afterward about "the valuable results which might be expected to follow a decided advantage gained over the enemy in Maryland or Pennsylvania," an obvious expression of his belief that a victory on Union soil could deliver a blow to Union will. In a conversation during the march north, Major General Isaac Trimble recorded that Lee "laid his spread fingers upon the map between Gettysburg and Emmitsburg and said, 'Somewhere hereabout, we will fight a great battle, and if successful, will secure our independence and win the war.'" Interestingly, according to Allan, Lee actually expected to remain in the North until the autumn, "to move about, to manoeuver & alarm the enemy, threaten their cities, hit any blows he might be able to do without risking a general battle, & then towards Fall return nearer his base."[13]

There was a political prong of this offensive as well. Davis wanted Vice President Alexander Stephens to accompany the army. His inspiration was the diplomat Nicholas Trist traveling with Winfield Scott's forces in the Mexican War. Stephens didn't arrive in Richmond before Lee marched, but he wouldn't have gone anyway, believing his arrival with an army was not conducive to any negotiations. Instead, he would be dispatched to Virginia, where he would wait on a ship off Fortress Monroe. Lincoln refused to see him.[14]

Even if he failed to achieve his strategic objectives, Lee hoped that his moves would at least bear some significant operational fruit. Lee's after-action report on the Gettysburg campaign gives the most succinct view of his operational objectives: "It was determined to draw [the Union army] from the position, and if practicable to transfer the scene of hostilities beyond the Potomac." This also meant clearing the Shenandoah of the Union forces under Milroy. Moreover, if the campaign didn't produce a situation that led to the end of the war, he "hoped that we should at least so far disturb the plan for the summer campaign as to prevent its execution during the season of active operations."[15] Lee also hoped a diversion mounted by Imboden's men in northwestern Virginia would help the planned move into the Shenandoah, and he was glad when he discovered Imboden moving "promptly...towards the Potomac."[16] Allan later wrote that in 1863 "Lee went North to break up the Federal campaign against Richmond; to relieve Virginia, to feed his army, to win such advantages as might be in reach of the smaller army when his more powerful adversary was hampered by the defence not of one but of several large cities."[17] Strategically and operationally, Lee had solid objectives. Achieving them became the rub.

The Union Prepares

ON THE SEVENTH OF MAY, Secretary of War Stanton wrote to a number of key Union military and political figures about the post-Chancellorsville situation in the east. His wire included the following: "The Army of the

Potomac will speedily resume offensive operations."[18] He proved optimistic—as well as wrong. The Army of the Potomac would now largely fight defensively for the next year.

Both Hooker and Lincoln initially had hoped otherwise. Though bloodied at Chancellorsville (suffering 17,000 casualties to the Rebels' 13,000), the Army of the Potomac remained a formidable host; infantry strength alone numbered 80,000. Hooker's defeat, though, had devastated the president. "I shall never forget that picture of despair," journalist Noah Brooks wrote of the May 6 moment when Lincoln entered the room bearing the tragic telegram with the news. Lincoln's face, "usually sallow, was ashen in hue." He gave Brooks the note and told him to read it. The "dispirited and ghostlike" Lincoln, his face as gray as the chamber's wallpaper, paced back and forth across the room, hands gripped behind his back, crying, "My God! my God! What will the country say! What will the country say!"[19]

Distraught over the possible public reaction, Lincoln and Halleck made a quick visit to Hooker's army the same day.[20] Lincoln wasted little time grieving. On the seventh, he penned the following to the commander of the Army of the Potomac: "What next? If possible I would be very glad of another movement early enough to give us some benefit from the fact of the enemies['] communications being broken, but neither for this reason or any other, do I wish anything done in desperation or rashness. An early movement would also help to supersede the bad moral effect of the recent one, which is sure to be considerably injurious." He added, "Have you already in your mind a plan wholly, or partially formed? If you have, prosecute it without interference from me. If you have not, please inform me, so that I, incompetent as I may be, can try [to] assist in the formation of some plan for the Army."[21]

Hooker replied that he had to look over the state of his force and think about it. By the thirteenth he had decided to again cross the Rappahannock, but his letter announcing this to Lincoln betrayed little confidence. It listed obstacles: expired enlistments had cost him 23,000 men, reducing his infantry strength to the aforementioned 80,000; Longstreet's corps was in Richmond and could easily support Lee; the Union troops in the areas around Washington, Baltimore, and the upper Potomac in general were out of position to be any use.[22]

Lincoln summoned Hooker to Washington. The president decided that the opportunity presented by the battering of the Rebel communications had now passed. Afterward, he wrote Hooker, "It does not now appear probable to me that you can gain anything by an early renewal of the attempt to cross the Rappahannock. I therefore shall not complain if you do no more for a time than to keep the enemy at bay, and out of other mischief by menaces and occasional cavalry raids, if practicable, and to put your own army in good condition again." But he also added a caveat: if Hooker saw an opportunity to attack, he was to take it.[23]

The Campaign Unfolds

LEE PLANNED TO MAKE his own opportunity. On June 10, 1863, he dispatched Lieutenant General Richard Ewell's corps to the Shenandoah Valley. He delayed the movements of his main army because of reports of enemy activity on the North Carolina coast, as well as in Virginia between the James and Rappahannock rivers. He worried that "it may now be too late to accomplish all that was desired."[24]

When Lee put the rest of his army in motion he tried to deceive the enemy as to his intentions and gave great leeway to his subordinate commanders in making their respective advances.[25] He told Ewell to move on Hagerstown, Maryland, northwest of Harpers Ferry, but instructed him to "give out that your movement is for the purpose of enveloping Harper's Ferry," and ordered Longstreet to make use of the same ruse.[26]

Once Ewell's corps crossed the Potomac, Harrisburg became the operational objective of Lee's advance. Here they could destroy the railroad bridge across the Susquehanna River, severing the rail connection between Washington and the West. On the evening of June 28, as the Confederates prepared to move against the Pennsylvania capital, they received word from Longstreet's spy, Henry Thomas Harrison, of the Union army having crossed the Potomac. The information caused Lee to abandon his drive on Harrisburg and prepare to meet the Federal threat.[27]

Lee's efforts to mask his advance failed. The Union knew he planned to march northward even before Ewell started for the Valley. The Richmond papers also proved helpful. Lee's actual intentions remained unclear to the Federal high command, but they watched and prepared. By late May, the Union commands in the Shenandoah, at West Point, Virginia, and on the Rappahannock knew something was up.[28]

The problem was what to do about it. The root of the difficulty with engineering a Union response is found in a note Halleck sent to General John A. Dix at Fortress Monroe: "As General Hooker reports direct to the President, I know not what he intends to do."[29] The general in chief did not control the Army of the Potomac. This meant it was nearly impossible to coordinate the

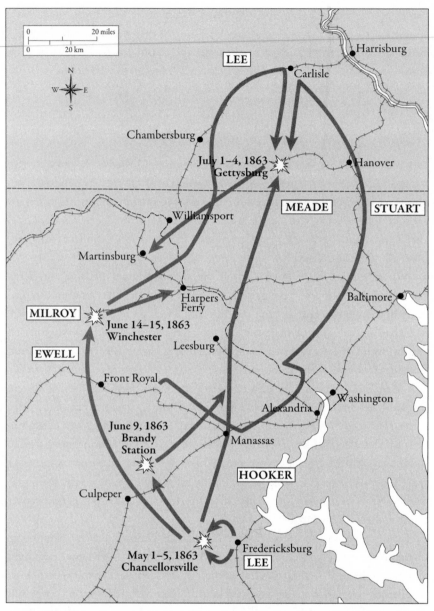

The Gettysburg Campaign. Adapted from Aaron Sheehan-Dean, *Concise Historical Atlas of the U.S. Civil War* (Oxford: Oxford University Press, 2009), 57.

actions of the various Union forces stretching from the Shenandoah to the Atlantic coast. This also made it improbable that the Union armies in the West would act in unison with those in the East. This lack of consistent coordination and information exchange gave the Confederates breathing spells. Plus, it limited the actions of subordinate commanders. For example, on May 30, General Milroy in the Shenandoah believed that Lee's army was concentrated against Hooker, and he suggested mounting a diversion in the valley.[30] He did not yet know that Lee's entire army was already marching in his direction, and this despite the fact that on March 31 Hooker had believed Lee was not with the Confederate forces to his front because Lee had not replied to a note sent a week before.[31] Late in the first week of June, Hooker observed the Rebels breaking up their camps. He believed Lee was going to either cross the Potomac and strike north, as he had the previous summer, or try to put the Army of Northern Virginia between Washington and Hooker's force. Then, in an oddly worded statement, Hooker told Lincoln, "As I am liable to be called on to make a movement with the utmost promptitude, I desire that I may be informed as early as practicable of the views of the Government concerning this army." Hooker wrote Lincoln that his instructions from Halleck were to protect Washington and Harpers Ferry, "operating as to be able to punish any force of the enemy sent against them." Hooker anticipated that the enemy would head toward the Potomac, and it was now his opinion that "it is my duty to pitch into his rear." "In view of these contemplated movements of the enemy, I cannot too forcibly impress upon the mind of His Excellency the President the necessity of having one commander for all of the troops whose operations can have an influence on those of Lee's army." Hooker complained that under the current system each of the commanders was "in ignorance of the movements of the others; at least such is my situation."[32]

Hooker's letter to Lincoln raised several warning flags, chief among them being Hooker's apparent loss of confidence in himself. The general, after suggesting he "pitch into" the rear of Lee's army, wondered in his note whether it was "within the spirit of his instructions to do so." Sir Frederick Maurice said of this that "a general who asks questions of that kind of his political chief shows that he had not a plan in which he believes, and is eager to have someone else to share his responsibilities."[33] Previously, Lincoln had told Hooker to act when he had the opportunity, yet the general was afraid to take the initiative without Lincoln's blessing. He also pointed out the same problem that Halleck had identified: the divided nature of the Union command structure in the Eastern Theater. Command is hard at any time; divided commands make the management of an already difficult situation even harder, generally producing paralysis. Hooker did at least present a plan for fighting the enemy, "to pitch into his rear." This might allow the mass of the Union army to hit a portion of the Confederate force.

The replies of his superiors simply made things worse. Both Lincoln and Halleck feared the effect of Hooker's having to fight the Rebel force in the entrenchments around Fredericksburg. Lincoln offered his advice: "In one word, I would not take any risk of being entangled upon the river, like an ox jumped half over a fence and liable to be torn by dogs front and rear, without a fair chance to gore one way or kick the other. If Lee would come to my side of the river, I would keep on the same side, and fight him or act on the defense, according as might be my estimate of his strength relatively to my own."[34]

This came with a great caveat: Lincoln said that he couldn't comment on Hooker's intended move because he lacked the military knowledge and had therefore given the matter over to Halleck to decide.[35] Halleck's rambling reply said both a great deal and nothing, which was normal for Halleck. He noted that Hooker's original instructions gave him the freedom to do what he wanted as long as Washington and Harpers Ferry remained secure. To Hooker's proposed move, he wired that he thought Lee's march gave Hooker "great advantages upon his flank to cut him in two, and fight his divided forces. Would it not be more advantageous to fight his movable column first, instead of first attacking his intrenchments, with your own forces separated by the Rappahannock?" In other words, Halleck offered no judgment on Hooker's plan, proposed another, and then attached to it intimation that Washington didn't have enough troops to defend it against a Confederate attack because the garrison didn't match the numbers that the earlier commission had determined necessary to hold the city. Because the safety of the capital partially depended upon Hooker's army, Halleck replied, "It would, therefore, seem perilous to permit Lee's main force to move upon the Potomac while your army is attacking an intrenched position on the other side of the Rappahannock."[36] This was a vote against Hooker's plan but not an order to forgo it. Halleck, as always, decided not to decide.

His insistence on the weakness of Washington's poor state of defense was also deeply disingenuous. Halleck had participated in a recent review of the city's military state in an effort to supply reinforcements for Hooker's army. Halleck may have believed the forces inadequate, but his own report said that his view of this was based upon the assumption that the Army of the Potomac was doing nothing. If it crossed the Rappahannock above Fredericksburg, troops could actually be removed from the city. If the army won a victory after it crossed, this would secure Washington and Maryland. But when composing his assessment, Halleck expected the Army of the Potomac to sit for a while.[37]

"Of course your movements must depend in a great measure upon those made by Lee," Halleck went on, suggesting that Lee might try to pin Hooker with the bulk of the Army of Northern Virginia while launching a raid into Pennsylvania and Maryland. Halleck promised that the troops in the Valley and at West Point would be given orders to help Hooker as he wished. He ended his note with a jab at Hooker as well as the past commanders of the Army of the Potomac: "Lee will probably move light and rapidly. Your movable force should be prepared to do the same."[38]

But Halleck gave no orders; indeed, he thought it wasn't his place to do so. Lincoln also dispatched none, believing he should bow to Halleck's superior military wisdom. Hooker lacked the confidence to act on his own. He sat, and the opportunity to wrest control of the summer campaign by striking Lee's rear passed untaken.[39] The Union command system was broken.

The Confederate forces in Hooker's fore continued to thin. And the Union leaders stepped up preparation for a Confederate raid into Pennsylvania.[40] Hooker proposed another move, writing Lincoln on June 10. He had clear information that Confederate cavalry commander Major General J. E. B. Stuart intended to mount a raid. Hooker was unsure whether the Confederates would send a large number of their infantry along with the cavalry, but his information forced him to consider this possibility. If this occurred, Hooker believed, the Rebels could leave little behind to stop him. "If it should be found to be the case," he wrote Lincoln, "will it not promote the true interest of the cause for me to march to Richmond at once?... If left to operate from my own judgment," he added, "with my present information, I do not hesitate to say that I should adopt this course as being the most speedy and certain mode of giving the rebellion a mortal blow. I desire that you will give it your reflection."[41]

Lincoln reflected and swiftly replied that he thought otherwise. "If left to me," he wrote, "I would not go south of Rappahannock upon Lee's moving north of it. If you had Richmond invested to-day, you would not be able to take it in twenty days: meanwhile your communications, and with them your army, would be ruined." He then repeated what he had been trying to drum into his generals' heads for more than a year: "I think Lee's army, and not Richmond, is your sure objective point." He went on: "If he comes toward the Upper Potomac, follow on his flank and on his inside track, shortening your lines while he lengthens his. Fight him, too, when opportunity offers. If he stays where he is, fret him and fret him."[42] Hooker, like many of Lincoln's generals, remained fixed on geographical objectives, rather than on one of the true keys to victory: the destruction of Lee's army.

But was Lincoln's refusal to allow Hooker to try to take Richmond another missed Union opportunity? A first question was whether it was even possible. Confederate brigadier general Edward Porter Alexander insisted after the war that not only was it possible, but it would have been the correct Union action, as well as "sure & easy."[43] The loss of Richmond would not have immediately destroyed the South's will or ability to resist, but it would have struck a severe blow at its capability of doing so. Without Richmond, Lee believed, he would have to fight the war from North Carolina. This would have meant the loss of Virginia and the subsequent loss of much of Lee's army, considering the predilection of Confederate troops from Union-controlled areas to desert, to not return from paroles, and even to enlist under the Union's banner. With Richmond in its hands, the Union could draw supplies from the James River. Lee would have had to attack Washington, a difficult and probably impossible task, or try to retake Richmond, all while his supplies dwindled. Or he would have had to escape south.

None of Lee's options was good. Strategically, Lincoln was right to target Lee's army, but in this case he might indeed have missed a chance to destroy Lee's army—indirectly. After his experience with McClellan, however, Lincoln did not trust any general who wanted to do anything other than fight the Army of Northern Virginia. He also feared that the Union army would become involved in a siege, as the Confederacy could have stripped other areas to try to save Richmond, though at some cost.

For what it was worth, Halleck agreed with Lincoln. He had come around to Lincoln's idea of how to fight the war. He urged attacks on Lee's army, insisting, as had the president, that the Army of Northern Virginia, not Richmond, was Hooker's objective. Additionally, Halleck had adopted Lincoln's habit of telling generals that the excuses they gave for failure and inaction did not seem to afflict their Confederate counterparts.[44]

Two days later, Hooker had solid information that just what he deemed necessary to put his plan into action had taken place: the bulk of Lee's army had moved into the Shenandoah Valley. "The instructions of the President," Hooker wrote to Halleck, "approved by yourself, and your original letter of instructions, compel me, in view of this movement of the enemy, to transfer the operations of this army from the line of the Aquia to the Orange and Alexandria Railroad."[45]

By the middle of June the Union position in the Shenandoah began to collapse. Lee's advance corps had surrounded Milroy's troops at Winchester, about 30 miles southwest of Harpers Ferry, and another Union garrison in Martinsburg, roughly 25 miles north of Winchester. Lincoln asked Hooker to try to relieve them, suggesting, "If the head of Lee's army is at Martinsburg and the tail of it on the Plank road between Fredericksburg and Chancellorsville, the animal must be very slim somewhere. Could you not break him?"[46] Hooker didn't think so. In fact, he didn't believe the reports and wanted to make no move before he had more solid intelligence.[47]

Lincoln, on the other hand, felt certain of his information and actively tried to get the endangered Union forces out of the enemy's reach. Since Halleck refused to play general in chief, the president had to do the job. He continued to try to convince Hooker of the truth of what was happening in the Valley, finally succeeding on June 15. A testy and seemingly disillusioned Hooker talked about possible moves, eventually recommending on the sixteenth that the Union cavalry be pushed across the Potomac into Maryland, with the infantry following. But in two dispatches he expressed doubt that his superiors wanted his opinion. Meanwhile, Halleck told Hooker, "Your army is entirely free to operate as you desire against Lee's army, so long as you keep his main army from Washington." Lincoln disliked Hooker's proposal, considering it defensive and believing that it "seems to abandon the fair chance now presented of breaking the enemy's long and necessarily slim line, stretched now from the Rappahannock to Pennsylvania." He conceded, however, that Hooker might be right. Lincoln called out 100,000 militia the same day.[48]

Hooker's morale was collapsing as fast as the Union's effort to stop Lee's advance. "You have long been aware, Mr. President, that I have not enjoyed the confidence of the major-general commanding the army," Hooker wrote, adding that any success in future operations would rest upon "our relations to be more dependent upon each other than heretofore." Hooker continued almost forlornly, telling Lincoln that it might still be possible to keep Lee's army from uniting, but that time was running out.[49]

Lincoln tried to reassure his faltering general. "I believe you are aware that since you took command of the army I have not believed you had any chance to effect anything till now," he told him. "As it looks to me, Lee's now returning toward Harper's Ferry gives you back the chance that I thought McClellan lost last fall. Quite possibly I was wrong both then and now; but, in the great responsibility resting upon me, I cannot be entirely silent. Now, all I ask is that you will be in such mood that we can get into our action the best cordial judgment of yourself and General Halleck, with my poor mite added, if indeed he and you shall think it entitled to any consideration at all."[50]

Confusion continued to reign in the Union high command: confusion as to the whereabouts of Lee's army, confusion regarding how to meet it when this was determined, confusion as to who commanded where and commanded what. The correspondence between Halleck and Hooker especially speaks to this. Lincoln sought to clear at least some of this away by placing Hooker firmly and clearly under Halleck's command, something, he insisted, that had been the case all along.[51]

Lee, meanwhile, marched on. By June 18 he knew that Hooker had moved his army away from the Rappahannock, though he remained unsure of his adversary's intentions. Ewell by this time had also taken Winchester and Martinsburg and reached the Potomac, inflicting nearly 4,000 casualties on the enemy while suffering only a few hundred.[52] On the nineteenth, Ewell crossed into Pennsylvania. Lee remained unsure how the Union planned to oppose the Confederates. (Given that they themselves did not know, this is hardly surprising.) Moreover, as the army neared the Virginia-Maryland border its difficulties in procuring supplies increased, making Lee unsure of the course of any future movement. He told Imboden to move north of the Potomac and into Pennsylvania if he was able. He also sought to make use of General Sam Jones's forces as well, telling him to threaten western Virginia and keep his eyes open for a favorable opportunity to convert his demonstration into a "real attack." At the very least, Lee believed, Jones would tie down troops that might be sent as reinforcements against the Army of Northern Virginia.[53]

As the Confederate army moved farther into enemy territory, the supply situation concerned Lee more and more. He wrote to Ewell, telling him that advancing would depend upon "the quantity of supplies obtained in that country." Ewell should use his cavalry to gather provisions. But Lee, as was typical of him, also gave him freedom of action, revealing the fluid nature of the general plan for his movement north: "Your progress and direction will of course depend upon development of circumstances. If Harrisburg comes within your means capture it."[54]

On June 23, Lincoln, Stanton, Halleck, and Hooker met at the War Department. Rather than help them coordinate a reply, the meeting seems to have produced more confusion, particularly about just which troops Hooker commanded, as well as the departmental lines. The muddle went on.[55]

When he returned to the Army of the Potomac, one of Hooker's engineering officers, Brigadier General G. K. Warren, who had recently provided stellar information on the road networks and possible Potomac fords, responded to a request from Hooker to give an assessment of the situation. Warren insisted that Hooker should immediately move his army to Harpers Ferry. Lee's army was reportedly there, half of it across the river "and threatening to advance upon Harrisburg." This spot would give the Union an easily supplied position too strong for the enemy to assault and from which they could protect Washington and Baltimore, "the shortest line to reach Lee's army," and the option to attack Lee's communications "if he advances." They could also "throw overwhelming forces on either portion of his army that he allows the river to divide." The position granted control of the route through South Mountain (one useful for attacking Lee) and prevented the Rebel general from detaching units to invade Pennsylvania because doing so would weaken him too much to face the Army of the Potomac. In his last point Warren wrote, "These opinions are based upon the idea that we are not to try and go round his army, and drive it out of Maryland, as we did last year, but to paralyze all its movements by threatening its flank and rear if it advances, and gain time to collect re-enforcements sufficient to render us the stronger army of the two, if we are not so already."[56]

It seems that Hooker had decided, at least for the moment, that some version of this was what he would do, but he maintained his usual habit of holding his own counsel. He dispatched troops to Harpers Ferry and ordered what amounted to a 15,000-man force of observation to Frederick, Maryland. He also had a contingency in his mind that echoed an earlier idea, one he noted on the twenty-fourth: "If the enemy should conclude not to throw any additional force over the river, I desire to make Washington secure, and, with all the force I can muster, strike for his line of retreat in the direction of Richmond." This was for naught; his army began crossing the Potomac the next day.[57]

Hooker went to Harpers Ferry. Once he had reached this key rail, river, and road junction, he decided that the troops there should be withdrawn and told Halleck so. He planned to use them to hit Lee's communications by attacking any elements of the Army of Northern Virginia not across the Potomac. But Halleck, believing it critical to hold Harpers Ferry and its environs tightly, opposed the idea. Feeling rebuffed, and also probably misunderstanding Halleck's instructions, Hooker (in a "peevish" act, as one historian put it) tendered his resignation.[58] He also sent a dispatch to Lincoln that included a phrase that must have raised the specter of McClellan in the president's head: "I state these facts that there may not be expected of me more than I have material to do with."[59] Just exactly what Hooker had planned to do, and the true reason for his resignation, remains unresolved.

The Union wasted no time replacing Hooker. Major General George Gordon Meade became the latest commander of the Army of the Potomac the same day. Meade was a tough, ill-tempered, defensive-minded Pennsylvanian whose irascibleness earned him the nickname "Old Snapping Turtle." A West Point graduate, he had served in the Mexican War and fought in all the Union eastern campaigns since the Peninsula. Halleck wired that he would "not be hampered by any minute instructions from these headquarters.... You will, however, keep in view the important fact that the Army of the Potomac is the covering army of Washington as well as the army of operation against the invading forces of the rebels." He therefore "ordered" Meade to "maneuver and fight in such a manner as to cover the capital and also Baltimore, as far as circumstances will admit. Should General Lee move upon either of these places, it is expected that you will either anticipate him or arrive with him so as to give him battle." He also assured Meade that "all forces within the sphere of your operations will be held subject to your orders."[60]

Meade replied: "As a soldier, I obey it, and to the utmost of my ability will execute it." Meade added that though he was "in ignorance of the exact condition of the troops and position of the enemy," he planned to advance toward the Susquehanna River, protecting Washington and Baltimore, and that if the enemy failed to cross the river or advanced toward the latter, he would "give him battle." The next day he wired Halleck that "if circumstances permit it," he would attack Lee. Meade understood his true objective, Lee's army, and made another remark that must have warmed Lincoln's heart: "My main point being to find and fight the enemy."[61]

Lincoln and Halleck also tried to get the troops in the Peninsula under Major General John A. Dix at Fortress Monroe in Hampton, Virginia, into the fight. They brought up units from North Carolina to reinforce Dix, who sent one force toward Richmond and another to try to cut the railroads supplying the city. The navy also made a push up the James River. Not a little anxiety erupted in the Confederate capital from these moves. Nothing much came of this though, and D. H. Hill, the Confederate general in the field opposite Dix, summed up the situation: "Where have the Yankees gone? The design on Richmond was not a feint but a faint."[62]

As both armies marched, Lee revived an idea he had presented to Davis earlier in the year, proposing it as a deception plan. He believed that because it was summer it was unlikely the Union would act in Georgia and along the Carolina coasts, thus making it safe to withdraw troops from there and use them in Virginia. He suggested organizing them as a new army under Beauregard at Culpeper Courthouse that could then threaten Washington. This, Lee insisted, "would not only effect a diversion most favorable for this army, but would I think, relieve us of any apprehension of an attack upon Richmond during our absence." Lee understood Lincoln's concern for Washington and thought that it might be used to advantage: "The well known anxiety of the Northern Government for the safety of its capital would induce it to retain a large force for its defence, and thus sensibly relieve the opposition to our advance." He believed that this threat, combined with success by his army, might even convince the Union to recall troops from the West. Lee suggested Beauregard for the command, believing that using him would make it appear that big things were brewing. If the government was uncomfortable removing the troops he had suggested, he felt that even a small force under Beauregard drawn from troops in North Carolina and Richmond would produce profitable results.[63] Edward Porter Alexander offered a cogent criticism of Lee's effort here, providing a window into some of the flawed operational and strategic concepts feeding the Rebel offensive: "The weak feature was that Lee did not have under his own control the troops which he desired to move. Davis had indeed proposed to him to control all the troops on the Atlantic slope; but Lee insisted even on being relieved of the department south of the James, under D. H. Hill. He did not take the War Dept. into his confidence at first, hoping to accomplish his purpose by gradual suggestion and request. The process was too slow, and the result was unfortunate."[64]

In Lee's mind, the Union reactions to the movements of his army strengthened his argument for this new force under Beauregard. He thought Lincoln's call for 100,000 men to defend Pennsylvania's borders, as well as the Union concentration of forces in Maryland, clearly revealed Northern anxiety over the safety of Washington. He also had a report that Burnside's forces had been recalled from Kentucky. In this Lee saw an opportunity for Buckner and Bragg to do something in Ohio, while also noting that if the Federals were concentrating against his army, "it will result in our accomplishing nothing, and being compelled to return to Virginia." The realization of this made him push again for the creation of an army under Beauregard at Culpeper Courthouse.[65]

In fact, the response to Lincoln's June 15 call for 100,000 men was weak. On June 26, he allowed Pennsylvania's governor, Andrew G. Curtin, to reduce the service requirement from six months to ninety days, and the Keystone State gathered 24,000 men to the colors over the next three weeks.[66]

The idea of a diversion in his favor and a movement in the West must have played heavily in Lee's mind on June 25, because he sent a second letter to Davis that day in which he again urged the creation of this new army.

He also insisted that if a report on Burnside's withdrawal was true, this presented an opportunity for a combined movement by Buckner and Sam Jones. If they couldn't do this, they could be withdrawn to provide reinforcements for Johnston or Bragg, or as part of the Culpeper Courthouse army, or even operate in western Virginia. "It should never be forgotten that our concentration at any point compels that of the enemy," he told Davis, "and his numbers being limited, tends to relieve all other threatened localities."[67] This statement reveals much of Lee's view of the strategic implications, and the necessity, of Confederate concentrations.

There was never any chance of the Confederacy creating the diversionary army Lee so desired. His request surprised Cooper as well as Davis, neither of whom remembered hearing anything of the idea before receiving Lee's most recent missives on the subject. They had no troops for a new army at Culpeper Courthouse, partially because of Union pressure then being exerted on Richmond via the forces on the Peninsula. Moreover, Davis, pressed to find troops for the West as well as the East, had recently been told by Beauregard that he had no more men to send to Johnston and could spare none for Lee's diversionary army.[68]

Beauregard had problems of his own, but took the time to write Johnston about the situation. He criticized the government's strategy in general and Lee in particular, asking, "Of what earthly use is that 'raid' of Lee's army into Maryland, in violation of all the principles of war? Is it going to end the struggle, take Washington, or save the Mississippi Valley?" He thought the better choice was sitting on the defensive in Virginia and sending Longstreet and his 20,000 men to prop up Bragg. Added to the 10,000 men Beauregard had already dispatched, the Louisianan argued that they "could have then crushed Rosecrans," afterward allowing the movement of 50,000 men against Memphis and Fort Pillow and to Johnston's aid.[69]

Here was a rare circumstance when Beauregard's complaints merited discussion. Indeed, what good was Lee's "raid," as Beauregard termed it, not realizing that Lee intended more? Was it worth losing control of the Mississippi? The South lacked sufficient manpower to invade the North and counter the intense Union pressure in the West, but the question is what would have happened had the South sent Longstreet to Tennessee to face Rosecrans while the Army of Northern Virginia stood on the defensive. Longstreet himself had suggested something similar to this in the wake of Chancellorsville, and Edward Porter Alexander believed that this would have been the South's best move. Secretary of War Seddon didn't believe that this would force Grant from his path; Longstreet insisted that Confederate success would see Grant receive orders to come to Rosecrans's aid. One must decide for Seddon in this case. Lee, for his part, had no desire to go to Tennessee and didn't want Longstreet or his men sent either. He had his mind set on going north.[70]

But what of Beauregard's other option—reinforcing Johnston and relieving Vicksburg? According to Alexander, Longstreet's corps (13,000, not the 20,000 Beauregard believed) combined with Johnston's army would have given the Confederacy a field army of 38,000 men. Another 5,000 at Knoxville also could have been added, making 43,000. Pemberton had about 30,000. Together, these would have stood a chance against Grant's 60,000.[71] There certainly would have been problems moving and feeding such a force, but saving Vicksburg and, more important, Pemberton's army—and by extension the South's strategic position in the West—might have made the effort worthwhile. The South's losing Vicksburg meant the Union changed the focus of its western campaign to middle Tennessee and Georgia, the heart of the Deep South. Holding Vicksburg would have bought the South time. There was no guarantee that the Confederates could pull off such a move, but when one measures the risks versus the *likely* rewards of Lee's invasion when compared to an effort to save Vicksburg, one must conclude that attacking Grant would have been the wiser choice if—and this was certainly not guaranteed—the South could shift the necessary troops in time

Adding to the Confederate difficulties was the Union capture of Davis's dispatch to Lee telling him that the South lacked the troops for his Culpeper Courthouse army, a note that also detailed other weaknesses. The information encouraged the Federals to once again make what proved a failed attempt to take Charleston. Union troops landed on Morris Island on July 10, supported by a squadron of four monitors. They took half the island but were repulsed with grievous losses when attacking Fort Wagner the next day. Additionally, the report Lee had about Burnside turned out to be half right. Of Burnside's troops, about 8,600 had been withdrawn from Lexington, Kentucky; they were sent not against Lee but to Vicksburg.[72]

On June 25, Lee concluded that he had insufficient troops to protect his communications and decided to abandon them (something reminiscent of Grant on his advance to Vicksburg), a move inspired by a captured report that Hooker was making preparations to shift the Union army north of the Potomac. He also gave Davis his operational objectives: "I think I can throw Genl Hooker's army across the Potomac and draw troops from the south, embarrassing their plan of campaign in a measure, if I can do nothing more and have to return."[73] Word of Hooker's movement also induced Lee to conclude that the time had arrived for the concentration of his army, especially since his cavalry had failed to provide him with proper information on Hooker's intent.[74]

At this point, Lee had accomplished the primary operational objective of his campaign: the Union army was north of the Potomac. By advancing further, Lee went beyond what Clausewitz calls the "culminating point," the point at which he could hold his gains or derive any benefit. If he had stopped at this moment and assumed the defensive, his chances of a successful summer campaign would have increased. Instead, he pushed on, accumulating more risk than would be within his army's ability to address and reaching for something that was both more and less than what he held.[75]

DURING THE FIRST THREE DAYS in July, the Army of Northern Virginia (75,000 troops) and the Army of the Potomac (93,500 troops), two of the best military forces Americans have ever fielded, fought the Battle of Gettysburg on a fishhook-shaped, hill-studded field. Lee had planned to fight when he moved north and even projected that the combatants might come to blows in the vicinity of the small Pennsylvania village, but what unfolded was not according to his plan. One of the big reasons for this was that during his march Lee lacked sound information on the enemy's dispositions. His cavalry commander, J. E. B. Stuart, neglected the primary duty of cavalry in the nineteenth century—reconnaissance—for a ride around the Union army and the seizure of supplies. Lee's army marched into Pennsylvania half blind.[76]

Tactically, Lee had a clear idea of how he intended to meet the enemy, telling Isaac Trimble, "My plan is to throw an overwhelming force against the enemy's advance, as soon as I learn the road they take, crush them, and following up the sweep, beat them in detail, and in a few hours throw the whole Army into disorder and probably create a panic by separate sweeps, and joining them [in] time to concentrate in large forces."[77] But this required finding the enemy first and with the mass of his troops as well.

Confederate and Union forces stumbled upon each other at Gettysburg on the morning of July 1. This wasn't how Lee wanted the fight to begin, piecemeal, and when he arrived at the scene at around two o'clock in the afternoon he held back his men. But then units of Ewell's corps began to arrive, and Lee drove the Union troops from the town. They regrouped on nearby high ground, Cemetery Hill, which Lee decided had to be taken immediately. He ordered Ewell to clear them off.[78]

As Ewell prepared, Longstreet and Lee met on Seminary Ridge, opposite the enemy. Longstreet advised moving around the Union forces and placing their army between the enemy and Washington, D.C., thus forcing the

Union to attack. Lee decided against this, electing to seize the opportunity to strike.[79]

Ewell, meanwhile, hesitated, waiting for the third and final division of his corps to arrive. His attack never went off, and Lee decided to shift the main assault to the opposite flank of the Union army using Longstreet's troops, and to do it the next day. Longstreet again suggested a southward move and a tactical defensive. Lee declined. Instead, he decided to attack both flanks of the Union forces, Ewell against the north, Longstreet against the south. Lee's last corps, A. P. Hill's, would demonstrate in the center to keep the Union troops there occupied. Lee hoped to fight before Meade's entire army was assembled.[80]

The next day, July 2, Longstreet dithered. This gave Meade time to bring in more troops and for Union forces to occupy the heights of Little Round Top, stretching the Union line farther southward than the Confederates at first realized. When the Confederates did attack, their assaults on both the northern and southern ends of the Union line went off too slowly, and piecemeal, with units habitually failing to support one another. The Federals also countered well, Meade and his subordinates feeding in reinforcements to rebuff Longstreet's blow at the right time.[81]

That night a dozen Union generals convened a midnight war council. Unanimously, they chose to fight. Meade also predicted Lee's next throw, telling Major General John Gibbon, who commanded the corps in the Union center, "If Lee attacks to-morrow it will be in *your front*." Gibbon asked for Meade's reasoning. The general replied: "Because he has made attacks on both our flanks and failed, and if he concludes to try it again it will be on our center."[82]

The next morning, Longstreet again suggested moving south and fighting a defensive battle. Lee informed him that it was logistically impossible. An army dependent upon feeding itself from the enemy's country has to keep moving. It couldn't sit, hoping for the enemy to attack. Lee hit Meade's center, on Cemetery Ridge, with the remaining fresh division of Longstreet's corps, Major General George Pickett's, and other units pulled from A. P. Hill's corps. Lee's tactical plan included two other elements as well. In combination with what became famous as Pickett's Charge, Stuart's cavalry was to storm into the Union center from the rear while Ewell's men attacked the Union's northern wing. None of this came off as planned. Early morning Union attacks thwarted Ewell's efforts, and Federal cavalry fought Stuart to a standstill 3 miles from his objective. The preparatory Confederate artillery bombardment began at one o'clock in the afternoon, and shortly afterward 15,000 men stepped off across Gettysburg's green fields toward

Cemetery Ridge—and into a brilliant, blue-birthed fire. Emory Thomas wrote: "For long moments the Confederates transformed the blood and filth of war into spectacle." But spectacle isn't enough. Meade's men repulsed the attack. The entire grand event had taken only an hour.[83]

"IT HAD NOT BEEN INTENDED to deliver a general battle so far from our base unless attacked," Lee wrote later, "but coming unexpectedly upon the whole Federal Army, to withdraw through the mountains with our extensive trains would have been difficult and dangerous." Moreover, Lee believed that he couldn't simply wait for an attack, since there was no way of collecting enough supplies for his army so long as the Union held the "mountain passes." As he put it, a battle had therefore "become in a measure unavoidable."[84] Lee insisted that he was merely seizing an opportunity presented him and in some ways forced upon him by circumstance.

Unavoidable or not, the battle was a devastating loss to the South. Lee's casualties, killed, wounded, prisoners, and deserters, numbered as many as 28,000—a full third of his army.[85] Meade's victory over Lee (a fact sometimes seemingly forgotten in discussions of Gettysburg) stopped the Confederate offensive. It forced Lee to abandon his strategy of trying to break the Union's will by winning a decisive battle, and he had to retreat. And it gave the North a chance to win the war. Lincoln had early seen a great possibility for the Union cause, telling New Jersey's governor, Joel Parker, on June 30 that "I really think the attitude of the enemies['] army in Pennsylvania presents us the best opportunity we have had since the war began."[86]

Lee elected "to withdraw to the west side of the mountains." He made this decision for two reasons. First, "numerous bodies of local and other troops…watched the passes" and therefore prevented his army from gathering the supplies so critical for its continued existence. The second reason was his inability to carry the Union position at Gettysburg.[87] During its retreat, Lee's army fell victim to what Clausewitz defined as "friction"; it struck in the form of bad weather.

It had rained "almost without intermission" from the moment Lee's army entered Maryland, impeding the Confederates' movements. It had even delayed the initial crossing for two days: rising waters made the Potomac impossible to ford. Lee was not unprepared for this eventuality, having built a pontoon bridge at Falling Waters, near Williamsport, Maryland, but Union cavalry severely damaged it on July 4, making it unusable, and stranding Lee's army north of the Potomac until they could build a new bridge.[88] Here, Meade was given one of the best opportunities of the entire conflict to destroy an enemy army.

Lee realized the danger of his position, and wrote a number of letters to his wife and his president in which he seems to be preparing both of them, particularly Davis, for impending disaster. His Hagerstown correspondence is filled with increased invocations of God's providence and has the ring of a man surrendering himself to his fate: "I had calculated upon the river remaining fordable during the summer," he wrote Davis on July 8, "so as to enable me to recross at my pleasure." But he could no longer do so. "I shall therefore have to accept battle if the enemy offers it, whether I wish to or not, and as the result is in the hands of the Sovereign Ruler of the Universe, and known to Him only, I deem it prudent to make every arrangement in our power to meet any emergency that may arise." Again, he called for the formation of a diversionary army under Beauregard and for it to mount a demonstration against Washington. Lee believed this would not only protect Richmond (which was out of his immediate power to do) but also lessen Union pressure on his own forces.[89]

As he waited for the river to fall, Lee relayed reports to Davis of the approaching enemy and repeated his warning that if the Union army drew close and insisted upon fighting, he would have no choice. He said they had plenty of ammunition, the bigger problem being "to procure subsistence" for his troops as well as his animals. Feeding his men grew more troublesome in the succeeding days. By the twelfth, the river had fallen far enough to begin building a bridge. This still did not lighten the tone of Lee's letters. He had word of Union forces gathering in Antietam Valley and told Davis, "But for the power he possesses of accumulating troops, I should be willing to await his attack, except that in our restricted limits the means of obtaining subsistence is becoming precarious."[90]

He lamented the high waters, insisting that if this had not happened, he could have crossed the river when he reached it. Aside from that, however, he tried to put a happy spin on the situation, arguing that the major operational objectives had been accomplished: "The Army of the Potomac had been thrown north of that river, the forces invading the coasts of North Carolina and Virginia had been diminished, their plan of the present campaign broken up, and, before new arrangements could have been made for its resumption, the summer would have been ended."[91]

The Snapping Turtle's Weak Bite

IN THE WAKE OF PICKETT'S CHARGE—the pivotal event of the last day of the bloody engagement at Gettysburg, in which the South suffered

50 percent casualties—Meade telegraphed Halleck, telling him, among other things, that "the army is in fine spirits." His tune had already changed by the next day. Lee began to withdraw, and Meade told Halleck that his army was "worn out by long marches and three days' hard fighting" and not ready to engage the enemy again. Here Meade condemns with his own hand his failure to immediately pursue. Of course, the Union army had fought no harder, had marched no farther, and had no worse a supply situation than the foe that faced it. Moreover, he had already told Halleck that he would pursue Lee "on his flanks." Meade started to move on the fifth but then hesitated, struck by indecision and uncertain of the enemy's intent.[92]

Meade seems to have been the only important figure in the Union high command that did not sense the immense opportunity before him. Union cavalry had burned the Confederate pontoon bridge over the Potomac the day Lee commenced his retreat, Lee's only path home, and the enemy army was at Meade's mercy. Halleck and Stanton began trying to move troops in Pennsylvania, Fortress Monroe, North Carolina, and other areas against Lee's communications. The capture of some of Lee's dispatches told the Union leaders that the area between Lee's army and Richmond had been largely denuded of Confederate forces.[93] Halleck urged an advance by Burnside's troops in eastern Kentucky and Tennessee. Stanton flogged Rosecrans onward, telling him, "Lee's army overthrown; Grant victorious. You and your noble army now have the chance to give the finishing blow to the rebellion. Will you neglect the chance?" In fact, Rosecrans would. He replied, testily and somewhat irrelevantly, "You do not appear to observe the fact that this noble army has driven the rebels from Middle Tennessee, of which my dispatches advised you."[94]

Lincoln saw the opportunity to destroy a defeated army far from its base, one he feared would be allowed to slip away and with it a chance to win the war. After receiving word of Grant's capture of Vicksburg, he told Halleck, "Now, if General Meade can complete his work, so gloriously prosecuted thus far, by the literal or substantial destruction of Lee's army, the rebellion will be over."[95] To the president, the twin shocks would end the war.

Meade didn't keep Lincoln's confidence long. On July 4 Meade issued General Orders No. 68, his congratulatory note to his troops for their hard-fought victory. In it he said that the job was not finished and that "the Commanding General looks to the Army for greater efforts to drive from our soil every vestige of the presence of the enemy." When he saw the telegram and some others that followed, a deeply frustrated Lincoln minced no words in his response. "I left the telegraph office a good deal dissatisfied," he told Halleck, and reminded the general of the presidential hatred of Meade's reference to driving the invaders from Union soil. Later, Lincoln said to his secretary, John Hay, "Will our Generals never get that idea out of their heads? The whole country is *our* soil." Worse, Lincoln had a note from a Union general about the Confederates crossing their wounded over the Potomac "without saying why he does not stop it, or even intimating a thought that it ought to be stopped." He had another wire revealing that Meade's army "is halted because it is believed the rebels are concentrating 'on the road toward Hagerstown, beyond Fairfield,' and is not to move until it is ascertained that the rebels intend to evacuate Cumberland Valley." This did not give Lincoln assurance. "These things all appear to me to be connected with a purpose to cover Baltimore and Washington, and to get the enemy across the river again without a further collision, and they do not appear connected with a purpose to prevent his crossing and to destroy him. I do fear the former purpose is acted upon and the latter is rejected."[96]

Despite Lincoln's discontent, Meade still dragged his feet, and this in the teeth of two orders from Halleck on July 7 to attack Lee's army before it found the Potomac's banks. Halleck pushed him along again on the eighth—once more with Lincoln's backing.[97]

The poverty of the pursuit surprised the Confederates. "Up to now," wrote Edward Porter Alexander, who provided the artillery support for Pickett's Charge, "the enemy had pursued us as a mule goes on the chase of a grizzly bear—as if catching up with us was the last thing he wanted to do." But Meade waited. He found Lee strongly dug in and "hesitated to attack him without some examination of the mode of approaching him." Unfortunately, Halleck gave him an out by telling him to attack only when he had all his force up. Meade promised to strike on the thirteenth—"unless something intervenes to prevent it," he insisted.[98] Inevitably, something would.

Meanwhile, Lincoln continued haunting the telegraph office, just as he had during the entirety of Lee's invasion. On July 11 he had been optimistic. However, when he received Meade's note about attacking the next day if nothing prevented it, Lincoln "paced the room wringing his hands and saying: 'They will be ready to fight a magnificent battle when there is no enemy there to fight.'" The next day, July 13, John Hay noted Lincoln's worried state and wrote: "Nothing can save them, if Meade does his duty. I doubt him. He is an engineer."[99]

Lincoln was right to doubt. Meade polled his corps commanders. They argued against making an assault, taking counsel of their fears. Meade bent to their wishes and insisted to Halleck that he lacked the authority to attack before investigating things further. Halleck quickly disabused him of this notion, but he failed to order Meade to strike, or to take responsibility for it himself. "You are strong enough to attack and defeat the enemy before he can effect a crossing. Act upon your own judgment and make your generals execute your orders. Call no council of war. It is proverbial that councils of war never fight. Re-enforcements are pushed on as rapidly as possible. Do not let the enemy escape."[100]

On the morning of the fourteenth the Union probed Lee's lines and found that he had withdrawn across the river during the night. Halleck told Meade of Lincoln's "great dissatisfaction" that Lee had escaped. Meade insisted that he had done all he could and asked to be relieved, citing the president's "undeserved censure." Halleck told him that there was no censure involved, only the desire to encourage him to pursue. Meade remarked in a letter to his wife, in a very McClellan-like defensive manner, "This is exactly what I expected; unless I did impracticable things, fault would be found with me."[101]

Lincoln suffered more than displeasure—anger, frustration, and even despair struck the man who had labored so hard to keep the Union together. Robert Todd Lincoln, the president's son, said his father cried upon learning Lee had escaped across the Potomac. Despite orders from Halleck, despite a possible secret order from Lincoln on July 10 that ordered Meade to take the risk (receiving the glory for success, and assigning Lincoln the blame for failure), the Confederates were gone, escaped—just as Lincoln "had dreaded yet expected." Lincoln told John Hay, "Our Army held the war in the hollow of their hand & they would not close it." He told his son Robert, "If I had gone up there I could have whipped them myself." Hay added: "I know he had that idea."[102]

THE GETTYSBURG CAMPAIGN was a disaster for the Confederacy and gained them nothing, and Lee admitted that he returned to the South far sooner than he had anticipated. Yet Lee and Davis insisted they derived some success from the venture. Lee wrote that since leaving the Rappahannock River they had "relieved" the Shenandoah Valley and drawn the Union army north of the Potomac. Lee took the blame for the Gettysburg defeat but noted to Davis that in his opinion his army had "achieved under the guidance of the Most High a general success, though it did not win a victory." These do not seem the words of a man who believes he has just presided over a debacle. Davis wrote that "though not defeated at Gettysburg, we had suffered a check."[103] Their words are, at best, a form of self-deception. Lee's failure had robbed him of much of his offensive power.

The "What if Lee had won?" question has always swirled around Gettysburg; it has been the subject of novels as well as serious histories.[104] Though not universal, the standard meme is that a Confederate victory in the battle would have brought a Southern victory in the war. Davis contended so, telling an interviewer in 1881 that "the moral effect of that victory would have brought peace."[105] This seems unlikely. Lee had defeated Union armies before, yet the war had continued. Defeating Meade only would have added one more to the list of Union generals who found their careers ruined by Lee. The rank and file of the Union army certainly would have had no inclination to quit. James McPherson describes them as hard, self-confident men with "a flinty self-reliance."[106] Moreover, Lincoln would have been no more inclined to end the war because of a Union defeat than a Union victory. Some argument could be made that Union public opinion would have suffered a blow, but public opinion was now used to Lee winning battles. And Grant's capture of Vicksburg, the South's "Gibraltar of the West," certainly would have provided a salve to the wound of any defeat in Pennsylvania.

Even had Lee had won at Gettysburg, barring some utterly miraculous occurrence, he could not have remained in the North for very long, arguably forfeiting much of the political benefit of a victory by withdrawing toward his base. What ensured his retreat under any circumstances was his difficulty in procuring food and fodder. As we've seen, he was having trouble feeding his men during the march through Virginia, though this had changed once they reached the North and began foraging.[107] After the battle, as a result of Lincoln's call for short-term volunteers, it became difficult for the Confederates to gather supplies because of small bands of Union troops.[108] Lee's adjutant Walter Herron Taylor wrote on July 17, "Indeed had we been eminently successful at Gettysburg, in all probability we would have been obliged to make the same movements we have."[109] A victory over Meade would not have solved his supply problems.

So what was the result of the Gettysburg campaign and this most famous of Civil War battles? Was it the "High Tide of the Confederacy," as it is often called? Lee and Davis certainly didn't see it that way. The Confederacy's high tide, if there was one, was the beginning of the war, when they held more territory than they would at any other time during the conflict. After First Manassas, the tide began to ebb. Though in many ways an example of brilliant operational execution because of his ability to move his force so deeply into the enemy's land, Lee's 1863 summer campaign has to be judged a strategic failure, in spite of Lee's and Davis's contentions otherwise. This is not just because of the Confederacy's tactical defeat but also because the invasion fulfilled neither the strategic nor the operational objectives its commander set for it, and, most important, because it did nothing to improve the South's strategic situation. Lee had intended for his invasion to draw the enemy out of Virginia, which it did, but only for a short time. By July 26, Lee was already writing of his fear that "we shall soon have them back again."[110] Lee had also believed his move would convince the Union to pull troops from the Carolinas. Again, this it did, but the Union had enough men to meet any threat that Lee could present, while maintaining a presence in the Carolinas. Finally, and most important, Lee's invasion failed to strike the blow at Union public opinion he had hoped it would deliver; arguably, it had precisely the opposite effect. Had he never gone north, this benefit would not have accrued to the Union. In the end, the Gettysburg campaign did little for the South other than destroy much of Lee's army, injuring his ability to counter later Union moves and weakening the Confederacy's powers of resistance; the casualties could not be replaced.

It also could have been worse. Lee had, after all, escaped. Afterward, Lincoln wrote Meade a letter that he never sent (his habit when he was working out his thoughts on a matter). He was grateful to Meade, though also deeply disappointed. The note provides a succinct picture not only of Lincoln's views but also of Meade's strategic, operational, and tactical failures. Lincoln noted that after defeating the enemy at Gettysburg, Meade did not "pressingly pursue him." Worse, even though Lee's retreat was blocked by the swollen Potomac, Meade simply "stood and let the flood run down, bridges be built, and the enemy move away at his leisure, without attacking him." Lincoln continued, "I do not believe you appreciate the magnitude of the misfortune involved in Lee's escape. He was within your easy grasp, and to have closed upon him would, in connection with our other late successes, have ended the war. As it is, the war will be prolonged indefinitely.... Your golden opportunity is gone, and I am distressed immeasureably because of it."[111]

In a letter to General O. O. Howard, Lincoln expressed similar sentiments, telling Howard that he was "deeply mortified" by Lee's escape across the Potomac, when destroying his army would have been "perfectly easy." Lincoln was convinced that "Gen. Meade and his noble army had expended all the skill, and toil, and blood, up to the ripe harvest, and then let the crop go to waste." Lincoln went on: "Perhaps my mortification was heightened because I had always believed—making my belief a hobby possibly—that the main rebel army going North of the Potomac, could never return, if well attended to."[112]

The rank and file of the Army of the Potomac shared the president's dissatisfaction. The soldiers coined a verse about Meade, which they added to others about McDowell, Banks, Pope, Burnside, and McClellan, sung to the tune of "When Johnny Comes Marching Home":

> Next came General Meade, a slow old plug,
> Hurrah! Hurrah!
> Next came General Meade, a slow old plug,
> Hurrah! Hurrah!
> Next came General Meade, a slow old plug,
> For he let them get away at Gettysburg,
> And we'll all drink stone blind—
> Johnny, fill up the bowl.[113]

Lincoln composed his own poem, written perhaps when he had found a better mood:

> Gen. Lees invasion of the North written by himself—
> In eighteen sixty three, with pomp,
>   and mighty swell,
> Me and Jeff's Confederacy, went
>   forth to sack Phil-del,
> The Yankees they got arter us, and
>   giv us particular hell,
> And we skedaddled back again,
>   and didn't sack Phil-del.[114]

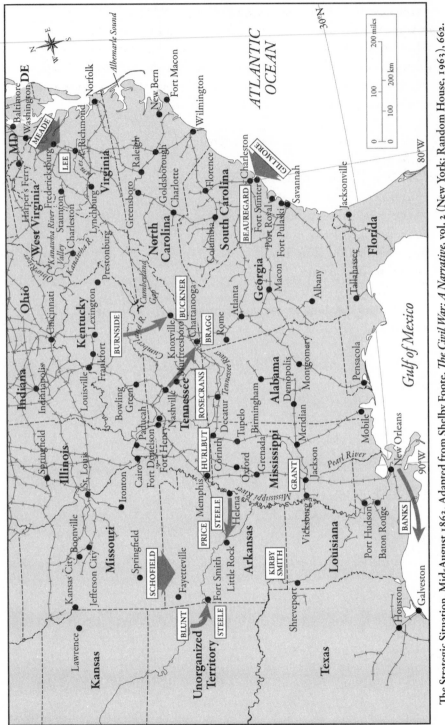

The Strategic Situation, Mid-August 1863. Adapted from Shelby Foote, *The Civil War: A Narrative*, vol. 2 (New York: Random House, 1963), 662.

17

The Autumn of 1863

PLAYING THE DEEP GAME

*I have, before this, said that Lincoln is a better General than
Halleck, but I don't think that this is saying much.*
—NOAH BROOKS, Journalist, January 1, 1854

THE UNION LEFT GRANT to go to seed not long after his great victory at
Vicksburg. For nearly three months he did not exercise a major command,
particularly one in the field, and saw his army broken up and scattered from
Chattanooga to Arkansas to Louisiana. "I am anxiously waiting for some
general plan of operations from Washington," he complained in late July. "It
is important that the troops of different departments should act in concert;
hence the necessity of general instructions coming from one head."[1]

Halleck decided that the Mississippi River would provide a base for
future Union operations. Vicksburg and Port Hudson would be held by
garrisons, freeing troops for the field. Halleck intended these garrisons to
consist of black troops, and told Grant to recruit as many as possible. But
the bigger problem remained: what next? Halleck worried that if Johnston
joined Bragg, more of Grant's forces than just those Grant had borrowed
from Burnside would have to go to Rosecrans's aid. Halleck also mulled
over the possibility of driving the Confederates from Louisiana, or clearing
Arkansas. If they could be forced from these states, he believed, Texas would
follow "almost of its own accord." But Halleck sent no orders, only options.
He closed a note to Grant: "Wherever the enemy concentrates we must concentrate to oppose him."[2]

Grant, as always, looked forward. He wrote Halleck asking whether he
should send troops to support a move Banks planned against Texas. Halleck
rejected the idea, insisting that the first order of business was to "clean out"
the other states. The first place he ordered action was in Arkansas.[3]

Major General John Schofield, commander of the Department of the
Missouri, a New Yorker, 1853 West Point graduate, and veteran of numerous western operations, had Arkansas as his responsibility. Much of his force
had been stripped away to support Rosecrans and Grant. He could do little

until the Union cleared the Mississippi and his men had returned. After this, however, Schofield immediately launched a two-pronged drive into the state, one led predominantly by Major General Frederick Steele. It was hardly a blitzkrieg. Steele jumped off on August 10. His forces took Little Rock on September 10, driving off the Confederate forces commanded by Sterling Price. After a brutal August 19 Confederate raid on Lawrence, Kansas, which included Jesse James and in which the Confederates murdered nearly 200 unarmed men, Schofield had adopted a system of establishing local militia to keep guerrillas in check in Missouri. This, coupled with a strategy of expelling relatives of known guerrillas and anyone supporting them, plus their slaves, helped secure most of Arkansas for the Union, though they did suffer some subsequent Rebel raids.[4]

Grant continued to wait for Halleck to decide his fate. Meanwhile, he launched raids against surrounding areas of the countryside aimed at destroying mills, railroads, and anything else useful to the Confederate war effort. One, against Grenada in north-central Mississippi, proved particularly successful. Moreover, when he pulled Sherman's troops back from Jackson, he told him to "leave nothing of value for the enemy to carry on war with."[5] With Sherman's eager assistance, Grant inaugurated a Union raiding strategy that would become an element of the evolving Union strategy of exhaustion. By 1864, some Union armies in the West would forage to their target destination, eating up the countryside on the way there and on the way back, while destroying resources and industrial capabilities useful to the Confederates. These expeditions would also recruit slaves to the Union army, sometimes even forcing them into the ranks.[6]

Grant agreed to send the necessary troops to support the Arkansas expedition, but he had a different idea about what his next target should be: Mobile. Halleck disagreed. He still wanted to focus on "cleaning up," and wanted Johnston "disposed of." Once they could withdraw troops from Vicksburg, Missouri, and Port Hudson, they could turn their focus to Mobile or Texas. Before receiving this note, Grant had again recommended a drive on Mobile to Halleck, but by this time things were even more out of Halleck's hands than usual.[7]

The War in Virginia

LEE'S DEFEAT AT GETTYSBURG, and the disaster he nearly met during the retreat, did not temper his aggressiveness. As his army withdrew deeper into Virginia, he looked, unsuccessfully, for opportunities to fight Meade.

But he had to fall back farther and farther, slowly giving up his gains of the summer.[8] In early August, taking advice from Davis about assuming a position in close cooperation with the forces defending Richmond, Lee camped on the south bank of the Rapidan River at Culpeper Courthouse.[9] The end of August found him still eager to try Meade again. He told Longstreet, "I can see nothing better to be done than to endeavor to bring General Meade out and use our efforts to crush his army while in its present condition."[10]

Meade had followed Lee, harassing him with cavalry and keeping in close contact with the ever-watchful administration. Near the end of July, when he inquired whether he should enter the Shenandoah Valley, Halleck made sure to remind the general of his true mission: "Lee's army is the objective point."[11]

But Lincoln, at least for a moment, had changed his mind. After years of pleading with the various commanders of the Army of the Potomac to fight the eastern Confederates, Lincoln changed his tune, or at least some of his notes. He wrote Halleck that though Meade was under the impression that they were demanding he "bring on a general engagement with Lee as soon as possible," that was not the case. "If he could not safely engage Lee at Williamsport, it seems absurd to suppose he can safely engage him now, when he has scarcely more than two thirds of the force he had at Williamsport, while it must be, that Lee has been re-inforced." He admitted that he had wanted Meade to pursue Lee across the Potomac but that moment had passed and he was now against pressing him to attack.[12] Lincoln had not regained much faith in his new commander.

Meade responded that he indeed thought the administration expected him to fight Lee at the first chance and that Lincoln had been misinformed about Meade's numbers; he possessed nearly as many troops as he had had at Williamsport. But the same day that Halleck forwarded Lincoln's note, he sent another telling Meade that the government might have to take some of his troops to help enforce the draft (there had been riots in New York and a few other places) and that therefore Meade should leave off chasing Lee and stop at the Rappahannock.[13] Needless to say, this left Meade confused as to what exactly his superiors wanted him to do. He asked for clarification. "Keep up a threatening attitude," Halleck told him, "but do not advance."[14]

Part of what motivated Lincoln was undoubtedly a desire to avoid forcing Meade into an action in which the general saw little hope of success. But bigger concerns, domestic as well as international, afflicted the president. These would begin occupying his time and in the process exert a negative influence on the course of Union strategy. The New York draft riots were quickly put down, resolving the domestic problem. Mexico furnished the stickier international one.

Mexico's default on its foreign loans, and the subsequent French intervention, lit a fire that the Lincoln administration determined had to be put out. They feared French ambitions in Mexico and against Texas, and also saw a chance at strengthening the blockade, which remained porous via the Mexican frontier. The day before Halleck issued the halt order to Meade, Lincoln had already revived with Stanton the idea of a Texas expedition, telling him, "I believe no local object is now more desirable."[15]

Two days later, Halleck instructed the Union commander in New Orleans, Nathaniel Banks, to prepare to mount an operation against Texas; they hadn't yet decided whether it would be by land or sea. He suggested Indianola and Galveston as points of attack. Just a week before, Halleck had wired Banks that "Texas and Mobile will present themselves to your attention." Halleck much preferred the Texas option and ordered Banks to prepare for such a move while clearing the Rebels from Louisiana's southwestern reaches.[16]

Banks, like Grant, had already decided where he wanted to go next, and it certainly wasn't Texas. Both preferred to take Mobile, one of the few remaining significant Confederate ports, as well as a key rail junction. Banks's original orders from Halleck had actually included a command to seize Mobile Bay, something he came to deem critical, and for good reason. "The possession of Mobile gives the Government the control of the Alabama River and the line of railways east and west from Charleston and Savannah to Vicksburg, via Montgomery," Banks argued, "and places the whole of Mississippi and Southern Alabama in position to resume at will their place in the Union." Should the Confederacy lose Mobile, it would lose its only port on the Gulf, aside from Galveston, which was not connected to the Rebel railroad net. "The operation need not last more than thirty days, and can scarcely interfere with any other movements east or west."[17]

Lincoln soon seconded Halleck's note to Banks, favoring Texas. He also sent a letter to Grant explaining the demands of state that forced the cancellation of their preferred move. Halleck, at least, did not waste the chance of deceiving the Rebels into thinking that Mobile was the next target.[18]

Halleck now clarified what the administration wanted of Banks: the U.S. flag planted somewhere on Texas soil. Halleck provided few specifics and left Banks to decide whether he should mount an overland campaign or an amphibious one. He disparaged the earlier idea of landing at Galveston or Indianola, preferring a course Banks had previously suggested: moving up the Red River, crossing northern Louisiana, and entering north Texas along this route. Halleck saw advantages here. "In the first place," Halleck wired, "by adopting the line of the Red River, you retain your connection with your own base, and separate still more the two points of the rebel Confederacy." This would also sever northern Louisiana and southern Arkansas entirely from supplies and reinforcements from Texas; "they are already cut off from the rebel States east of the Mississippi." As always, Halleck suggested; he did not order.[19]

Banks, having not yet received clear direction from Washington, continued discussing the Mobile operation with Grant, providing, as a side note, an incisive analysis of the strategic situation. He believed the position of Joe Johnston's army in Morton, Mississippi (35 miles east of Jackson), untenable because of pressure from Rosecrans. Moreover, considering "the present shattered conditions of the rebel armies, the right, center, and left having all been disastrously defeated," if Rosecrans was pushed southward and Charleston fell to the army and navy and became the base for an interior thrust, it would trap the forces of Bragg and Johnston between Rosecrans in Tennessee, Grant in northern Mississippi, and Banks in New Orleans. "I do not believe that that condition of things can be maintained," he concluded.[20] In other words, pressure from different points exerted upon the South would cause it to collapse—an idea rooted in McClellan's original strategic plan, then pushed by Lincoln, and now including variations from other pens. The Union leadership had failed to make this happen in the spring of 1862 when they had the chance; this occasion would prove no different.

Grant also saw advantages in seizing Mobile. It would force Bragg to send troops to counter it, and if the Confederates failed "to meet this fire in his rear," the Union forces, using Mobile as their base, could tear up much of the country that fed and supplied Lee's army. Moreover, if the administration did want a foothold in Texas, Grant believed it would be better simply to put troops in Brownsville, which was on the coast as well as the Texas-Mexico border.[21]

Lincoln and Seward had other ideas. They had initiated the Texas expedition for *raisons d'état*, as well as to meet domestic political concerns. Clausewitz argued the merits of a relationship in which the political leaders set policy and the military leaders did what they could to enact it. Such are also the traditional roles of the civilian and military forces in American society. But the Union command, including Lincoln and Seward, had lost sight of the main goal. Texas certainly mattered, but winning the war against the Confederacy, and winning it as quickly as possible at the least cost, mattered far more. This would remove all domestic as well as foreign political difficulties. In August

1863, the Confederacy was in desperate need of a breather. The Union gave them one by diverting its attention to peripheral theaters. Lincoln halted Meade. Lincoln and Halleck ordered Banks west. Halleck detached forces from Grant to clean out Arkansas—"tidying up," he called it. Clearing these areas did not noticeably impair the Confederacy's ability to resist; a thrust at the heart would have. Nor did these moves strike at the Confederate center of gravity, which Lincoln identified at the same time he was ensuring that Banks went in the wrong direction: "The strength of the rebellion, is its military— its army." He wrote this in August 1863.[22] All of this meant that Lee would be left alone, which was never a good thing.

In early August, Meade received orders to stop pursuing Lee. "I am quite sure if I was to advance now," Meade grumbled in a letter to his wife a few days later, "he [Lee] would fall back to Richmond." He added, aptly, "As the question never will be settled till their military power is destroyed, I think it unfortunate we do not take advantage of their present depression."[23]

By early September, Lee expressed some limited optimism regarding what he could do to Meade, even after Longstreet's troops went west to support Bragg (about which we will hear more shortly). "If I was a little stronger," he told Davis, "I think I could drive Meade's army under cover of the fortifications of Washington before he gathers more reinforcements." But Lee included a critical caveat: should Meade get all of his reinforcements, Lee might be forced to return to Richmond. "The blow at Rosecrans should be made promptly and Longstreet returned," he wrote.[24]

However, as September lengthened, Lee grew increasingly convinced that the Union was concentrating against him. He was upset by the loss of his troops to the West, believing that he needed them and that they had "gone where they will do no good." Moreover, since Burnside had unexpectedly gone to Knoxville, Lee believed that he would not join with Rosecrans but instead drive back Samuel Jones's forces in Abingdon, Virginia (near the Virginia/North Carolina/Tennessee border), thereby helping Meade's advance against Lee. A worried Lee agreed with Davis's assessment that if Rosecrans and Burnside did unite at Chattanooga, the enemy would be so strong that the only way to dislodge them would be an attack on their communications.[25]

Lee was right to feel uneasy. On September 15, Halleck suddenly seemed to remember that the Union had an army in Virginia, an awakening fueled by events in Tennessee. Halleck wrote Meade that "preparations should be made to at least threaten Lee, and, if possible, cut off a slice of his army. I do not think the exact condition of affairs is sufficiently ascertained to authorize any very considerable advance. I will write more fully to-day." These vaguely worded instructions provoked intervention and explanation by the ever-watchful Lincoln and clarification by Halleck. "The main objects are to threaten Lee's position," Halleck told Meade, "to ascertain more certainly the actual condition of affairs in his army, and, if possible, to cut off some portion of it by a sudden raid, if that be practicable." They also wanted hard information as to whether Confederate troops had truly gone to Tennessee. As he wrote Meade, this had direct bearing on the operations of Burnside, who was ordered to move toward Chattanooga, joining up with Rosecrans to face Johnston and Bragg and thus leaving "East Tennessee comparatively open on the Virginia side."[26]

Moreover, while instructing Meade to "threaten Lee" and try to "cut off a slice of his army," Halleck told him to expect very little in the way of reinforcements. While urging Meade to avoid doing anything rash, he pointed out that if Lee's force was "very considerably reduced, something may be done to weaken him or force him still farther back."[27] Considering his opponent, rashness would be needed to accomplish either.

Halleck took the added step of enclosing a message Lincoln had sent him regarding Meade: "My opinion is that he should move upon Lee at once in manner of general attack, leaving to developments whether he will make it a real attack. I think this would develop Lee's real condition and purposes better than the cavalry alone can do."[28]

Meade replied that Longstreet's corps had indeed left Lee's army and that the Army of the Potomac would cross the Rappahannock River. He was not, however, optimistic about drawing Lee out of his trenches and into a fight. Moreover, Meade immediately began to fear that if they were wrong about how many men had been taken from Lee's army, Lee might try to put his forces between the Army of the Potomac and Washington.[29]

Meade advanced because he believed Lee had weakened his army and would withdraw to Richmond if "threatened," but Lee took up a strong position behind the Rapidan River. Meade thought his forces insufficient to fight a battle and then advance, and he was unwilling to run the risk without clearer orders from his superiors.[30]

Lincoln, always on the lookout for communications from the Army of the Potomac, gave his view of what Meade should do. He also assessed the Union's strategic and operational situation in the East, offering a foreshadowing of things to come. As ever, he felt forced to submit to whoever was in the field regarding the best course of action. Nonetheless, he recognized the Union advantage and smelled opportunity. "These two armies confront each other across a small river, substantially midway between the two Capitals, each defending it's [*sic*] own Capital, and menacing the other. Gen. Meade estimates the enemies['] infantry in front of him at not less than forty thousand. Suppose we add fifty per cent to this, for cavalry, artillery, and extra duty men stretching as far as Richmond, making the whole force of the enemy sixty thousand. Gen. Meade, as shown by the returns, has with him, and between him and Washington, of the same classes of well men, over ninety thousand. Neither can bring the whole of his men into a battle; but each can bring as large a per centage in as the other. For a battle, then, Gen. Meade has three men to Gen. Lee's two. Yet, it having been determined that choosing ground, and standing on the defensive, gives so great advantage that the three can not safely attack the two, the three are left simply standing on the defensive also. If the enemies['] sixty thousand are sufficient to keep our ninety thousand away from Richmond, why, by the same rule, may not forty thousand of ours keep their sixty thousand away from Washington, leaving us fifty thousand to put to some other use?" However, to "avoid misunderstanding," Lincoln made it clear that he was against forcing the enemy back slowly to his Richmond trenches. This, he felt, was a mistake. He recalled that "his last attempt upon Richmond" had been to try to get McClellan to march on the city when he was closer to the Confederate capital than the Rebel army was. "Since then I have constantly desired the Army of the Potomac, to make Lee's army, and not Richmond, it's [*sic*] objective point."[31]

Halleck sent along to Meade Lincoln's note, as well as one of his own. As usual, Halleck gave no orders. He told Meade to fight if he thought he could, but if he was to do something, he should do it before the troops on detached service with Bragg returned. He also repeated Lincoln's key instruction to keep in mind that the Confederate army, not its capital, was the "objective point" and that he was to "do it as much harm as possible with as little injury as possible" to his own forces. Meade remained unimpressed. "As I expected," the general told Mrs. Meade, "no decisive answer was sent to me, but I was told to act in accordance with my own judgment." Talks in Washington followed. Meade thwarted an attempt to reduce his forces—or at least thought he had. He made plans for an offensive, but then received word that the administration considered his army too large for defensive purposes and was taking part of it away.[32]

Word that two corps had been taken from Meade and sent to Rosecrans provoked Lee into action. He decided to maneuver Meade out of the Union position at Culpeper Courthouse and try to turn his flank in a manner similar to what he had done to Pope the previous year. He told John D. Imboden in the Shenandoah Valley to support this by pushing as much as he was able.[33]

Lee put his army in motion on October 9, 1863. Meade withdrew over the Rappahannock River. "I am still moving with the view of throwing him further back towards Washington," Lee wrote. On October 14 Lee attacked Meade's rear guard at Bristoe Station. Meade's forces stung him, then withdrew, leaving the field to the Confederates.[34]

Lee's movements, though, worried the Union high command; they feared he would mount yet another invasion of the North. Stanton and Halleck scrambled to collect troops to prevent this.[35] Clearly, Lee's previous aggressive actions had garnered him a distinct psychological advantage over his foes. Halleck had also decided that it was time for Meade to fight Lee and pushed the general to do so. Lincoln did the same, sending word to Meade that he himself would bear the responsibility for any unfavorable results.[36]

In the face of Lee's push, Meade retreated to Centreville, a position Lee considered too strong to assault. Lee could do no more, however much he wanted to. Logistically, he was at the end of his tether. His army was in sad shape. He told his wife that "thousands were barefooted, thousands with fragments of shoes, & all without overcoats, blankets or warm clothing. I could not bear to expose them to certain suffering, on an uncertain issue." He told the Confederate quartermaster general that only his "unwillingness to expose the men to the hardships" had forced him to return to a position on the Rappahannock. "I should otherwise have endeavored to detain General Meade near the Potomac, if I could not throw him to the north side."[37]

Lee's rebuff at Gettysburg had not dampened his aggressiveness, nor had it given him much fear of Meade. Meade gave his adversary his due. "This was a deep game, and I am free to admit that in the playing of it he has gotten the better of me."[38]

Meanwhile, Halleck pressed Meade to fight. By this point, however, he held Meade and the Army of Potomac in contempt, something made clear by his letters. To another general, Halleck remarked that if "a general is unwilling to fight, he is not likely to gain a victory. That army fights well when attacked, but all its generals have been unwilling to attack, even very inferior numbers. It certainly is a very strange phenomenon." The Old Snapping Turtle had no qualms about biting back and told Halleck that if he had any orders to convey he should do so; if not, and if Halleck didn't trust him, he would hand over his stars. Halleck backed down.[39]

Meade, though, did advance, upsetting Lee's plans. Lee had hoped to reinforce Imboden so he could strike at the Baltimore and Ohio Railroad, which connected Harpers Ferry with Baltimore. But this did not prevent him from insisting upon action from his other forces. He told Sam Jones to move against eastern Tennessee because that might "attract the attention of the enemy in northwestern Virginia, so as to prevent a combination of his forces upon General Imboden." He wanted action in general, preferring Jones to move against Knoxville, if possible, to secure the Virginia and Tennessee Railroad, but if this could not be done he wanted him to march into northwestern Virginia in conjunction with Imboden to attack the railroad there. "It behooves us to be active," he wrote, "to give the enemy no rest, and to prevent his reinforcing his army about Chattanooga, which now seems to be the important point of his operations." Lee wrote much to Jones, hoping "to inspire him."[40]

The Union commanders continued their back-and-forth, Halleck and Lincoln keeping a tight leash on Meade while at the same time urging him to attack and suggesting plans and movements, including a push in conjunction with raids against the Confederate railroad and bridges between Lee's army and Richmond. A meeting between Meade and Lincoln on October 23 did nothing to alter the odd situation. Meade's superiors simply did not trust him. He held the same view of them, believing the politicians were after him. Meade slowly pushed south, and he did fight, but he refused to take big gambles, and his superiors refused to force him.[41]

Throughout the month of November, Lee and Meade probed and danced, Lee concluding that "our capital is the great point of attack of the enemy in the eastern portion of the Confederacy." The pressure forced Lee back over the Rapidan River; then winter gripped the theater.[42]

The South Considers Its Options

THE LOSS OF VICKSBURG left Jefferson Davis distraught. After receiving word of its fall he asked Johnston for an explanation. Johnston replied that his forces had been too weak and that he had been unable to move on Vicksburg until the end of June because of transportation problems, reasons he had earlier related to the secretary of war. "I then moved toward Vicksburg to attempt to extricate the garrison," Johnston wrote, "but could not devise a plan until after reconnoitering, for which I was too late."[43]

After Vicksburg fell, Port Hudson was not far behind, surrendering on July 8. Johnston made no effort to relieve it. He did advise Franklin Gardner, the post's commander, to pull his forces out and also hoped Richard Taylor would do something. (Johnston spent a lot of time hoping others would do something.)[44]

Immediately after Vicksburg's surrender, Grant sent Sherman to drive Johnston's forces from Jackson, Mississippi, issuing the orders before Vicksburg's defenders had time to lower the Confederate flag. Sherman, as always, proved eager to strike another blow. After word of the surrender came he wired Grant: "Already are my orders out to give one big huzza and sling the knapsack for new fields."[45] With the capture of Vicksburg and Port Hudson, the Union had achieved strategic dominance in the West. Control of the Mississippi provided a supply route the Confederates could not cut and an untouchable springboard for operations into Confederate territory.

The Confederacy's situation in the region went from bad to worse, both in the field and in the realm of civil-military relations. Davis looked for some type of counterthrust by his forces, but desertion plagued Johnston's army. Davis and his Confederacy resorted to a Southern version of the *levée en masse* in an effort to summon enough men to the colors.[46]

Davis was particularly upset with Johnston. He wanted to relieve him, but politically this wasn't feasible, as Johnston had strong supporters in the Confederate Congress, particularly Congressman Louis Wigfall, and was also a popular figure in the Confederacy. Davis did reorganize the command structure in the West, separating the commands of Bragg and Johnston and reducing Johnston's area to southern Alabama, Mississippi, and a piece of western Tennessee.[47]

Davis also continued what had become a feud with Johnston over just what the general had commanded by dispatching a multipage letter to Johnston on the matter. He laid out a lawyerly (and pedantic) case consisting of thirty-four points, undeniably proving his brief, but missing the greater point: that he had a general who would neither fight nor exercise his command prerogative. Plus, with the reorganization of the western Rebel commands, none of this mattered. At root, the problem was that Davis and Johnston simply despised each other. Davis hated Johnston for all the ills he had brought upon him, and Johnston's hatred of Davis "amounts to a religion," as Mary Chesnut wrote in her diary. "With him it colors all things." Johnston supplied an equally detailed and pointless reply.[48] Their feelings meant that they could not maintain a professional detachment, and this directly interfered with the South's prosecution of the war, mirroring the relationship between Lincoln and McClellan—and with similar results.

Davis was not the only one critical of Johnston. Bragg also weighed in after Vicksburg's surrender, noting that he too had wondered why Johnston was falling back, "yielding ground we cannot recover, and without which we cannot survive. By this time this whole army could have been in Mississippi and a victory won. As it is, we may expect to be destroyed in detail."[49]

But one can also critique the criticism. Rosecrans's advance in late June seems to support Johnston's point that pulling the troops from Tennessee meant deciding between Vicksburg and Tennessee, or more specifically Vicksburg and Chattanooga, the latter a critical rail connection between the eastern and western Confederacy, as well as the portal to the Deep South. Bragg's complaint about leaving Pemberton's army in Vicksburg to be captured is more difficult to refute, raising the question of whether the Confederates should have left smaller garrisons at Vicksburg and Port Hudson to free up more men for a field army, thus improving their chances of stopping Grant. But in addition to his own predisposition against offensive action, Johnston had real transportation and supply problems to overcome. Having a larger army would have multiplied these issues. Nonetheless, a larger army would have made thwarting Grant more likely. Moreover, freedom to maneuver gives one the chance to seize the initiative, something that the South never had in Mississippi once Grant bottled up Pemberton in Vicksburg. Had Johnston and Pemberton coordinated their attacks on Grant, they might have succeeded. But given that Pemberton and Johnston could not communicate freely and Johnston could not muster enough forces to strike Grant, the South was forced to yield the initiative to the North, and Vicksburg became a prison.

In July, Johnston placed the blame for Confederate failure in the West, particularly the fall of Vicksburg, on Pemberton. He had ordered the city evacuated (Port Hudson as well), but "General Pemberton set aside this order under the advice of a council of war." In other words, Pemberton was guilty because he did not abandon his position. But one can also imagine the recriminations if Pemberton, a Northern-born Confederate general that many Southerners already viewed with suspicion, had marched away from the "Confederate Gibraltar." Pemberton had no good choice. Still, obeying Johnston's order to break out was probably the best of those he did have. Better to risk the army and lose the city than to lose both.

As Johnston retreated, Davis wanted to know what the general now intended. "My purpose is to hold as much of the country as I can," Johnston replied, "and to retire farther only when compelled to do so. Should the enemy cross Pearl River, I will oppose his advance, and, unless you forbid it, order General Bragg to join me to give battle." This did not satisfy Davis. He told Lee as much, noting that Johnston's "vague purposes" were reminiscent of what he had supplied when "he held his army before Richmond."[50]

Davis was desperate for Lee's advice during the trying time after the Vicksburg disaster. Lee had already offered his opinion on the West, advising the selection and fortification of a suitable spot on the Mississippi River, one that could be held by a small garrison, thereby freeing the bulk of the region's forces for active operations against the enemy.[51] This was also what Bragg had suggested.

The Confederate generals in the West had other ideas. On July 26, Polk proposed to Davis a plan for a Confederate offensive in Tennessee. He recommended the concentration of most of Johnston's forces with Bragg's in Chattanooga, adding Buckner's as well. This, he believed, would give them 70,000–80,000 men with which to crush Rosecrans and move across Tennessee, cutting Grant's supply lines. They could advance all the way to Memphis, reestablishing communications with the Trans-Mississippi, and attack Grant from the north. The only downside Polk saw to his plan was that Alabama would be left open to the enemy, but this was a risk he believed had to be taken.[52]

Polk's proposal was deeply flawed. He was seeking to make use of what became the standard Confederate response to a Union push: concentration of forces. But the essence of Polk's plan was to ask the impossible while assuming the enemy would not react. Marching the length of Tennessee would have taxed even Union logistics, which were formidable. Moreover, the Confederates had no hope of finding the supplies and transportation necessary for such a move. Even if successful and unopposed, the offensive would not have separated Grant from his supplies; the North controlled the Mississippi. Lastly, nothing would prevent Grant from destroying the communications of the advancing Confederates by simply blocking any routes of retreat.

The South was already considering a counteroffensive when Polk dispatched his note. On August 1, Adjutant General Cooper asked whether Bragg could attack if reinforced with Johnston's army.[53] Bragg consulted with Johnston and quickly decided that even if they joined forces they lacked sufficient resources to mount a northern-bound offensive. "The defensive seems to be our only alternative," Bragg concluded, "and that is a sad one." Davis, obviously disappointed, sided with his general. "However desirable a movement may be, it is never safe to do more than suggest it to a commanding general, and it would be unwise to order its execution by one who foretold failure."[54]

The War in Tennessee

GETTING UNION GENERAL ROSECRANS to move always required the largest of Archimedes's levers. By late July, his recalcitrance had pushed the administration to the limits of its patience. Halleck bluntly relayed the administration's dissatisfaction and told him to lighten his baggage, live off the land, and move his army against the enemy before Johnston's forces united with Bragg's. Halleck also pushed Burnside to make the perpetually planned movement into eastern Tennessee, and wanted them moving together, Rosecrans against Bragg, and Burnside into eastern Tennessee.[55]

This effort had been delayed by a cavalry raid that carried John Hunt Morgan and his men into Ohio (in disobedience of his orders from Bragg). In a ride that Morgan believed was the means of thwarting both Burnside and Rosecrans, he succeeded only in wrecking his command and making himself a Federal prisoner.[56]

Unperturbed, Rosecrans told Halleck that his ambition was "something like your own—to discharge my duty to God and our country." He advised Halleck that "whenever the Government can replace me by a commander in whom they have more confidence, they ought to do so, and take the responsibility of the result." He also supplied a soliloquy on the various supply and communication obstacles facing his army.[57]

Halleck lost patience. He informed Rosecrans that his forces had to move forward "without further delay." Rosecrans was to send him daily reports about his progress until he crossed the Tennessee River. Old Rosy asked whether Halleck really meant for him to march immediately, or if he had the commander's discretion to move when he felt ready. Halleck replied that the orders to advance were "peremptory." He simultaneously ordered Burnside to advance on Knoxville.[58]

Burnside promised obedience. Rosecrans pled unreadiness and difficulty and asked to be relieved if the order was not modified. Halleck barked some more, but not loudly enough to get Rosecrans to budge. On the positive side, Rosecrans and Burnside did try to coordinate their movements and make them mutually supporting. Rosecrans even appealed to Lincoln, who backed Halleck. Burnside's campaign jumped off on August 15. Rosecrans began crossing the Cumberland Mountains the next day, aiming at Chattanooga.[59]

In the midst of the Union move, Davis asked Bragg whether he could unify his forces and throw them against one column of the Union advance, thereby defusing the threat. Bragg could not save Chattanooga, but he did intend to fight, hoping to meet Rosecrans with his whole force when the point of attack was revealed. Bragg asked for help. It came from Johnston, as well as in the form of paroled prisoners, some of whom had been at Vicksburg. Davis dispatched his aide-de-camp Colonel James Chesnut to the governors of Georgia and Alabama to convince them to send men to Bragg because the best way to defend Alabama and Georgia was by strengthening the Confederate forces in Tennessee.[60]

Davis sent another aide, Colonel W. P. Johnston, to Tennessee and Georgia in early September on a fact-finding mission. Davis hoped that General Sam Jones's forces, as they advanced west, would give freedom of action to the troops of Brigadier General William Preston, allowing these units to get in the rear of Burnside's army. Davis wanted the "junction" of Bragg's and Buckner's forces in eastern Tennessee so that they could attack one of the advancing Union columns before they were in "supporting distance of each other," with the help of reinforcements coming from Johnston's army, as well as Georgia and Alabama. Davis was very concerned about what Bragg and Buckner might accomplish, telling an aide that that the duo "will realize how necessary it is for every consideration that we should have a success against the enemy in that quarter." It would be "disastrous" to lose the mountainous regions that guarded the entrance to Georgia and Alabama, which could serve as a basis for regaining control of middle Tennessee and southern Kentucky.[61] Davis saw the South as having its back against the wall in the West—and he was right. Losing the passes of north Georgia would be a disaster, opening the way into the Deep South.

The Union advances unhinged the Confederate position in Tennessee. Burnside's troops took Knoxville on September 2 unopposed, severing the important and direct rail line between Richmond and Chattanooga. Six days later, they took Cumberland Gap. Meanwhile, Rosecrans pushed his army through the mountain passes in three separated columns, a move similar to the one that had forced Bragg to retreat to Chattanooga in June. He masked some of his intent with a well-executed deception that included nightly fires at every potential crossing along 40 miles of the Tennessee River. This, and fast marching, undermined the Confederate defensive positions.[62]

Bragg retreated, gathering his reinforcements as he did so. The lack of supplies in the area forced him, as he put it, to "maneuver between the enemy and our supplies," but as he marched he looked for a chance to attack. Davis was convinced that Rosecrans intended to force Bragg out of Chattanooga and then combine forces with Burnside. He urged Bragg to attack one or the other, defeating them in detail, meaning destroying one and then turning against the survivor. On September 6, Bragg wrote Davis: "Rosecrans' army has certainly crossed Tennessee River. Reported now as moving toward Rome. We shall move on him promptly."[63]

In support of his operations against Rosecrans, Bragg ordered Cumberland Gap abandoned, the destruction of all stores there that could not be removed, and the retreat of its defenders toward Abingdon, Virginia. Davis rescinded the order, believing that Bragg and Buckner were unaware of the true situation there. The area had been reinforced, and Davis advised the department commander, Sam Jones, to advance, but also gave him discretion to do as he thought best. Jones sought to hold his corner of Tennessee in order to keep at least a portion of Burnside's men from fighting Bragg.[64]

Help, though, was on the way to Bragg from another quarter—the Army of Northern Virginia—in the form of Longstreet's corps. The decision to send this force arose from a Richmond conference held at the end of August and the start of September. The Confederacy's leaders, reeling from reverses in both the Eastern and Western Theaters, believed they could not afford another in their center. Longstreet was eager for the change, believing that the Confederates' best opportunities lay in the West. They also discussed sending Lee, who professed a willingness to go, if Davis desired it, while insisting the department would be better commanded by someone already on the scene and familiar with the situation.[65]

Davis didn't make Lee go, partly because he feared his absence from Virginia. This created one of the great what-ifs of the Civil War. What if Lee had taken command of the Army of Tennessee? The theater certainly would have benefited from his leadership and organizational skill, as well as from his reputation, which Davis estimated as being worth more than a corps.[66] But had Lee been in command at Chickamauga instead of Bragg, the outcome might have allowed the Confederates to clear at least parts of Tennessee and forestall a future Union advance. Such a victory might have been enough to delay the Union's offensive into Georgia and the subsequent capture of Atlanta, an event that sealed Lincoln's reelection and the South's doom.

On the other hand, Lee's transfer also might have changed nothing; the Army of Tennessee, despite its bravery and sacrifice, was not the Army of Northern Virginia, and the terrain of Tennessee made it more difficult to move and feed forces there than in Virginia. Nonetheless, Davis probably should have made Lee go, at least for a season. The South needed to recoup some of its disastrous losses of the summer of 1863, and that autumn was its last chance to do so.

His communications threatened by Rosecrans's advance, Bragg abandoned Chattanooga. The Federals took the city on September 9. As Rosecrans pushed beyond the city, Halleck, unsure of the truth to reports that the Rebels had sent part of Bragg's army to Lee, put the brakes on Rosecrans's advance on September 11, planning to give orders for future movement soon. He directed Burnside to take the gaps in the mountains of North Carolina and link up with Rosecrans with at least his cavalry. Rosecrans thought it more likely that reinforcements were coming to Bragg. This was confirmed on the fourteenth. Meanwhile, Rosecrans worried about an attack on his communications. Halleck responded by ordering Burnside to push as many troops as possible to Chattanooga to reinforce Rosecrans and ordered Old Rosy to prevent Bragg from getting back into middle Tennessee. Halleck also began coordinating other forces to meet a possible counterthrust by Bragg by taking troops from the various commands farther west. Optimism arose in some quarters of future success by Rosecrans. Former journalist and now assistant secretary of war Henry Dana wrote Stanton, "This army has now gained a position from which it can effectually advance upon Rome and Atlanta, and deliver there the finishing blow of the war."[67]

Halleck waited for the Rebel counteroffensive to break. He first expected it to land on Meade in Virginia, but by September 15 he was certain that the Rebels were massing against Rosecrans and Burnside. He told Meade, "The enemy probably saw that if you and Rosecrans could hold your present position till Grant and Banks cleaned out the States west of the Mississippi, the fate of the rebellion would be sealed."[68] Halleck was overreaching a bit, but he had revealed exactly the shift in Union strategic thinking. The emphasis, for a while, was moving to peripheral operations.

Reinforced by Buckner as well as units from Joe Johnston's army, Bragg had decided to attack. Rosecrans's widely dispersed forces, moving through the mountain like three fingers, had given Bragg the chance to smash one, then move on to the next, defeating the enemy in detail. But unclear orders from Bragg, combined with his subordinates' mistrust, allowed the fore of the Union advance, a corps under George Thomas, to escape. Still, the opportunity to hit another Union prong remained. Bragg decided to do this, but then waited five days. His hesitation gave Rosecrans time to concentrate his divided forces; Bragg lost his chance. The Battle of Chickamauga, the third-bloodiest engagement of the Civil War, took place on September 19 and 20. The Union forces held off the Confederates on the first day. But then more Rebel troops arrived in the form of Longstreet's corps. Longstreet's men delivered a solid blow against the Union center on the second day of the fight, crumpling the Federal line. A retreat began, Rosecrans and some of his staff leading the way. Only the corps of George Thomas, who ever since has been known as the "Rock of Chickamauga," stood firm; they withdrew that night, unimpeded, after having done much to save Rosecrans's army. Both sides had about 60,000 men engaged. The North suffered 16,000 casualties, the South 18,000. Though a Confederate victory, it was not complete. Like Meade after

Gettysburg, Bragg failed to follow the retreating Rosecrans, provoking consternation from Longstreet and the accusation that Bragg had thrown away a
great opportunity. The Confederates then besieged the Union army in Chattanooga, Bragg hoping to starve them out.[69]

Rosecrans's defeat caused not a little worry in Washington (not to mention in Chattanooga). Rosecrans sounded the alarm, and Lincoln tried to
take matters in hand, ordering Burnside to march for Chattanooga. He
told Rosecrans, "Be of good cheer," and bade him take up a solid position
until Burnside could come to his relief. Lincoln considered it critical to
hold Chattanooga or its environs because "it keeps all Tennessee clear of
the enemy, and also breaks one of his most important Railroad lines." He
told Halleck that they had to do the "utmost of our ability" to help Rosecrans. "If he can only maintain this position," Lincoln concluded, "without
more, the rebellion can only eke out a short and feeble existence, as an
animal sometimes may with a thorn in its vitals." This was a conclusion
that McClellan had come to two years earlier when he first took up his
command in Washington. Halleck issued a typically loathsome reply, telling the president that he had given basically the same instructions ten days
before.[70]

The problem became getting Burnside to march to Rosecrans's relief.
Burnside asked for clarification of his orders: was he supposed to abandon his
gains in eastern Tennessee? Lincoln composed an angry response to the former commander of the Army of the Potomac. But as he so often did, Lincoln
folded the note away and dispatched something more constructive. "Hold
your present positions, and send Rosecrans what you can spare, in the quickest and safest way."[71]

Meanwhile, Halleck continued stripping the western commands to save
Chattanooga. He took troops from Sherman, who, in what for the Ohioan
passed for optimism, replied, "I doubt if our re-enforcement to Rosecrans can
reach him in time to do good." Sherman also supplied an alternative plan, suggesting that the "Texas expedition" and "all our available forces" be directed
at Mobile and at destroying the Mobile and Ohio railroad: "This would force
Joe Johnston to make very heavy detachments from Bragg." Halleck concurred, but nothing came of this.[72]

Burnside responded with three different plans, asking Halleck to decide
between them, and also sending them to Rosecrans. Halleck, as always,
refused to decide. He wired Burnside: "I can only repeat what I have so often
urged, the importance of your connecting with General Rosecrans's army
on the north side of the [Tennessee] river, so as to command the crossings."

Rosecrans wanted Burnside to implement his first suggestion, which was to abandon eastern Tennessee, except for Cumberland Gap, and push 20,000 troops to Rosecrans along the north bank of the Tennessee. Burnside asked Halleck if he should do as Rosecrans wanted.[73]

Meanwhile, bigger things had been brewing in the Union high command. Almost two weeks before, on September 19, Lincoln penned his extended analysis of the Eastern Theater in which he concluded that he could pull forces from the Army of the Potomac to use elsewhere. This same day, Bragg shattered a wing of Rosecrans's army. An anxious White House meeting occurred in the midnight hours of September 23–24 at which Stanton suggested using the rail lines to ship 30,000 men from Meade's army to the West, promising it could be done in five days. Lincoln, though skeptical of his secretary of war's timeline, approved the move. Stanton delivered—though not quite as quickly as promised—and moved 20,000 men west.[74]

Lincoln kept his eye on Rosecrans while the movement took place. The general's behavior in the aftermath of Chickamauga worried the president. He said Rosecrans was "confused and stunned like a duck hit on the head." Lincoln assured him that "if we can hold Chattanooga and East Tennessee, I think the rebellion must dwindle and die. I think you and Burnside can do this, and hence doing so is your main object." But he also told him that since Bragg's army was staring him in the face he had the opportunity to "menace or attack" it at any time and suggested that this might be the quickest way to end the Rebel assaults on his communications.[75]

The Confederates also saw opportunities. Lee hoped Bragg would operate on the enemy's communications and take advantage of what he had won. If he did so, Lee believed, Longstreet could move into Tennessee and "open that country," then combine with General Sam Jones's troops and rejoin Lee's army as quickly as possible to face what Lee saw as the growing power of General Meade.[76]

The initial Confederate response, however, was Bragg and his generals fighting among themselves. Bragg had Leonidas Polk forced out for failing to obey orders and others transferred to different commands. Many of the remainder, including Longstreet, summoned the nerve to petition the government for Bragg's removal but not the moral courage to admit authorship of the indictment. Davis visited the army and heard many complaints, but when he departed Bragg remained the commander. He could think of no better alternative. Other quarrels followed.[77]

Despite these troubles, Bragg tried to figure out how to pry the Federals out of Chattanooga. The works were too strong to storm, so Bragg tried to starve them out by mounting cavalry raids against the city's supply lines. Three such efforts produced very little. Meanwhile, Bragg tightened the Confederate noose around the city. The administration prodded him to advance; Bragg sat.[78]

On October 11, 1863, Davis, Bragg, and Longstreet met. Longstreet wanted to take Bridgeport, Alabama, a key point for the Federals to keep Chattanooga in supply, while Bragg pushed for implementation of a plan suggested by Beauregard to bring in men from Johnston and Lee, cross the Tennessee River north of Chattanooga, and force the Union out. Davis liked Beauregard's idea and admitted its virtue, but he refused to further weaken Lee. A successful Union attack on October 28–29 secured the Federals' communications with Bridgeport.[79]

A few days later, Davis confirmed his hopes in an overly revealing interview with a newspaper. The paper reported that Davis was "very anxious that we should gain the possession of Tennessee as soon as convenient, and winter [the army] in Kentucky, if possible." Another quoted Davis as saying "that his purpose was to 'snatch' Tennessee from the clutch of the Abolitionists."[80] Davis had adopted a bad habit of telling reporters what Confederate armies in the West planned to do.

The next Confederate offensive move came, as it so often did, at Davis's prompting. Davis advised Bragg to look for an opportunity to attack Rosecrans in detail if he moved from Chattanooga. But he also had ambitious objectives to be accomplished before the fall campaign season ended. He was happy with Bragg's efforts at clearing the Union forces from eastern Tennessee thus far, but hoped to see that area recovered and Bragg's reestablishment of his communications with Virginia. As always, the problem of supplies loomed, and Davis also wanted Bragg to redeem as much of the lost areas of Tennessee as possible in order to feed his army. He told him to consider dispatching Longstreet to drive out Burnside and recapture Knoxville. He also promised additional troops from commands farther west and discussed the ubiquitous efforts at cooperation with Sam Jones. Nonetheless, Davis expected little from this much-discussed but isolated quarter of the Confederate realm, and little could ever come from here. But this did not stop him from trying. Davis deemed success in eastern Tennessee imperative, writing at one point "how disastrous it would be to lose possession of that mountain region which covers the entrance into Georgia & Alabama & constitutes our best base for the recovery of Middle Tennessee & Southern Kentucky."[81]

When the decision was made, however, Bragg wasted no time in sending Longstreet on his way, and Longstreet wasted no time going. He made bitter remarks against Bragg, accusing him of refusing to grasp opportunities when they arose; Chickamauga remained a particular sore point. He had already grown to hate Bragg as much as did those generals who had served with him far longer. Longstreet was not optimistic, believing the effort had little chance of success because his force of 12,000 was too small. He thought 20,000 men would allow him to deal quickly with Burnside. But Bragg would have had to withdraw from around Chattanooga and find a better defensive position in order to spare sufficient troops. This he was unwilling to do. "We thus expose both to failure and really take no chance to ourselves of great results," Longstreet insisted. Edward Porter Alexander, who was in Longstreet's corps, agreed. Historian Craig Symonds cogently observed: "This was a particularly foolish dispersion of force, for it left Bragg with only about 36,000 men to besiege a Federal Army that had grown to nearly 80,000."[82]

Longstreet's observation revealed a pivotal problem with the Confederate command in the West. Lee realized that the South's inferior manpower forced it to undertake greater risks for the chance of benefit. The South simply did not have the ability to protect everything against a numerically superior enemy. And yet if the Confederacy was to have any chance of turning the tide on any front, it had to take risks.

Grant Moves East

GRANT BIDED HIS TIME through the summer and early fall. Events elsewhere were working to raise his status even higher. Before Longstreet's move to eastern Tennessee became apparent, there were major stirrings in the Union high command. The most important had to do with Rosecrans's fate. Defeated at Chickamauga and besieged by the Confederates in Chattanooga, he was also under siege from Assistant Secretary of War Henry Dana. Dana notified Washington of the lack of support, both in the ranks and among his immediate subordinates, for Rosecrans. Previously, Lincoln had had the problem of a replacement. Now he found one in Grant. On October 16, Halleck told Grant to go to Nashville and take charge, giving him permission to relieve Rosecrans or not. The administration even created a new department, consolidating three into one, all under Grant.[83]

Grant wasted no time when he took up his new command, issuing orders even before he arrived. "Hold Chattanooga at all hazards," he wired Thomas on October 19. "I will be there as soon as possible." "I will hold the town till we starve," Thomas replied. Grant ordered Burnside to repair the routes coming into Chattanooga and push in supplies, as well as to prepare the key points in eastern Tennessee so they could be held with as few men as possible. Grant had already removed Rosecrans.[84]

Meanwhile, Halleck laid out for Grant what Rosecrans and Burnside were supposed to be accomplishing in eastern Tennessee and what had been done so far to reach these objectives. Moving together, they were meant to achieve the administration's long-cherished goal of freeing eastern Tennessee while cutting an important Rebel railroad and robbing the Confederates of access to areas producing important foodstuffs and raw materials. Taking Chattanooga supported this. But, Halleck said, Rosecrans was instructed only to hold on to the mountain passes and no more. "In other words, the main objects of the campaign were the restoration of East Tennessee to the Union, and by holding the two extremities of the valley to secure it from rebel invasion." Then things fell apart because the Rebels attacked. Halleck gave Grant very little direction, merely telling him to retake the Lookout Mountain passes, "which should never have been given up."[85]

Grant reached Chattanooga on the night of October 23. Seeing opportunity as well as danger, he hurried Sherman along. Later, Grant wrote about how desperate the supply situation had been when he arrived and how close the enemy gripped the Union forces in Chattanooga—so close, he complained, that they "have been able to send Longstreet off, before my eyes, and I have not been able to move a foot to stop his advance up the Tennessee Valley against Burnside."[86]

In Chattanooga, Grant determined to secure his supply lines and prepare his troops for a forward movement. Acting on plans conceived before he arrived, Grant's forces cleared the Confederates out of Bridgeport, as we saw earlier, securing his supply lines. Then, reinforced by troops from the east under Hooker, he prepared to attack.[87]

Burnside, meanwhile, worried about Confederate forces concentrating against him. Grant tried to coordinate his movements with Burnside's and to get Halleck to push troops into what was now the new state of West Virginia to take pressure off his fellow general. Halleck asked if Grant could cut the rail lines supporting Bragg, preventing him from massing against Burnside. Grant committed to doing all he could to keep the Rebels from advancing on Burnside from the southwest, just as soon as he had supplies.[88]

Meanwhile, Grant began thinking about launching cavalry raids against the railroads east of Atlanta. Halleck was thinking along the same line: "How would it do for Sherman or a cavalry force to threaten Rome or Atlanta, moving by Warrenton and Jacksonville? If Bragg's communication can be cut off, he cannot supply an army in East Tennessee." Grant replied that he planned to recapture Lookout Mountain when Sherman arrived, but he also planned to hit the enemy's communications with cavalry as soon as possible. Longstreet's appearance scotched this plan. Grant wanted to attack immediately, but Sherman hadn't yet arrived. Grant told Burnside to hold. He would send Sherman to relieve him while Grant moved against Bragg's army.[89] Burnside though, would have to wait a bit first. Grant had more pressing work for Sherman and his men.

In mid-November, Davis had urged Bragg to attack before the Union could bring up reinforcements, just as Grant was now doing. Bragg had not done so.[90] Grant opened his offensive on November 23, having gathered 70,000 troops to face Bragg's now perhaps 40,000 men holding the hills ringing the southern and southeastern rim of Chattanooga. Grant's plan was to have George Thomas test and pin the center of the Confederate force while Hooker did the same to the Rebel left. Sherman would then land the coup de grâce against the Confederate right on the northern end of Missionary Ridge, the intention being to crumple that flank and roll up the Confederate line. Thomas and his men did their job well when the attack kicked off on the twenty-third. Hooker followed up their success with one of his own on the twenty-fourth, his progress aided by a heavy mist that engulfed the battlefield. Sherman launched his prong the next day, but heavy resistance from the single division of Confederate major general Patrick R. Cleburne stymied the Union forces and had Grant worrying about a Confederate counterattack. To regain the initiative, Grant ordered Thomas to push the Confederate center. He did, and his men overran the Confederate positions immediately to their front. Then, without any orders and seized by no one knows what—euphoria, adrenaline, or perhaps simply enthusiasm—the troops charged to the top of Missionary Ridge, shattering the Confederate center. Bragg's army collapsed and began streaming from the field. The Rebels retreated first to Chickamauga, then south to Ringgold, Georgia, before reaching Dalton, Georgia, by the twenty-seventh.[91]

As Bragg retreated, Davis told Longstreet to help Bragg if it was at all possible. It wasn't. The Union victory over Bragg had severed the rail links between Bragg and Longstreet, whose offensive had culminated in a series of failed attacks against Knoxville on the twenty-ninth. Davis became afraid that the Union would now move against Longstreet to relieve Burnside and destroy Longstreet's army as it did so. This forced Longstreet's withdrawal, and he went into winter quarters near Morristown, Tennessee.[92]

After the defeat at Chickamauga, Bragg confessed to Davis, "The disaster admits of no palliation, and is justly disparaging to me as a commander." Nonetheless, Bragg made the case that the fault was not entirely his. Bragg's response contrasts sharply with Lee's after Gettysburg, in which Lee offered his resignation and shouldered all the blame. Bragg pointed the finger at his subordinates.[93] Change would once again come to the Army of Tennessee.

A week later, Lincoln gave his own assessment of the situation in Tennessee, one based upon an inaccurate account of Longstreet's withdrawal. Lincoln believed that if the Army of the Potomac "was good for anything," it could move troops down to Lynchburg and catch Longstreet. "Can anybody doubt, if Grant were here in command that he would catch him? There is not a man in the whole Union who would for a moment doubt it." Nonetheless, Lincoln did not yet want to bring Grant from the west. He also saw Sherman's linking up with Burnside as pivotal, calling it "one of the most important gains of the war—the difference between Burnside saved and Burnside lost is one of the greatest advantages of the war—it secures us East Tennessee."[94]

The Gift of Time

CONFEDERATE MILITARY STRATEGY was reaching perhaps its lowest point. Despite intense debate and discussion, very little emerged that might be deemed valuable. No one had figured out how to win the war, and indeed, the leaders generally were not asking this question. At best, they thought operationally, and when they did, the plans were often outlandish, showing no understanding of logistics, geography, and time. Longstreet's dispatch west provides a case in point. The idea was rooted in Longstreet's original proposal to send a force to Tennessee in an effort to save Vicksburg before Lee's army marched into Pennsylvania. This would have linked the armies of Bragg and Johnston to destroy Rosecrans and then allowed a drive for Cincinnati. Alexander thought well of this idea, saying it "must be pronounced by all military critics to have been much our safest play."[95]

Other voices echoed this plan. The West allowed more room for maneuver, and the South was certainly losing the war there. A successful campaign to defeat Rosecrans might have resulted in the recovery of Tennessee, a place that would have provided food, fodder, industry, and, perhaps most important, fresh troops.

Nonetheless, as historian Charles P. Roland argues, even had the Confederates managed to destroy Rosecrans's army—an unlikely event considering the immense difficulty in doing this in any war—the plan assumed inaction on the Union's part.[96] The North had proved that it could quickly move troops from the Potomac to Tennessee. The forces under Grant, Banks, Meade, and Steele also would have not remained idle. The chances of a Confederate army reaching Cincinnati, as Longstreet hoped, were very slim indeed.

Union strategy in the last half of 1863 was no more distinguished. The Federals failed to capitalize on the victories at Gettysburg and Vicksburg, as well as the advantage gained by Rosecrans when he maneuvered Bragg out of Tullahoma and Chattanooga. Coordination from the top was slow, ineffective, and generally counterproductive. The biggest failure was a shift to a focus on secondary theaters that mattered very little, leaving the major Confederate armies a chance to rest, rebuild, and rearm. The Trans-Mississippi was not a critical region, nor was Texas. The Union had the chance to apply simultaneous pressure at a number of different points in the fall of 1863, perhaps resulting in the collapse of its enemy. Instead, it nibbled at the edges, giving the enemy what he needed most: time.

18

The Siren Song of Tennessee

THE WINTER OF 1863–64

If the enemy gain temporary advantage
the war will be protracted.

—ULYSSES S. GRANT, February 9, 1864

THE WINTER OF 1863–64 featured an intense period of debate among the civilian and military leaders of both sides regarding their next military moves in the West. The North came up with a number of operational plans to keep its forces on the advance. Davis also looked to the offensive, hoping this could redeem Southern fortunes. Numerous ideas flowed from Confederate pens, few of them practical. Both sides remained obsessed with Tennessee. Lincoln held to his sympathies with the suppressed loyalists of the state's eastern reaches, while Davis remained determined to regain its lost fields. "Every consideration rejects the policy of voluntarily surrendering any portion of our territory," he wrote once regarding Arkansas.[1] This certainly applied even more to Tennessee, an area of the Confederate heartland that before the war had served as the South's larder, and the resources of which a weakening Confederacy needed even more now.

IN THE WAKE of his Chattanooga debacle, in which Grant broke Bragg's army, the Confederate general wrote to Davis that he thought it unlikely the Union would move and indeed "cannot assail us here for some weeks." "What, then, shall be our policy [strategy]?" Bragg asked, then answered his own question. "Let us concentrate all our available men, unite them with this gallant little army, still full of zeal and burning to redeem its lost character and prestige, and with our greatest and best leader at the head, yourself, if practicable, march the whole upon the enemy and crush him in his power and his glory." But then he revealed the core issues: doing this would buoy flagging public opinion and, "what is more important, give us subsistence, without which I do not see how we are to remain united."[2]

Lee's view of what the South should do in the West was similar. He feared Grant's victories around Chattanooga opened a route for the Union to strike at key Southern manufacturing and supply centers in the Deep South. He urged concentration "under the best commander," suggesting Beauregard, "to ensure the discomfiture of Grant's army." Only this, he insisted, would secure the Atlantic coast against a potential advance from Chattanooga.[3]

Davis had his own thoughts about the South's next moves, but first he had to find a replacement for Bragg. The general offered his resignation on November 28; Davis quickly took it. Lee and Davis met in Richmond in December 1863. Lee again refused to go west, insisting it would undermine the effectiveness of the Army of Northern Virginia.[4] On the sixteenth, after much agonizing, and despite opposition by others within the hierarchy, Davis put Joe Johnston in Bragg's old post. Benjamin thought Johnston too much of a defensive fighter, and most of the other members of Davis's cabinet campaigned against the general. But Secretary of War Seddon and a core of others supported him. Davis made the appointment with great reluctance, fearing Johnston's "tendencies to a Fabian policy [strategy]," meaning of course avoidance of battle. The personal and professional differences between them contributed to Davis's reluctance, as did Johnston's association with an anti-Davis political bloc headed by one of Davis's most bitter critics, Congressman Louis T. Wigfall. His only other real choice was Beauregard, another political enemy whom Davis despised even more than he did Johnston. The problems with Beauregard, as we've seen, dated to before First Bull Run.[5]

Davis and Seddon made clear to Johnston what they expected of him: they wanted offensive action, and they wanted it now, before the Union could firm up its position in Tennessee. Davis sent a personal note to Johnston shortly before Christmas that made this very clear. The South needed to regain the lost areas for supply reasons. Moreover, success would restore the prestige of the army and prevent "the dispiriting and injurious results that must attend a season of inactivity."[6]

After his arrival in Dalton, Georgia, Johnston told Davis that offensive operations to recover the lost territory would be difficult. To mount any advance he needed more men, which Seddon had already told him was impossible. Moreover, Johnston insisted that taking the offensive meant moving into either middle or eastern Tennessee. Doing the former meant attacking Chattanooga, which Johnston described as a "fortress," as well as overcoming some other obstacles: the Tennessee River, the Cumberland Mountains, and, most important, an enemy army that was twice as large. He believed attacking from northern Mississippi a better choice.[7] Johnston would return to this again and again, even though it would have exposed Georgia to invasion. Moreover, Johnston judged an advance impossible because he could not accumulate sufficient supplies (Seddon did forewarn him about the supply difficulties). The general also predicted that as a result of not advancing he would suffer the same scorn that had been piled upon his predecessor, Bragg.[8]

"I can see no other mode of taking the offensive here than to beat the enemy when he advances, and then move forward," Johnston wrote. "But to make victory probable, the army must be strengthened." Johnston and a bloc of his generals offered a solution to part of this: impressing slaves to replace noncombatants. Using them in such jobs as cooks and laborers, he argued, would free more white men for combat units.[9]

These issues raise two points. Johnston's noting that he had to await and then defeat a Union push before he could attack is sometimes interpreted as symbolic of an offensive-defensive strategy. Johnston's response was a tactical one, not strategic, nor even operational. There was no strategy here—and nothing offensive.

The suggestion about impressing slaves was deeply revealing. The Confederacy constantly suffered manpower shortages, exacerbated by the lengthening of the war. The path from using slaves as supportive labor to arming them and putting them in the ranks was long and contentious, but one that in the war's closing days the South took.[10]

Davis gave Johnston his head and tried to help him as much as he could. He made sure Polk, who commanded in Mississippi, understood that he should cooperate with Johnston and that Johnston understood he could move any of the troops in his own department, including those in Mobile, as he saw fit. He also gave Johnston the freedom to attack along his north Mississippi route if he wished.[11]

This proved too little. Johnston soon concluded not only that his army could not take the offensive but also that the enemy might force them back because he lacked sufficient food, fodder, and shoes (Confederate armies were perpetually poorly shod). But Johnston did continue discussing offensive operations, offering different possible avenues of advance into Tennessee: moving from Rome, Georgia, via Huntsville, Alabama, or retracing the route of Bragg's retreat. Johnston had no confidence in the second path because it would necessitate an enormous train of supply wagons, as well as the added obstacles of rough terrain and attacking Chattanooga. He believed the Mississippi option offered the best base for moving into western Tennessee because it conferred the advantage of drawing supplies from the more abundant resources of these two areas. Johnston also told Davis: "These ideas are expressed not from opinion of their own value, but in the hope of turning your thoughts to this important subject, for my instruction."[12] This last phrase, "for my instruction," raises key questions. Johnston seems to be asking Davis to tell him what to do.

By February 1, 1864, Johnston suspected that the enemy was about to move against Rome (which was what Grant had ordered his subordinates to try to get the enemy to think in order to support a Union advance in Mississippi). Johnston told Davis that if this happened, the Confederates would be forced to evacuate Dalton, Georgia, on the railroad about 30 miles southeast of Chattanooga. He had already begun contemplating retreat and again insisted upon the impossibility of offensive operations because of his army's inferior size and lack of readiness. For the third time he returned to the idea of launching an offensive from northern Mississippi. He saw this as the only chance of carrying the war back into middle Tennessee, and then only if he could collect an army larger than the combined forces that he and Polk possessed.[13]

The Confederacy's other primary military commander also considered offensive moves, the difference being that he had a record of acting. On February 3, 1864, Lee broached the idea of spring action, arguing, "If we could take the initiative and fall upon them unexpectedly we might derange their plans and embarrass them the whole summer." He believed there were only two points east of the Mississippi where this could be done. The first was in Tennessee. Here Longstreet, if given more support or provided with more mobility by mounting his infantry on horses and mules, could advance into Kentucky, where he could supply himself. This would also cut Grant's lines of communication and force him to draw units from Johnston's front. The troops to strengthen Longstreet would have to come from Johnston's, Lee's, or Beauregard's armies.[14]

Lee's second plan involved his uniting with Longstreet's men "secretly and rapidly," and forcing Meade's army, which was in the Culpeper area, back to Washington, so frightening and upsetting the Union that they would cancel any operations they had planned. "We are not in a condition, and never have been, in my opinion," Lee wrote, "to invade the enemy's country with a prospect of permanent benefit. But we can alarm and embarrass him to some extent and thus prevent his undertaking anything of magnitude against us." Lee's ideas had not changed from the year before: seize the initiative, keep the enemy off balance. He pushed Davis to make a decision. "Time," he insisted, "is an important element to our success."[15] Both of Lee's suggestions undoubtedly were influenced by an earlier proposal made by Longstreet to mount his corps and secretly return it to Virginia as part of an attack against Meade's forces in Virginia, or even Washington itself.[16]

Longstreet's operational thinking was active during this time, partly because Davis was asking him for ideas. His most fevered schemes involved the West, the desire—indeed, even need—for the return of which haunted the Confederates. Longstreet wanted to invade Kentucky and believed that if Johnston held in north Georgia, the Union would have to withdraw from eastern Tennessee and gather reinforcements before again taking up offensive operations. Writing from his Morristown base in eastern Tennessee, Longstreet asked "that every available cavalry soldier in Georgia, Alabama, Mississippi, and West Tennessee" be sent against Chattanooga's rail lines and any Union cavalry in this area, and then link up with Longstreet in Kentucky. Meanwhile, Johnston's army, since it could not advance over the winter, might take the place of the Army of Northern Virginia, which Lee would then bring west to form part of Longstreet's advance. At the same time, Lee's cavalry would destroy the Baltimore and Ohio Railroad.[17]

Lee told Longstreet the plan presented too many difficulties (which seems a polite reply to such an outlandish proposal). "Until the enemy gives indications of his intentions it is difficult to say what is best to be done," Lee replied, "unless we could ourselves take the initiative, which if possible should be done."[18] It reminds one of a scheme by Beauregard, who in February 1862, as previously noted, proposed hastily raising and assembling 40,000 men and marching from Columbus, Kentucky, to "take Cairo, Paducah, the mouths of the Tennessee and Cumberland Rivers, and most probably be able to take also Saint Louis by the river."[19]

In mid-February, Lee again returned to the idea of offensive operations. He believed it "very important" for the South to recapture Tennessee, as well as to take the initiative before the North could "open the campaign." He also admitted to having little information on fronts other than his own. In Virginia, at least, he believed that if he had proper supplies and effective horses he could "disturb the quiet of the enemy & drive him to the Potomac."[20]

Davis Takes Control

SHERMAN LEFT VICKSBURG on February 3, intent upon destroying Meridian, Mississippi, and its connecting railways. Grant had also given him leeway to move on Mobile if he thought it possible. Polk, his Confederate opponent, soon got wind of what was going on and appealed to Johnston and Davis for help. Davis instructed Johnston to do what he could to help Polk and prevent the Union from reaching the Gulf and establishing a new base (they believed he aimed at Mobile). Johnston, for his part, thought Polk's cavalry could prevent the enemy from reaching Mobile because of the wagon train it would need to do so. Davis's orders to Johnston became more urgent. Johnston insisted he could not stop them; there was not enough time. Plus, this would require two-thirds of his army, which meant abandoning his Georgia lines.[21]

Displeased, Davis chastised Johnston. Johnston replied with sarcasm: "Wagons would be required for movements of the army, as we could not expect the enemy to await our arrival and give us battle at the terminus of the railroad."[22]

Davis told Polk to hold close to the advancing enemy in order to prevent them from foraging, while watching them carefully in case their move toward Mobile was a feint. Polk, unable to oppose the Union advance, fell back into Alabama. Meanwhile, in an extraordinary act of what today would be termed micromanagement, Davis ordered Johnston to reinforce Polk with a specific corps and even wrote directly to its commander.[23]

Lieutenant General William J. Hardee, the man whom Davis designated to go to Polk's aid, did not think the move a good one because it endangered Atlanta, unless Davis also planned on mounting the proposed offensive from Mississippi. He reported that Sherman was not marching on Mobile and predicted, accurately, that the Union general would tear up the Mobile and Ohio Railroad and withdraw to Jackson.[24]

Davis continued pressing Johnston to help Polk. "Promptitude, I have to repeat, is essential," he said. "To hesitate is to fail." The same day Davis received a report about the Union army being at two places in north Georgia and revoked the order for Johnston to support Polk. Two brigades had reached Polk, too late to do anything, as Johnston had predicted.[25]

During this whole chaotic to-and-fro to meet a Union raid, Davis had assumed de facto operational control of the relevant Confederate forces. Moreover, he instructed Polk to tell his cavalry commanders that after they dispersed the enemy's horsemen they should hold the Union foot soldiers in place until Polk could bring up his own infantry.[26] From Richmond, via telegraph, Davis was trying to exercise tactical control of an army in Mississippi, effectively depriving the field commander of his authority and responsibility, and failing to take advantage of Polk's situational awareness. Leaders reduced to such a state will exhibit none of the individual initiative so critical to success. Sun Tzu himself warned against this. "Now there are three ways in which a ruler can bring misfortune upon his army," he observed. "When ignorant that the army should not advance, to order an advance or ignorant that it should not retire, to order a retirement. This is described as 'hobbling the army.'...When ignorant of military affairs, to participate in their administration. This causes the officers to be perplexed....When ignorant of command problems to share in the exercise of responsibilities. This engenders doubts in the minds of the officers."[27]

Davis was unapologetic. Later, he insisted that if Johnston had obeyed his orders, the troops sent to reinforce Polk would have been in time to prevent Sherman from advancing on Meridian, destroyed Sherman's army, and prevented the invasion of Georgia.[28]

AS DAVIS AND JOHNSTON SPARRED over command, Longstreet tried to gather support for an offensive into Union-controlled Tennessee. Longstreet's previous effort to pull something together there had been rebuffed by his own chief. He was undeterred; indeed, on this issue, he would and could not be budged. A note from Lee in which he asked whether Longstreet could act with Johnston to drive the enemy from Tennessee proved the catalyst for an exhausting discussion of Confederate offensive options.[29]

Despite difficulties keeping his army supplied and fed—principally because of the Confederacy's eroding rail capacity—Longstreet wanted to invade Kentucky. He temporarily resurrected his idea of mounting his men and applied it to the Bluegrass State. He wrote Lee on February 21, "If I can get on the railroad between Louisville and Nashville I can hold Kentucky, I think. At all events, I can hold it long enough to force the enemy to quit Tennessee and allow General Johnston to advance and regain it." He only needed an additional 9,500 mules and their respective accoutrements to add to the 2,500 he would take from his current force. Secretary of War Seddon endorsed the idea and offered cavalry support from Forrest and Wheeler, operating in the rear of Chattanooga to cut the city's supply lines, and a movement by the Confederate cavalry in West Virginia. We might call this Longstreet's "Abingdon Plan"—named for the place where he would need to pre-stage supplies in Virginia along the railroad between Lynchburg, Virginia, and Knoxville.[30]

As Longstreet peddled his proposal, Davis decided to fix all of the Confederacy's command difficulties. On February 23, Bragg was brought in to help Davis with the war's administrative burdens. His position was an undefined one. Bragg considered himself a kind of chief of staff and busied himself investigating the conscription bureau, the prisoner of war system, and other such matters. He was not made the commander of the South's armies, though many at the time thought so. Davis remained the Confederacy's de facto commanding general. If nothing else, the appointment of Bragg demonstrated Davis's complete tone-deafness in regard to public opinion. The press, and seemingly nearly everyone else in the South, condemned the move.[31]

The subject in Richmond became a spring offensive in the West, and Longstreet remained eager to be the one supplying the operational plan. He was optimistic about the results of a spring campaign, believing it might allow the South to sue for peace with the North. He also thought Confederate success would hurt Union morale and help prevent Lincoln from being reelected. The alternative was four more years of war.[32]

The question was, however, what kind of move to make. In early March, Davis, with Bragg's assistance, tried to coordinate an advance by Johnston's and Longstreet's forces into eastern and central Tennessee with the aim of cutting Union communications. Longstreet proposed two routes for his army, one above and one below Knoxville, and a junction of their forces near Madisonville, Tennessee, midway between Chattanooga and Knoxville. This scheme died quickly because of the possibility that a Union movement behind Johnston would cut off both Confederate armies, forcing them to either disperse or surrender.[33] Longstreet kept trying.

A week earlier, at the end of February, Longstreet had asked Davis for permission to implement his Abingdon Plan. He received a curt reply from Cooper, the adjutant general, telling him to use his own discretion. In a March 7 note to Beauregard, Longstreet returned to his idea of mounting his command and putting his force astride the Union railroads between Louisville and Nashville.[34]

Longstreet's idea was impractical from the start. The Confederate commissary could not provide the necessary corn, and Davis vetoed it both because they lacked the necessary mounts and because it separated the Confederate forces by too great a distance.[35] None of this prevented Longstreet from clinging to his ridiculous scheme.

Lee suggested that the forces of Johnston and Longstreet push into Tennessee, uniting at Sparta, which was roughly equidistant from Nashville, Knoxville, and Chattanooga. They could then decide the best track to pursue. Their presence at Sparta would force the evacuation of Knoxville and Chattanooga, thereby allowing the Confederates to mass against one of these two Union forces and defeat the enemy in detail. The plan resembled Bragg's 1862 enterprise. "A victory gained there would open the country to you to the Ohio," Lee told Longstreet. "Study the subject, communicate with Johnston, and endeavor to accomplish it, or something better."[36]

Davis remained eager for a Confederate offensive aimed at middle Tennessee and even Kentucky. This would be the South's "great effort," he insisted, calling for action "as early as possible." He adopted a slightly modified version of Lee's aforementioned plan. Davis wanted to concentrate Longstreet's and

Johnston's forces near Maryville, Tennessee, south of Knoxville, and advance into the state, driving on Sparta, "where, with your united forces, you will be between the enemy's divided forces at Chattanooga, Knoxville, and Nashville, and be in condition to strike either one of them, or move forward into Kentucky, as events may determine." Supporting this would be a demonstration, or a genuine movement from northern Mississippi into central or western Tennessee.[37]

In mid-March, Johnston received a note from Bragg telling him to be ready. He responded that this implied some plan of campaign, of which he had not been informed. Bragg wrote Johnston that the government had previously ordered him to prepare to move and now they were going to tell him what to do, but only in a general sense. Bragg then presented the government's evolving plan, which centered upon attacking Union communications, specifically the railroad between Nashville and Chattanooga. They would concentrate the forces of Johnston and Longstreet at Kingston, on the banks of the Tennessee River, severing Knoxville's rail supply link with Chattanooga. This would isolate Union forces in both Chattanooga and Knoxville. A cavalry raid into western Tennessee would support the main moves. Should the enemy fail to come out and fight, Johnston was to advance to Sparta, where his army could live off the land. All of this would force the Union to withdraw to the Cumberland River. Bragg also pointed out the damage to the Union position if Johnston could seize Nashville.[38]

Bragg did at least ask for Johnston's view of the idea. Johnston gave it, though he thought no more of this proposal than he had of Longstreet's scheme of early March to unite their respective forces at Madisonville and move west. Johnston found Kingston an impossible objective, one the enemy could more easily reach, which would allow them to defeat the Confederates before they joined hands. His army lacked the necessary transportation, and even if he did have it, he didn't think it a good idea to take along what would be required for such a move. Johnston also believed part of the country through which they wanted him to march too picked over to supply his troops. Moreover, if he did fight a battle in such reaches, a defeat would mean the utter destruction of his army.[39]

On the morning of March 14, before Johnston sent his reply, Lee and Longstreet met with Davis, Seddon, and Bragg. Beforehand, Lee had encouraged Longstreet to present his Abingdon Plan, which now involved uniting his forces with Beauregard's and advancing into Kentucky. Longstreet insisted that Davis particularly disliked the fact that Longstreet's proposal included a field command for Beauregard. Nothing came of the morning meeting, but in afternoon talks Bragg recommended to Lee and Longstreet the aforementioned two-pronged Johnston-Longstreet offensive aimed at Nashville, the very one Johnston subsequently rebuffed. Essentially, the leaders decided nothing except that they "should take the initiative."[40]

A few days later, Longstreet sent Davis a long letter that included some argument in favor of his old idea of mounting his troops, but then offered two counterproposals. The first was concentrating with Johnston's army all the troops from Mississippi, Beauregard's command, and Longstreet's—an overwhelming force, in other words—and driving straight into central Tennessee. Still, he insisted that concentrating the army near Abingdon, Virginia, and then sending them through Pound Gap and into Kentucky remained the "strongest and most effective move." Longstreet felt that at a minimum this would regain part of Tennessee, but he was confident it would allow an advance into Kentucky. Tied to this would be action by Confederate cavalry against Union rear areas. This would, he wrote, "put an end to the war."[41]

Others chimed in to influence the Confederacy's operations in the West. Lieutenant General John Bell Hood, a brave but not necessarily brilliant veteran of Lee's army and now a corps commander under Johnston, wrote Seddon, urging the concentration of the forces of Polk, Loring, Johnston, and Longstreet, "which, I think, should be sufficient to defeat and destroy all the Federals on this side of the Ohio River." Hood also sent Bragg his plan, which was to "concentrate and fall upon the enemy before he is ready. That way, we shall beat him badly and regain our lost territory."[42]

A large number of people tried to decide the fate of Johnston's army, usually without bothering to get his opinion and generally unencumbered by rational thought. All of them were violating a primary rule of war: the autonomy of the commander in the field.

Johnston had his own idea about a drive into Tennessee. He suggested combining Longstreet's forces with his own, except for the cavalry, which would strike to the east and north of Knoxville. Meanwhile, an advance element of this new larger army would enter eastern Tennessee near Chattanooga to cut its communications with Knoxville. This would "virtually isolate" Knoxville and force the enemy to fight to relieve it. The advance force and the main army would stay close enough to coordinate their activities and maintain their supply line to Dalton. If things went badly, the Confederates could fall back on their supply lines; if things went well, they could follow the Union forces into central Tennessee. Johnston also suggested a move into middle Tennessee by way of northern Alabama.[43]

Johnston's plan was more sensible than most of the others swirling around. But all of them amounted to nothing more than tactical and operational wool-gathering, for Johnston contended he could do nothing before the Union was ready to move and attacked him, which he considered to his advantage.[44] He had returned to his original idea and foreshadowed how he would fight the coming campaign.

Longstreet, meanwhile, kept trying to get approval for his plan to throw his and Beauregard's forces into Kentucky through Pound Gap and even sought Lee's help. His superior was apparently not enthused with Longstreet's idea. Longstreet wrote Lee, "You complain of my excess of confidence, but I think that it is based upon good judgment and a proper appreciation of our difficulties."[45]

A number of blows toppled Longstreet's castle in the air. Beauregard balked, citing his lack of animals and saddles and the fact that Longstreet's scheme required the abandonment of their lines of communications, which violated one of the "maxims of war" (and Beauregard always paid attention to these, at least in his correspondence; here, though, he was correct). More-over, in December Beauregard had presented his own plan, which involved concentrating Confederate troops with Longstreet, or at Dalton or Rome, Georgia, and then throwing them into middle Tennessee.[46]

The next shock came in the supply arena. Longstreet simply could not easily keep his men and animals fed, and he actually worried about starva-tion.[47] If he could barely supply his own men and animals, it is doubtful that he could have procured what a larger force needed.

Davis also buried any hope of Longstreet seeing one of his plans enacted. He vetoed the idea of mounting his entire command as impractical, first because of the lack of horses and mules, and second, because of the impossibility of provid-ing them with forage. He then introduced Longstreet's other designs to Confed-erate logistic and strategic reality: to move the troops required from Beauregard, even if they were available—and they were not—would consume the railroad capacity that fed Lee's army. Moreover, gathering the other forces he wanted from Mobile and farther west meant leaving valuable and productive areas open to Union attack. Davis seemingly preferred the plan that he had previously dis-patched via Bragg for uniting Johnston's and Longstreet's forces.[48]

In early April, Bragg, concerned that they were running out of time in the west, suggested to Davis that Johnston's Army of Tennessee be reinforced by troops from Polk's department and Johnston forced to mount an attack the general had earlier proposed on Ringgold, Georgia, and Cleveland, Tennessee, towns south and east of Chattanooga respectively. Bragg wanted to support this by having Buckner threaten Knoxville and Forrest move into or menace middle Tennessee while Brigadier General Phillip D. Roddey pinned the Union forces in northern Alabama.[49]

In an effort to get Johnston to act, Davis sent Brigadier General W. N. Pendleton to Dalton to make sure Johnston understood the president's desires. Davis wanted immediate action:

First. To take the enemy at disadvantage while weakened, it is believed, by sending troops to Virginia, and having others absent still on furlough.

Second. To break up his plans by anticipating and frustrating his combinations.

Third. So to press him here as to prevent his heavier massing in Virginia.

Fourth. To beat him, it is hoped, and greatly gain strength in supplies, men, and productive territory.

Fifth. To prevent the waste of the army incident to inactivity.

Sixth. To inspirit it and the country, and to depress the enemy, involving the greatest results.

Seventh. To obviate the necessity of falling back likely to occur if the enemy be allowed to consummate his own plans.[50]

Johnston insisted that he, too, wanted action, and he promised an aggressive movement as soon as he was able, but the offensive that Davis now suggested differed from previous ones, and Johnston thought it impossible to meet the enemy "far beyond Chattanooga." He had good reasons as well. The opposing forces had not been weakened and dramatically outnumbered his. Plus, he lacked the necessary supply train and the troops to protect it in an advance, as well as any means of securing provender in the face of the enemy. Moreover, not only was the Union preparing to attack him, but if Johnston did advance it meant the destruction of his army, which would leave Georgia open to the enemy.[51]

Johnston made a counterproposal. He would stand on the defensive until his army was strengthened, waiting for a chance to strike at the Union forces (which was what he had been saying since taking up his new command in December 1863). When ready, he would attack the enemy at Ringgold, Georgia. If successful, he would move on Cleveland, cut the railroad, reach the Tennessee River, and isolate eastern Tennessee. Supporting this would be cavalry raids into middle Tennessee, forcing an evacuation of the Tennessee Valley and allowing a further advance into Tennessee. If this failed to pan out, Johnston would fight the enemy near Rome and, if he defeated them, advance to the Ohio. Pendleton agreed with Johnston's assessment of the growing Union strength and recommended the concentration of troops in north Georgia. Under the circumstances, he believed that Johnston's plan was the most promising.[52]

None of these operational plans had any chance of success as presented, not only because of the sheer impossibility of their execution in the face of Union strength and action but also because Johnston was never going to try any of them. Johnston was much like McClellan in this respect. Plus, he would need more of everything, especially men, before he could accomplish anything, particularly against a Union host the size of which some Confederates estimated at around 80,000. In early April, Johnston fielded only about 40,000 men.[53]

On April 2, 1864, Bragg succinctly summed up the result of the nearly interminable wrangling among the Confederate high command, of which he was a part: "The forward movement against the enemy, so much desired, and which promised such large results, has been so long delayed that he has been enabled to make combinations which render it now inexpedient, if not impracticable, unless we can beat him on this side the Tennessee River."[54]

The Union Dithers; Grant Decides

IN DECEMBER 1863, Lincoln had sent his annual address to Congress. Things certainly looked better for the Union cause than they had the year before. He noted success in keeping foreign powers out of the war, the reinforcing of the blockade, and the actions of the U.S. Navy, which had taken more than 1,000 blockade runners thus far. He harked back to 1862, when "the rebellion had been pressed back into reduced limits, yet the tone of public feeling and opinion, at home and abroad, was not satisfactory." Eleven months had changed much, he told Congress. The Union had cut the Confederacy in half by seizing the Mississippi and taken much territory from its grip. He noted other achievements: most of Tennessee and Arkansas were cleared of Rebels, and emancipation had turned rebel slaves into Union soldiers. Lincoln even spoke of reconstruction, the return of rebellious states to the Union. He issued a proclamation to this effect the same day, one that included an amnesty for anyone taking an oath of allegiance.[55] The proclamation was Lincoln at his best—political strategy directly supporting the objective of maintaining the Union.

Lincoln's political objectives, as always, would exercise an influence on military events, some that the generals did not necessarily want. Reconstruction would be one of these. For example, in February 1864 Brigadier General James H. Wilson, one of Grant's former subordinates, complained to Grant from Washington of the diversion of troops to help reestablish loyal state governments. He believed the priority should be destroying the Confederate forces first.[56] In terms of strategy, Wilson was correct. But Lincoln determined the administration's priorities.

Grant would not have disagreed with Wilson, but he was also a general who uncomplainingly obeyed the dictates of his political masters. After driving Bragg's army from around Chattanooga, he received new orders from Washington, which included relieving Burnside in Knoxville. Grant sent Sherman to do this but believed it prevented his own pursuit of Bragg's broken army deeper into Georgia.[57]

Even as Sherman's troops marched into eastern Tennessee, Grant planned his next move. Believing a winter campaign nearly impossible from Chattanooga, he revived the idea of attacking Mobile. He did not want his troops idle, nor to give the South time to catch its breath. He proposed landing 35,000 men at Pascagoula, Mississippi, and using this as a base to either capture or isolate Mobile and then raid into Georgia and Alabama. He also had high hopes for the operation, telling Halleck, "It seems to me this move would secure the entire States of Alabama and Mississippi and a part of Georgia, or force Lee to abandon Virginia and North Carolina. Without his force the enemy have not got army enough to resist the army I can take."[58]

The president and secretary of war loved the idea of Grant attacking Mobile, but lust for eastern Tennessee exerted its pull, and they worried about Longstreet's army nesting in the Tennessee hills. "If Longstreet were expelled from that country you could start for Mobile at once," said Henry Dana, by whose hand Grant had sent word of his proposal. But how to remove him? Grant had sent his thoughts on this as well: push the Army of the Potomac, as this would see Longstreet recalled. Grant's superiors agreed, Dana said, "but from that army nothing is to be hoped under its present commander," meaning, of course, Meade. Grant had also included a solution for this: replace Meade with W. F. "Baldy" Smith or Sherman. His superiors liked this as well and said they had already decided that Meade had to go and that Smith would replace him. But this never happened. Both Halleck and Stanton determined that the disputatious Smith was unsuitable for such a position.[59]

In his response to Dana's visit, Halleck summed up all that Grant was doing and planning to do in December 1863. "As I understand from your dispatch of the 7th, and from conversations with Mr. Dana," Halleck wrote, "you propose, first, to expel the enemy from eastern Tennessee, and to provide against his return into the valley; second, to either force the rebels farther back into Georgia, or to provide against their return by that line into Tennessee; third, to clean out western Tennessee, and, fourth, to move a force down the Mississippi and operate against Mobile." The administration decided the first three should be done; then they would talk about the fourth.[60]

Grant went to work. Even before Halleck dispatched the above, Grant had already issued the orders to build up the necessary supplies for a campaign in eastern Tennessee, telling Halleck that if Longstreet wasn't driven from Abingdon and the railroad destroyed, "I do not think it unlikely that the last great battle of the war will be fought in East Tennessee." In January, he sent Sherman west to Memphis, giving him three objectives: to clear out the Rebel forces in various areas, destroy Confederate railroads and industrial sites, and secure peaceful transit of the Mississippi. Sherman soon led the raid against Meridian that so worried Polk, Davis, and Johnston. Grant also clarified his thinking to Halleck, reassuring him that he did not intend to move against Mobile until eastern Tennessee was secured and "West Tennessee and the State of Mississippi so visited that large armies cannot traverse there this winter."[61]

Before he went to Mississippi, Sherman discussed with Grant an idea for how the Union should conduct its campaign in the West. He wrote his friend Halleck that "holding possession of any part of the interior" of Mississippi and Louisiana was a mistake, because it required a large army "wasted in detachments."[62] In the West, instead of trying to hold everything, the Union would garrison only key points. They then began marching armies toward important Confederate possessions, tearing up the railroads and eating up the countryside on the way, destroying everything of military value once they reached their objective, and then marching out by another route. The Union strategy of exhaustion was now in full force.

Before Sherman went off to burn Meridian, Mississippi, Halleck and Grant firmed up Grant's future plans. Part of this included extending Grant's command area to Arkansas, thus giving him greater reach and control. Halleck had at first hoped for cooperation between the Arkansas troops, Sherman, and Banks in order to clear the Rebels completely from Arkansas and hold the Red River. But Banks had been sent to Texas, where in November he captured Brownsville and then followed up by seizing some other minor sites, and Halleck now wondered if it would not be better to push more troops westward, destroying Confederate resistance west of the Mississippi. This done, most of the troops could then be withdrawn. To do this, Sherman would have to be sent to bolster the Union forces in Texas and Arkansas. Halleck asked Grant to consider this, adding that of course these plans were "subordinate and subsequent to" what Grant had proposed for eastern and western Tennessee.[63]

At about the same time, Grant received permission from the War Department to do whatever he wished, including launching his Mobile expedition, as long as he made sure eastern Tennessee was safe. Grant, as always, had views of his own. After visiting the much coveted region and observing firsthand the supply and logistical nightmare it presented (the roads were horrendous), something made worse by temperatures around zero, he pronounced any immediate move in force against Longstreet impossible. He had already dispatched Sherman, of course, and told Halleck that he could not spare the large number of troops necessary for the actions proposed west of the Mississippi. After taking Meridian, Sherman could push on to Mobile if it seemed feasible. Meanwhile, Grant would threaten the Confederate army in his front; furloughs granted to reenlisting veterans had weakened his army too much to permit anything else. Grant also proposed that his army advance southward to Mobile, via Montgomery and Atlanta, drawing their supply from the Tennessee River.[64]

Halleck, on the other hand, believed that they should mass all the troops that could be spared from Virginia and the Atlantic coastal enclaves under Banks and Grant. Over the winter, they could get a firm hold on Arkansas, Louisiana, Mississippi, and Tennessee, and ensure that the Confederate forces in Texas caused no more problems. (There was scant chance of the latter. In January 1863 all the Confederate forces for Texas, New Mexico, and Arizona amounted to only 9,322 men.) Then in spring, either concentrated or acting in support of one another, they could "inflict some terrible blows upon the rebels." Halleck also worried that the situation in eastern Tennessee would "prevent the accomplishment of these objects, or at least a part of them, this winter, and that we must soon prepare for a spring campaign."[65]

The administration, though, remained deeply concerned about the fate of Chattanooga and eastern Tennessee. Holding Chattanooga and its mountain pass environs guarded the flanks of Tennessee and Kentucky and prevented any Confederate invasion of these states. Halleck agreed with Grant about wanting to have the freedom to dictate the arena of the next campaign, but Halleck reminded him of the administration's long-standing desire to control eastern Tennessee.[66] Holding eastern Tennessee would garner almost no military benefits, but Lincoln deemed it a political necessity.

Late January 1864 saw Grant's first formal statement on operations in the Eastern Theater. He had habitually refrained from offering any such comments because it was not his command area and no one had ever asked him. But now Halleck was asking. Grant recommended shifting the focus away from Virginia by massing 60,000 troops farther south. "I would suggest Raleigh, N.C.," he wrote, "as the objective point and Suffolk as the starting point. Raleigh once secured, I would make New Berne [*sic*] the base of supplies until Wilmington is secured." He saw many benefits here. First, he thought, it would force an evacuation of Virginia and, "indirectly, of Eastern Tennessee." This would open to Union armies untouched regions where they could "partially live upon the country" while also taking potential stores from the Confederates. Second, Grant was convinced that scores of North Carolina troops would then desert and head home. Third, it would give the North "possession of many negroes who are now indirectly aiding the rebellion." Fourth, it would distract the enemy from their plans and force them to fight someplace they never expected. Fifth, it would "effectually blockade Wilmington, the port now of more value to the enemy than all the balance of their seacoast." Lastly, it would immediately shift operations to a warmer climate, thereby avoiding "months of inactivity."[67]

Sir Julian Corbett, the naval theorist, would have approved of such an ambitious application of power against an enemy's weak sea flank. Halleck was not so easily impressed. Such a move had been often contemplated, he told Grant, and just as often rejected. The problem was getting enough men. Weakening Meade's army of 70,000 to obtain 30,000 of the necessary troops would leave Maryland open to another invasion, and this still left the problem of assembling the other 30,000. Plus, the Washington garrison of 18,000 was only about half of what had been previously determined safe. Moreover, Halleck believed, this operation wouldn't force Lee to abandon Virginia. Instead, Union public opinion would demand Grant's withdrawal to defend the north.[68]

Halleck also revealed his dissatisfaction with the Union's overall conduct of the war (he obviously had forgotten who had been general in chief since July 1862). Halleck thought the various coastal operations wasted moves and particularly opposed the various attempts to take Charleston. The Union only had so many soldiers, and Halleck had been trying to get those that ended up fighting at Charleston used against Texas or Mobile. "And now these troops are sent upon another expedition," he complained to Grant, meaning used to push along the reconstruction of Florida, "which, in my opinion, can produce no military result." He admitted that the seizure of ports helped the navy enforce the blockade, but he thought it would be better to use the troops on a more important line. "We have given too much attention to cutting the toe nails of our enemy instead of grasping his throat."[69]

Most important, Halleck repeated Lincoln's thesis, which had become his own: "I have never considered Richmond as the necessary objective point of the Army of the Potomac; that point is Lee's army." Richmond, Halleck insisted, would not fall until "Lee's army was defeated or driven away."[70]

Halleck offered a cogent assessment of other strategic and operational matters. Once the "affairs of East Tennessee are settled," he argued, the next Union campaign should be directed "against the armies of Lee and Johnston." He recalled that everyone had failed to take Richmond: McClellan via the Peninsula,

Burnside, Hooker, and Meade "by the shorter and more direct route." McClellan had had the best shot at it, having the largest army, but "these facts in themselves prove nothing in favor of either route, and to decide the question we must recur to fundamental principles in regard to interior and exterior lines, objective points covering armies, divided forces, &c. These fundamental principles require, in my opinion, that all our available forces in the east should be concentrated against Lee's army." But Halleck believed they would not take Richmond and could not "operate advantageously on any point from the Atlantic coast," until they could "destroy or disperse" Lee's army, and the closer to Washington that was done "the better for us." "If we cannot defeat him here with our combined force, we cannot hope to do so elsewhere with a divided army."[71]

Meanwhile, Grant's plans changed, something Halleck had predicted in his note. Major General John G. Foster pointed out to Grant that if they forced Longstreet out of eastern Tennessee, his army would move someplace where it might do the Confederates some good. The problem of supplying their own army in the area also worried Foster. Grant decided to leave Longstreet alone. Instead, he struck into north Georgia, sending troops of Thomas's corps against Dalton. Later, particularly when Longstreet began to withdraw, he pushed troops under Major General John M. Schofield against him, convinced that exerting pressure against the Confederate forces on his front via Thomas and Schofield would give Sherman's Mississippi raid a better chance of success. Grant believed that the expeditions of Sherman and Thomas, if as successful as he expected, would lay the groundwork for his spring campaign.[72]

Like the Confederate planning debates taking place at the same time, much of the Union discussion was for naught. On February 29, 1864, Lincoln nominated Grant for the rank of lieutenant general, at the time the highest grade (the others being brigadier and major general, in that order). Lincoln did not do this lightly. He always kept an eye on his political back, and with the presidential election on the horizon he had no desire to bestow such power and fame upon one who might then be a rival. So before promoting Grant he did some checking about the general's political ambitions. To his great pleasure he discovered Grant had none. Both parties had already tried and failed to drag Grant into the political arena. In response to one of these fizzled efforts Grant wrote: "Nothing likely to happen would pain me so much as to see my name used in connection with a political office."[73]

Grant shortly took over from Halleck the mantle of general in chief. To him fell the task of constructing a strategy for destroying the rebellion. On February 1, 1864, Lincoln had already done something that would help Grant along this path: he had ordered the conscription of another 500,000 men.[74]

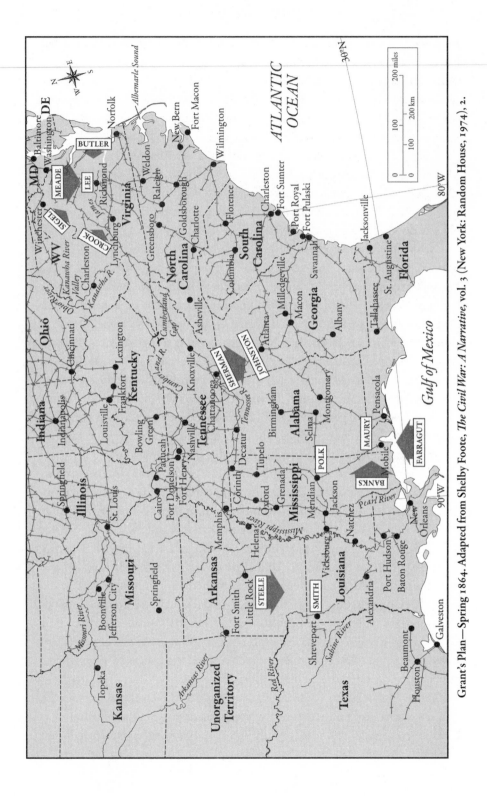

Grant's Plan—Spring 1864. Adapted from Shelby Foote, *The Civil War: A Narrative*, vol. 3 (New York: Random House, 1974), 2.

Decision and Desperation, 1864

*Tell the young women to send me all their beaux.
I want them at once.*

—ROBERT E. LEE, September 18, 1864

*I would give a sentiment, but just now I am not in a
sentimental mood.*

—ABRAHAM LINCOLN, May 7, 1864

WHEN GRANT FIRST MET LINCOLN alone, the president told him that he had never wanted to interfere in military matters, but the lack of activity on the part of Union commanders had combined with public pressure to make intervention necessary. Lincoln also told him he didn't want to know the general's intentions, then proceeded to pull out a well-marked map and suggest a campaign plan for Virginia. "He pointed out on the map two streams which empty into the Potomac," Grant recalled, "and suggested that the army might be moved on boats and landed between the mouths of these two streams. We would then have the Potomac to bring our supplies, and the tributaries would protect our flanks while we moved out.... I listened respectfully," Grant wrote, "but did not suggest that the same streams would protect Lee's flanks while he was shutting us up."[1] Grant had a plan of his own.

LIKE MCCLELLAN AND LINCOLN, Grant came early to an understanding of the necessity and the advantage of Union armies working together against the Confederate forces. He characterized the operations of the eastern and western Union armies as the efforts of a "balky team, no two ever pulling together," with the result that it allowed the enemy to take advantage of his interior lines to move troops, furlough them, or allow them to work "producing for the support of their armies." He was also convinced that there would be no lasting peace "until the military power of the rebellion was entirely broken." On March 15 he wrote Banks that it was critical that "all the armies act as much in concert as possible." "I therefore determined, first, to use the greatest number of troops practicable against the armed force of the enemy," Grant wrote after the war, "preventing him from using the same force at different seasons against first one and then another of our armies, and the possibility of repose for refitting and producing necessary supplies for carrying on resistance; second, to hammer continuously against the armed force of the enemy and his resources, until by mere attrition, if in no other way, there should be nothing left to him but an equal submission with the loyal section of our common country to the constitution and laws of the land. These views have been kept constantly in mind, and orders given and campaigns made to carry them out."[2] Here Grant laid out his strategy for winning the war and delivering the Union political objective: use offensive action to pin the enemy, kill his armies, and destroy his resources, eliminating his ability to prosecute the war.

To accomplish this Grant developed a plan for an offensive composed of multiple and simultaneously moving prongs intended to nullify the Confederate ability to use their interior lines to mass against an individual Union thrust. "It is my design," he told Sherman, "if the enemy keep quiet and allow me to take the initiative in the spring campaign, to work all parts of the army together and somewhat toward a common center." Grant wanted General Nathaniel Banks to quickly finish his ongoing operation against Shreveport, Louisiana, and move against Mobile. He was to strengthen his forces by abandoning Texas, except for a garrison at the mouth of the Rio Grande, and strip his other posts to gather an army of at least 25,000. Admiral Farragut was to assist him with a fleet. If Banks could not do this quickly, he was to abandon the operation.[3]

Grant instructed Major General Benjamin Butler to land his forces on the Virginia coast south of the James River, then aim at Richmond, cooperating with the advance of the Army of the Potomac and, if possible, cutting the Confederate railroads near Hicksford. Grant needed naval cooperation for this move.[4]

Grant planned to be with the Army of Potomac, though Meade technically remained its operational commander. He designated Lee's army as this force's "objective point," telling Meade "that wherever Lee went he would go also."[5] Grant intended for Meade's army to fight Lee between the two capitals, but if Lee fell back to Richmond, Grant would form a juncture with Butler's force, the two of them then drawing their supplies from a base on the James River. As McClellan did before him, Grant ordered pre-campaign preparations in case he had to lay siege to Richmond.[6]

He ordered Major General Franz Sigel to move up the Shenandoah Valley with orders to "occupy the attention of a large force, and thereby hold them from re-enforcing elsewhere, or . . . inflict a blow upon the enemy's resources, which will materially aid us." His men were also to destroy the Virginia and Tennessee Railroad.[7]

He told Sherman to move against Johnston's army and get as deeply into Southern territory as possible, wreaking as much havoc on their resources as he could. Moreover, Sherman was to keep the enemy from shifting troops to Lee while Grant endeavored to perform the same service for Sherman by keeping Confederate forces in the East from reinforcing Johnston's army. Initially, Grant hoped for all these forces to move on April 25, 1864, except for Banks. Subsequently he ordered "a general movement of the armies" no later than May 4.[8] To gather the men for this, Grant ordered the stripping of nonessential areas.[9]

Lincoln liked Grant's idea. It coincided well with his own oft-stated view of how to fight the war: simultaneous pressure at different points. "Those not skinning can hold a leg," Lincoln said. Grant appreciated this turn of phrase so much he borrowed it for one of his own notes. Sherman was also pleased. "That we are now all to act in a common plan, converging on a common center, looks like enlightened war."[10]

Before the campaign began, Grant wrote a letter to Lincoln thanking the president, the administration, and the secretary of war for their continual support. He remarked that since being appointed lieutenant general he had been "astonished" that everything he had asked for had been done "without even an explanation being asked." He closed the note by telling Lincoln: "Should my success be less than I desire, and expect, the least I can say is, the fault is not with you."[11]

Even before the offensive began, however, Grant had enjoyed Lincoln's confidence in a way unlike any other Union general. "The particulars of your plans I neither know nor seek to know," the president wrote. "You are vigorous and self-reliant; and, pleased with this, I wish not to obtrude any constraints or restraints upon you."[12] It is difficult to imagine Lincoln penning such a note to any of Grant's predecessors. Generally, he had insisted upon knowing the plans of his generals; if they had none, sometimes he provided one. For the first time since McClellan's arrival, Lincoln had delegated the burden of directing the war to someone else. Though he gave Grant free rein, he still kept a close eye on military operations, as we will see, and did not shy from interference if he deemed it necessary.

When Grant launched the spring campaign, he planned to finish the war by November. But to do this, he had to overcome determined Confederate resistance in both the Eastern and Western Theaters. The West he left to Sherman's capable hands. In the East, he took the reins, seeking first "to break the military power of the rebellion and capture the enemy's important strongholds." Because of this, he thought it vitally important that Butler take Richmond; only the "capture of Lee's army," Grant believed, would do more to accomplish the Union's goals in the East. But Grant's plan also had operational contingencies. If Butler failed, Grant wrote, "it was my determination, by hard fighting, either to compel Lee to retreat or to so cripple him that he could not detach a large force to go north and still retain enough for the defense of Richmond. It was well understood by both Generals Butler and Meade before starting on the campaign that it was my intention to put both their armies south of the James River in case of failure to destroy Lee without it."[13]

Grant's instructions to Butler had first emphasized the importance of capturing Richmond, Grant thinking this likely unless it was reinforced. Verbally, he also told Butler to tear up the railroads and seize Petersburg. Moreover, since the Army of the Potomac was moving simultaneously, this would make it dangerous for Lee to send troops against Butler, Grant believing the Confederates had no other units they could bring to Richmond "in time to meet a rapid movement from the north of James River."[14]

Clearly seen in Grant's plan are the elements that had brought success to Union arms in the first three years of the conflict: simultaneous pressure and movement at a number of different points and the pinning and attacking of Confederate armies. Ultimately, Grant's great offensive would bring the Union victory, but not as soon as Grant had hoped. Two factors contributed to the protraction of the struggle: bungling by three of Grant's subordinate commanders and the Confederacy's adoption of a defensive strategy that aimed at stopping Union penetration of the Confederate heartland.

The Atlanta Campaign

TO RUN THE DRIVE INTO GEORGIA, Grant had an excellent subordinate in Sherman. Together they had learned to fight the war, and together they proved instrumental in winning it for the Union. Sherman replaced Grant as the commander of the Military Division of the Mississippi (a conglomeration of four Union departments), based at Nashville, Tennessee, on March 18, 1864.[15]

Sherman's operational objective was the army of Joe Johnston, "go where it might," and he promised Grant that he would not let "side issues" divert him from hitting Johnston and doing as much damage as he could to Rebel resources. Sherman also thought ahead. Once Johnston withdrew behind the Chattahoochee River, he planned to launch a cavalry raid against the

Montgomery-Georgia Railroad, breaking it. Moreover, he intended to not only keep Johnston from sending troops against Grant but also keep him from dispatching elements to counter Banks. Sherman hoped Banks would take Mobile, thereby opening up the Alabama River, which would subsequently ease Sherman's supply problems. But he was not too worried if this did not happen, and foreshadowed his later campaign by writing, "Georgia has a million inhabitants. If they can live, we should not starve. If the enemy interrupt our communications, I will be absolved from all obligations to subsist on our own resources, and will feel perfectly justified in taking whatever and wherever we can find."[16]

The Union generals who failed to execute their prongs of Grant's strategy had let down their cause before; they at least proved consistent. Banks was out of the game before it began and never launched toward Mobile. Instead, he presided over the disastrous Red River campaign. It was planned as a thirty-day operation to knock the Trans-Mississippi out of the war. Doing so would support Lincoln's political strategy of organizing new governments by helping the establishment of a reconstructed Louisiana. Banks, though, bungled the operation, which should have been completed in time for him to participate in Grant's spring offensive, and was defeated by a dramatically inferior Confederate force. The last of Banks's men returned from the expedition in late May, too late to participate in the big push. Banks was fired.[17]

Like Sherman, Lee also thought in terms of knocking the enemy about. By late March he had concluded that when the Union acted it was most likely to be against Longstreet's forces in Kentucky or Johnston in Georgia, but he thought the blow would probably be against Johnston. As usual with Lee, he recommended an aggressive response: attacking Sherman's forces. He believed that by doing this, Johnston's army "might entirely frustrate the enemy's plans by defeating him."[18]

Davis also believed offensive action the solution and grew increasingly irritated by Johnston's lack of aggression. By April 13, he was convinced that the continual postponement of any advance had decreased the utility of such a move. He was also frustrated that Johnston had failed to move quickly enough to forestall reported Union preparations for offensive operations in Virginia and North Carolina that targeted Richmond. This had been the "primary object" of "threatening movements" by Johnston's army. He was well informed about Johnston's transportation problems, from the general, from his staff, and from his own investigators. But Davis also operated under the false impression that the Union was stripping forces from Sherman to reinforce the East. Johnston disabused him of this notion. Nevertheless, Davis wanted offensive action immediately and believed Johnston had missed his best chance by not acting during the winter.[19]

Johnston said he didn't oppose an offensive; he simply insisted upon launching it on his terms, not ones imposed by Richmond. He needed more troops and thought that Longstreet's forces in Tennessee, as well as Polk's in Mississippi, should be brought to his army. Longstreet went back to Virginia, but Polk's troops were ordered to Johnston in May.[20]

When Sherman assumed his new command, Johnston's forces were entrenched at Dalton. Johnston, Sherman said, "seemed to be acting purely on the defensive, so that we had time and leisure to take all our measures deliberately and fully." This seemed to prove the point raised by Davis and Lee about leaving Sherman undisturbed. This was critical because it gave Sherman time to prepare. Moreover, "the great question of the campaign," Sherman later wrote, "was one of supplies." His army's logistics lines stretched from Chattanooga through Nashville to Louisville, each leg of which the Union had to guard against Confederate raiders. This line lengthened with the advance into Georgia.[21]

The basic issue with the Atlanta campaign was this: should the South stand on the defensive, as Johnston insisted, or should it attack, as Davis and Lee believed? Both approaches had their advantages as well as their problems and raised other questions: If defense was the answer, what kind of defense? If offense, what kind of offense?

By standing completely on the defensive, tactically, operationally, and strategically, Johnston surrendered the initiative to the enemy and gave Sherman time to prepare at his leisure. But a full-scale attack against Sherman's army, which outnumbered Johnston's by two to one, was not the answer either, as Hood would show later. It is likely that Johnston's best course of offensive action was raids on Sherman's supply lines. This was what Johnston tried to do, producing constant worry for Sherman.[22]

When the campaign began, Johnston ordered Forrest to strike for central Tennessee and tear up the railroads feeding Sherman's army. But Sherman had ordered 8,000 men from Memphis to hunt him down. Forrest defeated this Federal force, which was twice his size, at Brice's Crossroads on June 10 by rolling up both the enemy's flanks. The Federals suffered more than 2,200 casualties, and their commander, Brigadier General S. D. Sturgis, never received another command. But they did keep Forrest out of Tennessee. This was too late to help Johnston, though, and an angry Sherman dispatched a larger force of 14,000, insisting they would "follow Forrest to the death, if it cost 10,000 lives and breaks the Treasury." They failed to kill Forrest, but they defeated him at Tupelo, Mississippi, wounding the famous cavalry leader and removing him temporarily from the field. The Confederates, though, were losing the cavalry advantage they had thus far enjoyed. All of this, and Union raids, prevented the destruction of Sherman's supply lines, as did Sherman's constructing blockhouses at each bridge and posting infantry at the stations. Moreover, Sherman's railroad crews carried ample replacement material and learned to repair breaches with a speed and efficiency that stunned the Confederates.[23]

Any substantial success could have delayed the start of Sherman's campaign, or at least limited its strength and ability to sustain an offensive. The South needed to buy time to allow war weariness in the North to increase. After three years of war, the North seemed no closer to winning the war in the summer of 1864 than it had after First Bull Run. Plus in the two months after the beginning of Grant's grand offensive, the Union would suffer 90,000 casualties—without producing any readily apparent gains.[24] Moreover, inflicting on Sherman's army cumulative delays of one month might have placed the critical fall of Atlanta after the 1864 Union election. With Sherman stalled at Atlanta and Grant stuck before Richmond and Petersburg, Lincoln might have gone down to defeat and McClellan become president. There is little doubt that McClellan would have failed to prosecute the war with sufficient vigor to secure victory.

In the first twelve days of Sherman's campaign his forces tramped and fought their way half the distance to Atlanta. In the face of the Union advance Johnston continued falling back. He kept close to the enemy, as Davis had instructed, the South mirroring the Union strategy of holding tight to the foe to prevent him from reinforcing the other theater—a good example of a symmetrical response. In the six days before May 20, Johnston withdrew 32 miles. The Confederates repulsed the Union attacks, and Johnston planned one of his own for May 15. This was never launched because the Union threatened Johnston's communications. Another Confederate counterattack was stopped in mid-move by a false report that the Union had turned the South's right flank. Johnston explained to Davis that he had been searching for an opportunity to attack, but Sherman dug in at the end of each flank movement, making any assault too risky.[25] Davis must have seen the old Joe Johnston of the Peninsula Campaign rising from Georgia's piney woods.

By the end of May, Sherman's army had forced the Confederates out of "Dalton, Resaca, Cassville, Allatoona, and Dallas," and advanced 100 miles south of Chattanooga. The fighting was bitter, the terrain was rough, and both sides made constant use of entrenchments, increasing the casualties in any attack. On one occasion Sherman told Halleck, "The whole country is one vast fort." Generally, Sherman insisted, the attacker fared the worst.[26]

In early June, Bragg surveyed the situation facing the Confederacy. He wrote Davis, "As the entire available force of the Confederacy is now concentrated with our two main armies, I see no solution of this difficulty but in victory over one of the enemy's armies before the combination can be fully perfected." He sent Johnston a copy of the note, remarking, "From this you will see the work on hand, and be able to judge better than I can what should be our policy [strategy]."[27]

Davis and Bragg did all they could to get men to Johnston, and Davis remained convinced that Johnston had a chance of success if he attacked before the Union finished reinforcing. By the end of June, though, there were simply no more men to send him. On June 10, Johnston had 61,772 men present for duty, but his rosters carried 137,931 men. Georgia militia of 7,000–10,000 also supported him, and 1,500 cavalry were en route to his army.[28]

In June, despite the near omnipresence of rain, Sherman "pressed operations with the utmost earnestness." His goal was to stay in constant contact with the Confederate forces, giving them no chance for a respite, and moving around (or turning) one of his flanks, seeking to cut both the Confederates' lines of communications and any path of retreat. Unlike many generals, Civil War or otherwise, Sherman did not worship battle and carried no visions of Austerlitz in his often melancholy head. "Its glory is all moonshine," he wrote; "even success the most brilliant is over dead and mangled bodies, with the anguish and lamentation of distant families." But on June 27, Sherman decided he could stretch his lines no more and launched an attack at Kennesaw Mountain. He and his other commanding generals had concluded that "there was no alternative but to attack 'fortified lines,' a thing carefully avoided up to that time." The Confederates repulsed the assault. The fighting went on; indeed, Sherman termed the period from June 10 until July 3 "a continuous battle."[29]

When Johnston fell back from Kennesaw Mountain on his way to the Chattahoochee River, Davis grew deeply concerned. He worried that if Johnston crossed the Chattahoochee, this would enable the Union to cut Johnston's communications with Alabama and then take advantage of northern Alabama's weak defenses to destroy the area's mines and industry. Davis feared that if Atlanta fell, the North would again sunder the Confederacy, as it had when Vicksburg surrendered.[30]

Johnston insisted that his retreat was slow and that he kept Bragg abreast of every change of position. Meanwhile, Joseph E. Brown, Georgia's petu-lant, half-mad governor, grew increasingly and understandably anxious about Sherman's advance. He pushed Davis to send more troops and to have cav-alry attack Sherman's supply lines. Johnston was thinking on similar lines and asked Davis if 4,000 of the supposedly 16,000 Confederate cavalry in Alabama and Mississippi could attack the railroad supplying Sherman from Dalton and force his retreat. Governor T. H. Watts of Alabama echoed the plea.[31]

Davis's reply was damning of Johnston, Brown, and anyone else accusing him of inaction. He reminded Johnston that he knew good and well there were no such 16,000 cavalry and that much of what had been there had already been sent to reinforce *him*. Use them for his proposed raid, Davis said. "If it be practicable for distant cavalry," he growled, "it must be more so for that which is near."[32]

Johnston's reply was not nearly as cutting and seems almost humble by comparison. He said his information on numbers had come from General Polk and that Johnston had not made a detachment to attack Sherman's lines of supply because of the great disparity in forces between the opposing armies. Employing the 4,000 cavalry against Sherman's communications, he insisted, was a way not only of forcing Sherman to retreat but also of saving the Department of Mississippi.[33]

Governor Brown sought another means of strengthening Johnston's army and saving his state: he decreed what equated to a *levée en masse*. Brown (with a few exceptions) summoned to the colors all men in the Georgia reserve mili-tia between the ages of sixteen and seventeen, all those fifty to fifty-five, and all free white men between seventeen and fifty who had not been subject to conscription. "Georgians," Brown cried in his proclamation, "you must re-enforce General Johnston's army and aid in driving back the enemy, or he will drive you back to the Atlantic, burn your cities and public buildings, destroy your property, and devastate the fair fields of your noble State."[34] He must have been reading Sherman's notes.

Brown got another prominent Georgian to intervene with the Confeder-ate government on Georgia's behalf—Confederate senator Benjamin H. Hill. Hill offered to visit Davis to try to get more resources for Georgia's defense, but insisted upon seeing Johnston first to get an understanding of the situa-tion. During their interview, Johnston repeated his belief that the only way Sherman could be expelled from Georgia was by destroying the railroad in his rear, thereby cutting off his supplies. Hill saw the situation as desperate,

one of life or death for the Confederacy, and told Johnston that by continuously falling back he would eventually lose all his supply lines; at some point
Sherman would "finally pen you up in Atlanta" and cut the railroads to the
west and south of the city, leaving all the area from which Lee's and Johnston's
armies drew their supplies at the mercy of the Union. The result, Hill told
him, would be that "Richmond and the whole country will be captured."
Johnston responded that there would be a horrible fight before this occurred.
Hill wrote: "This was the only point at which my mind received the impression that General Johnston would fight anyhow, or except under the condition previously mentioned."[35]

Hill also told Johnston of the benefits of throwing Sherman out of Georgia:
Tennessee and Kentucky regained, the failure of Lincoln's reelection bid, and the
war quickly ended on Southern conditions. "All, then, is lost by Sherman's success," Hill said, "and all is gained by Sherman's defeat." Then he asked Johnston
if he had understood correctly the general's insistence that the only way to stop
Sherman was the proposed Confederate cavalry attack on his rear areas; Johnston
replied that he had. Hill wrote: "I then expressed some apprehension that there
would not be time for its execution; that the time was certainly passing rapidly.
General Johnston thought it might be done. General Hood thought the time was
passing, if it had not already passed. We all agreed that no time was to be lost."[36]

Hill met with Davis in Richmond on July 1 and repeated Johnston's request
for forces to cut Sherman's supply lines in order to push the Union into a
battle. Hill also wanted to make sure Davis understood fully what was going
on in Georgia. Davis told Hill how "long ago" he had ordered Morgan (who
had escaped from Federal captivity in November) to move against Sherman's
rear, moving from Abingdon through eastern Tennessee. But Morgan convinced Davis that if he was allowed to go through Kentucky, he could recruit
men and gather horses. Davis agreed but had cause to regret it. Morgan suffered defeat, and the raid came to nothing. During the meeting Davis asked
Hill, "How long did you understand Gen. Johnston to say he could hold
Sherman north of the Chattahoochee river?" "From fifty-four to sixty days,"
Hill replied, basing his answer upon a count he had made, to which Johnston
had assented. But when he gave Davis the numbers, "thereupon the President
read me a dispatch from Gen. Johnston, announcing that he had crossed or
was crossing the Chattahoochee river!"[37]

Later, Davis recalled his insistence that Johnston fight, as well as his fear
that if the Confederates fell back too far it would enable the Union to send
raids through parts of Alabama and Georgia denuded of troops and cut Johnston's communications. "At last he fell back to Kennesaw Mountain & then to

the Chattahootchie [*sic*]. *There I lost all hope of a battle.*" Before this, Johnston had refused to fight Sherman's army unless it was outside its entrenchments; Sherman refused to give him the chance. And Johnston resorted to falling back when flanked.[38]

Davis sent Bragg to investigate. Bragg, in his inimitable fashion, wrote Davis: "I cannot learn that he has any more plan for the future than he has had in the past." Bragg later told Davis that the only answer was to throw the Union back across the Chattahoochee River by attacking his flank while cavalry struck his lines of communication. Lieutenant General John Bell Hood and Major General Joseph Wheeler, respectively corps and cavalry commanders under Johnston, agreed with Bragg. "But the emergency is so pressing & the danger so great," Bragg continued, "I think troops should at once be drawn from the Trans Mississippi to hold the Trans Chatahoochie [*sic*] Department." Hood, behind Johnston's back, also urged offensive action, as well as the movement of at least half of Kirby Smith's troops from the Trans-Mississippi Department to reinforce Johnston's Army of Tennessee. He believed these forces necessary for following up any success gained against Sherman. Indeed, newspapers in both the North and the South even reported the movement of Smith's forces.[39]

Others suggested similar transfers from the Trans-Mississippi in the wake of the Union drawdown in the region. In late June, J. Henry Behan, a Confederate commissary officer writing from Meridian (or at least what was left of it), suggested to Davis that the forces under Magruder, Taylor, and Price could advance through Arkansas and Missouri, then into Kentucky and Tennessee, "destroying depots at Nashville, cutting supply lines at Chattanooga, and uniting with Hood to 'capture the whole of the Yankee army under Sherman.'" Davis sent the note to Bragg, who liked the plan but pronounced it beyond the South's capability. Seddon agreed and suggested using the force "in sustaining resistance or revolt" in Kentucky or the Northwest instead. Davis killed the whole matter by late August, believing from his last correspondence with Smith that the general simply lacked the means to do what Behan suggested.[40]

Davis asked Johnston what he planned to do. Johnston replied that since the enemy had twice his number in troops, the only choice was staying "on the defensive." Operations would be reactive, responding to what the North was doing. The general idea would be "mainly to watch for an opportunity to fight to advantage. We are trying to put Atlanta in condition to be held for a day or two by the Georgia militia, that army movements may be freer and wider." This was the last straw for Davis. He fired Johnston on July 17, the stated reason being his failure to stop Sherman's advance. He was replaced by John Bell Hood. Hood, Hardee, and Lieutenant General Alexander P. Stewart, Johnston's corps commanders, asked that this decision be delayed, the situation being so critical, until the issue of Atlanta had been decided. Davis refused, so Hood took command. When queried for his advice on Johnston's replacement, Lee called Hood "a good fighter" but said that "Genl Hardee had more experience in managing an army." Bragg insisted that "Hood is the man."[41]

Later, Davis agreed with critics that he should have relieved Johnston sooner, but reminded a correspondent that the decision not to remove the general was based upon the information Davis possessed at the time. He insisted that had he known Johnston would abandon the mountainous areas of Georgia and retreat to Atlanta, he would have relieved him, "as it was my opinion then, as clearly as now, that Atlanta could be best defended by holding some of the strong positions to the North of it."[42]

Johnston handed over his command on the eighteenth and offered a bitter defense of his actions: "As to the alleged cause of my removal, I assert that Sherman's army is much stronger compared with that of Tennessee than Grant's compared with that of Northern Virginia. Yet the enemy has been compelled to advance much more slowly to the vicinity of Atlanta than to that of Richmond and Petersburg, and has penetrated much deeper into Virginia than into Georgia."[43] He later strengthened his defensive arguments, insisting in an August 13, 1864, letter that his approach was similar to Lee's and that after the Battle of the Wilderness Lee "adopted precisely the course which I followed and gained great glory by it," retreating "much more rapidly or rather less slowly." He insisted, "I therefore thought and still think my plan of operations correct."[44]

Davis had his own assessment. He had great respect for Johnston's military ability, which accounts for Davis's appointment of the general to high command on three separate occasions during the war, and even, seemingly, some sympathy for him. While maintaining that Johnston's personal bravery was above dispute, "he seems to think that his *army is not for the defense of the country, but that he must at all hazard protect his army*."[45] On another occasion, shortly before relieving Johnston, Davis expressed similar feelings, remarking that while there was "not a better fighter in the army if he will only fight," Johnston's great problem was a "want of confidence." "He can not realize his own power."[46]

The War in the East

IN LATE MARCH 1864, Lee received Union newspaper reports that Grant's first important drive would be against Richmond. He first thought the announcements of Grant setting up house with the Army of the

Potomac a trick and confessed to having considered the news a "stratagem to attract our attention here, while he was left unmolested in dealing us a blow from the West." To Lee, Grant's presence meant the concentration of Union forces and the surety that the primary Union blow would fall upon Virginia. Lee soon gave his estimate of future Union operations, and of his new opponent. He knew that troops were gathering at Annapolis under Burnside, which made him suspect an attack on the Peninsula or via North Carolina. "It behooves us to be on alert, or we will be deceived. You know that is part of Grant's tactics. He deceived Pemberton when he turned him, and in this last move of Sherman threw dust in Polk's eyes." He believed Grant's presence meant a large force thrown against him on one or more lines of advance. "Unless we can take the initiative in the West to disturb their plans," he wrote, "we shall have to concentrate to meet him." The hungry winter of 1863–64 had not dulled Lee's aggressive side, nor his belief in the advantages conferred by offensive action. "If a good move could be made before they are ready to execute their plans, we would confound their schemes and break them up."[47]

As always, Lee read his enemy well. He believed that Grant was sure to move the Army of the Potomac against Richmond, while Burnside's army would be thrown on the Confederate flank. He also had "indications" that the Union would put more troops into the Shenandoah Valley. He reiterated his concerns to Davis, insisting that "if an aggressive movement can be made in the West it will disconcert their plans & oblige them to conform to ours." If this could not be done, Lee advised that Longstreet's forces be made ready to enter the valley or reinforce Lee. He also asked for the return of all troops detached from the Army of Northern Virginia.[48]

Bragg assured Lee that the government was doing everything it could to shore up his position. Longstreet went back to Virginia, but Bragg dashed any hopes Lee had for a western offensive, telling Lee that since Johnston had not come up with a plan to move into Tennessee, diverting enemy troops from the East, the strategy "necessarily became defensive."[49]

Lee, as he labored to decipher the enemy's intent, worried about his supply situation. He deemed critical the maintenance of the railroads supplying his troops. Their destruction would make it impossible for him to maintain his position and might force his withdrawal into North Carolina.[50] Lee knew these fragile rail lines were his army's Achilles' heel, and he would return again and again to this concern. Cutting these would also make holding the Confederate capital impossible. His enemy realized this as well.

By mid-April, Lee developed a detailed picture of Grant's plan for his spring campaign in the Eastern Theater. Lee painted for Davis a strategic canvas where a large Union army would cross the Rappahannock, aiming at Richmond, while another advanced from Annapolis to take the Confederate capital "in flank or rear." Union troops and ironclads at Charleston would come to the James River. The Red River campaign's failure made Mobile secure, allowing Johnston to draw reinforcements from there. Moreover, the Confederates also soon knew of Sigel's anticipated offensive in the Shenandoah. Lee proved incorrect about some of the specific enemy forces involved and where they would be used (such as Burnside's command), but he had successfully deciphered some of the major elements of the Union's 1864 strategy. Confederate intelligence sources were not providing completely accurate information, but they were doing pretty well.[51]

To meet the coming Union offensive, Lee called upon Davis to scrape men from everywhere so that he could attack. "If Richmond could be held secure against the attack from the east," he told Davis, "I would propose that I draw Longstreet to me & move right against the enemy on the Rappahannock. Should God give us a crowning victory there, all their plans would be dissipated, & their troops now collecting on the waters of the Chesapeake will be recalled to the defence of Washington." Lee forecast bad results if he had to withdraw. He believed local offensive action the solution; it could upset Grant's plans, and he habitually sought to keep the enemy off balance. For the rest of April, Lee struggled to get more men for his army and to get Imboden's forces in northwestern Virginia to move against the Baltimore and Ohio Railroad before the Union could properly protect it.[52]

Realizing the threat to Richmond, Lee tried to get Beauregard moved to the Petersburg area at the head of troops from the Carolinas. Instead, Beauregard was put in charge of yet another new military department based at Weldon, North Carolina. The road to Richmond through Petersburg was left open. Moreover, troops Lee had detached to North Carolina were still involved in the siege of New Bern.[53]

Grant, as Lee had learned, went with the Army of the Potomac. Operationally, Grant's idea from the start had been "to beat Lee's army north of Richmond if possible." After that, he would destroy his lines of communication north of the James, cross the army over the river, and then "besiege Lee in Richmond, or follow him south if he should retreat." Grant, though, had had high expectations for Butler's thrust against Richmond, hoping that the capture of the city might have decisive results, at least in the war's Eastern Theater. But if Butler did not take Richmond, Grant had also mapped out a second course: "hard fighting" that would force Lee to retreat or "so cripple him that he could not detach a large force to go north and still retain enough for the defense of Richmond."[54]

On May 5, Grant launched his arm of the Union's great spring offensive, embarking upon a campaign that would last until Lee's surrender on April 9, 1865. The day before, May 4, Lee had sent word that Grant's army was on the move. He told Davis: "It seems to me that the great efforts of the enemy here and in Georgia have begun, and that the necessity of our concentration at both points is immediate and imperative." Here again, Lee offered his standard tactical, operational, and strategic riposte: concentration at the decisive point. But to Lee, this also always ensured his freedom of maneuver and thus opened up other opportunities.[55]

Upon hearing of the Union advance, Longstreet suggested something that Grant had feared: moving around the Union right. This would place the Confederate army between Grant's forces and the Union capital, threatening both Washington and the Union rear.[56] Lee didn't choose this route, but he did put his forces in motion to meet the enemy and placed all the units in the valley under the command of Major General John C. Breckinridge, a Mexican War veteran, vice president in the Buchanan administration, and former senator, telling him to fight the Union forces pushing up the Valley, "or by some movement to draw [them] back before they get on my left."[57]

Both Grant and Lee hoped to catch their enemy in motion and force a battle. The armies stumbled into each other, resulting in a confused struggle on May 5–6 that became known as the Battle of the Wilderness. Around 100,000 Union troops tangled with Lee's 60,000 Confederates on fields choked with heavy Virginia undergrowth. Weapon blasts set the brush ablaze, burning to death many of the wounded. But the tough terrain helped prevent the Union from effectively bringing its superior numbers to bear. On the second day Longstreet's corps appeared just in time to prevent a Union breakthrough on the southern end of the battlefield, then came within a whisper of making one of their own. The attack faltered when two Rebel units fired into each other, wounding Longstreet. Meanwhile, Confederate forces on the northern flank of the fight also came close to crushing the Union flank; darkness stopped this. Lee inflicted 17,600 casualties on the enemy for about 11,000 of his own.[58]

Tactically, the Battle of the Wilderness was a defeat for the Union. But Grant had immediately accomplished one of the strategic objectives of his advance: pinning Lee's army. In the battle's wake, Grant raised the whole spirit of the Army of the Potomac when he turned Lee's flank to the east and headed south.[59] Grant also inaugurated something new for the Civil War: continuous battle. Previously, particularly in the East, the armies had tangled for a few days and then withdrew. No more.[60]

The greatest failure in the Union offensive came at the hands of Benjamin Butler. Before the campaign, an enthusiastic Butler had promised he would move even if he had only ten men and said he wouldn't stop to dig in. He had orders to establish a strong position after landing and then drive on Richmond. The operation provided an excellent opportunity to penetrate the South's defenses while Grant tied down the bulk of Confederate manpower in the East, especially Lee's army. Moreover, Davis had not heeded advice from Lee to protect the areas between Richmond and Petersburg against a Union descent, making it possible for Butler to land against very thin opposition. But to pay off, such a gambit needed a vigorous commander, which Butler was not. Coming ashore on May 5 and gaining, as Grant termed it "complete surprise," Butler entrenched on May 6, set up a base for drawing supply, and tore up some of the important rail lines. He even launched a successful attack that took the Confederates' first lines on Drewry's Bluff. But his army did not advance. Grant was not pleased. Butler's failure allowed Beauregard time to gather forces from the Carolinas, bring them to Virginia, counterattack Butler on the sixteenth, and then entrench themselves while protecting the vital railroad into Richmond and the city itself. As a result, Butler's army, Grant wrote later, "though in a position of great security, was as completely shut off from further operations directly against Richmond as if it had been in a bottle strongly corked. It required but a comparatively small force of the enemy to hold it there."[61]

Butler had faced only light resistance, and his orders were to drive to Richmond. At a minimum, he could have burned the city, destroying Lee's logistical base and strategic position. His failure to execute his orders probably prolonged the war, thus costing tens of thousands of lives.

Meanwhile, Grant pushed. Believing Lee would stay in his works in the wake of the Wilderness, he attempted to steal a night march on May 7. If he could beat the Confederates to Spotsylvania, he could get between Lee and Richmond. Alerted to activity in the Union lines, Lee got to Spotsylvania first, which made the difference. A week of bloody fighting followed. The combat included a May 12 attack by 20,000 Federal troops against a salient, or bulge in the Confederate lines, known as "Bloody Angle." It was stopped only because of a secondary line of entrenchments. Losses were 4,100 to 6,820, the Federals getting the worst of it. Tactically, Lee managed the battle very well.

His men also dug the most intricate system of trenches in history up to this point. They stopped Grant, but not for long.[62]

Sigel's drive into the Shenandoah also did not go as Grant had hoped. Lee told Breckinridge that it would be "very desirable" if he could throw back the enemy forces there and then join Lee. Breckinridge proceeded to do so. He defeated the Union forces under Sigel at New Market, Virginia, on May 15, but then Lee altered his orders, telling Breckinridge to press the Union forces down the valley and pursue them into Maryland if it was possible but to make preparations to join Lee if it was not, and if the valley could be defended without him. Lee thought the former provided the most benefit to Confederate arms.[63] Breckenridge joined Lee, temporarily.

After Sigel's defeat, Grant gave Major General David Hunter the command, ordering him to advance to Charlottesville and Lynchburg, living off the country and tearing up the region's canals and railroads before withdrawing and joining the Army of the Potomac.[64]

Grant's strategy for 1864 also included raids. In early May, Grant launched an enormous cavalry raid, 10,000 strong, toward Richmond to tear up Confederate communications, destroy their supplies, and "whip Stuart." Commanded by Sheridan, it lasted sixteen days. Most significantly, it led to the death of the aforementioned Confederate cavalry general, who was mortally wounded at Yellow Tavern on May 11. Sheridan made another raid in June that prevented Lee from shifting troops to Petersburg, and Hunter launched another in the Shenandoah.[65] Such raids, though useful, would not win the North the campaign, nor were they intended to.

Meanwhile, Lee's casualties began mounting, whittling away at his ability to maneuver. He needed more men. Davis suggested he pull the troops from the valley, but Lee believed this too dangerous because it would leave the Union forces there unopposed. By mid-May Davis got very serious about gathering troops for Lee and ordered up units from farther south, as well as reserves from Virginia and North Carolina. Lee pushed Davis to concentrate and told him the choice was between fighting north of the capital or at Richmond itself.[66]

On May 21, Grant once again turned Lee's flank and headed south. He moved his force in a wide semicircular route southeastward, again striving to place his army between Lee and Richmond. Lee had anticipated the move. "But the enemy," Grant wrote, "again having the shorter line and being in possession of the main roads, was enabled to reach the North Anna in advance of us, and took position behind it." Lee told his wife two days later, "We have the advantage of being nearer our supplies & less liable to have our communications, trains,

&c., cut by his cavalry & he is getting farther from his base. Still I begrudge every step he makes towards Richmond."[67]

The strategy Grant was now pursuing, attrition, was not one he preferred, but he had been prepared to try it if his hand was forced. Maneuver had failed, in Grant's theater as well as Sherman's, and Grant especially had little choice but to simply grind away at the enemy's capacity to continue the fight.[68] The constraints of the terrain; the enemy's adoption of a defensive strategy that tactically included heavy use of fortifications; the skill of the Confederate commander, Lee, who showed a marked ability to guess Grant's next move; the failure of Butler's offensive—all of this left Grant little choice.[69]

Some have branded Grant's fight against Lee a strategy of annihilation. This was simply not the case. Strategically, the Union was pursuing attrition; Grant himself called it this. Grant was not seeking a single, climactic battle. Moreover, Grant had no illusions about the campaign in Virginia. He realized the bitter necessity of desperate fighting if the Union wanted to bring the war to a close. He wrote later: "The losses inflicted, and endured, were destined to be severe; but the armies now confronting each other had already been in deadly conflict for a period of three years, with immense losses…and neither had made any real progress toward accomplishing the final end." What lay ahead was a campaign that "was destined to result in heavier losses, to both armies, in a given time, than any previously suffered; but the carnage was to be limited to a single year, and to accomplish all that had been anticipated or desired at the beginning in that time."[70] Grant originally intended the campaign to end the war by November; the Confederates insisted otherwise. But his larger point was a good one, for the longer the war continued, the more the casualties mounted. The sooner it ended, the quicker the dying would end as well.

There was great risk in Grant's approach. Attrition takes time, which is the greatest of enemies to political leaders waging war. The populace will endure casualties for only so long. There will come a point at which they will simply cry no, the value of the object, in Clausewitz's words, having exceeded the cost they are willing to pay. A people will reach this point more quickly when they do not see battlefield results demonstrating clear steps on the road to success. The side choosing to implement an attrition strategy must also prove able to outlast their opponent in terms of will and resources. The weaker in either of these arenas may yield first.

Grant kept moving, though Lee's quick replies gave the Union few openings. Lee maneuvered his forces so that "whatever route he pursues I am in a position to move against him, and shall endeavor to engage him while in motion." His plan was also to stay near enough to Richmond to cooperate with Beauregard if necessary. But he was more interested in getting help than in giving it, insisting that in regard to Grant's army, "it seems our best policy [strategy] to unite upon it and endeavor to crush it."[71]

Lee was unaware that Beauregard had already submitted proposals for cooperation between the two forces. Beauregard, always good for a plan, suggested on May 14 that Lee fall back to the Chickahominy, perhaps even to the lines around Richmond, and send Beauregard 15,000 men with which to wipe out Butler. Then Beauregard could join Lee with 25,000 men, which would permit the destruction of Grant. Bragg forwarded the plan to Davis, accompanied by a withering commentary that included the fact that it would necessitate Lee's withdrawing 60 miles in the face of 8,000 Union cavalry, risking the destruction of his army. Other possible lesser catastrophes included the fall of Petersburg, the loss of the railroad supplying Lee's army, and the enemy's capture of the region necessary for its future supply. Minor details, certainly. Bragg went on to insist that the force Beauregard had under his control was sufficient for destroying Butler if it was simply used effectively (whatever that meant in Bragg-speak).[72]

Four days later, Beauregard submitted another plan entailing cooperation with Lee. It too involved Lee falling back to the Chickahominy to draw in Grant. Beauregard would take 15,000 men, unite with Breckinridge, and together they would hit Grant's flank with 20,000 men, ensuring the defeat of the Union army. All of this would be done quickly enough to allow Beauregard to return with reinforcements from Lee's army and drive Butler away.[73]

"If 15,000 men can be spared for the flank movement proposed," Davis observed, "certainly 10,000 may be sent to re-enforce General Lee. If that be done immediately General Lee's correspondence warrants the belief that he will defeat the enemy in Northern Virginia." Bragg certainly agreed and dispatched a staff officer and appropriate transportation to Drewry's Bluff to get Beauregard's troops on the move. The Creole general resisted, giving Bragg the plan for a counteroffensive that Beauregard insisted would result in the expulsion of all of Butler's force—if the troops remained with him. Bragg refused and Beauregard bowed. Davis explained to Beauregard the importance of defeating Grant and hoped that the Confederate forces confronting Butler would be able to join Lee before Butler's troops united with Grant.[74]

Lee continued to try to pull men to his hard-pressed force. As Grant began evacuating Butler, Lee told Davis: "If this army is unable to resist Grant, the troops under Genl Beauregard and in the city will be unable to defend it."[75] By the beginning of June, Lee concluded that the time had arrived for Confederate offensive action. He wrote Lieutenant General A. P. Hill that they needed to attack in order to keep the Federals from setting up a siege of Richmond, for if that happened, it would be only a matter of time before the capital fell. But nothing came of this.[76]

In the second week of June, Bragg recommended to Davis a different Confederate approach: driving the Union forces out of the Shenandoah Valley, thus opening the road to Washington. Davis sent the comment along to Lee. Lee agreed about driving the enemy out of the valley but said it would take one corps to do so. Lee would do it if it was "deemed prudent to hazard the defense of Richmond," which would be the result of taking away troops for the valley. This idea evolved, Lee hoping that Jubal Early's presence in the valley would not only make Lee's position more secure but also provide the Army of Northern Virginia with some relief. Later, Lee explained what he intended in his orders to Early, who was to attack, chase the enemy down the valley if possible, and, "if opportunity offered, to follow him into Maryland." This would drive the Union from the Shenandoah, while also threatening Washington and Baltimore, and force Grant to "weaken himself so much for their protection" that he would be vulnerable to attack—or be forced to attack.[77] The South now launched an operational diversion in the Shenandoah.

Defeated by Early at Lynchburg on June 18, Union general Hunter retreated northwest, up the Kanawha River, toward Lexington, instead of toward Charlottesville, supply driving his move. This took his army out of the theater of action. Hunter's escape disappointed Lee, but he still believed the best option was for Early to push down the valley. Lee told Davis, "I still think it is our policy [strategy] to draw the attention of the enemy to his own territory. It may force Grant to attack me, or weaken his force."[78] Early, with around 15,000 men, crossed into Maryland on July 6. After demanding and getting a $200,000 ransom from the inhabitants of Frederick, Maryland, Early pushed on toward the capital. Union major general Lew Wallace, a Shiloh veteran who is most famous for having penned *Ben Hur*, assembled a scratch force of 2,000 men to oppose him. He did this on his own, being convinced that Halleck would never allow it. Wallace marched his men to the Monocacy River, just east of Frederick, where he was reinforced by 5,000 men sent by Grant. After a sharp fight, Early captured nearly all of Wallace's little army, drove off the rest, and pushed to the outskirts of Washington. But the invaders were spent. Captain William Whitehurst Old, Early's aide-de-camp, wrote on July 11: "Troops much broken down by excessive heat, long marches, dusty roads and the exceedingly dry country through which we passed." The next night, they began their retreat.[79]

Lincoln saw in Early's advance not impending disaster (though that is exactly what many saw) but rather a chance to destroy a Confederate army. Nonetheless, he was unwilling to trust the safety of the capital to other hands. He summoned Grant, as well as reinforcements, and told his general in chief, "Now, what I think is that you should provide to retain your hold where you are, certainly, and bring the rest with you personally, and make a vigorous effort to destroy the enemy's force in this vicinity. I think there is really a fair chance to do this if the movement is prompt." Grant did not come, believing his absence from the main front would have a bad effect. He did send a corps to reinforce Washington and told Lincoln that he had "great faith that the enemy will never be able to get back with much of his force."[80]

Grant proved mistaken. The cumbersome Union command structure had the forces opposing Early in four separate commands. Moreover, Grant did not take a firm hold on the situation, and his inaction led to a rebuke from Lincoln. The response to Early's diversion marked a rare intervention on the part of Lincoln in Grant's conduct of the war. Generally Lincoln left Grant alone, but this time he corrected his general in chief, and it was a needed admonition.[81]

In early August, Grant reorganized the Union forces around Washington into the Middle Military Division. He told Halleck that he wanted Sheridan put in command with instructions to "put himself south of the enemy and follow him to the death. Wherever the enemy goes let our troops go also." Lincoln, when he saw the dispatch, heartily approved, remarking, "This, I think, is exactly right as to how our forces should move." But it is clear that Lincoln had no confidence that Grant's subordinates would do the job unless the general in chief peered over their shoulders. Evidence of this appears in his instruction to Grant to "please look over the dispatches you may have rece[i]ved from here, even since you made that order, and discover, if you can, that there is any idea in the head of any one here of 'putting our army *South* of the enemy' or of following him to the '*death*' in any direction. I repeat to you, it will be neither done nor attempted, unless you watch it every day, and hour, and force it." Grant replied that he would leave within two hours and headed for the Monocacy. Moreover, to limit reinforcements to Early and assist Sheridan's counteroffensive in the Shenandoah (about which we will see more in the next chapter), Grant ordered a movement on the north side of the James River with the intent of threatening Richmond and keeping the Confederates in their trenches.[82] Lee proved partially correct: Grant weakened his forces in response to Early's efforts.

On August 4, Lee told Davis that he had information that Grant was reinforcing the Union forces in the valley with the probable intention of overrunning Early and finishing the Shenandoah's destruction. He urged the dispatch of reinforcements to hold the valley and its valuable railroad connection into Richmond. Two days later, Lee tried to counter the Union thrust by sending troops to middle Virginia to cooperate with Early. Lee believed it necessary to have Confederate units operating north of the Rappahannock. He even discussed their demonstrating against Washington, if given the opportunity. Lee wanted action, writing that "any enterprise that can be undertaken to injure the enemy, distract or separate his forces, embarrass his communications on the Potomac or on land is desirable." But Lee lacked the forces to properly do this. Union action on his flanks was robbing him of both troops and his freedom to move and maneuver.[83]

In the end, the Union failed to trap Early as Lincoln had hoped (and feared wouldn't happen) and in spite of his efforts. It must have appeared tothe president that the Union generals once again had bungled a chance to destroy a Confederate army away from its base, just as they had done during the Antietam and Gettysburg campaigns.

Meanwhile, the campaign ground on, and the casualties mounted with bloody actions at places such as Cold Harbor, where 60,000 Union troops, in an assault that dwarfed Pickett's Charge, attacked a heavily fortified Rebel position and suffered 3,500 casualties in eight minutes. After this repulse, Grant again turned south. He crossed the James River, stealing a march on Lee, who was caught off guard. This buoyed Lincoln. "I begin to see it," he wired Grant. "You will succeed. God bless you all." Grant advanced on Petersburg, hoping to take the lightly held city before the Confederates caught wind of his intent. Slow action on the part of his subordinates cost the Union its chance. By June 16, both sides had entrenched outside the city. In six weeks, Grant had suffered 60,000 casualties to the South's probably 33,000.[84] But Grant's could be replaced.

Northern morale was depressed by losses that seemed to have delivered nothing more than putting the Army of the Potomac where it had been two years earlier. Journalist Noah Brooks wrote: "The great public, like a spoiled child, refuses to be comforted, because Richmond is not taken forthwith, and because we do not meet with an unbroken success at every point."[85] But Lincoln did not share their feelings. He certainly did not like the casualties, but he began to believe that finally he had a general who would succeed. In the wake of Fredericksburg he had lamented the fact that he could not find a general who understood the war's bloody arithmetic. In Grant, Lincoln had a general who understood that the people were weary of the war, that it was costing $4 million a day, and that prolonging it would kill even more men, particularly with the approach of summer and the deadly diseases that accompanied its onset.[86]

From June 19, 1864, Petersburg was effectively under siege. Grant began launching operations to the south of Petersburg to cut the city's supply and communications lines, and to the north of the James River to endanger Richmond or cut the Virginia Central Railroad. By the end of the month, Lee worried more about the state of his supplies than about fending off Grant. Indeed, he feared that this might force him to attack Grant's trenches, something he had no desire to do because of the casualties he would incur. He worried about his communications as well.[87]

Lee tried to do other things to stop the Union offensive. In late July, he sought to dispatch Morgan in a raid against the Baltimore and Ohio Railroad and into Pennsylvania, but illness kept Morgan from going. Lee did launch raids with cavalry into Maryland and Pennsylvania. He talked with Ewell about finding some way of interfering with Union navigation of the James River and considered sending a force, mounted and with long-range guns, across the lines south of the Potomac in the hopes of stirring up the leadership in Washington.[88] Always he looked for ways to knock the enemy off balance and disturb his plans.

By late July, Lee believed it was time for aggressive action. "We cannot afford to sit down in front of the enemy and allow him to entrench himself wherever he pleases," he wrote. But as the month wore on he became increasingly frustrated: "Where are we to get sufficient troops to oppose Grant? He is bringing to him now the 19th Corps, & will bring every man he can get. His talent & strategy consists in accumulating overwhelming numbers."[89] Such is the application of attrition.

By choosing to target the Confederate armies, Grant revealed what he deemed the South's chief center of gravity. He did not seek a decisive battle (though surely he would have taken it if it was offered), nor was he seeking merely the seizure of a specific location. He sought to win the war and would do this by destroying his enemy's ability to fight it.

The Full Fury of Modern War

I am going into the very bowels of the Confederacy,
and propose to leave a trail that will be recognized
fifty years hence.

—WILLIAM TECUMSEH SHERMAN, October 19, 1864

THERE ARE MANY WHO BRAND the Civil War the first "modern" conflict. They are right in many respects, for it displays the hallmarks of that type of war: mass armies, partially created by conscription; the mobilization of industry, including its control, particularly in the South, by a central government; and the respective efforts to sway public opinion. The execution of the struggle also supports this argument: trench warfare, such as that around Richmond and Petersburg; turreted ironclad and steam-powered warships; rifles; early machine guns; mines, both on land and in coastal waters; the wire (telegraph) first strung around trenches at Port Hudson in 1863. All of this points to the kind of war that would be fought in the following century.

But there were also throwbacks to the past: the use of irregulars, particularly by the South, to wage *petite guerre*, or partisan war, against the Union's rear areas and lines of communication; the Union's medieval, even ancient practice of destroying the enemy's resources—burning his crops and cities, driving his people from their lands, taking his slaves and peasants and making them their own. This strategy of exhaustion, as well as killing enemy armies, became a key component of Union victory.

Nonetheless, the "modern conflict" argument seems the most convincing when addressing that most modern of concerns among democratic nations, something upon which everything else depended: winning an election.

The Election of 1864

AS THE END OF AUGUST drew near, Grant's army remained stalled outside Richmond and Petersburg; Sherman's forces stood before Atlanta. The November elections loomed. Lincoln had again received the Republican nomination for president (though Republicans campaigned as the National

Union Party). Their platform included a call for a constitutional amendment outlawing slavery. Lincoln deemed this "a lifting and necessary conclusion to the final success of the Union." No longer was the policy objective merely maintaining the Union. With the inclusion of abolition in the party's platform, emancipation, which had begun as a military measure, evolved into an additional political objective. The Republican Party's platform also laid out terms for ending the war: "the determination of the government of the United States not to compromise with rebels, or to offer them any terms of peace, except such as may be based upon an unconditional surrender of their hostility and a return to their just allegiance to the Constitution and laws of the United States."[1]

Lincoln considered the election critical, believing that it would decide the "weal or woe of this great nation." Though McClellan, the Democratic Party candidate, officially favored continuing the war against the rebellion, Lincoln believed that McClellan's election would result in a Union defeat. He argued that "the rebel armies cannot be destroyed with Democratic strategy" because the Democrats intended to prosecute the war by turning out of the army between 100,000 and 200,000 blacks bearing arms for the Union. "These men will be disbanded," Lincoln insisted, "returned to slavery & we will have to fight two nations instead of one.... You cannot concilliate [*sic*] the South, when the mastery & control of millions of blacks makes them sure of ultimate success. You cannot concilliate the South, when you place yourself in such a position, that they see they can achieve their independence. The war democrat depends upon conciliation.... Abandon all the posts now possessed by black men surrender all these advantages to the enemy, & we would be compelled to abandon the war in 3 weeks.... But no human power can subdue this rebellion without using the Emancipation lever as I have done," continued Lincoln. "Freedom has given us the control of 200,000 able bodied men, born & raised on southern soil. It will give us more yet."[2]

This clearly shows that Lincoln's primary war aim was preserving the Union. Moreover, we see his determination to do whatever is necessary to achieve this goal and to take responsibility for it—an example of moral courage. Lincoln's remarks also demonstrated his awareness that the balance of strength between the two combatants necessitated the use of black troops to achieve victory. Certainly the Union had many advantages, but these did not guarantee success.

Though Lincoln had his party's support, he was not so sure about the voters. In late August 1864, he expressed deep doubts about his reelection, noting that if he lost, it would be his "duty to so co-operate with the President elect, as to save the Union between the election and the inauguration; as he will have secured his election on such ground that he can not possibly save it afterwards." Seward thought that McClellan, in the end, would have done nothing, an assessment with which Lincoln agreed. "At the least," the president replied, "I should have done my duty and have stood clear before my own conscience."[3] Lincoln had no reason to worry. His reelection, and hence the Union, would be saved by a red-haired general from Ohio and the intervention of Jefferson Davis.

The South saw opportunities in the Union presidential contest. Previously, Davis had tried to take advantage of Northern dissent during the 1862 congressional elections. The proclamation he prepared for Bragg and Lee was part of this. Many Southerners believed a presidential victory by a "Peace Democrat" (or Copperhead) their best hope of gaining independence. Moreover, like many in the South, Davis was emboldened by the anti-Union, anti-war, and anti-Lincoln activities of the Copperheads of the Northwest, as well as by (exaggerated) reports of Northern membership in secret societies. In the spring and summer of 1864, Davis and his advisors hatched a plan to try to influence the election in the South's favor.[4]

Davis sent agents to Canada and the North to negotiate with figures amenable to peace. Some had instructions to meddle in Union politics, others to attempt to free Confederate prisoners. Still others bribed newspapers to argue for peace and gave money to sympathetic political campaigns. Some even plotted to stage an uprising at the Democratic convention in Chicago, and a few figured in negotiations that caused Lincoln political injury, though not enough to cost him the election.[5]

These efforts were worthy elements of grand strategy, if misguided ones, and cost the Confederacy little. There were also problems. Historian Larry Nelson argues persuasively that Davis mismanaged the endeavor, partly because he did not really think much would come of it and partly because he feared the election of a peace candidate would *discourage* the South from continuing the war instead of encourage it. Seceded states might see in McClellan's election and subsequent policy of conciliation (or perhaps appeasement) a chance to return to the Union with slavery intact. This would kill the Confederacy.[6]

There were larger issues here as well, those of linkage between military and political strategies and between the various strategies and the political objective. The South's best hope of winning the war had now become its protraction. The optimal way to do this was to sit on the strategic defensive. In his assessment of

Johnston's defense of Georgia, Grant wrote: "I think his policy [strategy] was the best one that could have been pursued by the whole South—protract the war, which was all that was necessary to enable them to gain recognition in the end." He also pointed out, correctly, that "the North was already growing weary."[7]

Grant, however, was misinformed about what was really going on in the Confederate high command and with Johnston in particular. His attributing to Johnston a conscious decision to pursue a strategy of protraction was too generous; there was no such determination. Johnston had adopted his approach out of weakness and inclination, nothing else. Plus, foreign recognition was all but impossible. Nonetheless, Grant did hit on something: a strategy of protracting the war was what the South *should* have tried. Again, though, there was the issue of linkage. Davis did not coordinate the political and military efforts of the South in order to deny sufficient Union military success before the presidential election. Davis's action in Georgia clearly shows this.

On July 17, 1864, Jefferson Davis replaced Johnston with John Bell Hood. After Hood's first attack, Sherman met with Hood's West Point classmate, Union major general John Schofield. From Schofield he learned of Hood's reckless courage; Sherman warned his army to expect action. "This was just what we wanted," he insisted later, "to fight in open ground on any thing like equal terms, instead of being forced to run up against prepared intrenchments." Sherman judged Johnston's management of his defensive campaign "cautious but prudent."[8]

Despite this, on July 19 the Union forces were advancing against such light opposition that Sherman believed the South intended to evacuate Atlanta. Then Hood struck. Over an eight-day period beginning on July 20, Hood launched three furious assaults. The Confederates succeeded in preventing a move by one of Sherman's units to cut the remaining railroad south of Atlanta. However, Hood, or rather his army, paid the price, suffering 15,000 casualties to Sherman's 6,000, losses the South could not make good. Moreover, the bloodbath meant that Sherman's now vastly superior force could stretch around Hood's Atlanta positions, trapping him the way Pemberton had been ensnared by Grant in Vicksburg.[9]

When Hood's men took to their parapets once again, Sherman turned his attention to what proved to be the difficult task of cutting the last of Atlanta's rail links, especially the one south of Atlanta with Macon. He wrote that gaining the Macon Railroad "would, in my judgment, result in the capture of Atlanta." Though he preferred to destroy Hood's army, given that this "Gate-City of the South" was "full of foundries, arsenals, and machine-shops," he believed its fall would be the "death-knell of the Southern Confederacy."[10]

Sherman was wrong about Atlanta but right about what was truly important: Hood's army. And indeed, Sherman did keep this in mind, even as he contemplated ways to take Atlanta. He sent cavalry to try to cut the Macon-Atlanta rail line in the hopes that it would force Hood to evacuate Atlanta, which would not only deliver the city but also give Sherman the chance to "catch Hood in the confusion of retreat." The raiders, though successful in making a small breach in the rails, did no lasting damage. Sherman then made the bold decision to march his army south of Atlanta. At first the Confederates thought the Yankees had withdrawn. They soon discovered otherwise. Hood responded by attacking Sherman at Jonesborough, south of Atlanta, on August 30. The Union repulsed the assault, inflicting heavy casualties, then launched an attack of their own the following day. Hood, realizing that he faced being cornered and destroyed, abandoned Atlanta on September 1, 1864.[11]

Hood's offensive proved a great mistake. Grant later wrote that he thought Johnston had acted "very wisely" by preserving his men and saving as much territory as he could without engaging in a decisive battle "in which all might be lost." As Sherman advanced, his army became spread out until, "if this had been continued, it would have been easy to destroy it in detail."[12] Had Hood preserved his strength, he could have continued to stretch his lines, as Lee was then doing around Richmond, perhaps stifling Sherman, as Lee had Grant. This might have kept Atlanta in the South's hands until the election. But Davis had dictated otherwise. He had placed Hood in command and insisted upon the offensive. It was a critical and perhaps even fatal miscalculation.

The fall of Atlanta damaged Confederate rail communications and logistics, though not mortally. The strategic implications were what mattered most. Sherman delivered to the Union cause a triumph it desperately needed, one that heartened the Union and ensured Lincoln's reelection.[13] But Sherman had not yet achieved the strategic objectives of his campaign: he had not destroyed Johnston's (now Hood's) army. He had penetrated into the enemy's country and by taking Atlanta had destroyed a chunk of the South's war-making ability, but many Confederate resources remained untouched. Sherman would soon do better on both his charges.

War Writ Large: Sherman's March

WHILE ON A SPEAKING TOUR of the Deep South in the fall of 1864, Davis took for his chief topics Sherman and his army, and what the South intended to do about them. Despite the fall of Atlanta, Davis spread an optimistic message to the crowds gathering to hear his words. He told the people of Macon on September 23, 1864, that "Sherman cannot keep up his long line of communication, and retreat sooner or later, he must." He elaborated on his claim with an allusion to the past, insisting that Sherman's army would share the same fate as Napoleon's during its retreat from Moscow. In a speech in Montgomery, Davis told the audience to expect no help from abroad and that military victory was the best way to encourage the peace party in the North.[14]

Davis also began to talk publicly about the Confederacy's future military response to Sherman. He revealed Hood's intention to take the offensive within thirty days (though Davis sometimes varied the details). He propagandized that Atlanta would become "a perfect Moscow of defeat" and that Sherman would be driven out of Georgia, Tennessee, and Kentucky, and even back across the Ohio River. "Then we shall have thousands of recruits...that will so augment our armies that our foes will sue for peace." The next month was crucial to ultimate Confederate success, Davis insisted, and pointed to the coming Union presidential election and the hope that Southern victories would contribute to the triumph of a northern peace candidate. Not to be outdone, Beauregard and Hood also gave speeches announcing that Hood's army was heading toward Tennessee.[15]

Both Grant and Sherman appreciated the forewarning. It certainly eased their planning. Before Sherman marched on Atlanta, the only subsequent operation that he and Grant had discussed was a drive on Mobile. Grant, though, did not intend to see Sherman idle. "We want to keep the enemy constantly pressed to the end of the war," he wrote on September 10. "If we give him no peace whilst the war lasts, the end cannot be distant." The Union had just taken "all of Mobile Bay that is valuable" (Grant referred to Farragut's famous dash into the harbor and the Union's seizure of the city's key forts, all of which occurred during the first week in August), and Grant proposed that Sherman move against Augusta, Georgia. He also asked for Sherman's ideas. "Cump" suggested a deeper march into Georgia. Simultaneously, Grant would keep extending his line around Lee's positions in Petersburg to cut the railroads while he sent a force of infantry and ironclads against Wilmington, North Carolina, winning control of this port. But he didn't think he could begin these operations until October 5 and wanted to know what Sherman would do.[16]

Sherman was not sure. He wrote Grant on September 20 that he "would not hesitate to cross the State of Georgia with 60,000 men, hauling some stores and depending on the country for the balance." But he believed the better move would be for Union forces to take Wilmington, then Savannah, while others struck inland to attack Columbus, Georgia. Meanwhile, Sherman would "keep Hood employed" and prepare "for a march on Augusta, Columbia, and Charleston," as soon as Wilmington and Savannah fell.[17]

Already the germ of an idea was growing. It grew enough so that on October 1 Sherman could ask Grant, "Why would it not do for me to leave Tennessee to the force which Thomas has, and the reserves soon to come to Nashville, and for me to destroy Atlanta, and then march across Georgia to Savannah or Charleston, breaking roads and doing irreparable damage?" Upon hearing of this, Halleck broke character by promptly sending Grant a note listing eight reasons why this was a bad idea.[18] Grant ignored him. What worried Grant about Sherman implementing such a plan was Hood's army. This, however, soon took care of itself.

In an 1879 letter, Davis recalled that in September 1864 he had advised Hood to move his army to some point along the railroad between Chattanooga and Atlanta and dig in. "This it was supposed would compel Sherman to move to attack him, and if he insisted upon retaining possession of Atlanta would necessitate the division of his forces."[19]

Hood refused Davis's counsel (some consider *disobeyed* a better descriptor) and decided that he would draw Sherman as near as possible to Tennessee's border, convincing the Union general to divide his forces even further. Hood withdrew to northern Alabama, establishing his base at Gadsden. On October 22 he struck out for Tennessee, crossing the Tennessee River on November 13 and camping at Florence, Alabama, before moving into the Volunteer State. Among Hood's explanations for his action was that he did not receive until the twelfth Davis's November 7 command to attack Sherman, but his president's order was in many ways a reiteration of the instructions Hood had received in person in September. Moreover, Hood believed that pursuing Sherman would be seen by his troops as a retreat, with subsequently poor effects upon morale. Davis's orders also contained at least one deviation from reality: he expected that after Hood defeated Sherman's forces in detail, Hood could advance to the Ohio River.[20]

Meanwhile, Beauregard, whose command had been absorbed by Lee, took command of the Military Division of the West on October 17. This was basically Johnston's old department. His job was to organize the efforts of Confederate forces in Georgia, Tennessee, Alabama, Mississippi, and eastern Louisiana. This included Hood's army.[21]

By October 10, Sherman knew Hood was withdrawing west and asked Grant if the time had come to unfold their plan. Grant thought that if

Sherman "cut loose," Hood's army would not threaten him but instead strike for Nashville. His preference was for destroying Hood's army, "but I must trust to your own judgment." He warned Sherman that the move would be unsupported because Grant could not spare the men from his army to take Savannah.[22]

None of this discouraged Sherman. He resolved to move south, believing that Hood's army would then be forced to follow *him*. "Instead of being on the defensive," Sherman insisted, "I would be on the offensive; instead of guessing at what he means to do, he would have to guess at my plans. The difference in war is full 25 per cent [meaning that being on the offensive increased his strength]. I can make Savannah, Charleston, or the mouth of the Chattahoochee."[23]

"Your dispatch of to-day received," Grant replied. "If you are satisfied the trip to the sea-coast can be made, holding the line of the Tennessee firmly, you may make it, destroying all the railroad south of Dalton or Chattanooga, as you think best." Lincoln, though, was not so enthused and worried that this risked Sherman's army. But he let Grant decide.[24]

Over the next month they prepared and hashed out the details. Sherman laid out the strategic and operational context as well as the strategic objectives. His plan was strategy at its grandest. He was striking directly at the Confederacy's will, its leadership, its ability to wage war, and any slim chance it possessed of acquiring allies. "I propose to act in such a manner against the material resources of the South as utterly to negative Davis boasted threat and promises of protection," he wrote Grant. "If we can march a well-appointed army right through his territory, it is a demonstration to the world, foreign and domestic, that we have a power which Davis cannot resist. This may not be war, but rather statesmanship."[25]

Sherman saw three possible objective points for his march: Mobile, Apalachicola, and the coast of Charleston or Savannah. Important in his choice was his insistence that the army be capable of acting against the enemy afterward. Going to Apalachicola "would leave the army in a bad position for future movements." Striking for the coast, he told Grant, "would have a material effect upon your campaign in Virginia," which demonstrated his consideration of supporting Grant's efforts. Before he embarked, he would destroy Atlanta, as well as the railroad between there and Dalton.[26]

Sherman's 60,000 men lit their torches and marched out of Atlanta on November 14. Sherman wrote a brother general: "I will be off in a few days on a worse raid than our Meridian raid was, and you may look for a great howl against the brute Sherman." Grant provided support for this move by ordering a series of raids. Major General Edward Canby launched troops from Vicksburg and Baton Rouge to cut railroads and pin Confederate troops. Another force went inland from the Union Department of the South to tear up the railroads between Savannah and Charleston.[27]

The Confederacy searched for ways to counter Sherman's March. Governor Brown of Georgia ordered a "levy *en masse*" of every male between sixteen and fifty-five in the state able to bear arms (railroad workers, telegraphers, and office-holding clergy being exempt). Davis asked Lee for advice in dealing with Sherman, who he thought aimed at Macon. Lee speculated that Sherman's objective was Savannah, and believed the population had to turn out to stop him. He recommended the burning of all bridges and destruction of all roads and supplies within Sherman's reach, and putting in the field under Hardee an army gathered from Charleston, Savannah, and other areas. Davis agreed, and told Brigadier General William M. Browne "that every effort will be made, by destroying bridges, felling trees, planting subterra shells [land mines], and otherwise, to obstruct the advance of the enemy. All supplies which are likely to fall into the enemy's hands will be destroyed." He also wanted Forrest's cavalry sent to impede Sherman's foraging, if it wasn't too late.[28]

By November 19, Hardee had reports from prisoners that Sherman was indeed heading for Savannah, but via Augusta, where Hardee began gathering what forces he could. Davis ordered all industrial machinery removed from the city, though he preferred the "repulse of the enemy" to evacuation. Beauregard, writing from West Point, Mississippi, believed that "positions should be defended only so long as not to risk safety of troops and materials required for active operations in the field. Meanwhile remove to safe locality all Government property on line of enemy's march, and consume or destroy all supplies within his reach." Davis dispatched Bragg to Augusta and ordered him to coordinate with Hardee in Savannah.[29]

By the twenty-fourth, Beauregard concluded that Sherman was moving to the Atlantic coast to reinforce Grant, and he pushed Hood to "take offensive and crush enemy's force in Middle Tennessee soon as practicable, to relieve Lee." Beauregard insisted that enough troops could be gathered in Georgia to destroy Sherman's army, which he estimated at about 40,000. Beauregard said Hood's offensive was the best use of that general's troops under the circumstances and that the defeat of Thomas's army in Tennessee by Hood "would compel Sherman, should he reach the coast of Georgia or South Carolina, to repair at once to the defence of Kentucky and perhaps Ohio, and thus prevent him from reinforcing Grant."[30]

Grant thought otherwise. "The blindness of the enemy, however, in ignoring his [Sherman's] movement, and sending Hood's army, the only considerable force he had west of Richmond and east of the Mississippi River, northward on an offensive campaign, left the whole country open and Sherman's route to his own choice."[31] In other words, the Confederates had completely surrendered the initiative to the Union.

On December 2, Beauregard wrote to Kirby Smith, the commander of the Trans-Mississippi, asking him to move in order to provide support for Hood's Tennessee offensive. He requested that Smith either send Hood two divisions or "threaten" Missouri in order to prevent Union troops that were reported going from there to Thomas from leaving. "I beg to urge upon you prompt and decisive action," Beauregard wrote. "The fate of the country may depend upon the result of Hood's campaign in Tennessee." Beauregard feared that success on Sherman's part might force Lee to abandon Richmond, and he thought that triumph by Hood in Tennessee or Kentucky would offset the loss of the Confederate capital. To help Hood's chances Beauregard wanted Smith to mount a diversion or reinforce Hood. A few days later, Seddon sent Smith similar instructions.[32]

This was desperation. The Confederate high command had a terrible time communicating with the Trans-Mississippi. In late December 1864, Davis was responding to letters Kirby Smith had sent in August.[33] Expecting any prompt, coordinated action from here was ludicrous.

Even worse for the Confederate cause were the results of Hood's misadventure. He had only half destroyed the Army of Tennessee around Atlanta. He impaled its weakened remains on the Union forces at Franklin, Tennessee, then advanced to Nashville, only to be overwhelmed by a Union counterattack on December 15. The 18,000 weary survivors of a once-mighty Confederate force withdrew into Mississippi. Lincoln, his ever watchful eye on military events, wired Major General George Thomas, of Chickamauga fame: "You made a magnificent beginning. A grand consummation is within your easy reach. Do not let it slip." Grant agreed. "Push the enemy now," he told Thomas, "and give him no rest until he is entirely destroyed."[34]

By December 9, Beauregard had begun losing hope that the South could keep Savannah. He determined that preserving Confederate forces was more important than holding cities and told Hardee to abandon Savannah if keeping it meant the destruction of his troops, a move Richmond backed. Beauregard simply lacked the men to stop Sherman.[35] Preserving the army was the best response available to the Confederates. Without it, they had no options at all. Even with it, they still had very few.

To help prevent the fall of Savannah, Davis asked Lee to detach men from his army. Lee balked, but agreed to send them if the government ordered it. Lee's insistence that he could not spare any men proved that Grant's strategy was working: Lee's forces were pinned by Grant, allowing Sherman freedom of movement. The Confederates' order to evacuate Savannah went out on December 19; the withdrawal began the next day.[36]

The truth was that the war was ending for the South, and its leadership had been reduced to grasping for straws. Hood had finished destroying most of his army at Nashville a few days before. Sherman could not be stopped from tearing the guts out of South Carolina. Moreover, Sherman's success devastated public support for the war in Georgia. One observer speculated in January 1865 that "if the railroad communication with Richmond is once effectually broken it will be difficult to rally this state."[37]

The Gray Wolf at Bay

LEE'S FORCES FARED BETTER than Georgia, but not much. On August 19, Union troops permanently destroyed a section of the Weldon Railroad at Globe Tavern. Confederate attacks proved unable to retrieve the position. The South now controlled only one railroad into Richmond, the Danville line. Lee concluded that Grant intended to drive the Confederates from their positions by cutting their supplies, and he pressed for the stockpiling of corn and the utmost effort in protecting this route.[38]

Secretary of War Seddon promised that all would be done to protect the railroad, but warned Lee that the Confederates faced a dire logistical situation. There were sufficient supplies in the South of oats and wheat, but deliveries were being delayed by raids. Moreover, supplies were strained by the fact that the South had to feed both Lee's and Hood's army from sources in the same region. Seddon warned him to not expect corn before the next crop came in, and that this crop was expected to be bad.[39] The Union strategy of exhaustion was taking its toll.

Lee's manpower situation was even worse. "Unless some measures can be devised to replace our losses," he told Seddon, "the consequences may be disastrous." He tried to make it clear that if the government could not fill his rapidly thinning ranks, the war was lost. Lee could do little more than rush men from spot to spot to plug holes, which was wearing them down. Lee wanted every man possible brought into the ranks and told Davis it was time to replace white military noncombatants with slaves.[40]

In October, Grant began pushing his units westward, south of Petersburg, forcing Lee to further thin his lines to meet the Union move. As winter
descended, the armies dug in. They skirmished some, but mostly fought the
weather. The Confederates also battled hunger. Grant waited for spring.[41]

Meanwhile, the Shenandoah Valley—so often the scene of stunning
Confederate success—became a place of Confederate disaster. In early August,
after returning from his Richmond raid and in the wake of the Hunter debacle,
Grant named Phil Sheridan commander of the Middle Military Division, which
encompassed the Shenandoah. Grant wanted continuous pressure on the Rebels and the destruction of their supplies. "Give the enemy no rest," he ordered
Sheridan on August 26. "Do all the damage to railroads and crops you can. Carry
off stock of all descriptions, and negroes, so as to prevent further planting. If the
war is to last another year, we want the Shenandoah Valley to remain a barren
waste." Sheridan went to work. Moreover, with Grant's approval, he attacked
and defeated Early's forces at Winchester on September 19. He defeated Early
again at Fisher's Hill three days later, breaking the Confederate forces in the
area. Sheridan suggested he withdraw back to Winchester, tearing up everything as he went, and send reinforcements to Grant, who promptly agreed.[42]

Famously, Sheridan wrote of his exploits that "the whole country from
the Blue Ridge to the North Mountains has been made untenable for a rebel
army." He cataloged the devastation: "I have destroyed over 2,000 barns, filled
with wheat, hay, and farming implements; over 70 mills, filled with flour and
wheat; have driven in front of the army over 4[,000] head of stock, and have
killed and issued to the troops not less than 3,000 sheep.... The people here
are getting sick of the war."[43]

On October 19, reinforced by Lee, Early launched a surprise attack on
Sheridan's forces at Cedar Creek, about 150 miles to the west of Richmond.
Early planned his attack well, and by skillfully deploying his men he was able
to bring the bulk of his force against one of Sheridan's flanks. The Confederates initially scored a stunning success, sending the Federals reeling, but
Early thought the Union would abandon the field, and so he failed to press
his advantage. Sheridan, who had not been present when the fight began,
returned at around ten-thirty. He counterattacked late in the afternoon, driving away Early's army.[44]

Early's 18,000 Confederates had come within a hairsbreadth of defeating
30,000 Federals, but the tactical and operational defensive would have been a
better choice for the Confederates in the Valley. After this the military forces
of both sides began leaving the desolated Shenandoah.[45]

Sheridan's valley operation presents in microcosm the application of the Union's strategy of exhaustion. Sheridan not only attacked Confederate armies but damaged their logistical base, destroyed their communications lines, and hammered civilian morale. Sheridan's campaign, like Sherman's, damaged the Confederacy's will *and* resources.[46]

Sherman's Other War

WHEN SHERMAN'S "BUMMERS" (as his men came to be called during their march to the sea) fetched up on the Georgia coast, they found Union ships waiting.[47] One had a note from Grant telling Sherman to bring his army north by ship and help finish Lee. Sherman had a few minor details to tie up first, such as taking Savannah. But this went quickly enough. He made the city a Christmas present to Lincoln. The president thanked and congratulated him, then added: "But what next? I suppose it will be safer if I leave Gen. Grant and yourself to decide."[48]

Even before Savannah fell, Grant had changed his mind about shipping Sherman's army north. The fact that all the demands upon sea transport would have meant a two-month delay played a large part in this. He told Sherman to suggest another course. "I do sincerely believe that the whole United States, North and South," Sherman replied, "would rejoice to have this army turned loose on South Carolina to devastate that State, in the manner we have done in Georgia, and it would have a direct and immediate bearing on your campaign in Virginia." Grant told him to go. "Break up the railroads in South and North Carolina," he added, "and join the armies operating against Richmond as soon as you can."[49]

Sherman made his preparation to begin the second stage of his grand march. His men looked forward to it. He told Halleck, "The whole army is burning with an insatiable desire to wreak vengeance upon South Carolina. I almost tremble at her fate, but feel that she deserves all that seems in store for her." He also revealed the effect he believed such a move would have. "I attach more importance to these deep incisions into the enemy's country, because this war differs from European wars in this particular. We are not only fighting hostile armies, but a hostile people, and must make old and young, rich and poor, feel the hard hand of war, as well as their organized armies." Sherman understood the nature of the war and of the enemy the Union faced. He had reached this conclusion early in the struggle and wrote as early as August 1861 that he thought the Union would have to kill most of the Southern men capable of bearing arms.[50]

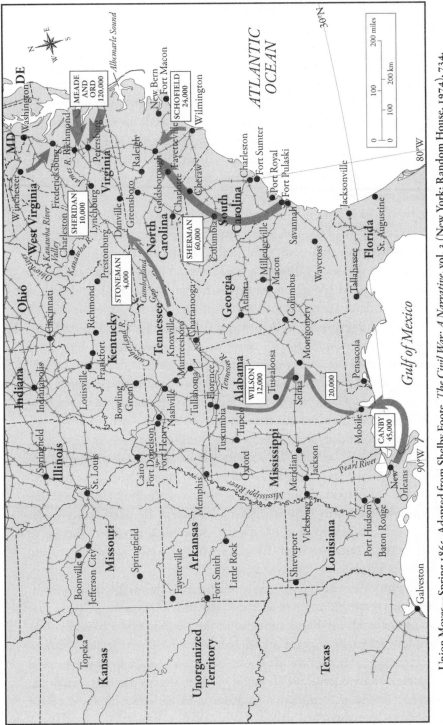

Union Moves—Spring 1865. Adapted from Shelby Foote, *The Civil War: A Narrative*, vol. 3 (New York: Random House, 1974), 734.

On December 31, Sherman told Halleck that he intended to invade South Carolina, aiming at Port Royal or its vicinity. "I do not think I can employ better strategy than I have hitherto done," he said, "namely, make a good ready and then move rapidly to my objective, avoiding a battle at points where I would be encumbered by wounded, but striking boldly and quickly when my objective is reached." He would "conduct war as though it could only terminate with the destruction of the enemy and the occupation of all his strategic points." Lincoln, ever vigilant, told Stanton, "It has occurred to me to say that while Gen. Sherman's *get a good ready* is appreciated, and is not to be overlooked, *time*, now that the enemy is wavering, is more important than ever before."[51]

In January 1865, Grant cemented the plans for what would be the last multipronged offensive of the war. Sherman's course, as we've seen, was laid out. Grant would remain locked with Lee's army. On January 18 he ordered Major General Edward Canby, in New Orleans, to head into Alabama and attack Mobile, Selma, and Montgomery, destroying any Confederate industry in these cities and busting up the railroads. This would be supported by another cavalry force coming south from Tennessee. In the valley in February, Sheridan would be again set loose, his objective soon becoming Lynchburg and the destruction of its canal and the nearby railroads. Cavalry under George Stoneman would also mount a raid from eastern Tennessee into North Carolina and Virginia. Grant had 600,000 men to do this, and a reserve force of another 300,000. The Confederates had perhaps 160,000 men. Shelby Foote, appropriately, branded this "Grant's Close-Out Plan."[52]

Sherman set off on February 1, 1865. Grant had prepared a number of subsidiary operations. Having lost confidence in Thomas because of his lackluster pursuit of Hood, Grant shipped Schofield's corps from Thomas's army in Tennessee to North Carolina. There, supported by naval forces under Porter, Schofield pushed up the Cape Fear River. Grant ordered Thomas to launch a cavalry raid into South Carolina, which was later redirected toward Lynchburg, Virginia.[53]

To counter Sherman's coming drive northward, Davis suggested that Beauregard concentrate his troops so as to menace the Union's path to Charleston, as well as maintain communications with Augusta, which was basically what Lee had suggested. Beauregard considered this unfeasible, believing he lacked the forces. Moreover, this would uncover the seacoast and allow the Union to march on Charleston. He put his forces on three already partially completed lines of defense between the Savannah River and Charleston, hoping to retard or even stop Sherman.[54]

At the end of December, Beauregard was sent to the Army of Tennessee. The command devolved upon Hardee, who was instructed to hold Charleston if he could, but to save the army if it became a choice between its destruction and the city's fall. Hardee planned to hold a line along the railroad running from Charleston to the Savannah River. "I am acting strictly on the defensive," he wrote Davis, "and unless heavily re-enforced must continue to do so."[55]

Hardee's reply demonstrated the core problem the Confederates faced in countering Sherman: a lack of men. The Confederacy struggled to fill the gaps with militia, reserves, and reinforcements from other commands.[56] The Confederate armies were simply breaking down, and some of this was due to the collapsing home front as families pled for their absent men to return and save them from chaos and starvation. Davis, in the wake of Atlanta's fall, made a speaking tour of Georgia and the Carolinas. On September 23, 1864, he told a crowd in Macon that Georgia had few remaining men from eighteen to forty-five to put into the ranks. His audience also heard a stunning revelation: two-thirds of Confederate soldiers were absent, "some sick," Davis said, "some wounded, but most of them absent without leave." Davis didn't exaggerate. Absenteeism, for all reasons, ran to 49 percent in the Army of Tennessee and 60 percent in the Army of Northern Virginia. In another speech Davis said there were a quarter of a million deserters "on the books of the war department."[57]

In 1865 the situation was worse. The only significant source of men for the defense of South Carolina was Hood's defeated army. Before his relief, Beauregard ordered Hood to begin sending elements east. Hood's army was demoralized and disorganized. This and the dilapidated condition of the rails and roads between Alabama and Augusta led Beauregard to remark that "no re-enforcements can be sent in time to General Hardee from that army."[58]

Despite Beauregard's report, and a subsequent warning that weakening the Army of Tennessee would endanger Mobile, Montgomery, and many other areas of Alabama, Davis ordered the bulk of Hood's old command east to join Hardee. "Sherman's campaign has produced bad effect on our people," Davis wrote. "Success against his future operations is needful to reanimate public confidence." Beauregard headed to South Carolina. The remnants of the Army of Tennessee followed in dribs and drabs without any clear overall leader, since the command responsibilities had become mixed and confused.[59]

Confederate efforts at finding more men proved not enough. By January 20, Hardee was warning that he would have to evacuate Charleston unless he was reinforced with 10,000 men. Lee argued for the city's abandonment if it could not be held. He also hoped that by gathering all of the men in Georgia and South Carolina, the Confederates could slow Sherman enough for Hood's old command to reach South Carolina.[60]

On February 2, the major Confederate generals commanding opposite Sherman, Beauregard, Hardee, D. H. Hill, and G. W. Smith, met at Green's Cut Station, Georgia. They thought that by the tenth or eleventh they could assemble 33,450 men to oppose what they believed was Sherman's advance toward Branchville, South Carolina, which occupied a central position nearly equidistant from Augusta, Charleston, and Columbia. Moreover, "during the pending negotiations for peace," meaning the talks then ongoing at Hampton Roads, "it was thought of the highest importance to hold Charleston and Augusta, as long as it was humanly possible." The dominant elements of their plan were to hold the line of the Combahee River as long as they could. If the enemy penetrated this, Hardee's forces would fall back on Charleston, fighting all the way, while Wheeler would split his cavalry and block movement to Columbia and Augusta. If the enemy pressed on to Charleston, Hardee would fall back to Columbia, combining his forces with those under Beauregard, who was to take up the Congaree River line southeast of Columbia.[61]

Beauregard explained everything to Davis. "The view presented is more discouraging than I had anticipated," Davis replied. The number of troops was lower than the Confederate president had expected. He put Beauregard back in command and told him to ask Governors Brown of Georgia and McGrath of South Carolina for more men. "You will realize the necessity for the rapid concentration of your forces," he told Beauregard, "and, if possible, the defeat of the enemy at some point south and east of Branchville and Augusta. To give time for such concentration and for the arrival of re-enforcements, every available means must be employed to delay the advance of the enemy, and, by operating on his lines of communication, to interfere with his supplies."[62]

But Davis's order to attack Sherman's lines of supply and communication was moot when given, and Beauregard knew it. The generals' conference of February 2 had clearly revealed this, as well as the advantages of what Sherman was doing: "The enemy moving with a certain number of days' rations for all his troops, with the hope of establishing a new base at Charleston after its fall, has in reality no lines of communication which can be threatened or cut. His overpowering force enables him to move into the interior of the country like an ordinary movable column." Beauregard made this clear to Davis.[63]

Upon taking up yet another new command, Beauregard outlined for Davis the problems he faced. "Our forces, about 20,000 effective infantry and artillery, more or less demoralized, occupy a circumference of about 240 miles from Charleston to Augusta. The enemy, well organized and disciplined, and flushed with success, numbering nearly double our force, is concentrated upon one point (Columbia) of that circumference. Unless I can concentrate rapidly here, or in my rear, all available troops, the result cannot be long doubtful." On February 14, Beauregard ordered the evacuation of Charleston in an effort to concentrate troops in the field. The Confederates began leaving two days later.[64]

All of this was for nothing. By February 15, Sherman's army was 20 miles from the South Carolina capital. Two days later, they began destroying manufacturing facilities, government buildings, and railroads in Columbia. Then they moved on, leaving the city in flames.[65]

In late February, insanity seemed to strike Beauregard. He proposed a plan that called for concentrating an army of "at least 35,000" against Sherman to defeat him and then Grant. Afterward, the army would "march on Washington to dictate a peace." Meanwhile, fearing Beauregard might place his army in a position where it would be captured, Davis sent Chief of Engineers Jeremy F. Gilmer, a friend of Beauregard's since their West Point days, to check on the general. Later Davis said he had given Gilmer oral instructions and a confidential note (now lost) to relieve Beauregard if the general did not withdraw toward Charlotte as told. Gilmer did not recall that Davis told him to take Beauregard's command in the event of disobedience, but this didn't matter; Beauregard did as ordered.[66]

Beauregard believed Sherman was advancing on Charlotte from Columbia and Alston and would reach Charlotte before Beauregard's forces could concentrate there. Beauregard then projected that "General Sherman will thence move on Greensborough, Danville, and Petersburg; or, if short of supplies, on Raleigh and Weldon, to form a junction with General Schofield." Lee did not think that Sherman could cover the route Beauregard projected if Confederate troops acted. "They can, at least, destroy or remove all provisions in his route, which I have again directed General Beauregard to do.... Everything on his route and Schofield's should be removed." Lee believed the Confederates wouldn't be able to meet Sherman in battle before the enemy reached Roanoke, Virginia. And he worried about what was coming, telling Davis that Richmond could not be held unless the "enemy can be beaten." "I think it prudent that preparations be made at all these points in anticipation of what may be necessary to be done."[67]

By this point, Lee commanded the Confederacy's armed forces. The Confederate Congress had made him commander in chief on February 6, a slap in

Davis's face, but one delivered nearly four years too late to benefit the Confederacy. February also saw a new secretary of war, John C. Breckinridge. When Lee took command of all the armies of the Confederacy, he wrote to Davis, insisting he must ask for the replacement of army commanders who failed or were neglectful. Since the army needed more men, he asked Davis to approve a general pardon for deserters returning within thirty days and that it be made public that this was the last such amnesty. Those who already had been pardoned for this crime, as well as those who had entered Union service, would not be eligible. Lee wanted it issued in his name instead of Davis's because the last such pardon (these had been many and frequent) had been in Davis's name, and Lee feared that repeating this would convince people that yet another one was in the wind.[68]

Lee's army had survived a desperate winter, but the New Year found them in horrendous straits. By the end of January, desertion plagued his force. Lee judged poor rations and lack of pay the primary causes. His army's suffering from insufficient food and forage became a constant refrain for Lee in early 1865. He warned his superiors: "Taking these facts in connection with the paucity of our numbers, you must not be surprised if calamity befalls us." By early February, Lee had accepted the impossibility of holding his more than 30 miles of defensive works around Richmond and Petersburg and took to destroying his correspondence after acting upon it.[69]

Lee now directed the war against Sherman as well as Grant. To deal with Sherman he urged concentration of all the forces in the Southern Department and an attack on Sherman to at least "embarrass" him if they could not stop his march. The Rebel generals had been unsuccessfully trying to do this since Sherman left Savannah. Lee told Bragg: "If you cannot arrest progress of enemy, concentrate your troops, hang upon his flanks, cripple and retard him, leaving no supplies in his route. Be bold and judicious."[70]

Lee also returned Joseph Johnston to command, placing Beauregard under him. Davis had not bowed to earlier pressure to once again appoint Johnston to an active post and agreed only because Lee wanted it. Johnston complained that Lee had done it too late and should have acted when he first became the commander in chief of the Confederate army, "if at all." Johnston also apparently at first feared that he had been placed in the position by Davis to serve as a "scapegoat" for the looming Southern defeat. The truth was that Davis was angry about the appointment, which gave Johnston tremendous pleasure.[71]

Johnston was one of the keys in a desperate fallback plan Lee concocted to stop Sherman. "I know of no one who had so much the confidence of the troops and people as General Johnston," he wrote Davis, "and believe he has capacity for the command." He insisted he would do everything he could to strengthen Johnston and, "should he be forced to cross the Roanoke, unite with him in a blow against Sherman before the latter can join General Grant." This would mean abandoning their position on the James River. Lee told Johnston, "I need not say that the first thing to be done is to concentrate all our forces and bring out every available man." Lee also pointed out to Johnston the danger of not stopping Sherman. If they couldn't halt him before he reached Greensboro or Danville, Lee's army would have to move.[72]

When he put Johnston in command, Lee ordered the immediate concentration of Confederate forces to drive back Sherman. "It is too late to expect me to concentrate troops capable of driving back Sherman," Johnston replied.[73] This was his habitual response, but this time he was right. It was indeed too late.

Three days later, Johnston described the impossibility of carrying out Lee's order to concentrate in the face of overwhelming Union superiority. He thought that if the approximately 25,000 forces he could gather united with Bragg around Fayetteville, North Carolina, they might stand a chance against Sherman. What followed was a convoluted and ultimately hopeless effort to combine the forces of Bragg, Hardee, Beauregard, and others under Johnston's command. He also suggested to Lee to divide his army, with half protecting Richmond and the other half joining with him to "crush Sherman." "We might then turn upon Grant."[74]

After taking Columbia, Sherman set out for Goldsborough, North Carolina. His objective did not become clear to the Confederates until mid-March, but this did not prevent them from trying to stop him in, as James McPherson put it, "the forlorn-hope style that had become Southern strategy." Johnston tried to pull together his scattered command in the hopes of checking Sherman; Lee believed "the effect would be of the greatest value."[75]

As Sherman's goal remained elusive, the mystery multiplied the effects of his move. Lee worried that Sherman aimed at Raleigh, which would cut the railroads and result in starvation for both Confederate armies. He urged Johnston to attack Sherman if he had a chance of success. But the Confederates also worried that Sherman was headed for Goldsborough, and sought to protect it. Johnston balked at facing Sherman's entire force in battle, believing himself outnumbered and outclassed—unless Lee's situation forced him. He was right on both points, far more than he realized. He believed Sherman had about 45,000 men, but the Union general had around 60,000 plus cavalry, as well as 30,000 more under Schofield marching from Wilmington.[76]

Johnston's plan, Lee informed Davis, was "to avoid a general engagement and endeavor to strike the enemy in detail." "The greatest calamity that could befall us," he continued, "is the destruction of our armies. If they can be maintained, we may recover from our reverses; but if lost we have no resource."[77] Lee was trying to maintain the Confederacy's center of gravity, its army; as long as he did so, the war would go on.

Hardee fought a part of Sherman's force near Averasboro, north of Fayetteville, on March 15, and then withdrew. The Confederates learned from this that Sherman's army was divided into two wings. Johnston concentrated his forces at Bentonville on March 19 and attacked the left. In the beginning, things went well for the Confederates. But the attack stalled. Sherman brought up more men and counterattacked on the twenty-first. The Confederates began to withdraw, and Sherman let them, seeing no need to waste the lives of his men fighting Johnston when he aimed at bigger things—helping Grant crush Lee's army.[78]

In the wake of Bentonville, Johnston cabled Lee: "Evening and night of 21st enemy moved toward Goldsborough, where Schofield joined him, and yesterday we came here. Sherman's course cannot be hindered by the small force I have. I can do no more than annoy him. I respectfully suggest that it is no longer a question whether you leave present position; you have only to decide where to meet Sherman. I will be near him." Lee asked him for the location he thought best to fight Sherman. Johnston suggested "this side" of the Roanoke River.[79]

By March 1865, Union forces were moving against the remaining vital points of the South. Sheridan's cavalry had advanced down the Shenandoah to White House; an army under Canby advanced on Mobile; and two raids dug into Alabama, while another struck via east Tennessee at Lynchburg. In the West, Grant had an army under Pope preparing to move against the Trans-Mississippi. Sherman's army continued happily tearing the guts out of South Carolina, while Grant's troops stared across the trench lines at Lee's pinned forces. Grant wrote later that "at this time the greatest source of uneasiness for me was the fear that the enemy would leave his strong lines about Petersburg and Richmond for the purpose of uniting with Johnston, before he was driven from them by battle or I was prepared to make an effectual pursuit."[80] He resolved to keep this from happening.

War Termination

*Gen. Sheridan says "If the thing is pressed I think that Lee
will surrender." Let the thing be pressed.*

—ABRAHAM LINCOLN, April 7, 1865

THE ENDINGS OF WARS are seldom clean. This is partly because the timing of their cessation is so unpredictable, and partly because too often little
thought is given to how to close the hostilities. The press of fighting the
war consumes so much energy that securing the peace for which one has
fought is too often neglected. When terminating a war there are two things
to keep in mind: how far to go militarily and what to ask for politically.
Both of these issues exerted a heavy influence on the ending of America's
Civil War.

Peace Overtures

IN DECEMBER 1863, the thoughts of some of the Confederacy's leaders turned to peace instead of war. Governor Zebulon B. Vance of North
Carolina urged the opening of negotiations. Davis explained to him
the impossibility of the success of any such attempt, recounting to him
Richmond's three previous failed efforts to launch such discussions with
Lincoln's government: Washington's refusal to accept the Confederate
commissioners sent before the outbreak of war; General Winfield Scott's
reception on Lincoln's behalf of a letter from Davis, to which the Union
gave no reply; and the rebuffed June 1863 effort of Confederate vice president Alexander Stephens.[1]

Davis explained to Vance the "despot" Lincoln's unwillingness to negotiate and his insistence upon complete surrender of all their slaves, with the
result that they would be in bondage to their former chattel. Lincoln, Davis
went on, had made it clear "that his purpose in his message and proclamation
was to shut out all hope that he would *ever* treat with us on *any* terms" short
of dissolving the Confederacy and its armies, taking an oath of allegiance,
and emancipating its slaves. Peace, Davis insisted, on terms other than "abject
submission to the enemy...is now impossible." The only way the South could

get acceptable terms was to convince the enemy that it could not subjugate them.[2]

On the most important matters Davis understood Lincoln's war aims very well. Earlier Lincoln would have made peace had the South simply disbanded its armies and the men returned home, but the opportunity for the South to end the war and keep its slaves had passed. The real obstacle was that Davis was unwilling to accept a peace that did not include Confederate independence.

There were other negotiating efforts as well. When the time of Johnston's departure from command of the Army of Tennessee neared, Horace Greeley, the famous newspaperman, arranged a meeting at Niagara Falls with Confederate agents working out of Ontario, Canada. What Greeley did not know was that he was being manipulated by the Confederate participants C. C. Clay Jr. and J. P. Holcombe, who had no real power to negotiate. The South had no interest in returning to the Union or making peace without being let go. These men hoped to "throw upon" the Union government "the odium of putting an end to all hope of negotiation, or of assuming a position which would enable our Government to approach it without compromising its own dignity." They intentionally clouded the South's stance on territorial integrity and "the authority of the states to manage their own social institutions," that is, slavery. Lincoln knew better than to trust them, but politically he felt he had no choice but to have someone see them. He gave Greeley the job.[3]

While Greeley negotiated in Niagara, Lincoln embarked upon his own effort, dispatching two emissaries to Davis to discover his terms for peace. Lincoln did this as a sop to the North's peace party and gave the agents, James F. Jaquess and James R. Gilmore, no official status or protection. They met with Davis and Benjamin on the night of July 17, 1864. The Confederate president ended the meeting after two hours, having no real desire to talk with anyone lacking official credentials. He sent the envoys on their way, telling them the South intended to have "Independence...or extermination."[4]

During this interview, Davis remarked, "We are not waging an offensive war, except so far as it is offensive-defensive,—that is, so far as we are forced to invade you to prevent your invading us."[5] Some would argue that this constitutes evidence of Davis having pursued an offensive-defensive strategy. The problem is that there is no evidence to support that contention other than this statement, one obviously delivered to justify the South's military actions to Lincoln's emissaries.[6]

Negotiating While Fighting:
The Hampton Roads Conference

FRANK BLAIR SR., the father of the Lincoln administration's former post-master general, Montgomery Blair, and one of the founders of the Republican Party, had been a friend of Davis's before the war, and approached Lincoln in December 1863 about visiting Davis and trying to make peace. Lincoln told him to bide his time until the Union forces had taken Savannah. Blair dutifully returned at the proper time, and Lincoln let him go south. After a second visit, and in response to a letter from Lincoln detailing the president's willingness to accept some Confederate emissaries, Blair returned with word of Davis's apparent willingness to negotiate an end to the conflict.[7]

Lincoln agreed to a conference with the Confederate delegates, Alexander Stephens, Robert M. Hunter, and John A. Campbell, but made it clear to Grant that this should not interfere with any of the general's plans, insisting that Grant fight while the negotiations proceeded. He reiterated his point on February 1, telling the general, "Let nothing which is transpiring change, hinder, or delay your military movements." Grant promised that there would be no "armistice."[8]

Lincoln dispatched Secretary of State Seward but gave him little leash. He instructed him to make sure the Rebels understood that three things were considered "indispensable": "1st, the restoration of the national authority throughout all the States; 2d, no receding by the Executive of the United States on the slavery question from the position assumed thereon in the late annual message to Congress, and in the preceding documents; 3d, no cessation of hostilities short of an end of the war and the disbanding of all the forces hostile to the Government." Anything that did not clash with the above would be considered. Lincoln wanted their words reported to him and told Seward matter-of-factly: "You will not assume to definitely consummate anything."[9] As always, Lincoln maintained an iron grip over matters political.

Seward arrived at Fortress Monroe to meet the Confederates on February 1. The whole effort nearly collapsed at this point over whether the Confederates had come to negotiate the fate of "one common country" or "two countries." Lincoln had insisted upon the former; Davis wanted the latter. Grant, who spoke with the Rebel commissioners, believed not seeing them would have an ill effect on the Union and telegraphed his views to Lincoln. The president bent and rendezvoused with the emissaries at Hampton Roads on February 3, 1865. Some of the press pilloried him for agreeing to the meeting.[10]

During the encounter Lincoln's opponents made no commitments but pressed for an armistice. Lincoln held fast. He would grant no stoppage of hostilities that was not an end to the war and did not include the disbanding of the Confederate armies and Southern recognition of the end of slavery.[11]

Nothing came of the Hampton Roads Conference, but one must give Lincoln credit for having understood the danger of granting what the Confederate representatives wanted. "An armistice," he had written in September 1864, "—a cessation of hostilities—is the end of the struggle, and the insurgents would be in peaceable possession of all that has been struggled for." He realized it would give the South a breather and that there might be difficulty restarting the fighting should the South still insist upon secession. Lincoln kept his political objectives clearly in view and made sure his negotiations and military pressure aligned with this. Sun Tzu gave some useful advice to keep him mind when negotiating with your foe: "When the enemy's envoys speak in humble terms, but he continues his preparations, he will advance.... When their language is deceptive but the enemy pretentiously advances, he will retreat.... When the envoys speak in apologetic terms, he wishes a respite.... When without a previous understanding the enemy asks for a truce, he is plotting."[12]

Negotiating with the Enemy: The Ord Talks

IN THE WAKE of the failed Hampton Roads Conference, Union major general E. O. C. Ord, convinced that the political leaders were afraid to talk peace, decided that the soldiers should. He met with his old friend Longstreet on February 25, 1865, and suggested that Grant and Lee discuss terms. Longstreet, Lee, Davis, and Breckinridge conferred in Richmond on the twenty-sixth and agreed to take up Ord's idea. Lee felt no optimism about Grant proposing any terms other than return to the Union, and he was unsure if this was acceptable to the people of the South.[13]

Grant went up the chain of command to Lincoln. The president was not as understanding as Ord and decisively asserted his prerogative. "You are not to decide, discuss, or confer upon any political question," he told Grant. Moreover, he ordered him not to meet with Lee unless it was to discuss the surrender of Lee's army, or on "some minor and purely military matter." Grant obeyed, telling Lee on March 4 that he had no authority to discuss the proposed matters; that rested with the president.[14]

The Confederacy's Impending Collapse

IN EARLY MARCH 1865, Breckinridge, the new Confederate secretary of war, asked Lee to give his assessment of the military condition of the South. Lee gave him no reason for optimism. He began by saying, "It must be apparent to every one that it is full of peril and requires prompt action." He then recited a litany of problems, beginning with the near bankruptcy of the Confederacy's supply base. "Unless the men and animals can be subsisted," he insisted, "the army cannot be kept together, and our present lines must be abandoned. Nor can it be moved to any other position where it can operate to advantage without provisions to enable it to move in a body." The only solution he saw was contributions from the people, but the usefulness of this would be governed by the available transport. Lee worried that his supply position would soon force the abandonment of their positions around Richmond and Petersburg, but he did not believe that this was necessarily a fatal blow to the Confederate cause.[15]

Lee went on to note the numerical inferiority of Johnston's army compared with its foe; he had little hope of it gaining any success. He felt the same way about the other portions of the Confederacy east of the Mississippi. "While the military situation is not favorable," Lee said, "it is not worse than the superior numbers and resources of the enemy justified us in expecting from the beginning. Indeed, the legitimate military consequences of that superiority have been postponed longer than we had reason to anticipate. Everything," Lee wrote, "in my opinion, has depended and still depends upon the disposition and feelings of the people."[16]

Historians Clifford Dowdey and Louis Manarin insist that Lee, Breckinridge, Longstreet, and others realized the sad state of the South's strategic position, but none of these men "was willing to assume the responsibility of trying to convince Davis of this."[17] This may have been true, but it ignores the pivotal point: Davis was not ready to end the war on any terms other than independence for the South. He might negotiate because it could gain the South an advantage, but his mind was fixed. The killing therefore went on.

Surrendering Lee's Army

ON MARCH 24, 1865, GRANT ISSUED orders for an offensive against Lee to begin on the twenty-ninth. Sheridan's cavalry would attack Lee's communications while major elements of the Army of the Potomac moved to the south of Petersburg. Sherman, by this time, had his army at Goldsborough, North Carolina, and he and Grant had discussed the possibility of Sherman moving to help Grant against Lee. Sherman planned to "threaten Raleigh" but then turn and cross the Roanoke River and attack the railroads supporting Richmond and Petersburg. Despite the immensity of Union progress, Grant still had his fears. "I was firmly convinced that Sherman's crossing the Roanoke would be the signal for Lee to leave. With Johnston and him combined, a long, tedious, and expensive campaign, consuming most of the summer, might become necessary....I therefore determined not to delay the movement ordered."[18]

On March 29, 1865, the Army of the Potomac unwound itself one last time. Lincoln was there. "I hope you will stay to see it out," Stanton told him. "If you are on the ground there will be no pause." Grant didn't pause. His lines broken, Lee abandoned Petersburg and Richmond on the night of April 2. Grant ordered a pursuit.[19]

Davis and Lee had discussed what to do in the event of the abandonment of Petersburg and Richmond. Lee rejected a suggestion delivered from Hood to withdraw into central Tennessee. The army had to move southward, in the direction of its source of supply and the homes of most of its men. They decided to try to unite with Johnston at Danville, Virginia, "the combined forces to be hurled upon Sherman in North Carolina, with the hope of defeating him before Grant could come to his relief. Then the more Southern States, freed from pressure and encouraged by this success, it was expected, would send large reinforcements to the army, and Grant, drawn far from his base of supplies into the midst of a hostile population, it was hoped, might yet be defeated, and Virginia be delivered from the invader."[20] But this was a pipe dream.

After Richmond fell, Davis issued a proclamation to the Confederacy in an effort to soften the blow. In this he made perhaps his most ridiculous statement related to strategy. To Davis the Confederacy was now "relieved from the necessity of guarding cities and particular points, important but not vital to our defence with our army free to move from point to point, and strike in detail the detachments and garrisons of the enemy." Confederate strategy had reached the level of farce. Of this statement Davis wrote later, "viewed by the light of subsequent events, it may fairly be said it was over-sanguine."[21]

Clearly, Lee had to come to terms with Grant or face annihilation. But even after abandoning Richmond and Petersburg, Lee did not immediately admit this. When he received a letter from Grant urging his surrender, he insisted that he did not think his situation as hopeless as the one Grant depicted but, in a confusing manner, wrote that he was willing to discuss the surrender of the troops under his command, though not that of the Army of Northern Virginia. On April 9, Lee wrote that he had received Grant's terms and was willing to talk. He surrendered his forces the same day.[22]

Later, Lee elaborated on the reasons for the collapse of his army. His troops, he said, lacked "boldness and decision," as well as the confidence that once characterized them. He believed this arose from the general "state of feeling" present in the country, which manifested in the pressure the men received to return home. When he withdrew his army from its line between Hatcher's Run and the Appomattox River on April 2, it simply disintegrated. In other words, at the end, Confederate public opinion collapsed, as well as the Confederate armies.[23]

Lee then gave Davis his assessment of the Confederacy's circumstances: "From what I have seen and learned, I believe an army cannot be organized or supported in Virginia, and as far as I know the condition of affairs, the country east of the Mississippi is morally and physically unable to maintain the contest unaided, with any hope of ultimate success." He then offered Davis an option, one obviously distasteful to Lee: "A partisan war may be continued, and hostilities protracted, causing individual suffering and the devastation of the country, but I see no prospect by that means of achieving a separate independence." He left it for Davis to decide, but "to save useless effusion of blood," Lee continued, "I would recommend measures to be taken for suspension of hostilities and the restoration of peace.[24]

Davis and His Cabinet Fight On

ON APRIL 10, DAVIS RECEIVED his first news of Lee's surrender at Appomattox. On April 12, after receiving official word, he wept. His government decamped from Danville, Virginia, for Greensboro, North Carolina. He told Johnston, "Let me hear from you there. I will have need to see you to confer as to future action." He told North Carolina's Governor Vance that an army that was willing to fight on would rally soldiers to it and "daily gather strength." He then set about trying to concentrate the remaining Confederate forces in the East on the Yadkin River in front of Salisbury, North Carolina.[25]

Meanwhile, Davis tried to gather forces from Georgia and Alabama to meet the Union thrusts in Alabama. Richard Taylor concentrated what forces he could at Columbus, Georgia, but Major General Dabney Maury was forced to evacuate Mobile. Taylor, though, was not sure what to do next. "Can unite everything with Cobb, in Georgia," Taylor wrote, "or cover supply region of Alabama and Mississippi and preserve communication with Mississippi River.

Enemy has power to occupy country south and east of Alabama River, as his large force engaged at Mobile is now liberated. Decision should be had at once as to which of the courses to adopt. Ignorant of the policy [strategy] of the Government, I cannot decide."[26]

Davis's reply was delusional. He expected to provide Taylor with men from Lee's old army, and remained a pedant obsessed with maintenance of his own military authority even when little remained to command. He told Howell Cobb, a former Georgia governor and now a Confederate general, "Exercise large discretionary power and report to me, that the proper orders, general and special, may be issued to ratify the action taken. In the meantime let it be understood that the organizations are temporary, or contingent, but made by my authority."[27]

Davis met with Beauregard, Johnston, and his cabinet on April 11–13. Beauregard gave a disheartening report, to which Davis responded with great though obviously misplaced optimism. The generals, as well as three cabinet members, Secretary of War Breckinridge, Secretary of the Navy Stephen Mallory, and Postmaster General John H. Reagan, did not share his feelings. Davis expressed views that staggered even Beauregard, insisting that the South still possessed vast resources and that a few weeks would see the Confederacy have the largest armies it had ever possessed. Three-quarters of the men in Lee's and Johnston's armies were at home when they were supposed to be in the ranks; they would now be gathered.[28] The Confederacy's Clausewitzian trinity had shattered: no rationality directed national policy, no passion for the struggle emanated from the people, and no creative spirit arose from its military remnants.

Surrendering Johnston's Army

AT THEIR APRIL 13 MEETING, Davis and his cabinet reached the consensus that they had to negotiate with Sherman. Johnston met with him near Hillsborough, North Carolina, on the seventeenth. Emissaries of Davis's government arrived the next day, and the agreement that followed was drawn up by Sherman. It included a cease-fire, disbandment of Confederate forces, recognition of the governments of the states of the South (if their respective leaders took the oath of allegiance), restoration of the Federal court system, and a general amnesty.[29] An armistice was secured, which lasted from April 18 to 26. But this was still not peace.

Pressure upon Davis to surrender began mounting from his official family. Benjamin, the Confederate secretary of state, cogently assessed the South's disastrous military situation for Davis. Lee's army was gone; the people no longer supported the war effort; desertion was rife in Johnston's army, which had fewer than 20,000 effectives; there were almost no sources of weapons, supplies, and powder. "The Confederacy is, in a word," Benjamin continued, "unable to continue the war by armies in the field, and the struggle can no longer be maintained in any other manner than by a guerrilla or partisan warfare. Such a warfare is not, in my opinion, desirable, nor does it promise any useful result." Benjamin thought it would do more damage to the people of the South than it would to the enemy, and in light of what the South's people had already endured, he doubted that they would be willing to prosecute such a war except under the most extreme duress. "Seeing no reasonable hope of our ability to conquer our independence," continued Benjamin, "admitting the undeniable fact that we have been vanquished in the war, it is my opinion that these terms should be accepted, being as favorable as any that we, as the defeated belligerent, have reason to expect or can hope to secure."[30]

Reagan urged Davis to accept Sherman's offer, as did Breckinridge, Mallory, and George Davis, the attorney general. Davis described the whole event as "one which is very painful for me to meet," but in the end he bowed to the pressure from his cabinet and told Johnston to accept Sherman's terms.[31]

Other events intervened, however. Lincoln was shot at Ford's Theater on the evening of April 14 and died the next morning. Andrew Johnson succeeded to the presidency. He disapproved of Sherman's offer and demanded Johnston's surrender based upon the articles given Lee at Appomattox. On April 24, Sherman told Johnston the Confederates had forty-eight hours to comply before he again took up the sword.[32]

Before the beginning of negotiations, Johnston and Davis had prepared for the possibility of the failure of the talks by determining a retreat route for Johnston's army, but Johnston elected to end the war by taking Sherman's offer. "Had I known that the surrender of the army was in Genl. Johnston's mind predetermined," Davis later insisted, "it would have given me no embarrassment to find a successor who would have had different ideas of the duty of a soldier to the government whose commission he bore, and who would not have failed to remember the obligations he avowed when that commission was accepted."[33]

Johnston really had little choice. With the signing of the armistice, many of his men had decided the war was over, or just about so, and several thousand deserted. Moreover, Johnston's commanders believed their men would not fight again. Johnston initiated negotiations with Sherman on the twenty-fifth and surrendered his army to Sherman the next day. Kirby Smith lowered the Confederate flag in the Trans-Mississippi a month later, on May 26.[34] The few remaining Confederate forces also soon left the field.

Assessing War Termination

LINCOLN HANDLED THE ENDING of the war masterfully. He set the political terms and kept military pressure on the enemy until they buckled. He also correctly matched the military means to achieving the Union's political ends. President Johnson did the same.

Any judgment of Davis must inevitably be harsher, and not just because the Confederates were defeated. It was obvious to any rational observer that after the surrender of Lee's army the Confederacy had lost the war. Moreover, since it was clear that a Union peace would not mean the extermination of the Southern people, there was no reason for him to push for continuing the struggle and to even consider carrying on the war from the Trans-Mississippi. Functionally, surrender for most whites in the South (except for some key political leaders) meant a return to the status quo antebellum, minus the ownership of slaves. Davis needlessly extended the war. This meant the bloodshed went on.

Conclusion

IN WAR'S SHADOW

*Now, gentlemen, that was true strategy because the enemy
was diverted from his purpose.*

—ABRAHAM LINCOLN, April 6, 1865

TO FOCUS PURELY ON MILITARY STRATEGY during the Civil War
may seem to some too coldly calculating an approach to a conflict that not
only took 620,000 lives but also defined both sides' fundamental vision of
their country—its past and its destiny—and had effects that endure to this
day. One of the reasons to study the past, however, is to learn from it. Otto
von Bismarck famously noted that "a fool learns from experience. A wise man
learns from the experience of others." This, in a small way, is what this book
is intended to do.

This is unapologetically top-down history, and the best place to start
a strategic evaluation of the antagonists is at the top, in the area of policy,
which, as I argued in the introduction, is the foundation from which strategy
flows. Ideally, in a democracy, the civilian leadership determines policy and
the military aligns its strategy to conform to it. In terms of the Civil War, this
meant the antagonists were Abraham Lincoln and Jefferson Davis. Obviously,
Lincoln was by far the more successful. He *always* kept the political objective
firmly in his mind, and he *always* ensured that his subordinates, military as
well as civilian, hewed to the administration's political course. For example,
he quickly and decisively checked Seward's grasping for power at the beginning of the war and later gave him clear parameters for talks with the Rebels.
He announced emancipation when he, rather than generals such as Frémont
and Hunter, had determined that its time had come. He refused to entertain
disingenuous Confederate negotiation attempts in 1864 and 1865, knowing
that their function was purely to thwart Union military efforts. He followed
the path of fighting while negotiating, for to do otherwise would have demonstrated weakness and undermined his source of leverage. He successfully
used military strength as a tool of policy.

Jefferson Davis, a man utterly determined to protect his military prerogative, failed to control the political realm. He allowed his generals to decide

when to extend the war into Kentucky, though this effectively destroyed the Confederacy's strategic position in the West. He knew what he wanted—independence—but he came up short in coordinating and guiding the various elements of Confederate national power to achievement of this objective.

Davis was deficient in a related field as well: appointing the right people to the right positions. Braxton Bragg's querulous nature and operational and battlefield mistakes effectively undermined his ability to command, yet Davis left him in charge of the Army of Tennessee. He believed he had no choice; such was not the case. He could have reached deeper into the Confederate bench, promoting a more junior leader, or he could have brought in someone from another army and weathered the political storm for doing so. Davis also erred in repeatedly placing Joseph Johnston in major positions of authority when the general's performance and behavior up to and during the Peninsula Campaign amply demonstrated that he lacked the temperament and skills necessary for higher command, as well as a willingness to obey orders.

By comparison, Lincoln dealt with the civil-military realm effectively, though he stumbled his way toward success. The tragically flawed—there seems no other phrase for it—relationship between him and McClellan remains a case in point. Lincoln deferred too long to his young general on pivotal issues, such as allowing him to determine the tempo of the war. He undermined his own authority by visiting McClellan instead of having McClellan visit him. Both of these things changed after Lincoln issued his famous January 27, 1862, order for all the armies to advance.[1]

Both Lincoln and Davis sometimes interfered more than they should have. Each occasionally undermined the authority of his commanders in the field, encouraging what Sun Tzu called paralysis and doubt.[2] Political interference in military affairs is often necessary, but as British author Sir Frederick Maurice writes, the leader should have the judgment to determine the proper kind of intervention.[3]

In the case of Lincoln this was particularly true in the conduct of the Peninsula Campaign. Lincoln is rightly admired for the hard line he took with his generals, and he learned far more about strategy than many of them. But his constant intervention in McClellan's Peninsula efforts, an adventure that Lincoln himself had approved, forced perpetual changes in the operational plan. This gave McClellan an excuse for inaction while heightening his already potent paranoia regarding the motives of his civilian superiors. Obviously, Lincoln meddled because he no longer trusted McClellan to act. Lincoln should have replaced him rather than keep him on and then try to exert control over military matters that he did not yet fully understand. This same problem of trust also arose with Meade in 1863–64, and the root of it was the same: a failure to act. As for Grant, Lincoln gave him more leeway, certainly, but never took his eyes off him and was not afraid to intervene, which his reaction to Early's 1864 raid proves. Lincoln had determined there was truth to the maxim French president Georges Clemenceau would utter more than a half century later: "War is too important to be left to the generals."

Davis also mistrusted many of his generals; they had given him good reason. An extreme example of the resulting interference was his attempt to direct the Confederate response to Sherman's 1864 Meridian raid from his desk in Richmond. Davis could have taken a page from Lincoln's book and learned to replace generals who consistently failed or did not do as they were ordered, but he never did.

Both sides often created ineffective command structures. The short period between McClellan's demotion and Halleck's ascension, during which Lincoln and Stanton tried to run the war, was a disastrous one for the Union. The multipronged Union strategy that McClellan was implementing simply collapsed, robbing the Union of a chance to secure victory in 1862. On the other hand, had the war ended that summer, Lincoln would not have arrived at the political moment that allowed him to free the slaves.

Retaining Halleck as general in chief for as long as Lincoln did was a mistake. One cannot fault him for making the appointment. It seemed perfectly reasonable, indeed even enlightened, at the time. Halleck had produced successes while others had failed. But when Halleck's irresoluteness became appallingly apparent, Lincoln should have relieved him. He decided that his general in chief was "little more than a first-rate clerk." And yet he kept him on. Halleck would have made a superb chief of staff for someone tough enough to make him do his job. Union major general Phil Kearny, who was killed at Second Manassas, thought one command solution would have been to appoint McClellan general in chief and place someone else at the head of the Army of the Potomac; he forecast disaster otherwise.[4] The establishment of the bizarre command arrangement that allowed Hooker to answer directly to Lincoln during his short tenure as head of the Army of the Potomac was also a terrible mistake that laid a foundation for disaster.

On the Confederate side, Davis made himself the de facto general in chief, a job for which he was miserably ill equipped. He jealously guarded his control over military affairs, reducing his five secretaries of war to administrative assistants and vetoing the Confederate Congress's efforts to create a general staff as well as appoint a true commanding general, someone the Confederacy desperately needed but got only in February 1865. By then, of course, it was too late.

Some blame for Confederate defeat is also occasionally placed on the Confederate military department system. Historian David M. Potter insists that it hindered cooperation between forces, sometimes producing artificial segmentation that contributed to disasters such as the loss of Vicksburg, where the system prevented the dispatch of aid from the Trans-Mississippi Department.[5] But as we've seen, the departmental system in no way prevented Davis from trying to bring troops from the Trans-Mississippi in an attempt to save Vicksburg. The system did impede effective collaboration between Bragg and Kirby Smith during their 1862 invasion, but this was a result of Davis's failure to grant Bragg's request to have Smith placed under his command. The system did have some other minor influences, but it was not an overbearing reason for Southern defeat. Moreover, the Union also had a departmental system that exerted friction on Union operations, a point generally overlooked in this argument.

The opposites in uniform exhibited a variety of responses to civilian control. Some deferred, such as Winfield Scott and Grant. Others rebelled, including Frémont and Leonidas Polk. Others treated their political masters with disdain; among these were McClellan, Joseph Johnston, and P. G. T. Beauregard. Other vacillated, hesitated, and complained, as did Halleck and Bragg. Still others managed their superiors well and learned to understand them, such as Robert E. Lee and (again) Grant. The reactions of the generals to their civilian masters often played out in microcosm with their military subordinates. Lee and Grant could work with those under them; Bragg could not. The personalities of these commanders and these various relationships influenced the nature of the war, its intensity, its scale, and thus the shape of its strategy and operations.

In addition to failing on the battlefield, McClellan also did not want to prosecute the war in the manner deemed necessary by his political superiors. He resisted the administration's judgment that it was necessary to seize or destroy Confederate property and force Southern civilians to feel the "hard hand of war." Disagreeing with his superiors was acceptable. But pushing back against their direct orders was not. At this point, someone had to bend or resign. McClellan yielded.

McClellan's resistance to accepting the administration's abandonment of conciliation for escalation relates directly to another point: he did not understand the nature of the war. McClellan wanted to wage war against the Confederate government and army and not have it touch Southern civilians. He failed to grasp that most of the white population of the South, and some of the black, opposed the Union. In the end, McClellan's strategic failure to prosecute the war vigorously protracted it and made escalation nearly inevitable. The result was precisely the kind of destruction that he had labored to prevent.

McClellan was not alone in this. Few leaders on either side really understood this war's essential nature, particularly in the beginning, and as a result, their respective strategic approaches were either shortsighted, counterproductive, or both. Sherman was the rarity, realizing very early on that the war would descend into horrific carnage. This was one of the things that drove him to what seems to have been a nervous breakdown in late 1861.[6]

BUT IF STRATEGY RESTS UPON POLICY, our focus necessarily returns to the policy makers. Lincoln came to his post knowing nothing of military affairs and having no pretensions that he did. Davis, a graduate of West Point, a Mexican War hero, and a former secretary of war, reached his office believing that he knew everything about strategy, campaigns, and tactics, and that not only did he not need to learn from his subordinates, they had nothing to teach him. Davis exercised an enormous amount of control over the Confederate war. He generally restrained ambitious subordinates such as Beauregard in the beginning. But when he decided in late 1862 that the Confederacy should go on the offensive, he saw to it that it did. He approved Lee's invasion in the summer of 1863. He shifted Longstreet to Tennessee later in the same year and made this the focus of Confederate operations. He made the decision to put Joe Johnston in command of the Army of Tennessee, thus dictating the Southern response to Sherman's 1864 invasion of Georgia.

But Davis failed as a strategist, an issue over which there has been much discussion.[7] Davis never produced any document with the wider-angled vision of Lincoln, Scott, McClellan, Bragg, or Grant. His habitual response to military problems was to concentrate and attack the enemy in detail. Davis could sometimes think operationally—within specific circumstances—but he was predominantly a tactician, which is not surprising considering his tendency to focus on detail. He never sat down with anyone and tried to figure out how to win the war, nor, in the vein of Lincoln, did he ever articulate a clear vision for how the South could achieve its political objective of independence.

Lincoln, too, could be a tactician, such as when he told Hooker to make sure he used all of his men when he had to fight. But Lincoln learned to focus on the larger issues. Early in the war he proposed operational plans to his generals—designs for advances against the enemy—and never stopped doing so, especially if they failed to come up with their own. More important, he could think strategically, such as with his idea of simultaneous offensives, a plan at which both he and McClellan arrived, albeit by different paths and seemingly independently. Lincoln possessed what is one of the greatest qualities in leadership: the ability to learn. Able rhetorically to soar above all others in his vision and evocation of the Union, he was also a ruthless pragmatist when it came to measures related to winning the war. He said once in 1862 that he "was pretty well cured of any objection to any measure, except want of adaptedness to putting down the rebellion." His record bears out his words.

Perhaps Lincoln's greatest strategic success was in deciphering the Confederacy's center of gravity, as he did in the summer of 1862: the Rebel army. Capturing Richmond was symbolically important and not without utility, but it was strategically unnecessary. The rebellion lived and moved with its army. The problem for Lincoln, though, became making his generals understand this.

Yet some of the claims of Lincoln's strategic mastery have been inflated. He is usually cast as a strong and decisive warlord who devised his own ideas for fighting the war and imposed them on his generals through sheer will. Moreover, there has been great insistence that Lincoln was a military genius, a master strategist. Yet his strategic ideas, barring emancipation, had virtually no impact on the course of the war. Lincoln's concept of simultaneous pressure is usually singled out as the key to eventual Union victory, but Lincoln never succeeded in getting his generals to implement his vision. Grant's strategy for 1864 was one the general had developed on his own, independent of his commander in chief. Lincoln concluded early that the Army of the Potomac should target and destroy Lee's army, but he never succeeded in getting McClellan, Burnside, Hooker, or Meade to do this. In the end, one of Lincoln's greatest military successes was the seizure of Norfolk, which was important but not critical to the war's outcome.

In truth, Lincoln doubted his own military ability; this doubt afflicted him with indecision in military affairs and therefore limited his strategic contributions. It is very likely that if he had indeed taken the field, as he himself admitted he was considering on at least two different occasions, he could have produced results that would rank him among the great military geniuses. Attorney General Edward Bates noted in his diary that Lincoln was "an excellent man, and, in the main wise, but he lacks *will* and *purpose*, and, I greatly fear he, has not *the power to command*."[8] In some ways events bear out Bates's critique.

Lincoln's genius lay where it all started—in the political realm. He navigated a perilous precipice throughout the war, struggling with infighting among domestic factions and threats from overseas. He managed these magnificently. He also clearly understood the relationship between military power and political ends. He held the political reins tight and saw to it that the military means were adjusted to policy ends. But this did not make him a great strategist.

There were others who possessed at least some strategic vision. Winfield Scott comes to mind. His Anaconda Plan may not have been what his superiors wanted and also was not based upon an accurate assessment of the enemy's willingness to fight, but it provided both an education for Lincoln and a firm foundation for the Union's strategic thinking. McClellan prepared strategic and operational plans that were often sweeping and original in content, if simultaneously and exasperatingly self-serving. McClellan's multipronged offensive strategy, in its basic concepts, was one of the Union's soundest approaches to fighting the war; it was also one that could have delivered an early Union triumph.

In the end, of course, Grant and Sherman provided the strategy that finally delivered victory over a skilled but far weaker opponent: constant, simultaneous pressure, exhaustion of the enemy's resources by raids, the destruction of his armies by attrition, and the crushing of his will via all of these. Of all the generals on both sides, none better understood the necessity of attacking the enemy's will to fight, or the means of doing so, than Sherman.

Strategic thinking in the South was almost nonexistent. The much-reviled Braxton Bragg produced his plan to strip fringe areas and concentrate. The problem for the South became how to use this power once it was assembled. The South chose to move to the strategic offensive in 1862, but with operational plans that were shoddy, as in the case of those in the West, or based upon a faulty understanding of the situation that actually faced them, as in the East.

Lee realized the strategic importance of Union public opinion to the North's continued prosecution of the war, and saw striking at it as a means of achieving the South's political objective. But he chose the wrong means of attacking what was certainly the Union's center of gravity. Winning a victory in the North would have given Lee only a victory in the North, not the war. Protracting the war, robbing the Union of success so that it became apparent to Union voters that Lincoln was failing them, was the best hope the South possessed. Lee knew the latter. He also understood the linkage between battlefield success or failure and public opinion, something most of his peers on either side failed to grasp. Strategically, however, Lee was given little opportunity to think or plan this way until it was too late to matter.

Operationally, it was a slightly different matter. McClellan's operational planning was in many ways superb. He formed clear objectives; he labored to coordinate ends and means; he saw to it that there were multiple supporting actions designed to disperse enemy strength; he ensured the protection of his forces while making it possible to damage the enemy; he guaranteed bases of supply and lines of communication. The problem was that often he simply couldn't execute his own plans, nor construct ones that were not almost entirely devoted to supporting the army he himself led. He was at the center of it all and intended to deliver the decisive blow.

Halleck occasionally provided solid operational planning, though he was a slave to theory, particularly the kind of theory formulated during the Napoleonic Wars. Clausewitz himself wrote that theory "is meant to educate the mind of the future commander."[9] In other words it was a learning tool, not a diktat. Old Brains had ingested much Jomini, but not enough to understand it fully. For example, a standard Halleck criticism of offensives at multiple points was that this violated the principle of concentration and forced the Union to operate on exterior lines, thus giving the Confederates the advantage of the stronger, interior position. The problem with this—one pointed out in Jomini's day—was that if one side possessed greatly superior numbers and a willingness to use them, it did not matter that they occupied the "exterior position." They could simply overwhelm the opponent.[10] Halleck lacked the ability to distinguish between the strategic and operational arenas, and the respective use of force in each realm.

Grant and Sherman both deserve high marks for their operational planning. They had clear objectives, ensured that their plans aligned with a larger strategy, and tried to inflict maximum damage upon the enemy while preserving their own forces. They were also flexible. They knew the rules, but they also knew when to chuck the rule book and do what worked. Grant's abandoning his supply lines on his march to Vicksburg showed this. Sherman's willingness after the fall of Atlanta not to rest on his laurels but to examine various options and keep things moving demonstrated his mental litheness. His march was a masterpiece of operational opportunism.

Generally, Confederate operational planning suffered. The objectives tended to be unclear, such as in the case of Bragg's and Kirby Smith's ill-fated fall 1862 offensive, or simply unobtainable unless one could bend the laws of physics (virtually anything from the warped quills of James Longstreet or P. G. T. Beauregard). Unsurprisingly, Lee emerges as the best of the Confederate operational warriors. He generally understood what he hoped to obtain by his actions (though he was often sloppy in relaying this). When

Lee moved, he tried to know what was going on with his own forces as well as those of the enemy. If he didn't know, he reacted swiftly as things became clearer. This was particularly true in 1862 and 1864. He consistently read the enemy commanders well and always found a way of maintaining a psychological superiority over them (a wonderful operational advantage). One of his few weaknesses—though arguably also a strength—was changing his plans on the march. The attempt to create a supplementary Richmond-based army under Beauregard during the Gettysburg campaign provides an example of something Lee should have sorted out before he went north.

This has been, as I said at the beginning, top-down history. For better or worse, military strategy begins and ends with those who formulate it, not those whose lives are put in jeopardy by its implementation. But I hope that something of the character of these leaders has emerged from my focus upon their thinking and planning, since that character directly affected the outcome of events.

And what were their outcomes? Lincoln, who strove so mightily to preserve the Union, of course did not live to see the consummation of his efforts. By conquering the South, Lincoln did what critics, doubters, and detractors had determined was impossible, and he did it even after it became far more difficult, involved, time-consuming, and costly than anyone (except Sherman) could imagine. Lincoln achieved his political objective; others would now have to win the peace. The Union embarked upon what became known as Reconstruction, and the Union army became responsible for what today would be classified as an enormous "post-hostility operation." By 1877, all of Winfield Scott's "Wayward Sisters" were home. Though the war abolished slavery, it did not bring equality. Black codes and Jim Crow ruled for another century.

Jefferson Davis survived the Confederacy's demise. Captured trying to flee to the Trans-Mississippi, he spent two years imprisoned at Fortress Monroe, then was released. He eventually settled at a plantation owned by a family friend in Beauvoir, Mississippi, where he proceeded to pen what must be one of the most self-justificatory memoirs in the history of the genre. He also continued to quarrel with Johnston and Beauregard; this part of the war never ended. He died in 1889.

Ulysses Simpson Grant continued as general in chief of the Union army. He became secretary of war in the Andrew Johnson administration, then served two terms as president, 1868–1876. Many in his administration were notoriously corrupt, though Grant himself was not. Mirroring his pre–Civil War days, he entered into a postwar business venture that failed. Diagnosed with throat cancer and financially destitute, he scrambled to write his famous memoir to provide for his wife. It became a best seller and a literary classic. Grant never saw it in print, passing away in 1885, a few days after writing the last page.[11]

William Tecumseh Sherman stayed in the army after the war, becoming a full general in March 1869. He assumed the post of general in chief from Grant a few days later and held the job for the next fourteen years, retiring in 1884.[12] Sherman also wrote a generally well-regarded memoir, though by some judgments a quirky one.

The war cost Robert E. Lee his home. His family plantation on the south bank of the Potomac was taken by the government and became Arlington National Cemetery. In August 1865 he accepted an appointment as president of Washington College in Lexington, Virginia, where he remained until his death in October 1870. The school subsequently became Washington and Lee University. He contemplated writing a history of the Army of Northern Virginia but unfortunately never did.[13]

Winfield Scott died a year after the end of the war. His successor as general in chief, George Brinton McClellan, returned to the business world after losing the 1864 presidential contest to Lincoln and was the chief engineer of New York City's Department of Docks from 1870 to 1872. He then tried politics again, winning election as New Jersey's governor, a post he held from 1878 to 1881. He died in 1887.[14]

McClellan's successor, Henry Wager Halleck, spent the few remaining years of his life in the army (he died in 1872). In April 1865, the Johnson administration sent him to Richmond to sort out the postwar situation there. One of his accomplishments was preserving much of the Confederate government's correspondence, laying the foundation for the later publication of the *Official Records*. His postwar assignments included managing the American military presence on the West Coast (which after 1867 included Alaska) and command of the Division of the South, based in Louisville, Kentucky.[15]

McClellan's successors to command of the Army of the Potomac, Ambrose Everett Burnside, Joseph Hooker, and George Gordon Meade, all served until the end of the war. Afterward, Burnside became governor of Rhode Island in 1866 and then a senator, dying in this post in 1881. Hooker retired from the army in 1868 after a stroke. He died in 1879. Immediately after the war Meade commanded the Division of the Atlantic, based in Philadelphia. He then ran Military District Number 3 (Alabama, Georgia, and Florida) before returning to the Philadelphia command. He died of pneumonia in 1872, age fifty-seven.[16]

McClellan's friend Don Carlos Buell left the army in 1864 and never returned to military service, despite Grant's efforts to have him reinstated. He became president of the Green River Iron Company and then a pension agent, dying in 1898.[17]

Joseph Eggleston Johnston went into the insurance business, as did so many other former generals, and served in Congress. He also wrote a memoir of the war that surpasses Davis's in its self-serving nature. Johnston's contemporaries deemed its often unsubstantiated attacks to have brought little favor on the man who was so obsessed with reputation. He died of pneumonia in 1891, having contracted the illness not long after attending Sherman's rain-drenched funeral.[18]

Pierre Gustave Toutant Beauregard went to work for a railroad and then supervised the Louisiana state lottery. (Considering the tenor of his operational plans, this latter post seems fitting.) He also wrote and helped write a number of works embellishing his exploits, lauding his genius, and attacking the greatest of Confederate enemies: Jefferson Davis.[19]

James Longstreet recovered from the wound he received in the Battle of the Wilderness to again command troops under Lee. After the war he went into insurance and then into the cotton business, and wrote a memoir typical of the age (meaning filled with inaccuracies). He also became the figure most blamed for the Southern defeat at Gettysburg, and, like many of his contemporaries, fired his own shots in postwar feuds. Worst of all in the eyes of most Confederates, he became a Republican.[20]

Edmund Kirby Smith initially fled to Cuba with many other Confederates. Missing his family, he returned to the United States, took the oath of allegiance, and eventually became a teacher in Sewanee, Tennessee.[21]

Braxton Bragg lost his Louisiana plantation and settled on his brother's land in Alabama for a while, then held a number of short-term appointments in industry, all of which ended because he quarreled with his co-workers. He dropped dead walking down the street in Galveston, Texas, in September 1876. He never wrote any accounts of his wartime service. "I dare not tell the truth," he once remarked, "and I dare not tell lies."[22]

The famous Rebel cavalry raiders went different routes. John Hunt Morgan did not survive the war, being killed by Union troops in Tennessee in September 1864. Joseph Wheeler became a congressman and later reentered the U.S. Army. He fought at San Juan Hill during the Spanish-American War and then served in the Philippines. Nathan Bedford Forrest, one of the war's true tactical geniuses (how many other cavalry commanders ever captured a steamship?), returned to being a planter but was unable to take up one of his old careers: slave trading. He did the next best thing—he helped found the Ku Klux Klan and may have been its first Grand Wizard.[23]

A number of former Union and Confederate officers ended up in the employ of the Egyptian army, including one of our minor characters, former Confederate general William Wing Loring, who served in both the Eastern and Western Theaters. He and a pair of other former Confederates were involved in a gunfight in the restaurant of the Hotel d'Europe in Alexandria, Egypt, in July 1872. The other protagonists were the American consul, George Butler, the nephew of the Union general Benjamin Butler, and two others, one of whom was a former Union officer.[24]

THE CONFLICT IN WHICH they all struggled is often considered the precursor to World War I, particularly because of the pervasive use of trench warfare in northern Virginia in 1864–65 and the sheer scale of carnage wrought by the weaponry either used or invented during war. While there is of course something to the analogy, the American Civil War mirrored past conflicts as much as it forecast future ones, having as many points of contact with the War of Independence as it did with the Great War. The political legacy of the first was critical. Many in the South saw themselves as following in the footsteps of the leaders of America's revolt against British rule. They were fighting for their freedom (which functionally meant the freedom to own slaves). The Confederacy's constitution was modeled almost verbatim on that conceived by the Founding Fathers.

There is also a more subtle military connection to the Revolution: in the military realm. For example, on a number of occasions Braxton Bragg made remarks about "partizan service," particularly in relation to the use of his cavalry against Union advances. Conventional thinking interprets this in the light of guerrilla warfare, particularly the modern version. But Bragg was actually recalling a mode of warfare from the eighteenth century, when it was a common practice to send units on detached service to harass the enemy, cut their supply lines, and so on. George Washington made this a key element of how he fought the British. Even Bragg's spelling of the term *partizan* is the eighteenth-century form.[25]

Braxton Bragg (as well as his wife, Elise, with whom he corresponded in detail on military matters) echoed the Revolutionary military experience in his discussions about a Fabian strategy, which offers a direct link with Washington. As early as 1778 British publications referred to Washington as the "American Fabius" because of his New Jersey campaign of 1776–77.[26]

Moreover, when one adds to this the example of Bragg's campaigns, particularly his invasion of Tennessee and Kentucky in the fall of 1862 and his efforts to maneuver Buell out of his positions by marching, one is led to propose that Bragg was trying to wage an eighteenth-century war.

Looking forward, the Civil War laid the foundation for teaching strategic thinking in the United States. Stephen B. Luce, a career naval officer and Civil War veteran, recalled a conversation he once had with Sherman regarding the seizure of Charleston. Sherman had commented that the navy had been pounding Charleston for three years, with no result. He told Luce that as soon as he cut the city's communications it would fall. Luce wrote, "After hearing General Sherman's clear exposition of the military situation the scales seemed to fall from my eyes." Luce realized that there were higher principles at work in warfare than simply the application of brute force. He embarked upon a quest to establish an institute that would seek strategic principles for warfare at sea and teach them to the service's officers; he also hoped to discover a "naval Jomini." This resulted in the founding in 1884 of the Naval War College in Newport, Rhode Island, and the assignment of another Civil War veteran, Alfred Thayer Mahan, as a faculty member. Mahan wrote one of the most impactful of all strategic works, *The Influence of Sea Power upon History, 1660–1783*, published in 1890. As many have pointed out, the book profoundly shaped American naval thinking for decades to come, convincing, among others, Secretary of the Navy Teddy Roosevelt to expand the country's naval power. It directed more than simply American strategy. It was hailed by the British as well as the Japanese. Kaiser Wilhelm II of Germany gave it great praise. Luce was also encouraged in his work by a contentious Civil War veteran and army officer, Emory Upton, a military intellectual in his own right who contributed much to the postwar interest in professionalism and education among his fellow officers. The army established its first staff college at Fort Leavenworth, Kansas, in 1881. The man responsible for this was Upton's mentor, William Tecumseh Sherman.[27]

BUT WHAT ABOUT the Civil War itself? Why did the Union win? Victory was not inevitable. James McPherson has astutely discussed the idea of contingency during this conflict, meaning "the recognition that at numerous critical points during the war, things might have gone altogether differently."[28] There is no doubt of the truth of this. The superiority of Union resources certainly played a part, but resources in and of themselves do not win wars. If such were the case, Great Britain would have triumphed over the American colonists, and the United States would have achieved success in Vietnam. The character of Lincoln certainly had much to do with Union victory. His determination kept the North fighting and the Union's cause alive.

The key reason was not individual heroism or personal courage, of which both sides had a tremendous supply. The Union triumphed in the end because it managed to develop strategic responses that addressed the nature of this particular war and the character of this particular enemy and then set about implementing them for as long as it took to achieve their political objective. The Confederacy never did—and perished.

Abbreviations

Bates, *Diary*
The Diary of Edward Bates, 1859–1866. Ed. Howard K. Beale. Washington, DC: USGPO, 1933.

B&L
Johnson, Robert U., and Clarence C. Buell, eds. *Battles and Leaders of the Civil War*. 4 vols. Edison, NJ: Castle, 1995.

Browning, *Diary*
The Diary of Orville Hickman Browning. Ed. Theodore C. Pease. 2 vols. Springfield: Illinois State Historical Library, 1925.

Chase, *Diaries*
Inside Lincoln's Cabinet: The Civil War Diaries of Salmon P. Chase. Ed. David Donald. New York: Longmans, Green, 1954.

CWL
The Collected Works of Abraham Lincoln. Ed. Roy P. Basler. 8 vols. Springfield, IL: Abraham Lincoln Association; New Brunswick, NJ: Rutgers University Press, 1953.

Davis Papers
The Papers of Jefferson Davis. Ed. Lynda Lasswell Crist, Mary Seaton Dix, and Kenneth H. Williams. 11 vols. to date. Baton Rouge: LSU Press, 1979–.

Grant Papers
The Papers of Ulysses S. Grant. Ed. John Y. Simon. 31 vols. Carbondale: Southern Illinois University Press, 1967–2009.

Hay, *Diary*
Inside Lincoln's White House: The Complete Civil War Diary of John Hay. Ed. Michael Burlingame and John R. T. Ettlinger. Carbondale: Southern Illinois University Press, 1997.

Lee's Dispatches
Lee's Dispatches: Unpublished Letters of General Robert E. Lee, C.S.A., to Jefferson Davis and the War Department of the Confederate States of America, 1862–65. Ed. Douglas Southall Freeman and Grady McWhiney. New York: G. P. Putnam's Sons, 1957.

McClellan Papers
The Civil War Papers of George B. McClellan: Selected Correspondence, 1860–1865. Ed. Stephen W. Sears. New York: Ticknor and Fields, 1989.

Messages and Papers
The Messages and Papers of Jefferson Davis and the Confederacy Including Diplomatic Correspondence, 1861–1865. Ed. James D. Richardson. 2 vols. New York: Chelsea House, 1966.

OR
U.S. Congress. *The War of the Rebellion: A Compilation of the Official Records of the Union and Confederate Armies*. 128 vols. Washington: GPO, 1880–1901. Version on CD-ROM: *The Civil War CD-ROM*. Ed. Phillip Oliver. Carmel: Guild Press of Indiana, 1996–2000.

ORN
U.S. Congress. *Official Records of the Union and Confederate Navies in the War of the Rebellion*. 30 vols. Washington, DC: GPO, 1894–1922.

ORS
Supplement to the Official Records of the Union and Confederate Armies. Ed. Jane B. Hewitt et al. 100 vols. Wilmington, NC: Broadfoot, 1994–1999.

Sherman's Civil War
Sherman's Civil War: Selected Correspondence of William T. Sherman, 1860–1865. Ed. Brooks D. Simpson and Jean V. Berlin. Chapel Hill: University of North Carolina Press, 1999.

Wartime Papers
The Wartime Papers of R. E. Lee. Ed. Clifford Dowdey and Louis H. Manarin. Boston: Little, Brown, 1961.

Welles, *Diary*
The Diary of Gideon Welles. 2 vols. Boston: Houghton and Mifflin, 1911.

Notes

INTRODUCTION

1. James M. McPherson, *Battle Cry of Freedom: The Civil War Era* (New York: Oxford University Press, 1987), ix; Brian Holden Reid, "The Civil War, 1861–5," in James C. Bradford, ed., *A Companion to American Military History* (Malden: Wiley-Blackwell, 2010), 1:99.

2. An example: Eliot Cohen, *The Supreme Command: Soldiers, Statesmen, and Leadership in Wartime* (New York: Free Press, 2002), 15–51.

3. Wallace P. Franz, "Two Letters on Strategy: Clausewitz' Contribution to the Operational Level of War," in Michael I. Handel, ed., *Clausewitz and Modern Strategy* (London: Frank Cass, 1986), 172.

4. See Christopher Bassford, *Clausewitz in English: The Reception of Clausewitz in Britain and America, 1815–1945* (Oxford: Oxford University Press, 1994).

5. Carl von Clausewitz, *On War*, ed. and trans. Michael Howard and Peter Paret (Princeton: Princeton University Press, 1976, 1984).

6. Ibid., 89.

7. Ibid., 177.

8. Antoine-Henri de Jomini, *The Art of War*, trans. G. H. Mendell and W. P. Craighill (Philadelphia: J. P. Lippincott, 1862; reprint, Westport, CT: Greenwood Press, 1978).

9. Baron [Antoine-Henri] de Jomini, *Précis de l'Art de la Guerre, ou Nouveau Traité Analytique des Principales Combinaisons de la Stratégie, de la Grande Tactique et de la Politique Militaire*, 2nd ed., 2 vols. (Bruxelles: Librairie Militaire de J.-B. Petit, 1838). This work first appeared in 1837.

10. Crane Brinton, Gordon A. Craig, and Felix Gilbert, "Jomini," in Edward Meade Earle, ed., *Makers of Modern Strategy: Military Thought from Machiavelli to Hitler* (Princeton: Princeton University Press, 1943), 84 n 10.

11. Jomini, *Art of War*, 62.

12. Michael I. Handel, *Masters of War: Classical Strategic Thought*, 2nd ed. (London: Frank Cass, 1996), 35–36.

13. Jomini, *Art of War*, 61.

14. Henry W. Halleck, *Elements of Military Art and Science, or Course of Instruction in Strategy, Fortification, Tactics of Battles, Etc.* (New York: D. Appleton, 1846); Antoine-Henri de Jomini, *Life of Napoleon*, trans. Henry W. Halleck, 4 vols. (New York: D. Van Nostrand, 1864).

15. Grady McWhiney, *Braxton Bragg and Confederate Defeat* (Tuscaloosa: University of Alabama Press, 1969, 1991), 17–21.

16. On misreading Jomini, see Azar Gat, *A History of Military Thought: From the Enlightenment to the Cold War* (Oxford: Oxford University Press, 2001), 129–31; on misreading Clausewitz, see David Kaiser, "Back to Clausewitz," *Journal of Strategic Studies* 32, 4 (Aug. 2009), 667–73.

17. U.S. Naval War College, College of Distance Education, *Strategy and War Syllabus* (Newport, RI: U.S. Naval War College, 2007), 15.

18. The term *national strategy* is often invoked for *grand strategy*, but its use leads to confusion between what is sought (the policy objective) and the route to getting there (the strategy). Moreover, all of the various strategies used are, by default, "national." I am indebted to George Baer for pointing this out.

19. Clausewitz, *On War*, 88–89.

20. Ibid., 92.

21. Ibid., 69.

22. William T. Sherman, "The Grand Strategy of the Last Year of the War," in Robert U. Johnson and Clarence C. Buell, eds., *Battles and Leaders of the Civil War* [hereafter *B&L*] (Edison, NJ: Castle, 1995), 4:247–59.

23. *Strategy and War Syllabus*, 15.

24. Clausewitz, *On War*, 595–97, 617.

25. U.S. Joint Chiefs of Staff, *Joint Operations*, Joint Publication 3–0 (Sept. 17, 2006, incorporating Change 1, Feb. 13, 2008), II-2; *Strategy and War Syllabus*, 15.

26. Jomini, *Art of War*, 61–62.

27. Ibid., 70.

28. Ibid., 93, 102–4, 106, 106n, 112–16. For an excellent graphic representation of interior and exterior lines, see Franz, "Two Letters on Strategy," 175.

29. Jomini, *Art of War*, 202–3.

30. Ibid., 89–90.

31. Clausewitz, *On War*, 204. Italics in the original.

32. The most important is Frank E. Vandiver, "Jefferson Davis and Confederate Strategy," in Avery O. Craven and Frank E. Vandiver, eds., *The American Tragedy: The Civil War in Retrospect* (Hampden-Sydney, VA: Hampden-Sydney College, 1959), 19–32. But the perpetuation of this is broad.

33. Jomini, *Art of War*, 62–63.

34. Beauregard to Bragg, Mar. 17, 1862, in Jane B. Hewitt et al., eds., *Supplement to the Official Records of the Union and Confederate Armies* [hereafter *ORS*] (Wilmington, NC: Broadfoot Publishing, 1994–99), 94:194–97; Beauregard report, Apr. 28, 1862, in U.S. Congress, *The War of the Rebellion: A Compilation of the Official Records of the Union and Confederate Armies*, 128 vols. (Washington, DC: GPO, 1880–1901); on CD-ROM as Phillip Oliver, ed., *The Civil War CD-ROM* (Carmel, IN: Guild Press of Indiana, 1996–2000) [hereafter *OR*; all *OR* notes are from series 1 unless otherwise noted], 10/2:458–59; Polk Perryville report, Nov. 1862, *OR*, 16/1:1109–12; Bragg to Cooper, May 20, 1863, *OR*, 16/1:1088–94; E. K. Smith to Cooper, Nov. 14, 1863, *OR*, 22/1:24–26; McPherson to Washburn, Apr. 29, 1864, *OR*, 32/3:536; Merritt to Russell, Oct. 24, 1864, *OR*, 43/1:448–52; Grant report, July 22, 1865, *OR*, 34/1:30.

35. Donald Stoker, "Confederate 'Grand Strategy,'" in *West Point Summer Seminar Projects in Military History* (West Point, NY: USMA, 2002).

1. Shelby Foote, *The Civil War: A Narrative*, vol. 1: *Fort Sumter to Perryville* (New York: Random House, 1958), 35; E. B. Long with Barbara Long, *The Civil War Day by Day: An Almanac, 1861–1865* (Garden City, NY: Doubleday, 1971), 35.

2. Long and Long, *Civil War*, 35–37.

3. McPherson, *Battle Cry*, 228–33; Avery O. Craven, "Why the Southern States Seceded," in George Harmon Knoles, ed., *The Crisis of the Union, 1860–1865* (New Orleans: LSU Press, 1965), 60–61, 63.

4. Winfield Scott, *Memoirs of Lieut.-Gen. Winfield Scott* (New York: Sheldon, 1864), 610–11.

5. John S. D. Eisenhower, *Agent of Destiny: The Life and Times of General Winfield Scott* (New York: Free Press, 1997), 346–47.

6. Timothy D. Johnson, *Winfield Scott: The Quest for Military Glory* (Lawrence: University of Kansas Press, 1998), 222–23.

7. Eisenhower, *Agent of Destiny*, 346–47.

8. Ibid., 348.

9. Jefferson Davis, *The Rise and Fall of Confederate Government* (New York: Thomas Yoseloff, 1958), 1:228.

10. Eisenhower, *Agent of Destiny*, 349.

11. Ibid., 351; Lincoln to Scott, Nov. 9, 1860, in *The Collected Works of Abraham Lincoln* [hereafter *CWL*], ed. Roy P. Basler (New Brunswick, NJ: Rutgers University Press, 1953), 4:137.

12. Foote, *Civil War*, 1:44.

13. Lincoln to Lyman Trumbull, Dec. 10, 1860, *CWL*, 4:149–50, 150 n. 1. Lincoln expressed the same sentiment in Lincoln to Kellogg, Dec. 11, 1860, and Lincoln to Washburne, Dec. 13, 1860, *CWL*, 4:150–51.

14. Lincoln to Francis P. Blair Sr., Dec. 21, 1860, *CWL*, 4:157–58.

15. *CWL*, 4:157–58 n. 1; Eisenhower, *Agent of Destiny*, 134–35.

16. Lincoln to Washburne, Dec. 21, 1860, *CWL*, 4:159. Lincoln repeated his insistence on the recapture of any lost forts in a letter to Hunter, Dec. 22, 1860, *CWL*, 4:159; see also Lincoln to Silvester, Dec. 22, 1860, *CWL*, 4:160, 160 n. 1.

17. Lincoln to Stephens, Dec. 22, 1860, *CWL*, 4:160–61. Italics in the original.

18. Lincoln to Webb, Dec. 29, 1860, *CWL*, 4:164–65, 165 n. 1.

19. Lincoln to Hale, Jan. 11, 1861, *CWL*, 4:172, 172 n. 1. In an interview Lincoln reiterated his unwillingness to be blackmailed into compromise, likening bending in the face of threats to the reduction of the U.S. government to a par with Mexico. See "Remarks Concerning Concessions to Secession" [c. Jan. 19–21, 1861], *CWL*, 4:175–76, 4:176 n. 1, published in the New York *Herald* on January 28, 1861, and reprinted later in the New York *Tribune* and the Chicago *Tribune*.

20. Farewell Address at Springfield, Illinois [A, B, and C versions], Feb. 11, 1861, *CWL*, 4:190–91.

21. Speech in Independence Hall, Philadelphia, Pennsylvania, Feb. 22, 1861, *CWL*, 4:240–41.

22. Eisenhower, *Agent of Destiny*, 356.

23. Ibid., 356–57. Scott is accused of softening his position on secession, and some, even at the time, cite Scott's insistence to Lincoln that he "would blow them to hell." But Scott made this statement in reference to attempts by the dissatisfied to disrupt the inauguration; it was not uttered in regard to secession itself. The quote is sometimes misunderstood. See Charles Winslow Eliot, *Winfield Scott: The Soldier and the Man* (New York: Macmillan, 1937), 696–97, and Eisenhower, *Agent of Destiny*, 356–58, 428 n. 6.

24. Scott to Seward, Mar. 3, 1861, in Scott, *Memoirs*, 2:625–28, Eliot, *Scott*, 697–98. The versions differ slightly.

25. Eisenhower, *Agent of Destiny*, 357; Eliot, *Scott*, 698–99.

26. Eliot, *Scott*, 700.

27. Ibid., 696; E. D. Townsend, *Anecdotes of the Civil War in the United States* (New York: D. Appleton, 1884), 55–56.

28. Seward quoted in Eliot, *Scott*, 696.

29. David Herbert Donald, *Lincoln* (New York: Simon & Schuster, 1996), 260.

30. Eliot, *Scott*, 696–97.

31. Townsend, *Anecdotes*, 55–56.

32. Eliot, *Scott*, 699–700; Emory M. Thomas, *Confederate Nation: 1861–1865* (New York: Harper Torchbooks, 1979), 88–89.

33. On this last point see Mark Grimsley, *The Hard Hand of War: Union Military Policy Toward Southern Civilians* (Cambridge: Cambridge University Press, 1997).

34. First Inaugural Address—Final Text, Mar. 4, 1861, *CWL*, 4:262–71. Lincoln also reaffirmed the constitutionality of the fugitive slave laws.

35. Ibid. Lincoln deleted "treasonable" in favor of "revolutionary," *CWL*, 4:265.

36. Ibid.

37. Ibid. Italics in the original.

38. Lynda Lasswell Crist, Mary Seaton Dix, and Kenneth H. Williams, eds., *The Papers of Jefferson Davis* [hereafter *Davis Papers*] (Baton Rouge: LSU Press, 1979–), 8:58.

39. Inaugural Address, Feb. 22, 1862, *Davis Papers*, 8:58–62. Union general Ulysses S. Grant had captured Forts Henry and Donelson a few weeks before, leading to the collapse of the South's defenses in the West.

40. Archer Jones, *Confederate Strategy from Shiloh to Vicksburg* (Baton Rouge: LSU Press, 1991), 20–21.

41. Robert G. Tanner, *Retreat to Victory? Confederate Strategy Reconsidered* (Washington, DC: Scholarly Resources, 2002), 3.

42. James D. Richardson, ed., *The Messages and Papers of Jefferson Davis and the Confederacy Including Diplomatic Correspondence, 1861–1865* (New York: Chelsea House, 1966), 1:xiii; Burton J. Hendrick, *Statesman of the Lost Cause: Jefferson Davis and His Cabinet* (New York: Literary Guild of America, 1939), 49–51; Mark M. Boatner III, *The Civil War Dictionary* (New York: David McKay, 1959), 168; McPherson, *Battle Cry*, 70–77.

43. Speech at Atlanta, Feb. 16, 1861, *Davis Papers*, 7:43–44.

44. Davis to Carroll, Mar. 1, 1861, *Davis Papers*, 7:64–65. See Hendrick, *Statesman of the Lost Cause*, 46–47.

45. "A Proclamation," Feb. 14, 1862, *Messages and Papers*, 1:67.

46. Victor Brooks and Robert Hohwald, *How America Fought Its Wars: Military Strategy from the American Revolution to the Civil War* (Conshohocken, PA: Combined, 1999), 296.

47. "Inaugural Address," Feb. 18, 1861, *Davis Papers*, 7:45–60.

48. Ibid., 7:47.

49. Message to Congress, Apr. 29, 1861, *Messages and Papers*, 1:82.

CHAPTER 2

1. Toombs, Rhett, and Marten to Davis, Feb. 9, 1861, *Davis Papers*, 7:36, 38; quoted in Steven E. Woodworth, *Jefferson Davis and His Generals: The Failure of Confederate Command in the West* (Lawrence: University Press of Kansas, 1990), 13.

2. Davis to Clayton, Jan. 30, Davis to Lincoln, July 6, 1861, *Davis Papers*, 7:221–22, 27–28.

3. "To the Speaker of the House," Mar. 14, 1862, *Messages and Papers*, 1:215–16 and 457–65.

4. Woodworth, *Jefferson Davis*, 10–11; David M. Potter, "Jefferson Davis and the Political Factors in Confederate Defeat," in David Herbert Donald, ed., *Why the North Won the Civil War* (New York: Simon & Schuster, 1996), 104–5; Davis to Varina Davis, May 16, 1862, *Davis Papers*, 8:178–79.

5. Davis to Pickens, Feb. 20, 1861, *Davis Papers*, 7:55; Russell F. Weigley, *A Great Civil War: A Military and Political History, 1861–1865* (Bloomington: Indiana University Press, 2000), 31.

6. Weigley, *Civil War*, 32.

7. Ibid., 35; Richard N. Current, "God and the Strongest Battalions," in *Why the North Won*, 33; Davis, *Rise and Fall*, 1:316.

8. Weigley, *Civil War*, 35; Davis, *Rise and Fall*, 1:315; Herman Hattaway and Archer Jones, *How the North Won: A Military History of the Civil War* (Urbana: University of Illinois Press, 1991), 58–59.

9. Richard E. Beringer, Herman Hattaway, Archer Jones, and William N. Still Jr., *Why the South Lost the Civil War* (Athens: University of Georgia Press, 1986), 118–19.

10. Interview with William H. Russell, May [7], 1861, *Davis Papers*, 7:153–54.

11. Craig L. Symonds, "Lincoln and the Strategy of Union," *Naval War College Review*, Mar.–Apr. 1975, 63–64; Hattaway and Jones, *How the North Won*, 114; Thomas L. Livermore, *Numbers and Losses in the Civil War, 1861–65* (Boston: Houghton, Mifflin, 1900), 63.

12. Richard M. McMurry, *Two Great Rebel Armies: An Essay in Confederate Military History* (Chapel Hill: University of North Carolina Press, 1989), 91–92, 97–104; McPherson, *Battle Cry*, 322–23; Davis, *Rise and Fall*, 1:301.

13. Potter, "Davis and Political Factors," 96–97; Current, "God and the Strongest Battalions," 27.

14. Davis, *Rise and Fall*, 1:263–65, 265n.

15. Memorandum, Mar. 15, and "Commissioners in Reply to Mr. Seward," Apr. 9, 1861, *Messages and Papers*, 1:85–86, 88–93; Davis, *Rise and Fall*, 1:266, 278, 676–78, and postscript, Apr. 8, 1861, 1:679–80; Bruce Catton, *The Centennial History of the Civil War*, vol. 1: *The Coming Fury* (New York: Doubleday, 1961), 258.

16. Davis, *Rise and Fall*, 1:270.

17. Jones, *Confederate Strategy*, 19; George A. Bruce, "Lee and the Strategy of the Civil War," in Gary W. Gallagher, ed., *Lee the Soldier* (Lincoln: University of Nebraska Press, 1996), 125; Potter, "Davis and Political Factors," 107.

18. Jones, *Confederate Strategy*, 20–21.

19. Ibid., 20.

20. Potter, "Davis and Political Factors," 106.

21. McPherson, *Battle Cry*, 337.

22. Woodworth, *Jefferson Davis*, 5–11; Hattaway and Jones, *How the North Won*, 113; Potter, "Davis and Political Factors," 106–7; *Messages and Papers*, 1:xxv–xxvi.

23. *Messages and Papers*, 1:xxv–xxvi; quoted in *Davis Papers*, 11:594.

24. Dean B. Mahin, *One War at a Time: The International Dimensions of the Civil War* (Washington, DC: Brassey's, 1999), 19–20.

25. *Davis Papers*, 7:49; Norman A. Graebner, "Northern Diplomacy and European Neutrality," in *Why the North Won*, 67; Brown interview, May 17, 1861, *ORS*, 93:157–61.

26. Douglas B. Ball, *Financial Failure and Confederate Defeat* (Urbana: University of Illinois Press, 1991), 12.

27. Current, "God and the Strongest Battalions," 27.

28. Ball, *Financial Failure*, 90.

29. Potter, "Jefferson Davis and the Political Factors," 97; Current, "God and the Strongest Battalions," 25.

30. *Messages and Papers*, 1:xxvi; Current, "God and the Strongest Battalions," 26.

31. Mahin, *One War at a Time*, 21.

32. Ball, *Financial Failure*, 109 n. 145.

33. Current, "God and the Strongest Battalions," 27.

34. Potter, "Jefferson Davis and the Political Factors," 98–99.

35. Ball, *Financial Failure*, 88.

36. Graebner, "Northern Diplomacy," 67.

37. Davis, *Rise and Fall*, 1:315.

38. Clausewitz, *On War*, 86–87.

39. Current, "God and the Strongest Battalions," 26.

40. *Messages and Papers*, 1:xxxvi–xxxvii.

41. Ibid., 1:xxxvii.

42. Ibid., 1:xxxvii–xxxviii.

43. Weigley, *Civil War*, 70–71; Hendrick, *Statesmen*, 140–41; Messages and Papers, 1:xxxviii.

44. Weigley, *Civil War*, 77–80; McPherson, *Battle Cry*, 389–91; Kenneth Bourne, "British Preparations for War with the North," *English Historical Review* 76, 301 (Oct. 1961): 600–32.

45. Weigley, *Civil War*, 81; Lee to his wife, Dec. 25, 1861, in Clifford Dowdey and Louis H. Manarin, eds., *The Wartime Papers of R. E. Lee* [hereafter *Wartime Papers*] (Boston: Little, Brown, 1961), 96. See also Lee to G. W. C. Lee, Dec. 29, 1861, *Wartime Papers*, 98.

46. Graebner, "Northern Diplomacy," 70, 79.

47. Davis to Campbell, Apr. 6, 1861, *Davis Papers*, 7:92–93; Boatner, *Dictionary*, 793. Davis insisted that the *Star of the West* had been armed, but it was not, ibid.; Woodworth, *Jefferson Davis*, 13.

48. Quoted in U. S. Grant III, "Military Strategy of the Civil War," *Military Affairs* 22, 1 (Spring 1958): 16–17. This article must be used with some care because it contains a number of errors. I have used its direct quotes.

49. Edwin C. Fishel, *Secret War for the Union* (Boston: Houghton and Mifflin, 1996), 16; Lincoln to Chew, Apr. 6, 1861, *CWL*, 4:323–24 and n. 1; Weigley, *Civil War*, 20–21.

50. McPherson, *Battle Cry*, 271–72, 272 n. 78. There is much debate about whether or not Lincoln baited the Confederates into firing the first shots.

51. Message to Congress, Apr. 8, 1861, *Messages and Papers*, 1:63, 73, 76–77, 79; Davis, *Rise and Fall*, 1:326; "Proclamation Calling Militia and Convening Congress," Apr. 15, 1861, *CWL*, 4:331–32; Weigley, *Civil War*, 24–25; Boatner, *Dictionary*, 729.

52. "An Act Recognizing the Existence of War Between the United States and the Confederate States, and Concerning Letters of Marque," May 6, 1861, *Messages and Papers*, 1:104–5.

53. James M. McPherson and William J. Cooper Jr., "Introduction," in James M. McPherson and William J. Cooper Jr., eds., *Writing the Civil War: The Quest to Understand* (Columbia: University of South Carolina Press, 1998), 5.

CHAPTER 3

1. T. Harry Williams, *Lincoln and His Generals* (New York: Knopf, 1952), 16; Potter, "Davis and Political Factors," 110.

2. "Proclamation of Blockade," Apr. 19 and 27, "Proclamation Forbidding Intercourse with Rebel States," Aug. 16, 1861, *CWL*, 4:338–39, 346–47, 487–89.

3. Quoted in Michael Burlingame and John R. T. Ettlinger, eds., *Inside Lincoln's White House: The Complete Civil War Diary of John Hay* [hereafter Hay, *Diary*] (Carbondale: Southern Illinois University Press, 1997), 11.

4. Williams, *Lincoln and His Generals*, 16.

5. Weigley, *Civil War*, xx–xxi.

6. Theodore Ropp, "Anacondas Anyone?" *Military Affairs* 27, 2 (Summer 1963): 72–73.

7. McClellan to Scott, Apr. 27, 1861, *OR*, 51/1:338–39; McClellan to Scott, Apr. 27, 1861, in Stephen W. Sears, ed., *The Civil War Papers of George B. McClellan: Selected Correspondence, 1860–1865* [hereafter *McClellan Papers*] (New York: Ticknor and Fields, 1989), 12.

8. McClellan to Scott, Apr. 27, 1861, *OR*, 51/1:338–39; McClellan to Scott, Apr. 27, 1861, *McClellan Papers*, 12.

9. Scott to Lincoln, May 2, 1861, "Indorsement [*sic*] on McClellan to Scott," Apr. 27, 1861, *OR*, 51/1:339.

10. Scott to McClellan, May 3, 21, 1861, *OR*, 51/1:369–70, 386–87.

11. Williams, *Lincoln and His Generals*, 18; Archer Jones, "Military Means, Political Ends: Strategy," in Gabor S. Boritt, ed., *Why the Confederacy Lost* (New York: Oxford University Press, 1992), 46.

12. Williams, *Lincoln and His Generals*, 18.

13. Weigley, *Civil War*, 25; Thomas J. Goss, *The War Within the Union High Command* (Lawrence: University Press of Kansas, 2003), 34–36, 49.

14. Boatner, *Dictionary*, 732; Graebner, "Northern Diplomacy," 61.

15. Boatner, *Dictionary*, 732; Graebner, "Northern Diplomacy," 63–64.

16. Scott to McClellan, May 3, 1861, *OR*, 51/1:369–70.

17. Williams, *Lincoln and His Generals*, 20–21.

18. Theodore C. Pease, ed., *The Diary of Orville Hickman Browning* [hereafter Browning, *Diary*] (Springfield: Illinois State Historical Library, 1925), 1:447–48.

19. Message to Congress in Special Session, July 4, 1861, *CWL*, 4:432–33.

20. Hattaway and Jones, *How the North Won*, 31, 40; Beringer et al., *How the South Lost*, 110; Bruce Catton, *The Army of the Potomac*, vol. 1: *Mr. Lincoln's Army* (New York: Doubleday, 1962), 30, 43–44.

21. Beringer et al., *How the South Lost*, 109, 111; Boatner, *Dictionary*, 441; Craig L. Symonds, *Joseph E. Johnston: A Civil War Biography* (New York: Norton, 1992), 67–70.

22. McDowell to Townsend, [c. June 24,] 1861, *OR*, 2:719–21; *Report of the Joint Committee on the Conduct of the War, 1863* (Washington, DC: GPO, 1863), 2:35–36; *B&L*, 2:144; Williams, *Lincoln and His Generals*, 20–21. T. Harry Williams, among others, insists that the Union aimed at Richmond. McDowell says otherwise.

23. Eliot, *Scott*, 727; Williams, *Lincoln and His Generals*, 20; McDowell to Townsend, June 24, 1861, *OR*, 2:718–19.

24. Fishel, *Secret War*, 31; McDowell to Townsend, June 24, 1861, *OR*, 2:718–19.

25. Beauregard to Davis, June 12, 1861, *Davis Papers*, 7:197–98. "President" in the address lines of all *OR* reports has been changed to "Davis" or "Lincoln" as applicable.

26. Davis to Beauregard, June 13, 1861, *Davis Papers*, 7:199–200.

27. Davis to J. E. Johnston, July 13, 1861, *Davis Papers*, 7:238–39.

28. Beringer et al., *How the South Lost*, 111, 114; Williams, *Lincoln and His Generals*, 20.

29. McClellan to Scott, [July 17, 1861], *McClellan Papers*, 59.

30. Scott to McClellan, July 18, 1861, *OR*, 2:743.

31. McClellan to Randolph B. Marcy, [c. July 21, 1861], *McClellan Papers*, 64.

32. J. E. Johnston Report, Oct. 14, 1861, *OR* 2:473–74.

33. J. E. Johnston to Davis, Aug. 3, 1861, *Davis Papers*, 7:258, 272–74.

34. Beringer et al., *How the South Lost*, 116.

35. Symonds, *Johnston*, 5; William C. Davis, *Jefferson Davis: The Man and His Hour* (New York: Harper Perennial, 1991), 530; Steven E. Woodworth, *Davis and Lee at War* (Lawrence: University Press of Kansas, 1995), 31–36, 47–49.

36. *OR*, 4:93; *B&L*, 2:700; Foote, *Civil War*, 1:294; Steven Woodworth and Kenneth Winkle, *Atlas of the Civil War* (New York: Oxford University Press, 2004), 96; Boatner, *Dictionary*, 591.

37. "Memoranda of Military Policy Suggested by the Bull Run Defeat," July 23, 1861, *CWL*, 4:457–58, 458 n. 2.

CHAPTER 4

1. Weigley, *Civil War*, 40; McPherson, *Battle Cry*, 284.

2. Weigley, *Civil War*, 40; McPherson, *Battle Cry*, 284.

3. Emory M. Thomas, *Confederate Nation: 1861–1865* (New York: Harper Torchbooks, 1979), 89–90.

4. Davis to Bragg, Apr. 3, 1861, *Davis Papers*, 7:85–86.

5. Message to Congress in Special Session, July 4, 1861, *CWL*, 4:428.

6. Lincoln to Browning, Sept. 22, 1861, *CWL*, 4:531–33.

7. Thomas, *Confederate Nation*, 89; McPherson, *Battle Cry*, 287.

8. Hudson Strode, *Jefferson Davis*, vol. 2: *Confederate President* (New York: Harcourt, Brace, 1959), 5.

9. Quoted in *Davis Papers*, 7:387.

10. Thomas, *Confederate Nation*, 89.

11. Williams, *Lincoln and His Generals*, 33–34.

12. Ibid., 34–35.

13. Ibid., 35.

14. Strode, *Davis*, 2:86.

15. Weigley, *Civil War*, 40–43; Reynolds to Davis, June 3, 1861, *Davis Papers*, 7:188–89, 189 n. 1, 190 n. 4.

16. Williams, *Lincoln and His Generals*, 35–37.

17. Frémont Proclamation, Aug. 30, 1861, *OR*, 3:466–67.

18. Nicolay Memorandum, Sept. 17, 1861, in *With Lincoln in the White House: Letters, Memoranda, and Other Writings of John G. Nicolay, 1860–1865*, ed. Michael Burlingame (Carbondale: Southern Illinois University Press, 2000), 56–58.

19. Lincoln to Frémont, Sept. 2, 1861, *CWL*, 4:506.

20. Frémont to Lincoln, Sept. 8, 1861, *OR*, 3:477–78.

21. Lincoln to Frémont, Sept. 11, 1861, *CWL*, 4:517–18.

22. Williams, *Lincoln and His Generals*, 36–40; David J. Eicher, *The Longest Night: A Military History of the Civil War* (New York: Touchstone, 2001), 131.

23. Lincoln to David Hunter, Oct. 24, 1861, *CWL*, 5:1–2; Hay, *Diary*, 28–29.

24. Dennison, Yates, and Morton Memorial, May 24, 1861, *OR*, 52/1:146–47; [Scott], "Remarks on a Memorial," May 29, 1861, *OR*, 52/1:147–48.

25. Weigley, *Civil War*, 45–47; Buckner on Crittenden's Lincoln memo, July 10, 1861, *ORS*, 93:377–78.

26. Magoffin to Davis, Aug. 1861, *OR*, 4:378.

27. Davis to Magoffin, Aug. 28, 1861, *OR*, 4:396–97.

28. Pillow to Polk, Aug. 28, 1861, *OR*, 3:685–87.

29. Polk to Magoffin, Sept. 1, 1861, *OR*, 4:179.

30. Harris to Davis, Sept. 4, 1861, *Davis Papers*, 7:325; Polk to Harris, Sept. 4, 1861, *OR*, 4:180.

31. Harris to Polk, Sept. 4, 1861, *OR*, 4:180.

32. Polk to Harris, Sept. 4, 1861, *OR*, 4:180.

33. Message of Nov. 18, 1861, *Messages and Papers*, 1:137–38.

34. *Davis Papers*, 7:325; Walker to Polk, Sept. 4, 1861, *OR*, 4:180; Walker to Harris, Sept. 5, 1861, *OR*, 4:189; Polk to Davis, Sept. 4, 1861, *OR*, 4:181; Davis to Polk, Sept. 4, 1861, *OR*, 4:181; Boatner, *Dictionary*, 885. See also *ORS*, 93:358–59, 365–66.

35. Buckner to Cooper, Sept. 13, 1861, *OR*, 4:189–90; Harris to Davis, Sept. 13, 1861, *OR*, 4:190; Polk to Magoffin, Sept. 8, 1861, *OR*, 4:185; Davis to Harris, Sept. 13, 1861, *OR*, 4:190.

36. Boatner, *Dictionary*, 352–53; Charles Bracelen Flood, *Grant and Sherman: The Friendship that Won the Civil War* (New York: Harper Perennial, 2005), 7–9.

37. Craig L. Symonds, *A Battlefield Atlas of the Civil War*, 2nd ed. (Baltimore: Nautical and Aviation Publishing, 1983), 17.

38. Buckner to Cooper, Sept. 13, 1861, *OR*, 4:189–90; Woodworth, *Jefferson Davis*, 39.

39. Davis to Polk, Sept. 15, 1861, *OR*, 4:188; A.S. Johnston to Davis, Sept. 16, 1861, *OR*, 4:193–94.
40. A. S. Johnston to Davis, Sept. 16, 1861, *OR*, 4:193–94; Symonds, *Atlas*, 17.
41. Davis to Polk, Sept. 15, 1861, *OR*, 4:188.
42. Weigley, *Civil War*, 48.
43. Davis to Polk, Nov. 12, 1861, *OR*, 4:539.

CHAPTER 5

1. See Joseph L. Harsh, "On the McClellan Go Round," *Civil War History* 19 (June 1973): 101–18.
2. The primary modern studies are Stephen W. Sears, *George B. McClellan: The Young Napoleon* (New York: Ticknor and Fields, 1988) and Ethan S. Rafuse, *McClellan's War* (Bloomington: Indiana University Press, 2005). See also Ethan S. Rafuse, "McClellan and Halleck at War: The Struggle for Control of the Union War Effort in the West, November 1861–March 1862," *Civil War History* 49 (Mar. 2003): 32–51.
3. Joseph L. Harsh, "George Brinton McClellan and the Forgotten Alternative: An Introduction to the Conservative Strategy in the Civil War: April–August 1861," Ph.D. dissertation, Rice University, 1970, 107–10.
4. Sears, *McClellan*, 95; Stephen W. Sears, "Lincoln and McClellan," in Gabor S. Boritt, ed., *Lincoln's Generals* (New York: Oxford University Press, 1994), 6–7; Catton, *Mr. Lincoln's Army*, 58–59.
5. Harsh, "McClellan," 112–14; Boatner, *Dictionary*, 524.
6. John Russell Young, *Around the World with General Grant* (New York: Subscription Book Department, American News Company, 1879), 2:216–17, 463.
7. McClellan to Mary Ellen McClellan, July 27, 1861, *McClellan Papers*, 70.
8. Catton, *Mr. Lincoln's Army*, 61.
9. Stephen W. Sears, "Little Mac and the Historians," *North and South* 2, 3 (Mar. 1999): 66; Fishel, *Secret War*, 53–54.
10. Fishel, *Secret War*, 3, 8.
11. Catton, *Mr. Lincoln's Army*, 121–23; James M. McPherson, *Tried by War: Lincoln as Commander in Chief* (New York: Penguin, 2008), 47.
12. Harsh, "McClellan," 189–90.
13. Ibid., 191–92.
14. McPherson, *Battle Cry*, 494, 506; T. Harry Williams, "The Committee on the Conduct of the War: An Experiment in Civilian Control," *Journal of the American Military Institute* 3, 3 (Autumn 1939): 141–42.
15. Harsh, "McClellan," 184; Joseph L. Harsh, "Lincoln's Tarnished Brass: Conservative Strategies and the Attempt to Fight the Early Civil War as a Limited War," in *The Confederate High Command and Related Topics. The 1988 Deep Delta Civil War Symposium: Themes in Honor of T. Harry Williams*, ed. Roman J. Heleniak and Lawrence L. Hewitt (Shippensburg, PA: White Mane Publishing, 1990), 127.
16. Williams, *Lincoln and His Generals*, 29. Before this McClellan produced an extensive outline that is reprinted in Harsh, "McClellan," 210.
17. McClellan report, *OR*, 5:6–7.

18. Ibid., *OR*, 5:7.

19. Ibid.

20. Sir Julian Corbett, *Some Principles of Maritime Strategy*, Eric J. Grove, introduction and notes (Annapolis: Naval Institute Press, 1988; reprint, 1911), 61. For "European," I have substituted "Confederate."

21. McClellan report, *OR*, 5:7–8.

22. Ibid., 5:8–10.

23. Ibid., *OR*, 5:6.

24. Ibid.

25. Some various examples: Doris Kearns Goodwin, *Team of Rivals: The Political Genius of Abraham Lincoln* (New York: Simon & Schuster, 2006), 378; Rowena Reed, *Combined Operations of the Civil War* (Lincoln: University of Nebraska Press, 1978), 36–39; Sears "Lincoln and McClellan," 19; Sears, *McClellan*, 98–100, 129. For evidence of the plan's future importance see Sears, *McClellan Papers*, 95–97, 114–18, 147–48, and *OR*, 5:9–10.

26. Harsh, "McClellan," 185, 226.

27. McClellan to Mary Ellen McClellan, Aug. 2, 1861, *McClellan Papers*, 75–76.

28. McClellan to Scott, Aug. 8, 1861, *McClellan Papers*, 79–80. Italics in the original.

29. McClellan to Townsend, June 22, 1861, *McClellan Papers*, 33–34, 80 n. 1.

30. McClellan to Welles, Aug. 12, 1861, *McClellan Papers*, 83.

31. McClellan to Mary Ellen McClellan, [Aug.] 19, [1861], *McClellan Papers*, 87.

32. *McClellan Papers*, 69.

33. Fishel, *Secret War*, 104.

34. Sears, "Little Mac," 67.

35. Clausewitz, *On War*, 102–3.

36. McClellan to Cameron, Sept. 8, 1861, *McClellan Papers*, 95–97, 97–98 n. 1; *OR*, 5:587–89.

37. Weigley, *Civil War*, 67; Fishel, *Civil War*, 87.

38. Memorandum for a Plan of Campaign, [c. Oct. 1, 1861], *CWL*, 4:544–45.

39. L. Thomas to W. T. Sherman, L. Thomas to O. M. Mitchel, Oct. 10, 1861, *OR*, 4:299–301; *B&L*, 1:383.

40. McClellan report, *OR*, 5:9–11; McClellan to Cameron, [Oct. 31, 1861], *McClellan Papers*, 114–18, 118–19 nn. 3, 4, 8, 9, 10.

41. McClellan report, *OR*, 5:9–11; McClellan to Cameron, [Oct. 31, 1861], *McClellan Papers*, 114–18.

42. McClellan report, *OR*, 5:35.

43. McClellan to Barlow, Nov. 8, McClellan to Mary Ellen McClellan, Nov. 3, 17, [1861], *McClellan Papers*, 124, 127–28, 135–36, 136 n. 3.

44. Sears, "Lincoln and McClellan," 19. See also numerous letters in *McClellan Papers*.

45. Williams, *Lincoln and His Generals*, 47.

46. Foote, *Civil War*, 1:145; Catton, *Mr. Lincoln's Army*, 196; Boatner, *Dictionary*, 367; John F. Marszalek, *Commander of All Lincoln's Armies: A Life of General Henry Wager Halleck* (Cambridge, MA: Belknap, 2004), 146–48.

47. Foote, *Civil War*, 1:145; Boatner, *Dictionary*, 96–97.

48. McClellan to Halleck, Nov. 11, 1861, *McClellan Papers*, 130–31, 131 n. 1; *OR*, 3:568–69.

49. Lincoln to Hunter, Oct. 24, 1861, *OR*, 3:553–54; Hay, *Diary*, 28–29.
50. Williams, *Lincoln and His Generals*, 47–48.
51. Thomas Scott to Guthrie, Nov. 10, 1861, *OR*, 4:349.
52. McClellan to Buell, Nov. 7, 12, 1861, *McClellan Papers*, 125–26, 131–32; [McClellan] to Buell, Nov. 7, 1861, *OR*, 4:342. Buell may not have received McClellan's November 7, 1861, letter, though Sears suggests it formed the basis for talks between Buell and McClellan. Buell received McClellan's letter of November 12. *McClellan Papers*, 126 n. 1.
53. McClellan to Buell, Nov. 25, 1861, *OR*, 7:447.
54. McClellan to Buell, Nov. 27, 1861, *OR*, 7:450.
55. Williams, *Lincoln and His Generals*, 48–49.
56. Buell to McClellan, Nov. 27, 1861, *OR*, 7:450–52.
57. Williams, *Lincoln and His Generals*, 49.
58. Ibid., 49.
59. McClellan to Buell, Nov. 29, 1861, *OR*, 7:457–58; McClellan to Buell, [Dec. 2, 1861], *McClellan Papers*, 138–39.
60. McClellan to Buell, Dec. 3, 5, 1861, *OR*, 7:468, 473; McClellan to Buell, Dec. 3, 1861, *McClellan Papers*, 140, 140–41 n. 1; Johnston and Maynard to Buell, Dec. 7, 1861, *OR*, 7:480.
61. Halleck to McClellan, Nov. 27, Dec. 6, 1861, *OR*, 8:382, 408. Halleck actually says " 'On to Richmond' policy," but he is really describing what today we would term strategy, not policy.
62. McClellan to Halleck, Dec. 10, 1861, *McClellan Papers*, 143–44, 144 n. 2; *OR*, 8:419.
63. McClellan to Halleck, Dec. 10, McClellan to Hunter, Dec. 11, 1861, *McClellan Papers*, 143–45, 144 n. 2, 145 nn. 1, 2; *OR*, 8:419.
64. McClellan to Halleck, Dec. 10, 1861, *McClellan Papers*, 143–44; *OR*, 8:419.
65. Buell to McClellan, Dec. 10, 1861, *OR*, 7:487–88.

CHAPTER 6

1. Eliot, *Scott*, 741; Harsh, "McClellan," 214; Harsh, "Lincoln's Tarnished Brass," 133.
2. Kevin J. Weddle, "The Blockade Board of 1861 and Union Naval Strategy," *Civil War History* 48, 2 (2002): 134, 139 n. 49, 139–42; *B&L*, 1:632.
3. McClellan to Cameron, Sept. 6, 1861, *McClellan Papers*, 92–93. McClellan had been actively thinking about the utility of gunboats and waterborne artillery since at least May 1861; McClellan to Rodgers, May 19, 1861, *McClellan Papers*, 21–22.
4. *B&L*, 1: 632–40, 660–61; McClellan to Mary Ellen McClellan, Nov. 18, 1861, *McClellan Papers*, 136, 137 n. 1.
5. *B&L*, 1:669; Foote, *Civil War*, 1:225; McClellan to Burnside, Jan. 7, 1862, *McClellan Papers*, 148–50; *OR*, 9:352–53.
6. William L. Barney, *Flawed Victory: A New Perspective on the Civil War* (New York: Praeger, 1975), 33–35.
7. Harsh, "McClellan," 221–22; Harsh, "Lincoln's Tarnished Brass," 135–36.
8. *B&L*, 1:639–40.
9. Harsh, "Lincoln's Tarnished Brass," 36.

10. Barnard, Memorandum for McClellan, c. Dec. 1, 1861, *OR*, 5:671–73.

11. Ibid.

12. Lincoln to McClellan, [c. Dec. 1, 1861], *CWL*, 5:34.

13. McClellan to Lincoln, Dec. 10, [1861], *McClellan Papers*, 143, 143 n. 1; Lincoln to McClellan, [c. Dec. 1, 1861], *CWL*, 5:34, 34–35 nn. 1–5; Sears, "Lincoln and McClellan," 20–21.

14. Lincoln to Halleck, Dec. 31, 1861, Jan. 1, 1862, *OR*, 7:524, 926.

15. McClellan to Halleck, Jan. 3, 1862, *McClellan Papers*, 146–47; *OR*, 7:527–28.

16. Buell to Halleck, Jan. 3, 1862, *OR*, 7:529–30.

17. Lincoln to Buell, Jan. 4, 1862, *OR*, 7:530; Buell to Lincoln, Jan. 5, 1862, *OR*, 7:530–31.

18. Lincoln to Buell, Jan. 6, 1862, *OR*, 7:927–28.

19. McClellan to Buell, Jan. 6, 1861, *McClellan Papers*, 147–48. Italics in the original.

20. Lincoln to Buell, Jan. 6, 1862, *OR*, 7:927–28.

21. For earlier examples, see McClellan to Buell, Nov. 27, Dec. 3, 5, 1861, *OR*, 7:450, 468, 474.

22. Halleck to Lincoln, Jan. 6, 1862, *OR*, 7:532–33.

23. Symonds, *Atlas*, 16.

24. Lincoln indorsement on Halleck to Lincoln, Jan. 6, 1862, *OR*, 7:532–33.

25. Lincoln to Buell, Jan. 7, 1862, *OR*, 7:535.

26. Buell to Thomas, Dec. 29, 1861, *OR*, 7:522; Buell to McClellan, Jan. 13, 1862, *OR*, 7:548–49; Hattaway and Jones, *How the North Won*, 62.

27. Halleck to Grant, Jan. 6, 1862, *OR*, 7:533–34; *The Papers of Ulysses S. Grant*, ed. John Y. Simon (Carbondale: Southern Illinois University Press, 1967–2005), 3:xiv; McClellan to Halleck, Jan. 3, 1862, *OR*, 7:527–28.

28. Grant, General Orders No. 3, Jan. 13, 1862, *Grant Papers*, 4:45–46.

29. Ulysses S. Grant, *Memoirs and Selected Letters: Personal Memoirs of U. S. Grant. Selected Letters, 1839–1865* (New York: Literary Classics, 1990), 189.

30. Ibid., 189–90; Grant note, Jan. 11, 1862, *Grant Papers*, 4:34, 34–35nn.

31. Grant, *Memoirs*, 189–90; Grant to Kelton, Jan. 20, 1862, *Grant Papers*, 4:74–75, 75 n. 2; Grant to Mary Grant, Jan. 23, 1862, *Grant Papers*, 4:96–97, 97 n. 2.

32. Rafuse, *McClellan's War*, 169–70.

33. Quoted in M. C. Meigs, "General M. C. Meigs on the Conduct of the Civil War," *American Historical Review* 26, 2 (Jan. 1921): 292.

34. Meigs, "General M. C. Meigs," 292–93; Donald, *Lincoln*, 330; McDowell quoted in William Swinton, *Campaigns of the Army of the Potomac* (New York: University Publishing, 1870), 80–81. Italics in the original.

35. McDowell quoted in Swinton, *Campaigns*, 81; Donald, *Lincoln*, 330.

36. McDowell quoted in Swinton, *Campaigns*, 81.

37. Ibid., 82–83.

38. Ibid., 84.

39. Ibid., 84–85; Meigs, "General M. C. Meigs," 292–93.

40. Meigs, "General M. C. Meigs," 293.

41. McPherson, *Tried by War*, 67.

42. David Homer Bates, *Lincoln in the Telegraph Office: Recollections of the United States Military Telegraph Corps During the Civil War* (Lincoln: University of Nebraska Press, 1995), 399–400.

43. Meigs, "General M. C. Meigs," 293.

44. Clausewitz, *On War*, 101–2.

45. McClellan to Buell, Jan. 13, 1862, *McClellan Papers*, 151–52.

46. Browning, *Diary*, 1:523.

47. Lincoln to Buell, Jan. 13, 1862, *CWL*, 5:98–99; *OR*, 7:928–29.

48. Ibid.

49. Memorandum for a Plan of Campaign, [c. Oct. 1, 1861], *CWL*, 4:544–45.

50. Jomini, *Art of War*, 89; T. Harry Williams, "Military Leadership in the North and South," in *Why the North Won*, 57.

51. Hattaway and Jones, *How the North Won*, 57.

52. Halleck to McClellan, Jan. 20, 1862, *OR*, 8:508–11.

53. Ibid.

54. Ibid.

55. Ibid.

56. Ibid.

57. McClellan to Stanton, [Jan. 26, 1862], *McClellan Papers*, 158 n. 1.

58. McClellan to Thomas, Jan. 25, 1862, *OR*, 6:677–78.

59. Meigs, "General M. C. Meigs," 298.

60. President's General War Order No. 1, Jan. 27, 1862, *CWL*, 5:111–12.

61. McClellan report, *OR*, 5:41; Hay, *Diary*, 35.

62. President's Special War Order No. 1, Jan. 31, 1862, *CWL*, 5:115.

63. McClellan report, *OR*, 5:41.

64. Ibid.; McClellan to Stanton, Jan. 31 [Feb. 3], 1862, *McClellan Papers*, 163–64, 170 n. 1.

65. McClellan to Stanton, Jan. 31 [Feb. 3], 1862, *McClellan Papers*, 163–64.

66. Ibid.

67. Jomini, *Art of War*, 70–76.

68. McClellan to Stanton, Jan. 31 [Feb. 3], 1862, *McClellan Papers*, 164–66. These factors included the enemy's fortifications, their possession of a strong central position, weather delays, and bad roads.

69. Ibid., 166–67.

70. Ibid., 167.

71. Ibid.

72. Ibid.

73. Ibid., 167–68, 170.

74. Ibid., 168.

75. Ibid.

76. Ibid., 168–69. Italics in the original.

77. Ibid., 169–70. Italics in the original.

78. Lincoln to McClellan, Feb. 3, 1862, in McClellan report, *OR*, 5:41–42.

79. *McClellan Papers*, 171 n. 1; McClellan report, *OR*, 5:42.

80. Sears, "Lincoln and McClellan," 29.

81. Bruce, "Strategy of the Civil War," 424–25.

82. Weigley, *Civil War*, 93–94.

83. I am indebted to Mark Elam for making this point.

84. Harsh, "McClellan and the Forgotten Alternative."

CHAPTER 7

1. Hattaway and Jones, *How the North Won*, 18; Bern Andersen, "The Naval Strategy of the Civil War," *Military Affairs* 26, 1 (Spring 1962): 11, 13; Bern Andersen, *By Sea and by River: The Naval History of the Civil War* (New York: Da Capo, 1962), 10.
2. Andersen, "Naval Strategy," 11–12; Raimondo Luraghi, *A History of the Confederate Navy* (Annapolis: Naval Institute Press, 1996), 15.
3. Weddle, "The Blockade Board," 123–25.
4. Ibid., 125; Jones, *Union in Peril*, 50; Benjamin to Mason, Apr. 8, 1862, *ORN*, ser. 2, 3:379–84.
5. Weddle, "Blockade Board," 125–26; Richard S. West, *Mr. Lincoln's Navy* (New York: Longmans, Green, 1957), 53; Andersen, "Naval Strategy," 13.
6. Weddle, "Blockade Board," 125–33.
7. Quoted in ibid., 131–33.
8. Welles to Du Pont, Bache, Davis, and Barnard, June 25, 1861, in ibid., 134.
9. Ibid., 132.
10. Ibid., 135–38, 141.
11. Ibid., 135, 138; Long and Long, *Civil War*, 119.
12. Weddle, "Blockade Board," 138–40, 139 n. 49; *ORN*, ser. 1, 16:680–81.
13. Davis Proclamation, Apr. 17, 1861, *ORN*, ser. 2, 3:96–97.
14. Luraghi, *Confederate Navy*, 72–75, 376 n. 16; Long and Long, *Civil War*, 74.
15. Alfred Thayer Mahan, *The Influence of Sea Power upon History, 1660–1783* (New York: Dover, 1987), 42–44.
16. Mallory to Davis, Apr. 26, 1861, *ORN*, ser. 2, 2:51–55; Davis, *Rise and Fall*, 2:227; Luraghi, *Confederate Navy*, 32–33.
17. Bulloch, *Secret Service*, 33–34.
18. Mallory to Bulloch, May 9, 1861, *ORN*, ser. 2, 2:64–65.
19. Luraghi, *Confederate Navy*, 66.
20. Bulloch to Mallory, Aug. 13, 1861, *ORN*, ser. 2, 2:83–87; Bulloch, *Secret Service*, 260.
21. West, *Mr. Lincoln's Navy*, 259; Craig L. Symonds, *Lincoln and His Admirals: Abraham Lincoln, the U.S. Navy, and Civil War* (New York: Oxford University Press, 2008), 341–42; McPherson, *Battle Cry*, 547; Luraghi, *Confederate Navy*, 320.
22. McPherson, *Battle Cry*, 5, 315–16; Eicher, *Longest Night*, 695.
23. Mallory to Conrad, May 10, 1861, *ORN*, ser. 2, 2:67–69; Luraghi, *Confederate Navy*, 67–68.
24. Mallory to Conrad, May 9, 1861, *ORN*, ser. 2, 2:66; Howell to Davis, May 10, 1861, *ORN*, ser. 2, 2:66–7 (2 notes); [memorandum], undated, *ORN*, ser. 2, 2:122–23.
25. Mallory to North, May 17, 1861, *ORN*, ser. 2, 2:70–72.
26. Luraghi, *Confederate Navy*, 91–92; William N. Still Jr., "Confederate Naval Strategy," *Journal of Southern History* 27, 3 (Aug. 1961): 331.
27. Mallory to Davis, July 18, 1861, *ORN*, ser. 2, 2:76–79.
28. Ibid.; *ORN*, ser. 2, 1:783–85; [memorandum], undated, *ORN*, ser. 2, 2:122–23; Luraghi, *Confederate Navy*, 92–94, 109.
29. Mallory to Davis, Feb. 27, 1862, *ORN*, ser. 2, 2:149–54.
30. Mallory to Mitchell, Mar. 15, 1862, *ORN*, ser. 2, 1:466–67; Boatner, *Dictionary*, 561; Symonds, *Lincoln and His Admirals*, 136; McPherson, *Battle Cry*, 375.

31. Boatner, *Dictionary*, 476; Mark M. Boatner, III, *Encyclopedia of the American Revolution* (New York: David McKay, 1966), 607–9; Emory M. Thomas, *Robert E. Lee: A Biography* (New York: W. W. Norton, 1995), 180, 188; Still, "Confederate Naval Strategy," 331–32; *Wartime Papers*, 81; Luraghi, *Confederate Navy*, 187. See also Lee to Cooper, Jan. 8, 1862, *OR*, 6:367.

32. Luraghi, *Confederate Navy*, 68, 236–37, 239–40, 249; Timothy S. Wolters, "Electric Torpedoes in the Confederacy: Reconciling Conflicting Histories," *Journal of Military History* 72 (July 2008): 755–83; Davis, *Rise and Fall*, 2:207.

33. Luraghi, *Confederate Navy*, 252.

34. Ibid., 252–58; John J. Poluhowich, *Argonaut: The Submarine Legacy of Simon Lake* (College Station: Texas A&M University Press, 1999), 38.

35. Maury to Preston, Oct. 22, 1861, *ORN*, ser. 2, 2:99–105.

36. Luraghi, *Confederate Navy*, 241–42, 426 n. 51; [2 notes], Dec. 23, 1861, *ORN*, ser. 2, 2:117; Jay W. Simson, *Naval Strategies of the Civil War: Confederate Innovations and Federal Opportunism* (Nashville, TN: Cumberland House, 2001), 66.

37. Kenneth J. Hagan, *This People's Navy: The Making of American Sea Power* (New York: Free Press, 1991), 68–69.

38. Bern, "Naval Strategy," 17; Welles, *Diary*, 1:213–14.

39. Welles, *Diary*, 1:342.

40. Luraghi, *Confederate Navy*, 101–2; Andersen, *By Sea and by River*, 87–88; *B&L*, 1:338–39 and notes.

41. Luraghi, *Confederate Navy*, 103–4.

42. Bulloch to Mallory, Oct. 20, 1863, *ORN*, ser. 2, 2:507–11.

43. Welles, *Diary*, 1:247.

44. Andersen, *By Sea and by River*, 47.

45. Welles, *Diary*, 1:246, 248–62.

46. Andersen, "Naval Strategy," 18.

47. Ibid.; West, *Mr. Lincoln's Navy*, 277, 280.

48. West, *Mr. Lincoln's Navy*, 52, 54, 60; Du Pont et al. to Welles, July 16, 1861, *ORN*, ser. 1, 12:198–201.

49. Welles to Goldsborough, Sept. 18, 1861, *ORN*, ser. 1, 6:233–34.

50. Andersen, *By Sea and by River*, 228; West, *Mr. Lincoln's Navy*, 58.

51. George A. Bruce, "The Strategy of the Civil War," 396–99. Bruce also argued that the closure of these ports by early 1862 would have made it impossible for the South to keep enough troops in the field, armed and equipped, to continue the war beyond 1863. This flies in the face of what we now know about the South's development of an internal wartime arms industry.

52. Hattaway and Jones, *How the North Won*, 82.

53. Andersen, "Naval Strategy," 17.

54. Welles, *Diary*, 1:334–35; Beringer et al., *Why the South Lost*, 58–59, 63; William N. Still Jr., "A Naval Sieve: The Union Blockade in the Civil War," in William N. Still Jr., John M. Taylor, and Norman C. Delaney, eds., *Raiders and Blockaders: The Civil War Afloat* (Washington: Brassey's, 1998), 136–37; Andersen, *By Sea and by River*, 231.

55. Andersen, "Naval Strategy," 19–20.

56. Luraghi, *Confederate Navy*, xi; McPherson, *Battle Cry*, 381.

57. Mallory to Conrad, May 10, 1861, *ORN*, ser. 2, 2:67–69; Mallory to Mitchell, Mar. 15, 1862, *ORN*, ser. 2, 1:466–67; Mallory to Bulloch, July 18, 1864, *ORN*, ser. 2, 2:688–89.

58. William J. Fowler Jr., *Under Two Flags: The American Navy in the Civil War* (New York: W. W. Norton, 1990), 305.

59. Andersen, *By Sea and by River*, 230–31.

60. Andersen, "Naval Strategy," 19–20; Andersen, *By Sea and by River*, 231.

61. Rose Razaghian, "Financing the Civil War: The Confederacy's Financial Strategy," Yale ICF Working Paper no. 04–05 (Jan. 2005), 16, 19.

62. McPherson, *Battle Cry*, 382.

CHAPTER 8

1. Tilghman to Davis, Dec. 28, 1861, *OR*, 52/2:245–46.

2. Woodworth, *Davis and His Generals*, 46–51.

3. Grant to Frémont, Sept. 6, 1861, *Grant Papers*, 2:196–97, 3:245n; Woodworth, *Davis and His Generals*, 52, 56.

4. [A. S. Johnston] report, Mar. 17, 1862, *OR*, 7:922; Symonds, *Atlas*, 16–17.

5. Woodworth, *Davis and His Generals*, 53–55; Foote, *Civil War*, 1:172; St. John R. Liddell, "Liddell's Record of the Civil War," *Southern Bivouac* n.s. 1 (Dec. 1885), 416–19.

6. A. S. Johnston to Davis, Mar. 18, 1862, *OR*, 7:258–61; Woodworth, *Davis and His Generals*, 55.

7. Buell to McClellan, Nov. 27, 1861, *OR*, 7:450–52.

8. Benjamin Franklin Cooling, *Forts Henry and Donelson: The Key to the Confederate Heartland* (Knoxville: University of Tennessee Press, 1987), 65–66.

9. Whittlesey to Halleck, Nov. 20, 1861, *OR*, 7:440.

10. William T. Sherman, *Memoirs of General W. T. Sherman* (New York: Literary Classics, 1990), 238.

11. Halleck to McClellan, Jan. 20, 1862, *OR*, 8:508–11; Stephen E. Ambrose, "The Union Command System and the Donelson Campaign," *Military Affairs* 24, 2 (Summer 1960): 78–80.

12. Ambrose, "The Union Command System," 80.

13. Halleck to McClellan, Jan. 9, 1862, *OR*, 7:539–40; Foote to Halleck, Dec. 6, 1861, *OR*, 7:477; Flag Officer Foote had three ironclad gunboats at hand in early December.

14. Grant, *Memoirs*, 189–90; Grant to Halleck, [Jan.] 28, 1862, *Grant Papers*, 4:99, 99–100nn.

15. McClellan to Halleck and Buell, Jan. 29, 1862, *OR*, 7:571.

16. *McClellan Papers*, 160 n. 1; Ambrose, "The Union Command System," 81; Halleck to McClellan, Feb. 6, 1862, *OR*, 7:586–7.

17. Grant, *Memoirs*, 190; Halleck to Grant, Feb. 1, 1862, *OR*, 7:577.

18. Buell to McClellan, Feb. 1, 1862, *OR*, 7:931–33.

19. Ibid.

20. See Halleck to Lincoln, Jan. 7, 1862, *OR*, 7:535.

21. Grant, *Memoirs*, 190–92.

22. Halleck to Buell, Feb. 5, 1862, *OR*, 7:583.

23. Buell to Halleck, Feb. 5, 1862, *OR*, 7:583.

24. Buell to McClellan, Feb. 5, 1862, *OR*, 7:585.

25. McClellan to Halleck, Feb. 6, 1862, *McClellan Papers*, 171–72; McClellan to Buell, [Feb. 6, 1862], *McClellan Papers*, 172; *OR*, 7:587.

26. Buell to McClellan, Feb. 6, 1862, *OR*, 7:587–88.

27. Halleck to McClellan, Feb. 6, 1862, *OR*, 7:587.

28. Halleck to McClellan, Feb. 7, 1862, *OR*, 7:590.

29. *Grant Papers*, 4:xiii.

30. Halleck to McClellan, Feb. 7, 1862, *OR*, 7:590–91.

31. McClellan to Halleck, Feb. 7, 1862, *OR*, 7:591.

32. McClellan to Buell, Feb. 7, 1862, *OR*, 7:593.

33. Halleck to Buell, Feb. 7, 1862, *OR*, 7:592.

34. Buell to McClellan, Feb. 7, 1862, *OR*, 7:593.

35. Buell to McClellan, Feb. 8, 1862, *OR*, 7:594.

36. McClellan to Halleck, Feb. 7, 1862, *OR*, 7:591.

37. Halleck to McClellan, Feb. 8, 1862, *OR*, 7:595.

38. McClellan to Halleck, Feb. 14, 1862, *OR*, 7:614.

39. Stanton to Buell, Feb. 9, 1862, *OR*, 7:937–38.

40. Buell to McClellan, Feb. 1, 1862, *OR*, 7:931–33.

41. Buell to Halleck, Feb. 12, 1862, *OR*, 7:607–8.

42. Halleck to McClellan, Feb. 15, 1862, *OR*, 7:616.

43. McClellan to Halleck, Feb. 15, 1862, *OR*, 7:617.

44. Halleck to McClellan, Feb. 15, 1862, *OR*, 7:617.

45. McClellan to Halleck, Feb. 15, 1862, *OR*, 7:617–18; McClellan report, *OR*, 5:6–7.

46. Buell to McClellan, Feb. 15, 1862, *OR*, 7:619–20; McClellan to Buell, Feb. 15, 1862, *OR*, 7:620.

47. Buell to Halleck, Feb. 15, 1862, *OR*, 7:621.

48. Halleck to Buell, Feb. 15, 1862, *OR*, 7:621–22.

49. Lincoln to Halleck, Feb. 16, 1862, *OR*, 7:624.

50. Halleck to McClellan, Feb. 16, 1862, *OR*, 7:625; McClellan to Halleck, Feb. 16, 1862, *OR*, 7:625.

51. McClellan to Buell, [Feb. 16?, 1862], *OR*, 7:626.

52. Halleck to McClellan, Feb. 16, 1862, *OR*, 7:627–28.

53. McClellan to Halleck, Feb. 17, 1862, *OR*, 7:628.

54. Halleck to McClellan, Feb. 17, 1862, *OR*, 7:628.

55. Buell to Halleck, Feb. 18 [17], 1862, *OR*, 7:940–41.

56. Halleck to Buell, Feb. 18, 1862, *OR*, 7:632.

57. Buell to Halleck, Feb. 18, 1862, *OR*, 7:632.

58. Halleck to Buell, Feb. 18, 1862, *OR*, 7:632–33.

59. Halleck to McClellan, Feb. 19, 1862, *OR*, 7:636.

60. Halleck to Thomas A. Scott, Feb. 19, 1862, *OR*, 7:637. See also Halleck to McClellan, Feb. 20, 1862, *OR*, 7:641.

61. Stanton to Halleck, Feb. 22, 1862, *OR*, 7:652; McClellan to Halleck, Feb. 21, 1862, *OR*, 7:645.

62. Halleck to Stanton, Feb. 23 [21], 1862, *OR*, 7:655.

63. Halleck to Thomas A. Scott, Feb. 20, 1862, *OR*, 7:642.

64. Halleck to Grant, Feb. 18, 1862, *OR*, 7:633; Foote to Cullum, Feb. 21, 1862, *OR*, 7:648.

65. Halleck to Thomas A. Scott, Feb. 21, 1862, *OR*, 7:648.

66. McClellan to Buell, Feb. 21, 1862, *OR*, 7:646.

67. Buell to Halleck, Feb. 21, 1862, *OR*, 7:650; Buell to Command Officer, United States Forces, Clarksville, Feb. 22, 1862, *OR*, 7:653.

68. Buell to McClellan, Feb. 23, 1862, *OR*, 7:656.

69. McClellan to Buell, Feb. 24, 1862, *OR*, 7:660.

70. McClellan to Halleck, Feb. 24, 1862, *OR*, 7:661. He also suggested some follow-on operations.

71. For relevant maps see Engle, *Buell*, 84; Weigley, *Civil War*, 97.

72. A. S. Johnston to Davis, Mar. 18, 1862, *OR*, 7:258–61; Woodworth, *Davis and His Generals*, 79; Long and Long, *Civil War*, 168–69.

73. A. S. Johnston to Davis, Mar. 18, 1862, *OR*, 7:258–61.

74. Ibid.

75. Weigley, *Civil War*, 108; McPherson, *Battle Cry*, 393, 402.

76. Weigley, *Civil War*, 112–13; Marszalek, *Halleck*, 119.

77. A. S. Johnston to Davis, Mar. 18, 1862, *OR*, 7:258–61.

78. Davis to [A. S. Johnston?], Mar. 12, 1862, *OR*, 7:257–58. See also Davis to A. S. Johnston, Mar. 12, 1862, *Davis Papers*, 8:92–94.

79. Price to Davis, Dec. 16, 1861, *OR*, 8:714–15.

80. Price to Polk, Dec. 23, 1861, *OR*, 8:729–31; Polk to Davis, Jan. 3, 1862, *OR*, 8:728–29.

81. Price to Polk, Dec. 23, 1861, *OR*, 8:729–31.

82. Polk to Davis, Jan. 3, 1862, *OR*, 8:728–29.

83. Halleck to McClellan, Jan. 30, 1862, *OR*, 7:571–72; Marszalek, *Halleck*, 116–17.

84. Benjamin to Price, Feb. 5, 1862, *OR*, 8:747–48.

85. Foote, *Civil War*, 1:277–78; Van Dorn to Price, Feb. 7, 1862, *OR*, 8:748–49.

86. Van Dorn to Price, Feb. 14, 1862, *OR*, 8:750–52; Foote, *Civil War*, 1:278. Van Dorn also proposed a contingency plan in case they could not take St. Louis.

87. Price to Jackson, Feb. 25, 1862, *OR*, 8:756–57; Foote, *Civil War*, 1:279–92; Weigley, *Civil War*, 102–3.

CHAPTER 9

1. Quoted in *Davis Papers*, 8:66.

2. Inaugural Address, Feb. 22, 1862, *Davis Papers*, 8:58–59; Inaugural Address, Feb. 22, 1862, *Messages and Papers*, 1:186. Clausewitz writes about "the nature of the war" and the "value of the object," *On War*, 88–89 and 92, respectively.

3. James I. Robertson Jr., "Braxton Bragg: The Lonely Patriot," in Gary W. Gallagher and Joseph T. Glatthaar, eds., *Leaders of the Lost Cause: New Perspectives on the Confederate High Command* (Mechanicsburg, PA: Stackpole, 2004), 71–73.

4. Bragg to Benjamin, Feb. 15, 1862, *OR*, 6:826–27.

5. Bragg to Beauregard, Feb. 27, 1862, *OR*, 6:836.

6. On this last point see Benjamin to Bragg, Feb. 18, 1862, *OR*, 6:828, and Bragg to Benjamin, Feb. 18, 1862, *OR*, 6:894.

7. *OR*, 7:889, 899–903, 908–9.

8. Benjamin to Bragg, Feb. 18, 1862, *OR*, 6:828.

9. Ibid.; Davis to Joseph Davis, Feb. 21, 1862, *Davis Papers*, 8:53.

10. Benjamin to Bragg, Feb. 18, 1862, *OR*, 6:828.

11. Benjamin to Hébert, Feb. 23, 1862, *OR*, 15:871.

12. A. S. Johnston to Benjamin, Feb. 25, 1862, *OR*, 7:426–27.

13. Ibid.

14. Davis to the Speaker of the House, Mar. 4, 1862, *OR*, ser. 4, 1:969–70. Benjamin put forward different numbers, which Davis gave to the Congress. See Benjamin to Davis, Mar. 4, 1862, *OR*, ser. 4, 1:970.

15. Davis to the Speaker of the House, Mar. 16, 1862, *OR*, ser. 4, 1:997.

16. Hattaway and Jones, *How the North Won*, 117; Douglas Southall Freeman, *R. E. Lee: A Biography*, 4 vols. (New York: Charles Scribner's Sons, 1935), 2:5–7.

17. A. S. Johnston to Davis, Mar. 25, 1862, *OR*, 10/2:361.

18. *Davis Papers*, 8:118 n. 3.

19. Davis to A. S. Johnston, Mar. 26, 1862, *Davis Papers*, 8:117.

20. McClellan to Buell, Feb. 25, 1862, *OR*, 7:664; McClellan to Halleck, Feb. 25, 1862, *OR*, 7:664.

21. Buell to Halleck, Feb. 26, 1862, *OR*, 7:668–69.

22. Buell to McClellan, Feb. 28, 1862, *OR*, 7:671.

23. Buell to McClellan, Mar. 1, 1862, *OR*, 7:945.

24. McClellan to Halleck, Mar. 2, 1862, *OR*, 7:678.

25. McClellan to Buell, Mar. 2, 1862, *OR*, 7:678.

26. McClellan to Halleck, Mar. 3, 1862, *OR*, 11/3:7–8.

27. Buell to McClellan, Mar. 3, 1862, *OR*, 7:679.

28. Buell to Halleck, Mar. 3, 1862, *OR*, 7:680.

29. Halleck to Buell, Mar. 4, 1862, *OR*, 7:682.

30. President's War Order No. 3, Mar. 11, 1862, *OR*, 10/2:28–29.

31. Buell to Halleck, Mar. 10, 1862, *OR*, 10/2:25.

32. Buell to Halleck, Mar. 10, 1862, *OR*, 10/2:27.

33. Buell to Scott, Mar. 7, 1862, *OR*, 10/2:611; Engle, *Buell*, 205; Buell to McClellan, Mar. 9, 1862, *OR*, 10/2:611–12.

34. Halleck to Buell, Mar. 13, 1862, *OR*, 10/2:33.

35. Buell to Halleck, Mar. 14, 1862, *OR*, 10/2:37–38.

36. Halleck to Buell, Mar. 14, 1862, *OR*, 10/2:38.

37. Buell to Halleck, Mar. 15, 1862, *OR*, 10/2:39.

38. Halleck to Buell, Mar. 16, 1862, *OR*, 10/2:42.

39. Halleck to Grant, Mar. 16, 1862, *OR*, 10/2:41.

40. Buell to Halleck, Mar. 17, 1862, *OR*, 10/2:44.

41. Halleck to Buell, Mar. 17, 1862, *OR*, 10/2:45.

42. Buell to Halleck, Mar. 23, 1862, *OR*, 10/2:60–61.

43. Halleck to Buell, Mar. 26, 1862, *OR*, 10/2:66.

44. A. S. Johnston to Davis, Apr. 3, 1862, *OR*, 10/2:387.

45. Davis to A. S. Johnston, Apr. 5, 1862, *OR*, 10/2:394.

46. Symonds, *Atlas*, 18–19.

47. Ibid., 19; Foote, *Civil War*, 1:339–40; Quoted in Williams, *Lincoln and His Generals*, 86.

48. Beauregard to Cooper, Apr. 9, 1862, *OR*, 10/2:403.

49. See Apr. 9, 10, 1862 correspondence, *OR*, 10/2: 404–7.

50. Lee to Beauregard, May 26, 1862, *OR*, 10/2:546.

51. Buell to Mitchel, Mar. 27, 1862, *OR*, 10/2:71–72.

52. Buell to Halleck, Mar. 28, 1862, *OR*, 10/2:75; Halleck to Buell, Mar. 29, 1862, *OR*, 10/2:77.

53. Stager to Stanton, Apr. 12, 1862, *OR*, 10/2:104.

54. Halleck to Stanton, Apr. 16, 1862, *OR*, 10/2:108.

55. Mitchel to Stanton, Apr. 17, 1862, *OR*, 10/2:111.

56. Buell to Mitchel, Apr. 19, 1862, *OR*, 10/2:114.

57. Mitchel to Chase, Apr. 19, 1862, *OR*, 10/2:115.

58. Stanton to Mitchel, Apr. 21, 1862, *OR*, 10/2:116–17.

59. Halleck to Lincoln, Apr. 22, 1862, *OR*, 10/2:117.

60. Mitchel to Stanton, Apr. 24, 1862, *OR*, 10/2:124; Mitchel to Buell, Apr. 24, 1862, *OR*, 10/2:124–25.

61. Mitchel to Stanton, Apr. 25, 1862, *OR*, 10/2:125. He knew of another 1,500 holding a nearby bridge, Mitchel to Stanton, Apr. 25, [1862], *OR*, 10/2:125–26.

62. Mitchel to Stanton, Apr. 25, [1862], *OR*, 10/2:125–26.

63. Mitchel to Buell, Apr. 27, [1862], *OR*, 10/2:133–34.

64. Mitchel to Buell, Apr. 20, 1862, *OR*, 10/2:619–20.

65. Mitchel to Buell, Apr. 27, [1862], *OR*, 10/2:134.

66. Mitchel to Stanton, May 4, 1862, *OR*, 10/2:161–62.

67. Mitchel to Stanton, May 1, 1862, *OR*, 10/2:155–56.

68. Stanton to Mitchel, May 1, 1862, *OR*, 10/2:156; Mitchel to Stanton, May 4, 1862, *OR*, 10/2:161–62.

69. Mitchel to Stanton, May 4, 1862, *OR*, 10/2:162–3 (2 notes).

70. Brown to Randolph, May 1, 1862, *OR*, 10/2:480.

71. Woodworth, *Davis and His Generals*, 126–28.

72. E. K. Smith to Washington, May 28, 1862, *OR*, 10/2:556–57.

73. Mitchel to Stanton, May 4, 1862, *OR*, 10/2:161–62.

74. E. K. Smith to Brown, May 27, 1862, *OR*, 10/2:554; E. K. Smith to Pemberton, May 27, 1862, *OR*, 10/2:554; Woodworth, *Davis and His Generals*, 126–28.

75. Hambright report, June 8, 1862, *OR*, 10/1:920–21.

76. Woodworth, *Davis and His Generals*, 126–28; E. K. Smith to Cooper, June 12, 1862, *OR*, 16/2:679; E. K. Smith to Cooper, June 12, 1862, *OR*, 16/2:679; Cooper to E. K. Smith, June 12, 1862, *OR*, 16/2:679.

77. Marszalek, *Halleck*, 121.

78. Ibid., 123–25; Halleck to Stanton, Apr. 8, 1862, *OR*, 10/2:98–99; Mitchel to Halleck, Apr. [14], 1862, *OR*, 10/2:618; Halleck to Pope, Apr. 22, 1862, *OR*, 10/2:117.

79. Foote, *Civil War*, 1:382–83.

80. Beauregard to Villepigue, May 28, 1862, *OR*, 10/1:902–3; Foote, *Civil War*, 1:383.

81. Beauregard to W. P. Johnston, June 22, 1862, *OR*, 10/1:774–77.

82. Ibid.

83. Davis to Varina Howell Davis, June 13, 1862, *Davis Papers*, 8:243–44.

84. Davis to W. P. Johnston, June 14, 1862, *OR*, 10/1:786.

85. W. P. Johnston to Davis, July 15, 1862, *OR*, 10/1:780–86.

86. Beauregard to Cooper, June 13, 1862, *OR*, 10/1:762–65.
87. Beauregard to Cooper, June 15, 1862, *OR*, 17/2:601; Davis to Bragg, June 20, 1862, *OR*, 17/2:614.
88. Davis to Varina Howell Davis, June 19, 1862, *Davis Papers*, 8:253–54; Foote, *Civil War*, 1:390.
89. McClellan to T. W. Sherman, Feb. 12, 14, 1862, *OR*, 6:224–25; McClellan indorsement on T. W. Sherman to Adj. Gen. U.S. Army, Feb. 15, 1862, *OR*, 6:226.
90. Foote, *Civil War*, 1:352.
91. Ibid, 353.
92. David D. Porter, *Incidents and Anecdotes of the Civil War* (New York: D. Appleton, 1885), 64–66; *B&L*, 2:24.
93. McPherson, *Battle Cry*, 418–21.
94. Porter, *Incidents*, 66.
95. Welles to Farragut, Jan. 20, 1862, *ORN*, ser. 1, 18:7–8.
96. Andersen, *By Sea*, 128; S. P. Lee to the Authorities at Vicksburg, May 18, 1862, *ORN*, ser. 1, 18:491; Autrey to Lee, May 18, 1862, *ORN*, ser. 1, 18:492.
97. Andersen, *By Sea*, 129; Farragut to Welles, May 30, 1862, *ORN*, ser. 1, 18:519–21; Lovell to Beauregard, May 25, 1862, *ORN*, ser. 1, 18:850; McPherson, *Battle Cry*, 421.
98. Andersen, *By Sea*, 129–30; Fox to Farragut, May 16, 1862, *ORN*, ser. 1, 18:498; Foote to C. H. Davis, May 9, 1862, *ORN*, ser. 1, 23:86; Fox to Farragut, May 17, 1862, *ORN*, ser. 1, 18:498–99; Welles to Farragut, May 19, 1862, *ORN*, ser. 1, 18:502.
99. Andersen, *By Sea*, 130–32; Farragut to Welles, May 30, 1862, *ORN*, ser. 1, 18:519–21; Butler to Stanton, June 1, 1862, *OR*, 15:447–50; Porter to Farragut, June 16, 1862, *ORN*, ser. 1, 18:558–59; Farragut to Welles, June 28, 1862, *ORN*, ser. 1, 18:588; Farragut to Halleck, [June 28, 1862], *ORN*, ser. 1, 18:590.
100. Halleck to Farragut, July 3, 1862, *ORN*, ser. 1, 18:593.
101. Stanton to Halleck, July 14, 1862, *ORN*, ser. 1, 18:636; Halleck to Stanton, July 15, 1862, *ORN*, ser. 1, 18:636.
102. Park to Davis, June 6, 1862, *ORN*, ser. 1, 23:121.
103. Farragut to [Bell], July 9, 1862, *ORN*, ser. 1, 18:632; Farragut to Welles, July, 10, 13, 1862, *ORN*, ser. 1, 18:594, 675.
104. Welles to Farragut, July 14, 1862, *ORN*, ser. 1, 18:595.
105. Welles, *Diary*, 1:71–72, 314.
106. McPherson, *Battle Cry*, 422.
107. Grant, *Memoirs*, 214–15.

CHAPTER 10

1. Davis to J. E. Johnston, *Davis Papers*, Feb. 28, 1862, 8:67–69, 69 n. 6.
2. Catton, *Mr. Lincoln's Army*, 85, 88.
3. Davis to J. E. Johnston, *Davis Papers*, Feb. 28, 1862, 8:67–69, 69 n. 7.
4. J. E. Johnston to Whiting, Mar. 15, 1862, *OR*, 5:1101–2 (two notes).
5. Boatner, *Dictionary*, 501; *Davis Papers*, 8:130 nn. 1, 2. See n. 2 for Confederate troop dispositions.
6. *McClellan Papers*, 204; Symonds, *Johnston*, 146.

7. President's General War Order No. 3, Mar. 8, 1862, *CWL*, 5:151; *OR*, 11/3:57–58.

8. Secretary of War to McClellan, Mar. 13, 1862, *CWL*, 5:157–58; Rafuse, *McClellan's War*, 196. See also "A Council of Generals," Mar. 13, 1862, *OR*, 11/3:58.

9. Stanton to McClellan, Mar. 13, 1862, *OR*, 5:750.

10. McClellan to Stanton, Mar. 19, 1862, *McClellan Papers*, 215–16; *OR*, 5:57–58.

11. Rafuse, *McClellan's War*, 200; Williams to Banks, Mar. 16, 1862, *OR*, 5:56; Catton, *Mr. Lincoln's Army*, 103–4; McClellan to Banks, [Mar. 16, 1862], *McClellan Papers*, 212; *OR*, 5:56.

12. McClellan to L. Thomas, Apr. 1, 1862, *McClellan Papers*, 222–23; McClellan report, *OR*, 5:60–61.

13. McClellan to L. Thomas, Mar. 13, 1862, *McClellan Papers*, 208 and n. 1.

14. McClellan to Burnside, Apr. 2, 1862, *McClellan Papers*, 224.

15. McClellan to Banks, Apr. 1, 1862, *McClellan Papers*, 220–21; *OR*, 5:59–60.

16. Rafuse, *McClellan's War*, 205–6; Wadsworth to Stanton, Apr. 2, 1862, *OR*, 11/3:60–61; Stanton to L. Thomas and Hitchcock, Apr. 2, 1862, *OR*, 11/3:57; L. Thomas to Hitchcock, Apr. 2, 1862, *OR*, 11/3:61–62.

17. Lincoln to Stanton, Apr. 3, 1862, *CWL*, 5:179.

18. McClellan to Mary Ellen McClellan, Apr. 6, [1862], *McClellan Papers*, 230.

19. McClellan to Rodgers, Apr. 6, 1862, *OR*, 11/3:75; Rafuse, *McClellan's War*, 203–5; Keyes to Harris, Apr. 7, 1862, *OR*, 11/1:13–14.

20. President's War Order No. 3, Mar. 11, 1862, *CWL*, 5:155.

21. Hay, *Diary*, 36; Weigley, *Civil War*, 122.

22. Rafuse, *McClellan's War*, 202; Stanton to McClellan, Mar. 31, 1862, *OR*, 11/3:52; McClellan to Sumner, Mar. 31, 1862, *OR*, 11/3:53; Lincoln to McClellan, Mar. 31, 1862, *CWL*, 5:175–76, 176 n. 1.

23. General Order No. 33, Apr. 3, 1862, in George B. McClellan, *McClellan's Own Story* (New York: Charles L. Webster, 1887; reprint, Sciutate, MA: DSI, 1998), 258–59; Sherman to John Sherman, May 12, 1862, in *Sherman's Civil War: Selected Correspondence of William T. Sherman, 1860–1865*, ed. Brooks D. Simpson and Jean V. Berlin (Chapel Hill: University of North Carolina Press, 1999), 217–19.

24. Magruder to Davis, Jan. 10, 1862, *OR*, 4:721.

25. Lee to J. E. Johnston, Mar. 28, 1862, *OR*, 11/3:408.

26. J. E. Johnston to Lee, Mar. 27, 28, 1862, *OR*, 11/3:405–6; Lee to J. E. Johnston, Mar. 28, 1862, *OR*, 11/3:408.

27. Lee to J. E. Johnston, Mar. 28, 1862, *OR*, 11/3:408.

28. Ibid., 408–9.

29. Symonds, *Johnston*, 146.

30. J. E. Johnston to Davis, Apr. 4, 1862, *Davis Papers*, 8:129, 130 n. 1; Lee to J. E. Johnston, Apr. 4, 1862, *OR*, 11/3:420; Symonds, *Johnston*, 149–50.

31. McClellan to Lincoln, Apr. 5, 1862, *OR*, 11/3:71.

32. Lincoln to McClellan, Apr. 6, 1862, *CWL*, 5:182.

33. Stanton to McClellan, Apr. 6, 1862, *OR*, 11/3:73.

34. McClellan to Mary Ellen McClellan, Apr. 8, [1862], *McClellan Papers*, 234.

35. Williams to Van Vliet, Apr. 5, 1862, *OR*, 11/3:71–72.

36. Rafuse, *McClellan's War*, 206.

37. L. Thomas to McClellan, Apr. 4, 1862, *OR*, 11/3:67–68.

38. McClellan to L. Thomas, Apr. 6, 1862, *OR*, 11/3:74.

39. Lincoln to McClellan, Apr. 9, 1862, *CWL*, 5:184–85.

40. McClellan to Lincoln, Apr. 6, 1862, *OR*, 11/3:73–74; McClellan to Stanton, Apr. 10, 1862, *OR*, 11/3:86; McClellan to Mary Ellen McClellan, Apr. 18, [1862], *McClellan Papers*, 240–41; McClellan to Goldsborough, Apr. 10, 1862, *OR*, 11/3:87 (second note).

41. Woodworth, *Davis and Lee*, 119.

42. Lincoln to McClellan, May 1, 1862, *CWL*, 5:203–4.

43. Davis to J. E. Johnston, May 1, 1862, *OR*, 11/3:484–85; Symonds, *Johnston*, 152–53.

44. *Davis Papers*, 11:596.

45. Woodworth, *Davis and Lee*, 118. In an uncharacteristic fit of aggressiveness, right before he withdrew his army Johnston proposed an immediate general Confederate offensive. The forces in the eastern theater crossing the Potomac, while everything in the western, gathered under Beauregard, struck across the Ohio, ibid., 119; Johnston to Lee, Apr. 30, 1862, *OR*, 11/3:477.

46. Chase, *Diaries*, 79–86; Donald, *Lincoln*, 350–51.

47. Davis to Varina Howell Davis, May 13, 1862, *Davis Papers*, 8:174 and n. 3.

48. *Davis Papers*, 8:174 nn. 2, 3. This meeting is sometimes mistakenly reported as having occurred on May 14; ibid.

49. Lee to J. E. Johnston, May 17, 1862, *Wartime Papers*, 175.

50. Lee to J. E. Johnston, May 18, 1862, *Wartime Papers*, 176.

51. Symonds, *Johnston*, 158; Woodworth, *Davis and Lee*, 130; Rafuse, *McClellan's War*, 211–14.

52. Stanton to McDowell, May 17, 1862, *OR*, 11/1:28.

53. McClellan to Stanton, May 8, 1862, *OR*, 11/3:150–51.

54. Lee to Jackson, Apr. 25, Lee to Ewell, Apr. 27, 1862, *Wartime Papers*, 156–57, 159.

55. Lee to Jackson, May 1, 1862, *Wartime Papers*, 162–63.

56. Lee to Jackson, May 16, 1862, *Wartime Papers*, 174–75.

57. Rafuse, *McClellan's War*, 215; McPherson, *Battle Cry*, 456–60; Lincoln to McClellan, May 24, 1862, *CWL*, 5:232.

58. Lincoln to Frémont, May 24, 1862, *CWL*, 5:230; *OR*, 12/1:643.

59. Lincoln to McDowell, May 24, 1862, *OR*, 12/3:219.

60. McDowell to Stanton, May 24, 1862, *OR*, 12/3:220.

61. Woodworth, *Davis and Lee*, 136–38.

62. McClellan report, *OR*, 11/1:28; Rafuse, *McClellan's War*, 216–19.

63. McDowell to Wadsworth, May 24, 1862, *OR*, 12/3:221.

64. Rafuse, *McClellan's War*, 215–16.

65. Nicolay to Lincoln, Oct. 17, 21, 1861, in Burlingame, ed., *With Lincoln*, 60.

66. Frémont to Lincoln, May 27, 1862, *OR*, 12/1:644.

67. Woodworth, *Davis and Lee*, 133–34; J. E. Johnston to Cooper, May 19, 1862, *OR*, 11/1:275–76.

68. Lee to J. E. Johnston, May 21, 22, 1862, *Wartime Papers*, 176–77.

69. J. E. Johnston to Lee, May 28, 1862, *OR*, 11/3:555.

70. Symonds, *Johnston*, 161; Rafuse, *McClellan's War*, 216.

71. Pendleton to J. E. Johnston, May 30, 1862, *OR*, 11/3:685.

72. J. E. Johnston to G. W. Smith, May 30, 1862, *OR*, 11/3:563.

73. Woodworth, *Davis and Lee*, 140–48; Symonds, *Atlas*, 30–31; Boatner, *Dictionary*, 272–73, 490; Douglas Southall Freeman, *Lee's Lieutenants: A Study in Command* (New York: Charles Scribner's Sons, 1944), 3:310.

74. Davis to Lee, June 1, 1862, *OR*, 11/3:568–69.

75. Lee to Davis, June 5, 1862, *Wartime Papers*, 183–84. It is not clear that Lee originated the idea of reinforcing Jackson; see *Lee's Dispatches: Unpublished Letters of General Robert E. Lee, C.S.A. to Jefferson Davis and the War Department of the Confederate States of America, 1862–65*, ed. Douglas Southall Freeman and Grady McWhiney (New York: G. P. Putnam's Sons, 1957), xiv, 6 n. 1.

76. Lee to G. W. C. Lee, Feb. 28, 1863, *Wartime Papers*, 410–12.

77. Lee to Randolph, June 5, 1862, *OR*, 12/3:905–6.

78. Lee to Jackson, June 8, 1862, *OR*, 12/3:908.

79. Lee to Randolph, June 9, 1862, *Wartime Papers*, 188.

80. Lee to Jackson, June 11, 1862, *OR*, 12/3:910; Lee to Davis, June 10, 1862, *Wartime Papers*, 188; *OR*, 51/2:1074.

81. Jackson to Lee and Lee's and Davis's indorsements, June 13, 1862, *Wartime Papers*, 193.

82. Lee to Jackson, June 16, 1862, *OR*, 12/3:913.

83. Lee to Cooper, Battle Report on the Seven Days, Mar. 6, 1863, *Wartime Papers*, 212.

84. Lincoln to McClellan, May 25, 1862, *CWL*, 5:235–36.

85. *McClellan Papers*, 282; McClellan report, 11/1:50.

86. McDowell to McClellan, June 8, 1862, *OR*, 11/3:220–21.

87. McClellan to Lincoln, May 25, 1862, *OR*, 11/1:32; L. Thomas to McDowell, June 8, 1862, *OR*, 12/3:354; Lincoln to Frémont, June 15, 16, 1862, *CWL*, 5:27–74; see also *OR* 12/1:542, 655.

88. Lincoln to McClellan, June 18, 1862, *CWL*, 5:276.

89. For McClellan's illness, see Rafuse, *McClellan's War*, 216–17.

90. McClellan to Stanton, June 25, 1862, *OR*, 11/1:51; *Lee's Dispatches*, 16n3.

91. Symonds, *Atlas*, 35; Eicher, *The Longest Night*, 280–83; McPherson, *Battle Cry*, 466.

92. Symonds, *Atlas*, 36–37; Eicher, *The Longest Night*, 284–97; Rafuse, *McClellan's War*, 227.

93. Lee to Cooper, Battle Report on the Seven Days, Mar. 6, 1863, *Wartime Papers*, 221.

94. Russell F. Weigley, *The American Way of War: A History of United States Military Strategy and Policy* (Bloomington: Indiana University Press, 1973), 106, 108–14.

95. Lee to Seddon, Jan. 10, 1863, *Wartime Papers*, 388–90. I am indebted to Michael W. Jones for making this point regarding the actions of generals.

96. Davis, *Rise and Fall*, 2:132. The supposed existence of this Confederate strategy is refuted in detail in Stoker, "There Was No Offensive-Defensive Confederate Strategy," 177–208.

97. General Orders No. 75, July 7, 1862, *Wartime Papers*, 210.

98. Eicher, *The Longest Night*, 296; Weigley, *The American Way of War*, 107–18, 126–27.

99. Davis to Varina Howell Davis, July 6, 1862, *Davis Papers*, 8:280–81.

100. Quoted in *Davis Papers*, 8:282.

101. Rafuse, *McClellan's War*, 217–18.

102. Quoted in *CWL*, 5:284 n. 1.

103. Lincoln to Seward, June 28, 1862, *CWL*, 5:291–92.

104. Call for 300,000 Volunteers, July 1, 1862, *CWL*, 5:296–97.

105. Order Constituting the Army of Virginia, June 26, 1862, *CWL*, 5:287; Williams, *Lincoln and His Generals*, 121–23.

106. Quoted in Boatner, *Dictionary*, 658–60.

107. Lincoln to Burnside, June 28, 1862, *CWL*, 5:288.

108. Lincoln to McClellan, June 26, 1862, *OR*, 11/3:259.

109. Lincoln to McClellan, July 4, 1862, *CWL*, 5:305–6.

110. McClellan to Lincoln, July 2, [1862], *McClellan Papers*, 329, 331–32.

111. Memorandum of Interviews Between Lincoln and Officers of the Army of the Potomac, July 8–9, 1862, *CWL*, 5:309–12; Heintzelman journal, *ORS*, 2:94.

112. Quoted in *Davis Papers*, 8:162–63, 262.

113. Quoted in ibid., 8:286.

114. Quoted in ibid., 8:287.

115. Davis to Forsyth, July 18, 1862, *Davis Papers*, 8:293.

116. Ibid.

117. Ibid.

118. Stanton to Halleck, July 11, 1862, *OR*, 17/2:90; Halleck report, *OR*, 12/2:4; Marszalek, *Halleck*, 136.

119. Marszalek, *Halleck*, 136–37.

120. Ibid., 138.

121. Ibid., 139–40; Halleck to McClellan, Aug. 3, 1862, *OR*, 11/1:80–81; McClellan to Halleck, Aug. 4, 1862, *OR*, 12/2:8–9.

122. Marszalek, *Halleck*, 140–42.

123. Quoted in Graebner, "Northern Diplomacy," 69, 72–73.

124. Jones, *Union in Peril*, 4.

125. Darryl Lyman, *Civil War Quotations* (Conshohocken, PA: Combined Books, 1995), 147.

126. Bulloch, *Secret Service*, 610, n for 76.

127. *Davis Papers*, 8:279 n. 4.

128. Lee to Davis, July 18, 1862, *OR*, 51/2:1074–5; Lee to Jackson, July 23, 1862, *OR*, 12/3:916–17.

129. Symonds, *Atlas*, 39; Lee to Jackson, July 23, 1862, *Wartime Papers*, 235.

130. Lee to Davis, July 26, 1862, *Lee's Dispatches*, 38–40; Lee to Jackson, July 27, 1862, *Wartime Papers*, 239–40.

131. Lee to Randolph, July 28, 1862, *Wartime Papers*, 240–41.

132. Lee to Clark, Aug. 8, 1862, *Wartime Papers*, 249.

133. Lee to Randolph, Aug. 14, 1862, *Wartime Papers*, 252.

134. Lee to Longstreet, Aug. 14, 1862, *Wartime Papers*, 252–53.

135. Lee to Smith, Aug. 14, 1862, *Wartime Papers*, 254–55; *Davis Papers*, 8:343.

136. Lee to Davis, Aug. 17, 1862, *OR*, 51/2:1075–76.

137. Lee to Davis, Aug. 23, 1862, *Davis Papers*, 8:354–55, 355 nn. 1, 3, 5.

138. Lee to Davis, Aug. 23, 1862, *Davis Papers*, 8:354–55.

139. Lee to Davis, Aug. 24, Lee to his wife, Aug. 25, 1862, *Wartime Papers*, 264–65.

140. Lee to Davis, Aug. 23, 1862, *Davis Papers*, 8:354–55; Lee to Cooper, Apr. 18, 1863, *Wartime Papers*, 270–75.

141. Lee to Davis, *Wartime Papers*, Aug. 24, 1862, 263; Lee to Randolph, Aug. 25, 1862, *OR*, 12/3:943.

142. Lee to Randolph, Aug. 25, 1862, *OR*, 12/3:943.

143. Halleck to McClellan, Aug. 20, 1862, *OR*, 11/3:379–80; Marszalek, *Halleck*, 140–43; McPherson, *Battle Cry*, 528.

144. McClellan to Lincoln, Aug. 29, 1862, *McClellan Papers*, 416.

145. Lincoln to McClellan, Aug. 29, 1862, *CWL*, 5:399; Marszalek, *Halleck*, 144–45.

146. Hay, *Diary*, 36–39; Welles, *Diary*, 1:115.

147. Lee to Davis, Aug. 30, 1862, *Wartime Papers*, 266–68.

148. Symonds, *Atlas*, 38–41.

149. Lee to Davis, Sept. 3, 1862, *Wartime Papers*, 228–29, 269–70.

150. Nicolay to Bates, July 13, 1862, in Burlingame, ed., *With Lincoln*, 85.

151. Jones, *Union in Peril*, 164.

152. McClellan to Lincoln, Apr. 20, 1862, *McClellan Papers*, 244–45.

153. McClellan report, *OR*, 11/1:37.

154. Sun Tzu, *The Art of War*, trans. Samuel B. Griffith (New York: Oxford University Press, 1971), 81.

155. Quoted in Marszalek, *Halleck*, 138.

CHAPTER 11

1. Halleck to Buell, June 2, 1862, *OR*, 10/2:243–44 (two notes).

2. Halleck to Buell, May 31, June 1, 4, 1862, *OR*, 10/2:232–3 (two notes) 236, 254; Engle, *Buell*, 251–52.

3. McClellan in Lincoln to Halleck, June 5, 1862, *OR*, 10/1:670.

4. Johnson to Halleck, June 5, 1862, *OR*, 10/2:261.

5. Thomas to Halleck, Oct. 30, 1862, *OR*, 16/2:657.

6. Halleck to Lincoln, June 7, 1862, *OR*, 10/1:670.

7. Buell to Halleck, June 6, 1862, *OR*, 10/2:263–64; Halleck to Buell, June 6, 1862, *OR*, 10/2:264–5 (two notes).

8. Halleck to Buell, June 6, 1862, *OR*, 10/2:264–65.

9. Mitchel to Buell, June 7, 1862, *OR*, 10/2:271–72; Mitchel to Fry, June 7, 1862, *OR*, 10/2:271.

10. Lincoln to Halleck, June 8, 1862, *OR*, 10/2:277.

11. Halleck to Stanton, June 9, 1862, *OR*, 10/1:670–71.

12. Halleck to Stanton, June 9, 1862, *OR*, 10/1:671.

13. Stanton to Halleck, June 9, 1862, *OR*, 10/1:671. Lincoln was also pleased; Stanton to Halleck, June 11, 1862, *OR*, 16/2:8.

14. Halleck to Buell, June 9, 1862, *OR*, 10/2:280–81.

15. Mitchel to Halleck, June 9, 1862, *OR*, 10/2:282–83.

16. Buell to Halleck, June 9, 1862, *OR*, 10/2:280.

17. Mitchel in Buell to Halleck, June 9, 1862, *OR*, 10/2:280.

18. Mitchel to Halleck, June 9, 1862, *OR*, 10/2:282–83.

19. Stanton to Buell, June 9, 1863, *OR*, 10/2:285.

20. Buell to Stanton, June 9, 1862, *OR*, 10/2:285–86.

21. Special Field Orders No. 90, June 10, 1862, *OR*, 17/2:3; Marszalek, *Halleck*, 126.

22. Halleck to Stanton, June 12, 1862, *OR*, 16/2:14.

23. Halleck to Buell, June 11, 1862, *OR*, 16/2:9.

24. Mitchel to Buell, June 11, 1862, *OR*, 16/2:10.

25. Buell to Halleck, June 17, 1862, *OR*, 16/2:33.

26. Halleck to Buell, June 17, 1862, *OR*, 16/2:33–34.

27. Lincoln to Halleck, June 18, 1862, *OR*, 16/2:37.

28. Morgan to Stanton and Buell, June 18, 1862, *OR*, 16/2:38.

29. Halleck to Lincoln, June 21, 1862, *OR*, 16/2:43.

30. Stanton to Mitchel, June 21, 1862, *OR*, 16/2:46.

31. Stanton to Halleck, June 28, 1862, *OR*, 16/2:69–70.

32. Halleck to Buell, June 12, 1862, *OR*, 16/2:16.

33. Halleck to Stanton, June 16, 1862, *OR*, 16/2:26–27.

34. Halleck to Stanton, June 30, 1862, *OR*, 16/2:74–75.

35. Stanton to Halleck, June 30, 1862, *OR*, 16/2:75.

36. Lincoln to Halleck, June 30, 1862, *OR*, 16/2:75.

37. Halleck to Buell, June 30 (two notes), July 1, 1862 *OR*, 16/2:75, 77, 82; Halleck to McClernand, June 30, 1862, *OR*, 16/2:76; Halleck to Stanton, July 1, 1862, *OR*, 16/2:81–82.

38. Halleck to Lincoln, July 1, 1862, *OR*, 16/2:82; Halleck to Stanton, July 1, 1862, *OR*, 16/2:82; Lincoln to Halleck, July 2, 1862, *OR*, 16/2:88.

39. Lincoln to Halleck, July 4, 1862, *OR*, 11/3:294; also *OR*, 16/2:95.

40. Halleck to Lincoln, July 5, 1862, *OR*, 16/2:95.

41. Lincoln to Halleck, July 6, 1862, *OR*, 16/2:100.

42. *Davis Papers*, 8:251.

43. Ruggles to Bragg, and Bragg to Ruggles, June 20, 1862, *OR*, 17/2:614.

44. Davis to Varina Davis, June 25, 1862, *Davis Papers*, 8:268–69.

45. Johnston to Davis, July 15, 1862, *OR*, 10/1:780–85.

46. Thomas Connelly, *Army of the Heartland: The Army of Tennessee, 1861–1862* (Baton Rouge: LSU Press, 1967), 196–97.

47. E. K. Smith to Davis, July 14, 1862, *OR*, 16/2:726–27.

48. Boatner, *Dictionary*, 288–89, 567.

49. E. K. Smith to Cooper, July 19, 1862, *OR*, 16/2:729; E. K. Smith to Bragg, July 20, 1862, *OR*, 16/2:730; E. K. Smith to Cooper, July 21, 1862, *OR*, 16/2:730–31.

50. Quoted in *Davis Papers*, 8:296.

51. Lee to Davis, July 26, 1862, *Lee's Dispatches*, 38–40, 40–41 n. 7.

52. Quoted in McWhiney, *Bragg*, 1:267–68.

53. Bragg to Davis, July 21, 22, 1862, *OR*, 52/2:330.

54. Special Orders No.4, July 21, 1862, *OR*, 16/2:731.

55. Bragg to Beauregard, July 22, 1862, *OR*, 52/2:330–31.

56. Bragg to Cooper, July 23, 1862, *OR*, 17/2:655–56.

57. Buell Court of Inquiry, Apr. 24, 1863, *OR*, 16/1:711; Davis to E. K. Smith, July 25, 1862, *Davis Papers*, 8:305–6.

58. E. K. Smith to Bragg, July 24, 1862, *OR*, 16/2:734–35.

59. [Bragg] to Cooper, Aug. 1, 1862, *OR*, 16/2:741.

60. Ibid.

61. Davis to Bragg, Aug. 5, 1862, *OR*, 52/2:334–36. Davis wrote of eastern Tennessee in this note, but his relation of this to Grant, and the then military situation, makes one think he meant western Tennessee.

62. McWhiney, *Bragg*, 1:273–74; E. K. Smith to Bragg, Aug. 9, 1862, *OR*, 16/2:748.

63. Bragg to E. K. Smith, Aug. 12, 1862, *OR*, 16/2:754–55; McWhiney, *Bragg*, 1:274.

64. Bragg to E. K. Smith, Aug. 12, 15, 1862, *OR*, 16/2:754–55, 758–59; McWhiney, *Bragg*, 1:274.

65. Halleck to Buell, July 8, 1862, *OR*, 16/2:104.

66. Buell to Halleck, July 11, 12, 1862, *OR*, 16/2:122–23, 127–28.

67. Halleck to Buell, July 12, 1862, *OR*, 16/2:128.

68. Buell to Halleck, July 13, 14, 1862, *OR*, 16/2:136, 143.

69. Halleck to Buell, July 14, 1862, *OR*, 16/2:143.

70. Halleck to Lincoln, July 15, 1862, *OR*, 16/2:150–51; Buell to Halleck, July 16, 1862, *OR*, 16/2:159; Halleck to Thomas, July 16, 1862, *OR*, 16/2:160; Halleck to Sherman, July 16, 1862, *OR*, 17/2:100.

71. Donald, *Lincoln*, 361; Marszalek, *Halleck*, 127–28.

72. Marszalek, *Halleck*, 126, 128.

73. Halleck to Lincoln, July 10, 1862, *OR*, 16/2:117; Marszalek, *Halleck*, 127–28.

74. The order was originally issued on July 22, 1862; General Orders No. 109, Aug. 16, 1862, *OR*, ser. 3, 2:397.

75. Quoted in *Grant Papers*, 5:226–27nn.; Italics in the original.

76. Halleck to Grant, Aug. 2, 1862, *OR*, 17/2:150.

77. Grant to Rosecrans, Aug. 10, 1862, *Grant Papers*, 5:282–83.

78. General Orders No. 107, Aug. 15, 1862, *OR*, ser. 3, 2:388.

79. Halleck to Sherman, Aug. 25, 1862, *OR*, 17/2:186.

80. Grant to Halleck, Aug. 1, [1862], *Grant Papers*, 5:257; *OR* 17/2:148.

81. Grant to Blair, Aug. 8, 1862, *Grant Papers*, 5:276–77, 257ff.

82. Halleck to Butler, Aug. 7, 1862, *OR*, 15:544; Halleck to Curtis, Aug. 7, 1862, *OR*, 13:544.

83. Halleck to Sherman, Aug. 25, 1862, *OR*, 17/2:186.

84. Ibid.; Halleck to Buell, Aug. 6, 12, 18 [*sic*], 1862, *OR*, 16/2:266, 314–15, 324.

85. Catton, *Grant Moves South*, 299, 304.

86. Van Dorn report, Sept. 9, 1862, *OR*, 15:15–19.

87. Ibid.

88. Van Dorn to Davis, Aug. 2, 1862, *OR*, 52/2:334.

89. Davis to Van Dorn, Aug. 4, 1862, *OR*, 15:794.

90. Van Dorn report, Sept. 9, 1862, *OR*, 15:15–19.

91. Breckenridge report, Sept. 30, 1862, *OR*, 15:76–81; Van Dorn report, Sept. 9, 1862, *OR*, 15:15–19.

92. Anderson, *By Sea and by River*, 135; Van Dorn report, Sept. 9, 1862, *OR*, 15:15–19.

93. *OR*, 15:15–19; Long and Long, *Civil War*, 253; Foote, *Civil War*, 1:581–82.

94. Oliver P. Temple, *East Tennessee and the Civil War* (Cincinnati: Robert Clarke, 1899), 460–61.

95. Browning, *Diary*, 1:562.

450

CHAPTER 12

1. Foote, *Civil War*, 1:648–49; Weigley, *Civil War*, 142–44; quoted in Welles, *Diary*, 1:113; quoted in Hay, *Diary*, 38–39.

2. Thomas, *Lee*, 257; Davis to Lee, Bragg, and E. K. Smith, Sept. 12, 1862, in *Jefferson Davis: The Essential Writings*, ed. William J. Cooper Jr. (New York: Modern Library, 2003), 260–62. Lee's proclamation differed from Davis's. See Lee to the People of Maryland, Sept. 8, 1862, *Wartime Papers*, 299–300.

3. John B. Jones, *A Rebel War Clerk's Diary*, ed. Earl Schenck Miers (New York: Sagamore Press, 1958), 36.

4. Davis to Lee, Sept. [?] 7, 1862, *OR*, 19/2:598–99; Davis to Lee, Bragg, and E. K. Smith, Sept. 12, 1862, in *Jefferson Davis: The Essential Writings*, 260–62.

5. Lee to Davis, Sept. 3, 1862, *Wartime Papers*, 292–93.

6. Ibid.

7. Lee to Davis, Sept. 4, 6, 12, 1862, *Wartime Papers*, 288, 294–96, 304–5.

8. William Allan, "Memoranda of Conversations with Robert E. Lee," Apr. 15, 1868, in Gary W. Gallagher, ed., *Lee the Soldier* (Lincoln: University of Nebraska Press, 1996), 13; Lee to Davis, Sept. 5, 6, 1862, *Wartime Papers*, 295–96.

9. Quoted in *B&L*, 2:605–6; Special Orders No. 191, Sept. 9, 1862, *Wartime Papers*, 301–2.

10. Lee to Gustavus Smith, Sept. 7, 1862, *Wartime Papers*, 297.

11. Lee to Davis, Sept. 7, 1862, *Wartime Papers*, 297–98.

12. Lee to Davis, Sept. 8, 1862, *Wartime Papers*, 301.

13. Lee to Davis, Sept. 13, 1862, *Davis Papers*, 8:387–88; *Wartime Papers*, 288; Lee to Davis, Sept. 23, 1862, *OR*, 19/2:622–23.

14. Lee to Davis, Sept. 12, 1862, *Wartime Papers*, 288, 304–5.

15. Special Orders No. 191, Sept. 9, 1862, *Wartime Papers*, 301–3; McClellan to Halleck, Sept. 13, 1862, *OR*, 19/2:281–82.

16. Quoted in Williams, *Lincoln and His Generals*, 166; Lee to Cooper, Lee report on the Antietam/Sharpsburg Campaign, Aug. 19, 1863, *Wartime Papers*, 315, 317.

17. Weigley, *Civil War*, 148–49.

18. Ibid., 153; Symonds, *Atlas*, 45; Boatner, *Dictionary*, 20–21.

19. Lee to Cooper, Lee report on the Antietam/Sharpsburg Campaign, Aug. 19, 1863, *Wartime Papers*, 322.

20. Sears, "Lincoln and McClellan," 42.

21. Lincoln to Treat, Nov. 19, 1862, *CWL*, 5:501–2.

22. Lee to Davis, Sept. 21, 1862, *OR*, 19/1:142–43; Lee to Davis, Sept. 25, 1862, *OR*, 19/2:626–27; Lee to Loring, Sept. 25, 1862, *OR*, 19/2:625–26.

23. Randolph to Lee, Oct. 14, 1862, *OR*, 19/2:665; Lee to Randolph, Oct. 15, 1862, *OR*, 19/2:666; Lee to Loring, *OR*, Oct. 15, 16, 1862, 19/2:666–68.

24. Lee to Davis, Sept. 25, 1862, *OR*, 19/2:626–27.

25. Davis to Lee, Sept. 28, 1862, *Davis Papers*, 8:408–9.

26. Halleck to McClellan, Sept. 26, 1862, *OR*, 19/2:360; McClellan planned to take Harpers Ferry and prepare the army for its next campaign.

27. McClellan to Mary Ellen McClellan, Sept. 20, 1862 (two notes), *McClellan Papers*, 473–74, 474n, 476.

28. Weigley, *Civil War*, 92–94, 161–62.

29. Donald, *Lincoln*, 387.

30. Halleck to McClellan, Oct. 6, 1862, *OR*, 19/1:10–11.

31. McClellan to Halleck, Oct. 7, 1862, *OR*, 19/1:11–12; Donald, *Lincoln*, 387.

32. Lincoln to McClellan, Oct. 13, 1862, *CWL*, 5:460–61.

33. Ibid.

34. Lincoln to McClellan, Sept. 15, 1862, *CWL*, 5:426.

35. Lincoln to McClellan, Oct. 13, 1862, *CWL*, 5:460–61; Donald, *Lincoln*, 388–90; Nicolay to Bates, Nov. 9, 1862, in Burlingame, ed., *With Lincoln*, 90–91.

36. Van Dorn to Davis, Aug. 11, 1862, *OR*, 52/2:340.

37. *Davis Papers*, 8:328. Marshall wrote to Davis on August 7, 1862.

38. Boatner, *Dictionary*, 777; E. K. Smith to Bragg, Aug. 20, 1862, *OR*, 16/2:766–67; E. K. Smith to Bragg, Aug. 24, 1862, *OR*, 16/2:775–76.

39. E. K. Smith to Davis, Aug. 21, 1862, *OR*, 16/2:768–69.

40. E. K. Smith to Cooper, Aug. 24, 1862, *OR*, 16/2:777–78.

41. *Davis Papers*, 8:301.

42. Marshall to Bragg, Aug. 28, 1862, *OR*, 52/2:342–43.

43. Marshall to Randolph, Sept. 7, 1862, *OR*, 52/2:346–48.

44. Ibid., and Randolph indorsement, *OR*, 52/2:346–48.

45. Long and Long, *Civil War*, 256; Bragg to Price, Aug. 27, 1862, *OR*, 16/2:782–83.

46. Buell to Nelson, Aug. 10, 1862, *OR*, 16/2:304.

47. Buell to Halleck, Aug. 10, 1862, *OR*, 16/2:307; Halleck to Buell, Aug. 12, 1862, *OR*, 16/2:314.

48. Buell to Grant, Aug. 13, 1862, *OR*, 16/2:325.

49. Grant to Halleck, Aug. 14, 1862, *OR*, 16/2:333.

50. Halleck to Buell, Aug. 18, 1862, *OR*, 16/2:360; Buell to Halleck, Aug. 18, 1862, *OR*, 16/2:360–61.

51. Nelson to Halleck, Aug. 23, 1862, *OR*, 16/2:394; Halleck to Nelson, Aug. 23, 1862, *OR*, 16/2:394; Halleck to Wright, Aug. 23, 1862, *OR*, 16/2:404–5.

52. Buell to Halleck, Aug. 24, 1862, *OR*, 16/2:406–7.

53. Buell to Halleck, Aug. 25, 1862, *OR*, 16/2:416–17.

54. Halleck to Wright, Aug. 25, 1862, *OR*, 16/2:421.

55. Buell to Rousseau for Johnson, Aug. 30, 1862, *OR*, 16/2:451.

56. Foote, *Civil War*, 1:654.

57. Quoted in McWhiney, *Bragg*, 281.

58. Ibid., 283–86.

59. Buell to Thomas, Aug. 31, 1862, *OR*, 16/2:463; Buell to Halleck, Sept. 2, 14, 26, 1862, *OR*, 16/2:470–71, 515, 546; Halleck to Buell, Sept. 2, 20, 1862, *OR*, 16/2:471, 530; Buell to Wright, Sept. 14, 1862, *OR*, 16/2:516; Buell to Gilbert, in Nelson to Wright, Sept. 19, 1862, *OR*, 16/2:527; McWhiney, *Bragg*, 294.

60. Davis to Bragg, Sept. 19, 1862, *OR*, 17/2:707; Randolph to Van Dorn, Sept. 19, 1862, *OR*, 17/2:707.

61. Van Dorn report, Oct. 20, 1862, *OR*, 17/1:376–82; Van Dorn to Price, Sept. 17, 18, 24, 1862, *OR*, 17/2:705–6, 711; Price to Van Dorn, Sept. 17, 19 (two notes), 1862, *OR*, 17/2:705–8.

62. Van Dorn to Price, Sept. 24, 1862, *OR*, 17/2:711–12.

63. I am indebted to Mark Elam for making this point.

64. Grant to Halleck, Sept. 16, 1862, *OR*, 17/2:220.

65. Halleck to Grant, Sept. 17, 1862, *OR*, 17/2:222.

66. Foote, *Civil War*, 1:717–20; Van Dorn report, Oct. 20, 1862, *OR*, 17/1:376–82; Boatner, *Dictionary*, 176, 428–29.

67. Price to Harris, Sept. 28, 1862, *OR*, 17/2:714; Randolph to Van Dorn, Sept. 29, 1862, *OR*, 17/2:715; Randolph to Pemberton, Sept. 29, 1862, *OR*, 17/2:716–17.

68. Foote, *Civil War*, 1:720–21.

69. Bragg to Adjutant General, Sept. 25, 1862, *OR*, 16/2:876; Connelly, *Army of the Heartland*, 274.

70. McWhiney, *Bragg*, 286–94.

71. Bragg, "To the People of the Northwest," Sept. 26, 1862, *OR*, 52/2:363–65.

72. Foote, *Civil War*, 1:711–12.

73. Halleck to McKibbin, Sept. 24, 1862, *OR*, 16/2:538; General Orders No. 138, Sept. 23, 1862, *OR*, 16/2:539; Thomas to Halleck, Sept. 29, 1862, *OR*, 16/2:555; Halleck to Buell and Thomas, Sept. 29, 1862, *OR*, 16/2:555; Crittenden et al. to Lincoln, Sept. 29, 1862, *OR*, 16/2:557–58; Foote, *Civil War*, 1:715.

74. Halleck to Buell, Oct. 2, 1862, *OR*, 16/2:564.

75. Buell to Halleck, Oct. 3, 1862, *OR*, 16/2:566.

76. Foote, *Civil War*, 1:716.

77. Ibid., 1:712–13, 726–41; McWhiney, *Bragg*, 297, 307–20; Bragg to Davis, Oct. 12, 1862, *OR*, 16/1:1087–88; Symonds, *Atlas*, 46–47; Boatner, *Dictionary*, 643–44.

78. Van Dorn report, Oct. 20, 1862, *OR*, 17/1:376–82; Van Dorn to Randolph, Oct. 7, 1862, *OR*, 17/1:375–76; Boatner, *Dictionary*, 176–77.

79. McWhiney, *Bragg*, 321–22.

80. Diary of John Euclid Magee, *ORS*, 2:217–18.

81. McWhiney, *Bragg*, 321–33.

82. Ibid., 334.

83. Buell to Halleck, Oct. 16, 17, 1862, *OR*, 16/2:619, 621–22.

84. Halleck to Buell, Oct. 18, 19, 1862, *OR*, 16/2:623, 626–27.

85. Halleck to Pope, Aug. 29, 1862, *OR*, 12/3:724.

86. Buell to Halleck, Oct. 22, 1862, *OR*, 16/2:636–37 (dated Oct. 20 in the Buell Commission).

87. Halleck to Buell, Oct. 23 [22], 1862, *OR*, 16/2:638; Donald, *Lincoln*, 389; Halleck to Rosecrans, Oct. 24, 1862, *OR*, 26/2:640–41.

88. Nicolay to Bates, Oct. 16, 1862, in Burlingame, ed., *With Lincoln*, 89.

89. Grant, *Memoirs*, 256–57.

90. Lincoln to McClellan, Oct. 13, 1862, *CWL*, 5:460–61.

91. Bragg to Adjutant-General, Oct. 12, 1862, *OR*, 16/1:1087–8.

92. Boatner, *Dictionary*, 21, 177, 428–29; Connelly, *Army of the Heartland*, 274; Randolph to Lee, Oct. 25, 1862, 19/2:681–82.

93. Foote, *Civil War*, 1:712.

94. McWhiney, *Bragg*, 335.

95. Thomas to Davis, Nov. 8, 1862, *OR*, 20/2:395.

CHAPTER 13

1. Halleck to Curtis, Aug. 7, 1862, *OR*, 13:544.

2. Catton, *Grant Moves South*, 321.

3. Boatner, *Dictionary*, 750; Flood, *Grant and Sherman*, 21–22.

4. Sherman to Grant, Oct. 4, 1862, *OR*, 17/2:259–62.

5. Grant to Halleck, Oct. 26, 1862, *Grant Papers*, 6:199–201.

6. Halleck to Grant, Nov. 3, 1862, *OR*, 17/1:467; Halleck to Curtis, Nov. 3, 1862, *OR*, 13:778; Curtis to Halleck, Nov. 4, 1862, *OR*, 13:779.

7. Halleck to Banks, Nov. 9, 1862, *OR*, 15:590–91.

8. Ibid.

9. Ibid.

10. Ibid.

11. Catton, *Grant Moves South*, 324–26, 522 n. 1; McClernand to Lincoln, Sept. 28, 1862, *OR*, 17/2:849–53.

12. Catton, *Grant Moves South*, 326–27; Hattaway and Jones, *How the North Won*, 293–94.

13. Lincoln to Banks, Nov. 22, 1862, *CWL*, 5:505–6; Hattaway and Jones, *How the North Won*, 325.

14. Halleck to Rosecrans, Oct. 24, 1862, *OR*, 16/2:640–41; Halleck to Wright, Oct. 4, 1862, *OR*, 16/2:574; Wright to Halleck, Oct. 5, 1862, *OR*, 16/2:574.

15. Foote, *Civil War*, 1:227; Williams, *Lincoln and His Generals*, 179–80.

16. Halleck to Burnside, Nov. 5, 1862, *OR*, 19/2:546.

17. Burnside to Cullum, Nov. 7, 1862, *OR*, 19/2:552–54.

18. Ibid.

19. Marszalek, *Halleck*, 156; Halleck to Burnside, Nov. 14, 1862, *OR*, 19/2:579.

20. Halleck to Banks, Nov. 4, 1862, *OR*, Ser. 3, 2:736–37.

21. Lincoln to Schurz, Nov. 24, 1862, *CWL*, 5:509–10.

22. Davis to E. K. Smith, Oct. 29, 1862, *Davis Papers*, 8:468–70.

23. Davis to Bragg, Oct. 17, 1862, *Davis Papers*, 8:448–49.

24. Davis to Holmes, Oct. 21, 1862, *Davis Papers*, 8:454–55.

25. Ibid., 8:454–56.

26. Davis wrote this on Oct. 25, 1862; *Davis Papers*, 8:465.

27. Bragg to Davis, Oct. 23, 1862, *OR*, 52/2:382.

28. Davis to E. K. Smith, Oct. 29, 1862, *Davis Papers*, 8:468–70.

29. McWhiney, *Bragg*, 325–26; Cooper to E. K. Smith, Nov. 1, 1862, *OR*, 20/2:384; Cooper to Bragg, Nov. 1, 1862, *OR*, 20/2:384–85; Woodworth, *Davis and His Generals*, 167–69.

30. McWhiney, *Bragg*, 337; Bragg to Cooper, Nov. 3, 1862, *OR*, 20/2:386–87; Bragg to Pemberton, Nov. 7, 1863, *OR*, 20/2:394.

31. Bragg to Davis, Nov. 24, 1862, *Davis Papers*, 8:509–11, 511 n. 1; Woodworth, *Davis and His Generals*, 168–69.

32. Bragg to Davis, Nov. 24, 1862, *Davis Papers*, 8:509–11; Woodworth, *Davis and His Generals*, 169.

33. Lee to Jackson, Nov. 9, Lee to Randolph, Nov. 10, Lee to G. W. C. Lee, Nov. 10, 1862, *Wartime Papers*, 330–33.

34. Lee to Randolph, Nov. 17, 1862, *Wartime Papers*, 337–38.
35. *Davis Papers*, 8:498.
36. Lee to Jackson, Nov. 12, 25, Lee to Davis, Nov. 20, 25, 1862, *Wartime Papers*, 333–34, 341, 345–47; Hattaway and Jones, *How the North Won*, 303.
37. Lee to Jackson, Nov. 28, Dec. 2, 1862, *Wartime Papers*, 349–51.
38. Lee to Davis, Dec. 6, 1862, *Wartime Papers*, 352–53.
39. Davis to Lee, Dec. 8, 1862, *Davis Papers*, 8:533–35.
40. Marszalek, *Halleck*, 156; Lincoln to Burnside, Nov. 25, 1862, *CWL*, 5:511.
41. Lincoln to Halleck, Nov. 27, 1862, *CWL*, 5:514–15.
42. Marszalek, *Halleck*, 156; Welles, *Diary*, 1:121.
43. Marszalek, *Halleck*, 156–57.
44. McPherson, *Battle Cry*, 570–74; Marszalek, *Halleck*, 156; Symonds, *Atlas*, 55.
45. Lee to Seddon, Dec. 16, 1862, *Wartime Papers*, 363–64.
46. Quoted in Mark E. Neely, "Wilderness and the Cult of Manliness: Hooker," in *Lincoln's Generals*, Gabor S. Boritt, ed. (New York: Oxford University Press, 1994), 59–60; quoted in Gabor S. Boritt, "'Unfinished Work': Lincoln, Meade, and Gettysburg," in Boritt, ed., *Lincoln's Generals*, 107–8.
47. Lincoln to Halleck, Sept. 19, 1863, *CWL*, 6:466–68.
48. Hay, *Diary*, 38.
49. Meigs to Burnside, Dec. 30, 1862, *OR*, 21:916–18.
50. Franklin and W. F. Smith to Lincoln, Dec. 20, 1862, *OR*, 21:868–70; Lincoln to Franklin and W. F. Smith, Dec. 22, 1862, *CWL*, 6:15–16 and nn. 1–2.
51. Barnard to Kelton, Nov. 28, 1862, *OR*, 21/807–8.
52. Lincoln to Halleck, Jan. 1, 1863, *CWL*, 6:31; *OR*, 21/940.
53. Halleck to Stanton, Jan. 1, 1863, *OR*, 21:940–41.
54. Burnside to Lincoln, Jan. 1, 1863, *OR*, 21:941–42.
55. Halleck to Burnside, Jan. 7, 1863, *OR*, 21:953–54.
56. McPherson, *Battle Cry*, 584–85.
57. Grimsley, *The Hard Hand of War*, 101.
58. Halleck to Rosecrans, Oct. 24, 1862, *OR*, 16/2, 640–41.
59. Rosecrans to Halleck, Nov. 11, 17, 1862, *OR*, 20/2:35–36, 59.
60. Halleck to Rosecrans, Nov. 27, Dec. 4, 1862, *OR*, 20/2:102, 117–18; Foote, *Civil War*, 1:768–69.
61. Rosecrans to Halleck, Dec. 4, 1862, *OR*, 20/2:118.
62. Halleck to Rosecrans, Dec. 5, 1862, *OR*, 20/2:123–24.
63. Ibid.
64. Rosecrans to Halleck, Dec. 10, 1862, *OR*, 20/2: 150.
65. Bragg to Cooper, Jan. 8, 1863, *OR*, 17/1:591–92.
66. Symonds, *Atlas*, 49.
67. Hattaway and Jones, *How the North Won*, 324–25.
68. General Orders, No. 159, Oct. 16, 1862, *OR*, 17/2:278; Grant, *Memoirs*, 283–87; Grant to Halleck, Nov. 2, 1862, *OR*, 17/1:466–67.
69. Grant, *Memoirs*, 288; Grant to Sherman, Dec. 8, 1862 (two notes), *Grant Papers*, 6:404, 406–7.
70. Grant to Halleck, Dec. 8, 1862, *OR*, 17/1:474; Grant, *Memoirs*, 288–89.

71. Christopher S. Dwyer, "Raiding Strategy: As Applied by the Western Confederate Cavalry in the American Civil War," *Journal of Military History* 63, 2 (Apr. 1999): 271; Grant to Halleck, Dec. 21, 1862, *Grant Papers*, 7:83; Hattaway and Jones, *How the North Won*, 311; Grant, *Memoirs*, 289–91; Forrest to Brent, Dec. 24, 1862, *OR*, 17/1:594–97.

72. Dwyer, "Raiding Strategy," 272; Grant, *Memoirs*, 289–91; Grimsley, *The Hard Hand of War*, 101.

73. Sherman to John Sherman, Dec. 14, 1862, *Sherman's Civil War*, 344–46.

74. Hattaway and Jones, *How the North Won*, 311–14; Long and Long, *Civil War*, 301.

75. Sherman to John Sherman, Jan. 6, [1863], *Sherman's Civil War*, 351–53.

76. Sherman to Halleck, Jan. 5, 1863, *OR*, 17/1:613–14; McClernand to Curtis, Jan. 8, 1863, *OR*, 17/2:545–46; Sherman to Ellen Ewing Sherman, Jan. 12, 1863, *Sherman's Civil War*, 353.

77. Lincoln to Greeley, Aug. 22, 1862, *CWL*, 5:388–89.

78. Quoted in Jones, *The Union in Peril*, 139, 141–42.

79. Grimsley, *The Hard Hand of War*, 123–24; Allen C. Guelzo, *Lincoln's Emancipation Proclamation: The End of Slavery in America* (New York: Simon & Schuster, 2004), 30.

80. Grimsley, *The Hard Hand of War*, 130–32.

81. Message to Congress, Apr. 16, 1862, *CWL*, 5:192; Guelzo, *Lincoln's Emancipation Proclamation*, 88.

82. Grimsley, *The Hard Hand of War*, 134; extracts from General Orders No. 91, July 17, 1862, *OR*, ser. 3, 2:280–82.

83. Guelzo, *Lincoln's Emancipation Proclamation*, 44–54, 71, 73–75.

84. Ibid., 55–56; Message to Congress, Mar. 6, 1862, *CWL*, 5:144–46; Lincoln to Raymond, Mar. 9, 1862, *CWL*, 5:152–53; Lincoln to McDougal, Mar. 14, 1862, *CWL*, 5:160–61; Appeal to Border State Representatives to Favor Compensated Emancipation, July 12, 1862, *CWL*, 5:317–19.

85. Address on Colonization to a Deputation of Negroes, Aug. 14, 1862, *CWL*, 5:370–75.

86. Annual Message to Congress, Dec. 1, 1862, *CWL*, 5:518–37.

87. Account of the Emancipation Proclamation Related Verbally by the President to the Artist F. B. Carpenter, Feb. 6, 1864, in *Abraham Lincoln: Complete Works*, ed. John G. Nicolay and John Hay (New York: Century, 1907), 2:479; Guelzo, *Lincoln's Emancipation Proclamation*, 151–53.

88. Preliminary Emancipation Proclamation, Sept. 22, 1862, *CWL*, 5:433–36.

89. Emancipation Proclamation, Jan. 1, 1863, *CWL*, 6:28–30.

90. Guelzo, *Lincoln's Emancipation Proclamation*, 24–25.

91. Emancipation Proclamation, Jan. 1, 1863, *CWL*, 6:28–30.

92. Sun Tzu, *The Art of War*, 76.

93. Quoted in Guelzo, *Lincoln's Emancipation Proclamation*, 171–72.

94. Lincoln to Johnson, Mar. 26, 1863, *CWL*, 6:149–50.

95. Lincoln to Banks, Mar. 29, 1863, *CWL*, 6:154–55.

96. Reply to Members of the Presbyterian General Assembly, June 2, 1863, *CWL*, 6:245–46.

97. Graebner, "Northern Diplomacy," 68; Guelzo, *Lincoln's Emancipation Proclamation*, 225.

98. Guelzo, *Lincoln's Emancipation Proclamation*, 16–19, 158–59, 175, 185, 187–88, 222.

99. Ibid., 210, 214–15; Grimsley, *The Hard Hand of War*, 138.

100. Interview with Alexander W. Randall and Joseph T. Mills, Aug. 19, 1864, *CWL*, 7:506–8; McPherson, *Battle Cry*, 769–70 and n. 35.
101. Lincoln to Hodges, Apr. 4, 1864, *CWL*, 7:281–82.
102. Meigs to Burnside, Jan. 12, 1863, *OR*, 21:965–67.
103. Memorandum on Furloughs, Nov. 1862, *CWL*, 5:484.

CHAPTER 14

1. *Davis Papers*, 8:xii–xiii.
2. *Wartime Papers*, 125.
3. Davis to Varina Howell Davis, May 16, 1862, *Davis Papers*, 8:178–79, 449 n. 3.
4. Lee to Seddon, Jan. 10, 1863, *Wartime Papers*, 388–90.
5. Speech at Jackson, Dec. 26, 1862, *Davis Papers*, 8:575.
6. Davis to Holmes, Dec. 21[?], 1862, *OR*, 52/2:397–99; ibid., *Davis Papers*, 8:560–62.
7. McPherson, *Battle Cry*, 593.
8. Davis to Holmes, Dec. 21[?], 1862, *OR*, 52/2:397–99; speech at Jackson, Dec. 26, 1862, *Davis Papers*, 8:576–77, 579.
9. Davis to Holmes, Dec. 21[?], 1862, *OR*, 52/2:397–99.
10. Speech at Jackson, Dec. 26, 1862, *Davis Papers*, 8:576–77, 579.
11. Special Orders No. 275, Nov. 24, 1862, *OR*, 17/2:757–58; Davis to Lee, Dec. 8, 1862, *Davis Papers*, 8:533–35.
12. Johnston to Cooper, Nov. 25, 162, *OR*, 20/2:424.
13. Davis to J. E. Johnston, [Dec. 8, 1862?], *Davis Papers*, 8:529 and n. 5.
14. *Davis Papers*, 8:550 n. 6.
15. Holmes to J. E. Johnston, Dec. 29, 1862, *OR*, 17/2:810–11; Holmes to Davis, Dec. 29, 1862, *Davis Papers*, 8:584–86, 587 n. 8; Eicher, *Longest Night*, 392–95.
16. J. E. Johnston to Davis, Dec. 22, 1862, *OR*, 17/2:800–1.
17. Jones, *Diary*, 131; Symonds, *Atlas*, 49; J. E. Johnston to Davis, Dec. 22, 1862, *OR*, 17/2:800–1.
18. J. E. Johnston to Davis, Dec. 22, 1862, *OR*, 17/2:800–801.
19. J. E. Johnston to Davis, Jan. 2, 6, 1863, *OR*, 17/2:823, 827.
20. Speech at Richmond, Jan. 5, 1863, *Davis Papers*, 9:12.
21. J. E. Johnston to Cooper, Jan. 6, 1863, *OR*, 20/2:487; J. E. Johnston to Davis, Jan. 7, 1863, *OR*, 20/2:487–88; Davis to J. E. Johnston, Jan. 8, 1863, *OR*, 52/2:404; quoted in *Davis Papers*, 8:551 n. 5.
22. Bragg to J. E. Johnston, Jan. 11, 1863, *OR*, 20/2:492–93.
23. Bragg to Ewell, Jan. 14, 1863, *OR*, 52/2:407.
24. Davis to J. E. Johnston, Jan. 22, 1863, *OR*, 23/2:613–14.
25. J. E. Johnston to Davis, Feb. 3, 12, 1863, *Davis Papers*, 9:48–49, 59–60.
26. Maynard to Halleck, Jan. 10, 1863, *OR*, 20/2:313; Johnson to Lincoln, Jan. 11, 1863, *OR*, 20/2:317.
27. Rosecrans to Stanton, Jan. 11, 1863, *OR*, 20/2:317; Rosecrans to Halleck, Jan. 11, 1863, *OR*, 20/2:318; Hattaway and Jones, *How the North Won*, 356–58.
28. Halleck to Rosecrans, Jan. 14, 1863, *OR*, 20/2:328; Halleck to Wright, Jan. 15, 1863, *OR*, 20/2:332; Wright to Rosecrans, Jan. 16, 1863, *OR*, 20/2:333; Wright to Granger, Jan. 16, 1863, *OR*, 20/2:334. For Wright's dispositions, see Wright to Cullum, Jan. 20, 1863, *OR*, 20/2:342.

29. Rosecrans to Halleck, Jan. 29, 1863, *OR*, 23/2:20–21; Reynolds to Flynt, Feb. 10, 1863, *OR*, 23/2:54–57; Thomas, Feb. 11, 1863, indorsement on ibid.

30. Halleck to Rosecrans, Mar. 5, 1863, *OR*, 23/2:107–9. This also has Halleck's instructions for dealing with various classes of citizens, loyal and disloyal.

31. Halleck to Rosecrans, Jan. 30, 1863, *OR*, 23/2:23.

32. Ibid.

33. Rosecrans to Halleck, Feb. 12, 1863, *OR*, 23/2:59.

34. Rosecrans to Halleck, Feb. 1, 2, 1863, *OR*, 23/2:31, 33–34; Lincoln to Halleck, Feb. 14, Lincoln to Rosecrans, Feb. 17, 1863, *CWL*, 6: 105, 108–9.

35. Rosecrans to Wright, Mar. 13, 1863, *OR*, 23/2:143.

36. Wright to Cullum, Mar. 15, 1863, *OR*, 23/2:143–46; Halleck to Burnside, Mar. 16, 1863, *OR*, 23/2:147.

37. Halleck to Burnside, Mar. 23, 1863, *OR*, 23/2:162–64.

38. Ibid.; Halleck to Rosecrans, Mar. 25, 1863, *OR*, 23/2:171; Rosecrans to Halleck, Mar. 25, 1863, *OR*, 23/2:172.

39. Halleck to Burnside, Mar. 25, 1863, *OR*, 23/2:172; Burnside to Halleck, Mar. 26, 1863, *OR*, 23/2: 175–76; Rosecrans to Burnside, Mar. 30, 1863, *OR*, 23/2:193; Burnside to Rosecrans, Mar. 30, 1863, *OR*, 23/2:193; Burnside to Halleck, Mar. 30, 1862, *OR*, 23/1:166.

40. Halleck to Burnside, Mar. 30, 1863, *OR*, 23/2:193; Burnside to Halleck, Apr. 1, 1863, *OR*, 23/1:166–67; Halleck report, *OR*, 23/1:6; Burnside report, *OR*, 23/1:11–12; Burnside to Rosecrans, Apr. 6, 1863, *OR*, 23/2:217.

41. Meigs to Rosecrans, May 1, 1863, *OR*, 23/2:301–4.

42. Halleck to Burnside and Rosecrans, May 18, 1863, *OR*, 23/2:337; Rosecrans to Halleck, May 21, 1863, *OR*, 23/2:351.

43. Lincoln to Rosecrans, May 28, 1863, *CWL*, 6:236; *OR*, 23/2:369.

44. Rosecrans to Lincoln, May 28, 1863, *OR*, 23/2:369.

45. Rosecrans to Burnside, May 28, 29, 1863, *OR*, 23/2:370, 372.

46. Johnson to Lincoln, May 29, 1863, *OR*, 23/2:372.

47. Rosecrans to Burnside, May 31, 1863, *OR*, 23/2:376.

48. Halleck to Burnside, June 3, 1863, *OR*, 23/2:383–84 (two notes); Halleck to Rosecrans, June 3, 1863, *OR*, 23/2:383; Burnside to Halleck, June 3, 1863, *OR*, 23/2:384.

49. *OR*, 23/2:394–97, 402–7, 409–11, 413–15, 417–18.

50. Palmer to Goddard, June 9, 1863, *OR*, 23/2:407–9; Stanley to Goddard, June 9, 1863, *OR*, 23/2:411–13.

51. Garfield to Rosecrans, June 12, 1863, *OR*, 23/2:420–24.

52. Rosecrans to Halleck, June 11, 1863, *OR*, 23/1:8.

53. Halleck to Rosecrans, June 12, 1863, *OR*, 23/1:8.

54. Ibid.

55. Rosecrans to Halleck, June 21, 1863, *OR*, 23/1:9.

56. Halleck to Rosecrans, June 16, 1863, *OR*, 23/1:10.

57. Rosecrans to Halleck, June 16, 1863, *OR*, 23/1:10.

58. Burnside to Rosecrans, June 17, 1863, *OR*, 23/2:436; Burnside to Halleck, June 20, 1863, *OR*, 23/2:440.

59. Rosecrans to Burnside, June 17, 1863, *OR*, 23/2:436.

60. Halleck to Burnside, June 18, 1863, *OR*, 23/2:438.

61. Burnside to Rosecrans, June 19, 1863, *OR*, 23/2:438–39.
62. Eicher, *Longest Night*, 496; Foote, *Civil War*, 2:665–67; *B&L*, 3:635; Halleck report, *OR*, 23/1:9.
63. Halleck to Grant, Jan. 3, 6, 1863, *OR*, 17/1:479–80; *OR*, 17/2:542.
64. Grant to Halleck, Jan. 9, 1863, *OR*, 17/2:549.
65. Grant, *Memoirs*, 293–95; Grant to McClernand, Jan. 11, 1863, *OR*, 17/2:553–54; Halleck to Grant, Jan. 12, 1863, *OR*, 17/2:555; Grant to Gorman, Jan. 12, 1863, *OR*, 17/2:555.
66. Grant, *Memoirs*, 295; Grant to Halleck, Jan. 20, 1863, *OR*, 17/2:573.
67. Grant to Halleck, Jan. 20, 1863, *OR*, 24/1:8–9; Halleck to Grant, Jan. 21, 25, 1863, *OR*, 24/1:9–10; Grant to Gorman, Jan. 21, 1863, *OR*, 24/3:5–6.
68. McClernand to Lincoln, Dec. 17, 1862 (similar to Stanton), Jan. 16, 1863, *OR*, 17/2: 420, 566–67.
69. Catton, *Grant Moves South*, 376–84; Weigley. *Civil War*, 264.
70. Halleck to Grant, Mar. 20, 1863, *OR*, 24/1:22.
71. Halleck to Grant, Mar. 31, 1863, *OR*, 24/3:156–57.
72. Grant to Steele, Apr. 11, 1863, *OR*, 24/3:186–87.
73. Sherman to Tod, Mar. 12, 1863, *Sherman's Civil War*, 415–17.
74. Grant to Halleck, Apr. 4, 1863, *Grant Papers*, 8:10–12; *OR* 24/1:25–26; Grant, *Memoirs*, 305–6.
75. Halleck to Grant, Apr. 2, 1863, *OR*, 24/1:25.
76. Davis to J. E. Johnston, Jan. 8, 1863, *OR*, 52/2:404.
77. J. E. Johnston to Davis, Jan. 10–31, 1863, *Davis Papers*, 9:19.
78. Polk to Davis, Feb. 4, 1863, *OR*, 20/1:698–99.
79. J. E. Johnston to Davis, Jan. 10–31, 1863, *Davis Papers*, 9:19.
80. Davis to J. E. Johnston, Jan. 22, 1863, *OR*, 23/2:613–14.
81. Seddon to J. E. Johnston, Feb. 5, 1863, *OR*, 23/2:626–27.
82. Ibid.
83. Davis to J. E. Johnston, Feb. 19, 1863, *Davis Papers*, 9:66–57.
84. J. E. Johnston to Davis, Mar. 2, 1863, *Davis Papers*, 9:86–87.
85. Seddon to J. E. Johnston, Mar. 3, 1863, *OR*, 23/2:658–59.
86. Ibid.
87. *Wartime Papers*, 375.
88. Lee to Seddon, Jan. 5, Lee to Davis, Jan. 6, 1863, *Wartime Papers*, 376, 385–88.
89. Lee to Seddon, Jan. 5, 1863, *Wartime Papers*, 376–78, 385–87.
90. *B&L*, 4:53–54; Symonds, *Lincoln and His Admirals*, 200–202; Welles, *Diary*, 1:276, 313–14.
91. Symonds, *Lincoln and His Admirals*, 202–3.
92. Ibid., 204–6, 208–9.
93. Ibid., 208–11; *B&L*, 4:10.
94. Lee to Seddon, Apr. 9, 1863, *Wartime Papers*, 429–30.
95. Ibid.
96. Lee to Davis, Apr. 16, 1863, *Wartime Papers*, 434–35.
97. Lee to Cooper, Apr. 16, 1863, *Wartime Papers*, 433–34.
98. Lee to his wife, Apr. 19, 1863, *Wartime Papers*, 437–38. Lee also hoped that 1863 would see the foundations for supplying his army firmly established.

99. Lincoln to Hooker, Jan. 26, 1863, *CWL*, 6:78–79.

100. Marszalek, *Halleck*, 165; Heintzelman journal, *ORS*, 3:447; Hay, *Diary*, 80; Lincoln to Hooker, Jan. 26, 1863, *CWL*, 6:78–79.

101. Marszalek, *Halleck*, 166.

102. McPherson, *Battle Cry*, 585; Halleck to Hooker, Jan. 31, 1863, *OR*, 25/2:12; Walter A. Hebert, *Fighting Joe Hooker* (Indianapolis: Bobbs-Merrill, 1944), 170.

103. Halleck to Hooker, Jan. 31, 1863, *OR*, 25/2:12; Halleck to Burnside, Jan. 7, 1863, *OR*, 25/2:13.

104. Hebert, *Hooker*, 171, 185–87.

105. Halleck to Hooker, Mar. 27, 1863, *OR*, 25/2:158; Hebert, *Hooker*, 187; Hooker to Stanton, Apr. 2, 1863, *OR*, 25/2:187–88.

106. Donald, *Lincoln*, 433–34; Kent R. Greenfield, *American Strategy in World War II: A Reconsideration* (Malabar, FL: Krieger, 1983), 56–58.

107. Memorandum on Joseph Hooker's Plan of Campaign Against Richmond, [c. Apr. 6–10, 1863], *CWL*, 6:164–65.

108. *B&L*, 3:119–20, 155.

109. Hebert, *Hooker*, 187; Hooker to Lincoln, Apr. 11, 1863, *OR*, 25/2, 199–200; Meigs to Burnside, Dec. 30, 1862, *OR*, 21:916–18; Archer Jones, *Civil War Command and Strategy: The Process of Victory and Defeat* (New York: Free Press, 1992), 156–57.

110. Lincoln to Hooker, Apr. 12, 1863, *CWL*, 6:169; Hooker to Lincoln, Apr. 15 (two notes), 17, 1863, *OR*, 25/2:213–14, 220; Lincoln to Hooker, Apr. 15, 1863, *OR*, 25/2:214; *B&L*, 3:155–56.

111. Milroy to Schenck, Feb. 10, 1863, *OR*, 25/2:63–64.

112. Halleck to Hooker, Hooker to Halleck, Mar. 6, 1863, *OR*, 25/2:127–28.

113. Halleck to Schenck, Mar. 7, 1863, *OR*, 25/2:132.

114. Roberts to Halleck, Mar. 14, 1863, *OR*, 25/2:136–37.

115. W. E. Jones to Lee, Jan. 26, 1863, *OR*, 25/2:605–6; Lee to W. E. Jones, Jan. 27, Feb. 2, 1863, *OR*, 25/2:598, 606; Lee to Seddon, Feb. 2, 1863, *OR*, 25/2:604–5; Seddon to Sam Jones, Feb. 13, 1863, *OR*, 25/2:620–21.

116. Imboden to Lee, Mar. 2, 1863, *OR*, 25/2:652–53; Lee to Imboden, Mar. 11, 1863, *OR*, 25/2:661; Lee to Sam Jones, Mar. 11, 21, 1863, *OR*, 25/2:661, 679–81; Lee to W. E. Jones, Mar. 26, 1863, *OR*, 25/2:684–85; Boatner, *Dictionary*, 445.

117. Halleck to Hooker, Mar. 16, 1863, *OR*, 25/2:139; Halleck to Schenck, Mar. 16, 1863, *OR*, 25/2:139.

118. Hooker to Stanton, Mar. 16, 1863, *OR*, 25/2:140; Halleck to Hooker, Mar. 16, 1863, *OR*, 25/2:140.

119. Various correspondence, April and May 1863, *OR*, 25/2.

120. Schenck to Milroy, Apr. 19, 1863, *OR*, 25/2:230.

121. Halleck to Dix, Apr. 17, 1863, *OR*, 25/2:225–26.

122. Dix to Halleck, Apr. 18, 1863, *OR*, 25/2:226; Hooker to Stanton, Apr. 18, 1863, *OR*, 25/2:226; Stanton to Hooker, Apr. 18, 1863, *OR*, 25/2:226; Jomini, *Art of War*, 93.

123. Williams, *Lincoln and His Generals*, 234; Hooker to Lincoln, Apr. 27, 1863, *CWL*, 6:190 n. 1; Williams to Sedgwick, Apr. 27, 1863, *OR*, 23/2:268; Lincoln to Hooker, Apr. 28, 1863, *CWL*, 6:189–90.

124. Symonds, *Atlas*, 59–61.

125. Lee to Seddon, May 6, Lee to Longstreet, May 7, 1863, Lee to Hood, May 21, *Wartime Papers*, 377–78, 456, 458, 490; Welles, *Diary*, 1:335–36.

126. Heintzelman journal, *ORS*, 4:469–70; Hooker to Peck or Dix, Apr. 29, 1863, *OR*, 25/2:293.

CHAPTER 15

1. J. E. Johnston to Davis, Feb. 12, 1863, *Davis Papers*, 9:59–60, 61 n. 8; Boatner, *Dictionary*, 871.

2. Davis to J. E. Johnston, Mar. 16, 1863, *OR*, 23/2:713.

3. J. E. Johnston to Davis, Mar. 28, 1863, *OR*, 23/2:726–27.

4. J. E. Johnston to Davis, Apr. 10, 1863, *Davis Papers*, 9:137–38.

5. Seddon to J. E. Johnston, May 9, 1863, *OR*, 24/1:215; J. E. Johnston to Seddon, May 9, 1863, *OR*, 24/1:215.

6. Halleck to Grant, Apr. 2, 1863, *OR*, 24/1:25.

7. Grant to Halleck, Apr. 4, 1863, *OR*, 24/1:25–26.

8. Catton, *Grant Moves South*, 412–13; Sherman to Ellen Ewing Sherman, Apr. 10, 23, 1863, *Sherman's Civil War*, 445–48, 455–57; Clausewitz, *On War*, 101–2.

9. Grant, *Memoirs*, 309; Grant to McClernand, Apr. 12, 13, 1863, *Grant Papers*, 8:56–57, 63; *OR*, 24/3:188–89; Grant to Halleck, Apr. 12, 1863, *OR*, 24/1:29.

10. Grant to Halleck, Apr. 17, 1863, *Grant Papers*, 8:85; Grant, *Memoirs*, 307–10; Special Orders No. 110, Apr. 20, 1863, *OR*, 24/3:212–14.

11. Grant, *Memoirs*, 315.

12. Catton, *Grant Moves South*, 421–23; Grant, *Memoirs*, 318.

13. Grant to Sherman, Apr. 27, 1863, *OR*, 24/3:240.

14. Sherman to Grant, Apr. 28, 1863, *OR*, 24/3:242–43.

15. Catton, *Grant Moves South*, 424–25; Grant, *Memoirs*, 321.

16. Clausewitz, *On War*, 456–59; Grant to Julia Dent Grant, Apr. 28, 1863, *Grant Papers*, 8:132–33; Grant to Sherman, May 3, 1863, *OR*, 24/3:268–69; Grant to Halleck, May 3, 1863, *OR*, 24/1:32–34; Grant, *Memoirs*, 322–23; Catton, *Grant Moves South*, 425–26.

17. Catton, *Grant Moves South*, 432–33; Grant, *Memoirs*, 328; Grant to Sherman, May 3, 1863, *OR*, 24/3:268–69; Grant to Halleck, May 3, 1863, *OR*, 24/1:32–34.

18. Grant to McClernand, May 4, 1863, *Grant Papers*, 8:156.

19. Grant to Halleck, May 6, 1863, *Grant Papers*, 8:169; OR 24/1:35.

20. Grant to Hurlbut, May 5, 1863, *Grant Papers*, 8:159–60.

21. Grant to Steele, Apr. 11, 1863, *Grant Papers*, 8:49.

22. Grant, *Memoirs*, 328; Grant to Sherman, May 9, 1863, *Grant Papers*, 8:183–84.

23. Grant, *Memoirs*, 328.

24. Catton, *Grant Moves South*, 435, 439.

25. Symonds, *Johnston*, 201–2, 205; J. E. Johnston to Seddon, May 13, 16, 1863, *OR*, 24/1:215.

26. *Davis Papers*, 9:189; Symonds, *Johnston*, 207–8.

27. Grant to Sherman, May 12, 1863, and Grant to Blair, May 14, 1863, *Grant Papers*, 8:207–8, 213–14; Symonds, *Johnston*, 208; Grant, *Memoirs*, 332.

28. Pemberton to J. E. Johnston, May 17, 1862, *OR*, 24/1:217–18; J. E. Johnston to Pemberton, May 14, 1863, *OR*, 24/3:877–78.

29. J. E. Johnston to Pemberton, May 14, 15, 1863, *OR*, 24/3:877–78, 882; Symonds, *Johnston*, 209.

30. Grant, *Memoirs*, 338–39; Catton, *Grant Moves South*, 441, 443–45; *Davis Papers*, 9:189.

31. Davis indorsement on J. E. Johnston to Seddon, May 16, 1863, *OR*, 24/1:215–16.

32. J. E. Johnston to Seddon, May 16, 1863, *OR*, 24/1:215–16.

33. J. E. Johnston to Cooper, May 17, 18, 1863, *OR*, 24/1:216–17; J. E. Johnston to Pemberton, May 17, 1863, *OR*, 24/3:888; Pemberton to J. E. Johnston, May 18, 1863, *OR*, 24/3:889–90; J. E. Johnston to Seddon, May 27, 1863, *OR*, 24/1:220–23.

34. Jones, *Diary*, 212; Walter Herron Taylor to his brother Dick, July 17, 1863, in *Lee's Adjutant: The Wartime Letters of Colonel Walter Herron Taylor, 1862–1865*, ed. R. Lockwood Tower (Columbia: University of South Carolina Press, 1995), 59–63.

35. J. E. Johnston to Cooper, May 18, [1863], *OR*, 24/1:218; Davis to Bragg, May 22, 1863, *OR*, 24/1:191.

36. Grant, *Memoirs*, 338; Catton, *Grant Moves South*, 445, 450–53.

37. Lincoln to Arnold, May 26, 1863, *CWL*, 6:230–31.

38. Seddon to J. E. Johnston, May 23, 1863, *OR*, 24/1:219; Bragg to Davis, May 23, 1863, *OR*, 24/1:192; Symonds, *Johnston*, 211.

39. J. E. Johnston to Gardner, May 19, 1862, *OR*, 24/3:896–97.

40. *Davis Papers*, 9:183. See also Davis to Pettus, May 18, 1863, *OR*, 52/2:472.

41. Pettus to Davis, May 18, 1863, *OR*, 52/2:472–73. In the wake of the passage of conscription, Davis's correspondence generally reveals a Confederate tendency to rely upon the militia for local defense.

42. J. E. Johnston to Davis, May 23, 1863, *OR*, 24/1:192.

43. Davis to J. E. Johnston, May 24, 1863, *OR*, 24/1:193; ibid., *Davis Papers*, 9:189.

44. J. E. Johnston to Seddon, May 27, 1863, *OR*, 24/1:220–23.

45. Various, May 28–June 2, 1863, *OR*, 24/1:194–224.

46. Davis to Lee, May 26, 1863, *Davis Papers*, 9:191–93.

47. J. E. Johnston to Seddon, June 4, 5, 1863, *OR*, 24/1:224–25; Seddon to J. E. Johnston, June 3, 5, 1863, *OR*, 24/1:223–24.

48. Davis to Holmes, Jan. 28, 1863, *OR*, 53:846–47; Jeff Prushankin, *A Crisis in Confederate Command: Edmund Kirby Smith, Richard Taylor, and the Army of the Trans-Mississippi* (Baton Rouge: LSU Press, 2005), 15.

49. Holmes to Davis, Apr. 8, 1863, *Davis Papers*, 9:130–32.

50. Symonds, *Johnston*, 199–200; Prushankin, *Crisis*, 36.

51. Davis to E. K. Smith, May 8, June 3, 1863, *Davis Papers*, 9:171–72.

52. Davis to Holmes, Feb. 26, 1863, *Davis Papers*, 9:74–76.

53. E. K. Smith to Davis, June 16, 1863, *Davis Papers*, 9:220–23.

54. Seddon to J. E. Johnston, May 23, 1863, *OR*, 24/1:219.

55. J. E. Johnston to E. K. Smith, May 31, June 3, 1863, *OR*, 24/3:998.

56. *Davis Papers*, 9:224 n. 20; Prushankin, *Crisis*, 34–35.

57. *Davis Papers*, 9:224 n. 20; Prushankin, *Crisis*, 42–45.

58. *Davis Papers*, 9:224 n. 20; J. E. Johnston to E. K. Smith, June 26, 1863, *OR*, 24/3:979; E. K. Smith to Davis, June 16, 1863, *Davis Papers*, 9:220–23.

59. Davis to E. K. Smith, July 2, 1863, *OR*, 22/2:902.

60. Walker to E. K. Smith, July 3, 1863, *OR*, 24/3:999–1000.

61. E. K. Smith to J. E. Johnston, July 4, 1863, *OR*, 22/2:904.

62. Prushankin, *Crisis*, 47.

63. J. E. Johnston to Seddon, June 12, 1863, *OR*, 24/1:226.

64. J. E. Johnston to Seddon, June 15, 1863, *OR*, 24/1:227.

65. Seddon to J. E. Johnston, June 16, 1863, *OR*, 24/1:227.

66. J. E. Johnston to Davis, June 16, 1863, *OR*, 24/1:196.

67. J. E. Johnston to Seddon, June 19[18], 1863, *OR*, 24/1:227.

68. Davis to Bragg, June 17, 1863, *OR*, 24/1:196–97.

69. Seddon to J. E. Johnston, June 21, 1863, *OR*, 24/1:228 (two notes); J. E. Johnston to Seddon, June 24, 1863, *OR*, 24/1:229.

70. Harvie to Joseph [R.] Davis, June 21, 1863, *OR*, 24/3:969–71. *Davis Papers*, 9:242 n. 10 says that this letter is incorrectly addressed to J. E. Davis.

71. McPherson, *Battle Cry*, 634–36.

72. Harvie to Joseph [R.] Davis, June 21, 1863, *OR*, 24/3:969–71; Elgee to Taylor, June 22, 1863, *OR*, 24/3:998–99; McPherson, *Battle Cry*, 635–36.

73. *Davis Papers*, 9:265 n. 4.

74. *Davis Papers*, 9:264–65 n. 3; McPherson, *Battle Cry*, 636; Bruce Catton, *This Hallowed Ground: The Story of the Union Side of the Civil War* (Hertfordshire, UK: Wordsworth Military Library, 1998), 269.

75. McPherson, *Battle Cry*, 636–37.

76. Lincoln to Grant, July 13, 1863, *CWL*, 6:326.

77. Grant, *Memoirs*, 381.

CHAPTER 16

1. E. P. Alexander, *Fighting for the Confederacy: The Personal Recollections of General Edward Porter Alexander*, ed. Gary Gallagher (Chapel Hill: University of North Carolina Press, 1989), 219.

2. J. E. Johnston to Cooper, May 1, 1863, *OR*, 24/1:214.

3. Lee to Seddon, May 10, 1863, *Wartime Papers*, 482.

4. *Davis Papers*, 9:179; Lee to Seddon, Apr. 9, May 11, 1863, *Wartime Papers*, 429–30, 483–84.

5. Lee to D. H. Hill, May 16, and Lee to Seddon, May 20, June 8, 1863, *Wartime Papers*, 485–86, 489–90, 504–5.

6. Seddon to Lee, June 10, 1863, *OR*, 27/3:882.

7. Lee to Davis, June 10, 1863, *Wartime Papers*, 507–9.

8. *Davis Papers*, 244 n. 5; Jones, *Diary*, 229–30; Boatner, *Dictionary*, 864.

9. Walter H. Taylor, *General Lee: His Campaigns in Virginia, 1861–1865, with Personal Reminiscences* (Norfolk: Nussbaum, 1906), 179–80. See also Walter H. Taylor, *Four Years with General Lee*, ed. James I. Robertson (Bloomington: Indiana University Press, 1996), 90–91.

10. Allan, "Memoranda," in Gallagher, ed., *Lee the Soldier*, 13.

11. Taylor, *General Lee*, 180.

12. Frederick Maurice, ed., *Lee's Aide-de-Camp: Charles Marshall* (Lincoln: University of Nebraska Press, 2000), 63–76.

13. Davis, *Rise and Fall*, 2:437–38; Allan, "Memoranda," in Gallagher, ed., *Lee the Soldier*, 13–14; Lee to Cooper, Battle Report of Gettysburg Campaign, Jan. 20, 1864, *Wartime Papers*, 569–70; Trimble to Bachelder, Feb. 8, 1883, *ORS*, 5:432–35.

14. James McPherson, *This Mighty Scourge: Perspectives on the Civil War* (New York: Oxford University Press, 2007), 84–85.

15. Lee to Cooper, Battle Report of Gettysburg Campaign, Jan. 20, 1864, *Wartime Papers*, 569–70; see also Taylor, *General Lee*, 180.

16. Lee to Imboden, June 10, 1863, *Wartime Papers*, 510.

17. William Allan, "Campaigns in Virginia, Maryland, and Pennsylvania, 1862–1863," paper read May 9, 1887, in *Papers of the Military Historical Society of Massachusetts* (Boston: Military Historical Society of Massachusetts, 1903), 3:446–47.

18. Stanton to Burnside, May 7, 1863, *OR*, 25/2:437–38 (similar to Grant, Dix, Pope, Rosecrans, various governors, etc.).

19. Quoted in Noah Brooks, *Washington in Lincoln's Time* (New York: Century, 1895), 57–58; Donald, *Lincoln*, 435–36; McPherson, *Battle* Cry, 645; Hooker to Lincoln, May 13, 1863, *OR*, 25/2:473.

20. Stanton to Hooker, May 6, 1863, *OR*, 25/2:435; Donald, *Lincoln*, 438.

21. Lincoln to Hooker, May 7, 1863, *CWL*, 6:201.

22. Hooker to Lincoln, May 7, 13, 1863, *OR* 25/2:438, 473; Freeman Cleaves, *Meade of Gettysburg* (Norman: University of Oklahoma Press, 1960), 115.

23. Lincoln to Hooker, May 13, 1863, *OR*, 25/2:474; Lincoln to Hooker, May 14, 1863, *CWL*, 6:217–18; *OR*, 25/2:479.

24. Lee to Davis, June 15, 1863, *Wartime Papers*, 514–15.

25. For an example, see Lee to A. P. Hill, June 16, 1863, *Wartime Papers*, 517.

26. Lee to Ewell and Lee to Longstreet, June 17, 1863, *Wartime Papers*, 518–19.

27. *Davis Papers*, 9:261 n. 3; McPherson, *This Mighty Scourge*, 85.

28. For examples of warning letters, see *OR*, 25/2:509–10; Stanton to Halleck, May 23, 1863, *OR*, 25/2:514; Hooker to Chase, May 25, 1863, *OR*, 25/2:524; Hooker to Stanton, May 27, 28, 1863, *OR*, 25/2:527, 542–43; Sharpe to Williams, May 27, 1863, *OR*, 25/2:528; Milroy to Schenck, May 27, 1863, *OR*, 25/2:531; Halleck to Dix, May 28, 1863, *OR*, 25/2:531; Hebert, *Hooker*, 232–33.

29. Halleck to Dix, May 28, 1863, *OR*, 25/2:531.

30. Milroy to Schenck, May 30, 1863, *OR*, 25/2:569–70.

31. Hooker to Dix, May 31, 1863, *OR*, 25/2:574.

32. Hooker to Lincoln, June 5, 1863, *OR*, 27/1:30.

33. Maurice, "Lincoln as a Strategist," 165–66.

34. Lincoln to Hooker, June 5, 1863, *CWL*, 6:249; *OR*, 27/1:31.

35. Lincoln to Hooker, June 5, 1863, *CWL*, 6:249.

36. Halleck to Hooker, June 5, 1863, *OR*, 27/1:31–32.

37. Halleck to Stanton, May 18, 1863, *OR*, 25/2:504–6.

38. Halleck to Hooker, June 5, 1863, *OR*, 27/1:31–32.

39. Ibid. Hebert, *Hooker*, 234, also insists it would have been a good move for Hooker to attack, but disagrees with my assessment of other issues.

40. Hooker to Dix, June 9, 1863, *OR*, 27/1:34; Hebert, *Hooker*, 234–35.

41. Hooker to Lincoln, June 10, 1863, *OR*, 27/1:34–35.

42. Lincoln to Hooker, June 10, 1863, *OR*, 27/1:35.

43. Alexander, *Fighting for the Confederacy*, 276.

44. Halleck to Hooker, June 11, 1863, *OR*, 27/1:35; Neely, "Hooker," 66.

45. Hooker to Halleck, June 13, 1863, *OR*, 27/1:38.

46. Lincoln to Hooker, June 14, 1863, *OR*, 27/1:39.

47. Hooker to Lincoln, June 14, 1863, *OR*, 27/1:39–40.

48. Lincoln to Hooker, June 14, 15, 1863, *OR*, 27/1:40, 43; Lincoln to Kelley, Schenck, and Tyler, June 14, Lincoln to Hooker, June 16, 1863, *CWL*, 6:274–75, 280; Hooker to Lincoln, June 15, 16, 1863, *OR*, 27/1:43–44; Halleck to Hooker, June 15, 1863, *OR*, 27/1:41–42; Lincoln Proclamation, June 15, 1863, *OR*, 27/3:136–37.

49. Hooker to Lincoln, June 16, 1863, *OR*, 27/1:45.

50. Lincoln to Hooker, June 16, 1863, *CWL*, 6:281–82.

51. Hebert, *Hooker*, 238–41; various notes, *OR*, 27/1:45–53; Lincoln to Hooker, June 16, 1863, *CWL*, 6:282 and n. 1.

52. Lee to Davis, June 18, 1863, *Wartime Papers*, 519–20; Jeffrey C. Hall, *The Stand of the U.S. Army at Gettysburg* (Bloomington: Indiana University Press, 2003), 6.

53. Lee to Davis, June 19, Lee to Imboden and Lee to Sam Jones, June 20, 1863, *Wartime Papers*, 520–23.

54. Lee to Ewell, June 22, 1863, *Wartime Papers*, 524–25.

55. Kenneth P. Williams, *Lincoln Finds a General: A Military Study of the Civil War* (New York: Macmillan, 1949–59), 2:638, 839 n. 94.

56. Ibid., 2:639–40; Warren to Hooker, June 24, 1862, *OR*, 27/3:292.

57. Hooker to Halleck, June 24, 1863, *OR*, 27/1:55–56; Williams, *Lincoln Finds a General*, 2:640–41.

58. Williams, *Lincoln Finds a General*, 2:646–50; Marszalek, *Halleck*, 174–75; Hebert, *Hooker*, 244–45; Hooker to Halleck, June 27, 1863, *OR*, 27/1:60.

59. Hooker to Halleck (copy to president), June 27, 1863, *OR*, 27/1:59.

60. Halleck to Meade, June 27, 1863, *OR*, 27/1:61; Boatner, *Dictionary*, 539.

61. Meade to Halleck, June 28, 29, 1863, *OR*, 27/1:61–62, 66–67.

62. Hattaway and Jones, *How the North Won*, 401–2; Long and Long, *Civil War*, 375; D. H. Hill to Seddon, July 5, 1863, *OR*, 27/3:972–73.

63. Woodworth, *Davis and Lee*, 228; Lee to Davis, June 23, 1863, *Wartime Papers*, 527–28.

64. E. P. Alexander, *Military Memoirs of a Confederate*, intro. and notes by T. Harry Williams (Bloomington: Indiana University Press, 1962), 366.

65. Lee to Davis, June 25, 1863, *Wartime Papers*, 530–31.

66. *Davis Papers*, 9:245 n. 7.

67. Lee to Davis, June 25, 1863, *Wartime Papers*, 532–33.

68. Davis to Lee, June 28, 1863, *Davis Papers*, 9:239–40, 247–49, 249 n. 1; Cooper to Lee, June 29, 1863, *OR*, 27/1:75–76.

69. Beauregard to J. E. Johnston, July 1, 1863, *OR*, 28/2:173–74.

70. Alexander, *Military Memoirs*, 364–65.

71. Ibid.

72. Davis to Lee, June 28, 1863, *Davis Papers*, 9: 245 n. 13, 247–49, 249 n. 1; Butterfield to Halleck, July 3, 1863, *OR*, 27/1:75–77; Symonds, *Lincoln and His Admirals*, 242–44; Long and Long, *Civil War*, 382–83.

73. Lee to Davis, June 25, 1863, *Wartime Papers*, 530–31; *Davis Papers*, 9:245 n. 13.

74. Lee to Cooper, Battle Report of Gettysburg Campaign, Jan. 20, 1864, *Wartime Papers*, 574.

75. Clausewitz, *On War*, 572–73.

76. Thomas, *Lee*, 292–93, 295.

77. Trimble to Bachelder, Feb. 8, 1883, *ORS*, 5:432–35.

78. Thomas, *Lee*, 295.

79. Ibid., 296.

80. Ibid., 296–97.

81. Ibid., 297–98; McPherson, *Battle Cry*, 657, 659–660.

82. Quoted in *B&L*, 3:313–14; McPherson, *Battle Cry*, 660–61.

83. Thomas, *Lee*, 298–300; Freeman, *Lee*, 3:117; *B&L*, 3:406; McPherson, *Battle Cry*, 661–63.

84. Lee to Cooper, Battle Report of Gettysburg Campaign, Jan. 20, 1864, *Wartime Papers*, 576.

85. Thomas, *Lee*, 304.

86. Lincoln to Parker, June 30, 1863, *CWL*, 6:311–12.

87. Lee to Davis, July 7, 1863, *Wartime Papers*, 540–41.

88. Lee to Davis, July 7, 1863, Lee to Cooper, Battle Report of Gettysburg Campaign, Jan. 20, 1864, *Wartime* Papers, 540–41, 582; *Davis Papers*, 9:267 n. 2.

89. Lee to Davis, July 8, Lee to his wife, July 12, 1863, *Wartime Papers*, 543–44, 547–48.

90. Lee to Davis, July 10, 12, Lee to his wife, July 15, 1863, *Wartime Papers*, 545, 548, 551.

91. Lee to Davis, July 12 1863, *Wartime Papers*, 548.

92. Meade to Halleck, July 3, 4, 5, 1863, *OR*, 27/1:74–75, 78–79; Meade to Comm. Off. 6th Corps, July 6, 1863, *The Life and Letters of George Gordon Meade* (New York: Charles Scribner's Sons, 1913), 2:126.

93. Stanton to L. Thomas, July 4, 1863, *OR*, 27/3:525; L. Thomas to Stanton, July 4, 1863, *OR*, 27/3:525; Halleck to Kelly, July 4, 1863, *OR*, 27/3:528; Stanton to Dix, July 4, 1863, *OR*, 27/3:529; Halleck to Meade, July 5, 1863, *OR*, 27/1:79–80.

94. Halleck to Burnside, July 6, 1863, *OR*, 23/2:517; Burnside to Halleck, July 6, 1863, *OR*, 23/1:633–34; Stanton to Rosecrans, July 7, 1863, *OR*, 23/2:518; Rosecrans to Stanton, July 7, 1863, *OR*, 23/2:518.

95. Lincoln to Halleck, [July 7, 1863], *CWL*, 6:319.

96. General Orders, No. 68, July 4, 1863, Meade, *Life and Letters*, 2:122–23; Lincoln to Halleck, July 6, 1863, *CWL*, 6:318; quoted in Hay, *Diary*, 62.

97. Halleck to Meade, July 7, 1863, *OR*, 27/1:82–83; Halleck to Meade, July 8, 1863, *OR*, 27/3:605.

98. Alexander, *Fighting for the Confederacy*, 270–71; Halleck to Meade, July 10, 1863, *OR*, 27/1:89; Meade to Halleck, July 12, 1863, *OR*, 27/1:91.

99. Hay, *Diary*, 61–62; David Homer Bates, *Lincoln in the Telegraph Office: Recollections of the United States Military Telegraph Corps During the Civil War* (Lincoln: University of Nebraska Press, 1995), 156–57.

100. Meade to Mrs. Meade, July 14, 1863, *Life and Letters*, 2:134; Meade to Halleck, July 13, 1863, *OR*, 27/1:91–92; Halleck to Meade, July 13, 1863, *OR*, 27/1:92.

101. Halleck to Meade and Meade to Halleck, July 14, 1863, *OR*, 27/1:92–93; Meade to Mrs. Meade, July 14, 1863, *Life and Letters*, 2:134.

102. Gabor S. Boritt, "'Unfinished Work': Lincoln, Meade, and Gettysburg," in Boritt, ed., *Lincoln's Generals*, 83, 98–99, 212–13 n. 32; quoted in Hay, *Diary*, 63–65, 302–5, nn. 67–73.

103. Lee to his wife, July 15, Lee to Davis, July 31, 1863, *Wartime Papers*, 551, 565; quoted in *Davis Papers*, 9:259.

104. See, among others, Newt Gingrich and William Forstchen, *Gettysburg: A Novel of the Civil War* (New York: Thomas Dunne Books, 2003).

105. Quoted in *Davis Papers*, 9:259.

106. McPherson, *Battle Cry*, 652.

107. Lee to Davis, June 19, 1863, *Wartime Papers*, 520; Kent Masterson Brown, *Retreat from Gettysburg: Lee, Logistics, and the Gettysburg Campaign* (Chapel Hill: University of North Carolina Press, 2005), esp. 33–35.

108. Lee to Davis, July 7, 1863, *Wartime Papers*, 540–41.

109. Taylor to his brother Dick, July 17, 1863, in *Lee's Adjutant: The Wartime Letters of Colonel Walter Herron Taylor, 1862–1865*, ed. R. Lockwood Tower (Columbia: University of South Carolina Press, 1995), 59–63.

110. Lee to Margaret Stuart, July 26, 1863, *Wartime Papers*, 561.

111. Lincoln to Meade, July 14, 1863, *CWL*, 6:327–28.

112. Lincoln to Howard, July 21, 1863, *CWL*, 6:341.

113. Quoted in Boritt, "Meade," 119–20.

114. Verses on Lee's invasion of the North, [July 19, 1863], *The Collected Works of Abraham Lincoln. Supplement, 1832–1865*, ed. Roy P. Basler (Westport, CT: Greenwood, 1974), 194, 195 n. 1.

CHAPTER 17

1. Foote, *Civil War*, 2:769; Grant to Webster, July 26, 1863, *OR*, 24/3:552–53.

2. Halleck to Grant, July 11, 1863, *OR*, 24/3:497–98.

3. Grant to Halleck, July 11, 1863, *OR*, 24/3:498–99; Halleck to Grant, July 15, 1863, *OR*, 24/3:513 (two notes).

4. Schofield report, *OR*, 22/1:12–17; McPherson, *This Mighty Scourge*, 88–89.

5. Grant, *Memoirs*, 389; Foote, *Civil War*, 2:769–70; Grant to Sherman, July 18, 1863, *OR*, 24/3:528.

6. Grimsley, *Hard Hand of War*, 159, 162–63; Hattaway and Jones, *How the North Won*, 489–90; Grant to Halleck, July 24, 1863, *OR*, 24/3:546–47; Grant to Crocker, Aug. 28, 1863, *OR*, ser. 3, 3:735.

7. Grant to Halleck, July 18, 24, 1863, *OR*, 24/3:529–30, 546–47; Halleck to Grant, July 22, 1863, *OR*, 24/3:542.

8. Lee to Imboden, July 21, 1863, *Wartime Papers*, 556–57.

9. Davis to Lee, Aug. 2, 1863, *Davis Papers*, 317–19, 319 n. 4.

10. Lee to Longstreet, Aug. 31, 1863, *Wartime Papers*, 594.

11. Meade to Halleck, July 26, 1863, *OR*, 27/1:101; Halleck to Meade, July 27, 1863, *OR*, 27/1:101.

12. Lincoln to Halleck, July 29, 1863, *CWL*, 6:354.

13. Meade to Halleck, July 30, 1863, *OR*, 27/1:106–7; Halleck to Meade, July 29, 1863, *OR*, 27/1:105–6; Boatner, *Dictionary*, 245–46.

14. Meade to Halleck, July 30, 1863, *OR*, 27/1:106–7; Halleck to Meade, July 30, 1863, *OR*, 27/1:108; Meade to Mrs. Meade, Aug. 3, 1863, *Life and Letters*, 2:141.

15. Lincoln to Stanton, July 29, 1863, *CWL*, 6:354–55, 355 n. 1; *OR*, 26/1:659.

16. Halleck to Banks, July 24, 31, 1863, *OR*, 26/1:652–53, 664.

17. Halleck to Banks, Nov. 9, 1862, *OR*, 15:590–91; Banks to Halleck, Aug. 1, 1863, *OR*, 26/1:666; Grant to Halleck, Aug. 1, 1863, *OR*, 24/3:569; Foote, *Civil War*, 2:770.

18. Lincoln to Banks, Aug. 5, 1863, *CWL*, 6:364–65; Lincoln to Grant, Aug. 9, 1863, *OR*, 24/3:584; Halleck to Grant, Aug. 3, 1863, *OR*, 24/3:571.

19. Halleck to Banks, Aug. 10, 1863, *OR*, 26/1:673.

20. Banks to Grant, Aug. 10, 1863, *OR*, 26/1:673–74; Symonds, *Johnston*, 219.

21. Grant, *Memoirs*, 388.

22. Lincoln to Conkling, Aug. 26, 1863, *CWL*, 6:406–10.

23. Meade to Mrs. Meade, Aug. 3, 6, 1863, *Life and Letters*, 2:141–42; Meade to Halleck, Aug. 4, 1863, *OR*, 27/1:114.

24. Lee to Davis, Sept. 11, 1863, *Wartime Papers*, 599.

25. Lee to Davis, Sept. 14, 18, 1863, *Wartime Papers*, 600–2; *OR*, 29/2:730–31.

26. Halleck to Meade, Sept. 15, 1863, *OR*, 29/2:186–87 (two notes); Lincoln to Halleck, Sept. 15, 1863, *CWL*, 6:450.

27. Halleck to Meade, Sept. 15, 1863, *OR*, 29/2:186–87.

28. Lincoln to Halleck, Sept. 15, 1863, *OR*, 29/2:187.

29. Meade to Halleck, Sept. 15, 16, 1863, *OR*, 29/2:187–88, 195–96; Meade to Mrs. Meade, Sept. 16, 1863, *Life and Letters*, 2:149–50.

30. Meade to Mrs. Meade, Sept. 19, 24, 1863, *Life and Letters*, 2:150–51; Meade to Halleck, Sept. 18, 1863, 29/2:201–2.

31. Lincoln to Halleck, Sept. 19, 1863, *CWL*, 6:466–68.

32. Halleck to Meade, Sept. 19, 1863, *OR*, 29/2:206–7; Meade to Mrs. Meade, Sept. 19, 24, 1863, *Life and Letters*, 2:150–51.

33. Lee to Davis, Sept. 30, 1863, *OR*, 29/2:757–58; Lee to Imboden, Oct. 9, 1863, *Wartime Papers*, 587, 607.

34. Lee to Seddon, Oct. 11, 13, 17, 1863, *Wartime Papers*, 587, 607–9; Meade to Halleck, Oct. 14, 15, 1863, *OR*, 29/2:314, 326.

35. Meade to Halleck, Oct. 13, 1863, *OR*, 29/2:305–6; various, *OR*, 29/2:307–19.

36. Halleck to Meade, Oct. 15, 1863, *OR*, 29/2:328; Lincoln to Halleck, Oct. 16, 1863, *CWL*, 6:518.

37. Lee to Davis, Oct. 17, Lee to Lawton, Lee to his wife, Oct. 19, 1863, *Wartime Papers*, 608–11.

38. Meade to Mrs. Meade, Oct. 21, 1863, *Life and Letters*, 2:154.

39. Halleck to Meade, Oct. 18, 19, Meade to Halleck, Oct. 18, 1863, *OR*, 29/2:345–46 (two notes), 354; Halleck to Foster, Oct. 10, 1863, *OR*, 29/2:277–78.

40. Meade to Halleck, Oct. 20, 1863, *OR*, 29/2:358–59; Lee to Sam Jones, Nov. 2, 1863, *Wartime Papers*, 617–18, 638.

41. The key letters in this mess: Lincoln to Halleck, Oct. 24, 1863, *CWL*, 6:534; Meade to Mrs. Meade, Oct. 23, 1863, *Life and Letters*, 2:154; Halleck to Foster, Oct. 20, 1863, *OR*, 29/2:361; Meade to Halleck, Oct. 21, 24, Nov. 2, 4, 1863, *OR*, 29/2:361–62, 376–77,

409–10, 415; Halleck to Foster, Oct. 21, 1863, *OR*, 29/2:366; Halleck to Meade, Oct. 24, Nov. 3, 1863, *OR*, 29/2:375, 412.

42. Lee to Seddon, Oct. 28, 1863, Lee to Davis, Nov. 10, Lee to his wife, Nov. 11, 1863, *Wartime Papers*, 588, 616–17, 620–22.

43. Davis to J. E. Johnston, July 8, 1863, *Davis Papers*, 9:264–65; J. E. Johnston to Davis, July 9, 1863, *OR*, 24/1:199.

44. *Davis Papers*, 9:265 n. 5.

45. Grant to Sherman, July 3, 1863, *OR*, 24/3:460–61 (two notes); Sherman to Grant, July 3, 4, 1863, *OR*, 24/3:461, 472.

46. Davis to J. E. Johnston, July 9, 1863, *OR*, 24/1:199–200; J. E. Johnston to Davis, July 11, 1863, *OR*, 24/1:200; Proclamation by the President, July 15, 1863, *OR*, ser. 4, 2:635.

47. Symonds, *Johnston*, 219–20.

48. Davis to J. E. Johnston, July 15, 1863, *OR*, 24/1, 202–7; Symonds, *Johnston*, 220; *Davis Papers*, 9:264 n. 1; Mary Chesnut, quoted in ibid.; J. E. Johnston to Davis, Aug. 8, 1863, *OR*, 24/1:209–13.

49. Bragg to [Beauregard], July 21, 1863, *OR*, 23/2:920.

50. J. E. Johnston to Seddon, Nov. 1, 1863, *OR*, 24/1:238–49; Davis to J. E. Johnston, July 18, 1863, *OR*, 24/1:208; J. E. Johnston to Davis, July 19, 1863, *OR*, 24/1:208; Davis to Lee, July 21, 1863, *Davis Papers*, 9:294–95.

51. Davis to Lee, July 28, 1863, *Davis Papers*, 9:307–9; Lee to Davis, July 16, 1863, *Wartime Papers*, 552–53.

52. Polk to Davis, July 26, 1863, *OR*, 23/2:932–33. Polk reiterated his ideas to Davis on August 9, *Davis Papers*, 9:335.

53. Cooper to Bragg, Aug. 1, 1863, *OR*, 23/2:948.

54. Bragg to Cooper, Aug. 2, 5 (2 notes), 1863, *OR*, 23/2:948, 952–53; Bragg to J. E. Johnston, Aug. 5, 1863, *OR*, 52/2:514; Davis indorsement, Aug. 10, 1863, on Bragg to Cooper, Aug. 5, 1863, *OR*, 23/2:952–53.

55. Halleck to Rosecrans, July 24, 1863, *OR*, 23/2:552 (two notes); Halleck to Burnside, July 24, 1863, *OR*, 23/2:553; Burnside to Halleck, July 24, 1863, *OR*, 23/2:553; *OR*, 23/2:254–58.

56. Foote, *Civil War*, 2:678–83.

57. Rosecrans to [Halleck], Aug. 1, 1863, *OR*, 23/2:585–86.

58. Halleck to Rosecrans, Aug. 4, 5, 1863, *OR*, 23/2:592; Rosecrans to Halleck, Aug. 4, 1863, *OR*, 23/2:592; Halleck to Burnside, Aug. 5, 1863, *OR*, 23/2:593.

59. Burnside to Halleck, Aug. 6, 1863, *OR*, 23/2:593–94; Rosecrans to Halleck, Aug. 6, 7, 1863, *OR*, 23/2:594, 597; Halleck to Rosecrans, Aug. 7, 9, 1863, *OR*, 23/2:597, 601–2; Rosecrans to Burnside, Aug. 7, 1863, *OR*, 23/2:598; Burnside to Rosecrans, Aug. 8, 1863, *OR*, 23/2:600; Foote, *Civil War*, 2:677; Halleck report, *OR*, 30/1:33; Lincoln to Rosecrans, Aug. 10, 1863, *CWL*, 6:377–78.

60. Davis to Bragg, Aug. 19, 1863, *OR*, 52/2:517; Bragg to Davis, Aug. 23, 1863, *OR*, 52/2:517; Bragg to Cooper, Aug. 22, 1863, *OR*, 30/4:531; Mackall to Hill, Aug. 22, 1863, *OR*, 30/4:531; Cooper to J. E. Johnston, Aug. 22, 1863, *OR*, 30/4:529; Davis to W. P. Johnston, Sept. 3, 1863, *Davis Papers*, 9:366–67; Davis to Chesnut, Aug. 31, 1863, *OR*, 52/2:520.

61. Davis to W. P. Johnston, Sept. 3, 1863, *Davis Papers*, 9:366–67.

62. Foote, *Civil War*, 2:684–9; Long and Long, *Civil War*, 403.

63. Bragg to Cooper, Sept. 4, 1863, *OR*, 30/2:21; Davis to Bragg, Sept. 5, 1863, *OR*, 52/2:521, 524; Bragg to Davis, Sept. 6, 1863, *OR*, 52/2:522.

64. Buckner to Sam Jones, Sept. 6, 1863, *OR*, 30/4:618; Sam Jones to Davis, Sept. 21, 1863, *OR*, 52/2:527–28.

65. Lee to Davis, Sept. 6, 1863, *OR*, 29/2:700–1; Lee to Davis, Aug. 24, Sept. 6, 1863, *Wartime Papers*, 593–94, 596; *Davis Papers*, 9:387 n. 11; Foote, *Civil War*, 2:695.

66. Davis to Lee, Sept. [8], 1863, 29/2:702.

67. Long and Long, *Civil War*, 407; Halleck report, *OR*, 30/1:34–35, 37; Rosecrans to Halleck, Sept. 4, 1863, *OR*, 30/3:339; Halleck to Burnside, Sept. 13, 1863, Halleck to Rosecrans, Sept. 13, 1863, *OR*, 30/1:35; Halleck to Hurlbut, Halleck to Grant or Sherman, Sept. 13, 1863, *OR*, 30/1:35–36; Halleck to Grant, Sept. 17, 1863, *OR*, 30/3:693–94; [Dana to Stanton], Sept. 14, 1863, *OR*, 30/1:186–87.

68. Halleck to Meade, Sept. 15, 1863, *OR*, 30/2:186–87.

69. Symonds, *Atlas*, 73; McPherson, *Battle Cry*, 675; Foote, *Civil War*, 2:692–93. For Bragg's report, see Bragg to Cooper, Sept. 24, 1863, *OR*, 30/2:23–25.

70. Lincoln to Burnside, Sept. 21, 1863, *OR*, 30/1:146; Lincoln to Rosecrans, Sept. 21, 22, Lincoln to Halleck, Sept. 21, 1863, *CWL*, 6:470–74; *OR*, 30/1:146, 148; Halleck to Lincoln, Sept. 21, 1863, *OR*, 30/1:148.

71. Burnside to Halleck, Sept. 27, 1863, *OR*, 30/3:904–5; Lincoln to Burnside, Sept. 25, 27, 1863, *CWL*, 6:480–81, 481nn, 484.

72. Rawlins to Sherman, Sept. 22, 1863, *OR*, 30/1:161–62; Sherman to Rawlins, Sept. 22, 1863, *OR*, 30/3:773; Halleck to Burnside, Sept. 27, 1863, *OR*, 30/3:906.

73. Burnside to Halleck, Sept. 30, 1863, *OR*, 30/3:954–55; Burnside to Rosecrans, Sept. 30, 1863, *OR*, 30/3:955–56; Halleck to Burnside, Oct. 3, 1863, *OR*, 30/4:72; Burnside to Halleck, Oct. 4, 1863, *OR*, 30/4:96.

74. Lincoln to Halleck, Sept. 19, 1863, *CWL*, 6:466–68; Donald, *Lincoln*, 457–58.

75. Lyman, *Civil War Quotations*, 154; Lincoln to Rosecrans, Oct. 4, 1863, *CWL*, 6:498; *OR*, 30/4:79.

76. Lee to Davis, Sept. 23, 1863, *Wartime Papers*, 602–4.

77. Judith Lee Hallock, *Braxton Bragg and Confederate Defeat* (Tuscaloosa: University of Alabama Press, 1991), 2:88–108.

78. Hallock, *Bragg*, 2:110–13, 120; Bragg to Cooper, Oct. 3, 1863, *OR*, 30/4:726.

79. *Davis Papers*, 10:38 n. 4.

80. Quoted in *Davis Papers*, 10:23 n. 4. Italics in the original.

81. Davis to Bragg, Oct. 29, Davis to W. P. Johnston, Sept. 3, 1863, *Davis Papers*, 9:366–67, 10:36–38; *OR*, 52/2:554–55.

82. Davis to Bragg, Oct. 29, 1863, *Davis Papers*, 10:36–38, 39 n. 7; Bragg to Longstreet, Nov. 4, 1863, *OR*, 31/3:634–35; Longstreet to Buckner, Nov. 5, 1863, *OR*, 52/2:559–60; Alexander, *Fighting for the Confederacy*, 311; Symonds, *Johnston*, 247.

83. Foote, *Civil War*, 2:766–68; [Dana to Stanton], Sept. 30, Oct. 12, 1863, *OR*, 30/1:204–5, 214–15; Halleck to Grant, Oct. 16, 1863, *OR*, 30/4:404; General Order No. 337, Oct. 16, 1863, *OR*, 30/4:404; Grant to Julia Dent Grant, Nov. 2, 1863, *Grant Papers*, 9:352–53.

84. Grant to Thomas, Oct. 19, 1863, *OR*, 30/4:479; Thomas to Grant, Oct. 19, 1863, *OR*, 30/4:479; Grant to Burnside, Oct. 20, 1863, *OR*, 31/1:681; *Grant Papers*, 9:298 notes.

85. Halleck to Grant, Oct. 20, 1863, *OR*, 31/1:667–69.

86. Grant to Halleck, Oct. 26, Grant to Sherman, Oct. 24, 1863, *OR*, 31/1:713, 739–40; Grant to Riggin, [Nov. 18, 1863], *Grant Papers*, 9:413.

87. Grant to Halleck, Oct. 26, 28, 1863, *OR*, 31/1:56, 739–40.; Symonds, *Atlas*, 75.

88. Grant to Halleck, Oct. 28, 30, 1863, *OR*, 31/1:767–68, 784; Grant to Burnside, Oct. 28, 1863, *OR*, 31/1:770; Halleck to Grant, Oct. 29, 1863, *OR*, 31/1:774.

89. Grant to Burnside, Nov. 3, 8, 14, 1863, *OR*, 31/3:35, 88, 145–46; Halleck to Grant, Nov. 5, 1863, *OR*, 31/3:48; Grant to Halleck, Nov. 6, 1863, *OR*, 31/3:63.

90. G. W. C. Lee to Bragg, Nov. 11, 1863, *OR*, 52/2:562–63; Davis to Bragg, Nov. 19, 1863, *OR*, 52/2:563; Bragg to Davis, Nov. 20, 1863, *OR*, 31/3:723.

91. Symonds, *Atlas*, 75; Davis *Papers*, 10:76 n. 2.

92. Davis to Ransom, Nov. 27, 1863, *OR*, 52/2:564; Longstreet to Davis, Nov. 30, 1863, *OR*, 31/3:767–68; W. P. Johnston to Longstreet, Dec. 2, 1863, *OR*, 52/2:566–67; *Davis Papers*, 10:76 n. 4.

93. Bragg to Davis, Dec. 1, 1863, *Davis Papers*, 10:94–95; Bragg to Davis, Dec. 2, 1863, *OR*, 52/2:567–68.

94. Quoted in "Memorandum," Dec. 7, 1863, Burlingame, ed., *With Lincoln*, 121.

95. *B&L*, 3:245–46; Alexander, *Fighting for the Confederacy*, 219.

96. Charles P. Roland, "The Generalship of Robert E. Lee," in Gallagher, ed., *Lee the Soldier*, 170–71.

CHAPTER 18

1. Davis to R. W. Johnston, July 14, 1863, *Davis Papers* 9:276–77.

2. Bragg to Davis, Dec. 2, 1863, *OR*, 52/2:567–68.

3. Lee to Davis, Dec. 3, 1863, *OR*, 29/2:858–59.

4. *Wartime Papers*, 637.

5. Quoted in *Davis Papers*, 10:119.

6. Davis to J. E. Johnston, Dec. 16, 1863, *OR*, 31/3:835–36; Seddon to J. E. Johnston, Dec. 18, 1863, *OR*, 31/3:842–43; Davis to J. E. Johnston, Dec. 23, 1863, *Davis Papers*, 10:121–22.

7. J. E. Johnston to Davis, Jan. 2, 1864, 32/2:510–11.

8. Quoted in *Davis Papers*, 10:121 n. 2; Seddon to J. E. Johnston, Dec. 18, 1863, *OR*, 31/3:842–43.

9. J. E. Johnston to Davis, Jan. 2, 1864, *OR*, 32/2:510–11.

10. On this see Bruce Levine, *Confederate Emancipation: Southern Plans to Free and Arm Slaves During the Civil War* (Oxford: Oxford University Press, 2006).

11. Davis to J. E. Johnston, Jan. 14, 1864, *OR*, 32/2:554.

12. J. E. Johnston to Davis, Jan. 15, 1864, *Davis Papers*, 10:174–75.

13. J. E. Johnston to Davis, Feb. 1, 1864, *Davis Papers*, 215–16, 216 n. 2.

14. Lee to Davis, Feb. 3, 1864, *OR*, 32/2:667.

15. Ibid.

16. Longstreet to Lee, Jan. 10, 1864, *OR*, 32/2:541–42.

17. Freeman, *Lee*, 3:260; Longstreet to Lee, Feb. 2, 1864, *OR*, 32/2:652–54.

18. Lee to Longstreet, Feb. 17, 1864, *OR*, 32/2:760–61.

19. Beauregard, Confidential Circular, Feb. 21, 1862, *OR*, 7:899–900; Beauregard to Van Dorn, Feb. 21, 1862, *OR*, 7:900–1.

20. Lee to Davis, Feb. 18, 1864, *Davis Papers*, 10:241.

21. *Davis Papers*, 10:235 nn. 2, 3; Davis to J. E. Johnston, Feb. 11, 1864, *OR*, 32/2:716; J. E. Johnston to Polk, Feb. 11, 1864, *OR*, 32/2:716; Davis to Polk, Feb. 13, 1864, *OR*, 32/2:729; J. E. Johnston to Davis, Feb. 13, 1864, *OR*, 32/2:729; Davis to J. E. Johnston, Feb. 13, 15, 1864, *OR*, 52/2:619–20.

22. Davis to J. E. Johnston, Feb. 15, 1864, *OR*, 52/2:619–20; J. E. Johnston to Davis, Feb. 16, 1864, *OR*, 32/2:751–52.

23. Davis to Polk, Feb. 16, 1864, *OR*, 32/2:751; Polk to J. E. Johnston, Feb. 13, 1864, *OR*, 32/2:729–30; Davis to J. E. Johnston, Feb. 17, 1864, *OR*, 52/2:621; Davis to Hardee, Feb. 17, 1864, *OR*, 52/2:621.

24. Hardee to Davis, Feb. 20, 1864, *OR*, 52/2:625–26 (two notes).

25. *OR*, 32/2:798–99; *OR*, 52/2:627.

26. Davis to Polk, Feb. 23, 1864 (second note), *OR*, 52/2:628.

27. Sun Tzu, *The Art of War*, 81.

28. Davis interview with William D. Gale, July 30, 1864, *Davis Papers*, 10:571.

29. Lee to Longstreet, Feb. 17, 1864, *OR*, 32/2:760–61.

30. Lawton to Lee, Feb. 17, 1864, *OR*, 32/2:762; Longstreet to Lee, Feb. 21, 1864, *OR*, 32/2:790; Longstreet to Seddon, Feb. 22, 1864, *OR*, 32/2:791–92; Freeman, *Lee's Lieutenants*, 3:307.

31. General Orders No. 23, Feb. 24, 1864, *OR*, 32/2:799; Hallock, *Bragg*, 2:165–66; Davis, *Davis*, 541–42.

32. Longstreet to Cooper, Mar. 19, 1864, *OR*, 32/2:655; *OR*, 32/3:679–80.

33. Longstreet to G. W. C. Lee, Mar. 5, 1864, *OR*, 32/3:586–87; Longstreet to J. E. Johnston, Mar. 5, 1864, *OR*, 32/3:587; ibid., *OR*, 52/2:634.

34. Longstreet to Davis, Cooper to Longstreet, Feb. 29, 1864, *OR*, 32/2:818; Freeman, *Lee's Lieutenant's*, 3:307–8; Longstreet to Beauregard, Mar. 7, 1864, *OR*, 32/3:590–91.

35. Lawton to Longstreet, Mar. 9, 1864, *OR*, 32/3:598–99; Davis to Longstreet, Mar. 7, 1864, *OR*, 52/2:634–35.

36. Lee to Longstreet, Mar. 8, 1864, *OR*, 32/3:594–95.

37. Davis to Longstreet, Mar. 7, 1864, *OR*, 52/2:634–35.

38. J. E. Johnston to Bragg, Mar. 12, 1864, *OR*, 32/3:613–14; Bragg to J. E. Johnston, Mar. 12, 1864, *OR*, 32/3:614–15.

39. Bragg to J. E. Johnston, Mar. 12, 1864, *OR*, 32/3:614–15; J. E. Johnston to Bragg, Mar. 16, 19, 1864, *OR*, 32/3:636–37, 653–54; Sale memorandum, Mar. 19, 1864, *OR*, 52/2:642–44.

40. Jeffrey Wert, *General James Longstreet: The Confederacy's Most Controversial Soldier—A Biography* (New York: Simon & Schuster), 369–70; Freeman, *Lee's Lieutenants*, 3:308–9; James Longstreet, *From Manassas to Appomattox: Memoirs of the Civil War in America* (Old Saybrook, CT: Konecky and Konecky, 2003), 544–45; quoted in *Davis Papers*, 10:290. Longstreet does not mention mounting his men in his memoirs.

41. Longstreet to Davis, Mar. 16, 1864, *OR*, 32/3:637–41.

42. Hood to Seddon, Mar. 10, 1864, *OR*, 32/3:607; Hood to Davis, Mar. 7, 1864, *OR*, 32/3:606–7; Hood to Bragg, Mar. 10, 1864, *OR*, 32/3:607–8; John Bell Hood, *Advance and Retreat: Personal Experiences in the United States and Confederate States Armies* (Lincoln: Bison/University of Nebraska Press, 1996), 67–68. Hood also discusses here Davis's desire for a spring offensive into Tennessee by Johnston's army.

43. Sale memorandum, Mar. 19, 1864, *OR*, 52/2:642–44.

44. Ibid.

45. Longstreet to J. E. Johnston, Mar. 16, 1864, *OR*, 32/3:637; Longstreet to Lee, Mar. 16, 1864, *OR*, 32/3:641–42. For the plan in detail, see Longstreet to Davis, Mar. 16, 1864, *OR*, 32/3:637–41.

46. Jordan to Longstreet, Mar. 19, 1864, *OR*, 32/3:656–57.

47. *Davis Papers*, 10:290; Longstreet to Cooper, Mar. 19, 1864, *OR*, 32/3:655; Longstreet to Bragg, Mar. 22, 1864, *OR*, 32/3:667–68.

48. Davis to Longstreet, Mar. 25, 1864, *OR*, 32/3:674–76; Freeman, *Lee's Lieutenants,* 3:309–10.

49. Bragg to Davis, Apr. 2, 1864, *OR*, 38/3:624–25.

50. Pendleton memorandum, Apr. 16, 1864, *OR*, 38/3:622–24.

51. Ibid.

52. Ibid.

53. B. S. Ewell to Bragg, Apr. 20, 1864, *OR*, 38/3:626; Pendleton memorandum, Apr. 16, 1864, *OR*, 38/3:622–24.

54. Bragg to Davis, Apr. 2, 1864, *OR*, 38/3:624–25.

55. Annual Message to Congress and Proclamation of Amnesty and Reconstruction, Dec. 8, 1863, *CWL*, 7: 36–53, 53–56.

56. *Grant Papers*, 10:141–42nn.

57. Grant to J. R. Jones, Dec. 5, 1863, *Grant Papers*, 9:495–96; Grant, *Memoirs*, 457–58.

58. Grant to McPherson, Dec. 1, 1863, *Grant Papers*, 9:480–81; [Dana] to Stanton, Nov. 29, 1863, *OR*, 31/2:71–72; Grant to Halleck, Dec. 7, 1863, *OR*, 31/3:349–50.

59. [Dana] to Stanton, Dec. 12, 1863, *OR*, 31/2:73; Dana to Grant, Dec. 21, 1863, *OR*, 31/3:457–58; Bruce Catton, *Grant Takes Command* (Boston: Little, Brown, 1969), 98–99.

60. Halleck to Grant, Dec. 21, 1863, *OR*, 31/3:458.

61. Grant to Halleck, Dec. 17, 23, 1863, *OR*, 31/3: 429–30, 473; Grant, *Memoirs*, 463–64.

62. Sherman to Halleck, Dec. 26, 1863, *OR*, 31/3:497–98.

63. Halleck to Steele, Jan. 7, Halleck to Grant, Jan. 8, 1864, *OR*, 32/2:40–43; Foote, *Civil War*, 2:871–72.

64. Dana to Grant, Jan. 10, 1864, *OR*, 32/2:58; Grant to Halleck, Jan. 15, 1864, *OR*, 32/2:99–101; Grant, *Memoirs*, 459; Weigley, *Civil War*, 324.

65. Halleck to Grant, Jan. 17, 1864, *OR*, 32/2:122–23; Livermore, *Numbers and Losses*, 45.

66. Halleck to Grant, Jan. 18, 1864, *OR*, 32/2:126–27.

67. Halleck to Grant, Jan. 8, 1864, *OR*, 32/2:40–42; Grant to Halleck, Jan. 15, 1864, *OR*, 32/2:99–101; Grant to Halleck, Jan. 19, 1864, *OR*, 33:394–95.

68. Halleck to Grant, Feb. 17, 1864, *OR*, 32/2:411–13.

69. Ibid.; Lincoln to Gilmore, Jan. 13, 1864, *CWL*, 7:126.

70. Halleck to Grant, Feb. 17, 1864, *OR*, 32/2:411–13.

71. Ibid.

72. Grant, *Memoirs*, 466; Grant to Thomas, Feb. 12, 18, 1864, *OR*, 32/2:373, 421; Grant to Halleck, Feb. 12, 1864, *OR*, 32/2:374–75; Grant to Schofield, Feb. 24, 1864, 32/2:456; Grant to Thomas, Feb. 13, Grant to Ingalls, Feb. 16, 1864, *Grant Papers*, 10:119–20, 131–32.

73. Lincoln to the United States Senate, Feb. 29, 1864, in *The Collected Works of Abraham Lincoln. Supplement*, ed. Basler, 226; Donald, *Lincoln*, 490–91; Grant to Burns, Dec. 17, 1863, *Grant Papers*, 9:541.

74. Order for Draft of 500,000 Men, Feb. 1, 1864, *CWL*, 7:164.

CHAPTER 19

1. Grant, *Memoirs*, 473–74. Interestingly, this plan does not appear in Lincoln's published correspondence.

2. Grant to Banks, Mar. 15, 1864, *OR*, 34/2:610–11; Grant report, *OR*, 34/1:8–9.

3. Grant to Sherman, Apr. 4, 1864, *OR*, 32/3:245–46; Grant report, *OR*, 34/1:11.

4. Grant to Butler, Apr. 2, 16, 1864, *OR*, 33:794–95, 885–86; Grant report, *OR*, 34/1:11; Grant to Halleck, Apr. 8, 1864, *OR*, 33:821.

5. Grant to Meade, Apr. 9, 1864, *OR*, 33:827–29; Grant to Butler, Apr. 2, 1864, *OR*, 33:794–95; Grant report, *OR*, 34/1:11; Grant to Sherman, Apr. 4, 1864, *OR*, 32/3:245–46.

6. Grant to Butler, Apr. 18, 1864, *OR*, 33:904–5; Grant to Halleck, Apr. 29, 1864, *OR*, 33:1017–18; Grant to Meade, Apr. 17, 1864, *OR*, 33:889.

7. Grant to Sigel, Apr. 15, 1864, *OR*, 33:874; Grant to Sherman, Apr. 4, 1864, *OR*, 32/3:245–46.

8. Grant report, *OR*, 34/1:10, 13; Grant to Sherman, Apr. 4, 1864, *OR*, 32/3:245–46.

9. For examples see Grant to Rosecrans, Mar. 26, 1864, *OR*, 34/2:740–41, and Halleck to Grant, May 2, 1864, *OR*, 36/2:328–29.

10. Quoted in Hay, *Diary*, 194; Grant to Sherman, Apr. 4, 1864, *OR*, 32/3:245–46; Sherman to Grant, Apr. 10, 1864, *OR*, 32/3:312–14.

11. Grant to Lincoln, *Grant Papers*, May 1, 1864, 10:380.

12. Lincoln to Grant, Apr. 30, 1864, *CWL*, 7:324–25.

13. McPherson, *Battle Cry*, 721; Grant report, *OR*, 34/1:13–14.

14. Grant report, *OR*, 34/1:14.

15. Sherman, *Memoirs*, 463. Sherman's memoirs should be read in light of the chapter on this work in Albert Castel, *Winning and Losing the Civil War: Essays and Stories* (Columbia: University of South Carolina Press, 1996).

16. Sherman to Grant, Apr. 10, 1864, in Sherman, *Memoirs*, 489, 491–92.

17. Hattaway and Jones, *Why the North Won*, 519–22; Boatner, *Dictionary*, 689.

18. Lee to Davis, Mar. 25, 1864, *Davis Papers*, 10:295–97.

19. *Davis Papers*, 10:339–40; B. S. Ewell to J. E. Johnston, Apr. 29, 1864, *OR*, 32/3:840–41; Symonds, *Johnston*, 264–67. Ewell had been sent to Richmond on April 8 to explain to Davis that Johnston planned to go on the offensive when properly prepared. He arrived in Richmond on April 12.

20. Symonds, *Johnston*, 267; Davis to Lee, May 20, 1864, *OR*, 51/2:950–52.

21. Sherman, *Memoirs*, 464–67.

22. Ibid., 520, 523.

23. McPherson, *Battle Cry*, 748–49; Sherman, *Memoirs*, 523; Sherman to Stanton, June 15, 1864, *OR*, 39/2:121; Boatner, *Dictionary*, 85; Hattaway and Jones, *How the North Won*, 612.

24. McPherson, *Battle Cry*, 750.

25. Ibid., 745; J. E. Johnston to Davis, May 20, 21, 1864, *OR*, 38/4:728, 736; Davis to Lee, May 20, 1864, *OR*, 51/2:950–52.

26. Sherman, *Memoirs*, 515, 526, 530.

27. Bragg to Davis, June 4, 1864, *OR*, 38/4:762; Bragg to J. E. Johnston, June 7, 1864, *OR*, 38/4:762.

28. Bragg to Davis, June 29, 1864, *OR*, 38/4:805; Davis to Brown, June 29, 1864, *OR*, 52/2:680.

29. Sherman, *Memoirs*, 527, 530–31, 533; Basil H. Liddell Hart, *Sherman: Soldier, Realist, American*, 402, quoted in McPherson, *Battle Cry*, 744.

30. Davis to J. E. Johnston, July 7, 1864, *Davis Papers*, 10:503, 504 nn. 1, 4.

31. Brown to Davis, June 28, 1864, *OR*, 52/2:680–81; J. E. Johnston to Davis, July 8, 1864, *OR*, 38/5:868–69; Watts to Davis, July 4, 1864, *Davis Papers*, 10:498–99, 508–9.

32. Davis to J. E. Johnston, July 11, 1864, *OR*, 38/5:875.

33. J. E. Johnston to Davis, July 12, 1864, *OR*, 52/2:692.

34. Brown Proclamation, July 9, 1864, *OR*, 52/2:688–91.

35. Boatner, *Dictionary*, 400; Seddon to B. H. Hill, July 13, 1864, *OR*, 52/2:693–95; B. H. Hill to Seddon, July 14, 1864, *OR*, 52/2:704–7.

36. B. H. Hill to Seddon, July 14, 1864, *OR*, 52/2:704–7.

37. Quoted in *Davis Papers*, 10:513; Boatner, 566.

38. Quoted in interview with William D. Gale, July 30, 1864, *Davis Papers*, 10:570; B. H. Hill to Seddon, July 14, 1864, *OR*, 52/2:704–7.

39. Davis to Bragg, July 9, 1864, *OR*, 39/2:695–96; Bragg to Davis, July 15, 1864, *OR*, 38/5:881; Hood to Bragg, July 14, 1864, *OR*, 38/5:879–80; Bragg to Davis, July 15, 1864, *Davis Papers*, 10:523–25, 527 n. 11.

40. *Davis Papers*, 10:554; Davis, Bragg, and Seddon indorsements on Behan to Davis, July 23, 1864, *OR*, 41/2:1022–23.

41. Davis to J. E. Johnston, July 16, 1864, *OR*, 38/5:882; J. E. Johnston to Davis, July 16, 1864, *OR*, 38/5:883; Davis to Hood, July 18, 1864, *OR*, 38/5:888; Cooper to J. E. Johnston, July 17, 1864, 38/5:885; Hood, Hardee, and Stewart to Davis, July 18, 1864, *OR*, 52/2:708–9; Davis to Lee, July 12, 1864, *OR*, 52/2:692; Lee to Davis, July 12, 1864, *Davis Papers*, 10:517; quoted in *Davis Papers*, 10:523.

42. Davis to H. V. Johnston, Sept. 18, 1864, *Davis Papers*, 11:50–51.

43. J. E. Johnston to Cooper, July 18, 1864, *OR*, 38/5:888.

44. Quoted in *Davis Papers*, 10:499–500 n. 1.

45. Quoted in interview with William D. Gale, July 30, 1864, *Davis Papers*, 10:569–71.

46. Quoted in *Davis Papers*, 10:573 n. 10.

47. Lee to Davis, Mar. 25, Lee to Longstreet, Mar. 28, Lee to G. W. C. Lee, Mar. 29, 1864, *Wartime Papers*, 682–87, 639.

48. Lee to G. W. C. Lee, Mar. 29, Lee to Davis, Mar. 30, 1864, *Wartime Papers*, 685–90.

49. Bragg to Lee, Apr. 8, 1864, *OR*, 51/2:1076–77.

50. Lee to Davis, Apr. 12, 1864, *Wartime Papers*, 698.

51. *Davis Papers*, 10:350 n. 7, 352; Lee to Davis, Apr. 15, 1864, *Wartime Papers*, 699–700.

52. Lee to Davis, Apr. 15, Lee to Bragg, Apr. 16, Lee to Imboden, Apr. 18, Lee to Davis, Apr. 29, 30, Lee to G. W. C. Lee, Apr. 30, 1864, *Wartime Papers*, 699–700, 703–4, 706–9; *Davis Papers*, 10:351–52 n. 19.

53. *Wartime Papers*, 640.

54. Grant report, *OR*, 34/1:14–15, 18–19.

55. Bruce, "Strategy of the Civil War," 437; Lee to Bragg, May 4, 1864, *OR*, 51/2:887; Lee to Davis, May 4, 1864, *Wartime Papers*, 711, 719–20.

56. *Davis Papers*, 10:351–52 n. 19, 10:392 n. 12.

57. Lee to Breckinridge, May 4, 1864, *Wartime Papers*, 718–19 (two notes).

58. *Davis Papers*, 10:392 n. 14; Symonds, *Atlas*, 83; A. Young, "Numbers and Losses in the Armies of Northern Virginia, *North & South* 3, no. 3 (Mar. 2000): 26.

59. Grant report, *OR*, 34/1:10; Hattaway and Jones, *How the North Won*, 539, 545.

60. Alexander, *Fighting for the Confederacy*, 346.

61. *Grant Papers*, 10:329–30 notes; Grant report, *OR*, 34/1:16–17, 24–25; Butler to Stanton, May 9, 1864, *OR*, 34/1:16; *Wartime Papers*, 711–12.

62. *Davis Papers*, 10:404–5 n. 5; *Wartime Papers*, 715–16; Boatner, *Dictionary*, 783–89.

63. Lee to Breckinridge, May 14, 16, 1864, *Wartime Papers*, 729, 731–32.

64. Grant report, *OR*, 34/1:20–21; Grant to Halleck, May 25, 1864, *OR*, 34/1:20–21.

65. Hattaway and Jones, *How the North Won*, 554, 574–75; Lee to Hampton, June 18, 1864, *Wartime Papers*, 792–93; Boatner, *Dictionary*, 749–50.

66. *Davis Papers*, 10:418–19; Lee to Davis, May 12, 13, 18, 1864, *Wartime Papers*, 728–29, 733, 716.

67. Symonds, *Atlas*, 89; Grant report, *OR*, 34/1:15; Lee to his wife, May 23, 1864, *Wartime Papers*, 716, 748.

68. Grant report, *OR*, 34/1:9.

69. Hattaway and Jones, *How the North Won*, 558–62, 564–67, 570.

70. Grant, *Memoirs*, 512.

71. Lee to Davis, May 23, 1864, *Wartime Papers*, 739, 747–48.

72. *Wartime Papers*, 739; Beauregard to Bragg, May 14, 1864, *OR*, 36/2:1024; Bragg to Davis, May 19, 1864, *OR*, 36/2:1024–5.

73. Beauregard memorandum, May 18, 1864, *OR*, 36/2:1021–2.

74. Davis to Bragg, May 19, 1864, *OR*, 51/2:945, indorsement on Beauregard memorandum, *OR*, 51/2:945; Bragg to Davis, May 19, 1864, *OR*, 51/2:945–46; Bragg to Beauregard, May 19, 1864, *OR*, 51/2:947; Beauregard to Bragg, May 19, 1864, *OR*, 51/2:947; Davis to Lee, May 20, 1864, *OR*, 51/2:950–52; Davis to Beauregard, May 20, 1864, *OR*, 51/2:952–53.

75. Lee to Davis, May 29, 30, Lee to Bragg, May 30, Lee to Beauregard, June 1, 1864 (two notes), *Wartime Papers*, 756–59, 761.

76. Lee to Davis, May 29, 30, Lee to Bragg, May 30, Lee to Beauregard, June 1 (two notes), Lee to A. P. Hill, June—, 1864, *Wartime Papers*, 756–61 Symonds, *Atlas*, 89.

77. *Davis Papers*, 10:462, 468 n. 4; Breckinridge to Bragg, June 11, 1864, and indorsements of Bragg and Davis, *OR*, 51/2:1002–3; Lee to Davis, June 11, 15, 1864, Lee to Seddon, July 19, *Wartime Papers*, 774–75, 782–83, 822–23.

78. Lee to Davis, June 26, 29, 1864, *Wartime Papers*, 806–8, 811; Grant report, *OR*, 34/1:20–21; Boatner, *Dictionary*, 255.

79. McPherson, *Battle Cry*, 756; Symonds, *Atlas*, 93; Journal of William Whitehurst Old, *ORS*, 7:274.

80. Hattaway and Jones, *How the North Won*, 601–2; Lincoln to Grant, July 10, 1864, *OR*, 37/2:155; Grant to Lincoln, July 10, 1864, *OR*, 37/2:155–56.

81. Boatner, *Dictionary*, 256; John Y. Simon, "Grant, Lincoln, and Unconditional Surrender," in *Lincoln's Generals*, Boritt, ed., 178–81.

82. Grant report, *OR*, 34/1:25; Grant to Halleck, August 1, 1864, *OR*, 37/2:558; Lincoln to Grant, Aug. 3, 1864, *CWL*, 7:476; Grant, *Memoirs*, 2:616–17.

83. Davis to Lee, Aug. 4, 1864, *OR*, 42/2:1161–62; Lee to Anderson, Lee to Hampton, Aug. 11, 1864, *Wartime Papers*, 799, 832–33.

84. Hattaway and Jones, *How the North Won*, 589–90; Freeman, *Lee*, 3:398; Symonds, *Atlas*, 91; Grant to Halleck, June 14, 1864, *OR*, 40/2:18–19; Lincoln to Grant, June 15, 1864, *CWL*, 7:393; Gordon C. Rhea, *Cold Harbor: Grant and Lee, May 26–June 3, 1863*, 2nd ed. (Baton Rouge: LSU Press, 2008), 362; A. Young, "Numbers and Losses in the Armies of Northern Virginia, *North & South* 3, no. 3 (Mar. 2000): 27.

85. Brooks, May 19, 1864, in Burlingame, ed., *Lincoln Observed*, 109–10.

86. Hattaway and Jones, *How the North Won*, 590–94; Neely, "The Wilderness," 60.

87. Lee to Davis, June 26, July 5, 1864, *Wartime Papers*, 797, 806–8, 814–15.

88. Lee to Secretary of War, July 28, 1864, *OR*, 37/2:602; Davis to Lee, Aug. 4, 1864, *OR*, 42/2:1161–2; Lee to Davis, July 23, Lee to G. W. C. Lee, July 24, 1864, *Wartime Papers*, 823–26.

89. Lee to Ewell, July 24, Lee to G. W. C. Lee, July 24, 1864, *Wartime Papers*, 824–26.

CHAPTER 20

1. Reply to the Committee Notifying Lincoln of His Renomination, June 9, 1864, *CWL*, 7:380, quoted in 381–82nn; Boatner, *Dictionary*, 582.

2. Interview with Alexander W. Randall and Joseph T. Mills, Aug. 19, 1864, *CWL*, 7:506–8.

3. Memorandum Concerning His Probable Failure of Re-election, Aug. 23, 1864, *CWL*, 7:514–15, quoted in notes.

4. Larry E. Nelson, *Bullets, Ballots, and Rhetoric: Confederate Policy for the United States Presidential Contest of 1864* (Tuscaloosa: University of Alabama Press, 1980), xi, 18–20.

5. Ibid., 20, 24, 89, 110–11.

6. Ibid., 28, 129.

7. Grant, *Memoirs*, 632–33.

8. McPherson, *Battle Cry*, 753; Sherman, *Memoirs*, 543–44, 549.

9. Sherman, *Memoirs*, 544; McPherson, *Battle Cry*, 754–55; Symonds, *Atlas*, 97.

10. Sherman, *Memoirs*, 573.

11. Ibid., 577; McPherson, *Battle Cry*, 774.

12. Grant, *Memoirs*, 632.

13. Hattaway and Jones, *How the North Won*, 623; McPherson, *Battle Cry*, 774–75.

14. Speeches at Macon and Montgomery, Sept. 23, 29, 1864, *Davis Papers*, 11:61, 75.

15. Speeches at Palmetto, Montgomery, Columbia, and Greensboro, Sept. 26, 29, Oct. 4, 5, 1864, *Davis Papers*, 11:71, 74, 83, 85, 87, 91–92, 208–9 nn. 1, 5.

16. Grant to Halleck, Oct. 4, 1864, *OR*, 39/3:63–64; Grant to Sherman, Sept. 10, 12, 1864, in Grant, *Memoirs*, 634–36; Symonds, *Lincoln and His Admirals*, 328–29; Boatner, *Dictionary*, 298–99.

17. Sherman to Grant, Sept. 20, 1864, *Sherman's Civil War*, 722–24.

18. Sherman to Grant, Oct. 1, 1864, *OR*, 39/3:3; Halleck to Grant, Oct. 2, 1864, *OR*, 39/3:25–26.

19. *Davis Papers*, 11:146 n. 9.

20. Hood to Seddon, Oct. 19, 1864, *OR*, 39/3:831; Hood to Taylor, Oct. 20, 1864, *OR*, 39/3:835; Beauregard to Cooper, Oct. 22, 1864, *OR*, 39/3:841; Davis to Hood, Nov. 7, 1864, *Davis Papers*, 11:145, 145–46 nn. 6, 9, 11.

21. Boatner, *Dictionary*, 55, 241; Alfred Roman, *The Military Operations of General Beauregard* (New York: Da Capo Press, 1994), 2:283.

22. Grant to Sherman, Oct. 11, 1864, *OR*, 34/1:36; Grant to Sherman, Oct. 11, 1864, *OR*, 39/3:202.

23. Sherman to Grant, Oct. 11, 1864, *OR*, 39/3:202.

24. Grant to Sherman, Oct. 11, 1864, *OR*, 39/3:202; Stanton to Grant, Oct. 12, 1864, *OR*, 39/3:222.

25. Sherman to Grant, Nov. 6, 1864, *OR*, 39/3:658–61.

26. Ibid.

27. Sherman to Smith, Nov. 2, 1864, *OR*, 39/3:596; Grant report, *OR*, 34/1:36–37.

28. Brown proclamation, Nov. 19, 1864, *OR*, 53:375–76; Davis to Lee, Nov. 18, 1864, *OR*, 53:375; Lee to Davis, Nov. 19, 1864, *OR*, 44:869; Davis to Browne, Nov. 22, 1864, *OR*, 44:880–81.

29. Hardee to McLaws, Nov. 19, 1864 (two notes), *OR*, 44:871; Hardee to Cooper, Nov. 21, 1864, *OR*, 44:877; Davis to Fry, Nov. 22, 1864, *OR*, 44:883; Beauregard to Wheeler, Nov. 20, 1864, *OR*, 44:874; Davis to Bragg, Nov. 22, 1864, *OR*, 42/3:1225.

30. Beauregard to Hood, Nov. 24, 1864, *OR*, 44:890; Beauregard to Davis, Dec. 6, 1864, *Davis Papers*, 11:207–8; *OR*, 44:931–33.

31. Grant report, *OR*, 34/1:36.

32. Beauregard to E. K. Smith, Dec. 2, 1864, *OR*, 44:918–19; Seddon to E. K. Smith via Hardee, Dec. 7, 1864, *OR*, 41/1:123.

33. Davis to E. K. Smith, Dec. 24, 1864, *OR*, 41/1:123–24.

34. Symonds, *Atlas*, 99; Lincoln to Thomas, Dec. 16, 1864, *CWL*, 8:169; Grant to Thomas, Dec. 15, 1864, *OR*, 45/2:195.

35. Beauregard to Hardee, Dec. 8, 9, 1864, *OR*, 44:940, 942; Beauregard to Cooper, Dec. 15, 1864, *OR*, 44:959; Cooper to Beauregard, Dec. 17, 1864, *OR*, 44:963.

36. Davis to Bonham, Dec. 12, 1864, *OR*, 44:952; Roy [Confidential Circular], Dec. 19, 1864, *OR*, 44:967; *Davis Papers*, 11:221 n. 20.

37. Fry to Davis, Jan. 8, 1865, *Davis Papers*, 11: 293.

38. Lee to Seddon, Aug. 21, Lee to Davis, Aug. 22, 1864, *Wartime Papers*, 798, 841–43.

39. Seddon to Lee, Aug. 23, 1864, *OR*, 42/2:1199.

40. Lee to Seddon, Aug. 23, Lee to Davis, Sept. 2, 1864, *Wartime Papers*, 843–44, 847–48; Lee to Davis, Sept. 2, 1864, *OR* 42/2:1228–30.

41. *Wartime Papers*, 801; Symonds, *Atlas*, 104–5; Grant, *Memoirs*, 630–31.

42. Boatner, *Dictionary*, 744–45, 748; Grant to Sheridan, Aug. 26, 1864, *OR*, 43/1:916–17.

43. Sheridan to Grant, Oct. 7, 1864, *OR*, 43/2:307–8.

44. Boatner, *Dictionary*, 132–34; Wartime *Papers*, 800.

45. Boatner, *Dictionary*, 134, 744; Hattaway and Jones, *How the North Won*, 619–20.

46. Grimsley, *The Hard Hand of War*, 168.

47. With apologies to the great historian John Marszalek, from whom I have stolen this title.

48. Grant to Sherman, Dec. 6, 1864, *OR*, 44:636–37; Lincoln to Sherman, Dec. 26, 1864, *CWL*, 8:181–82.

49. Grant to Sherman, Dec. 18, 27, 1864, *OR*, 44:740–41; 820–21; Sherman to Grant, Dec. 18, 1864, *OR*, 44:742–43. On the same day Halleck sent Sherman a note suggesting just such a move, *OR*, 44:741.

50. Sherman to Halleck, Dec. 24, 1864, *OR*, 44:798–800; Sherman to Mary Ellen Sherman, Aug. 3, 1861, *Sherman's Civil War*, 126.

51. Sherman to Halleck, Dec. 31, 1864, *OR*, 44:842; Lincoln to Stanton, Jan. 5, 1865, *CWL*, 8:201.

52. Grant, *Memoirs*, 673–76; Boatner, *Dictionary*, 801; Foote, *Civil War*, 3:737–39.

53. Grant to Sherman, Jan. 21, 1865, in Grant, *Memoirs*, 673–74; Grant report, *OR*, 34/1:44–45.

54. Davis to Beauregard, Dec. 20, 1864, *OR*, 44:969; Lee to Davis, Dec. 19, 1864, *OR*, 44:966; Beauregard indorsement, Dec. 24, 1864, on Chisholm, Dec. 20, 1864, *OR*, 44:969–70.

55. Beauregard to Hardee, Dec. 31, 1864, *OR*, 44:1009–10; Davis to Hardee, Jan. 7, 1865, *OR*, 47/2:997; Hardee to Davis, Jan. 8, 1865, *OR*, 47/2:999–1000.

56. De Sassure, et al to Seddon, Dec. [?], 1864, Lee indorsement, Feb. 11, 1865, *OR*, 44:1011–12; Davis to Hardee, Jan. 7, 1865, *OR*, 47/2:997; *Davis Papers*, 11:329.

57. Speeches at Macon and Palmetto, Sept. 23, 1864, *Davis Papers*, 11:62–63, 66 n. 18, 70–71; quoted in ibid.

58. Beauregard to Davis, Dec. 24, 1864, 44:984–85; Davis to Hardee, Jan. 11, 1865, *OR*, 47/2:1003; Beauregard to Davis, Jan. 13, 1865, *OR*, 45/2:780.

59. Davis to Taylor, Jan. 12, 1865, *OR*, 45/2:778–79; Beauregard to Davis, Jan. 17, 1865, *OR*, 45/2:789; *Davis Papers*, 11:303 n. 3.

60. *Davis Papers*, 11:343, 346.

61. Brent report, Feb. 3, 1865, *OR*, 47/2:1083–84.

62. Beauregard to Davis, Feb. 3, 1865 (two notes), *OR*, 47/2:1083–4; Davis to Beauregard, Feb. 4, 1865, *OR*, 47/2:1090.

63. Brent report, Feb. 3, 1865, *OR*, 47/2:1084–85; *Davis Papers*, 11:376.

64. Beauregard to Lee, Feb. 16, 1865, 47/2:1202; *Davis Papers*, 11:402–3; Hardee to Beauregard, Feb. 16, 1865, 47/2:1205.

65. *Davis Papers*, 11:400 n. 3; Grant report, *OR*, 34/1:44.

66. Beauregard to Davis, Feb. 21, 1865, 47/2:1238; *Davis Papers*, 11:423 n. 12.

67. Lee to Davis, Feb. 19, 1865, *OR*, 53/412–13.

68. Lee to Davis, Feb. 9, 1865, *Wartime Papers*, 802, 898, 892–93.

69. Lee to Seddon, Jan. 27, Feb. 8, Lee to Miles, Feb. 9, 1865, *Wartime Papers*, 886–87, 898, 890, 891.

70. Lee to Davis, Feb. 23, 1865, *OR*, 53:413; Lee to Davis, Feb. 23, 1865, *Davis Papers*, 11:421; Lee to Bragg, Feb. 22, 1865, *OR*, 47/2:1249.

71. Lee to Davis, Feb. 23, 1865, *Davis Papers*, 11:421, 422 n. 5.

72. Lee to Davis, Feb. 23, 1865, *OR*, 53:413; Lee to J. E. Johnston, Feb. 23, 1865, *OR*, 47/2:1256–7.

73. Lee to J. E. Johnston, Feb. 22, 1865, *OR*, 47/2:1247; Johnston to Lee, Feb. 22, 1865, *OR*, 47/2:1247.

74. J. E. Johnston to Lee, Feb. 25, 1865, *OR*, 47/1:1050–1. For examples of the efforts at concentration see J. E. Johnston to Lee, Mar. 1, 1865, *OR*, 47/1:1051; *OR*, 47/2:1314–18, 1321, 1325.

75. McPherson, *Battle Cry*, 830; J. E. Johnston to Bragg, Mar. 10, 1865, *OR*, 47/2:1363; Lee to Vance, Mar. 9, 1865, *OR*, 47/2:1353–4.

76. Lee to J. E. Johnston, [Mar. 11, 1865?], *OR*, 47/2:1372; J. E. Johnston to Lee, Mar. 11, 1865, *OR*, 47/2:1372–3; J. E. Johnston to Lee, Mar. 12, 1865, *OR*, 47/2:1380; *Davis Papers*, 11:440 n. 3.

77. Lee to Davis, Mar. 14, 1865, *OR*, 53:414; Lee to J. E. Johnston, Mar. 15, 1865, *OR*, 47/2:1395–6.

78. J. E. Johnston to Lee, Mar. 20, 1865, *OR*, 47/2:1440; J. E. Johnston to Lee, Mar. 27, 1865, *OR*, 47/1:1055–57; McPherson, *Battle Cry*, 830; *Davis Papers*, 11:440 n. 2.

79. J. E. Johnston to Lee, Mar. 23, 1865, *OR*, 47/2:1453–54; Lee to J. E. Johnston, Mar. 23, 1865, *OR*, 47/2:1454; J. E. Johnston to Lee, Mar. 24, 1865, *OR*, 47/1:1055.

80. Grant report, *OR*, 34/1:48.

CHAPTER 21

1. Davis to Vance, Jan. 8, 1864, *Davis Papers*, 10:158–60; Nelson, *Bullets*, 37.

2. Davis to Vance, Jan. 8, 1864, *Davis Papers*, 10:160–61.

3. Clay and Holcombe to Davis, July 25, 1864, *Davis Papers*, 10:559, 560–61; Steven E. Woodworth, "The Last Function of Government: Confederate Collapse and Negotiated Peace," in *The Collapse of the Confederacy*, ed. Mark Grimsley and Brooks D. Simpson (Lincoln: University of Nebraska Press, 2001), 18–21. See also Memorandum on Clement C. Clay, [c. July 25], 1864, *CWL*, 7:459–60.

4. Quoted in *Davis Papers*, 10:559–60; Lincoln to Wakeman, July 25, 1864, *CWL*, 7:461.

5. Quoted in *Davis Papers*, 10:533; Edmund Kirke [James Gilmore], *Down in Tennessee, and Back by Way of Richmond* (New York: Carleton, 1864), 270.

6. See Stoker, "There Was No Offensive-Defensive Confederate Strategy," 13–19.

7. Burlingame, ed., *Lincoln Observed*, 159–63; Donald, *Lincoln*, 556–57; Woodworth, "The Last Function," 27–30.

8. Stanton to Grant, Jan. 30, Lincoln to Grant, Feb. 1, Grant to Lincoln, Feb. 1, 1865, *Messages and Papers*, 1:525–26.

9. Lincoln to Seward, Jan. 31, 1865, *Messages and Papers*, 1:525; Burlingame, ed. *Lincoln Observed*, 160.

10. George Baker, ed., *The Works of William H. Seward* (Boston: Houghton, Mifflin, 1890), 5:171–73; Woodworth, "The Last Function," 30–31; Burlingame, ed. *Lincoln Observed*, 160–61.

11. Nicolay to Bates, Feb. 4, 1865, Burlingame, ed., *With Lincoln*, 172–73.

12. Lincoln to Schermerhorn, Sept. 12, 1864, *CWL*, 8:1–2; Sun Tzu, *The Art of War*, 119–20.

13. Longstreet to Lee, Mar. 1, 1865, *OR*, 46/2:1275–6; *Davis Papers*, 11:428 n. 2; Lee to Davis, Mar. 2, 1865, *Wartime Papers*, 911.

14. Stanton [Lincoln] to Grant, Mar. 3, 1865, *CWL*, 8:330–31; *Davis Papers*, 11:428 n. 3; *Wartime Papers*, 898.

15. Lee to Breckinridge, Mar. 9, 1865, *OR*, 46/2:1295–6.

16. Ibid.

17. *Wartime Papers*, 897–98.

18. Grant to Meade, Ord, and Sheridan, Mar. 24, 1865, *OR*, 34/1:48–50; Grant report, *OR*, 34/1:50.

19. Grant report, *OR*, 34/1:51; Lincoln to Stanton, Mar. 30, 1865, *CWL*, 8:377–78; Stanton to Lincoln, Mar. 31, 1865, *OR*, 46/3:332; Grant to Bowers, Apr. 3, 1865, *OR*, 46/3:509; Grant to Sherman, Apr. 3, 1865, *OR*, 46/3:510.

20. Davis, *Rise and Fall*, 2:648–49.

21. Davis to the People of the Confederate States of America, Apr. 4, 1865, in *Davis: The Essential Writings*, 363–65; Davis, *Rise and Fall*, 2:676–78.

22. Lee to Grant, Apr. 7, 8, 9 (four notes), 1865, *Wartime Papers*, 931–34.

23. Lee to Davis, Apr. 20, 1865, *Wartime Papers*, 938–39.

24. Ibid.

25. Davis to J. E. Johnston, Apr. 10, 11 (two notes), 1865, *OR*, 47/3:777, 787–88; Harrison to Mrs. Davis, Apr. 12, 1865, *OR*, 46/3:1393–94; *Davis Papers*, 11:541; Davis to Vance, Apr. 11, 1865, *OR*, 47/3:786–87; Davis to Walker, Apr. 11, 1865, *OR*, 47/3:787.

26. Cobb to Davis, Apr. 6, 1865, *OR*, 49/2:1208; Davis to Taylor, Apr. 7, 1865, *OR*, 49/2:1212; Davis to Cobb, Apr. 7, 1865, *OR*, 49/2:1212; Davis to Wofford, Apr. 7, 1865, *OR*, 49/2:1213; Davis to Adams, Apr. 8, 1865, *OR*, 49/2:1220; Taylor to Sec. of War, Apr. 20, 1865, *OR*, 49/2:1255.

27. Davis to Cobb, Apr. 21, 1865, *OR*, 49/2:1257.

28. *Davis Papers*, 11:540, 562 n. 13.

29. Ibid., 11:552. For the terms of the agreement, see also G. Davis to Davis, Apr. 22, 1865, *OR*, 47/3:827–28.

30. Benjamin to Davis, Apr. 22, 1865, 47/3:821–23.

31. Reagan to Davis, Apr. 22, 1865, *OR*, 47/3:823–26; G. Davis to Davis, Apr. 22, 1865, *OR*, 47/3:827–28; Breckinridge to Davis, Apr. 23, 1865, *OR*, 47/3:830–31; Mallory to Davis, Apr. 24, 1865, *OR*, 47/3:832–34; Davis to Varina Davis, Apr. 23, 1865, *Davis Papers*, 11:558–59; Davis to J. E. Johnston, Apr. 24, 1865, *OR*, 47/3:834; Boatner, *Dictionary*, 225.

32. Donald, *Lincoln*, 594–99; *Davis Papers*, 11:562 n. 15; J. E. Johnston to Breckinridge, Apr. 24, 1865, *OR*, 47/3:835; Sherman, *Memoirs*, 844–51.

33. Quoted in *Davis Papers*, 11:562 n. 12; J. E. Johnston, General Orders No. 18, Apr. 27, 1865, *OR*, 47/3:843–44.

34. J. E. Johnston to Breckinridge, Apr. 25, 1865 (second note), *OR*, 47/3:836; *Davis Papers*, 11:562 n. 12; J. E. Johnston, General Orders No. 18, Apr. 27, 1865, *OR*, 47/3:843–44; Davis, *Rise and Fall*, 2:698.

CONCLUSION: IN WAR'S SHADOW

1. Hay, *Diary*, 35.

2. Sun Tzu, *Art of War*, 81.

3. Maurice, "Lincoln as a Strategist," 164.

4. Lyman, *Civil War Quotations*, 130.

5. Potter, "Davis and Political Factors," 108–9.

6. Sherman to Ellen Sherman, July 16, Aug. 3, [Aug. 20–27], Nov. 1, 1861, *Sherman's Civil War*, 113–14, 116–18, 126, 135, 154–55.

7. Some examples: Frank E. Vandiver, "Jefferson Davis and Confederate Strategy," in *The American Tragedy: The Civil War in Retrospected*. ed. Avery O. Craven and Frank E. Vandiver (Hampden-Sydney, VA: Hampden-Sydney College, 1959), 19–32; Joseph G. Dawson III, "Jefferson Davis and the Confederacy's 'Offensive-Defensive' Strategy in the U.S. Civil War," *Journal of Military History* 73 (Apr. 2009): 591–607, 611–13.

8. Quoted in Donald, *Lincoln*, 328.

9. Clausewitz, *On War*, 141.

10. Gat, *A History of Military Thought*, 122–23.

11. Boatner, *Dictionary*, 352–53.

12. Ibid., 751.

13. Gary W. Gallagher, "'A Great General Is So Rare': Robert E. Lee and the Confederacy," in *Leaders of the Lost Cause*, Gallagher and Glatthaar, eds., 32–34.

14. Boatner, *Dictionary*, 524.

15. Marszalek, *Halleck*, 227–48.

16. Boatner, *Dictionary*, 107, 409, 539–40.

17. Ibid., 96.

18. Robert K. Krick, "'Snarl and Sneer and Quarrel': General Joseph E. Johnston and an Obsession with Rank," in *Leaders of the Lost Cause*, Gallagher and Glatthaar, eds., 193–95; Boatner, *Dictionary*, 441.

19. Charles P. Roland, "P. G. T. Beauregard," in *Leaders of the Lost Cause*, Gallagher and Glatthaar, eds., 64–68; Boatner, *Dictionary*, 54–55.

20. Boatner, *Dictionary*, 491.

21. Joseph T. Glatthaar, "Edmund Kirby Smith," in *Leaders of the Lost Cause*, Gallagher and Glatthaar, eds., 239. He died in 1893.

22. Quoted in Robertson, "Braxton Bragg," 92–94.

23. Boatner, *Dictionary*, 288–89, 567, 910.

24. John P. Dunn, "An American Fracas in Egypt—The Butler Affair of 1872," *Journal of the American Research Center in Egypt* 42 (2005–6): 159–60.

25. Bragg to Davis, Nov. 24, 1862, *Davis Papers*, 8:509–11; Washington's "Partizan War" began on Staten Island, see Council of War, [July 12, 1776], in *Papers of George Washington, Revolutionary War Series*, ed. Philander D. Chase et al. (Charlottesville: University Press of Virginia, 2002), 5:280.

26. J. Dodsley, *The Annual Register, or a View of the History, Politics, and Literature for the Year 1777* (London, 1778), 20.

27. Quoted in Gat, *A History of Military Thought*, 442–50; Weigley, *The American Way of War*, 168–73; Maurice Matloff, *American Military History* (Washington, DC: Office of the Chief of Military History, U.S. Army, 1969), 288–89.

28. McPherson, *Battle Cry*, 857–58.

Index

Note: Page references in *italics* denote maps.